Barcelona

timeout.com/barcelona

Penguin Books

PENGUIN BOOKS

Published by the Penguin Group
Penguin Books Ltd, 80 Strand, London WC2R ORL, England
Penguin Books USA Inc., 375 Hudson Street, New York, New York 10014, USA
Penguin Books Australia Ltd, 250 Camberwell Road, Camberwell, Victoria 3124, Australia
Penguin Books Canada Ltd, 10 Alcorn Avenue, Toronto, Ontario, Canada M4V 3B2
Penguin Books (NZ) Ltd, cnr Rosedale and Airborne Roads, Albany, Auckland, New Zealand

Penguin Books Ltd, Registered Offices: Harmondsworth, Middlesex, England

First published 1996
Second edition 1998
Third edition 2000
Fourth edition 2001
Fifth edition 2002
Sixth edition 2003

Seventh edition 2004
10 9 8 7 6 5 4 3 2 1

Colour reprographics by Icon, Crowne House, 56-58 Southwark Street, London SE1 1UN
Printed and bound by Cayfosa-Quebecor, Ctra. de Caldes, Km 3 08 130 Sta, Perpètua de Mogoda, Barcelona, Spain

Edited and designed by
Time Out Guides Limited
Universal House
251 Tottenham Court Road
London W1T 7AB
Tel + 44 (0)20 7813 3000
Fax + 44 (0)20 7813 6001
Email guides@timeout.com
www.timeout.com

Editorial
Editor Sally Davies
Deputy Editor Christi Daugherty
Listings Editors Cecily Doyle, Alix Leveugle
Copy Editor Lily Dunn
Proofreader Tamsin Shelton
Indexer Jonathan Cox

Editorial/Managing Director Peter Fiennes
Series Editor Ruth Jarvis
Deputy Series Editor Lesley McCave
Guides Co-ordinator Anna Norman
Accountant Sarah Bostock

Design
Art Director Mandy Martin
Acting Art Director Scott Moore
Acting Art Editor Tracey Ridgewell
Acting Senior Designer Astrid Kogler
Designer Sam Lands
Digital Imaging Dan Conway
Ad Make-up Charlotte Blythe

Picture Desk
Picture Editor Jael Marschner
Deputy Picture Editor Kit Burnet
Picture Researcher Alex Ortiz

Advertising
Sales Director Mark Phillips
International Sales Manager Ross Canadé
International Sales Executive James Tuson
Advertising Sales (Barcelona) Creative Media Group
Advertising Assistant Lucy Butler

Marketing
Marketing Manager Mandy Martinez
US Publicity & Marketing Associate Rosella Albanese

Production
Guides Production Director Mark Lamond
Production Controller Samantha Furniss

Time Out Group
Chairman Tony Elliott
Managing Director Mike Hardwick
Group Financial Director Richard Waterlow
Group Commercial Director Lesley Gill
Group Marketing Director Christine Cort
Group General Manager Nichola Coulthard
Group Art Director John Oakey
Online Managing Director David Pepper
Group Production Director Steve Proctor
Group IT Director Simon Chappell

Contributors
Introduction Sally Davies. **History** Nick Rider (*Who's who: Els Segadors* Alex Leigh). **Barcelona Today** Daniel Campi. **Architecture** Nick Rider (*Who's who: Ricard Bofill* Alex Leigh). **Picasso, Miró & Dalí** Jeffrey Swartz. **Where to Stay** Kirsten Foster, Alix Leveugle, Tara Stevens. **Sightseeing: Introduction** Sally Davies. **Barri Gòtic** Sally Davies (*The Jewish Quarter* John O'Donovan). **Raval** Nadia Feddo (*Writing on the wall* Kirsten Foster). **Sant Pere & the Born** Sally Davies. **Barceloneta & the Ports** Alex Leigh. **Montjuïc** Jeffrey Swartz. **The Eixample** Nadia Feddo. **Gràcia & Other Districts** Alex Leigh (*all features* John O'Donovan). **Restaurants** Sally Davies, Nadia Feddo (*One for the road* Richard Neill). **Cafés, Tapas & Bars** Sally Davies. **Shops & Services** Nadia Feddo. **Festivals & Events** Nadia Feddo. **Children** Alix Leveugle. **Film** Jonathan Bennett (*Top ten Spanish must-sees* Rob Stone). **Galleries** Jeffrey Swartz. **Gay & Lesbian** Sean O'Flynn, Quim Pujol. **Nightlife & Music** Kirsten Foster, Tara Stevens. **Performing Arts** *Classical Music & Opera* Jonathan Bennett. *Theatre* Nadia Feddo (*Who's who: Calixto Bieito* Isobel Mahoney). *Dance* Nuria Rodríguez. **Sport & Fitness** Alex Leigh.**Trips Out of Town** Sally Davies, Alex Leigh (*Far out food festivals* Nadia Feddo; *On the Piste* Rob Jones). **Directory** Rob Jones, Alix Leveugle (*Up in smoke* Andrew Losowsky).

Maps Mapworld, 71 Blandy Road, Henley on Thames, Oxon, RG9 1QB, and JS Graphics (john@jsgraphics.co.uk).

Photography Matei Glass, except: pages 6, 9, 10, 11, 16 and 22 AISA; page 13 Hulton Getty; page 25 AFP/Getty Images; page 229 Metro Tartan; page 298 courtesy of the Andorra Tourist Board.

The following images were provided by the featured establishments/artists: pages 42, 43, 44 and 266.

The Editor would like to thank: Al & Lucy Petrie, Alfonso Blanco, Andrew Dillon, Dante Battistella, David Noguer, Deirdre Branchflower, Diane O'Donovan, Dmitri Barsoukov, Ferran Barenblit, Jack Dollar, Jack Plowtree, Jane Mullane, Manel Baena, Montse Cabrero, Montse Muñoz, Montse Planas, Montse Pozo, Paul Martin, Quim Pujol, Sarah Guy, Silvia Pares, Steven Guest.

Contents

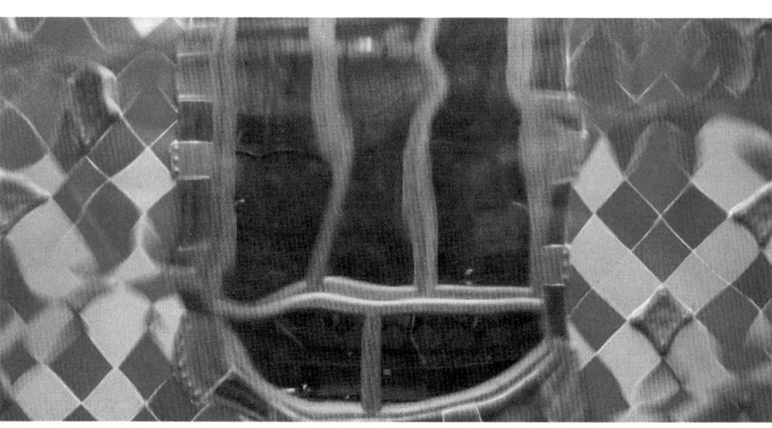

Introduction

Gaudí never really intended the Sagrada Família to be finished. Instead he saw its construction as an ongoing tribute to God, a chance for men to expiate for their sins through a constant striving for perfection. It seems right and fitting, then, that this has become the most enduring symbol of the city, for Barcelona, too, is a work in progress, an ever-expanding installation with citizens for curators. A prototype for democratic urbanism, the city is shaped by its people, and everyone is invited, and expected, to participate in every aspect, from naming the roads to proffering opinions on which of the Christmas street-lights were the most fabulous. This being Style City, supereminent designers were behind the lights in question, but *barcelonins* take such a keen interest in these matters that someone only has to design a new recycling system or a park bench and within days they will become a household name, regardless of whether anyone actually thought they were up to snuff.

Visitors, too, can have their say. Should you remain unmoved by Barcelona's sheer, epic beauty; indifferent to what writer Rose Macaulay called its 'tempestuous, surging, irrepressible life and brio'; to the history writ large in its buildings or to the eccentricities of its specialist shops and idiosyncratic museums – why then the city has a website where you can post your suggestions for improvement.

The trade-off for those in charge is that their whims and the more controversial of their plans are more likely to be tolerated. The forthcoming spectacular that is the Fòrum 2004, a lavish five-month exploration of diversity, peace and sustainable development, has raised many a sceptical eyebrow, not least for the millions of euros which have been poured into new buildings in connection with it, but an unwritten consent is granted nonetheless. Ricard Bofill's towering sail-shaped hotel, which will soon rise up alongside the breakwater and change the seafront inestimably, has provoked a similar response and yet it is allowed to go ahead. Quite simply, if the people of Barcelona don't like it, then they'll have it pulled down.

This defiance of the crude logic and rigid structures of town planning elsewhere extends beyond design and architecture, and brings with it a high degree of civic responsibility. Recent campaigns to promote *civisme* have included one that entreats Catalans to befriend an immigrant and encourage them to speak this dwindling language, thereby furthering two good causes in one go. Another asks people to tip the wink to a nearby policeman if they see anyone peeing in the street. Graffiti, too, is to be addressed, though it is far from the council's style to issue on-the-spot fines for spray-painting a 15th-century Gothic palace. Instead they will say 'Hey, look at that blank wall over there. That could use your contribution.'

And the very best of it is that in this unstinting struggle for the perfect city in which to live, its residents have created a playground for you, the tourist. Come and judge the results for yourself.

ABOUT THE TIME OUT CITY GUIDES

The *Time Out Barcelona Guide* is one of an expanding series of Time Out City Guides, now numbering more than 45, produced by the people behind London and New York's successful listings magazines. Our guides are all written and updated by resident experts who have striven to provide you with all the most up-to-date information you'll need to explore the city or read up on its background, whether you're a local or a first-time visitor. The guide contains detailed practical information, plus features that focus on unique aspects of the city.

THE LOWDOWN ON THE LISTINGS

Above all, we have tried to make this book as useful as possible. Addresses, telephone numbers, websites, transport information, opening times, admission prices and credit card details are included in our listings. And, as far as possible, we've given details of facilities, services and events, all checked and correct at the time we went to press. However, owners and managers can change their arrangements at any time, and often do. Many small shops and businesses in Barcelona do not keep precise opening hours and may close earlier or later than stated here. Similarly, arts programmes are often finalised very late, and liable to change. We would advise you whenever possible to phone ahead and check opening times, ticket prices and other particulars. While every effort has been made to ensure the accuracy of this guide, the publishers cannot accept responsibility for any errors it may contain.

PRICES AND PAYMENT

The prices given in this guide should be treated as guidelines, not gospel. If they vary wildly from those we've quoted, please write and let us know. We aim to give the best and most up-to-date advice, so we always want to know when you've been badly treated or overcharged. Wherever possible we have factored in the sales tax (IVA), which many restaurants and hotels leave out of their advertised rates.

We have listed prices in euros (€) throughout, and we have noted whether venues take credit cards, but have only listed the major cards – American Express (**AmEx**), Diners Club (**DC**), MasterCard (**MC**), Visa (**V**). Many businesses will also accept other cards, including **JCB**. Some shops, restaurants and attractions take travellers' cheques.

THE LIE OF THE LAND

We have divided the city into areas – simplified, for convenience, from the full complexity of Barcelona's geography – and the relevant area name is given with each venue listed in this guide. Wherever possible, a map reference is provided for every venue listed, indicating the page and grid reference for where it can be found in the street maps at the back of the book.

TELEPHONE NUMBERS

It is necessary to dial provincial area codes with all the numbers in Spain, even for local calls. Hence all normal Barcelona numbers begin 93, whether you're calling from inside or outside the city. From abroad, you must dial 34 (the international dialling code for Spain) followed by the number given in the book – which includes the initial 93. For more information on telephones and codes, *see p318*.

ESSENTIAL INFORMATION

For all the practical information you might need for visiting Barcelona, including emergency phone numbers and details of local transport, turn to the **Directory** chapter at the back of the guide. It starts on page 303.

LANGUAGE

Barcelona is a bilingual city; street signs, tourist information and menus can be in either Catalan or Spanish, and this is reflected in the guide. We have tried to use whichever is more commonly used or appropriate in each case.

Advertisers

We would like to stress that no establishment has been included in this guide because it has advertised in any of our publications and no payment of any kind has influenced any review. The opinions given in this book are those of *Time Out* writers and entirely independent.

MAPS

The map section of the book includes some overviews of the greater Barcelona area and its neighbourhoods; detailed street maps of the Eixample, the Raval, Gràcia and other districts, and a large-scale map of the Old City, with a comprehensive street index, a map of the entire region for planning trips out of town and maps of the local rail and metro networks. The maps start on page 331.

LET US KNOW WHAT YOU THINK

We hope you enjoy the *Time Out Barcelona Guide*, and we'd like to know what you think of it. We welcome tips for places that you consider we should include in future editions and take note of your criticism of our choices. There's a reader's reply card at the back of this book for your feedback – or you can email us at guides@timeout.com.

There is an online version of this guide, and guides to over 45 international cities, at **www.timeout.com**.

In Context

Features

History

There have been Romans and plagues and tyrants, but it's really all about Wilfred the Hairy.

The Romans founded Barcelona in about 15 BC, on the Mons Taber, a small hill between two streams that provided a good view of the Mediterranean, and which today is crowned by the cathedral. At the time, the plain around it was sparsely inhabited by the Laetani, an agrarian Iberian people who produced grain and honey, and gathered oysters. Then called Barcino, the town was smaller than Tarraco (Tarragona), the capital of the Roman province of Hispania Citerior, but it had the only harbour between there and Narbonne.

Like virtually every other Roman new town in Europe, Barcino was a fortified rectangle with a crossroads at its centre (where the Plaça Sant Jaume is today). It was a decidedly unimportant provincial town, but the rich plain provided it with a produce garden, and the sea gave it an incipient maritime trade. It acquired a Jewish community very soon after its foundation, and was associated with Christian martyrs, notably Barcelona's first patron saint, Santa Eulàlia. She was supposedly executed at the end of the third century via a series of revolting tortures that included being rolled naked in a sealed barrel full of glass shards down the alley now called Baixada (descent) de Santa Eulàlia.

The people of Barcino accepted Christianity shortly afterwards, in AD 312, together with the rest of the Roman Empire, which by then was under growing threat of invasion. In response, in the fourth century the town's rough defences were replaced with massive stone walls, many sections of which can still be seen today. It was these ramparts that ensured Barcelona's continuity, making the stronghold very desirable to later warlords (*see also p86* **Walk on: Roman remains**).

Nonetheless, defences like these could not prevent the empire's disintegration. In 415 Barcelona (as it became known) briefly became capital of the kingdom of the Visigoths, under their chieftain Ataülf. They soon moved on southwards to extend their control over the whole of the Iberian peninsula, and for the next 400 years the town was a neglected backwater. It was in this state when the Muslims swept across the peninsula after 711, easily crushing Goth resistance. They made little attempt to settle Catalonia, but much of the Christian population retreated into the Pyrenees, the first Catalan heartland. Then, at the end of the eighth century, the Franks drove south, against the Muslims, from across the mountains.

In 801 Charlemagne's son, Louis the Pious, took Barcelona and made it a bastion of the Marca Hispanica (Spanish March), which was the southern buffer of his father's empire. This gave Catalonia a trans-Pyrenean origin entirely different from that of the other Christian states in Spain; equally, it is for this reason that the closest relative of the Catalan language is Provençal, not Castilian.

When the Frankish princes returned to their main business further north, loyal counts were left behind to rule sections of the Catalan lands. At the end of the ninth century one of them, Count Guifré el Pilós ('Wilfred the Hairy'), managed to gain control over several of these Catalan counties from his base in Ripoll. By uniting them under his rule he laid the basis for a future Catalan state, and he founded the dynasty of Counts of Barcelona that reigned in an unbroken line until 1410. His successors would make Barcelona their capital, setting the seal on the city's future.

As a founding patriarch Wilfred is the stuff of legends, not the least of which is that he was the creator of the Catalan flag, the Quatre Barres four bars of red on a yellow background, also known as La Senyera. The story goes that he was fighting the Saracens alongside his lord, the Frankish emperor, when he was severely wounded; in recognition of Wilfred's heroism, the emperor dipped his fingers into his friend's blood and ran them down the Count's golden shield. Recorded facts make this story highly unlikely, but whatever its mythical origins the four red stripes symbol is first recorded on the tomb of Count Ramon Berenguer II from 1082, making the Quatre Barres the oldest national flag in Europe, predating its nearest competitor, in Denmark, by a century. What is not known is exactly in what way Wilfred was so hairy.

A century after Wilfred, in 985, a Muslim army attacked and sacked Barcelona. The hairy count's great-grandson, Count Borrell II, requested aid from his theoretical feudal lord, the Frankish king. He received no reply, and so repudiated all Frankish sovereignty over Catalonia. From then on – although the name was not yet in use – Catalonia was effectively independent, and the Counts of Barcelona were free to forge its destiny.

LAYING THE FOUNDATIONS

In the first century of the new millennium, Catalonia was consolidated as a political entity, and entered an era of great cultural richness. In the 1060s the country's distinctive legal code, the Usatges, was established. This was the great era of Catalan Romanesque art, with the building of the magnificent monasteries and churches of northern Catalonia, such as Sant Pere de Rodes near Figueres, and the painting of the glorious murals housed in the Museu Nacional on Montjuïc. There was also a flowering of scholarship at this time, that reflected Catalan contacts with northern Europe and with Islamic and Carolingian cultures. In Barcelona, shipbuilding and trade in grain and wine all expanded, and a new trade developed in textiles. The city grew both inside its old Roman walls and outside, where *vilanoves* (new towns) appeared at Sant Pere and La Ribera.

Catalonia was also gaining more territory from the Muslims to the south, beyond the Penedès, and – either through marriage or with Arab booty – large areas of what is now southern France. The most significant marriage, however, occurred in 1137, when Ramon Berenguer IV (1131-62) wed Petronella, heir to the throne of Aragon. This would, in the long term, bind Catalonia into Iberia. The uniting of the two dynasties created a powerful entity known as the Crown of Aragon, each element retaining its separate institutions, and ruled by monarchs known as the Count-Kings. Since Aragon was already a kingdom, it was given precedence and its name was often used to refer to the state, but the language used in the court was Catalan and the centre of government remained in Barcelona.

Ramon Berenguer IV also extended Catalan territory to its current frontiers in the Ebro valley. At the beginning of the next century, however, the dynasty lost virtually all its lands north of the Pyrenees to France, when Count-King Pere I 'the Catholic' was killed at the battle of Muret in 1213. This was a blessing in disguise. In future, the Catalan-Aragonese state would be oriented decisively towards the Mediterranean and the south, and was able to embark on two centuries of imperialism that would be equalled in vigour only by Barcelona's burgeoning commercial enterprise.

THE EMPIRE GROWS

Pere I's successor was the most expansionist of the Count-Kings. Jaume I 'the Conqueror' (1213-76) abandoned any idea of further adventures in Provence and joined decisively in the campaign against the Muslims to the south, taking Mallorca in 1229, Ibiza in 1235 and then, at much greater cost, Valencia in 1238. He made it another separate kingdom, the third part of the Crown of Aragon. Barcelona finally became the centre of an empire that spanned across the Mediterranean.

The city grew tremendously under Jaume I, and in the mid 13th century he ordered the building of a new, second wall, along the line of the Rambla and roughly encircling the area between there and the modern Parc de la

Ciutadella, thus bringing La Ribera and the other *vilanoves* within the city. In 1274 he also gave Barcelona a form of representative self-government, the Consell de Cent, a council of 100 chosen citizens, an institution that would last for more than 400 years. In Catalonia as a whole, royal powers were strictly limited by a parliament, the Corts, with a permanent standing committee, known as the Generalitat.

The Count-Kings commanded a powerful fleet and a mercenary army, centred on the Almogàvers, fast-moving bands of irregular warriors who had been hardened in the endless battles with the Muslims on the Catalan frontier. The stuff of another set of heroic legends, the Almogàvers made themselves feared equally by Christians and Muslims as they travelled the Mediterranean conquering, plundering and enslaving in the name of God and the Crown of Aragon.

In 1282, Pere II 'the Great' sent his armies into Sicily; Catalan domination over the island would last for nearly 150 years. The Catalan empire reached its greatest strength under Jaume II 'the Just' (1291-1327). Corsica (1323) and Sardinia (1324) were added to the Crown of Aragon, although the latter would never submit to Catalan rule and would from then on be a constant focus of revolt.

THE GOLDEN AGE

The Crown of Aragon was often at war with Arab rulers, but its capital flourished through commerce with every part of the Mediterranean, Christian and Muslim. Catalan ships also sailed into the Atlantic, to England and Flanders. Their ventures were actively supported by the Count-Kings and burghers of Barcelona, and regulated by the first-ever code of maritime law, known as the *Llibre del Consolat de Mar* (written 1258-72), the influence of which extended far beyond their own territories. By the late 13th century, around 130 consulates ringed the Mediterranean, engaged in a complex system of trade.

Not surprisingly, this age of power and prestige was also the great era of building in medieval Barcelona. The Count-Kings' imperial conquests may have been ephemeral, but their talent for permanence in building can still be seen today. Between 1290 and 1340, the construction of most of Barcelona's best known Gothic buildings was initiated. Religious edifices such as the cathedral, Santa Maria del Mar and Santa Maria del Pi were matched by civil buildings such as the Saló de Tinell and the Llotja, the old market and stock exchange. As a result, Barcelona today contains the most important collection of historic Gothic civil architecture anywhere in Europe.

Borrell II, Count of Barcelona. *See p7.*

The ships of the Catalan navy were built in the monumental Drassanes (shipyards), begun by Pere II and completed under Pere III, in 1378. In 1359, Pere III also built the third, final city wall, along the line of the modern Paral.lel, Ronda Sant Pau and Ronda Sant Antoni. This gave the 'old city' of Barcelona its definitive shape. La Ribera, 'the waterfront', was the centre of trade and industry in 14th-century Barcelona. Once unloaded at the beach, wares were taken to the Llotja. Just inland, the Carrer Montcada was the street par excellence where newly enriched merchants could display their wealth in opulent Gothic palaces. All around were the workers of the various craft guilds, grouped together in their own streets.

The Catalan 'Golden Age' was also an era of cultural greatness. Catalonia was one of the first areas in Europe to use its vernacular language, as well as Latin, in written form and as a language of culture. The oldest written texts in Catalan are the *Homílies d'Organyà*, 12th-century translations from the Bible. The court and the aristocracy seem very early to have attained an unusual level of literacy, and Jaume I wrote his own autobiography, the *Llibre dels Feits* or 'Book of Deeds', dramatically recounting his achievements and conquests.

Ramon Berenguer and his wife. *See p7.*

Incipient Catalan literature was given a vital thrust by the unique figure of Ramon Llull (1235-1316). After a debauched youth, he experienced a series of religious visions and became the first man in post-Roman Europe to write philosophy in a vernacular language. Steeped in Arabic and Hebrew writings, he brought together Christian, Islamic, Jewish and classical ideas, and wrote a vast amount on other subjects – from theories of chivalry to poetry and visionary tales. In doing so Llull effectively created Catalan as a literary language. Catalan translations were undertaken from Greek and Latin, chroniclers like Ramon Muntaner recorded the exploits of Count-Kings and Almogàvers, and in 1490, in the twilight of the Golden Age, the Valencian Joanot Martorell published *Tirant lo Blanc,* a bawdy adventure that is considered the first European novel.

REVOLT AND COLLAPSE

The extraordinary prosperity of the medieval period did not last. The Count-Kings had overextended Barcelona's resources, and overinvested in far-off ports. By 1400, the effort to maintain their conquests by force, especially Sardinia, had exhausted the spirit and the coffers of the Catalan imperialist drive. The Black Death, which had arrived in the 1340s, had also had a devastating impact on Catalonia. This served only to intensify the bitterness of social conflicts between the aristocracy, merchants, peasants and the urban poor.

In 1410, Martí I 'the Humane' died without an heir, bringing to an end the line of Counts of Barcelona unbroken since Guifré el Pilós. After much deliberation the Crown of Aragon was finally passed to a member of a Castilian noble family, the Trastámaras: Fernando de Antequera (1410-16). In the 1460s, the effects of war and catastrophic famine led to a sudden collapse into violent and devastating civil war and peasant revolt. The population was depleted to such an extent that Barcelona would not regain the numbers it had had in 1400 (40,000) until the 18th century.

In 1469, an important union for Spain initiated a woeful period in Barcelona's history, dubbed by some Catalan historians the Decadència, which would lead to the end of Catalonia as a separate entity. In that year, Ferdinand of Aragon (reigned 1479-1516) married Isabella of Castile (1476-1506), and so united the different Spanish kingdoms, even though they would retain their separate institutions for another two centuries.

EAST OF EDEN

As Catalonia's fortunes had declined, so those of Castile to the west had risen. While Catalonia was impoverished and in chaos, Castile had become larger, richer, had a bigger population and was on the crest of a wave of expansion. In 1492, Granada, the last Muslim foothold in Spain, was conquered, Isabella decreed the expulsion of all Jews from Castile and Aragon, and Columbus discovered America.

It was Castile's seafaring orientation towards the Atlantic, as opposed to the Mediterranean, that confirmed Catalonia's decline. The discovery of the New World was a disaster for Catalan commerce: trade shifted decisively away from the Mediterranean, and Catalans were officially barred from participating in the exploitation of the new empire until the 1770s. The weight of Castile within the monarchy was increased, and it very soon became the clear seat of government.

In 1516, the Spanish crown passed to the House of Habsburg, in the shape of Ferdinand and Isabella's grandson, Emperor Charles V. His son, Philip II of Spain, established Madrid as the capital of all of his dominions in 1561. Catalonia was managed by appointed viceroys, and the power of its institutions increasingly restricted, with a down-at-heel aristocracy and a meagre cultural life.

Who's who Els Segadors

'Triumphant Catalonia will become rich and bountiful again' begins the Catalan national anthem, in formal, austere tones. Then it starts getting nasty: 'We shall drive out these arrogant and conceited people' it declares, and it outlines how, in no uncertain terms. 'A good blow of the sickle, defenders of the land, a good blow of the sickle.'

Els Segadors (*The Reapers*) is a particularly bloodthirsty 17th-century battlecry for Catalan independence from Spanish rule, which still causes political problems between Catalonia and the rest of Spain. It was written in the late 1600s to celebrate the Guerra dels Segadors, in which the Catalan peasantry rose up against Spanish troops billeted in their country, attacking them with their sickles, and marching on Barcelona.

Originally it had over 60 verses, and told in some detail the story of the abuses of the unwelcome soldiers and how they were avenged by the peasants. In 1892, during the flowering of Catalan nationalism, Francesc Alio devised new music for the words, and then in 1899 poet Emili Guanyavents wrote a shorter version of the lyrics to make it more memorable for the masses.

The song has a chequered past. It was banned by the dictatorship of Primo de Rivera (1923-30), became the unofficial anthem of the short-lived 'Catalan Republic' in the '30s and was banned again under Franco (1939-75). In periods when it wasn't allowed, the Catalans used other songs (such as *El Cant de la Senyera*) in its place, but as soon as Franco died, the anthem was struck up once again wherever Catalans felt the occasion demanded it. Finally, in 1993 it was officially declared to be the national anthem of the Catalan autonomous community.

Even so many in Madrid were affronted, when, in 2001 the Generalitat announced that *Els Segadors* would be taught to every schoolchild in Catalonia. Many Spaniards, including some living in Catalonia, would favour an action similar to that of 1931 when the Catalan Republic changed the words to make them less bloodthirsty. This bowdlerisation didn't work; everyone sang the old words anyway.

'Now is the time, reapers,' concludes the anthem, 'to be alert, because when another June comes we will sharpen our tools again. Our enemies should tremble to see our banner, because we're now cutting down stalks of wheat, but when the time is right our chains will follow.' With the 2003 Catalan elections placing separatist supporters in positions of power, Madrid might well add apprehensive to affronted.

It's anarchy!

On 1 May 1931, just two weeks after the start of Spain's Second Republic, some 150,000 people – in a city with a total population which was then not much over one million – met in the Ciutadella park to restate the aims of anarchism under the new regime. This was only one of the many huge anarchist rallies between 1910 and 1936, for Barcelona was then the only city in the world where anarchism, far from a fringe movement, was something nobody could ignore.

Anarchism first appeared in Barcelona amid the outburst of agitation that followed the fall of Isabel II in 1868, and was brought in by Giuseppe Fanelli, an Italian emissary of the Russian anarchist theorist Bakunin. It quickly gained an audience among the city's workers' societies, who were open to the idea that the only true socialism would be a society without central authority as well as without inequality. Catalans in particular, even if they were not nationalists, were used to seeing the Spanish state as a distant, incompetent entity, whose only functions were repressive ones.

Barcelona anarchism went through several different phases. It was most notorious in the 1890s, when anarchists launched terrorist attacks against the symbols of established society, most dramatically when a bomb was thrown down into the stalls of the Liceu opera house in 1893. These incidents were carried out by small groups or lone terrorists, and at this time anarchism was actually at a low point in terms of real popular support.

Anarchist influence really grew vastly after 1910, with the founding of the CNT union (Confederación Nacional del Trabajo) and the growth of anarchosyndicalism, the idea that a workers' union movement should take on the running of society.

The CNT was a distinctively obstreperous, combative union. With it came the cultivation of a particular attitude, that no grievance or injustice should ever be allowed to go by without some kind of response. CNT support grew massively during the economic crisis brought by World War I, and climaxed in the Canadiense general strike of February 1919, which brought Barcelona to a shuddering halt. This, though, caused an equally profound state of shock among respectable society and provoked an intransigent and violent response, in the 'gunmen years' that led up to Primo de Rivera's coup in 1923.

Union agitation was only part of anarchist activity. A central idea of Spanish anarchism was that a completely self-managed society could be brought about through constant collective organization. Anarchists set up co-operatives, schools and social centres, publishing houses and countless magazines, and were among the first to bring progressive ideas on education and sexuality into Spain. Many of these efforts were able to carry on under Primo's relatively lax dictatorship, and exploded into new life under the Republic.

At its 1931 peak the Catalan CNT had 400,000 members. A network of anarchist clubs or *ateneos libertarios* existed around Barcelona, organising regular *jiras libertarias*, mass outings to the countryside or the beach. Housing campaigns ensured that many of the poor paid no rent, and an anarchist-feminist movement gained momentum.

GRIM REAPERS

While Castilian Spain went through its 'Golden Century', Catalonia was left more and more on the margins. Worse was to come, however, in the following century, with the two national revolts, both heroic defeats that have since acquired a role in central Catalan mythology.

The problem for the Spanish monarchy was that, whereas Castile was an absolute monarchy and therefore could be taxed at will, in the former Aragonese territories, and especially Catalonia, royal authority kept coming up against a mass of local rights and privileges. As the Habsburgs' empire became bogged down in endless wars and expenses that not even American gold could meet, the Count-Duke of Olivares, the formidable great minister of King Philip IV (1621-65), resolved to extract more money and troops from the non-Castilian dominions of the crown. The Catalans, however, felt they were taxed quite enough already.

In 1640, a mass of peasants, later dubbed Els Segadors (the Reapers), gathered on the Rambla in Barcelona, outside the Porta Ferrissa (Iron Gate) in the second wall. They rioted against royal authority, surged into the city and seized and murdered the viceroy, the Marqués de Santa Coloma. This began the general uprising known as the Guerra dels Segadors, or the 'Reapers' War'. The authorities of the Generalitat, led by its president, Pau Claris, were fearful of the violence of the poor and, lacking the confidence

But Catalan anarchism faced its most dramatic moment, as would be expected, during the Civil War. This was its much longed-for opportunity to put into practice anarchist ideas, as Barcelona became the only city ever to undergo a predominantly libertarian socialist revolution. Factories, markets, cinemas, public services and more came under collective self-management, and taxis, instead of being black and yellow, were black and red. Some collectives, such as public transport, worked very well, while others stumbled from setback to setback. At the same time, the war put the CNT's ideas and resources under unprecedented pressure, as they were caught between unsympathetic 'allies' like the Communists and the greater threat of Franco. Ideals and morale were gradually ground down, and today, only glimmers of this world remain.

to declare Catalonia independent, appealed for protection from Louis XIII of France. French armies, however, were unable to defend Catalonia adequately, and in 1652 a destitute Barcelona capitulated to the equally exhausted army of Philip IV. In 1659, France and Spain made peace with a treaty that gave the Catalan territory of Roussillon, around Perpignan, to France. After the revolt, Philip IV and his ministers were surprisingly magnanimous, allowing the Catalans to retain what was left of their institutions despite their disloyalty.

THE REIGN IN SPAIN

Fifty years later came the second of the great national rebellions, in the War of the Spanish Succession, the last time Catalonia sought to regain its national freedom by force. In 1700, Charles II of Spain died without an heir. Castile accepted the grandson of Louis XIV of France, Philip of Anjou, as King Philip V of Spain (1700-46). However, the alternative candidate, the Archduke Charles of Austria, promised that he would restore the traditional rights of the former Aragonese territories, and so won their allegiance. He also had the support, in his fight against France, of Britain, Holland and Austria.

Once again, though, Catalonia backed the wrong horse, and was let down in its choice of allies. In 1713, Britain and the Dutch made a separate peace with France and withdrew their aid, leaving the Catalans stranded with no possibility of victory. After a 13-month siege in which every citizen was called to arms, Barcelona fell to the French and Spanish armies on 11 September 1714.

The most heroic defeat of all, this date marked the most decisive political reverse in Barcelona's history, and is now commemorated as Catalan National Day, the Diada. Some of Barcelona's resisters were buried next to the church of Santa Maria del Mar in the Born in the Fossar de les Moreres (Mulberry Graveyard), which is now a memorial.

In 1715, Philip V issued his decree of Nova Planta, abolishing all the remaining separate institutions of the Crown of Aragon and so, in effect, creating 'Spain' as a single, unitary state. Large-scale 'Castilianisation' of the country was initiated, and Castilian replaced the Catalan language in all official documents.

In Barcelona, extra measures were taken to keep the city under firm control. The crumbling medieval walls and the castle on Montjuïc were refurbished with new ramparts, and a massive new citadel was built on the eastern side of the old city, where the Parc de la Ciutadella is today. To make space for it, thousands of people had to be expelled from La Ribera and were forcibly rehoused in the Barceloneta, Barcelona's first-ever planned housing scheme, with its barrack-like street plan unmistakably provided by French military engineers. This citadel became the most hated symbol of the city's subordination.

RETAIL THERAPY

Politically subjugated and without a significant native ruling class, Catalonia nevertheless revived in the 18th century. Shipping picked up again, and in the last years of the 18th century Barcelona had a booming export trade to the New World in wines and spirits from Catalan vineyards, and textiles, wool and silk. In 1780, a merchant called Erasme de Gómina opened Barcelona's first true factory, a hand-powered weaving mill in C/Riera Alta with 800 workers. In the next decade, Catalan trade with Spanish America quadrupled; Barcelona's population had grown from around 30,000 in 1720 to close to 100,000 by the end of the century.

This prosperity was reflected in a new wave of building in the city. Neo-classical mansions appeared, notably on C/Ample and the Rambla. The greatest transformation, though, was in the Rambla itself. Until the 1770s, it had been no more than a dusty, dry riverbed where country people came to sell their produce, lined on the Raval side mostly with giant religious houses and on the other with Jaume I's second wall. In 1775, the Captain-General, the Marqués de la Mina, embarked on an ambitious scheme to demolish the wall and turn the Rambla into a paved promenade. Beyond the Rambla, the previously semi-rural Raval was swiftly becoming densely populated.

Barcelona's expansion was briefly interrupted by the French invasion of 1808. Napoleon sought to appeal to Catalans by offering them national recognition within his empire, but, curiously, met with very little response. After six years of turmoil, Barcelona's growing business class resumed its many projects in 1814, with the restoration of the Bourbon monarchy in the shape of Ferdinand VII.

GETTING UP STEAM

On his restoration, Ferdinand VII (1808-33) attempted to reinstate the absolute monarchy of his youth and reimpose his authority over Spain's American colonies, but failed to do either. On his death he was succeeded by his three-year-old daughter Isabel II (1833-68), but the throne was also claimed by his brother Carlos, who was strongly backed by the most reactionary sectors in the country.

To defend Isabel's rights, the Regent, Ferdinand's widow Queen María Cristina, was obliged to seek the support of liberals, and so granted a very limited form of constitution. Thus began Spain's Carlist Wars, which had a powerful impact in conservative rural Catalonia, where Don Carlos's faction won a considerable following, in part because of its support for traditional local rights and customs.

'Barcelona was rebellious, liberal, republican and free-thinking; utopian groups proliferated.'

While this see-saw struggle went on around the country, in Barcelona a liberal-minded local administration, freed from subordination to the military, was able to engage in some city planning, opening up the soon-to-be fashionable C/Ferran and Plaça Sant Jaume in the 1820s, and later adding the Plaça Reial. A fundamental change came in 1836, when the government in Madrid decreed the Desamortización (or the 'disentailment') of Spain's monasteries. In Barcelona, where convents and religious houses still took up great sections of the Raval and the Rambla, a huge area was freed for development.

Then the Rambla took on the appearance it roughly retains today, while the Raval, the main district for new industry in a Barcelona still contained within its walls, rapidly filled up with tenements and textile mills several storeys high. In 1832, the first steam-driven factory in Spain was built on C/Tallers, sparking resistance from hand-spinners and weavers.

Most of the city's factories then were still relatively small, however, and the Catalan manufacturers were very aware that they were at a disadvantage in competing with the industries of Britain and other countries to the north. Also, they did not have the city to themselves. Not only did the anti-industrial Carlists threaten from the countryside, but Barcelona soon became a centre of radical ideas. Its people were notably rebellious, and liberal, republican, free-thinking and even utopian socialist groups proliferated between sporadic bursts of repression. In 1842, a liberal revolt, the Jamancia, took over Barcelona, and barricades went up around the city. This would be the last occasion on which Barcelona was bombarded from the castle on Montjuïc, as the army struggled to regain control.

The Catalan language, by this time, had been relegated to secondary status, spoken in every street but rarely written or used in cultured discourse. Then, in 1833, Bonaventura Carles Aribau published his *Oda a la Pàtria*, a romantic eulogy in Catalan of the country, its language and its past. This poem had an extraordinary impact, and is still traditionally credited with initiating the Renaixença (rebirth) of Catalan heritage and culture. The year 1848 was a high point for Barcelona and Catalonia, with the inauguration of the first railway in Spain, from Barcelona to Mataró, and the opening of the Liceu opera house.

SETTING AN EIXAMPLE

The optimism of Barcelona's new middle class was counterpointed by two persistent obstacles: the weakness of the Spanish economy as a whole, and the instability of their own society, reflected in atrocious labour relations. No consideration was given to the manpower behind the industrial surge: the underpaid, overworked men, women and children who lived in appalling conditions in high-rise slums within the cramped city. In 1855, the first general strike took place in Barcelona. The Captain-General, Zapatero, inaugurating a long cycle of conflict, refused to permit any workers' organisations to function, and bloodily suppressed all resistance.

One response to the city's problems that had almost universal support in Barcelona was the demolition of the city walls, which had imposed a stifling restriction on its growth. For years, however, the Spanish state refused to relinquish this hold on the city. To find space, larger factories were established in villages around Barcelona, such as Sants and Poblenou. In 1854, permission finally came for the demolition of the citadel and the walls. The work began with enthusiastic popular participation, crowds of volunteers joining in at weekends. Barcelona at last broke out of the space it had occupied since the 14th century and spread outward into its new *eixample* (extension), to a controversial new plan by Ildefons Cerdà.

In 1868, Isabel II, once a symbol of liberalism, was overthrown by a progressive revolt. During the six years of upheaval that followed, power in Madrid would be held by the provisional government – a constitutional monarchy under an Italian prince and later a federal republic. Workers were free to organise, though, and in 1868 Giuseppe Fanelli brought the first anarchist ideas (*see p12*). In 1870, the first-ever Spanish workers' congress took place in Barcelona. The radical forces, though, were divided between many squabbling factions, while the established classes of society felt increasingly threatened and called for the restoration of order. The Republic proclaimed in 1873 was unable to establish its authority, and succumbed to a military coup less than a year later.

IF YOU BUILD IT, THEY WILL COME

In 1874 the Bourbon dynasty was restored to the Spanish throne in the person of Alfonso XII, son of Isabel II. Workers' organisations were again suppressed. The middle classes, however, felt their confidence renewed. The 1870s saw a frenzied boom in stock speculation, known as the *febre d'or* (gold fever), and the real take-off of building in the Eixample. From the 1880s, Modernisme became the preferred style of the new district, the perfect expression for the confidence and impetus of the industrial class. The first modern Catalanist political movement was founded by Valentí Almirall.

Barcelona felt it needed to show the world all that it had achieved, and that it was more than just a 'second city'. In 1885, an exhibition promoter named Eugenio Serrano de Casanova proposed to the city council the holding of an international exhibition, such as had been held successfully in London, Paris and Vienna. Serrano was a highly dubious character, who eventually made off with large amounts of public funds, but by the time this became clear the city fathers had fully committed themselves. The Universal Exhibition of 1888 was used as a pretext for the final conversion of the Ciutadella into a park; giant efforts had to be made to get everything ready in time, a feat that led the mayor, Francesc Rius i Taulet, to exclaim that 'the Catalan people are the yankees of Europe'. The first of Barcelona's three great efforts to demonstrate its status to the world, the 1888 Exhibition signified the consecration of the Modernista style, the end of provincial, dowdy Barcelona and its establishment as a modern-day city on the international map.

Characters departed

Barcelona's standing as a mecca for table-squatters is not a recent invention. The city has never hosted more eccentrics and oddities than during the golden age of Barcelona bohemia, from the 1880s to the Civil War. Here are three Ramblistes gone by.

José Fola Igúrbide

Around 1910 the most popular plays in the many theatres on the Paral.lel were those of José Fola Igúrbide. His sweeping dramas with titles like *The Sun of Humanity*, in which symbolic heroines called Idea or Strength struggled against oppression to redeem the human race, they were also pretty wordy, but this combination of melodrama and high ideals was a huge success among Barcelona's radicalised, revolutionary minded, working class audiences.

Fola was not just a playwright, for he also wrote equally big-brush philosophical works, like *The Harmonious Nature of Space*, and was a scientist and inventor. He claimed to have solved the problems of flight, and that the Wright brothers had stolen his ideas, and his shabby flat on Ronda Sant Antoni was full of hundreds of model aeroplanes.

THE CITY OF THE NEW CENTURY

The 1888 Exhibition left Barcelona with huge debts, a new look and plenty of reasons to believe in itself as a paradigm of progress. As 1900 approached, there were few cities in the world where the new century was regarded with greater anticipation than in Barcelona. The Catalan Renaixença continued, and acquired a more political tone. In 1892, the Bases de Manresa were drawn up, a draft plan for Catalan autonomy. Middle-class opinion was gradually becoming more sympathetic to political Catalanism, and then a decisive moment came in 1898, when the underlying weakness of the Spanish state was abruptly made plain, despite the superficial prosperity of the first years of the Bourbon restoration. Spain was manoeuvred into a short war with the United States, in which it very quickly lost its remaining empire in Cuba, the Philippines and Puerto Rico. Catalan industrialists were horrified at losing the lucrative Cuban market, and despaired of the ability of the state ever to actually reform itself. Many swung behind a conservative nationalist movement founded in 1901, the Lliga Regionalista (Regionalist League), led by Enric Prat de la Riba and the politician-financier Francesc Cambó. It promised both national revival and modern, efficient government.

When impatient theatre managers would call to ask when his plays would be delivered, Fola would play the guitar or run around the room demonstrating his models and babbling endlessly about flying machines. He died in the flu epidemic of 1918. His plays fell out of favour, except among Barcelona's anarchist theatre groups, for whom they remained favourites right up until 1936.

Lluís Capdevila

In the 1960s, this long-forgotten Catalan writer published in exile a memoir recalling a life of idleness of truly heroic proportions. A near-archetype of the local *culs de café* or 'café-arses', Capdevila was already partly familiar from other memoirs of the era: he aspired to be the classic bohemian, wearing a long cape, big hat and a monocle, and smoking a pipe for which he often couldn't afford any tobacco. He was theoretically a radical journalist, writing for tub-thumping revolutionary sheets called *Bohemios* or *Los Miserables*, but at best would scribble a few words between cabarets.

Capdevila's only homes were several bohemian cafés around La Rambla. Around 1917 his cronies noticed that he would disappear for weeks at a time, to re-emerge unusually well dressed. It transpired he had acquired a protector, a rich American called Marion who had decided wartime Paris was too drab and moved south. She was bisexual, and would alternate between lavish gowns and jewellery and tweeds and riding outfits. It was In the latter she once turned up one day on La Rambla to beat up Capdevila with a riding crop, also providing a great show for the other *culs de café*.

Santiago Rusiñol

If Fola and Capdevila were hand-to-mouth bohemians, Rusiñol – one of the most important Modernista painters – represented 'golden bohemia'. Not only did he inherit a textile fortune, but many of his paintings sold for high prices. He was generous with his money, and it was known that if you caught the great man on his way home in the early hours from his favourite café, the Lyon d'Or, to his Passeig de Gràcia flat, you could almost always touch him for a 'loan'.

Critics have long complained that Rusiñol's paintings and writings were often superficial. Artistic seriousness was perhaps not helped by his legendary and relentless commitment to having a good time. He once had to have a kidney removed during carnival time, and insisted that he be operated on wearing a false nose. He discovered Sitges for the outside world, and the Festes Modernistes he orchestrated there in the 1890s brought a new idea of sophisticated entertainment to Catalonia and ensured unheard-of publicity for the new artistic movement.

He left for a tour of Argentina as the new literary director of a theatre company, but disappeared on arrival, only to be discovered days later in a Buenos Aires café, where he'd acquired a circle of young followers. A statue of some Argentinian worthy was scheduled to be unveiled nearby, and Rusiñol suggested they inaugurate it themselves. He amassed a crowd, delivered a grand but nonsensical speech and was solidly applauded... much to the bemusement of the official inauguration party, which arrived on the scene a couple of hours later to a deserted stage.

At the same time, Barcelona continued to grow, fuelling Catalanist optimism. The city officially incorporated most of the surrounding smaller communities in 1897, and reached a population of over half a million, and in 1907 initiated the 'internal reform' of the old city by creating the Via Laietana which cut right through it. The street was expected to allow in more air and so make the streets less unhealthy.

Catalan letters were thriving: the Institut d'Estudis Catalans (Institute of Catalan Studies) was founded in 1906, and Pompeu Fabra set out to create the first Catalan dictionary. Above all, Barcelona had a vibrant artistic community, centred on Modernisme, consisting of great architects and established, wealthy painters such as Rusiñol and Casas, and also the penniless bohemians who gathered round them, like the young Picasso.

Barcelona's bohemians were also drawn to the increasingly wild nightlife of the Raval, where cabarets, bars and brothels multiplied at the end of the 19th century. Around the cabarets, though, were also the poorest of the working class, for whom conditions had only continued to decline. Barcelona had some of the worst overcrowding and highest mortality rates in Europe. Local philanthropists called for something to be done, but Barcelona was more associated with revolutionary politics and

violence than with peaceful social reform. In 1893 more than 20 people were killed in a series of anarchist terrorist attacks, including the notorious throwing of a bomb into the wealthy audience at the Liceu. The perpetrators acted alone, but the authorities seized the opportunity to round up the usual suspects – local anarchists and radicals – several of whom, known as the 'Martyrs of Montjuïc', were later tortured and executed in the castle above the city. One retaliation came in 1906, when a Catalan anarchist tried to assassinate King Alfonso XIII on his wedding day.

Anarchism was still only in a fledgling stage among workers in the 1900s, but rebellious attitudes, along with growing republican sentiment and a fierce hatred of the Catholic Church united the underclasses and led them to take to the barricades with little provocation.

In 1909 came the explosive outburst of the Setmana Tràgica (Tragic Week). It began as a protest against the conscription of troops for the colonial war in Morocco, but degenerated into a general riot, with the destruction of churches by excited mobs. Suspected culprits were summarily executed, as was the anarchist educationalist Francesc Ferrer, who was accused of 'moral responsibility' even though he was not even in Barcelona at the time.

These events dented the optimism of the Catalanists of the Lliga, but in 1914 they secured from Madrid the Mancomunitat, or administrative union, of the four Catalan provinces, the first joint government of any kind in Catalonia in 200 years. Its first president was Prat de la Riba, who would be succeeded on his death in 1917 by the architect Puig i Cadafalch. However, the Lliga's plans for an orderly Catalonia were to be obstructed by a further surge in social tensions.

CHAMPAGNE AND SOCIALISTS

Spain's neutral status during World War I gave a huge boost to the Spanish, and especially Catalan, economy. Exports soared as Catalonia's manufacturers made millions supplying uniforms to the French army. Barcelona's industry was at last able to diversify from textiles into engineering, chemicals and other more modern sectors.

Barcelona also became the most amenable place of refuge for anyone in Europe who wished to avoid the war. Its international refugee community, included artists Sonia and Robert Delaunay, Francis Picabia, Marie Laurencin and Albert Gleizes, and it was a bolt-hole for all kinds of low-life from around Europe. The Raval area was soon dubbed the Barrio Chino, 'Chinatown', definitively identifying it as an area of sin and perdition.

Some of the most regular patrons of the lavish new cabarets were industrialists, for many of the war profits were spent immediately in very conspicuous consumption. The war also set off massive inflation, driving people in their thousands from rural Spain into the big cities. Barcelona doubled in size in 20 years to become the largest city in Spain, and also the fulcrum of Spanish politics.

Workers' wages, meanwhile, had lost half their real value. The chief channel of protest in Barcelona was the anarchist workers' union, the Confederación Nacional del Trabajo (CNT), constituted in 1910, which gained half a million members in Catalonia by 1919. The CNT and the socialist Union General de Trabajadores (UGT) launched a joint general strike in 1917, roughly coordinated with a campaign by the Lliga and other liberal politicians for political reform. However, the politicians soon withdrew at the prospect of serious social unrest. Inflation continued to intensify, and in 1919 Barcelona was paralysed for more than two months by a CNT general strike over union recognition. Employers refused to recognise the CNT, and the most intransigent among them hired gunmen to get rid of union leaders. Union activists replied in kind, and virtual guerrilla warfare developed between the CNT, the employers and the state. More than 800 people were killed on the city's streets over five years.

In 1923, in response both to the chaos in the city and a crisis in the war in Morocco, the Captain-General of Barcelona, Miguel Primo de Rivera, staged a coup and established a military dictatorship under King Alfonso XIII. The CNT, was already exhausted, and was suppressed. Conservative Catalanists, longing for an end to disorder and the revolutionary threat, initially supported the coup, but were rewarded by the abolition of the Mancomunitat and a vindictive campaign by the Primo regime against the Catalan language and national symbols.

This, however, achieved the opposite of the desired effect, helping to radicalise and popularise Catalan nationalism. After the terrible struggles of the previous years, the 1920s were actually a time of notable prosperity for many in Barcelona, as some of the wealth recently accumulated filtered through the economy. This was also, though, a highly politicised society, in which new magazines and forums for discussion – despite the restrictions of the dictatorship – found a ready audience.

A prime motor of Barcelona's prosperity in the 1920s was the International Exhibition of 1929, the second of the city's great showcase events. It had been proposed by Cambó and Catalan business groups, but Primo de Rivera saw that it could also serve as a propaganda event for his regime. A huge number of public projects were undertaken in association with the main event, including the post office in Via Laietana, the Estació de França and Barcelona's first Metro line, from Plaça Catalunya to Plaça d'Espanya. Thousands of migrant workers came from southern Spain to build them, many living in decrepit housing or shanty towns on the city fringes. By 1930, Barcelona was very different from the place it had been in 1910; it contained more than a million people, and its urban sprawl had crossed into neighbouring towns such as Hospitalet and Santa Coloma.

For the Exhibition itself, Montjuïc and Plaça d'Espanya were comprehensively redeveloped, with grand halls by Puig i Cadafalch and other local architects in the style of the Catalan neo-classical movement Noucentisme, a backward-looking reaction to the excesses of Modernisme. They contrasted strikingly, though, with the German pavilion by Mies van der Rohe (the Pavelló Barcelona), which emphatically announced the trend toward rationalism.

THE REPUBLIC SUPPRESSED

Despite the Exhibition's success, in January 1930 Primo de Rivera resigned, exhausted. The King appointed another soldier, General Berenguer, as prime minister, with the mission of restoring stability. The dictatorship, though, had fatally discredited the old regime, and a protest movement spread across Catalonia against the monarchy. In early 1931, Berenguer called local elections as a first step towards a restoration of constitutional rule. The outcome was a complete surprise, for republicans were elected in all of Spain's cities. Ecstatic crowds poured into the streets, and Alfonso XIII abdicated. On 14 April 1931, the Second Spanish Republic was proclaimed.

The Republic came in amid real euphoria. This was especially true in Catalonia, where it was associated with hopes for both social change and national reaffirmation. The clear winner of the elections in the country had been the Esquerra Republicana, a leftist Catalanist group led by Francesc Macià. A raffish, elderly figure, Macià was one of the first politicians in Spain to win genuine affection from ordinary people. He declared Catalonia independent, but later agreed to accept autonomy within the Spanish Republic.

The Generalitat was re-established as a government that would, potentially, acquire wide powers. All aspects of Catalan culture were then in expansion, and a popular press in Catalan achieved a wide readership. Barcelona was a small but notable centre of the avant-garde. Miró and Dalí had already made their mark in painting; under the Republic, the Amics de l'Art Nou (ADLAN, Friends of New Art) group worked to promote contemporary art, while the GATCPAC architectural collective sought to work with the new authorities to bring rationalist architecture to Barcelona.

In Madrid, the Republic's first government was a coalition of republicans and socialists led by Manuel Azaña. Its overriding goal was to modernise Spanish society through liberal-democratic reforms, but as social tensions intensified the coalition collapsed, and a conservative republican party, with support from the traditional Spanish right, secured power shortly after new elections in 1933. For Catalonia, the prospect of a return to right-wing rule prompted fears that it would immediately abrogate the Generalitat's hard-won powers. On 6 October 1934, while a general strike was launched against the central government in Asturias and some other parts of Spain, Lluís Companys, leader of the Generalitat since Macià's death the previous year, declared Catalonia independent. This 'uprising', however, turned out to be something of a farce, for the Generalitat had no means of resisting the army, and the new 'Catalan Republic' was rapidly suppressed.

The Generalitat was suspended and its leaders imprisoned. Over the following year, fascism seemed to become a real threat for the left, as political positions became polarised throughout Spain. Then, in February 1936, elections were won by the Popular Front of the left across the country. The Generalitat was reinstated, and in Catalonia the next few months were surprisingly peaceful. In the rest of Spain, though, tensions were reaching bursting point, and right-wing politicians, refusing to accept the loss of power, talked openly of the need for the military to intervene. In July, the 1929 stadium on Montjuïc was to be the site of the Popular Olympics, a leftist alternative to the main Olympics of that year in Nazi Germany. On 18 July, the day of their inauguration, however, army generals launched a coup against the Republic and its left-wing governments, expecting no resistance.

UP IN ARMS

In Barcelona, militants from the unions and leftist parties, on alert for weeks, suddenly poured into the streets to oppose the troops in fierce fighting. Over the course of 19 July the military were gradually worn down, until it finally surrendered in the Hotel Colón on Plaça Catalunya (by the corner with Passeig de Gràcia, the site of which is now occupied by the Radio Nacional de España building). Opinions have always differed as to who could claim most credit for this remarkable popular victory:

workers' militants have claimed it was the 'people in arms' who defeated the army, while others stress the importance of the police remaining loyal to the Generalitat throughout the struggle. A likely answer is that they actually encouraged each other.

'Far from the front, Barcelona was the chief centre of the revolution.'

Tension released, the city was taken over by the revolution. People's militias of the CNT, different Marxist parties and other left-wing factions marched off to Aragon, led by streetfighters such as the anarchists Durruti and García Oliver, to continue the battle. The army rising had failed in Spain's major cities but won footholds in Castile, Aragon and the south, although in the heady atmosphere of Barcelona in July 1936 it was often assumed that their resistance could not last long, and that the people's victory was near inevitable.

Far from the front, Barcelona was the chief centre of the revolution in republican Spain, the only truly proletarian city. Its middle class avoided the streets, where, as Orwell recorded in his *Homage to Catalonia*, everyone you saw wore workers' clothing. Barcelona became a magnet for leftists from around the world, drawing writers André Malraux, Hemingway and Octavio Paz. All kinds of industries and public services were collectivised, including cinemas, the phone system and food distribution. Ad hoc 'control patrols' of the revolutionary militias roamed the streets supposedly checking for suspected right-wing agents and sometimes carrying out summary executions, a practice that was condemned by many leftist leaders.

The alliance between the different left-wing groups was unstable and riddled with tensions. The Communists, who had some extra leverage because the Soviet Union was the only country prepared to give the Spanish Republic arms, demanded the integration of these loosely organised militias into a conventional army under a strong central authority. The following months saw continual political infighting between the discontented CNT, the radical-Marxist party Partit Obrer d'Unificació Marxista (POUM), and the Communists. Co-operation broke down totally in May 1937, when republican and Communist troops seized the telephone building in Plaça Catalunya (on the corner of Portal de l'Àngel) from a CNT committee, sparking off the confused war-within-the-civil-war witnessed by Orwell from the roof of the Teatre Poliorama. A temporary agreement was patched up, but shortly afterwards the POUM was banned, and the CNT excluded from power. A new republican central government was formed under Dr Juan Negrín, a Socialist allied to the Communists.

After that, the war gradually became more of a conventional conflict. This did little, however, to improve the Republic's position, for the Nationalists under General Francisco Franco and their German and Italian allies had been continually gaining ground throughout it all. Madrid was under siege, and the capital of the Republic was moved to Valencia, and then to Barcelona, in November 1937.

Catalonia received thousands of refugees, as food shortages and the lack of armaments ground down morale. Barcelona also had the sad distinction of being the first major city in Europe to be subjected to sustained intensive bombing – to an extent that has rarely been appreciated – with heavy raids throughout 1938, especially by Italian bombers based in Mallorca. The Basque Country and Asturias had already fallen to Franco, and in March 1938 his troops reached the Mediterranean near Castellón, cutting the main Republican zone in two. The Republic had one last throw of the dice, in the Battle of the Ebro in summer 1938, when for months the Popular Army struggled to retake control of the river. After that, the Republic was exhausted. Barcelona fell to the Francoist army on 26 January 1939. Half a million refugees fled to France, to be interned in barbed-wire camps along the beaches.

THE FRANCO YEARS

In Catalonia the Franco regime was iron-fisted and especially vengeful. Thousands of Catalan republicans and leftists were executed, among them Generalitat President Lluís Companys; exile and deportation were the fate of thousands more. Publishing, teaching and any other public cultural expression in Catalan, including even speaking it in the street, were prohibited, and every Catalanist monument in the city was dismantled. All independent political activity was suspended, and the entire political and cultural development of the country during the previous century and a half was thus brought to an abrupt halt.

The epic of the Spanish Civil War is known worldwide; more present in the collective memory of Barcelona, though, is the long *posguerra* or post-war period, which lasted for nearly two decades after 1939. During those years, the city was impoverished, and food and electricity were rationed; it would not regain the standard of living of 1936 until the mid 1950s. Nevertheless, migrants in flight from the still more brutal poverty of

Josep Tarradellas fires up the crowds on his return to power. *See p23.*

the south flowed into the city, occupying precarious shanty towns around Montjuïc and other areas in the outskirts. Reconstruction work on the nearly 2,000 buildings destroyed by bombing was slow, and the regime built little during its first few years other than monumental showpieces and the vulgarly ornate basilica on top of Tibidabo, which was said to have been done to expiate Barcelona's 'sinful' role during the war.

Some underground political movements were able to operate – the anarchist Sabaté brothers carried on their own small-scale urban guerrilla campaign, and 1951 saw the last gasp of the pre-war labour movement in a general tram strike. Some Catalan high culture was tolerated, and the young Antoni Tàpies held his first exhibition in 1949. For many people, though, the only remaining focus of any collective excitement was Barcelona football club, which took on an extraordinary importance at this time, above all in its twice-yearly meetings with the 'team of the regime', Real Madrid.

As a fascist survivor, the Franco regime was subject to a UN embargo after World War II. Years of international isolation and attempted self-sufficiency came to an end in 1953, when the USA and the Vatican saw to it that this anti-communist state was at least partially re-admitted to the western fold. Even a limited opening to the outside world meant that foreign money finally began to enter the country, and the regime relaxed some control over its population. In 1959, the Plan de Estabilización (Stabilisation Plan), drawn up by Catholic technocrats of the Opus Dei, brought Spain definitively within the western economy, throwing its doors wide open to tourism and foreign investment. After years of austerity, tourist income at last brought the Europe-wide 1960s boom to Spain and set off change at an extraordinary pace.

Two years earlier, in 1957, José María de Porcioles was appointed Mayor of Barcelona, a post he would retain until 1973. Porcioles has since been regarded as the personification of the damage inflicted on the city by the Franco regime during its 1960s boom, and was accused of covering it with drab high-rises and road schemes without any concern for its character. Many valuable historic buildings – such as the grand cafés of the Plaça Catalunya – were torn down to make way for bland modern business blocks, and minimal attention was paid to collective amenities.

After the years of repression and the years of development, 1966 marked the beginning of what became known as *tardofranquisme*, 'late Francoism'. Having made its opening to the outside world, the regime was losing its grip, and labour, youth and student movements began to emerge from beneath the shroud of repression. Nevertheless, the Franco regime never hesitated to show its strength. Strikes and demonstrations were dealt with savagely, and just months before the dictator's death the last person to be executed in Spain by the traditional method of the garrotte, a Catalan anarchist named Puig Antich, went to his death in Barcelona.

In 1973, however, Franco's closest follower, Admiral Carrero Blanco, had been assassinated by a bomb planted by the Basque terrorist group ETA, leaving no one to guard over the core values of the regime. Change was in the air.

GENERALISIMO TO GENERALITAT

When Franco died on 20 November 1975, the people of Barcelona took to the streets in celebration, and not a bottle of cava was left in the city by evening. But no one knew quite what was about to happen. The Bourbon monarchy was restored, under King Juan Carlos, but his attitudes and intentions were not clear. In 1976, he charged a little-known Francoist bureaucrat, Adolfo Suárez, prime minister, with leading the country to democracy.

The first years of Spain's 'transition' were difficult. Nationalist and other demonstrations continued to be repressed by the police with considerable brutality, and far-right groups threatened less open violence. However, political parties were legalised, and June 1977 saw the first democratic elections since 1936. They were won across Spain by Suárez's own new party, the Union de Centro Democratico (UCD), and in Catalonia by a mixture of Socialists, Communists and nationalists.

It was, again, not clear how Suárez expected to deal with the demands of Catalonia, but shortly after the elections he surprised everyone by going to visit the president of the Generalitat in exile, a veteran pre-Civil War politician, Josep Tarradellas. His office was the only institution of the old Republic to be so recognised, perhaps because Suárez astutely identified in the old man a fellow conservative. Tarradellas was invited to return as provisional president of a restored Generalitat, and arrived amid huge crowds in October 1977.

The following year, the first free council elections since 1936 were held in Barcelona. They were won by the Socialist Party, with Narcís Serra as Mayor. The party has retained control of the council ever since. In 1980, elections to the restored the Generalitat were won by Jordi Pujol and his party, Convergència i Unió, who held power for the next 23 years.

CITY OF DESIGN

Inseparable from the restoration of democracy was a complete change in the city's atmosphere after 1975. New freedoms – in culture, sexuality, and work – were explored, and newly released energies expressed in a multitude of ways. Barcelona soon began to look different too, as the inherent dowdiness of the Franco years was swept away by a new Catalan style for the new Catalonia: postmodern, high-tech, punkish, comic strip, minimalist and tautly fashionable. For a time, street culture was highly politicised, but simultaneously it was also increasingly hedonistic. In the 1980s, design mania struck the city, a product of unbottled energies and a rebirth of Barcelona's artistic, artisan and architectural traditions.

This emphasis on a slick, fresh style first began on a street and underground level, but the special feature of Barcelona was the extent to which it was taken up by public authorities, and above all the Ajuntament, as a part of their drive to reverse the policies of the regime. The highly educated technocrats in the Socialist city administration began, gradually at first, to 'recover' the city from its neglected state, and in doing so enlisted the elite of the Catalan intellectual and artistic community in their support. No one epitomises this more than Oriol Bohigas, the architect and writer who was long the city's head of culture and chief planner. A programme of urban renewal was initiated, beginning with the open spaces, public art and low-level initiatives, such as the campaign in which hundreds of historic façades were given an overdue facelift.

This ambitious, emphatically modern approach to urban problems acquired much greater focus after Barcelona's bid to host the 1992 Olympic Games was accepted, in 1986. Far more than just a sports event, the Games were to be Barcelona's third great effort to cast aside suggestions of second-city status and show the world its wares. The exhibitions of 1888 and 1929 had seen developments in the Ciutadella and on and around Montjuïc; the Olympics provided an opening for work on a citywide scale. Taking advantage of the public and private investment the games would attract, Barcelona planned an all-new orientation of itself toward the sea, in a programme of urban renovation of a scope unseen in Europe since the years of reconstruction after World War II.

Along with the creation of the new Barcelona in bricks and mortar went the city-sponsored promotion of Barcelona-as-concept, a seductive cocktail of architecture, imagination, tradition, style, nightlife and primary colours. This was perhaps the most spectacular – certainly the most deliberate – of Barcelona's reinventions; it succeeded in large part because this image of creativity and vivacity simply fitted well with an idea of the city already held by many of its citizens – it was as if the drab decades had been just a bad collective dream.

Who's who Jordi Pujol

Even before the surprises of the result, the Catalan elections of November 2003 were always going to mark a change of era. For the first time in the history of Catalonia's autonomous government, the leading candidate to preside over it would not be Jordi Pujol. After 23 years in office and six successive election victories, aged 73, the President of the Generalitat was finally retiring, although no one would bet on not hearing from him again.

Pujol and the Generalitat had often seemed inseparable. The 1992 Olympics – one of modern Catalonia's finest hours – saw the epitome of the Pujol style. Spanish Prime Minister Felipe González was oddly absent from the big event, and King Juan Carlos spent much of his time with the Spanish sports teams. Jordi Pujol, on the other hand, was in the front rank welcoming visiting dignitaries to his country as Mr President. This typified a central aspect of the Pujol approach to Catalonia's place in the world, carried off with formidable bumptiousness: behave like the leader of an independent country and people start to treat you like one.

The Pujol name first became known in 1960, when he led a demonstration that embarrassed Franco during a visit by the dictator to Barcelona. This earned Pujol two years in prison and a solid reputation in the anti-Franco resistance, despite his conservative brand of Catalanism. After his release, he developed his central idea of *fer pais*, 'making a country': denied all political rights, Catalonia would have to rebuild itself through creating its own institutions of all kinds in civil society – publishing, finance, sports, culture, business and more. As a father of seven Pujol also made his own contribution by counteracting the remarkably low Catalan birthrate, something that all Catalan nationalists have long been gravely concerned about. With democracy post-1975 he soon emerged as the foremost leader of mainstream Catalan nationalism, and his Convergència i Unió was the near-inevitable winner of the first elections to the restored Generalitat in 1980.

Catalan politics in the Pujol era were never lacking in personality. Barcelona sophisticates often find the Pujol style of nostalgic, folkloric Catalanism infuriating, but it has never failed to strike a chord in many parts of Catalonia, and there's probably no other politician in Spain who's so good at pressing the flesh and connecting with his own grass roots. Pujolism also embodies, tacitly if not overtly, a certain kind of Catalan attitude: that of someone who has no real emotional identification with Spain whatsoever, but recognises the practical reasons for tolerating the status quo.

Popular belief holds that as time goes by, 'Spain' will gradually exert less and less influence over day-to-day Catalan life. This is one prime source of the remarkable animosity towards Pujol personally seen in many other parts of Spain – especially among the PP – where he's routinely accused of blackmail and is seen as being devious. For his Catalan faithful though, this combination of artfulness and determination has always been one of his particular areas of strength.

Inseparable from all this was Pasqual Maragall, mayor of Barcelona from 1982 to 1997, a tireless 'Mr Barcelona' who appeared in every possible forum to expound his vision of the role of cities, and intervened personally to set the guidelines for projects or secure the participation of major international architects. In the process, Barcelona, a byword for modern blight only a few years before, was turned into a reference point in urban affairs. Maragall also established a personal popularity well beyond that of his Catalan Socialist Party (PSC).

ENDGAMES

The Games were finally held in July-August 1992 and universally hailed as an outstanding success. Barcelona and Catalonia rode out Spain's post-1992 recession better than any other part of the country. The Ajuntament announced still more large-scale projects, such as the old Port and the Raval. Pasqual Maragall, however, was to stand down amid general surprise in 1997, after winning a fifth term. He was succeeded as Mayor by his then little-known deputy, Joan Clos, who has held on to the Ajuntament ever since. Maragall, meanwhile, sought to work his electoral magic beyond the city limits by becoming the Socialist candidate for president of the Generalitat in the 1999 elections. He would not succeed, as once again Pujol was to triumph, thanks in no small part to his several years of successful horse-trading with the then minority PP central government (*see above* **Who's who: Jordi Pujol**).

With the years, the limitations of Pujolism have become more visible. The restoration of the Catalan language has been its greatest achievement, but many feel that Generalitat policy has also needlessly alienated Castilian speakers. Pujol was at his most inflated in the years of minority governments in Madrid, when it looked as if he could present them with demands from the Generalitat in return for Convergència support. This scenario finally collapsed, though, when Aznar won a majority in 2000, although, in retrospect, it has looked like a significant miscalculation. Freed from the much-resented need for horse-trading with the nationalists, the Aznar government has displayed a new and often belligerent assertiveness, calling for Spain to regain a sense of 'national unity' and reaffirming the powers of central government in the face of a decentralisation process that, it clearly feels has gone too far.

The emergence of this brand of 'Spanish neo-nationalism' has shown that Spain is not just going to go away quietly.

In 2001 Jordi Pujol finally announced, two years in advance, that he would not be standing for another term, and named his then deputy, Artur Mas, as his chosen successor. When new regional elections finally came round on 16 November 2003, though, the results defied all predictions. Maragall, media frontrunner for months, seemed once again to have been disappointed, as the PSC won a few more votes than Convergència, but also gained fewer seats in the Catalan parliament. For a short while it appeared Mas had triumphed, until it became clear that the real winners of the night, taking seats off both the 'majors', were previously-fringe left-wing parties – the 'eco-communists' of the ICV and above all Esquerra Republicana (ERC). It is directly descended from the old Esquerra of the 1930s, and it all but doubled its vote, so that in some areas as much as one-fifth of voters supported a party that, at least theoretically, is in favour of total or partial Catalan independence, and also rejects the Spanish monarchy. A whole month of wrangling followed, until it was announced that the PSC had agreed to form a left-wing coalition with the ERC and ICV, bringing Convergència's apparently eternal hold on local power to an end. Maragall would finally get the Generalitat, but only in return for a commitment to push strongly for a new Autonomy Statute – an idea that the Madrid government immediately condemned. More surprises are all but guaranteed, along with, eventually, some very tough decisions.

Key events

c15 BC Barcino founded by Roman soldiers.
cAD 350 Roman stone city walls built.
415 Barcelona briefly capital of Visigoths.
719 Muslims attack and seize Barcelona.
801 Barcelona taken by Franks.
985 Muslims sack Barcelona; Count Borrell II renounces Frankish sovereignty.
1035-76 Count Ramon Berenguer I of Barcelona extends his possessions into southern France.
1137 Count Ramon Berenguer IV marries Petronella of Aragon, uniting the two states in the Crown of Aragon.
1213 Pere I is killed and virtually all his lands north of the Pyrenees are seized by France.
1229 Jaume I conquers Mallorca, then Ibiza (1235) and Valencia (1238); second city wall built in Barcelona.
1274 Consell de Cent, municipal government of Barcelona, established.
1282 Pere II conquers Sicily.
1298 Gothic cathedral begun. Population of city c40,000.
1323-4 Conquest of Corsica and Sardinia.
1347-8 Black Death cuts population by half.
1462-72 Catalan civil war.
1479 Ferdinand II inherits Crown of Aragon, and, along with his wife Isabella, unites the Spanish kingdoms.
1492 Final expulsion of Jews, and the discovery of America.
1522 Catalans refused permission to trade in America.
1640 Catalan national revolt, the Guerra dels Segadors.
1652 Barcelona falls to Spanish army.
1702 War of Spanish Succession begins.
1714 Barcelona falls to Franco-Spanish army after siege.
1715 Nova Planta decree abolishes Catalan institutions; new ramparts and citadel built around Barcelona. Population c33,000.
1808-13 French occupation.
1814 Restoration of Ferdinand VII.
1833 Aribau publishes *Oda a la Pàtria*, beginning of Catalan cultural renaissance. Carlist wars begin.
1836-7 Dissolution of Barcelona monasteries.
1842-4 Barcelona bombarded for the last time from Montjuïc, to quell Jamancia revolt.
1854 Demolition of Barcelona city walls.
1855 First general strike is violently suppressed.
1859 Cerdà plan for the Eixample approved.
1868 September: revolution overthrows Isabel II. November: the first anarchist meetings are held in Barcelona.
1873 First Spanish Republic.
1874 Bourbon monarchy restored under Alfonso XII.
1882 Work begins on construction of the Sagrada Família.
1888 Barcelona Universal Exhibition.
1899 FC Barcelona founded; as are the first electric trams.
1900 Population of Barcelona 537,354.
1909 Setmana Tràgica, anti-church and anti-army riots.
1910 CNT anarchist workers' union is founded.
1921 First Barcelona Metro line opened.
1923 Primo de Rivera establishes dictatorship in Spain.
1929 Barcelona International Exhibition.
1930 Population 1,005,565. Fall of Primo de Rivera.
1931 14 April: Second Spanish Republic begins.
1934 October: Generalitat attempts revolt against new right-wing government in Madrid, and is then suspended.
1936 February: Popular Front wins Spanish elections; Catalan Generalitat restored. 19 July: military uprising against left-wing government is defeated in Barcelona.
1937 May: fighting within the republican camp in Barcelona.
1939 26 January: Barcelona taken by Franco's army.
1959 Stabilisation Plan opens up Spanish economy.
1975 20 November: Franco dies.
1977 First democratic general elections in Spain since 1936; provisional Catalan Generalitat re-established.
1978 First democratic local elections in Barcelona won by Socialists.
1980 Generalitat fully re-established under Jordi Pujol.
1982 Pasqual Maragall becomes mayor.
1992 Olympic Games held in Barcelona.
1996 Partido Popular wins Spanish elections.
1997 Joan Clos replaces Maragall as mayor.
2000 Partido Popular wins absolute majority in the Madrid parliament.
2003 Coalition of left-wing parties wins control of Generalitat.

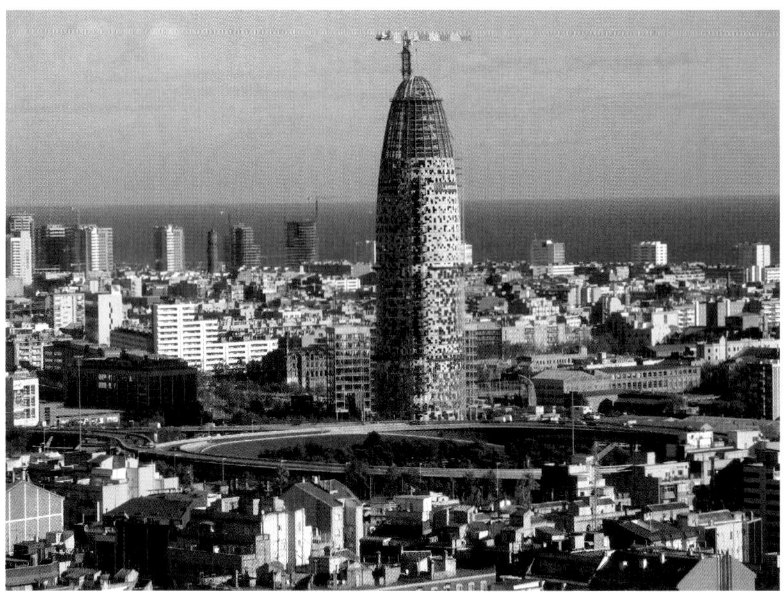

Barcelona Today

Reflecting on a year of solidarity and electoral surprises.

When the dust settled there was some disagreement about how many of Barcelona's residents really took to the streets on 15 February 2003 to protest against the imminent outbreak of war in Iraq. Two million, said the organisers; 200,000 counterclaimed the authorities in Madrid, to generalised derision. In fact a study by *El País*, using images taken by helicopter along the march and applying a 'three people per square metre' calculation, established the figure at a more reasonable 1.3 million. Whatever it was, it soon became clear that Barcelona had outdone London, Paris and New York, to hold the biggest anti-war demonstration in the world; an indication of the traditional enthusiasm with which the city's residents have always taken to the streets to protest peacefully, and not so peacefully (*see p12* **It's anarchy!**), against the powers that be – especially if those powers be in Madrid.

There was a nostalgic atmosphere on the march that day, as veteran anti-fascists rubbed shoulders with young anarchists, local celebrities, militant expats and tourists. Some felt that the old Barcelona was back and that the city was regaining its radical traditions after two decades of prosperity and political stability. But, the diversity of voices shouting '*¡No a la guerra!*' in February was a portrait of a Barcelona that had changed substantially since the big demonstrations of the early '80s; a city becoming more cosmopolitan and multicultural and beginning to discover the new and difficult challenges that this process entails.

NO PLACE LIKE HOME

Sit down with any *barceloní* for more than five minutes and the conversation will soon turn to the price of flats and the difficulty of buying one these days. The cost of a half-decent flat within central Barcelona has risen a back-breaking 60 per cent over the last three years, putting the price beyond the reach of most young couples on the lookout for independence – something that traditionally happens a lot later in Spain, where many of those aged 30 or

over are unembarrassed to enjoy the hospitality of *mamà*. Many are opting to move to the peripheries, choosing places like the urban sprawl of the huge satellite town L'Hospitalet, or the bucolic calm of La Floresta, only 20 minutes by train from Plaça Catalunya.

Meanwhile, vast shopping centres have sprung up in the suburbs, putting pressure on smaller shops in town and challenging the traditional notion of the Catalans as a nation of *botiguers* (shopkeepers). On central streets like C/Ferran, the old cafés are being replaced with fast-food chains and Irish pubs to cater for the transient tourists who now arrive en masse, and it is not uncommon to find local residents looking slightly bewildered by their own city. The new bête noir of Barcelona's residents is '*el especulador*' – the real estate entrepreneur who buys entire buildings in the centre of town, empties them of their unprofitable, old rent-paying residents and sells them on at an exorbitant price to those desperate for a place to call their own.

There is no doubt that life in the centre of Barcelona has changed substantially over the last few years, but arguably it has changed less than in most comparable European cities. Thanks to intervention by the council's famously hands-on urban planning authority, with initiatives that include rent-protected flats in the centre for young people and a moratorium on the granting of licences for big shops, Barcelona has managed to remain that rare thing among modern cities: a city with a centre where people actually want to live.

'CHARNEGO' POWER

In the 1960s, Barcelona's population swelled by nearly 50 per cent as hundreds of thousands of immigrants arrived from the poorer areas of Spain to work as cheap labour in the city's booming industries. Locals looked down upon these new arrivals, and the offensive epithet *charnego* was invented to describe them – a word derived from '*nocharnego*' or, 'someone that wanders the street at night'. An ethnic class system sprang up, dividing purebred Catalans from the Spaniards who served them in the bars, drove their taxis and worked in their factories. Now the children of these immigrants make up a substantial proportion of the population and are themselves Catalans, albeit with strong roots in other parts of Spain. Increasingly confident of their role within a new Catalan society, these are the people at the forefront of a cultural scene where *mestizaje* (the Spanish word for cultural and ethnic mix) is the new cool, typified by the wildly popular rumba-flamenco-hip hop fusion bands such as Ojos de Brujo or Manu Chao, heard everywhere.

But multiculturalism is a concept that sometimes sits uneasily in a small country that is intensely proud of its local traditions and has spent centuries defending them from the big Spanish brother next door. Some *catalanistes* have begun to voice concern that after the huge strides made since the end of the dictatorship, the 'normalisation' and promotion of Catalan as Barcelona's official language is in danger of taking a step back. Recent studies have shown that the vast majority of recent immigrants, mainly from Latin America, Pakistan and Eastern Europe – are choosing Spanish as their lingua franca, instead of Catalan. A recent campaign by the Generalitat urging local residents to 'adopt an immigrant' as a friend and give them free Catalan conversation classes did not prove a great success.

Yet, as the Catalan nationalist oligarchy wrings its hands and ex-President Jordi Pujol's wife worries aloud that 'our Romanesque churches will all become mosques', the reality on the streets tells a different story. In neighbourhoods like the Old City, Gràcia and Poble Sec, the inexorable transition to a new multiracial Barcelona is happening without any major headaches.

MAYOR NECESSITIES

Every year the Mayor gives a keynote speech to open the festivities of the four-day festival La Mercè, in honour of Barcelona's patron saint. Joan Clos, famous for his perfectly groomed, silver thatch and for previously having worked as an anaesthetist (his detractors have been known to suggest that he talked his patients to sleep) likes to make speeches (you can even find a 'best of' selection on the Barcelona council's website, www.bcn.es). Like a headmaster addressing his pupils at the end of term, in September 2003 Clos began by gently praising his citizens for their tolerance and optimism, but in the 'could do better' section made mention of the fact that Barcelona is slipping when it comes to *civisme*.

Barcelona council has sometimes been criticised for resembling a huge advertising agency in its efforts to define a 'Barcelona brand' and because of the money it devotes to campaigns – most successfully in the ubiquitous '*Barcelona, posa't guapa*' ('Barcelona, doll yourself up') campaign of the 1990s. Clos has announced that the next campaign will be dedicated to promoting *civisme*; in other words, stamping out such urban habits as shouting drunkenly in the streets, dumping rubbish about and pissing on your neighbour's doorstep. Volunteers will be forming 'civic brigades' that will take to the streets to 'inform and sensitize the uncivil' armed with leaflets and the power to

The **CiU** candidate declares 'Yes to Catalonia'. Catalonia declared 'No' to him.

issue small fines for bad behaviour. Barcelona's residents will tell you that most of the public nuisance is caused by visitors and the recently arrived, but some of the traditional habits that characterise the essence of the Mediterranean city (late opening hours, pavement cafés and improvised street parties) could conflict with the Mayor's efforts to create a more 'civilised' city.

POLITICS, POLICIES AND PACTS

For the first time since Franco's prolonged demise, the same political party is now in power in both the Generalitat (Catalonia's 800-year-old independent, autonomous government) and the Ajuntament (the city council). Socialist Pasqual Maragall, grandson of one of Barcelona's most famous poets, ex-Mayor of the city and scion of the left wing, intellectual Catalan elite traditionally distrusted in the rural heartlands, became President of Catalonia after weeks of uncertainty following an unclear result in the November 2003 local elections. In the end, the result hinged on the decision of a previously marginal radical Catalan nationalist party, the ERC, who had managed to double their parliamentary representation. This they achieved thanks largely to disillusionment with the two main parties and a clever policy of keeping their heads down while Maragall and his rival in the conservative CiU got stuck into each other with insults that ranged from the mild: *'corrupto'* (thief), to the serious: *'espanyolista'* (pro-Spaniard).

In the tradition of Catalan pragmatism and political doublespeak, ERC (Republican Left of Catalonia) prefer to call for a radical shake-up of the relationship between the autonomous regions and the Spanish state, instead of out and out independence; and nor are they particularly left-wing, regarded even by the more moderate of the socialists as traitors to the cause, more interested in nationalistic parochialism than social policy. In the end, ERC managed to surprise most by electing to form, alongside the Socialists and the Green Party, a three party 'progressive government' that gave Maragall the presidency, but more surprises were in store. Just as this guide was going to press, it become known that ERC's leader, Josep Carod Rovira, had held secret talks with ETA separatists, ostensibly to broker a peace deal, but without the knowledge of his party, let alone the new government. Carod resigned as Prime Minister, but with no obvious candidate to replace him, and Socialist leader, José Luis Rodríguez Zapatero, calling on his Catalan colleagues to end the alliance, the post – not to mention the future of the coalition – hung in the balance.

So, what do ERC actually stand for? By coincidence, 2003 was the year of the 25th anniversary of the Spanish constitution, the political agreement that was intended to finally end centuries of internecine arguments between Spain's nations by ceding autonomy, but leaving centralised power in Madrid and, essentially, keeping the notion of a Spanish state alive. However, things have changed since the rosy days of *la transición* and the right-wing ruling Popular Party now have a tight grip on the central government. For the PP, the constitution is perfect and inviolable and anyone suggesting otherwise is little better than a terrorist bent on the destruction of a nation. Parties like ERC are thriving on the divisiveness of Spanish politics and the intransigence that underlies both sides of the debate. For them, and for a host of other parties from the Basque country to Galicia, the Spanish constitution is 'a working paper' and needs to be rewritten to give more power to the autonomous regions, recognise the 'cultural difference' of each nation and (here's the rub) give them control of their own finances.

BADLANDS OF BARCELONA

Like most things in Spain, Barcelona's crime wave remains a seasonal phenomenon: when everyone is on holiday, the thieves are at work. Recent figures insist that street crime is dropping, but Barcelona's residents are increasingly concerned with their personal security and many believe that Barcelona is becoming a more dangerous place to live. In fact, a recent tragic case gave people the impression that Barcelona was becoming the South Bronx. A gang killed a young Colombian boy outside his school and the press sensed a juicy story when it soon emerged that a gang known as the Latin Kings had been active in the neighbourhood. Speculation was rife that young Ronny Tàpies had died as Barcelona's first victim of gangland violence. However, the Barcelona chapter of the Latin Kings – a gang inspired by Hispanics in LA – turned out to consist of a few teenage, Dominican tearaways with gangsta delusions. An unfortunate side effect of Ronny's death, however, was a further reinforcement of the public perception between immigration and crime. Police recently released figures that showed that 74 per cent of people arrested in the Old City had been immigrants. The fact that virtually all those arrested were '*sin papeles*' (illegal immigrants denied legal status and thus the possibility to look for work) was not lost on most people.

UN-RAVALLED

The Born area of Barcelona was recently described in the *New York Times* as 'cooler than Manhattan's Lower East Side'. Unfortunately, they got it wrong. The hippest area of Barcelona is now officially the Raval. As the Born got too expensive for anyone who isn't an advertising executive, and the tourist economy stripped it of its last vestiges of authenticity, the young and young at heart moved to the other side of La Rambla, to an area that has seen one of the most ambitious urban regeneration plans ever undertaken in Europe. Whole blocks of unsanitary and unstable buildings were torn down and a bright new *rambla* installed, to the delight of pram-pushing mothers and cricket-playing Pakistanis. A new street market now takes over the area on Saturdays and dreadlocks (fake and authentic) are becoming de rigueur. The Filmoteca is set to move from the stuffy Eixample to the area that is increasingly accepted as the centre of Barcelona's art scene.

'Anti-war sentiments united the city in a way difficult to imagine anywhere else.'

But while the area outdoes the rest of Barcelona in the hipness stakes it is also way ahead on some of the less desirable urban phenomena: crime, dirt, drugs and prostitution. The council's solution to give the Raval a further boost is not completely uncontroversial: it has decided to build a new five-star hotel on the Rambla to provide a new 'urban symbol' for the area. The Raval's residents, however, suspect otherwise. Why put a huge, ultra-posh hotel in a place where many tourists fear to tread? Do they want the Raval to go the way of the Born? Whatever happens, it won't go quietly.

WAR CRIES

Barcelona became the city of peace during the war. Balconies hung with anti-war slogans that ranged from the sublime 'Lee Harvey Oswald, where are you now the world needs you?' to the ridiculous 'Less bombs, more bums'. The *cacerolada*, a new form of civic protest, was imported from Argentina and at 10 o'clock every night Barcelona's residents, from grannies to squatters, took their kitchenware out on to their streets, rooftops and balconies and pounded the living daylights out of them for 15 perfect minutes of protest.

Of course, the council got in on this feeling of civic solidarity, producing thousands of funkily designed '*Barcelona per la pau*' ('Barcelona for peace') stickers that still sit in local government offices around the city. A peace camp was set up by pacifists in the Plaça Sant Jaume in front of the government offices and, remarkably, left alone by the police. These sentiments seemed to unite the whole city in a way that would be difficult to imagine anywhere else. Once again, Barcelona residents were demonstrating the 'Olympic spirit' that had made their city unique: solidarity, energy and a rare sense of civic pride. The question is: how will Barcelona harness that energy in the future?

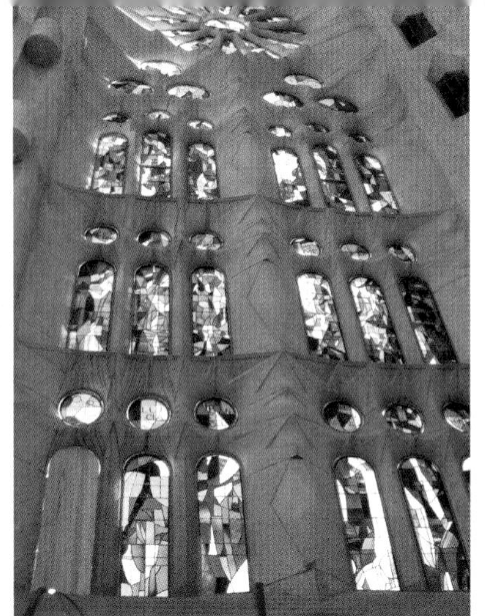

Architecture

The art of Barcelona.

Where other countries might use painting, music or other art forms to express their national identity, Catalonia has always used architecture, taking in ideas, attitudes and trends from abroad and assimilating them into a strong local culture. Those periods of greater Catalan freedom of action and self-expression, coupled with greater wealth, have bequeathed most of the city's finest architecture.

Catalan builders have always shown a liking for decorating surfaces, along with a concern with texture and the use of fine materials and finishes. This is combined with a simplicity of line and sense of sobriety often seen as distinguishing Catalan character from that of the rest of Spain. Other common elements are references to the traditional architecture of rural Catalonia – the large stone farmhouses, with chalet-type tile roofs, massive stone walls and round-arched doorways, a style maintained by anonymous builders for centuries – and to the powerful constructions of Catalan Romanesque and Gothic. There has also long been a close relationship between architects and craftsmen in the production of buildings, especially in the working of metal and wood.

Modern Catalans have an impressive sense of contributing to their architectural heritage in the present day, rather than preserving it as a relic. Contemporary buildings are daringly constructed alongside (or within) old ones, and this mix of old and new is a prime characteristic of many of the most successful projects seen in Barcelona over the past two decades. The importance of architecture is also reflected in public attitudes; Barcelona's citizens take a keen interest in their buildings. A range of architectural guides is available, some in English, and informative leaflets on building styles are also provided (in English) at tourist offices (*see p319*).

ROMAN TO GOTHIC

The Roman citadel of Barcino was founded on the hill of Mons Taber, just behind the cathedral, which to this day remains the religious and civic heart of the city. It left an important legacy in the fourth-century city wall, fragments of which are visible at many points around the Old City.

Barcelona's next occupiers, the Visigoths, left little in the city, although a trio of fine Visigothic churches survives nearby in Terrassa. When the Catalan state began to form under the Counts of Barcelona from the ninth century, the dominant architecture of this new community was massive, simple Romanesque. In the Pyrenean valleys there are hundreds of fine Romanesque buildings, notably at **Sant Pere de Rodes**, **Ripoll**, **Sant Joan de les Abadesses** and **Besalú**. There is, however, relatively little in Barcelona.

On the right-hand side of the cathedral, looking at the main façade, is the 13th-century **chapel of Santa Llúcia**, incorporated into the later building; tucked away near Plaça Catalunya is the **church of Santa Anna**; and in La Ribera there is the tiny travellers' chapel, the **Capella d'en Marcús**. The city's greatest Romanesque monument, though, is the beautifully plain 12th-century church and cloister of **Sant Pau del Camp**, built as part of a larger monastery.

By the 13th century, Barcelona was the capital of a trading empire, and was growing rapidly. The settlements – called *ravals* or *vilanoves* – that had sprung up outside the Roman walls were brought within the city by the building of Jaume I's second set of walls, which extended west to the Rambla.

This commercial growth and political eminence formed the background to the great flowering of Catalan Gothic (*see p34* **Novel Gothic**), with the construction of many of the city's most important civic and religious buildings. The **cathedral** was begun in 1298, in place of an 11th-century building. Work began on the **Ajuntament** (Casa de la Ciutat) and **Palau de la Generalitat** – later subject to extensive alteration – in 1372 and 1403 respectively. Major additions were made to the **Palau Reial** of the Catalan-Aragonese kings, especially the **Saló del Tinell** of 1359-62. The great hall of the Llotja was finished in 1380-92. Many of Barcelona's finest buildings were built or completed in these years, in the midst of the crisis that followed the Black Death.

The architecture of medieval Barcelona, at least that of its noble and merchant residences, can be seen at its best in the line of palaces along **Carrer Montcada**, next to Santa Maria. Built by the city's merchant elite at the height of their confidence and wealth, these conform to a very Mediterranean style of urban palace, and make maximum use of space. A plain exterior faces the street, with heavy doors opening into an imposing patio, on one side of which a grand external staircase leads to the main rooms on the first floor (*planta noble*), which often have elegant open loggias.

MARKING TIME

By the beginning of the 16th century, political and economic decline meant there were far fewer patrons for new building in the city. In the next 300 years a good deal was built, but rarely in any distinctively Catalan style, with the result that these structures have often been disregarded. In the 1550s, the **Palau del Lloctinent** was built for the royal viceroys on one side of Plaça del Rei, while in 1596 the present main façade was added to the

Modernisme

Manzana de la Discòrdia
Gaudí's utterly original Casa Batlló, Puig i Cadafalch's cautious, medievalist Casa Amatller and the lush curves of Domènech i Montaner's Casa Lleó Morera. *See p117.*

Palau de la Música Catalana
Domènech's extraordinary concert hall is the epitome of Modernisme; the explosion in tile, sculpture and glass makes any event here special. *See p39.*

Sagrada Família
Modernisme's most eccentric, ambitious monument. *See p124.*

Park Güell
An incomplete, tantalising vision of Gaudí's ideal world. *See p125.*

La Pedrera
Gaudí's most successful combination of imagination and radical architectural innovation. *See p121.*

Hotel España
Domènech designed the bar, Eusebi Arnau the curvaceous fireplace, and the main dining room is adorned with water nymph murals in paint and tile by Ramon Casas. *See p57.*

Palau Güell
Beyond the striking exterior is a wonderful Gaudí interior. *See p96.*

Parc de la Ciutadella
Domènech's 'Castle of Three Dragons' sums up the fairy-tale side of Modernisme, but is also highly innovative in its use of iron, glass and brick. *See p38.*

MNAC
Painting by Rusiñol, Casas and Nonell, and decorative art move here from the defunct Museu d'Art Modern, but nothing can be seen until autumn 2004. *See p114.*

Fàbrica Casaramona
Puig's former textile mill is a prime example of Modernista industrial building. *See p40.*

Hospital de Sant Pau
One of the most successful examples of the application of Modernista style and vivid decoration to a very practical purpose. *See p119.*

Novel Gothic

Catalan Gothic has provided the historic benchmark for all Catalan architecture, continually echoed and referred to in later buildings, from the medievalist Modernista fancies of Domènech i Montaner down to contemporary creations. It is a very distinctive style, with many characteristics that mark it off clearly from the more classic, northern European Gothic style.

Medieval cathedral-builders in France, England or Germany were intoxicated by leaping buttresses and the spaces between them, and the creation of soaring, airy space with lace-like windows to give a sense of weightlessness. Catalan Gothic, in contrast, is much simpler, even severe, and gives more emphasis to huge, solid stone walls between towers and columns than to empty space.

Generalitat, in an Italian Renaissance style. The Church also built lavishly, with baroque convents and churches along La Rambla, of which the **Betlem** (1680-1729), at the corner of C/Carme, is the most important survivor. Later baroque churches include **Sant Felip Neri** (1721-52) and **La Mercè** (1765-75).

Another addition, after the siege of Barcelona in 1714, was new military architecture, since the city was encased in ramparts and fortresses. Examples remaining include the **Castell de Montjuïc**, the buildings in the **Ciutadella**, and the **Barceloneta**.

A more positive 18th-century alteration was the conversion of the Rambla into a paved promenade, begun in 1775 with the demolition of Jaume I's second wall. Neo-classical palaces were built alongside: **La Virreina** and the **Palau Moja** (at the corner of C/Portaferrisa) both date from the 1770s. Also from that time but in a less classical style is the **Gremial dels Velers** (Candlemakers' Guild) at Via Laietana 50, with its two-coloured stucco decoration.

It was not, however, until the closure of the monasteries in the 1820s and '30s that major rebuilding on the Rambla could begin. Most of the first constructions that replaced them were still in international, neo-classical styles. The site that is now the **Mercat de la Boqueria** was first remodelled in 1836-40 as Plaça Sant Josep to a design by Francesc Daniel Molina, based on the English Regency style of John Nash. It is buried beneath the 1870s market building, but its Doric colonnade can still be

In façades, as much emphasis is given to horizontals as to verticals, and the octagonal towers at corners end in cornices and flat roofs, not in spires. Again, while French cathedrals often had entire façades covered in carved decoration, Catalans used such intricacies only sparingly, confining them usually to portals, arches, gargoyles and rose windows, all between great swathes of plain unforgiving stone wall.

The result is a building style that seems to be much more massive than it actually is. It also has much more of a monumental simplicity, to the extent that sometimes Catalan 14th-century buildings don't even seem Gothic at all (the original unfinished façade of Barcelona cathedral was deemed much too plain for 19th-century Barcelona, and so was finished off in the 1900s to the current far more ornate, French-influenced design). As art historian Robert Hughes has pointed out, many Catalan Gothic churches retain something of the cave about them. Many of them have no aisles but only a single wide nave. The classic example in Barcelona is the lovely, undervisited **Santa Maria del Pi** in Plaça del Pi (*see p81*). It was built between 1322 and 1453, and has a distinctly broad, squat and massive – rather than a lofty or soaring – grandeur.

The virtues of Catalan simplicity can be seen at their finest, though, in the supreme achievement of Catalan Gothic, **Santa Maria del Mar** in the Born (*pictured and see p98*). Inside this church, perfectly proportioned, elegant columns – exceptionally widely spaced for a medieval building – create an impression of quite staggering beauty despite their plainness, with a magical timelessness that truly goes beyond any dated style. A comparable civic building might be the **Drassanes**, built from 1378 as the royal shipyards (and now the Museu Marítim), which is really just a very beautiful shed, but its enormous parallel aisles make this one of the most imposing spaces in the city.

Another contrast with northern Gothic was that Catalan Gothic was more closely related to the previous great medieval architecture of Catalonia – the also plain Romanesque of **Sant Pau del Camp** or the Pyrenean churches – and, notably, to the folk architecture of the Catalan mountains, the building styles of the *masia* farmhouses that in their basics seem to have changed little in over 1,000 years. This can be seen particularly in many of the non-religious buildings of medieval Barcelona, in the giant arched stone doorway in the original façade of the **Ajuntament**, or in the beautifully shaded patios of the **Palau del Lloctinent** or the **Hospital de Santa Creu**.

Robust, elegant and practical, Catalan Gothic was also capable of technical much innovation. This can be seen at its best in another of the era's soaring achievements, the Saló del Tinell banqueting hall in the **Palau Reial**. Designed in 1359 by Pere III's court architect Guillem Carbonell, it consists of six giant arches supporting a timber roof. These still rank among the largest purely masonry arches in Europe. With plain walls at either end, the hall verges on minimalist, but the sheer scale and elegance of the arches give it tremendous splendour.

detected. Molina also designed the **Plaça Reial**, begun in 1848. Other fine examples from the same era are the colonnaded **Porxos d'en Xifré**, the 1836 blocks opposite the Llotja on Passeig Isabel II, by the Port Vell.

BIRTH OF THE MODERN CITY

In the 1850s, Barcelona was able to expand physically, with the demolition of the walls, and psychologically, with economic expansion and the cultural reawakening of the Catalan Renaixença. And from the first, one could see in operation one of the characteristics of modern Barcelona – audacious planning. The city would spread outwards and be connected up to Gràcia and other outlying towns through the great grid of the **Eixample**, designed by **Ildefons Cerdà** (1815-75). An engineer by trade, Cerdà was also a radical influenced by utopian socialist ideas, concerned with the cramped, unhealthy conditions of workers' housing in the old city.

With its love of straight lines and grids, his plan was closely related to visionary rationalist ideas of its time, as was the idea of placing two of its main avenues along a geographic parallel and a meridian. Cerdà's central aim was to alleviate over-population problems while encouraging social equality by using quadrangular blocks of a standard size, with strict building controls to ensure that they were built only on two sides, to a limited height, with a garden. Each district would be of 20 blocks, with all community necessities.

In the event, though, this idealised use of urban space was rarely achieved, for private developers regarded Cerdà's restrictions as pointless interference. Buildings exceeded planned heights, and all the blocks from Plaça Catalunya to the Diagonal were enclosed. Even the planned gardens failed to withstand the onslaught of construction.

However, the development of the Eixample did see the refinement of a specific type of building: the apartment block, with giant flats on the *principal* floor (first above the ground), often with large glassed-in galleries for the drawing room, and small flats above. In time, the interplay between the Eixample's straight lines and the disorderly tangle of the older city became an essential part of the city's identity.

MODERNISME

The influence of art nouveau across Europe and to the Americas became, between 1890 and 1914, the leading movement in the decorative arts. Here, its influence merged forcefully with the cultural and political movement of the Catalan Renaixença to produce what became known as Modernisme (used here in Catalan to avoid confusion with 'modernism' in English, which refers to 20th-century functional styles).

For all of Catalonia's many long and varied traditions in building and the arts, no style is as synonymous with it than Modernisme. This is in part due to the enormous modern popularity of its most famous proponent, Gaudí, and with its mix of unrestrained decoration, eccentric unpredictability, dedicated craftsmanship and solid practicality. Modernisme can also be seen as matching certain archetypes of Catalan character. It was a passionately nationalist expression that made use of Catalan traditions of design and craftwork. Artists strove to revalue the best of Catalan art, showing enormous interest in the Romanesque and Gothic of the Catalan Golden Age; Domènech i Muntaner, for example, combined iron frame construction with distinctive brick Catalan styles from the Middle Ages, regarding them as an 'expression of the Catalan earth'.

All art nouveau had a tendency to look backwards and forwards simultaneously, combining a love of decoration with new industrial techniques and materials, and so it was in Catalonia. Modernista architects, even as they constructed a nostalgic vision of the ideal Catalan motherland, plunged into experimentation with the newest technology.

Encouraged by wealthy patrons, they designed works of iron and glass, introduced electricity, water and gas piping to their building plans, were the first to tile bathroom and kitchen walls, made a point of allowing extensive natural light and fresh air into all rooms, and toyed with the most advanced, revolutionary expressionism.

Catalan Modernista creativity was at its peak from 1888 to 1908. The Eixample is the style's display case, with the greatest concentration of art nouveau in Europe, but Modernista buildings can be found in innumerable other locations: in streets behind the Avda Paral.lel or villas on Tibidabo, in shop interiors or dark hallways, in country town halls or the cava cellars of the Penedès.

'More than any other form of art nouveau, Modernisme extended into literature, thought and music.'

International interest in Gaudí often eclipses the fact that there were many other remarkable architects and designers working at that time, and Modernisme was much more than an architectural style. The movement included painters such as **Ramón Casas**, **Santiago Rusiñol** and **Isidre Nonell**, sculptors such as **Josep Llimona**, **Miquel Blay** and **Eusebi Arnau**, and furniture makers like the superb Mallorcan, **Gaspar Homar**; and, much more than any other form of art nouveau, it extended into literature, thought and music, marking a whole generation of Catalan writers, poets, composers and philosophers. Although it was in architecture that it found its most splendid expression, Modernisme was an artistic movement in the fullest sense of the word.

Seen as the genius of the Modernista movement, **Antoni Gaudí i Cornet** was really a one-off, an unclassifiable figure. His work was a product of the social and cultural context of the time, but also of his own unique perception of the world, together with a deep patriotic devotion to anything Catalan. Unlike Domènech i Montaner and Puig i Cadafalch, who were public figures who took an active part in politics and other fields, Gaudí, after being fairly sociable as a youth, became increasingly eccentric, leading a semi-monastic existence, lost in his own obsessions.

Born in Reus in 1852, he qualified as an architect in 1878. His first architectural work was as assistant to Josep Fontseré in the 1870s on the building of the **Parc de la Ciutadella** where the gates and fountain are attributed to him. Around the same time he also designed the lamp-posts in the **Plaça Reial**. His first major commission was for **Casa Vicens** in Gràcia, built between 1883 and 1888 for Manuel Vicens, a tile manufacturer. An orientalist fantasy, it is

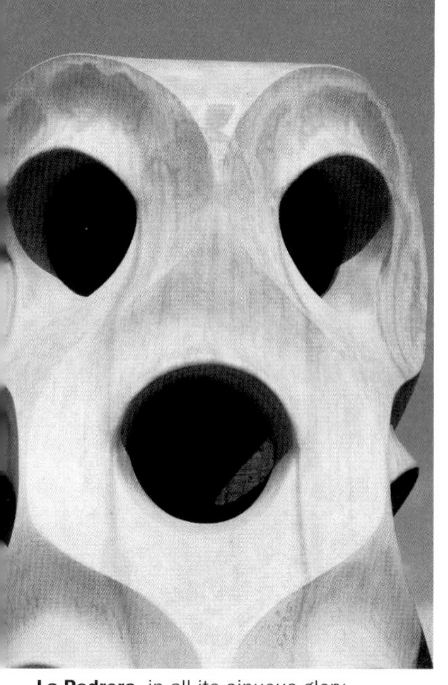
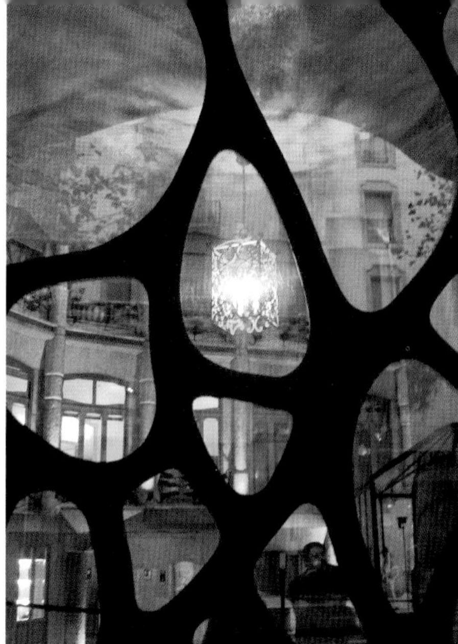

La Pedrera, in all its sinuous glory.

fairly conventional structurally, but Gaudí's control of the use of surface material already stands out in the neo-Moorish decoration, multicoloured tiling and the superbly elaborate ironwork on the gates. Gaudí's **Col.legi de les Teresianes** convent school (1888-9) is more restrained, but the clarity and fluidity of the building, with its simple finishes and use of light, is very appealing.

An event of crucial importance in Gaudí's life came in 1878, when he met Eusebi Güell, heir to one of the largest industrial fortunes in Catalonia. Güell had been impressed by Gaudí's early furniture, and the pair shared many ideas on religion, philanthropy and on the socially redemptive role of architecture. Güell placed utter confidence in his architect, allowing him to work with complete liberty. Gaudí produced several buildings for Güell, the first being the **Palau Güell** (1886-8), a darkly impressive, historicist building that firmly established his reputation, and the crypt at **Colònia Güell** outside Barcelona, one of his most structurally experimental and surprising buildings.

In 1883, Gaudí became involved in the design of the **Sagrada Família**, begun the previous year. He would eventually devote himself to it entirely. Gaudí was profoundly religious, and an extreme Catholic conservative; part of his obsession with the building was a belief that it would help redeem Barcelona from the sins of secularism and the modern era (some conservative Catalan Catholics have long campaigned for him to be made a saint). From 1908 until his death he worked on no other projects, often sleeping on site, a shabby, white-haired hermit, producing visionary ideas that his assistants had to interpret into drawings (on show in the museum alongside).

The Sagrada Família became the testing ground for Gaudí's ideas on structure and form, although he would live to see the completion of only the crypt, apse and nativity façade, with its representation of 30 species of plants. As his work matured he abandoned historicism and developed free-flowing, sinuous expressionist forms. His boyhood interest in nature began to take over from more architectural references, and what had previously provided external decorative motifs became the inspiration for the actual structure of his buildings.

In his greatest years, Gaudí combined other commissions with his cathedral. **La Pedrera**, begun in 1905, was his most complete project. It has an aquatic feel about it: the balconies resemble seaweed, and the undulating façade the sea, or rocks washed by it. Interior patios are in blues and greens, and the roof resembles an imaginary landscape inhabited by mysterious figures. The **Casa Batlló**, on the other side of Passeig de Gràcia, was an existing building that Gaudí remodelled in 1905-7; the roof looks like a reptilian creature perched high above the street. The symbolism of the façade is the source of endless speculation. Some link it to the myth of St George and the dragon; others maintain it is a

Who's who Ricard Bofill

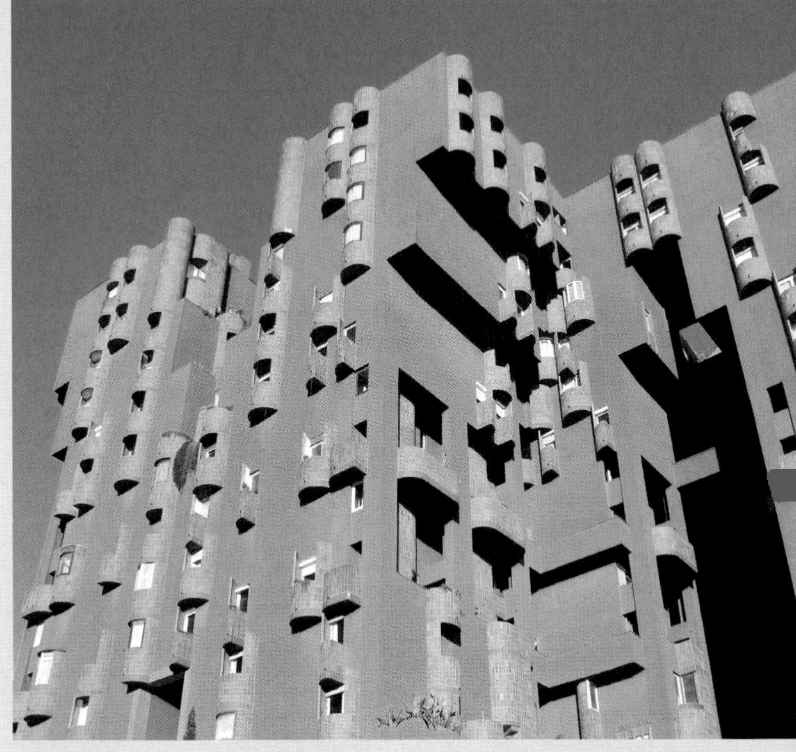

celebration of carnival, with its harlequin hat roof, its wrought-iron balcony 'masks' and the cascading, confetti-like tiles – this last element was an essential contribution of **Josep Maria Jujol**, who was, many believe, even more skilled than his master as a mosaicist.

Gaudí's later work has a uniquely dreamlike quality. His fascination with natural forms found full expression in the **Park Güell** (1900-14), where he blurred the distinction between natural and artificial forms in a series of colonnades winding up the hill. These paths lead up to the large central terrace projecting over a hall; a forest of distorted Doric columns planned as the marketplace for Güell's proposed 'garden city'. The terrace benches are covered in some of the finest examples of *trencadís* (broken mosaic work), again mostly by Jujol.

In June 1926, Antoni Gaudí was run over by a tram on the Gran Via. Nobody recognised the down-at-heel old man, and he was taken to a public ward in the old Hospital de Santa Creu in the Raval. When his identity was discovered, Barcelona gave its most famous architect a funeral so grand it was almost a state burial.

Modernista architecture received a vital, decisive boost around the turn of the century from the **Universal Exhibition of 1888**. The most important buildings for the show were planned by the famed **Lluís Domènech i Montaner** (1850-1923), who was then far more prominent than Gaudí as a propagandist for Modernisme in all its forms, and much more of a classic Modernista architect. Most of the Exhibition buildings no longer exist, but one that does is the **Castell dels Tres Dragons**

Ricard Bofill is one of the world-class stars of architecture, and is certainly one of the most controversial. He has designed flagship buildings in Paris, Chicago, Tokyo and Beijing, whole districts in Luxembourg, Warsaw and Madrid, and an entire town – Antigone – in the south of France. An eclectic with an eye for mixing styles, one of his current projects is a brand new capital city for Algeria. Yet in his home city (he was born in Barcelona in 1939, and continues to live and work here) he is still generally overlooked in the major architectural overhauls in which the city periodically indulges; and among intellectual circles the mention of his name often results in a grunt of disdain.

His first project in 1974 was a block of flats in the brutalist style – the Walden 7 complex in the suburbs of Sant Just (*pictured*). The idea was to create a community in which rich and poor (flats vary in size) live together using the same amenities; there's a bar and a chemist's, a betting shop and a vet. It didn't work; inside it's a gloomy labyrinth; inmates in their cells. From outside, the building's belly looms over you, a monster made of Lego. The further you are from it, however, the better it looks, a triumph of design over function.

Two constructions in the 1990s further tarnished Bofill's local reputation. Barcelona airport's international terminal, redesigned before the Olympics, looked beautiful when the extra tourists started coming in. Then the indoor palm trees died from lack of light and air and the paving started to crack... by 2002 *La Vanguardia* newspaper was talking about a 'Third World' amenity. Bofill wasn't, therefore, a popular choice in 1997 to design Catalonia's National Theatre.

But he did it anyway, and in a neo-classical style that was an affront to many Catalans who equate Doric columns with the Franco years. Still, it is a beautiful building. The power of the thick columns communes with the delicacy of the glass-and-scaffold façade. It also lights up spectacularly at night – highlighting to many the unfashionable classical symmetry of its elegant façade.

The architect attributes his unpopularity in Barcelona to the provincial obsession with fashion, and has stated that he would have done better for himself if he had been born in Washington or Beijing, where people are more 'broadminded'. He detests what he sarcastically calls the 'radical versatility' of the intellectual elite of Barcelona, whom he sees as radical only when the latest trend comes along.

Despite his against-the-flow opinions, Bofill has been chosen to design a building that will soon change the skyscape of Barcelona, a 100-metre (328-foot) hotel in the shape of a sail that will loom over Barceloneta beach. It will be one of the first things you will see from aeroplane or boat as you approach town, an important city landmark, and will mean the architect will leave a valuable legacy in his home city. Perhaps, too, there is a hint of more to come: Bofill has pointed his sail towards, not away from, Barcelona.

in the Ciutadella park, designed to be the exhibition restaurant and now the **Museu de Zoologia**. It already demonstrated many key features of Modernista style: the use of structural ironwork allowed greater freedom in the creation of openings, arches and windows; and plain brick, instead of the stucco usually applied to most buildings in Barcelona, was used in an exuberantly decorative manner.

Domènech was one of the first Modernista architects to develop the idea of the 'total work', working closely with large teams of craftsmen and designers on every aspect of a building. Not in vain was he dubbed 'the great orchestra conductor' by his many admirers.

His greatest creations are the **Hospital de Sant Pau**, built as small 'pavilions' within a garden to avoid the usual effect of a monolithic hospital, and the fabulous **Palau de la Música Catalana**, an extraordinary display of outrageous decoration. He also left quite a few impressive constructions in Reus, near Tarragona, notably the ornate mansions **Casa Navàs** and **Casa Rull**, as well as the spectacular pavilions of the **Institut Pere Mata**, a psychiatric hospital and forerunner of the Hospital de Sant Pau.

Third in the trio of leading Modernista architects was **Josep Puig i Cadafalch** (1867-1957), who showed a neo-Gothic influence in such buildings as the **Casa de les Punxes** (or the 'House of Spikes', officially the **Casa Terrades**) in the Diagonal, combined with many traditional Catalan touches. Nearby on Passeig de Sant Joan, at No.108, is another of his masterpieces, the **Casa Macaya**, its inner courtyard inspired by the medieval palaces of C/Montcada. Puig was responsible for some of the best industrial architecture of the time, an area in which Modernisme excelled: the Fundació La Caixa's cultural centre recently moved from Casa Macaya to another of Puig i Cadafalch's striking creations, the **Fábrica Casaramona** at Montjuïc, built as a textile mill, and outside Barcelona he designed the extraordinary **Caves Codorniu** wine cellars. His best-known work, however, is the **Casa Amatller**, between Domènech's **Casa Lleó Morera** and Gaudí's **Casa Batlló** in the **Manzana de la Discòrdia**.

'By 1910, Modernisme was too extreme for the middle class, and Gaudí's later buildings met with derision.'

These are the famous names of Modernista architecture, but there were many others, for the style caught on with extraordinary vigour throughout Catalonia. Some of the most engaging architects are the least known internationally. Impressive apartment blocks and mansions were built in the Eixample by **Joan Rubió i Bellver** (Casa Golferichs, Gran Via 491), **Salvador Valeri** (Casa Comalat, Avda Diagonal 442) and **Josep Vilaseca**. North of Barcelona is La Garriga, Catalonia's Baden-Baden, where MJ Raspall built exuberant summer houses for the rich and fashionable families of the time, and there are some dainty Modernista residences in many towns along the coast, such as Canet and Arenys de Mar. Some of the finest Modernista industrial architecture is in Terrassa, designed by the municipal architect **Lluís Moncunill** (1868-1931), while another local architect, **Cèsar Martinell**, built co-operative cellars that are true 'wine cathedrals' in Falset, Gandesa and many other towns in southern Catalonia.

THE 20TH CENTURY

By the 1910s, Modernisme had become too extreme for the Barcelona middle class, and the later buildings of Gaudí, for example, were met with derision. The new 'proper' style for Catalan architecture was Noucentisme, which stressed the importance of classical proportions. However, it failed to produce anything of much note: the main buildings that survive are those of the 1929 Exhibition, Barcelona's next 'big event', which was also the excuse for the bizarre, neo-baroque **Palau Nacional**.

The 1929 Exhibition also brought the city one of the most important buildings of the century: Mies van der Rohe's German Pavilion, the **Pavelló Barcelona**, rebuilt near its original location in 1986. Even today it is modern in its challenge to the conventional ideas of space, and its impact at the time was extraordinary. Mies had a strong influence on the main new trend in Catalan architecture of the 1930s, which, reacting against Modernisme and nearly all earlier Catalan styles, was quite emphatically functionalist. Its leading figures were **Josep Lluís Sert** and the **GATCPAC** collective (Group of Catalan Architects and Technicians for the Progress of Contemporary Architecture), who struggled to introduce the ideas of their friend Le Corbusier and of the International Style to local developers. Under the Republic, Sert built a sanatorium off C/Tallers, and the **Casa Bloc**, a workers' housing project at Passeig Torres i Bages 91-105 in Sant Andreu. In collaboration with Le Corbusier, the GATCPAC also produced a plan for the radical redesign of the whole of Barcelona as a 'functional city', the **Pla Macià** of 1933-4; drawings for the scheme present a Barcelona that looks more like a Soviet-era new town in Siberia, so few regret that it never got off the drawing board. In 1937, Sert also built the Spanish Republic's pavilion for that year's Paris Exhibition, since rebuilt in Barcelona as the **Pavelló de la República** in the Vall d'Hebron. His finest work, however, came much later, in the **Fundació Joan Miró**, built in the 1970s after he had spent many years in exile in the United States.

BARCELONA'S THIRD STYLE

The Franco years had an enormous impact on the city: as the economy expanded at breakneck pace in the 1960s, Barcelona received a massive influx of migrants, in a context of unchecked property speculation and of minimal planning controls. The city was ringed by a chaotic mass of high-rise suburbs. Another legacy of the era are some ostentatiously tall office blocks, especially on the Diagonal and around Plaça Francesc Macià.

Hence, when an all-new democratic city administration finally took over the reins of Barcelona at the end of the 1970s, there was a great deal for them to do. But, even though a generation of Catalan architects had been chafing at Francoist restrictions for years, the tone set early on, above all by Barcelona's ubiquitous chief planner Oriol Bohigas – who has also continued to design individual buildings as part of the MBM partnership with Josep Martorell and David Mackay – was one of 'architectural realism', with a powerful combination of imagination and practicality. Budgets were limited, so it was decided that resources should initially be concentrated not

The exquisite, flamboyant **Palau de la Música Catalana**. *See p39.*

on buildings, but the gaps between them – the public spaces – with a string of fresh, modern parks and squares, many of them incorporating original artwork. From this beginning, Barcelona placed itself in the forefront of international urban design.

Barcelona's renewal programme took on a far more ambitious shape with the award of the 1992 Olympics, helped by a booming economy in the late 1980s. Third and most spectacular of the city's great events, the Barcelona Games were intended to be stylish and innovative, but most of all to provide a focus for a sweeping renovation of the city, with emblematic new buildings and infrastructure projects linked by clear strategic planning.

The three main Olympic sites – **Vila Olímpica**, **Montjuïc** and **Vall d'Hebron** – are quite different. The Vila Olímpica had the most comprehensive masterplan, drawn up by Bohigas and MBM themselves, which sought to extend Cerdà's grid down to the seafront. The main project on Montjuïc was to be the transformation of the existing 1929 stadium, but alongside it there is also Arata Isozaki's **Palau Sant Jordi**, with its space-frame roof. Vall d'Hebron is the least successful of the three sites, but Esteve Bonell's **Velòdrom** is one of the finest (and earliest) of the sports buildings, built before the Olympic bid in 1984.

Not content with all the projects completed by 1992, the city continued to expand through the '90s, as one major scheme followed another. Post-1992, the main focus of activity shifted to the **Raval** and the **Port Vell** (old port), and then more recently to the Diagonal-Mar area in the north of the city. Many striking buildings are by local architects, such as Helio Piñón and Albert Viaplana, whose work combines fluid, elegant lines with a strikingly modern use of materials, from the controversial 1983 **Plaça dels Països Catalans** through daring transformations of historic buildings such as the Casa de la Caritat, now the **Centre de Cultura Contemporània**, and all-new projects like **Maremàgnum** in the port.

Other recent projects are all by international names: Richard Meier's bold white **MACBA**, and Norman Foster's **Torre de Collserola** on Tibidabo, one of many new emblems for Barcelona's skyline. Another major acquisition, the giant, box-like **Auditori**, is by a Madrid-based Spanish architect (a fairly rare thing in close-knit Barcelona), Rafael Moneo. And, finally, at the time of writing, Richard Rogers is hard at work converting the *mudéjar* arches of the **Las Arenas bullring** into a big and futuristic shopping and leisure centre for which the city has high hopes.

Most of the recent changes to the cityscape, however, are linked to the **Fòrum Universal de les Cultures** (*see p218* **Fòrum 2004**). The area at the mouth of the Besòs river, near where Avda Diagonal meets the sea, has been completely transformed for the occasion, most notably with the construction of a glittering triangular building, the **Edifici Fòrum**, which was designed by Herzog and de Meuron of Tate Modern fame. Nearby the late Catalan architect Enric Miralles (best known for the Scottish Parliament building) has created a fiercely modern and somewhat soulless park, the **Parc Diagonal-Mar**. Looming above from the Plaça de les Glòries is Jean Nouvel's blatantly phallic 142-metre (466-foot) office building, the **Torre Agbar**. All this dynamic new architecture has come to represent a third style incorporated into the city's identity, alongside Gothic and Modernisme. More diffuse and eclectic than either, it is not without its critics.

Personaje delante del sol. Miró.

Picasso, Miró & Dalí

Meet the holy trinity of Catalan art.

Catalonia has produced only a handful of world-renowned figures in modern culture. In literature it is hard to point to anyone who has become a household name outside Spain – perhaps because for much of the century it was virtually impossible to find success while writing in Catalan. The same goes for playwrights. In architecture, perhaps only Gaudí ranks among the finest. In classical music the Catalans have fared rather better, with the great cellist Pau Casals, and opera singers like Josep Carreras and Montserrat Caballé, but it is in the visual arts where Catalans can make their boldest claim, with Pablo Picasso (1881-1974), Joan Miró (1893-1983) and Salvador Dalí (1904-89) standing brightly above the rest.

The three will be forever associated with Barcelona's elevated role in early 20th-century avant-garde culture. This is a flattering bond, bolstered by the presence of the Museu Picasso (*see p99*) and the Fundació Miró (*see p111*), but should not be overplayed. Indeed, all of them would have their most creative times elsewhere: the discovery of cubism for Picasso, and the revelation of surrealism for Dalí and Miró, are more closely associated with their time in Paris, but there is no doubting the early influences of the periods they spent in Catalonia.

BEGINNINGS

Of the three, only Miró was born within the city walls. Today a small plaque commemorates the location of the family flat on the Passatge del Crèdit, which runs off C/Ferran. The son of a goldsmith and watchmaker, he would never lose that middle-class sense of propriety that kept his jacket tightly buttoned and his marriage and family life exemplary. Photos of his cherubic visage suggest a gentle disposition.

Picasso was born in Málaga in the south of Spain. Despite spending his teen years in Barcelona and six more decades in France he retained his Andalucian temperament, to which many credit his glowing vitality, his love of the bullfight, and his particularly complex and overanalysed relationship with women. Like Miró he was committed to the cause of democracy, producing the 20th century's most admired political painting, *Guernica*, for the Pavilion of the Republic at the 1937 Paris World Fair (where Miró also showed).

Dalí was a child of Figueres, the modest capital of the Empordà district to which he remained deeply attached all his life. When it came to art school, he shunned Barcelona and headed for Madrid, where he befriended Federico García Lorca and the filmmaker Luis Buñuel (with whom he directed *Un Chien Andalou* in 1928). Dalí's love for extravagant gestures and penchant for nonconformity – including his ambiguous sexuality, or in contrast, his suspicious comfortability with the Franco regime – could be attributed to a kind of studied provincialism. Happy to be an eternal outsider, he got away with the type of behaviour a well-reared child of the Barcelona bourgeoisie could not.

PASTURES NEW

Many clichés surround the idea of what an avant-garde artist was all about. One of the most enduring is that the cultural innovator of the early 20th century had to be an eminently cosmopolitan person, bound to the values of the

***Naturaleza muerta con cráneo de buey.* Picasso.**

metropolis. Yet Picasso, Miró and Dalí did some of their most important work in rural settings, isolated from the driving rhythms of the modern city. Anyone interested in following their footsteps will inevitably have to get their boots dirty. Even as a young man living between Barcelona and Paris, vividly portraying fin-de-siècle nightlife and café culture, Picasso was quick to seek retreat. Shortly after he had made his first cubist breakthrough with the painting *Les Demoiselles d'Avignon* in 1907, he hid out for a summer in the Pyrenean village of Gosol, where many of the guiding principles of cubist form were hammered out. A few years later he would return to the Tarragona town of Horta de Sant Joan, where he had gone as a teenager with a Barcelona art-school friend. Céret, a lovely town on the French side of the Pyrenees, was another early hangout. In all of these places he was to expand the cubist lexicon while connecting up with a more rustic side of the Catalan mindset, far from the family pressures of Barcelona and the pretences of Paris.

Miró, too, found refuge on the land. Though born an urbanite, by the 1920s he came to spend more and more time in his family's old stone farmhouse in Mont-roig, near Tarragona. Miró's hyper-realist depiction of the home (*The Farm*, 1921-2), completed in Paris, was purchased by Ernest Hemingway, who recognised it as the epitome of rural Spain. It is now in the National Gallery of Art in Washington DC.

Within a year this obsessive concern for detailing physical objects would explode into the magical dreamlike world of his first fully surrealist paintings. The moon, stars, birds and even the traditional Catalan peasant would be recurring motifs in his art throughout his career. In the mid 1950s Miró had his architect friend Josep Lluís Sert design a pristine white studio for him on the island of Mallorca. It would be hard to imagine the intense colours and delightful luminosity of Miró's more mature work without the full exposure to Mediterranean light made possible by these country workplaces.

Few artists of the 20th century were as loyally dedicated to a single vista as Dalí was to the scene at Cadaqués. A great number of his most worthy paintings have as their backdrop the small beach and tight, craggy cove of this once-obscure fishing village on Cap de Creus, about an hour from Figueres. He had first gone there as a child with his family, and later would entice a long list of illustrious creators

The Year of Dalí

To commemorate the centenary of Dalí's birth, 2004 has been declared the 'Year of Dalí', with several shows and special exhibitions to celebrate the occasion. The highlights include two shows in Barcelona; at the CaixaForum (*see p111*) is *Dalí: Mass Culture* from January to May, focusing on his creative use of mass media, advertising and pop consumerism. Meanwhile, over at the Miró Foundation there will be a more specialised exhibition from June to August on *The Yellow Manifesto*, co-authored by Dalí in 1928 and a key positioning document for his avant-garde ideas.

Worthwhile shows in Figueres, his former home town, include an exhibition on Dalí's connection with the Empordà region: from May to August *Dalí's Land* will be at the Museu de l'Empordà (Rambla 2, 972 502 305, closed Mon), while at the splendid toy museum, Museu dels Joguets (C/Sant Pere 1, 972 504 585, closed Mon), there will be a show on Dalí's youth running from April to September. Both spaces are just a short walk away from his museum, the Teatre-Museu Dalí (*see p293 and pictured right*).

No visit to Dalí's world would be complete without a trip to Cadaqués, with Dalí's home in nearby Port Lligat; the setting is marvellous. Only guided visits are offered, and bookings should be made well in advance (*see p293*). The Municipal Museum of Cadaqués will have a small exhibition of his early drawings from June to October. From March to November, at the castle in Púbol (*see p289*), near Girona, there will be a small exhibition of his drawings based on *Don Quixote*.

The Year of Dalí will also feature a number of performing arts events showing works for which he designed sets and costumes. The prestigious summer Perelada Castle Festival, just north of Figueres, will commemorate this aspect of the artist's work with productions of Manuel de Falla's ballet *The Three-Cornered Hat*, as well as Richard Strauss' *Salome*, in a new Peter Brook production. Contemporary dancer Ramón Oller has prepared three new choreographies based on music by Schubert and Wagner for ballets for which Dalí designed the sets during the time he spent in the USA. All of these will be presented in the Teatre El Jardí in Figueres.

– including García Lorca, Man Ray and Marcel Duchamp – to enjoy its beauty. Since the 1960s it has been a veritable mecca for those seeking inspiration. In the adjacent and even more isolated Port Lligat he ended up buying and restoring a fisherman's cottage, which can now be visited (*see p293*).

FINAL STROKES

Thus of the three, it was Miró who would retain the greatest loyalty to Barcelona. He had a clear idea that it should be the flagship of a much-beleaguered Catalan identity that he was eager to defend. When democracy was restored the city rewarded him with a number of public commissions, such as for the large sculpture in the Parc dels Escorxadors. The Miró Foundation, founded in 1975, has had its fine collection enhanced by donations from the artist's family, corroborating the relationship of mutual trust between Miró and his birthplace. Until the MACBA was finally opened in 1995, the Miró Foundation was the city's de facto museum of contemporary art. Though his final decades were spent working out of the fabulous studio just outside Palma de Mallorca (now a part of his foundation there), Miró chose to be buried in his hometown, and after passing away on the island his body was brought back to Barcelona. His tomb can be visited in the municipal cemetery on Montjuïc, just over the hill from his foundation.

Picasso, meanwhile, was banned from Franco's Spain for his political views (he had joined the French communist party in the 1950s), and so he was forced to make all the arrangements for his museum by proxy. He arranged to have his early work still in the hands of family members donated to the collection, and from the late '50s onward deliberately set aside work for it. Late in life it seemed Picasso had grown nostalgic about his fun-filled formative years in the city. Sadly, though, he would never visit the museum that bore his name, as he died in the south of France before Franco's dictatorship ended.

Dalí, always the showman, chose to be embalmed and buried right inside his namesake Figueres museum, where visitors are free to step on his tombstone. His final act of provocation, however, was to leave all of his remaining, uncommitted estate to the Spanish government, ignoring both the Figueres museum and the Generalitat. This means you have to travel to Madrid's Reina Sofia museum to view works like *Figure at a Window (The Artist's Sister)* from 1925, or his most famous masterpiece *The Great Masturbator* (1929), both paintings set in Cadaqués; an affront which many Catalans will never forgive.

Where to Stay

Features

Where to Stay

A snooze with a view.

Hotel options in Barcelona have seen a meteoric rise in the last few years, getting into pace with the city's growing popularity as a tourist and business destination. It is now bursting with hotels, from youth hostels or budget *pensiones* to luxurious five-stars. But it's true to say you don't get much bang for your euro these days, and price hikes have been spectacular. Most budget options feature strictly functional rooms and facilities, although there are exceptions. Mid-range options are especially uneven, as they tend to be either soulless business stop off points or pricier and slightly more comfortable versions of *pensiones*, with little middle ground.

A recent and welcome change in the hotel scene is the construction of a few more luxury boutique hotels, such as **Hotel Neri** (*see p51*), the **Hotel Constanza** (*see p68*) and the **Hotel Prestige** (*see p64*). On the other end, cheap and funky places, such as the **Hostal Gat Raval** (*see p55*), the **Pensió 2000** (*see p59*) and the **Gothic Point** and **Sea Point** (*see p74*) youth hostels bring in similar ideas of style and service at a much lower price.

In response to the shortage of hotel rooms, there has been an increase in the number of apartments on offer for short-term rental – for this and student and youth accommodation services, *see p73*.

SAFETY

Theft is a problem in some places, especially in lower-end establishments, but occasionally also in luxury ones. If you're sleeping cheap, you might want to travel with a padlock to lock your door, or at least lock up your bags. As a rule of thumb, check to see if youth hostel rooms have lockers if you're sharing with other people. Use hotel safes where possible.

STAR RATINGS AND PRICES

Accommodation in Catalonia is divided into two official categories: hotels (H) and *pensiones* (P). To be a hotel (star-rated one to five) a place must have en suite bathrooms in every room. Ratings are based on services and general quality (in that order) rather than price. *Pensiones*, usually cheaper and often family-run,

The spanking new **Hotel Neri** is at the heart of class and style. *See p51.*

are star-rated one or two, and are not required to have en suite bathrooms, though many do. Some *pensiones* are called *hostales*, but, confusingly, are not youth hostels; those are known as *albergues*.

As previously mentioned, rooms don't come cheap. For a double room per night, expect to pay €40-€65 for a budget *pensión*, €60-€160 for a mid-range establishment and from €160 to more than €450 for a five-star, top-of-the-range hotel. This is a guideline only, since prices can vary considerably depending on the time of year, demand and special offers. All hotel and *pensión* bills are subject to seven per cent IVA (value added tax) on top of the basic price; this is not normally included in the advertised rate.

Breakfast is not included in the price unless otherwise stated.

BOOKING A ROOM

It is quite difficult to find a room in Barcelona outside the winter months, especially in mid-range to budget establishments. Booking in advance – by at least two weeks, and more in summer – is strongly advised. Many of the cheaper hotels, however, will not accept reservations. Others may require you to guarantee your booking with credit card details or a deposit. It's worth calling a few days before your arrival to reconfirm the booking (get it in writing if you can – many readers have reported problems), and to check what the cancellation policy is.

To be sure of light or a view, ask for an outside room (*habitación exterior*), usually facing the street. Many of Barcelona's buildings are built around a central patio or airshaft, and the inside rooms (*habitación interior*) around them can be quite gloomy, albeit quieter. However, there are some cases where an inward-facing room is the best option because it will look on to large, open-air patios or gardens; we have tried to mention these where possible.

Barcelona On-Line

Gran Via de les Corts Catalanes 662, Eixample (93 343 79 93/fax 93 317 11 55/www.barcelona-on-line.es). Metro Passeig de Gràcia. **Open** 9am-7pm Mon-Fri; 9am-2pm Sat. **Map** p342 D5.

This booking agency can reserve hotel rooms and private apartments online, over the phone or at its Eixample office. The service is free and the staff multilingual. There is a cancellation fee if you cancel less than 48 hours before arrival.

Europerator

Gran Via de les Corts Catalanes 561, Eixample (93 451 03 32/fax 93 451 14 89/www.europerator.org). Metro Urgell. **Open** 9.30am-2pm, 4.30-7.30pm Mon-Fri; 9.30am-2pm Sat. **Credit** AmEx, MC, V. **Map** p342 C5.

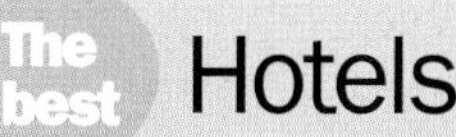

The best Hotels

Splashing out

Most hotel pools come with a view as they are usually on the roof. Float and gloat at views of Montjuïc from the **Barcelona Plaza** (*see p71*), the Med from the **Grand Marina** (*see p61*) and the city from **La Florida** (*see p72*).

Gadgets & gizmos

Get technotronic with handclap-operated CD players in the **Hotel Arts** (*see p59*), remote-controlled beds in the suites at the **Atrium Palace** (*see p63*) and plasma screen web TVs in **Hotel Axel** (*see p67*).

Old soaks

Bathing beauties should check in to **Hostal d'Uxelles** for Andalucían tiled bathrooms (*see p67*), the **Ritz** for 1919 mosaic 'Roman baths' (*see p67*) or the **Podium** for covetable bath goodies (*see p64*).

Space monkeys

Go out without leaving your hotel. **Alberg Mare de Déu de Montserrat** (*see p73*) and **Hotel Balmes** (*see p63*) offer green relief from cityitis in their leafy gardens. **Hostal Eden**'s suntrap terrace comes with its own barbecue set (*see p68*).

Staying in on the tiles

Modernista freaks will love **Hotel Nouvel**'s ornate ceilings (*see p51*), **Hostal Girona**'s tiled floors (*see p69*) and **Hotel España**'s murals by Ramon Casas (*see p57*).

A room search service dealing with hotels and *pensiones* along with apartments, aparthotels and rooms in private houses. Multilingual staff will waive booking fees or commission for *Time Out* readers.

Hotel Connect

28 St Alban's Lane, London, NW11 7QE (00 44 (0)20 8731 7000/fax 00 44 (0)20 8731 7003/ www.hotelconnect.co.uk). **Open** 8am-8pm Mon-Fri. **Credit** MC, V.

A London-based booking agency offering a selection of Barcelona hotels, rated from two to five stars. Reservations can be made online or by phone and offers are posted on the website each month. No booking fees and no commission.

TUI Viajes

Vestibule, Estació de Sants, Sants (93 491 44 63/ fax 93 491 35 32/www.tuiviajes.com). Metro Sants Estació. **Open** 8am-10pm daily. **Credit** AmEx, DC, MC, V. **Map** p341 A4.

visit barcelona
Vacation Rental Apartments
www.visit-bcn.com
+34.93.342 45 34

This agency can book a room for you at most of Barcelona's hotels and at some of the city's *pensiones*. You will be charged a fee of €3 per reservation, and you will be asked for a deposit. The rest of the payment is to be paid directly to the hotel.
Other locations throughout the city.

Barri Gòtic & La Rambla

Expensive

Hotel Colón

Avda de la Catedral 7 (93 301 14 04/fax 93 317 29 15/www.hotelcolon.es). Metro Jaume I or Urquinaona. **Rates** single €165.80; double €235.40; suite €374.50. **Credit** AmEx, MC, V. **Map** p344 B2.

Location doesn't get better than a room overlooking Barcelona's magnificent cathedral. The Colón maintains an air of colonial grandeur with its coral-coloured marble lobby, glossy wood and intimate lounge areas. Rooms are colourfully decorated with bright flower prints. Rooms on the sixth floor have terraces, providing the perfect setting to watch the cathedral light up at night.
Hotel services *Air-conditioning. Babysitting. Bar. Laundry. Limousine service. Restaurant.* **Room services** *Minibar. Room service (24hrs). Telephone. TV: pay movies/satellite.*
Other locations: **Hotel Regencia Colón** C/Sacristans 13, Barri Gòtic (93 318 98 58).

Hotel Le Meridien Barcelona

La Rambla 111 (93 318 62 00/fax 93 301 77 76/www.lemeridien-barcelona.com). Metro Catalunya or Liceu. **Rates** single €235.40-€374.50; double €278.20-€406.60; suite €444-€800. **Credit** AmEx, DC, MC, V. **Map** p344 A2.

A classic hotel, elegant and genteel, Le Meridien is famed for having the best and most expensive suites in town, attracting presidents and pop stars, including bad boys of pop Liam and Noel Gallagher. Despite its size (it has 212 rooms), it manages to retain a personal air with friendly, helpful staff. Rooms are done out in soothing sandstone with roam-about bathrooms. All are soundproofed and the best look out over the Rambla. There's a plush piano bar on the ground floor and a top-grade restaurant that's worth staying in for. Sometime in 2004 the hotel should have its own spa facilities in place, in the meantime, guests have free use of Holmes Place gym and spa, nearby.
Hotel services *Air-conditioning. Babysitting. Bar. Car park (€18.80/day). Concierge. Disabled: adapted rooms (4). Internet access. Laundry. Limousine service. Non-smoking rooms. Restaurant.* **Room services** *Minibar. Room service (24hrs). Telephone. TV: satellite. VCR/DVD (on request).*

Hotel Neri

C/Sant Sever 5 (93 304 06 55/fax 93 304 03 37/www.hotelneri.com). Metro Jaume I or Liceu. **Rates** single/double €149.80-€277.15; suite €174.40-€323.15. **Credit** AmEx, DC, MC, V. **Map** p345 B3.

Opened in summer 2003, this classy four-star, set in a converted 18th-century mansion, boasts high levels of personal service combined with cutting edge design. The scene is set in the reception area where reds, golds and slates make a dramatic impression. Rooms are decorated with neutral colours, natural materials (rough wood and unpolished marble) and large modern art canvases. Enormous plasma-screen TVs, DVD and CD players and wireless internet access mean gadget fiends need never leave the room. 'Superior' rooms on the third floor have private terraces, but all residents can use the hotel's roof terrace and solarium.
Hotel services *Air-conditioning. Bar. Laundry. Library. Lounge. Restaurant. Solarium. Wireless internet.* **Room services** *CD player. Minibar. Room service (24hrs). Telephone. TV: cable/VCR/DVD.*

Hotel Nouvel

C/Santa Anna 20 (93 301 82 74/fax 93 301 83 70/www.hotelnouvel.com). Metro Catalunya. **Rates** (incl breakfast) single €99.50-€112.40; double €163.70-€177.60; triple €196.90-€210.80. **Credit** MC, V. **Map** p342 D5.

Opened in 1917, this hotel has both charming staff and the ambience of a Modernista building. Stuffed with carriage lantern chandeliers, curved woodcarvings and ornate ceilings, it provides a window into Barcelona's turn-of-the-century prosperity. Most of the rooms have the original tiled floors, which contrast with thoroughly modern bathrooms. The best rooms have balconies, and there's a pleasant bar and restaurant with marble floors and a huge skylight, which is perfect for daytime or evening.
Hotel services *Air-conditioning. Disabled: adapted rooms (2). Laundry. Restaurant.* **Room services** *Telephone. TV: satellite.*

Hotel Rivoli Ramblas

La Rambla 128 (93 302 66 43/reservations 93 412 09 88/fax 93 317 50 53/www.rivolihotels.com). Catalunya or Liceu Metro. **Rates** single €188.40-€225.80; double €229-€270.80; suite €749. **Credit** AmEx, DC, MC, V. **Map** p344 A2.

The peaceful Rivoli is a world apart from the bustle on La Rambla outside. The rooms are comfortable and classy, with soundproofed windows blocking out most of the noise in the rooms facing La Rambla. The Blue Moon cocktail bar is a relaxing place to begin or end the evening. Residents can use the pool at nearby branch Hotel Ambassador (*see p55*).
Hotel services *Air-conditioning. Babysitting. Bar. Car park (€17.70/day). Disabled: adapted rooms (4). Fitness centre. Laundry. Non-smoking floor. Restaurant. Terrace.* **Room services** *Minibar. Room service (24hrs). Telephone. TV: satellite.*

Mid-range

Hostal Jardí

Plaça Sant Josep Oriol 1 (93 301 59 00/fax 93 342 57 33/hoteljardi@retemail.es). Metro Liceu. **Rates** single €68-€83; double €83. **Credit** AmEx, DC, MC, V. **Map** p345 A3.

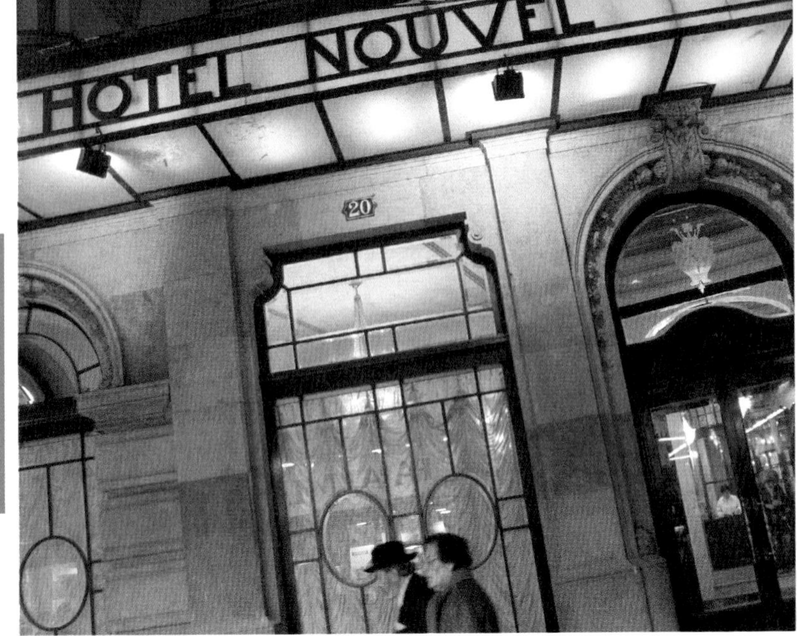

The stunning and original Modernista charm of the **Hotel Nouvel**. *See p51.*

The Hostal Jardí offers simple, unfussy accommodation in one of the most desirable locations in the Barri Gòtic. The lobby seems a touch clinical but rooms are clean and fresh, all with en suite bathrooms. And the best, which are worth the extra money, have balconies overlooking the pretty *plaça*.
Hotel services *Air-conditioning.* **Room services** *Telephone. TV.*

Hotel Barcelona House

C/Escudellers 19 (93 301 82 95/fax 93 412 41 29/ www.hotelbarcelonahouse.com). Metro Drassanes. **Rates** (incl breakfast) single €28.50-€46.70; double €52.70-€77.30; triple €85.40-€102.50. **Credit** MC, V. **Map** p345 A3-B3.
Treading a line between seedy and cool, like so much of the local neighbourhood, Barcelona House divides its rooms into the categories of 'standard', 'comfort' and 'charm'. Standard rooms can be small, dark and rather worse for wear, but are painted in bright colours, and have funky '50s furniture. Comfort rooms are newly renovated and have parquet flooring, good bathrooms and lots of space. Charm rooms are campy palaces of kitsch – pink walls, faux rococo bedsteads and floral motifs. This hotel is a good choice for nightlife-loving guests.
Hotel services *Laundry.* **Room services** *Air-conditioning (some rooms). Telephone (some rooms). TV (some rooms).*

Hotel Oriente

La Rambla 45-7 (93 302 25 58/fax 93 412 38 19/ www.husa.es). Metro Drassanes. **Rates** single €107-€133.80; double €133.80-€171.20; triple €165.90-€216.10. **Credit** AmEx, DC, MC, V. **Map** p343 A3.
Inaugurated in 1842 as Barcelona's first ever 'grand hotel', and still with an olde worlde ballroom and dining room, the Oriente aims to salvage the splendour of its heyday, while attaining 21st-century standards of comfort. A full-scale renovation is under way, and will probably last until 2005. This is a welcoming place; but peaceful it is not, with builders tinkering away inside. Rooms are being refurbished wing by wing: those that are complete are bright and spacious; those that aren't are shabby for the price, although the beds are new.
Hotel services *Bar. Internet access. Laundry.* **Room services** *Air-conditioning (renovated rooms). Telephone. TV: satellite.*

Budget

Hostal Fontanella

Via Laietana 71, 2º (tel/fax 93 317 59 43). Metro Urquinaona. **Rates** single €35.30-€42.80; double €52.50-€66.40; triple €73.40-€92.90; quadruple €91.80-€116.10. **Credit** AmEx, DC, MC, V. **Map** p337 B1.
The Fontanella is usefully located where the Gòtic meets the Born and the Eixample. Other than the splendid Modernista lift, it's all change as Mary Poppins meets Laura Ashley with the interior decor. Rooms are flowery, but clean and comfortable.
Hotel services *Laundry. Telephone.* **Room services** *TV: satellite.*

Hostal Lausanne

Avda Portal de l'Àngel 24 (93 302 11 39). Metro Catalunya. **Rates** single €25; double €45-€55; triple €75-€80. **No credit cards**. **Map** p344 B2.

Smack bang on one of downtown Barcelona's busiest shopping streets, the *hostal* occupies the first floor of a fine old building. Of the 17 basic rooms, only two have en suite bathrooms. While the furniture is dated, they are all clean enough and leave little room for complaint if you are just looking for a place to conk out. The back two rooms open out on to a large balcony. High ceilings, a spacious lounge and a predominantly student-based clientele make for a chilled-out atmosphere. The street is as quiet at night as it is frenzied during the day.
Hotel services *Lounge. Telephone. TV.*

Hostal Maldà

C/Pi 5, 1° 1ª (93 317 30 02). Metro Liceu. **Rates** single €12; double €27; triple €36. **No credit cards. Map** p344 B2.
This comfortable *pensión* in the heart of the Barri Gòtic is a find in every sense: access is through a shopping arcade, after which you receive a beaming welcome. There are no en suite facilities, but the four communal bathrooms are clean. The atmosphere is homey and some of the rooms preserve the old building's original coloured floor tiles. Rooms face either a pedestrian street of shops or a quiet, sunny patio.
Hotel services: *Lounge. Refrigerator. TV.*

Hostal Noya

La Rambla 133, 1° (93 301 48 31). Metro Catalunya. **Rates** single €20-€22; double €30-€35. **No credit cards. Map** p344 A2.
This is a cheerful cheapo with a smiling *mama* on hand to greet you. You'll find fake ferns in the doorways and handsome old tiles on the floor. The bathroom is white, weathered and worn, but very clean; just as well since there's only one between 12 rooms, along with a separate WC. Don't expect frills at this place, but it's a great base for travellers on a budget.
Hotel services *Payphone.*
Other locations: **Pension Bienestar** C/Quintana 3, Barri Gòtic (93 318 72 83).

Hostal Parisien

La Rambla 114 (tel/fax 93 301 62 83). Metro Liceu. **Rates** single €38-€48; double €57-€64. **No credit cards. Map** p344 A2.
An extrovert parrot called Fede greets guests in the lobby, which is done up in an odd jumble of knick-knacks. The 13 rooms (facing La Rambla or a narrow street at the back) are well kept, and the eight bathrooms have been recently refurbished. Service is friendly and the location is excellent, but the long-term residents mean it's hard to get a single room.
Hotel services *Lounge. Payphone. TV.*

Hostal Rembrandt

C/Portaferrissa 23, pral 1ª (tel/fax 93 318 10 11/ hostrembrandt@yahoo.es). Metro Liceu. **Rates** single €28; double €45-€60; triple €65-€75. **Credit** MC, V. **Map** p344 B2.
A charming 15-room *hostal*: fairly stylish (considering the price) with lots of wood panelling and soft lighting. Rooms out front can be a little noisy, but that's what you get in an excellent location .
Hotel services *Payphone. Refrigerator. TV.*

Hotel Toledano

La Rambla 138, 4° (93 301 08 72/fax 93 412 31 42/ www.hoteltoledano.com). Metro Catalunya. **Rates** single €31.50-€36; double €56.70; triple €75.80; quadruple €84.30. **Credit** AmEx, DC, MC, V. **Map** p344 A2.
This central and friendly hotel has been around since 1914, but all 17 rooms were renovated in 2003, and feel fresh as a daisy (though almost as small as one). Some have air-conditioning; others just have a small balcony. There are 11 more basic rooms in the sister *hostal* upstairs (same telephone number). It is high up, which means there is less noise than in many other hotels in the same area (there's a lift).
Hotel services *Internet access. Lounge.* **Room services** *Air-conditioning (some rooms). Telephone. TV: satellite.*

Location, location, location

Unsurprisingly, the highest concentration of hotels is to be found in the areas that make up the **Old City**: the Barri Gòtic, the Raval, and Sant Pere and the Born. While the narrow streets of these districts ooze Barcelona charm, watch your bag, as petty crime abounds. Hotels on or near **La Rambla** are convenient for many of the city's sights, but can be noisy and over-priced. For a better value and more peaceful hotel experience, try somewhere in the **Eixample**. The area's elegant 19th-century buildings, with their attractive architectural features (high ceilings, Modernista tiling and wrought-iron balconies) make for lovely hotels.

Poble Sec is a residential suburb bordered by Montjuïc and Avda Paral.lel – a somewhat seedy but historic avenue that was once the heart of Barcelona's theatre, nightlife and prostitution scene. It still has a couple of theatres and boasts some good bars, clubs and restaurants; and it is a good option if you are planning on spending time exploring Montjuïc or visiting the Fira exhibition halls. **Gràcia** is a lively, up-and-coming residential area in the north of the city, only a five- to ten-minute metro ride from the centre, with plenty of bars, restaurants and character. The **Zona Alta** is good if you're here on business, or want a taste of uptown chic.

flatsbydays.com
Enjoy Barcelona. Feel at home.
Log on to www.flatsbydays.com and discover your flat.
Rent a flat from us and enjoy the city to the max, with all the comfort and at the best price.
reservation@flatsbydays.com
Tel. +34 93 342 6481

APARTMENTS
RAMBLAS
BARCELONA APARTMENTS
SHORT-TERM RENTALS
CENTRALLY LOCATED
BEST PRICES IN TOWN
www.apartmentsramblas.com
+34 933017678

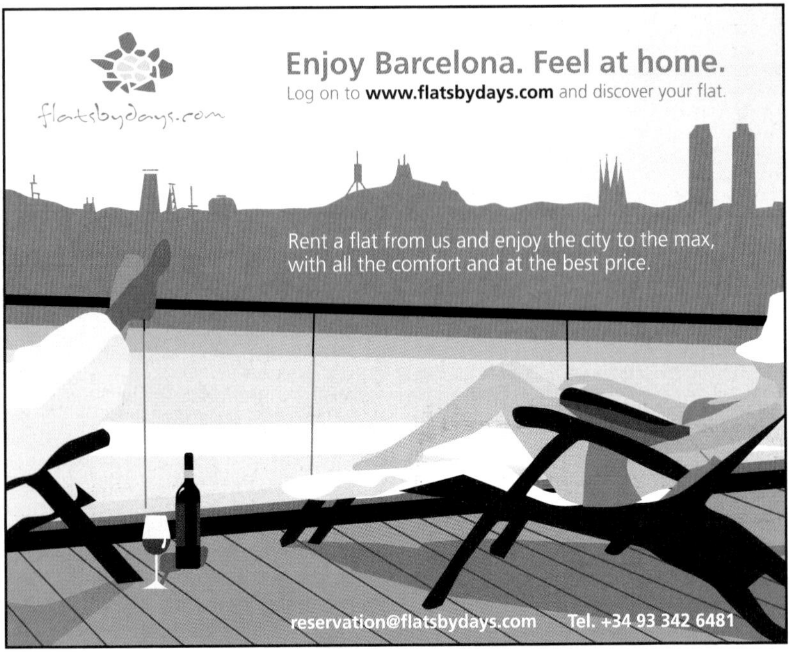

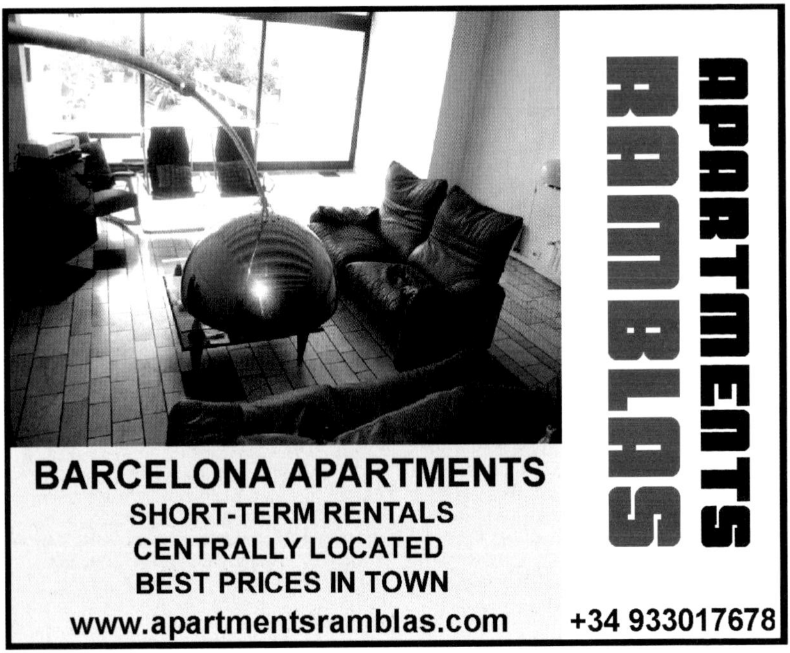

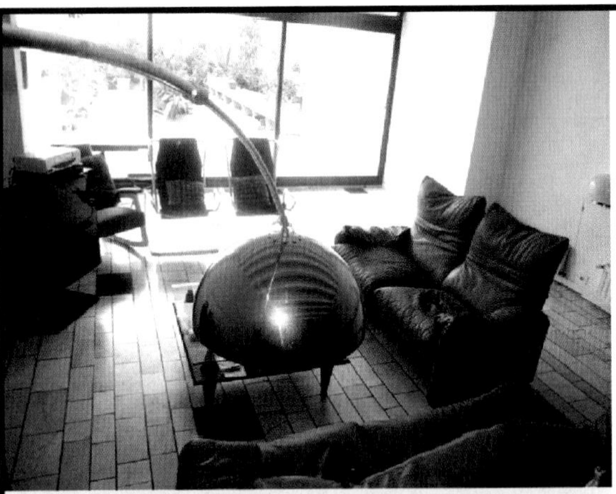

Pensión-Hostal Mari-Luz

C/Palau 4 (phone/fax 93 317 34 63/mariluz@menta.net). Metro Liceu. **Rates** double €40-€45; 4-6-person rooms €16 per person. **Credit** AmEx, DC, MC, V. **Map** p345 B3.

You have to climb several flights of a grand stone staircase to reach Mari-Luz and Simón's clean and friendly *pensión*. Stripped wood doors and old floor tiles add character to the otherwise plain but quiet rooms (some face a plant-filled inner courtyard). There are four-, five- and six-bed dorms (with lockers, without bath), as well as double and triple rooms (No.4 and No.6 have good en suite bathrooms). Guests can use the small kitchen in the mornings.

Hotel services *Lockers. Lounge. Payphone.*

Other locations: **Pensión Fernando** C/Ferran 31, Barri Gòtic (93 301 79 93).

Pensión Portugal

C/Josep Anselm Clavé 27 (93 342 60 61/fax 93 342 60 62/www.hostalportugal.com). Metro Drassanes. **Rates** single €30-€40; double €50-€65; triple €70-€80. **Credit** DC, MC, V. **Map** p342 D6.

A welcome new addition, the Portugal is owned by the same people as the Hostal-Residencia Ramos (*see p55*) and is equally friendly, spotlessly clean, no-frills accommodation. It also has the advantage of being tucked away at the back of the building, so it's generally very quiet, despite the young vibe.

Hotel services *Air-conditioning.* **Room services** *TV.*

Pensión Segre

C/Simó Oller 1, 1º (93 315 07 09). Metro Drassanes. **Rates** single €20; double €35-€45. **No credit cards**. **Map** p345 B4.

With its stuffed deer head at reception, and '70s brown and orange floor tiles, this friendly pensión is more than a little kitsch. Rooms are comfortable enough, some have private bathrooms and there's a small, functional lounge for catching up on Spanish TV. A bonus is the fairly tranquil street and the fact that you're spitting distance from the Port Vell.

Hotel services *Payphone.*

Pensión Vitoria

C/Palla 8, pral (tel/fax 93 302 08 34). Metro Liceu. **Rates** single €10-€15; double €30-€35; triple €30-€40. **Credit** MC, V. **Map** p344 B2.

Extremely basic facilities (which occasionally veer dangerously close to dingy) make for one of the most affordable budget options in the Old City. Nine doubles (two with en suite bathrooms) and two inward-facing singles are crammed into this *hostal* just off picturesque Plaça del Pi. It still tends to be booked out by those willing to sacrifice luxury for an excellent location and rates as low as they go.

Hotel services *TV.*

Residencia Victòria

C/Comtal 9, 1º 1ª (93 318 07 60/317 45 97/victoria@atriumhotels.com). Metro Catalunya. **Rates** single €29; double €39-€42; triple €52. **No credit cards**. **Map** p344 B2.

This spacious and peaceful *pensión* features rare extras such as communal cooking and washing facilities and a pleasant little outdoor terrace, which is lovely in the warm months. The rooms are basic, clean and light, with sinks but no en suite bathrooms. Personable service keeps the clientele coming back, so make sure to book early. Rooms must be paid for with cash on arrival.

Hotel services *Kitchen. Laundry. Lounge. Payphone. Terrace. TV.*

Raval

Expensive

Hotel Ambassador

C/Pintor Fortuny 13 (93 342 61 80/fax 93 302 79 77/www.rivolihotels.com). Metro Catalunya or Liceu. **Rates** single €215.10; double €270.20; junior suite €401.30; suite €749. **Credit** AmEx, DC, MC, V. **Map** p342 C5.

The Ambassador somehow managed to slip into obscurity after the 1992 Olympics despite its four stars. This is odd, because it's the only place on La Rambla with a rooftop pool and jacuzzi, though there's not much of a view. Recently refurbished, with a kitschy blend of water features, gold paint and smoked glass, a glittering colossus of a chandelier and a free-standing Modernista bar dominating the lounge area, the hotel has comfortable, sleek rooms with big, fat, comfortable beds.

Hotel services *Air-conditioning. Bar. Car park (€18/day). Disabled: adapted rooms (4). Fitness centre (gym/sauna). Internet access. Laundry. Non-smoking rooms. Pool (outdoor). Restaurant.* **Room services** *Dataport (some rooms). Minibar. Room service (noon-4pm, 8-11pm). Telephone. TV: cable.*

Mid-range

Hostal Gat Raval

C/Joaquín Costa 44, 2ª (93 481 66 70/fax 93 342 66 97/www.gataccommodation.com). Metro Universitat. **Rates** single €35.30-€41.70; double €51.50-€76. **Credit** AmEx, MC, V. **Map** p342 C5.

With its acid-green and black decor and internet facilities, the Gat Raval embodies everything that 21st-century budget accommodation should be. Smart, clean and funky with bright, sunshiney rooms each boasting a unique work by a local artist. Some have balconies while others, appropriately, have views of Richard Meier's MACBA. The only downside is that nearly all bathrooms are communal (though sparkling clean).

Hotel services *Internet access. Payphone.* **Room services** *TV.*

Hostal-Residencia Ramos

C/Hospital 36 (93 302 07 23/fax 93 302 04 30/www.hostalramos.com). Metro Liceu. **Rates** single €45-€50; double €65-€80; triple €84-€95. **Credit** DC, MC, V. **Map** p345 A3.

One of the best deals in the Raval for its pretty, black and white tiled entrance patio and friendly, family-run atmosphere. There's no air-conditioning, but plenty of windows and balconies keep it cool. Rooms are basic, but light and airy. The best rooms have balconies on to the *plaça*, but this can get noisy. All rooms have private bathrooms.
Hotel services *Air-conditioning.* **Room services** *Telephone. TV.*

Hotel España

C/Sant Pau 9-11 (93 318 17 58/fax 93 317 11 34/ www.hotelespanya.com). Metro Liceu. **Rates** (incl breakfast) single €50-€66; double €98; triple €130. **Credit** AmEx, DC, MC, V. **Map** p345 A3.
The España is a Modernista landmark, with lower floors designed by Domènech i Montaner in 1902. The main restaurant is decorated with floral tiling and elaborate woodwork, and the larger dining room beyond it features extravagant murals of river nymphs by Ramon Casas. The rooms can come as something of a disappointment after all this; they vary in size and some are poky and rather gloomy, although several open on to a bright interior patio.
Hotel services *Air-conditioning. Disabled: adapted rooms (2). Restaurant. TV room.* **Room services** *Telephone. TV: satellite.*

Hotel Gaudí

C/Nou de la Rambla 12 (93 317 90 32/fax 93 412 26 36/www.hotelgaudi.es). Metro Liceu. **Rates** (incl breakfast) single €101.70; double €139.10; triple €176.60; quadruple €203.30. **Credit** AmEx, DC, MC, V. **Map** p345 A3.
In a nod to the great architect himself (the Palau Güell is right opposite), the hotel has a replica of the Palace's roof in the lobby, but you can feast your eyes on the real thing if you book into one of the upper rooms with a terrace. Rooms are cool and comfortable, and all have good-sized bathrooms. A small restaurant nearby serves snacks.
Hotel services *Air-conditioning. Bar. Car park (€15/day). Disabled: adapted rooms (2). Fitness centre. Internet access. Laundry. Restaurant.* **Room services** *Room service (noon-midnight). Telephone. TV: satellite.*

Hotel Mesón Castilla

C/Valldonzella 5 (93 318 21 82/fax 93 412 40 20/ www.mesoncastilla.com). Metro Universitat. **Rates** (incl breakfast) single €101.70; double €130.60-€144.50; triple €171.20. **Credit** AmEx, DC, MC, V. **Map** p344 A1.
This chocolate-box hotel opened in 1952, before which it was a private house belonging to an aristocratic Catalan family. The hotel's public areas are crammed with antiques and curious artworks, but the rooms are fairly uniform, with cosy soft furnishings to contrast with the tiled floors. The best have tranquil terraces, and there's a delightful, plant-filled terrace off the breakfast room.
Hotel services *Air-conditioning. Car park (€20/day). Laundry. Terrace.* **Room services** *Telephone. TV: satellite.*

Hotel Peninsular

C/Sant Pau 34-6 (93 302 31 38/fax 93 412 36 99). Metro Liceu. **Rates** (incl breakfast) single €50; double €70; triple €85; quadruple €110. **No credit cards. Map** p344 A3.
This colonial-style hotel is housed in a building that once belonged to Augustinian monks. There's a pleasant cafeteria for breakfast, and an interior patio, which is great for catching up on postcard writing. The rooms, however, have seen better days; if you opt for a cheaper room using communal showers and toilets, expect the basics. One or two *Time Out* readers have reported incidents of theft from rooms, too, so be careful.
Hotel services *Air-conditioning. Iron. Terrace. TV room.* **Room services** *Telephone.*

Hotel Principal

C/Junta de Comerç 8 (93 318 89 74/fax 93 412 08 19/www.hotelprincipal.es). Metro Liceu. **Rates** (incl breakfast) single €65-€120; double €70-€140. **Credit** AmEx, DC, MC, V. **Map** p345 A3.
The Principal distinguishes itself by the ornate furniture in its 120 completely renovated rooms, all with good bathrooms. The best rooms are those facing the street (all of which have balconies), although there are a couple of late-opening bars nearby that can make them noisy. Usually a good bet, recently the Principal's reputation has started to slide with reports of theft from some of the rooms.
Hotel services *Air-conditioning. Bar. Disabled: adapted rooms (3). Internet access.* **Room services** *Telephone. TV: satellite.*

Hotel Rondas

C/Sant Erasme 19 (93 329 00 04/www.rondas.com.). Metro Sant Antoni. **Rates** single/double €65-€190; triple €80-€201.20. **Credit** AmEx, DC, MC, V. **Map** p342 C5.
The starstruck owner has papered the walls of the cafeteria with autographed photos of flamenco dancers, bullfighters, actors and musicians who have performed in Barcelona, not that they ever stayed here, necessarily. This was once an aparthotel and it still has that air about it, but it's not a bad bet for bargain deals (check the website), and the rooms are pleasant enough, with parquet floors.
Hotel services *Air-conditioning. Bar. Car park (€19.30/day). Concierge. Disabled: adapted room. Restaurant.* **Room services** *Minibar. Telephone. TV: satellite.*

Hotel Sant Agustí

Plaça Sant Agustí 3 (93 318 16 58/fax 93 317 29 28/www.hotelsa.com). Metro Liceu. **Rates** (incl breakfast) single €107-€117.70; double €142.30-€160.50; triple €171.20-€195.80. **Credit** AmEx, DC, MC, V. **Map** p345 A3.
With its buff, sandstone walls and huge, arched windows looking on to the *plaça*, not to mention the pink marble lobby filled with forest-green furniture, this imposing hotel is the Raval's handsomest. Housed in the former convent of St Augustine, it was converted into a hotel in 1840, and what might have been

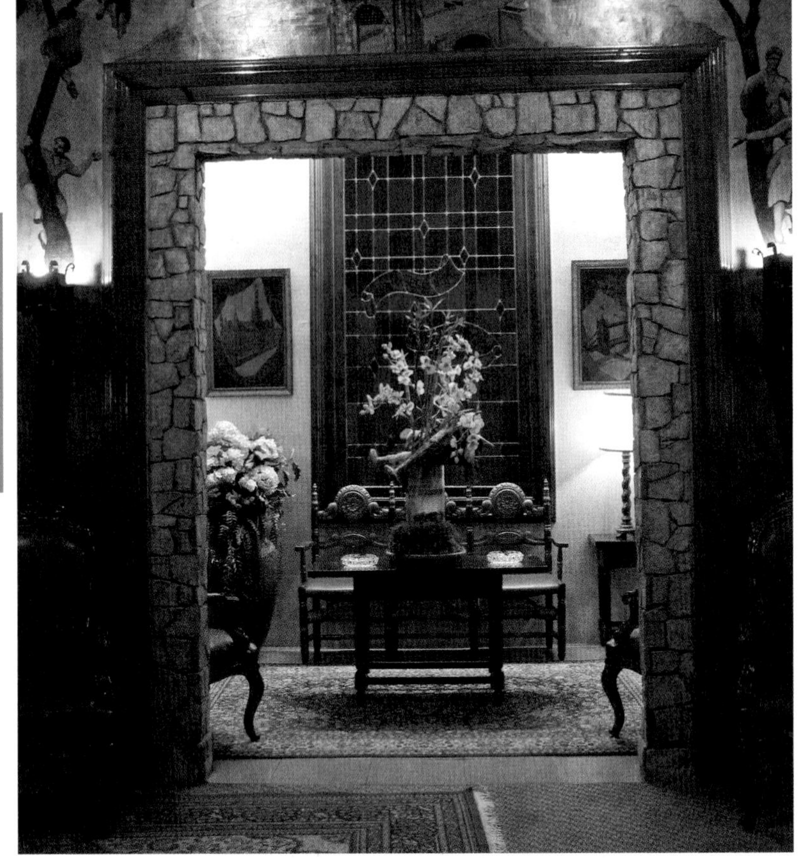

Hotel Mesón Castilla is a chocolate box of antiques and curious artworks. *See p57.*

bare-boned saintliness has been replaced with creature comforts. Rooms are cool, calm and comfortable, with classy oak beams, but, sadly, no soundproofing.
Hotel services *Air-conditioning. Babysitting. Bar. Disabled: adapted rooms (2). Internet access. Laundry. Restaurant (dinner only).* **Room services** *Minibar (some rooms). Telephone. TV: satellite.*

Budget

Hostal La Terrassa

C/Junta de Comerç 11 (93 302 51 74/fax 93 301 21 88). Metro Liceu. **Rates** single €20; double €30-€36; triple €48; quadruple €60. **Credit** DC, MC, V. **Map** p345 A3.
Clean, friendly and above all cheap, La Terrassa is a typical backpackers' joint and the top spot, apparently, for travelling skateboarders. There's no a/c but rooms have fans, it's kid-friendly and there's a scruffy terrace out back for soaking up the sun and making new friends over some cold beer.
Hotel services: *Payphone. Terrace.*

Hostal Opera

C/Sant Pau 20 (93 318 82 01). Metro Liceu. **Rates** single €35; double €55; triple €80. **Credit** MC, V. **Map** p345 A3.
As the name indicates, this *pensión* is situated right beside the Liceu opera house, just off La Rambla. All rooms have been renovated and enjoy abundant natural light, private bathrooms, central heating and air-conditioning. The rooms at the back of the hotel are the nicest and the quietest, so book early.
Hotel services *Air-conditioning. Disabled: adapted rooms (3). Internet access. TV room: satellite.*

Hosteria Grau

C/Ramelleres 27 (93 301 81 35/fax 93 317 68 25/ www.hostalgrau.com). Metro Catalunya. **Rates** single €30-€42.80; double €48.70-€70.10; triple €65.80-€88.30 ; apartment €74.90-€139.10. **Credit** AmEx, DC, MC, V. **Map** p344 A1.
Hosteria Grau is an utterly charming, family-run *hostal* that oozes character. It has a stunning tiled spiral staircase and fabulous 1970s style communal areas. And the open fireplace is a major luxury if

you're travelling in the chillier winter months. Roomwise, it's basic, comfortable and fairly quiet. If you're after self catering, the family also has apartments that are available for rent.
Hotel services *Bar. Internet access. Laundry. Payphone. TV room: satellite.*

Pensión Córdoba

C/Nou de la Rambla 1 1°1ª (93 302 50 52). Metro Drassanes or Liceu. **Rates** single €20; double €35. **No credit cards**. **Map** p342 C6.
Cute, clean and chintzy, this bare-bones pensión is on the second floor of a recently renovated building and is well located very close to the port (which is brilliant if you're catching an early morning ferry). Aside from which, Pensión Córdoba is simply a pleasant place to lay your head.

Sant Pere & the Born

Mid-range

Banys Orientals

C/Argenteria 37 (93 268 84 60/fax 93 268 84 61/ www.hotelbanysorientals.com). Metro Jaume I. **Rates** (incl breakfast) single €79.20-€92; double €95.20. **Credit** AmEx, DC, MC, V. **Map** p345 B3.
Banys Orientals exudes cool, from its location in the heart of the Born to the deeply stylish shades-of-grey minimalism of its rooms, and special touches such as complimentary mineral water on every floor, slide projections at the front desk and quirky fresh flower arrangements. A breath of fresh air in the city's hotel scene, Banys Orientals remains one of a kind, bringing together comfort, affordable rates (though another price hike is expected in July 2004), originality and style. There are plans to heat things up in 2004 by tapping into the eponymous thermal baths that lie underneath the hotel, thus creating a luxurious new service.
Hotel services *Air-conditioning. Disabled: adapted room. Restaurant.* **Room services** *Telephone. TV.*

Hotel Catalonia Princesa

C/Rec Comtal 16-18 (93 268 86 00/fax 93 268 84 91/www.hoteles-catalonia.es). Metro Arc de Triomf. **Rates** *single* €101.70-€171.20; *double* €123.10-€184.10. **Credit** AmEx, DC, MC, V. **Map** p344 C2.
This tasteful and comfortable hotel is housed in a pretty old building that used to be a textile factory. It has been well converted – all 89 rooms get excellent natural light; they face either the quiet street or a sunny atrium. Parquet floors and arched windows are elegant touches and the big bathrooms are a bonus. Be aware that the surrounding streets have their fair share of bagsnatchers, however.
Hotel services *Air conditioning. Bar. Disabled: adapted rooms (3). Laundry. Restaurant.* **Room services** *Dataport. Minibar. Room service (7-10.30am). Telephone. TV: (satellite).*

Budget

Hostal Orleans

Avda Marquès de l'Argentera 13 (93 319 73 82/ fax 93 319 22 19/www.hostalorleans.com). Metro Barceloneta. **Rates** single €24-€39; double €45-€55; triple €55-€68; quadruple €80. **Credit** AmEx, DC, MC, V. **Map** p341 E6.
This is a family-run *hostal* on a traffic-filled avenue near the Born and the port, with 18 recently refurbished en suite rooms. It's an unspectacular but dependable option with competitive rates, and rooms that feel less gloomy than those in many *hostales* in the same category. Air-conditioning is gradually being installed in all the rooms – you pay a €5 surcharge for it at present. Friendly owner Fina lights up an otherwise dismal lobby.
Hotel services *Laundry.* **Room services** *Air-conditioning (some rooms). Telephone. TV.*

Pensió 2000

C/Sant Pere Més Alt 6, 1° (93 310 74 66/fax 93 319 42 52/www.pensio2000.com). Metro Urquinaona. **Rates** single €38.50-€49.20; double €48.20-€62.10; third person €19.30; fourth person €16.20. **Credit** MC, V. **Map** p344 B2.
Friendly owners Manuela and Orlando run one of Barcelona's best value and most endearing *pensiones*. It has six bright and airy rooms in a charming old building opposite the Palau de la Música. Only two rooms are en suite, but communal facilities are sparkling clean. With its tall windows, buttercup-yellow walls and a lounge peppered with books and toys, this is a cheery sunbeam of a place, with a warm, relaxed atmosphere.
Hotel services *Laundry. Lounge. TV.* **Room services** *Room service (8-10.30am).*

Pensión Francia

C/Rera Palau 4 (93 319 03 76). Metro Barceloneta. **Rates** single €26.80; double €40.60-€53.50; triple €53.50-€64.20. **Credit** AmEx, MC, V. **Map** p345 C4.
Pensión Francia is central, surprisingly tranquil and pretty good value: the 14 rooms are clean, painted white and furnished with simple pine furniture, but some are very small. Some rooms have a shower, sink and toilet; others have one or more of these facilities outside the room. They are spread over two upper floors and there is no lift. It is excellently located just off a little square in the Born.
Hotel services *Payphone.* **Room services** *TV.*

Ports & shoreline

Expensive

Hotel Arts

C/Marina 19-21 (93 221 10 00/fax 93 221 10 70/ www.ritzcarlton.com). Metro Ciutadella-Vila Olímpica. **Rates** deluxe room €347.80-€481.50; executive room €449.40-€631.30; club deluxe room €535-€674.10; club suite €642-€834.60; apartment €1,284-€8,025. **Credit** AmEx, DC, MC, V. **Map** p343 F7.

The charming **Hosteria Grau** with its spiral staircase and open fire. *See p58.*

Plush robes and Bang & Olufsen CD players that open at a clap of the hands are just some of the luxurious perks awaiting guests at the Hotel Arts. Owned by the Ritz-Carlton, the 44-storey glass and steel hotel is only 100m from the beach, affording some of the pastel, contemporary rooms striking views of the sea. Even seasoned travellers are dazzled by the personal service, art-filled hallways and the city's only beachfront pool, overlooking Frank Gehry's bronze fish sculpture. The luxury duplex apartments have round-the-clock butlers.
Hotel services *Air-conditioning. Babysitting. Bar. Beauty salon. Business centre. Car park (€37.50/day). Concierge. Disabled: adapted rooms (5). Fitness centre. Garden. Hairdresser. Laundry. Limousine service. Non-smoking floors. Pool (outdoor). Restaurants.* **Room services** *CD player. Dataport. Fax (some rooms). Minibar. Room service (24hrs). Telephone. TV: satellite.*

Grand Marina Hotel

Edificio World Trade Center, Moll de Barcelona (93 603 90 30/fax 93 603 90 90/www.grandmarina hotel.com). Metro Drassanes. **Rates** single/double €401.30-€529.70; junior suite €727.60; suite (incl breakfast) €781.10-€1,685.30. **Credit** AmEx, DC, MC, V. **Map** p342 C7.
For business travellers, this five-star hotel in the World Trade Center at the end of the pier in Port Vell could not be more convenient. For tourists it's near the Old City, yet isolated from its chaos. All 235 rooms are spacious, with minimalist furnishings, jacuzzis and views over the sea or city. Five-star facilities include a rooftop gym and swimming pool, an elegant piano bar and a fine restaurant.
Hotel services *Air-conditioning. Bar. Beauty salon. Business centre. Car park (€22.50/day). Concierge. Disabled: adapted rooms (4). Fitness centre. Laundry. Limousine service. Non-smoking floor. Restaurants. Pool (outdoor). Terrace.* **Room services** *Minibar. Room service (24hrs). Telephone. TV: satellite.*

Hotel Duquesa de Cardona

Passeig Colom 12 (93 268 90 90/fax 93 268 29 31/ www.hduquesadecardona.com). Metro Drassanes or Jaume I. **Rates** single €144.50-€187.30; double €144.50-€235.40; junior suite €305-€358.50. **Credit** AmEx, DC, MC, V. **Map** p342 D6.
This 16th-century palace has been completely renovated to create an elegant boutique hotel. Natural materials – wood, leather and stone – are complemented by a soft colour scheme that reflects the original paintwork. Rooms at the front overlook Port Vell; those at the back compensate with larger bathrooms and a little less noise. If guests can't bear the ten-minute walk to the beach, they can take the lift to the roof terrace to sunbathe, cool off in the pool and take in amazing views.
Hotel services *Air-conditioning. Bar. Business centre. Disabled: adapted room. Lounge. Non-smoking rooms. Pool (outdoor). Restaurant. Terrace.* **Room services** *Dataport. Minibar. Room service (24hrs). Telephone. TV: satellite.*

Budget

Marina Folch

C/del Mar 16, pral (93 310 37 09/fax 93 310 53 27). Metro Barceloneta. **Rates** single €33; double €55; triple €67. **Credit** AmEx, DC, MC, V. **Map** p342 D7.

Petit Hotel
Barcelona's first official
Bed & Breakfast
c/ Laforja, 67 1º-2ª · 08021 Barcelona
Tel. 93 202 3663
www.petit-hotel.net
info@petit-hotel.net

BED & BREAKFAST
www.cityhall-bedandbreakfast.com
CITY HALL
telf: 0034.651.89.14.13
adress: c/ templers 6, Barcelona
at the center of Barcelona, by the City Hall House
from 20 €/person

low cost
hotels
with all the
frills in Barcelona!
from
£31

hotelconnect
the hotel specialist

A small family-run *hostal*, whose star attraction is its friendly owners. The ten rooms are all en suite, clean, decent-sized and comfortable, decked out in shades of sea blue – appropriate as it's in a quiet Barceloneta location, wonderful for the beach.
Hotel services *Air-conditioning.* **Room services** *TV.*

Poble Sec

Mid-range

Hotel Nuevo Triunfo

C/Cabanes 34 (93 442 59 33/fax 93 443 21 10/ www.hotelnuevotriunfo.com). Metro Paral.lel. **Rates** single €53.50-€74.90; double €85.60-€122. **Credit** AmEx, MC, V. **Map** p342 C6.
Located off a quiet residential street at the base of Montjuïc, the squeaky clean Nuevo Triunfo has 40 comfortable rooms, all simply decorated, with good bathrooms; some have leafy, private terraces. Intriguing old photos in the hallways depict the Avda Paral.lel of 100 years ago, and the tiny bar offers a basic continental breakfast. The friendly owners speak some English.
Hotel services *Air-conditioning. Disabled: adapted room.* **Room services** *Telephone. TV: cable.*

Budget

Hostal Restaurante Oliveta

C/Poeta Cabanyes 18 (93 329 23 16/july206@ hotmail.com). Metro Paral.lel. **Rates** single €30-€40; double €40-€60; extra person €15. **Credit** MC, V. **Map** p341 B6.
The Oliveta's six rooms are clean and basic with white walls and limited space – there's just enough room to walk around the beds. Just two rooms have en suites. The *hostal* is open 24 hours and there's a decent bar/restaurant downstairs where they claim you can crawl in for breakfast at any hour.
Hotel services *Air-conditioning. Restaurant.*

Eixample

Expensive

Hotel Atrium Palace

Gran Via de les Corts Catalanes 656 (93 342 80 00/ fax 93 342 80 01/www.apsishotels.com). Metro Passeig de Gràcia. **Rates** single €117.70-€181.90; double €128.40-€192.60; suite €214-€374.50. **Credit** AmEx, DC, MC, V. **Map** p342 D/E6.
This promising new face on the luxury hotel scene cuts a dashing, hyper-modern figure, even though it is in an attractive Eixample building that retains many original features. Light streams into the lobby from a skylight; stylish rooms are similarly bright and decked out in a minimalist attire of creams and browns. They sidestep sterility thanks to plenty of wood, splashes of cherry red and fresh flowers. This is high-tech heaven from the magnetic do not disturb signs to the interactive web TV, cordless keyboards and remote-controlled beds in the suites. Booking online gets you lower rates.
Hotel services *Air-conditioning. Business centre. Disabled: adapted rooms (2). Fitness centre. Laundry. Non-smoking floors (2). Pool (indoor). Restaurant. Wireless internet.* **Room services** *Dataport. Iron. Minibar. Telephone. TV: satellite/web TV.*
Other locations: **Hotel Aranea** Consell de Cent 444, Eixample (902 39 39 30); **Hotel Millenni** Ronda Sant Pau 14, Poble Sec (93 441 41 77).

Hotel Balmes

C/Mallorca 216 (tel/fax 93 451 19 14/ www.derbyhotels.es). Metro Passeig de Gràcia. **Rates** single €128.40-€187.50; double €142.30-€194.80. **Credit** AmEx, DC, MC, V. **Map** p338 C4.
The Balmes is a gem of a place with a chic, marble lobby lit up by artsy, twisted ropes of copper lanterns and African artworks. Parquet floors slung with rugs, and exposed brick walls give it a homey air, unusual for a hotel of this size. A lovely garden is hidden away at the back, complete with a swimming pool; some rooms have terraces overlooking it. No less than you would expect of the people who brought you the Claris (*see p63*).
Hotel services *Air-conditioning. Café. Garden. Laundry. Pool (outdoor). Restaurant.* **Room services** *Minibar. Telephone. TV: cable/pay movies.*

Hotel Catalonia Berna

C/Roger de Llúria 60 (93 272 00 50/58/ www.hoteles-catalonia.es). Metro Girona or Passeig de Gràcia. **Rates** single €132.70-€224.70; double €167-€259. **Credit** AmEx, DC, MC, V. **Map** p338 D4.
Opened in 2003, the Berna epitomises the Catalonia group's policy of restoring buildings of historical value in city centres to turn them into modern hotels. Its eye-catching exterior is a chunk of local history built in 1864 by Josep Cerdà. The Italian artist Raffaelo Beltramini painted the recently restored façade, with its brightly coloured allegorical figures representing Nature, Art and Science. The interior is another world and era: a swish, modern hotel. Some of the rooms are on the small side, but they are sleekly appointed throughout.
Hotel services *Air-conditioning. Bar. Car park (€16.10/day). Disabled: adapted rooms (4). Laundry. Restaurant.* **Room services** *Dataport. Minibar. Room service (7am-midnight). Safe. Telephone. TV: satellite.*

Hotel Claris

C/Pau Claris 150 (93 487 62 62/fax 93 215 79 70/ www.derbyhotels.es). Metro Passeig de Gràcia. **Rates** single €261.10-€358.50; double €288.90-€398.10; suite €486.70-€1,012.20. **Credit** AmEx, DC, MC, V. **Map** p338 D4.
This elegant 124-room hotel strikes an artful balance between the contemporary and antique, the trendy and the classical. Owner Jordi Clos displays part of his private art collection in the Claris's rooms and hallways, and pieces from the Museu Egipci – which

he runs – in a small exhibition on the first floor. In the bedrooms, antique artworks and chesterfield sofas sit alongside elegant modern furnishings by the in-house interior decorator, while Andy Warhol prints liven up the East 47 bar. Sidle past the glorious rooftop pool and solarium to the restaurant, and a DJ will mix a soundtrack to your dinner.
Hotel services *Air-conditioning. Babysitting. Bar. Business centre. Car park (€19.30/day). Disabled: adapted rooms (4). Fitness centre. Laundry. Limousine service. Non-smoking floor. Pool (outdoor). Restaurants.* **Room services** *CD player. Minibar. Room service (24hrs). Telephone. TV: pay movies/ satellite.*

Hotel Condes de Barcelona

Passeig de Gràcia 73-5 (93 467 47 86/fax 93 467 47 85/www.condesdebarcelona.com). Metro Passeig de Gràcia. **Rates** single €184-€315; double €199-€342; suite €588. **Credit** AmEx, DC, MC, V. **Map** p338 D4.
Made up of two buildings facing each other on C/Mallorca at the intersection of Passeig de Gràcia, the four-star, family-owned Condes has a split personality. The building on the north side occupies a 19th-century palace and has a somewhat dated, old-world feel. A plush dipping pool sits on the roof. The newer building was refurbished shortly before the '92 Olympics. Rooms on the seventh floor have terraces and a bird's-eye view of La Pedrera.
Hotel services *Air-conditioning. Bar. Car park (€17.20/day). Disabled: adapted rooms (2). Laundry. Non-smoking rooms. Pool (outdoor). Restaurant.* **Room services** *Dataport. Minibar. Room service (6am-midnight). Telephone. TV: pay movies/satellite.*

Hotel Inglaterra

C/Pelai 14 (93 505 11 00/fax 93 505 11 09/ www.hotel-inglaterra.com). Metro Universitat. **Rates** single €187.30-€219.40; double €235.40-€267.50. **Credit** AmEx, DC, MC, V. **Map** p344 A1.
With over 75 years in the business, the Inglaterra is one of the original 'designer' hotels and is surprisingly peaceful considering the hubbub of shoppers on the street outside. With blond wood hallways, and neat minimalist bedrooms with meditative Japanese characters sunk into the walls, it's simple and elegant. Star features include a leafy roof terrace and a comfortable living room and cafeteria.
Hotel services *Air-conditioning. Bar. Disabled: adapted room. Internet access. Laundry. Restaurant. Terrace.* **Room services** *Minibar. Room service (7.30am-11pm). Telephone. TV: satellite.*

Hotel Majestic

Passeig de Gràcia 68 (93 488 17 17/fax 93 487 97 90/www.hotelmajestic.es). Metro Passeig de Gràcia. **Rates** single/double €353.10-€433.40; suite €513.60-€620.60; apartment €4,173. **Credit** AmEx, DC, MC, V. **Map** p338 D4.
As plush and prestigious as they come, this grande dame of Barcelona's hotel scene offers as much sophistication and super-duper luxurious pampering as your heart can desire and your wallet can afford. Sumptuous rooms are decorated with classical flair, and all newly remodelled suites feature jacuzzis in their marble bathrooms and swanky toiletries by Italian label Etro. Guests can live the high life on the rooftop, indulging themselves in a panoply of perks, from the bright, spacious gym to the outdoor pool and the stunning views over the city from the sundeck. The Drolma restaurant is one of the finest in the city.
Hotel services *Air-conditioning. Babysitting. Bar. Business centre. Car park (€16.05/day). Concierge. Disabled: adapted rooms (4). Fitness centre. Laundry. Limousine service. Non-smoking floors (2). Pool (outdoor). Restaurant. Wireless internet.* **Room services** *Minibar. Room service (24hrs). Telephone. TV: pay movies/satellite.*

Hotel Onix Rambla Catalunya

Rambla Catalunya 24 (93 342 79 80/reservations 93 426 00 87/fax 93 342 51 52/www.hotelsonix.com). Metro Catalunya or Passeig de Gràcia. **Rates** single €149.80; double €160.50; triple €203.30. **Credit** AmEx, DC, MC, V. **Map** p342 D5.
This spanking new and seamlessly elegant hotel has a rooftop pool and views of the Collserola hills. Bedrooms have retained some original features, such as floor-to-ceiling windows, and are fairly plush. Elsewhere, the only things to break the starkness are a few well-chosen works of modern art.
Hotel services *Air-conditioning. Bar. Car park. Disabled: adapted rooms (1). Fitness centre. Laundry. Non-smoking rooms. Pool (outdoor).* **Room services**. *Minibar. Telephone. TV: satellite.*

Hotel Podium

C/Bailén 4-6 (93 265 02 02/reservations 902 11 51 16/fax 93 265 05 06/www.nh-hotels.com). Metro Arc de Triomf. **Rates** single/double €195.80-€215. **Credit** AmEx, DC, MC, V. **Map** p343 E5.
The quiet 145-room Podium is part of the reliable NH chain. The stylish lobby – with marble floors, original artwork and contemporary furniture – is stocked with international newspapers. The façade is from an early 20th-century duchess's palace, but the interior resembles a quirky office building, with green-stained wood-panelled walls. Superior rooms are split-level, with separate bathroom and toilet. The rooftop pool is a definite plus. Most guests are here on business, so rates fall at weekends.
Hotel services *Air-conditioning. Babysitting. Bar. Car park (€13.25/day). Disabled: adapted rooms (5). Fitness centre. Laundry. Limousine service. Non-smoking rooms. Pool (outdoor). Restaurant. Wireless internet.* **Room services** *Minibar. Room service (24hrs). Telephone. TV: pay movies/satellite.*

Hotel Prestige

Passeig de Gràcia 62 (93 272 41 80/fax 93 272 41 81/www.prestigehotels.com). Metro Passeig de Gràcia. **Rates** single/double €245-€333; junior suite €526.50. **Credit** AmEx, DC, MC, V. **Map** p338 D4.
Architect Josep Juanpere has taken this 1930s building and given it a modernist design to make it the coolest new hotel in Barcelona. As well as the Bang & Olufsen sound systems, Jacobsen telephones and

Big-name hunting

If you want to lay your head where movie stars and world leaders have rested theirs, Barcelona is just the place.

Likewise should you need a little historical flavour to your stay: any of the city's hotels seen their fair share of dramas, too, not least those which were confiscated during the Civil War for use as barracks or hospitals. Most didn't survive the experience. One iconic Barcelona hotel that did was the **Oriente** (*see p52*), which suffered severely from one of the last bombs of the war. After its recovery from the conflict, it became one of the hotels best loved by celebrities. Its proximity to the Liceu opera house (in fact, an underground tunnel joins the hotel to the theatre) means it was long a favourite with stars. Guests have included Mary Pickford and Errol Flynn, as well as Toscanini and Maria Callas.

The **Avenida Palace** (Gran Via de les Corts Catalanes 605-7) played its part in Spanish history in 1953, when it lodged George Train, chief of the Mission for the Mutual Assistance Treaty between the US and Spain. Maybe restful nights here persuaded Mr Train to arrange more than a billion dollars in US aid for Spain during the 1950s.

Today's stars (Oasis, Pavarotti, Michael Jackson and Eric Clapton) are more likely to stay at the thoroughly modern **Le Meridien** (*see p51*), although both Woody Allen and Madonna have been pampered at the elegant **Hotel Arts** (*see p59*).

The **Hotel Condes de Barcelona** (*see p64*) has fluffed up pillows for Isabel Allende, Lenny Kravitz, John Malkovich, Catherine Deneuve and Pedro Almodóvar.

One hotel still attracting the glamour set is the **Ritz** (*pictured, see also p67*). Previous heads on pillows here include the Duke of Windsor and Salvador Dalí. And then there's the recently rebuilt **La Florida** (*see p72*) on top of ol' Tibidabo. It is still working to win back guests of the calibre of writer Ernest Hemingway, though not, presumably, hoping to host many more like Himmler.

Ritz Hotel. *See p67.*

an intelligent lighting system in every room, there are oriental gardens. The hotel also provides the acclaimed 'Ask Me' service, where an expert concierge is constantly on hand with recommendations of bars, restaurants and shops in the area, or can book cinema tickets and hire cars for you.
Hotel services *Air-conditioning. Bar. Currency exchange. Disabled: adapted room. Non-smoking rooms.* **Room services** *Dataport. Minibar. Room service (24hrs). Telephone. TV: satellite.*

Ritz Hotel

Gran Via de les Corts Catalanes 668 (93 318 52 00/ fax 93 317 36 40/www.ritzbcn.com). Metro Passeig de Gràcia. **Rates** single €379.90; double €406.60; junior suite €508.30; suite €1,215.30. **Credit** AmEx, DC, MC, V. **Map** p342 D5.

The definition of grandeur, with more mirrors, gilt, brocade and chandeliers than most hotels would know what to do with. Open since 1919 (and renovated in 2002), the Ritz incorporates modern comforts into its ostentatiously traditional structure without sacrificing classic elegance. Hence, the mosaic 'roman baths' in some rooms now have the latest power showers. Chef Romain Fornell, the youngest ever to be awarded a Michelin star, heads up the kitchen in the sumptuous restaurant, Diana.
Hotel services *Air-conditioning. Babysitting. Bar. Business centre. Car park (€23.65/day). Concierge. Garden. Fitness centre. Hairdresser. Laundry. Limousine service. Non-smoking floors. Restaurant. Wireless internet.* **Room services** *Minibar. Room service (24hrs). Telephone. TV: satellite.*

Mid-range

Hotel Astoria

C/París 203 (93 209 83 11/fax 93 202 30 08/ www.derbyhotels.es). Metro Diagonal. **Rates** single €128.40-€176.55; double €142.30-€194.80. **Credit** AmEx, DC, MC, V. **Map** p345 B3.

Originally built in 1952 and renovated in the '90s by the Derby group (whose star is the Hotel Claris, *see p63*), the Astoria lobby features marble floors, leather armchairs and frescoes. Black and white chequered floors and a stylish bathroom spice up the standard business-class hotel rooms. The breakfast buffet is worth waking up for; look out for the original art deco posters at the restaurant's entrance.
Hotel services *Air-conditioning. Babysitting. Bar. Car park (€19.25/day). Fitness centre. Laundry. Limousine service. Non-smoking rooms. Restaurant.* **Room services** *Minibar. Room service (8am-11pm). Telephone. TV: satellite.*

Hostal Ciudad Condal

C/Mallorca 255, pral (93 215 10 40/fax 93 487 04 59). Metro Diagonal. **Rates** single €64.20-€80.30; double €101.70-€112.40; triple €128.40. **Credit** AmEx, DC, MC, V. **Map** p339 F4.

Even though it is located in a Modernista building dating back to 1891 by Josep Vilaseca i Casanovas, the Ciudad Condal is a fairly basic *hostal* that offers 15 clean and functional rooms. All rooms have private bathrooms and high ceilings. The best rooms look over a lush interior garden. There is no lift.
Hotel services *Bar. Car park (€16.10/day). Non-smoking rooms (4).* **Room services** *Telephone. TV.*

Hostal d'Uxelles

Gran Via de les Corts Catalanes 688, pral (93 265 25 60/fax 93 232 85 67/www.hotelduxelles.com). Metro Tetuán. **Rates** single €64.20; double €80.25; triple €105.90; quadruple €144.50. **Credit** AmEx, MC, V. **Map** p343 E5.

A delightfully pretty *hostal*, with high ceilings and (in some rooms) original tiled floors. The angels above reception are a hint of what is to come: pine floors and cream walls festooned with gilt framed mirrors and antique furnishings. Pastel colours are favoured, and curtains are draped above bedsteads. Rooms on the C/Girona side have terrace-balconies complete with plants. The whole effect is whimsically romantic. Breakfast is served in the bedrooms. The second wing, which echoes the first in ambience and decor, is housed in a building down the road.
Hotel services *Lounge.* **Room services** *Telephone. TV.*
Other locations: Hostal d'Uxelles 2 Gran Via de les Corts Catalanes 667, entl 2ª (same phone number).

Hotel Actual

C/Rosselló 238 (93 552 05 50/fax 93 552 05 55/ www.hotelactual.com). Metro Diagonal. **Rates** single €138; double €152. **Credit** AmEx, DC, MC, V. **Map** p338 D4.

A chic lobby with white leather sofas sets the stage for this boutique-style hotel owned by the Gimeno sisters, who have an eponymous design and household store nearby. The 29 rooms are creatively done up in a minimalist style, with black headboards, velvet curtains and grey slate bathrooms, and there is a reading room and bar. Some rooms look over Gaudí's La Pedrera.
Hotel services *Air-conditioning. Bar. Car park (€19.30/day). Disabled: adapted rooms (2). Laundry. Limousine service. Non-smoking rooms. Reading room.* **Room services** *Dataport. Minibar. Room service (7am-3pm). Telephone. TV: satellite.*

Hotel Axel

C/Aribau 33 (93 232 93 93/fax 93 323 93 94/ www.hotelaxel.com). Metro Universitat. **Rates** single €128.40-€176.60; double €176.60-€224.70; suite €315.70. **Credit** AmEx, MC, V. **Map** p342 C5.

This boutique hotel was originally a place for discerning gay clientele, but everyone is welcome. It has a white colour scheme, functional modular furniture and large square pillows. Superior rooms have Modernista balconies, huge beds and jacuzzis. Guests can dip in the rooftop pool, and use the computers in the library. Restaurant decor veers from black leather to crisp white linen via lush red velvet.
Hotel services *Air-conditioning. Bar. Business centre. Disabled: adapted rooms (2). Fitness centre. Pool (outdoor). Restaurant.* **Room services** *Dataport. Room service (24hrs). TV: satellite. Telephone.*

Barcelona's best-loved hotel makes a stunning comeback...

Hotel Constanza

C/Bruc 33 (93 270 19 10/fax 93 317 40 24/ www.hotelconstanza.com). Metro Urquinaona. **Rates** single €107-€117.70; double €128.40; triple €160.50. **Credit** AmEx, MC, V. **Map** p343 D5.

Here's a rarity: a chic, boutique hotel that doesn't cost the earth. Hotel Constanza is done out in white with the odd scarlet couch adding a splash of colour. Breakfast is served in a sleek, minimal dining room. Upstairs, wine-coloured corridors lead to sumptuous bedrooms, with dark wood and leather furnishings, huge pillows and high quality cotton sheets. Bathrooms are just as chic as the rooms and go overboard on the toiletries. Those at the back are quietest, and some have private terraces.

Hotel services *Air-conditioning.* **Room services** *Minibar. Telephone. TV: satellite.*

Hotel Ginebra

Rambla Catalunya 1, 3º 1ª (93 317 10 63/fax 93 317 55 65/hotelginebra@telefonica.net). Metro Catalunya. **Rates** single €42; double €70. **Credit** DC, MC, V. **Map** p344 B1.

With its rather grand entrance on the corner of Plaça Catalunya, a stay at Hotel Ginebra will give you a taste of what it's like to live in one of the Eixample's sprawling apartments. Unusual features include a small bar filled with an intriguing range of ancient liqueurs, and a chintzy living room. All 12 rooms are clean and comfortable, each with its own tiny bathroom. Ask for one of the best rooms that have small balconies that look over the square.

Hotel services *Air-conditioning. Snack bar.* **Room services** *Telephone. TV: satellite.*

Hotel Gran Via

Gran Via de les Corts Catalanes 642 (93 318 19 00/ fax 93 318 99 97/www.nnhotels.es). Metro Passeig de Gràcia. **Rates** single €80.30-€107; double €133.80; triple €171.20; quadruple €198. **Credit** AmEx, DC, MC, V. **Map** p342 D5.

The faded splendour of this old mansion (built in 1870 and converted into a hotel in 1936) has a certain unintentional charm. The paint is beginning to chip, and the rooms are on the spartan side, but they are ample and furnished with antiques. The impressive lobby is a flourish of grand columns, arches and gilt, and there is a pretty garden. Decor is resolutely old-fashioned, though more 1970s than 1870s.

Hotel services *Air-conditioning. Disabled: adapted (2). Internet access. Laundry.* **Room services** *Minibar. Telephone. TV: satellite.*

Budget

Hostal Central Barcelona

C/Diputació 246 (93 245 19 81/fax 93 231 83 07/ www.hostalcentralbarcelona.com). Metro Tetuán. **Rates** single €32.10-€42.80; double €57.80-€68.50; triple €73.85-€87.75. **Credit** MC, V. **Map** p343 E5.

Rooms have private balconies or galleries, high ceilings, chandeliers and are painted duck egg blue, with original tiles throughout. This is a great deal if you're looking for cheery, safe accommodation with a civilised ambience that puts many *hostales* to shame; free tea and coffee for example, a fridge full of cold drinks, water and fresh fruit, and helpful staff. Rooms overlooking the Ronda can be noisy, so bring earplugs or ask for a back room.

Hotel services *Air-conditioning. Fax. Iron. Snack bar. No smoking.*

Hostal Eden

C/Balmes 55, 1º (93 454 73 63/fax 93 452 66 21/ www.hostaleden.net). Metro Passeig de Gràcia. **Rates** single €35-€45; double €50-€65; triple €60-€75; quadruple €70-€85. **Credit** AmEx, MC, V. **Map** p338 D4.

It's not exactly luxurious, but this 32-room *pensión* does have its perks: free internet access and a new, large sunny patio. The best rooms are those with

...and the newly polished **La Florida** shines brighter than ever. *See p72.*

corner baths – especially Nos.114 and 115 at the rear, with large windows overlooking the patio. Room 103 is dark but good-sized and quirky, with a large bathroom up steps behind big sliding doors. Other rooms can be gloomy and cramped, noise travels between them, and the shared bathrooms are slightly shabby, but bright murals liven it up, and the atmosphere is warm and relaxed. A good deal, especially for groups of three or four. Note, there's no lift.
Hotel services *Internet access. Lounge. Payphone.* **Room services** *Air-conditioning (some rooms). TV.*

Hostal Girona

C/Girona 24, 1° 1ª (93 265 02 59/fax 93 265 85 32/ www.hostalgirona.com). Metro Urquinaona. **Rates** single €26.80-€37.50; double €48.20-€66.40. **Credit** MC, V. **Map** p344 C1.
Gorgeous and good value. Oozing with Eixample charm, this rare gem of a *hostal* combines prettily painted rooms, antiques, crystal chandeliers, coloured tiled floors and oriental rugs with a spectacular marble staircase. It has three wings, two of which have been refurbished and rooms made en suite; it is worth splashing out an extra few euros on these (although rooms in the older wing have en suite showers, and are not to be sniffed at). Outward-facing rooms tend to be brighter and more spacious.
Hotel services *Payphone.* **Room services** *TV: satellite.*

Hostal Goya

C/Pau Claris 74, 1° (93 302 25 65/fax 93 412 04 35/www.hostalgoya.com). Metro Urquinaona. **Rates** single €28.90-€34.30; double €47.10-€88.30. **Credit** MC, V. **Map** p342 D5.
This good-value *hostal* is being steadily transformed. The upper floor, which holds the reception and a large, stylish TV lounge, still has some unrenovated rooms with ancient bedspreads and woodchip-effect walls, but good bathrooms. Rooms without baths have robes and slippers provided for trips to the communal facilities. Renovated rooms on both floors are a pleasant surprise (if a little more expensive) with designer furnishings and creamy colour schemes. Most have new parquet flooring but some have their original Modernista floor tiles.
Hotel services *Air-conditioning (some rooms). Fax. Iron. TV room.*

Hostal-Residencia Oliva

Passeig de Gràcia 32, 4° (93 488 01 62/fax 93 487 04 97). Metro Passeig de Gràcia. **Rates** single €32.10; double €53.50-€64.20. **No credit cards**. **Map** p342 D5.
This is a very average *hostal* that distinguishes itself through its excellent location. This makes for good views but noisy rooms. Inward-looking rooms can feel stuffy. Facilities and furniture have seen better days, but it is all clean enough. Staff are a bit gruff but their bark is worse than their bite.
Hotel services *Lounge. Payphone.* **Room services** *TV.*

Hostal de Ribagorza

C/Trafalgar 39 (93 319 19 68/fax 93 319 19 68/ hostalribagorza@terra.es). Metro Urquinaona. **Rates** double €40-€60; triple €55-€70. **Credit** MC, V. **Map** p344 C2.
Lace curtains and fresh flowers are some of the special touches found at this *pensión* run by Pedro Iglesias and family. Located near the Palau de la Música, the Ribagorza is entered through an impressive Modernista lobby with unique carved wooden doors. The 11 rooms have televisions and lofty ceilings. Room 106 has a very nice light-filled gallery.
Hotel services *Payphone.* **Room services** *TV.*

Hostal San Remo

C/Ausiàs Marc 19, 1° 2ª (93 302 19 89/fax 93 301 07 74/www.hostalsanremo.com). Metro Urquinaona. **Rates** single €30; double €46-€56; triple €56-€78. **Credit** MC, V. **Map** p344 C1.

Friendly owner Roser (and her little dog) keeps this modest, seven-room *pensión* sparkling clean. Four of the rooms enjoy great street views and balconies, but all seven are an ample size and have old tiled floors and simple en suite bathrooms. The only exception is the popular triple/quadruple room whose bathroom is separate, though the room does have a seating area with a sofa.
Hotel services *Air-conditioning. Payphone.* **Room services** *TV.*

Residencia Australia

Ronda Universitat 11, 4° 1ª (93 317 41 77/fax 93 317 07 01/www.residenciaustralia.com). Metro Universitat. **Rates** single €28; double €45-€80. **Credit** MC, V. **Map** p344 A1.
Owner Maria fled Franco's Spain to Australia in the '50s, and returned after the generalismo's death to open this small, friendly, home-from-home *pensión*. There are just four rooms (one en suite); all are cosy and clean. There are two clean but basic communal bathrooms with showers. Note that there is a minimum two-night stay. The family also has an apartment nearby that can be booked if rooms are full.
Hotel services *Internet access.* **Room services** *Air-conditioning (some). Fridge (some). TV (some).*

Gràcia

Mid-range

Hotel Confort

Travessera de Gràcia 72 (93 238 68 28/fax 93 238 73 29/www.mediumhoteles.com). Metro Diagonal or Fontana. **Rates** single €104.90-€112.40; double €119.90. **Credit** AmEx, DC, MC, V. **Map** p338 D3.
Opened in 2001, the Confort still feels shiny and new, and is light-years ahead of other two-star establishments, with 36 simple but smart modern bedrooms with light wood furnishings and marble bathrooms. All the rooms get lots of light, thanks to several interior patios, and there is a bright dining room and lounge area, and a large leafy terrace.
Hotel services *Air-conditioning. Disabled: adapted room. Laundry.* **Room services** *Minibar. Telephone. TV: satellite.*

Budget

Acropolis Guest House

C/Verdi 254 (tel/fax 93 284 8187/ acropolis@telefonica.net). Metro Lesseps.
Rates single €25-€36; double €40-€50; triple €60-€70. **No credit cards**. **Map** p339 D3.
Neatness freaks abstain, but if the broken flowerpots and bric-a-brac strewn in the front garden make you smile rather than frown, there's a fair chance you'll love it here. Eight big, airy, spotless rooms have decent though minimal furniture, and some are en suite. Two share a large balcony; but that's nothing compared to the attic room with its roof terrace and spectacular views, making the schlep up the hill worth every minute. The ramshackle kitchen is communal, as is the chaotic garden.
Hotel services *Cooking facilities. No smoking. Payphone.*

Sants

Expensive

Hotel Catalonia Barcelona Plaza

Plaça d'Espanya 6-8 (93 426 26 00/fax 93 426 04 00/ www.hoteles-catalonia.es). Metro Espanya. **Rates** single €145.50-€224.70; double €183-€259. **Credit** AmEx, DC, MC, V. **Map** p341 A5.
This huge hotel overlooks the Fira (trade fair), and consequently the majority of guests are business travellers. Standard rooms are comfortable and well equipped but rather, well, standard. Suites are more impressive, if a little sombre, with separate sitting rooms and luxurious bathrooms. Some rooms overlook the Arenas bullring, currently being converted into a shopping centre (the noise from which isn't fully shut out in the lower rooms). A covered inner patio is the setting for an exceptional breakfast buffet, and there's a small gym and outdoor pool.
Hotel services *Air-conditioning. Babysitting. Bar. Business centre. Car park (€16.05/day). Disabled: adapted rooms (4). Fitness centre. Laundry. Limousine service. Pool (outdoor). Restaurant. Terrace.* **Room services** *Minibar. Room service (24hrs). Telephone. TV: pay movies/satellite.*

Mid-range

Hotel Onix Fira

C/Llançà 30 (93 426 00 87/fax 93 426 19 81/ www.hotelsonix.com). Metro Espanya. **Rates** single €85.60-€128.40; double €96.30-€160.50; triple €125.20-€199. **Credit** AmEx, DC, MC, V. **Map** p341 B5.
This 80-room hotel is an efficient, but rather clinical option. Piped music and salmon-pink bedding liven the fully equipped rooms, some of which overlook the Arena's bullring currently being (noisily) converted into a shopping centre; others face an interior patio. The roof has a tiny pool and two terraces.
Hotel services *Air-conditioning. Bar. Car park (€12.90). Disabled: adapted rooms (2). Laundry. Pool (outdoor).* **Room services** *Minibar. Room service (8am-11pm). Telephone. TV: satellite.*

Budget

Hostal Sofía

Avda Roma 1-3, entl (93 419 50 40/fax 93 430 69 43). Metro Sants Estaciò. **Rates** single €35; double €40-€50; triple €51-€60. **Credit** DC, MC, V. **Map** p341 B4.
Housed in an apartment block near the Sants station, Hostal Sofía offers simple, homely accommodation. The white walled, marble-floored rooms are

Hotel Constanza: a chic and cheapish boutique hotel. *See p68.*

plainly furnished, apart from the splash of brightly patterned bedspreads. Bathrooms, both en suite and communal, are clean and well appointed. There's a handy restaurant directly below the hostal where customers can enjoy breakfast.
Hotel services *Payphone.* **Room services** *TV (some rooms).*

Zona Alta

Expensive

La Florida

Carretera de Vallvidrera al Tibidabo 83-93 (93 259 30 00/fax 93 259 30 01/www.hotellaflorida.com). **Rates** single/double €274.50-€454.80; room with garden or terrace €530-€630; junior suite €775.80-€829.30; suite €829.30-€1,605. **Credit** AmEx, DC, MC, V.

From 1925 when it first opened through to the 1950s, La Florida was Barcelona's best hotel, frequented by royalty and film stars. Now, after a long renovation, it is open again, studded with well-chosen works by artists and designers like Rebecca Horn and Ben Jakober, who have also come up with inspired, individually designed suites for that special weekend. There's a magnificent steel pool that appears to fall from the mountainside into the Med, terraces, gardens, 360-degree views over the city, bracing walks in the Collserola hills, a five-star restaurant and a swanky jazz club. Getting a cab to take you back at night can be tricky, but there is a free shuttle service that can be arranged in advance. Check the website for good value mini breaks.

Hotel services *Air-conditioning. Babysitting. Bars. Business centre. Car park (€19.30/day). Concierge. Complimentary shuttle service. Disabled: adapted rooms (2). Fitness centre. Laundry. Non-smoking floor. Pool (outdoor/indoor). Restaurant.* **Room services** *Dataport. Minibar. Room service (24hrs). Telephone. TV: pay movies/satellite.*

Mid-range

Hotel Guillermo Tell

C/Guillem Tell 49 (93 415 40 00/fax 93 217 34 65/www.hotelguillermotell.com). Metro Fontana/FGC Plaça Molina. **Rates** single €82.40-€156.20; double €100-€174.40; suite €122-€232.20. **Credit** AmEx, DC, MC, V. **Map** p338 D2.

This striking, red-brick building opened in 2000 and still has an air of newness about it. The lobby is instantly welcoming, with music playing in the background and the smell of fresh coffee wafting through the open-plan breakfast room. Rooms are extremely comfortable, with cream and sky-blue furnishings and well-equipped bathrooms, with plenty of toiletries and fluffy towels.

Hotel services *Air-conditioning. Car park (€13/day). Disabled: adapted rooms (2). Laundry.* **Room services** *Minibar. Telephone. TV: satellite.*

Petit Hotel

C/Laforja 67, 1° 2ª (93 202 36 63/fax 93 202 34 95/www.petit-hotel.net). **Rates** (incl breakfast) single €66.40; double €83.50-€97.40; extra bed adult €28.90, under-12s €22.50. **Credit** AmEx, DC, MC, V. **Map** p338 C3.

Located in the chic neighbourhood of Sant Gervasi, this charming hotel has just four bedrooms (one en-suite, the others sharing two immaculate bathrooms), set around a smart, softly lit lounge. More like staying with friends than in a hotel, it is very popular with couples. Other pluses include a homey kitchen, where owners Rosa and Leo are happy to give insider information on the city. Unfortunately, you can't cook in the kitchen, but you can get breakfast all day from 8.30am. Petit Hotel is among the nicest alternative accommodation in the city.
Hotel services *Air-conditioning. Internet access. Laundry. Payphone.* **Room services** *Fridge. TV.*

Apartment hotels

Citadines

La Rambla 122 (93 270 11 11/fax 93 412 74 21/ www.citadines.com). Metro Catalunya. **Rates** studio €152-€171.20; apartment €214-€256.80; extra bed €20.40; linen kit €7.50-€10.70. **Credit** AmEx, DC, MC, V. **Map** p342 D5.

Situated in a prime location on the Rambla, Citadines offers 115 recently renovated studios and 16 one bedroom apartments (which all sleep four). One weekly clean is included in the price (there's an option to pay extra for the daily cleaning service). Breakfast is served in a cafeteria on the first floor, which looks out over La Rambla. This impeccable establishment is definitely a crowd-puller, with its mod cons and shiny fittings, but there is no denying the sterile sheen of the chain hotel.
Hotel services *Air-conditioning. Car park (€20/day). Disabled: adapted rooms (4). Laundry.* **Room services** *CD player (some rooms). Kitchenette. Telephone. TV: satellite.*

Hispanos Siete Suiza

C/Sicilia 255, Eixample (93 208 20 51/ fax 93 208 20 52/www.hispanos7suiza.com. Metro Sagrada Família. **Rates** (incl breakfast) apartments 1-2 people €192.60-€278.20; 3 people €224.70-€363.80; 4 people €256.80-€385.20; up to 6 people €385.20-€535. **Credit** AmEx, DC, MC, V. **Map** p339 F4.

The crème de la crème of apartment hotels, with 19 intimate-feeling but spacious apartments. Each has a kitchen and a sitting area with parquet floors, a terrace and two bedrooms. Not only are they cosy, tastefully decorated and well thought-out for longer stays and families, but the profits go to the cancer research foundation that runs the hotel. The foundation was set up by a local doctor, Dr Melchor Colet, when his wife died of cancer in 1974. The hotel opened after the doctor himself died, but still houses his collection of vintage cars (built by the Spanish manufacturer Hispanos Suiza).
Hotel services *Air-conditioning. Bar. Car park (€13/day). Disabled: adapted room. Laundry. Restaurant. Supermarket service.* **Room services** *Dataport. Minibar. Room service (24hr). Telephone. TV: satellite/DVD hire.*

Apartment & room rentals

Check all the small print (cancellation, cleaning and other fees, etc) carefully before handing over money. You may also want to check that there will be someone in Barcelona to give you assistance in case of any problems. As well as the sites listed below, also try www.loquo.com and www.expatriates.com.

Barcelona Living

C/Mallorca 264, 2° 2ª, Eixample (www.barcelona living.com). Metro Passeig de Gràcia. **Rates** 1-2 people €133.80-€176.60; 3 people €160.50-€203.30; 4 people €187.30-€230.10. **Credit** MC, V.

Barcelona Living is a small holiday apartment agency started by an Anglo-Spanish expat from Manchester. The main property is a lovely old building in the Born. Its four small but perfectly formed apartments have all been given a hip makeover, with exposed stone walls, and furniture alternating between retro chic and IKEA functionalism. Each apartment has one bedroom (a sofa bed can accommodate more sleepers), a fully equipped kitchen and a lounge with cable TV, stereo and phone.

Habit Servei

C/Muntaner 200, 2° 3ª, Eixample (93 209 50 45/ fax 93 414 54 25/www.habitservei.com). FGC Provença/Metro Hospital Clínic. **Open** 10am-2pm, 3-7.30pm Mon-Fri. **Credit** DC, MC, V. **Map** p338 C3.

This agency can find rooms in flats for visitors staying at least two weeks. Rates range from €300 to €390 a month for a flatshare, or around €300 for a room in a private house. Whole flats, with widely varying prices (from about €600 a month), are also available. The agency fee is €139 for a shared flat and €209 for an entire flat.

Oh-Barcelona

C/Fontanella 20, 2-D Eixample (93 302 03 79/fax 93 342 53 12/www.oh-barcelona.com). Metro Catalunya or Urquinaona. **Open** 8.30am-1.30pm, 2.30-5.30pm Mon-Fri. **Credit** AmEx, MC, V. **Map** 344 B1.

Oh-Barcelona is an agency for Spanish language courses as well as accommodation in apartments, shared flats and family homes. A credit card or bank transfer payment must be made before reservations are accepted, with the balance paid in cash on arrival.

Youth hostels

For student and youth services and websites that can take reservations for hostels, *see p317.*

Alberg Mare de Déu de Montserrat

Passeig de la Mare de Déu del Coll 41-51, Gràcia (93 210 51 51/fax 93 210 07 98/www.tujuca.com). Metro Vallcarca. **Open** *Hostel* 7am-midnight daily (ring for entry after hours). *Reception* 8am-3pm, 4.30-11pm daily. **Rates** (incl breakfast) under-25s €15.90; over-25s €19.40; sheets €2 per person. **Credit** AmEx, DC, MC,V.

Acropolis Guest House: quirky chaos for the more creative visitor. *See p71.*

This traditional hostel is housed in a beautiful old building that has alternately served as a private mansion, hospital and orphanage over the years. You can see echoes of its grand past in the tilework, painted cherubs and stained-glass windows. Some of the well-kept dorms have views of the city and the hostel's gorgeous gardens. IYHF cards are required for anyone wishing to stay.
Hotel services *Car park (free). Dining room. Disabled: adapted rooms. Games room. Internet access. Laundry. No smoking. Payphone. TV room.*

Barcelona Mar Youth Hostel

C/Sant Pau 80 (93 324 85 30/fax 93 324 85 31/ www.youthostel.com). Metro Para.lel. **Open** 24hrs daily. **Rates** (incl breakfast) €15.50-€21.50; sheets €2.50 per stay. **Credit** AmEx, MC, V. **Map** p342 C6.
This one's as cheap as chips, with pleasant communal areas, sparkling clean washrooms and handy on-site facilities such as laundry room and computer terminals with internet access. There are no individual rooms, only dorms stacked with bunk beds; though, in a token nod to privacy, all can be cordoned off by powder-blue drapes.
Hotel services *Bicycle rental. Disabled: adapted room. Internet access. Laundry. Non-smoking rooms (all). TV.* **Room services** *Lockers.*

Gothic Point

C/Vigatans 5, Born (93 268 78 08/fax 93 246 15 52/www.gothicpoint.com). Metro Jaume I.
Open 24hrs daily. **Rates** (incl breakfast) €16-€21 per person; sheets/blankets/towels (all €2/night).
Credit DC, MC, V. **Map** p345 B3.
Decor is colourful, staff are helpful and the reception walls are covered with info on clubs, bars, tours and so on. Dorms (six to 14 beds) are a bit cramped. An undersheet and pillowcase is provided, but anything else must be rented. Communal bathrooms are clean. Beach bums should stay at the sister hostel, Sea Point (Plaça del Mar 1-4, 93 224 70 75) on the seafront.
Hotel services *Air-conditioning. Disabled: adapted room. Fridge. Internet access (free). Lounge. Microwave. No smoking. Payphone. TV.* **Room services** *Lockers (€1.20).*

Itaca Alberg-Hostel

C/Ripoll 21, Barri Gòtic (93 301 97 51/www.itaca hostel.com). Metro Catalunya or Urquinaona.
Open *Reception* 7am-4am daily. **Rates** (incl sheets) dormitory €18; twin €44. **No credit cards**.
Map p344 B2.
This funky, colourful hostel is located on a very quiet street a stone's throw from the cathedral. Murals, sofas, and music in the lobby make for a welcoming atmosphere. There is a communal kitchen, a small breakfast room and shelves of books and games. Its 33 beds are in five airy dormitories, all with balconies. Bathroom facilities are clean.
Hotel services *Air-conditioning. Café. Dining room. Internet access. Kitchen. No smoking.* **Room services** *Lockers. Sheets.*

Campsites

For more information on campsites not far from the city, get the *Catalunya Campings* book from the tourist offices (*see p319*) or bookshops.

Estrella de Mar

Autovia de Castelldefels km 16.7, Castelldefels (93 633 07 84/fax 93 633 03 70). **Open** *Reception* 9am-2pm, 4-10pm daily. *Campsite* 7.30am-midnight daily.
Rates per person €4.70; €3.40 under-10s. Tent/caravan/car €4.70; Motorhome €8.85; electricity connection €4. **Credit** MC, V.

Camping Masnou

Carretera N2, km 633, El Masnou, Outer Limits (tel/fax 93 555 15 03). **Open** *Reception* Winter 9am-midday, 3-7pm daily. Summer 8am-10pm daily. *Campsite* 7am-11.30pm daily. **Rates** per person €5.35; €4.30 2-10s; free under-2s. **No credit cards**.

Sightseeing

Features

Introduction

Sights for sore eyes.

At the very heart of the Old City is the **Barri Gòtic** (Gothic Quarter), a twisting maze of interconnecting streets and buildings from Barcelona's Golden Age, and one of the best preserved medieval centres anywhere. Its streets grew inside the original Roman walls; then, as the city's own wealth increased in the Middle Ages, new communities developed outside the old Roman perimeter. These areas, **La Mercè**, **Sant Pere** and the **Born**, were brought within the city with the building of a second wall in the 13th century. The area south of this wall, on the other side of the riverbed later to become the Rambla, was the **Raval**, enclosed within a third city wall built in the 14th century.

Until the mid 19th century, Barcelona comprised little else. In the dramatic surge that followed the destruction of the city walls in 1860, small towns such as **Gràcia** and **Sants** were sucked into the city and the **Eixample** was built, devouring churches and convents in its path. With its long, straight streets, this became the city's second great characteristic district, and a showcase for the location of the greatest works of **Modernisme** – although there are others, such as the Park Güell, to be found in many parts of the city. Beyond the Eixample lie the green mountains of **Montjuïc** and, at the centre of the great ridge of the Serra de Collserola, **Tibidabo**, both towering above Barcelona and providing wonderful views.

GETTING AROUND

The Old City is easily walked (and almost impenetrable by public transport), but the metro system and buses are cheap, fast and easy to use. A funky way to get around the ports and beaches is the **Trixi** rickshaws. Running midday to 8pm, April to September, and costing €1.50 per person/kilometre, they can be hailed on the street, or booked on (mobile) 677 732 773/www.trixi.info.

Discount schemes

As well as the multi-tickets and discount cards described below, a ticket on the Bus Turístic (*see p179*) also includes a useful book of coupons that are valid against many of the city's top-rated attractions.

Articket

www.articketbcn.com **Rates** €15.

The Articket gives a discount of around 50% to six major museums and art galleries: **MNAC** (*see p114*), **MACBA** (*see p95*), the **Fundació Miró** (*see p111*), **Espai Gaudí-La Pedrera** (*see p121*), the **Fundació Tàpies** (*see p119*) and the **CCCB** (*see p95*). The ticket is valid for three months, and available from participating venues, tourist offices (*see p319*) and via Tel-entrada (*see p212*).

Barcelona Card

Rates *1 day* €17; €14 concessions. *2 days* €20; €17 concessions. *3 days* €23; €20 concessions. *4 days* €25; €22 concessions. *5 days* €27; €24 concessions.
One to five days of unlimited transport on the metro and buses, as well as discounts on the airport bus and cable cars, reduced entry to a wide variety of museums and attractions, and discounts at dozens of restaurants, bars and shops. It is sold in the airport, at tourist offices (*see p319*), L'Aquàrium (*see p223*), Casa Batlló (*see p117*), the Monument a Colom (*see p105*) and Sants railway station.

Ruta del Modernisme

Centre del Modernisme, Casa Amatller, Passeig de Gràcia 41, Eixample (93 488 01 39/www.bcn.es). Metro Passeig de Gràcia. **Open** 10am-7pm Mon-Sat; 10am-2pm Sun. **Rates** €7.50; €4 concessions. **No credit cards. Map** p340 D5.
Not a route, but a ticket, which includes a guidebook to many of the finest Modernista buildings in the city, and entitles the holder to 50% discount on entry to many of them. A guided tour of the façades of the Manzana de la Discòrdia (*see p117*) is also given. Ticket is valid for 30 days.

Tours

By bike

Barcelona by Bicycle

Un Cotxe Menys, C/Esparteria 3, Born (93 268 21 05). Metro Barceloneta. **Open** 10am-2pm Mon-Fri (call ahead for bike hire outside these times). **Tours** *Mar-Dec* 11am daily. **Rates** €22 incl guide & bike rental. **No credit cards. Map** p345 C3-4.
Straightforward bike hire runs from €6 for an hour to €70 per week, but tours of the city are also offered. Lasting three hours, they include a drink and are suitable for all ages. The meeting point is the Plaça Sant Jaume and booking is not essential.

► For more information on the **Fòrum 2004**, *see p218*.

Barcelona condensed

There are various solutions to limited time. Among other ideas, you could eschew the sights altogether and follow our **walks** on *pp86, 102 and 120* for the essence of the city. Or you could hop on either of the **tourist buses** (*see p79*) and let the sights come to you. But if you must fill two photo albums when you get home, here's how.

DAY ONE

Start with a stroll down **La Rambla**. Cut in to the **Plaça Reial**, admire Gaudí's lamp-posts and from there head to the heart of the **Barri Gòtic** and the **cathedral**. Crossing the Via Laietana takes you to the **Palau de la Música Catalana**, and marvel at the fantastic façade. From here head down into the Born proper, and perhaps tuck into some lunchtime tapas outside the majestic **Santa Maria del Mar**. From here it's a skip and a hop to the **Museu Picasso**. If you've any energy left, wander down to the **Port Vell**, **Barceloneta** and the **beach**, with its seafront restaurants.

DAY TWO

Head up the elegant **Passeig de Gràcia** to admire the contrasting masterpieces of the **Manzana de la Discòrdia**. A little further up is Gaudí's **La Pedrera**, with its Modernista apartment and staggeringly strange and beautiful roofscape. Backtrack slightly to catch a direct metro to Gaudí's most legendary work, the **Sagrada Família**. The Avda Gaudí has several places to grab a *bocadillo* and a beer, after which you could drop in to the stunning **Hospital Sant Pau**. From here hop in a cab (or a tourist bus) to the beautiful colours of Gaudí's **Park Güell**. The 24 bus will get you back to the centre in time for dinner.

DAY THREE

Venture into the Raval to see Richard Meier's striking **MACBA** and, nearby, the **CCCB**. Walk to the Ronda Sant Antoni to take a 55 bus up to **Montjuïc** and the **Fundació Miró**, which is also a good spot for lunch. From here you can walk to the **Olympic stadium** and then to the nearby **Jardí Botànic** for leafy tranquillity and spectacular views. Walk back past the Miró to get to the **cable car**, which will take you on a vertiginous ride to the **Port Vell** and the myriad seafood restaurants along Passeig Joan de Borbó.

Mike's Bike Tours

C/Escudellers 48 (93 301 36 12/www.mikes biketoursbarcelona.com). Metro Drassanes.
Tours *Mar-mid Apr* 12.30pm daily. *Mid Apr-July* 11.30am & 4.30pm daily. *Aug* 4pm daily. *Sept-mid Dec* 12.30pm daily. **Rates** €22. **No credit cards. Map** p345 A3.
Half-day bike tours of the Old City, Sagrada Família and Ciutadella park, with a pit-stop at the beach. Bike hire on its own is €5 per hour or €20 a day. From mid 2004 night tours and day trips outside the city will also be offered. All tours meet at the Monument a Colom (*see p105*).

By bus

Barcelona Tours

93 317 64 54. **Tours** 9am-9pm daily. Approx every 15-20mins Nov-May; approx every 8-10mins June-Oct. **Tickets** *1 day* €16; €10 4-14s. *2 days* €20; €13 4-14s. Free under-4s. Available on board bus. **No credit cards.**
As these bright orange open-topped buses make huge, one-way circuits of the city, a little forward planning is required. They are not as frequent as the Bus Turístic, and no discounts are offered to attractions, but they are far less crowded, and the recorded commentary, via headphones, is better informed. The entire route (without stopping) takes about three hours, so the latest you can begin a full tour, without getting off, is around 6pm.

Bus Turístic

Tours *Apr-Oct* 9am-9pm daily; approx every 6-10mins. *Nov-Mar* 9am-7pm daily; approx every 30mins. **Tickets** *1 day* €16; €10 concessions. *2 days* €20; €13 concessions. Free under-4s. Available from tourist offices or on board bus. **No credit cards.**

Top five Tips

Do be aware that most museums are closed on Mondays. The MACBA (*see p95*) is a notable exception.
Don't panic when you inevitably get lost in the winding streets of the Old City. Sooner or later you will emerge on La Rambla or the Via Laietana.
Do learn where La Rambla and the Via Laietana are. *See pp344-5.*
Don't carry anything you don't need. Leave your passport (but do carry a photocopy for ID), jewellery and credit cards in the hotel.
Do look down. Pavement plaques celebrate shops more than 60 years old, red discs alert passers-by to Modernista buildings or details, and other plaques identify individual trees of note.

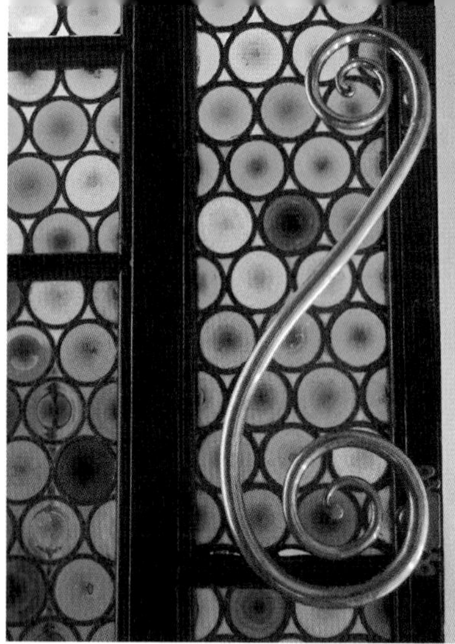

The Bus Turístic (white, splashed with colourful images of the sights) runs two circular routes, both passing through Plaça Catalunya: the northern (red) route passes La Pedrera, Sagrada Família, Park Güell, Tibidabo and Pedralbes; the southern (blue) route takes in Montjuïc, Port Vell, Vila Olímpica and the Barri Gòtic. Both are one-way. Ticket holders get discount vouchers for a range of attractions.

On foot

The **Travel Bar** (C/Boqueria 27, 93 342 52 52) organises city tours by bike on or foot, along with pub crawls. For gastronomic tours of Barcelona and further afield, contact **Saboroso** (93 451 50 10, www.saboroso.com).

Barcelona Walking Tours

906 301 282/93 368 97 30. **Tours** *Gothic* 10am (English), noon (Catalan/Spanish) Sat, Sun. *Picasso* 10.30am (English), 11.30am (Catalan/Spanish) Sat, Sun. **Tickets** *Gothic* €8; €3 concessions. Picasso €10; €5 concessions. €8; €3 concessions 1st Sun of mth. **No credit cards. Map** p344 B1.
Both the Gothic and the Picasso tours start at the tourist office in Plaça Catalunya, and from there wander through the Barri Gòtic. The Picasso tour then takes in the Born and the Museu Picasso, the price of which is included in the visit. Both tours take around 1½ hours (not including the museum visit). In such a walkable city, this is one of the better ways to take in the sights. Numbers are limited, so book ahead via the tourist offices.

My Favourite Things

mobile 637 265 405/678 542 753/www.myft.net.
Aiming to get you off the beaten track, and looking at the social and cultural aspects of the city, these are walking tours (€25-€30), with routes based on various themes from food to design and architecture. Phone or check out the funky website for details.

Barri Gòtic

Europe's most perfectly preserved medieval quarter.

The **Plaça Reial**, as seen by its many drunks. *See p83.*

Maps p344-p345

The two main hubs of the Barri Gòtic have represented the religious and political hearts of the city for over 2,000 years. The Gothic **cathedral** is the third cathedral to be built on the site; the first was built in the sixth century, and before that it was the location for part of the Roman temple, columns of which are still visible. The main square of the Old City is the Plaça Sant Jaume, where the main Roman axes – the *cardo maximus*, where C/Call becomes C/Llibreteria and later C/Carders, and the *decumanus maximus*, now called C/Bisbe and C/Ciutat – used to run. The Roman forum used to sit here, at the crossroads (*see p86* **Walk on: Roman remains**).

The square now contains the municipal government (**Ajuntament,** *see p83*) and Catalan regional government (**Palau de la Generalitat**, *see p87*) buildings, standing opposite each other. They have not always done so: the square was only opened up in 1823, after which the present dull neo-classical façade was added to the Ajuntament. That of the Generalitat is Renaissance, from 1598 to 1602. The greater part of both buildings, however, was built in the early 15th century, and both of their original main entrances open on to what was once the *decumanus maximus* at the side.

On this street is one of the most photographed features of the Barri Gòtic, the **bridge** across C/Bisbe from the Generalitat. It is actually a 20th-century addition, built to look old in 1928, when the idea of the neighbourhood as a 'Gothic Quarter' really took off. To help the image stick, a few enhancements were made. The **Casa dels Canonges** (a former set of canons' residences, and now Generalitat offices), on the other side of the bridge, has an equally medieval look, but had most of its Gothic touches added in the 1920s. Nevertheless, the area represents one of the most complete surviving ensembles of medieval buildings, from churches to houses, anywhere.

Many buildings around here represent history written in stone. In C/Santa Llúcia, just in front of the cathedral, is **Casa de l'Ardiaca**, originally a 15th-century residence for the archdeacon (*ardiaca*), with a superb tiled patio. Today it houses the city archives. It was renovated recently, but in a previous renovation in the 1870s, it acquired its curious letterbox by Domènech i Montaner showing swallows and a tortoise, believed by some to symbolise the contrast between the 'swiftness of justice and the law's delay', or by others, more prosaically, to be a reflection on the postal service.

On the other side of Plaça Nova from the Casa de l'Ardiaca is the **Col.legi d'Arquitectes**, with a sand-blasted frieze designed by Picasso (*see p85*). In front of the cathedral, on the right as you come out, is the **Museu Diocesà**, housing religious art (*see p85*), and around the side of the cathedral is the little-visited but fascinating **Museu Frederic Marès** (*see p87*).

A little further along is the 16th-century **Arxiu de la Corona d'Arago** building, named for the 'Archive of the Crown of Aragon' that was housed here until recently, but also known as the **Palau del Lloctinent** (Palace of the Lieutenant, or here, 'Viceroy'). It has a lovely Renaissance patio seen at its best during **L'Ou Com Balla** at Corpus Christi, when its fountain is garlanded with flowers and a hollowed-out eggshell placed on top. In less happy times, this was also the local headquarters for the Spanish Inquisition. The building was once part of the former royal palace (**Palau Reial**), and has another exit to the medieval palace square, the superbly preserved **Plaça del Rei**. Around the square are some of Barcelona's most historically important buildings – the **chapel of Santa Àgata**, the 16th-century watchtower (**Mirador del Rei Martí**) as well as the palace itself. Parts of the palace are said to date back to the tenth century, and there have been many remarkable additions to it since, notably the 14th-century Saló del Tinell, a medieval banqueting hall that is a definitive work of Catalan Gothic. It is here that Ferdinand and Isabella are said to have received Columbus on his return from America. Most of the sections of the Palau Reial now form part of the **Museu d'Història de la Ciutat** (*see p85*).

The narrow streets centred on C/Call once housed a rich Jewish ghetto (*call)*. At the corner of C/Sant Domènec del Call and C/Marlet is the medieval **synagogue**, recently restored and now open to the public (*see p82* **The Jewish quarter**). At C/Marlet 1 is a 12th-century inscription from a long-demolished house. Hebrew inscriptions can also be seen on stones set into the eastern wall of the **Plaça Sant Iu**, across from the cathedral, and at ankle level in the south-west corner of the Plaça del Rei. At the northern edge of the former *call* is the baroque **Sant Sever** church, to open to the public in 2004 as part of *Christus Splendor*, an exhibition of religious art from around Spain. Over 300 paintings are to be shown in the rooms at Sant Sever.

Near the centre of the *call* is the beautiful little **Plaça Sant Felip Neri**, with a fine baroque church and a soothing fountain. The damage from heavy artillery during the Spanish Civil War is still clearly visible. In fact the square is a relatively recent construction; the shoemakers' guild building (now housing the **Museu del Calçat** *see p85*) was moved here after the war, brick by brick, to make way for the Avda de la Catedral, while the tinkers' guild nearby was moved earlier last century when the Via Laietana was driven through the district. Close by are the leafily attractive **Plaça del Pi** and **Plaça Sant Josep Oriol**, where there are great pavement bars and artisanal weekend markets. The squares are separated by **Santa Maria del Pi**, one of Barcelona's most distinguished – but least visited – Gothic churches, with a magnificent rose window and spacious single nave. Opposite is the 17th-century neo-classical retailers' guildhall, with colourful sgraffiti added the following century.

Despite the expansion of Barcelona into the Eixample, the old centre has remained a hub of cultural, social and political life. In C/Montsió, a narrow street off Portal de l'Àngel, is the **Els Quatre Gats** café (*see p171*), legendary haunt of Picasso and other artists and bohemians, in a wonderful Modernista building designed by Puig i Cadafalch. Between C/Portaferrissa and Plaça del Pi lies **C/Petritxol**, one of the most charming streets of the Barri Gòtic, known for its traditional *granges* offering coffee and cakes, and also housing the **Sala Parés** (*see p232*), the city's oldest art gallery, where Rusiñol, Casas and the young Picasso all exhibited. On the other side of C/Portaferrissa, heading up C/Bot, is the newly done-up **Plaça Vila de Madrid**, where there are the excavated remains of a Roman necropolis, and a rare expanse of city-centre grass. Between here and the Plaça Catalunya is the marvellous little Romanesque church of **Santa Anna**, begun in 1141 as part of a monastery then outside the walls, and with an exquisite 14th-century cloister.

Back on the seaward side of the Barri Gòtic, if you walk from Plaça Sant Jaume up C/Ciutat, to the left of the Ajuntament, and turn down the narrow alley of C/Hércules, you will come to **Plaça Sant Just**, a fascinating old square with a Gothic water fountain from 1367 and the grand church of **Sants Just i Pastor**, built in the 14th century on the site of a chapel founded by Charlemagne's son Louis the Pious.

The once wealthy area between here and the port became steadily more run-down throughout the 20th century. It has a different atmosphere from the northern part of the Barri Gòtic; shabbier and with less prosperous shops. The city authorities made huge efforts to change this, particularly in the 1990s, when new squares were opened up: **Plaça George Orwell** on C/Escudellers, known as the 'Plaça del Trippy' by the youthful crowd that hangs out there, and the subject of much heated debate when CCTV was recently introduced (the irony of which was lost on no one), and **Plaça Joaquim Xirau**, off the Rambla. Another tactic was the siting of parts of the Universitat Pompeu Fabra on the lower Rambla. Just above is the neighbourhood's

The Jewish quarter

If walls could talk, the atmospheric alleys of the old Jewish quarter, or *call*, would tell of a once vibrant, learned community, of artisans and tradesmen, doctors and advisers to the Crown, of persecution by their stronger Christian neighbour, of expulsion, Inquisitors and execution. It is a past that is still very much to the fore with the discovery of what the Call's main synagogue until 1391, and its recent opening to the public. Increasingly in the public arena, too, are the demands of the Sephardic diaspora (descendants of those Jews who were expelled) for return of their nationality from the Spanish government.

There's little to suggest when Jews first arrived in Spain, although it is said that St Paul met resident Jews when he came to preach here. A community in Barcelona had probably already been established by the end of the second century. But after the decline and fall of the Roman empire, the supremacy of the Visigoths brought harsh anti-Semitic repression; by a decree of 694, all Jews were enslaved.

By the 13th century, the standing of the Jews had improved somewhat. They were allowed to own property, not only in the Call but also near to the Jewish cemetery on Montjuïc, although they were still required to wear easily recognisable dress. The intellectual esteem in which they were held in the city is demonstrated by the 'Disputation of Barcelona' of 1263 in which the rabbi Nahmanides and a friar argued their doctrinal differences before Jaume I for three days. It is said that the rabbi so impressed the King that he was given 300 pieces of silver.

During this golden time for medieval Jewry, the gates to the bustling Call were at either end of C/Call. The water supply came from a fountain on C/Sant Honorat, the eastern boundary of the quarter, and there was a school for women on C/Arc de Sant Ramon del Call (the western boundary). With numbers approaching 4,000, permission was given for a smaller community whose synagogue was on the site of the church of Sant Jaume on C/Ferran.

It's only in the last few years that historians have come to agree that the small basement in the building at C/Marlet 5 was the synagogue of the main Call. The extensive notes taken by a medieval tax collector called Jaume Colon on his meandering route around the Call, still preserved today, has allowed a detailed reconstruction of the area. The front of the building, slightly skewing the street, fulfils religious requirements by which the façade has to face Jerusalem; the two windows at knee height allow light to enter from that direction.

The 14th century brought utter disaster for the Jewish community. Failure of the wheat crop caused 10,000 deaths in the city in 1333 and in 1348 the Black Death arrived. Cycles of plague and famine occurred again and again, killing off an increasingly desperate populace. In 1391 the Catholic residents of the city, looking for somebody to blame for their ills, went on the rampage in the Call, massacring its residents.

The decline of the Call was mirrored by the economic decline of the whole city. Those Jews who could leave closed their businesses and did so. The remainder were either expelled en masse by Ferdinand and Isabel in 1492, or, having converted to Christianity, were subjected to the horrors of the Spanish Inquisition.

Sinagoga Shlomo Ben Adret

C/Marlet 5 (93 317 07 90/www.callde barcelona.org). Metro Jaume I or Liceu.
Open 11am-2.30pm, 4-7.30pm Tue-Sat; 11am-2.30pm Sun. **Admission** free (2 donation encouraged). **Map** p345 B3.

heart, the **Plaça Reial,** known for its bars and cheap hotels, and a favourite spot for a drink or an outdoor meal – provided you don't mind the odd drunk and are prepared to keep an eye on your bags. An addition from the 1840s, the *plaça* has the **Tres Gràcies** fountain in the centre and **lamp-posts** designed by the young Gaudí. On Sunday mornings a coin and stamp market is held here.

The grand porticoes of some of the buildings around the church of **La Mercè**, once the merchants' mansions, are testimony to the former wealth of the area before the building of the Eixample. There are also a dwindling number of lively *tascas* (small traditional tapas bars) on C/Mercè. Beyond C/Ample and the Mercè you emerge from narrow alleys on to the **Passeig de Colom**, where a few shipping offices and ships' chandlers still recall the dockside atmosphere of former decades. If the pretty **Plaça Duc de Medinaceli**, off to one side, looks familiar, it's probably because it was the setting for some scenes in Almodóvar's *All About My Mother*. Monolithic on Passeig de Colom is the army headquarters, the **Capitanía General**, with a façade that has the dubious distinction of being the one construction in Barcelona directly attributable to the dictatorship of Primo de Rivera.

Casa de l'Ardiaca. *See p81.*

Ajuntament (City Hall)

Plaça Sant Jaume (93 402 70 00/special visits 93 402 73 64/ww.bcn.es). Metro Liceu or Jaume I.
Open *Office* 8.30am-2.30pm Mon-Fri. *Visits* 10am-1.30pm Sun. **Admission** free. **Map** p345 B3.
The centrepiece and oldest part of the Casa de la Ciutat is the stately 15th-century Saló de Cent, flanked by the semicircular Saló de la Reina Regent, where council meetings are still held, and the Saló de Cròniques, spectacularly painted with murals by Josep Maria Sert. The Catalan Gothic old entrance on C/Ciutat contrasts with the rather dull 19th-century neo-classical façade on the main entrance. On Sundays there are guided tours (in different languages) every 20 minutes, or you can go it alone.

Cathedral

Pla de la Seu (93 315 15 54). Metro Jaume I.
Open *Combined ticket* 1.30-4.30pm daily. *Church* 8am-1.15pm, 5-7.30pm Mon-Fri; 8am-1.15pm, 5-6pm Sat; 8-9am, 5-6pm Sun. *Cloister* 9am-1.15pm, 5-7pm daily. *Museum* 10am-1pm daily. **Admission** *Combined ticket* €4. *Church & cloister* free. *Museum* €1. *Lift to roof* €2. *Choir* €1.50. **No credit cards**. **Map** p345 B3.
Based on a three-naved basilica that once stood on the site of the Roman forum, construction on the present-day cathedral began in 1298 and ended with the neo-Gothic façade added at the end of the 19th century. The building is predominantly Gothic, save the Romanesque chapel of Santa Llúcia to the right of the main façade. Aside from the glorious, light-filled

cloister, it is a slightly forbidding place, but contains many images, paintings and sculptures, and an intricately carved choir built in the 1390s. The cathedral museum, in the 17th-century chapter house, has paintings and sculptures, including works by the Gothic masters Jaume Huguet, Bernat Martorell and Bartolomé Bermejo. Santa Eulàlia, patron saint of Barcelona, lies in the dramatically lit crypt in an alabaster tomb carved with scenes from her martyrdom. To one side there is a lift to the roof, for a magnificent view of the Old City. A new combined ticket (*visita especial*) has a special timetable intended to keep tourists and worshippers from bothering one another. During the afternoons, ticketholders have the run of the cloister, church, choir and lift, and can enter some chapels and take photographs – something normally prohibited.

Centre Civic Pati Llimona

C/Regomir 3 (93 268 47 00). Metro Jaume I.
Open 9am-2pm, 4.30-8.30pm Mon-Fri; 10am-2pm Sat, Sun. **Exhibitions** 9am-2pm, 4.30-10pm Mon-Fri; 10am-2pm, 4-8pm Sat. Closed Aug. **Admission** free. **Map** p342 D5.

A building incorporating part of a round tower that dates from the first Roman settlement with later Roman baths and a 15th-century residence. The excavated foundations are visible from the street under glass. It is now used as a civic centre, with frequent exhibitions of photography.

Col.legi d'Arquitectes

Plaça Nova 5 (93 301 50 00/www.coac.net). Metro Jaume I. **Open** 10am-9pm Mon-Fri; 10am-2pm Sat. **Admission** free. **Map** p344 B2.

The architects' association is mainly of interest for its sand-blasted mural of Catalan folk scenes, designed by Picasso while in self-imposed exile in the 1950s and executed by other artists. Behind its atypical style is a story that when Picasso heard that Miró was also being considered he responded dismissively that he could easily do a Miró. For those of an architectural bent there are frequent, low-key exhibitions: see the website for details.

Museu del Calçat (Shoe Museum)

Plaça Sant Felip Neri 5 (93 301 45 33). Metro Jaume I. **Open** 11am-2pm Tue-Sun. **Admission** €2.50; €1.50 concessions; free under-7s. **No credit cards**. **Map** p345 B3.

A tiny off-beat museum of the type Barcelona does so well, and one of only three in the world, this footwear museum displays the cobbler's craft from Roman times to the present day. Embroidered slippers from the Arabic world, 17th-century musketeers' boots, and delicately hand-painted 18th-century party shoes are all highlights, along with the biggest shoe in the world, according to the *Guinness Book of Records*.

Museu Diocesà

Avda de la Catedral 4 (93 315 22 13). Metro Jaume I. **Open** 10am-2pm, 5-8pm Tue-Sat; 11am-2pm Sun. **Admission** €2; €1.50 concessions; free under-10s. **Credit** (shop only) MC, V. **Map** p344 B2.

Plaça Duc de Medinaceli. *See p83.*

A hotchpotch of religious art, punctuated with occasional exhibitions of unrelated themes, the Diocesan Museum is interesting for its 14th-century alabaster virgins, altarpieces by Bernat Martorell and wonderful Romanesque murals. The building itself is interesting, and includes the Pia Almoina, a former almshouse, stuck on to a Renaissance canon's residence, which in turn was built inside a Roman tower. In 2004, the museum, along with the church of Sant Sever nearby and Santa Maria del Mar (*see p103*), will display some of the hundreds of religious works collected for the Christus Splendor exhibition.

Museu d'Història de la Ciutat

Plaça del Rei 1 (93 315 11 11). Metro Jaume I.
Open *June-Sept* 10am-8pm Tue-Sat; 10am-3pm Sun. *Oct-May* 10am-2pm, 4-8pm Tue-Sat; 10am-3pm Sun. **Guided tours** by appointment. **Admission** €4; €2.50 concessions; free under-16s. Free 4-8pm 1st Sat of mth. **No credit cards**. **Map** p345 B3.

Walk on Roman remains

Duration: 45 minutes.

In 15 BC Roman soldiers established a colony on a small hill called the **Mons Taber**, later to become the settlement of **Barcino**. Medieval Barcelona and all subsequent buildings in the Barri Gòtic were constructed on top of the site, and many a local resident has set out to make over a bathroom and turned up a bit of ancient masonry. Barcino has had an unappreciated impact on every subsequent era: many of Barcelona's most familiar streets – C/Hospital, even the Passeig de Gràcia – follow the line of Roman roads. The best way to get an idea of the Roman town is to walk the line of its walls. Along the way all kinds of Roman remains can be found, poking out from where they were reused or built over by medieval and later builders.

A logical place to start a walk is at **C/Paradís**, between the cathedral and Plaça Sant Jaume, where a round millstone is set into the paving to mark what was believed to be the precise centre of the Mons Taber. It is here that you'll find the remains of the **Temple Romà d'Augusti** (*see p89*). Where C/Paradís meets the Plaça Sant Jaume was where Barcino's two main thoroughfares used to meet, and the road left, **C/Llibreteria**, began life as the **Cardus Maximus**, the main road to Rome. Just off this road is the Plaça del Rei and the extraordinary **Museu d'Història de la Ciutat**, below which you can visit the largest underground excavation of a Roman site in Europe.

Rejoining C/Llibreteria, turn left at **C/Tapineria** to reach **Plaça Ramon Berenguer el Gran** and the largest surviving stretch of ancient wall, incorporated into the medieval Palau Reial. Continue on along Tapineria, where there are many sections of Roman building, to **Avda de la Catedral**. The massive twin-drum gate on C/Bisbe, while often retouched, has not changed in its basic shape, at least at the base, since it was the main gate of the Roman town. To its left you can see fragments of an aqueduct, and at its front are Joan Brossa's bronze letters, spelling out 'Barcino'. If you take a detour up C/Capellans to **C/Duran i Bas**, you can see another four arches of a former aqueduct, and heading left and straight over the Avda Portal de l'Àngel is the Roman necropolis in **Plaça Vila de Madrid**, with the tombs clearly visible. In accordance with Roman custom these had to be outside the city walls.

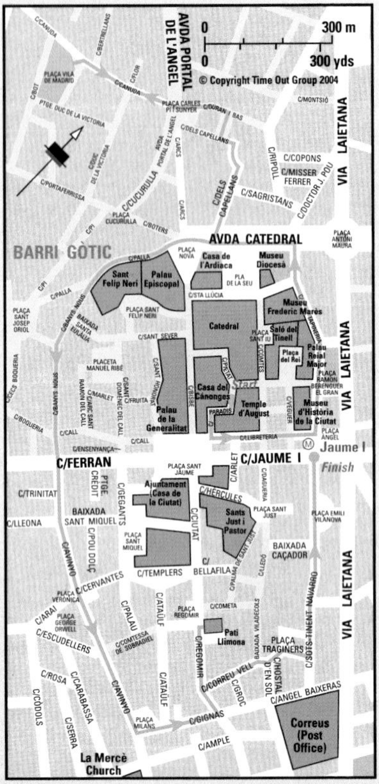

The City History Museum is part of a trio that includes the monastery at Pedralbes (*see p131*), and the Museu Verdaguer (*see p129*) – tickets are valid for all. From late 2004 tickets will also include entrance to the medieval remains found under the Born market (*see p98*). Extensive remains of the Roman city of Barcino form a giant labyrinthine cellar beneath the museum, with streets and villa layouts still visible. A visit takes you underground as far as the cathedral, beneath which there is a fourth-century baptistery (closed at the time of writing), and busts, monuments and other sculptures found in the excavations are on display. The admission fee also gives you access to the Santa Àgata chapel – with its 15th-century altarpiece by Jaume Huguet, one of the greatest Catalan painters in medieval times – and the majestic 14th-century Saló del Tinell (when there is no temporary exhibition held here). The Rei Martí watchtower is still closed to the public while it awaits reinforcement.

To complement the events of the Fòrum 2004, *The Human Condition* will explore the concept of peace through art from various periods of history, beneath the arches of the Saló del Tinell.

Museu Frederic Marès

Plaça Sant Iu 5-6 (93 310 58 00/www.museumares.bcn.es). Metro Jaume I. **Open** 10am-7pm Tue-Sat; 10am-3pm Sun. **Admission** €3; €1.50 concessions; free under-16s. Free 3-7pm Wed, 1st Sun of mth. **Guided tours** noon Sun. **Credit** (shop only) AmEx, MC, V. **Map** p345 B3.

This quirky and impressive museum is dedicated to Barcelona sculptor and collector Frederic Marès. Famously something of a kleptomaniac, Marès spent most of his 97 years gathering (by various means, evidently) every imaginable type of object. A drawn-out renovation programme is coming to an end, and has made the collections more accessible. The basement has reopened and contains an impressive selection of remains from ecclesiastical buildings dating back to Roman times; capitals, tombs, gargoyles, stone window frames and entire church portals, exquisitely carved. Part of the cloister from the now-disappeared Santa Clara monastery is also shown. The ground floor contains his extensive collection of Romanesque crucifixes, virgins and saints, while the first floor takes sculpture up to the 20th century. The Museu Sentimental on the second floor contains his most unusual collections: containing everything from iron keys, ceramics and tobacco pipes to pocket watches, early daguerreotypes and Torah pointers. The 'Ladies' Room' contains fans, sewing scissors, nutcrackers and perfume flasks, and is especially charming. Also on the second floor is Marès' study and library, now filled with sculptures, many of them his own. From May to September 2004, a temporary exhibition, *Objecte i Memòria*, looks at the human need to keep memory intact through the preservation of certain objects. From December 2005 Marès' collection of 19th-century paper theatres will be on show.

Palau de la Generalitat

Plaça Sant Jaume (93 402 46 17/www.gencat.es). Metro Liceu or Jaume I. **Guided tours** (subject to change) every 30mins 10.30am-1.30pm 2nd & 4th Sun of mth; also 9.30am-1pm, 4-7pm Mon, Thur, Fri-Sun by appointment. **Admission** free. **Map** p345 B3.

Like the Ajuntament, the Generalitat has a Gothic side entrance on C/Bisbe, with a beautiful relief of St George (Sant Jordi), patron saint of Catalonia, made by Pere Johan in 1418. Inside, the finest features are the first-floor Pati de Tarongers ('Orange Tree Patio'), which was to become the model for many patios in Barcelona, and the magnificent chapel of Sant Jordi of 1432-4, the masterpiece of Catalan architect Marc Safont. The Generalitat is traditionally open to the public on Sant Jordi (23 April), when its patios are spectacularly decorated with red roses, and queues are huge; it normally also opens on 11 September (Catalan National Day) and 24 September (La Mercè).

Temple Romà d'Augusti

C/Paradís 10 (93 315 11 11). Metro Jaume I. **Open** 10am-2pm, 4-8pm Tue-Sat; 10am-3pm Sun. **Admission** free. **Map** p342 D5.

Returning to the cathedral, turn right into **C/Palla**. A little way along, a large chunk of wall is visible. This was only discovered in the 1980s when a building was demolished. Palla runs into **C/Banys Nous**, where at No.16 there is a centre for disabled children, which inside contains a piece of wall with a relief of legs and feet (try to phone ahead, 93 318 14 81, for a viewing time). At No.4 is **La Granja** (*see p171*), a lovely old café with yet another stretch of Roman wall at the back. Beyond this is the junction with **C/Call**, the other end of the Cardus, and so the opposite side of the Roman town from Llibreteria-Tapineria. The staff of the clothes wholesalers at C/Call 1 are also used to people wandering in to examine their piece of Roman tower.

Carry on across C/Ferran and down **C/Avinyó**, which is the next continuation of the perimeter. At the back of **El Gallo Kiriko**, the Pakistani restaurant at No.19, there is a cosy cave-like dining room, two sides of which are formed by portions of the Roman wall.

From **C/Milans**, turn left when you get to **C/Gignás**. Near the junction with **C/Regomir** are remains of the fourth sea gate of the town, which would have faced the beach, and the Roman shipyard. Take a detour up C/Regomir to visit one of the most important relics of Barcino, the **Pati Llimona** (*see p85*), then continue walking up **C/Correu Vell** (where there are more fragments of wall) to reach one of the most impressive relics of Roman Barcelona in the small, shady **Plaça Traginers**: a Roman tower and one corner of the ancient wall, in a remarkable state of preservation despite having had a medieval house built on top of it.

Finally, turn up **C/Sots-Tinent Navarro,** with a massive stretch of Roman rampart, to end the walk at Plaça de l'Àngel.

The Centre Excursionista de Catalunya (a hiking club) contains four fluted Corinthian columns that formed the rear corner of the Temple of Augustus, built in the first century BC as the hub of the town's Forum. Opening hours can vary.

La Rambla

It used to be said that it was an obligation for every true Barcelona citizen to walk down the mile-long Rambla at least once a day. Nowadays, many locals have become weary with the place, tired of tawdry souvenir shops, and of elbowing through crowds of tourists, but this boulevard remains one of Barcelona's essential attractions. The multitude of human statues, fortune tellers, cardsharps, puppeteers, dancers and musicians might be infuriating to anyone late for work, but for those with a ringside seat at a pavement café it is nothing short of pure theatre.

The name derives from *ramla*, an Arabic word for sand, and originally this was a seasonal riverbed, running along the western edge of the 13th-century city. From the Middle Ages to the baroque era a great many churches and convents were built along this riverbed, some of which have given their names to sections of it: as one descends from Plaça Catalunya, it is successively called Rambla de Canaletes, Rambla dels Estudis (or dels Ocells), Rambla de Sant Josep (or de les Flors), Rambla dels Caputxins and Rambla de Santa Mònica. For this reason, many people refer to it in the plural, as Les Rambles.

The Rambla also served as the meeting ground for city and country dwellers, for on the far side of these church buildings lay the still scarcely built-up Raval, 'the city outside the walls', and rural Catalonia. At the **fountain** on the corner with C/Portaferrissa, colourful tiles depict the city gateway that once stood here (porta ferrissa means 'iron gate'). The space by the gates became a natural marketplace, and from these beginnings sprang **La Boqueria**, now the largest market in Europe.

The Rambla took on its recognisable present form between approximately 1770 and 1860. The second city wall came down in 1775, and the Rambla was gradually paved and turned into a boulevard. Seats were available along it to rent in the late 18th century. The avenue acquired its definitive shape after the closure of the monasteries in the 1830s, which made swathes of land available for new building. No longer on the city's edge, the Rambla became a wide path through its heart.

As well as having five names, the Rambla is divided into territories. The first part – at the top, by Plaça Catalunya – has belonged by unwritten agreement to groups of men perpetually engaged in a *tertulia*, a classic Iberian half-conversation, half-argument about anything from politics to football. The **Font de Canaletes** drinking fountain is beside them; if you drink from it, the legend goes, you'll return to Barcelona. Here, too, is where Barça fans converge in order to celebrate their increasingly rare triumphs.

Next comes perhaps the best-loved section of the boulevard, known as **Rambla de les Flors** for its line of magnificent flower stalls, open into the night. To the right is the **Palau de la Virreina** exhibition and cultural information centre (*see p319*), and the superb Boqueria market. A little further is the **Pla de l'Os** (or **Pla de la Boqueria**), centrepoint of the Rambla, with a pavement **mosaic** created in 1976 by Joan Miró. On the left, where more streets run off into the Barri Gòtic, is the extraordinary **Bruno Quadros** building (1883), with umbrellas on the wall and a Chinese dragon protruding over the street.

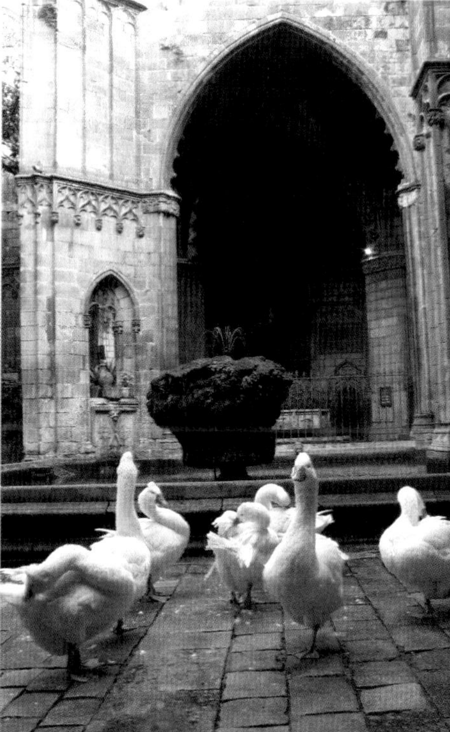

Security patrol at the **cathedral**. *See p83.*

Bruno Quadros building. *See p89.*

The lower half of the Ramblas is initially more restrained, flowing between the sober façade of the **Liceu** opera house and the rather more fin-de-siècle (architecturally and atmospherically) **Cafè de l'Opera** (*see p171*), Barcelona's second most famous café after the Zurich. On the right is C/Nou de la Rambla (where you'll find Gaudí's **Palau Güell**, *see p96*), and then the promenade widens into the **Rambla de Santa Mònica**. This area has traditionally been the centre of a thriving industry in prostitution, and although official clean-up efforts have reduced its visibility, single males walking at night can expect to be frequently approached. Renovations, including a 1980s arts centre, the **Centre d'Art Santa Mònica** (*see below*), have also done much to dilute the seediness of the area. Across the street is the unintentionally hilarious **Wax Museum** (*see p225*) and, at weekends, stalls selling bric-a-brac and craftwork. Then finally it's a short skip to the port, and the **Monument a Colom** (*see p105*).

Centre d'Art Santa Mònica

La Rambla 7 (93 316 28 10/www.cultura.gencat.es/casm). Metro Drassanes. **Open** 11am-8pm Tue-Sat; 11am-3pm Sun. **Admission** usually free. **Map** p345 A4.

Recent renovations by Albert Viaplana, one of the original architects to create this centre for visual arts from a 17th-century monastery back in 1988, have led to considerably more exhibition space. Other dynamic changes have included a new directorship and a move away from conventional all-encompassing exhibitions. Around 20 shows from artists local and international, famous and unknown, will now take place every year. From March to June 2004,Yamadú Canosa, Tere Recarens, Livia Flores and Costa Vece will appear, then Maria Eichhorn, Florian Göttke and João Tabarra from July to September.

Museu de l'Eròtica

La Rambla 96 bis (93 318 98 65/www.erotica-museum.com). Metro Liceu. **Open** *June-Sept* 10am-midnight daily. *Oct-May* 11am-9pm daily. **Admission** €7.50; €6.50 concessions. **Credit** AmEx, MC, V. **Map** p345 A3.

Let down by some horrendous airbrushed paintings of the maidens and serpents school (much like those found in Saddam's palace), the Erotica Museum does contain some genuine rarities. These include Japanese drawings, 19th-century engravings by German Peter Fendi and compelling photos of brothels in Barcelona's Barrio Chino in the decadent 1930s. Other curiosities include S&M apparatus and simulated erotic telephone lines, but until things are sharpened up, the Eròtica is something of an embarrassment in a city with true connoisseurship for the bawdy.

Palau de la Virreina

La Rambla 99 (93 301 77 75/www.bcn.es/cultura). Metro Liceu. **Open** 11am-2pm, 4-8.30pm Mon-Fri; 11am-8.30pm Sat; 11am-3pm Sun. **Admission** €3; €1.50 concessions; free under-16s. **No credit cards**. **Map** p344 A2.

This classical palace, with baroque features, takes its name from the widow of an unpopular former viceroy of Peru, who commissioned it and lived in it after its completion in the 1770s. The Virreina houses the city cultural department, and has information on events and shows around town, but also boasts strong programming in its two distinct exhibition spaces. Upstairs is dedicated to one-off exhibitions, with the smaller downstairs gallery focused on historical and contemporary photography. This will feature, from May to September 2004, a collection of previously unpublished photographs of Salvador Dalí, taken by his secretary. From July to September the upstairs space will show *The First Eros*, an exploration of eroticism among ancient cultures, which is to be followed by *Counterculture* from November to January 2005. This will look at alternative Barcelona, from hippie to punk, after Franco's death.

Raval

Artfully dodgy.

The mammoth, modern and marvellous **MACBA**. *See p95.*

This is the part of town that everyone warns you about. Jean Genet, seasoned pickpocket and notorious rent boy of the '20s, described the Raval as 'a multitude of dark, dirty, narrow streets,' where 'no one would have dreamed of cleaning his room, his belongings or his linen.' Flea-infested flophouses, junkies and a few shag-haggling prostitutes are part of the area's folklore but work has long been under way to purge – or at least conceal – the less desirable elements and replace them with that Barcelona panacea: some hi-design architecture.

Amid all the urban reform projects, the district survives today as a kind of choppy synthesis of stately heritage buildings, girly clubs, immigrant ghettoes, bohemian artistic circles and the hippest new hangouts around. As long as you leave your mink coat and jewellery in your hotel room, it can make for one of the more vibrant neighbourhoods in which to stroll, and while there are few major sights, there are correspondingly few tourists.

Ever on the margins, Raval (*arrabal* in Spanish) is a generic word adapted from the Arabic *ar-rabad* meaning 'outside the walls'. When a defensive wall was built down the north side of La Rambla in the 13th century the area now sandwiched between Avda Paral.lel and La Rambla was a sparsely populated green belt of garden plots. Over the centuries the land absorbed the functional spillover from the city in the form of monasteries, religious hospitals, prisons and virtually any noxious industry that citizens didn't want on their doorstep, including the likes of brickmaking or slaughtering. When industrialisation arrived in the 18th century this became Barcelona's working-class district, reaching an estimated density of over 100,000 people per square kilometre by the 1930s.

Nonetheless, in the late 18th century, this was the area where most land was available, and even more land came into use after liberal governments dissolved the monasteries in 1836 and early industry – mainly the textile mills –

Writing on the wall

In a city so conscious of its appearance and so proud of its architecture, it may seem a little odd to see so many surfaces scrawled with graffiti. But the attitude towards this 'art form' perfectly reflects Barcelona's mix of civic pride and *laissez faire* attitude. The city is famed for its political and artistic energies, both of which combine in this medium.

Graffiti was imported, along with hip-hop culture, to Barcelona from the US in the 1980s. But although you can still see the gaudy jagged tags of suburban b-boys on building sites and local trains, graffiti has moved away from its bad boy roots. Now, in its myriad forms, it is the expression of choice for the designers, musicians and professional protesters who make up the city's cosmopolitan creative set.

One of the figures most responsible for graffiti's new cool is stencil artist Banksy, who uses humour, intelligence and cheek to make political statements. His most famous Barcelona piece was a stencil of the five bar lines normally seen scratched on prison walls, only this time the cage was the elephant enclosure in Barcelona zoo. His latest scrawls include tigers breaking out of barcode cages and elephants carrying missiles. London-based Banksy is one of a growing number of European graffiti stars

mushroomed. Some of the bleak, barrack-like buildings known as *cases-fàbriques* (residential factories) can still be seen, such as the **Can Ricart** textile factory on C/Sant Oleguer. Here workers once lived in appallingly crowded slums devoid of ventilation or running water. Malnutrition, tuberculosis, scrofula and typhus kept the average life expectancy down to 40 years. It is no coincidence that the city's hospitals, sanatoriums and orphanages were based here. Then known to most people as the Quinto or 'Fifth District', this was also where the underclasses forged the centre of revolutionary Barcelona, a perennial breeding ground for anarchists and other radicals. Innumerable riots and revolts began here, and whole streets became no-go areas after dark.

Heroin's arrival in the late 1970s caused serious problems and the old, semi-tolerated petty criminality became more threatening, affecting the tourist trade. Spurred on by the approaching 1992 Olympics, the authorities made a clean sweep of the Chino and whole blocks associated with drug dealings or prostitution were demolished. The displaced families were often transferred to housing estates on the outskirts of town (out of sight and out of mind). A sports centre, a new police station and office blocks were constructed along with the pedestrianisation of some of the more visible streets.

Most dramatic was the plan to create a '*Raval obert al cel*' – a 'Raval open to the sky' – the most tangible result of which is the sweeping,

who visit Barcelona to 'bomb', attracted by the city's creative energy and its relatively forgiving attitude to graffiti.

The local council invites artists to decorate playgrounds and parks, and graffiti is often a part of visual arts festivals here. Colombian collective Joystick turned graffiti stickering into a performance art during the 2003 Zeppelin music festival. They invited the public to choose parts of the Raval with good sounds, then stickered the spot.

The stencil and the sticker have become the media of choice for the graffiti generation partly because they're easy and quick, aiding both the less artistic and the cowardly, and partly because of traditional associations with authority and commerce, ripe for subversion with an anti-commerical and anti-authority message. When Prime Minister Aznar declared support for the Iraq war, a flurry of anti-war statements appeared; you may still be able to see stencils of Aznar, Blair and Bush with clown noses. Joystick's archive of political stickers is now on the internet for anyone to print and paste.

Not all Barcelona graffiti is political. Parisian artist Miss Van is one of only a few female graffiti stars. Her larger-than-life, curvy, saucy girl characters add sexy colour to one of Barcelona's main 'halls' (expanses of wall given over to graffiti, often by a single group of artists) behind the busy Boqueria market. German Boris Hoppek scrawled his Klan-like chalk line characters around C/Doctor Dou so often that he eventually moved here. Work by local artist Pez is easily recognised by his trademark grinning fish. Another eponymous symbol is Xupet Negre's shiny black dummy – a gang of them clothed in hip hop gear hang out behind the Boqueria.

Freaklüb's distinctive character Aunara represents how far Barcelona graffiti can travel from its anarchist roots. A Japanese-style cartoon little girl with an outsize magical mop of orange hair, Aunara dominates another 'hall' opposite the CCCB. Yet this strangely expressionless character has taken her creators' talent off the streets and into the commercial world. The duo have created campaigns for Nokia and Camel, and decorated the walls of Gràcia bar Gusto. You can even buy Aunara products at the Raval art bookshop and gallery Ras, along with coasters decorated with Bert Hoppek's scrawl and T-shirts featuring Xupet Negre's dummy. Perhaps this is another aspect of the art that tunes into part of Barcelona's soul – its sensible, money-making side: why risk arrest and give your talent for free when there are people and brands out there willing to pay plenty of cold hard cash for just a little bit of street cool?

www.bcngraffiti.com General Barcelona graffiti; mainly in the old-skool freehand spray-can style.
www.banksy.co.uk Banksy's own site.
www.duncancumming.co.uk A good range of photos of Barcelona graffiti, especially good for stencils.
www.positivos.com/graffiti News, interviews, festival and exhibition listings from Spain.
www.woostercollective.com Includes Pez's guide to Barcelona and interview with the artists known as Freaklüb.

palm-lined Rambla del Raval, completed in 2000. This is a continuation of the Avda Drassanes, an earlier attempt to 'open up' the Raval in the 1960s. Entire blocks have vanished in its wake and bulldozers are next scheduled to plough a perpendicular extension to the Ronda de Sant Pau over municipal land that once held the Folch i Torres swimming pools (and before that, a women's prison). This will provide better access to the current grand project, **L'Illa de la Rambla del Raval**; a mega-complex halfway up the new *rambla* which will contain shops, protected housing, offices and the Filmoteca. The star of the piece, a glass-sheathed, elliptical, luxury hotel by Pere Puig, is intended to provide the area with a new, glittering landmark.

Some of these changes have been for the best, but their cumulative effect has been to leave parts of the Raval looking rather empty. Efforts to fill the new *rambla* include licences for new clubs and bars, Botero's deliciously bulging *Gat* (Cat) sculpture, and an ethnic Saturday street market, **Món Raval**. Its multicultural nature reflects the huge number of immigrants now living in the Raval – mainly Pakistanis, North Africans and Filipinos – who were originally attracted by the lower cost of housing in this area. The facelift has also raised the prices, though, and as the immigrants – often young men sleeping ten to a room – are gradually squeezed out, a wealthier community of arty western expats moves in, scattering the area with galleries, boutiques and cafés.

Upper Raval

This area never had such a louche reputation as the lower Raval and in recent years the plethora of late-night bars and restaurants has made it one of Barcelona's hippest places. The section between C/Carme and Plaça Catalunya was the early focus of cultural rejuvenation, a plan started in 1979. The epicentre is the Plaça dels Àngels, where the 16th-century **Convent dels Àngels** houses the **FAD** design institute and the remains of the gigantic almshouse, the **Casa de la Caritat**, since converted into the cultural complex of the **MACBA** and the **CCCB** (for both *see below*). When the MACBA opened in 1995, it seemed to embody everything the Raval was not: clean, white spaces and a rarefied world of high culture. It was initially mocked as an isolated block of culture, dropped into the middle of the slums like a social experiment. Over the years, though, the square has gradually become a focus for new restaurants, boutiques and galleries, pollinated by university students.

Below that is the part of the Raval that first took on an urban character – a long triangle defined by C/Hospital below and C/Carme above. The streets meet at the Plaça Pedró, where the tiny Romanesque chapel of **Sant Llàtzer** sits. From La Rambla, this area is accessed along either street or through the **Boqueria** market, itself the site of the Sant Josep monastery until the sale of church lands led to its destruction in the 1830s. Behind the Boqueria is the **Antic Hospital de la Santa Creu** (*see below*), which took in the city's sick from the 15th century until it finally closed in 1926. It now houses Catalonia's main library and the headquarters of the Institute of Catalan Studies, and **La Capella**, an attractive exhibition space. C/Carme is capped at the Rambla end by the 18th-century **church of Betlem** (Bethlehem) with its serpentine pillars and geometrically patterned façade. Its name features on many of the nearby shop signs and older residents still refer to this part of the Raval as Betlem.

Antic Hospital de la Santa Creu & La Capella

C/Carme 47-C/Hospital 56 (no phone). Metro Liceu. **Open** 9am-8pm Mon-Fri; 9am-2pm Sat. *La Capella* 5 *(93 442 71 71)* noon-2pm, 4-8pm Tue-Sat; 11am-2pm Sun. **Admission** free. **Map** p344 A2.

There was a hospital on this site from 1024, but in the 15th century it expanded to centralise all the city's hospitals and sanatoriums (with the exception of the Santa Margarida leper colony, which remained outside the city walls). By the 1920s it was hopelessly overstretched and its medical facilities moved uptown to the Hospital Sant Pau. One of the last patients was Gaudí, who died here in 1926.

Renovated in 2001, the buildings are some of the most majestic in the city, combining a 15th-century Gothic core with baroque and classical additions. The beautifully shady colonnaded courtyard is a popular spot for reading or eating lunch. The buildings are now given over to cultural institutions including the Massana Arts School; Catalonia's main library; the Institute of Catalan Studies and the Royal Academy of Medicine. Highlights include the neoclassical lecture theatre complete with revolving marble dissection table, and the entrance hall of the Casa de Convalescència. This is tiled with lovely baroque ceramic murals telling the story of Sant Pau (St Paul), including an artery-squirting decapitation scene. La Capella (the hospital chapel) was rescued from a sad fate as a warehouse and sensitively converted to an exhibition space for contemporary art.

CCCB (Centre de Cultura Contemporània de Barcelona)

C/Montalegre 5 (93 306 41 00/www.cccb.org). Metro Catalunya. **Open** *Mid June-mid Sept* 11am-8pm Tue-Sat; 11am-3pm Sun. *Mid Sept-mid June* 11am-2pm, 4-8pm Tue, Thur, Fri; 11am-8pm Wed, Sat; 11am-7pm Sun. **Admission** *1 exhibition* €4; €3 concessions & Wed. *2 exhibitions* €5.50; €4 concessions & Wed. Free under-16s. **Credit** MC, V. **Map** p344 A1.

In 1994 Spain's largest cultural centre was opened in the huge Casa de la Caritat, built in 1802 on the site of a medieval monastery to serve as the city's main workhouse. The massive façade and part of the courtyard remain from the original building, while the rest was rebuilt in dramatic contrast, all tilting glass and steel, by architects Piñón and Viaplana, in what could be seen as an echo of their Maremàgnum shopping centre (*see p188*).

As is so often the case in Barcelona, the CCCB's exhibitions tend to favour smart production values over actual information. Until May 2004 *The European Savage* examines western iconography of the wildman. From May to September *War* looks at the impact of conflict on society including works by Henry Moore, Dalí and Lichtenstein and there are countless spin-off exhibitions and lectures. As a contemporary culture centre it picks up whatever falls through the cracks elsewhere in Barcelona, including urban culture, early 20th-century art, and festivals ranging from the May festival of Asian cinema, to Dies de Dansa (*see p219*) and Sónar, the electronic music festival (*see p217*). The shop has a vast range of English-language publications on urban topics.

MACBA (Museu d'Art Contemporani de Barcelona)

Plaça dels Àngels 1 (93 412 08 10/www.macba.es). Metro Catalunya. **Open** *June-Sept* 11am-8pm Mon, Wed-Fri; 10am-8pm Sat; 10am-3pm Sun. *Oct-May* 11am-7.30pm Mon, Wed-Fri; 10am-8pm Sat; 10am-3pm Sun. **Guided tours** (Catalan/Spanish) 6pm Wed, Sat; noon Sun. **Admission** *Museum* €5.50; €4 concessions. *Temporary exhibitions* €4; €3 concessions. *Combined ticket* €7; €5.50 concessions. **Credit** MC, V. **Map** p344 A1.

Barcelona's answer to the Pompidou centre, the MACBA is a majestic iceberg floating in a sea of concrete, sparkling with Richard Meier's trademark white façades, plate glass and aluminium panels. Zigzag ramps lead visitors through vast halls. Its nouvelle cuisine version of art has been gradually fattened up by impressive donations since it opened in 1995, and the MACBA now holds its own.

The collection covers the second half of the 20th century, divided into four chronological sections. The earlier pieces are strong on Spanish expressionists such as Saura and Tàpies alongside Dubuffet, and Basque sculptors Jorge Oteiza and Eduardo Chillida. Works from the past 40 years are more international, with Joseph Beuys, Jean-Michel Basquiat and AR Penk. The contemporary Spanish collection includes a review of Catalan painting (Ferran García Sevilla, Miquel Barceló) and sculpture (Sergi Aguilar, Susana Solano).

Temporary shows in spring 2004 offer retrospectives of Tàpies and performance artist Vito Hannibal Acconci. From the end of May to the end of August the MACBA, in association with Fòrum 2004, pulls out all the stops for a huge exhibition focusing on the tension between Art and Utopia including works by Miró, Klee, Picasso, Jeff Wall and Marcel Duchamp among many others. For two to three months in autumn 2004, all three floors will be given over to the museum holdings.

Lower Raval

The lower half of the Raval, from C/Hospital downwards, is generally referred to as the **Barrio Chino** ('Barri Xino' in Catalan). The nickname was coined in the 1920s by a journalist comparing it to San Francisco's Chinatown, and referred to its underworld feel rather than to any Chinese population. In those days, swarms of drifters filled the bars and cheap *hostals* along streets such as Nou de la Rambla, where there were high-class cabarets and brothels for the rich and cheap porn pits for the poor. Many writers revelled in the sleaze, from Genet's *Thief's Journal* (1949) to André Pieyre de Mandiargues' *The Margin* (1967) and Raval-born Manuel Vázquez Montalbán's series of Carvalho detective books. Contemporary explorations of the Chino have been more hard-hitting, such as José Luís Guerín's excellent film *Work in Progress* (2001).

The main thoroughfare of the area, C/Nou de la Rambla, is home to Gaudí's first major project, **Palau Güell** (*see below*), built for his patron, Eusebi Güell. An intensely private, fortress-like edifice, it was an extension of Güell's parents' house on the more fashionable Rambla. Nearby, in C/Sant Pau, is another Modernista landmark, the **Hotel España** (*see p57*), designed by Domènech i Montaner, and at the end of the street, the Romanesque tenth-century church of **Sant Pau del Camp** (*see below*). Iberian remains dating to 200 BC have been found next to the edifice, marking it as one of the oldest parts of the city. At the lower end of the area were the **Drassanes** (shipyards), now home to the **Museu Marítim**. Along the Paral.lel side of this impressive Gothic building remains the only large section of Barcelona's 14th-century city wall.

Palau Güell

C/Nou de la Rambla 3-5 (93 317 39 74). Metro Liceu. **Guided tours** *Mar-Oct* 10am-6.15pm Mon-Sat. *Nov-Feb* 10am-4.30pm Mon-Sat. **Admission** €3; €1.50 concessions; free under-6s. **No credit cards. Map** p345 A3.

The façade of Gaudí's first major commission for his patron, Eusebi Güell, resembles a dark, Gothic fortress more than a palace. Inside, the paucity of exterior windows and fireplaces evokes a chilly troll's cave, as do the vast sheets of grey Garraf marble – taken from Güell's quarries – that cover the stairways, walls and even ceilings. Shoehorned into a narrow, six-storey sliver, the odd site was chosen as an extension of the family residence (now a hotel) on the Rambla, to which it is still connected by a passageway. It was built between 1886-90, and the seed ideas of Gaudí's later motifs are clearly visible: the fungiform brick capitals in the cellar are precursors of the organic stone passageways of Park Güell; the parabolic arches a rehearsal for the free structure of La Pedrera; the colourful tile mosaics on the chimney stacks an early exploration of the possibilities of the *trencadís* broken tile method. Highlights include the lavishly decorated roof terrace, the Mozarabic-style coffered ceiling of the visitors' parlour (surrounded by a secret passageway so that Güell could spy on his guests below), and his wife's oddly kitsch bedroom combining dark Gothic stonework with floral carpets and a tassled cowhide loveseat. Visits are still by guided tour only and can last well over an hour if you get a large group with lots of different languages. In general, mornings tend to be quieter than afternoons.

Sant Pau del Camp

C/Sant Pau 101 (93 441 00 01). Metro Paral.lel. **Open** 5-8pm Mon-Sat. **Admission** €1. **Map** p342 C6.

The name, St Paul-in-the-Field, reflects a time when the Raval was still countryside, and archaeologists date the construction of this little Romanesque church at well over 1,000 years ago. The date carved on the church's most prestigious headstone: that of Count Guifré II Borell, son of Wilfred the Hairy, and inheritor of all Barcelona and Girona, is 912AD. The impressive façade includes sculptures of fantastical flora and fauna along with human grotesques. The tiny cloister features some extraordinary Visigoth capitals and triple-lobed arches. Now restored after stints as a school in 1842, an army barracks from 1855-1890 and a bombsite in the Civil War, it has been declared a national monument.

Sant Pere & the Born

Where ecclesiastical treasures and chi-chi boutiques sit cheek by jowl.

Maps p344-p345

The last few years have been very kind to the districts of Sant Pere and the Born, and where moneyed Catalans once feared to tread, they now covet property. La Ribera (as the area is occasionally known) is used to the slings and arrows of fortune, and was witness to two historic acts of urban vandalism. The first came after the 1714 siege, when the victors, acting on the orders of Philip V, destroyed 1,000 houses, hospitals and monasteries to construct the fortress of the Ciutadella (Citadel). The second occurred when the Via Laietana was struck through the district in 1907, in line with the theory of 'ventilating' unsanitary city districts by driving wide avenues through them.

'Ribera' means waterfront, and recalls the time before permanent quays were built, when the shoreline reached much further inland. Originally contained, like the Barri Gòtic, within the second, 13th-century city wall, this is one of the most engaging districts of the Old City. In Barcelona's Golden Age, from the 12th century onwards, La Ribera was the favourite residential area of the city's merchant elite as well as the principal centre of commerce and trade. Sant Pere and the Born are divided by **C/Princesa**, running between the **Plaça de l'Àngel** (once called the Plaça del Blat, or 'wheat square'), the commercial and popular heart of the city where all grain was traded, and the lush **Parc de la Ciutadella** (*see p102*), built on the site of the hated citadel. The area north of C/Princesa is centred around the monastery of **Sant Pere de les Puelles**, which still stands, if greatly altered, in Plaça de Sant Pere. For centuries this was Barcelona's main centre of textile production, and to this day streets like Sant Pere Més Baix and Sant Pere Més Alt contain many textile wholesalers and retailers.

The area may be medieval in origin, but its finest monument is also one of the most extraordinary works of Modernisme – the **Palau de la Música Catalana** (*see p101*), facing C/Sant Pere Més Alt. Less noticed on the same street is a curious feature, the **Passatge de les Manufactures**, a 19th-century arcade between C/Sant Pere Més Alt and C/Ortigosa.

Sant Pere is currently undergoing dramatic renovation, with the gradual opening up of a continuation of the Avda Francesc Cambó, which will eventually swing around to meet with C/Allada-Vermell, a wide street formed when a block was demolished in 1994. The district's market, **Mercat de Santa Caterina** is one of Barcelona's oldest, and is being rebuilt to a design by the late Enric Miralles (who also famously designed the Scottish Parliament), and remains of the medieval **Santa Caterina convent** will be shown behind glass at one end. At the time of writing the gay colours of its floral roofing were already visible, but it is not due to be finished until mid 2004. In the meantime its stallholders have been relocated along Passeig Lluís Companys, by the park. Another convent nearby is the **Convent de Sant Agustí**, now a civic centre, on C/Comerç. The entrance contains *Deuce Coop*, a magical 'light sculpture' by James Turrell, which was commissioned by the Ajuntament in the 1980s and is best seen after dark.

Where C/Carders meets C/Montcada, is the Placeta d'en Marcús, with a small chapel, the 12th-century **Capella d'en Marcús**, built as part of an inn. It was founded by Bernat Marcús, who is said to have organised Europe's first postal service. It was from this chapel, then outside the city wall, that his riders set off for the north, and it also provided a refuge for them and other travellers who arrived after the city gates had closed for the night.

From this tiny square **C/Montcada**, one of the unmissable streets of old Barcelona, leads into the Born. It is lined with a succession of medieval merchants' mansions, the greatest of which house a variety of museums, including the **Museu Tèxtil** (*see p101*), the **Museu Barbier-Mueller** (*see p98*) of pre-Columbian art and, above all, the **Museu Picasso** (*see p99*). In 1148 land ceded to Guillem Ramon de Montcada became the site for the construction of this street, where the opulence of the many merchant-princes of the time is still very visible. The streets nearby were filled with workshops supplying anything the inhabitants needed, and these trades are commemorated in the names of many of the streets (*see p102* **Walk on: Medieval trading**).

'Born' originally meant 'joust' or 'list', and in the Middle Ages and for many centuries thereafter the neighbourhood's main artery, the **Passeig del Born**, was the centre for the city's festivals, processions, tournaments, carnivals and the burning of heretics by the

Exquisite detail of the **Palau de la Música Catalana**. *See p101.*

Inquisition. At one end of the square is the old **Born market**, a magnificent 1870s wrought-iron structure that used to be Barcelona's main wholesale food market. It closed in the 1970s, and the market was transferred elsewhere. Plans to turn it into a library were thwarted by the discovery of perfectly preserved medieval remains. The foundations of buildings razed by Philip V's troops were found to contain hundreds of objects, some domestic and some, like rusty bombs, suggesting the traumas of the period. By spring 2004 it is hoped that a viewing platform will have been erected on C/Fusina, and ultimately the remains will be incorporated into a cultural centre and museum.

At the other end of the Passeig from the market stands the greatest of all Catalan Gothic buildings, the magnificent basilica of **Santa Maria del Mar** (*see p103*). On one side of it, a square was opened in 1989 on the site where it is believed the last defenders of the city were executed after the city of Barcelona fell to the Spanish army in 1714. Called the **Fossar de les Moreres** (the 'Mulberry Graveyard'), the square is inscribed with patriotic poetry, and nationalist demonstrations converge here every year on Catalan National Day, 11 September. The 'eternal flame' sculpture is a more recent, and less popular, addition.

From here narrow streets lead to the **Plaça de les Olles** or the grand **Pla del Palau** and another symbol of La Ribera, **La Llotja** (the 'exchange'). Its neo-classical outer shell was added in the 18th century, but its core is a superb 1380s Gothic hall, sadly closed to the public, save for occasional functions organised through the Chamber of Commerce. Until the exchange moved to the Passeig de Gràcia in 1994, this was the oldest continuously functioning stock exchange in Europe.

Metrònom

C/Fusina 9 (93 268 42 98). Metro Arc de Triomf or Jaume I. **Open** 11am-2pm, 5-8pm Tue-Sat. Closed Aug. **Map** p345 C3.

Run by collector Rafael Tous, this was Barcelona's most lively art space back in the 1980s. After a brief hiatus, it has recently won back some of its original impetus, focusing on photography and multimedia installations. In 2004, the MetrònomLab project will promote media arts, new technology, electronic music and new choreography.

Museu Barbier-Mueller d'Art Precolombí

C/Montcada 14 (93 310 45 16/www.barbier-mueller.ch). Metro Jaume I. **Open** 10am-6pm Tue-Sat; 10am-3pm Sun. **Admission** €3; €1.50 concessions; free under-16s. Free 1st Sun of mth. **Credit** (shop only) AmEx, MC, V. **Map** p345 C3.

Renowned American scenographer and artist Robert Wilson has been commissioned to shake up the Barbier-Mueller's presentation of pre-Columbian art as part of the Fòrum 2004. Officially an exhibition entitled 'The Image of the Body', it will affect the whole museum, and aims to contextualise objects from the collection – specifically, representations of the human body – in thought-provoking ways. The regular, frequently changing selection of ancient tribal art in the museum is from the Barbier-Mueller in Geneva: here it concentrates solely on the Americas.

Museu de Ciències Naturals de la Ciutadella

Passeig Picasso, Parc de la Ciutadella (www.bcn.es/museuciencies 93 319 69 12). Metro Arc de Triomf. **Open** 10am-2pm Tue, Wed, Fri-Sun; 10am-6pm Thur. **Admission** *Combined ticket with temporary exhibition & Jardí Botànic* €4; €2 concessions. *Museums only* €3; €1.50 concessions. *Temporary exhibitions only* €3.50; €1.50 concessions. Free under-12s. Free 1st Sun of mth. **No credit cards. Map** p343 E6.

The Natural History Museum now comprises the the zoology and geology museums in the Parc de la Ciutadella. Both suffer from old-school presentation: dusty glass cases filled with moth-eaten stuffed animals and serried rows of rocks. The zoology museum is redeemed by its location in the 'Castell dels Tres Dragons', built by Domènech i Montaner as the café-restaurant for the 1888 Exhibition, and by its interesting temporary exhibitions. From June 2004 a year-long show with interactive exhibits will demonstrate the importance of biodiversity. The geology museum is for aficionados only, with a dry display of minerals, painstakingly classified, alongside explanations of geological phenomena found in Catalonia. More interesting is the selection from the museum's collection of 300,000 fossils, many found locally. A combined ticket now also grants entrance to the Jardí Botànic on Montjuïc (*see p113*).

Museu Picasso

C/Montcada 15-23 (93 319 63 10/www.museupicasso.bcn.es). Metro Jaume I. **Open** (last ticket 30mins before closing) 10am-8pm Tue-Sat; 10am-3pm Sun. **Admission** *Permanent collection only* €5; €2.50 concessions. *With temporary exhibition* €8; €4.70 concessions; free under-16s. Free (museum only) 1st Sun of mth. **Credit** (shop only) AmEx, MC, V. **Map** p345 C3.

As the Picasso Museum grew from its beginnings in the Palau Aguilar in 1963 to encompass a row of medieval mansions, the spread was felt to be somewhat disjointed. In 2003 a complete overhaul of the space corrected its many flaws, and created more

Crime watch

While Barcelona is by no means a dangerous city, bagsnatching and pickpocketing have ruined many a holiday. The city's thieves, however, have never really had much of a taste for violence, and prey almost entirely on the unwary. Anyone with their nose in a guidebook, camera round their neck or any ostentatious displays of wealth can expect to attract attention. Common sense is generally all it takes to maintain your happiness; keep your wallet in an inside pocket, leave your valuables in the hotel safe and make sure you can see your bag at all times.

Common ruses you might encounter involve asking for directions (the map serves as a useful screen while someone rummages in your bag), pretending to clean something off your shoulder, and a kind of over-friendliness which often can result in one hand on your shoulder and another in your pocket.

The current hotspots are **C/Montcada** in the Born, **C/Carders** in Sant Pere, **C/Escudellers** in the Barri Gòtic, and **C/Hospital** and **C/Sant Pau** in the Raval, but the whole of the Old City is prey to petty crime. The most sensible approach is not to become paranoid, but simply to carry only that which you wouldn't mind losing.

Let your troubles float away in the **Parc de la Ciutadella**. *See p102.*

room. The main entrance is now at the Palau Meca, and the exit at the Palau Aguilar. Temporary exhibitions are held under the magnificent coffered ceiling of the Palau Finestres, and in 2004 will include *Picasso: War and Peace* showing works inspired by his horror at the Spanish Civil War.

By no means an overview of the artist's work, the Museu Picasso is rather a record of the vital formative years that the young Picasso spent nearby at La Llotja art school (where his father taught), and later hanging out with Catalonia's *fin-de-siècle* avant-garde. The culmination of Picasso's early genius in *Les Demoiselles d'Avignon* (1907) and the first cubist paintings from the time (many of them done in Catalonia), as well as his collage and sculpture, are all completely absent. The founding of the museum is down to a key figure in Picasso's life, his friend and secretary Jaume Sabartés, who donated his own collection for the purpose. Tribute is paid with a room dedicated to Picasso's portraits of him (best known is the Blue Period painting of Sabartés wearing a white ruff), and Sabartés' own doodlings. The seamless presentation of Picasso's development from 1890 to 1904, from deft pre-adolescent portraits to sketchy landscapes to the intense innovations of his Blue Period, is unbeatable, then it leaps to a gallery of mature cubist paintings from 1917. The *pièce de résistance* is the complete series of 57 canvases based on Velázquez' famous *Las Meninas*, donated by Picasso himself, and now stretching through three rooms. The display later ends with a wonderful collection of ceramics donated by his widow.

Museu Tèxtil

C/Montcada 12 (93 319 76 03/www.museutextil.bcn.es). Metro Jaume I. **Open** 10am-6pm Tue-Sat; 10am-3pm Sun. **Admission** *Combined admission with Museu de Artes Decoratives and Museu de Ceràmica* €3.50; €2 concessions. Free under-16s; free 1st Sun of mth. **Credit** (shop only) AmEx, DC, MC, V. **Map** p345 C3.

The displays of the Textile and Clothing Museum occupy two adjacent buildings, the Palau Nadal and Palau dels Marquesos de Llió; the latter retains some of its 13th-century wooden ceilings. Items include medieval Hispano-Arab textiles, liturgical vestments and the city's lace and embroidery collection. The real highlight is the historic fashions – from baroque to 20th-century – that collector Manuel Rocamora donated in the 1960s, one of the finest collections of its type anywhere. Recent important donations include one from Spanish designer Cristóbal Balenciaga, famous for the 1958 baby doll dress and pill-box hat. The museum shop is a great place to pick up presents, and there's a wonderful café in the courtyard. At an unspecified date in the future, the museum is to move to a new Museu de Disseny (Design Museum) in the Plaça de les Glòries.

Museu de la Xocolata

Antic Convent de Sant Agustí, Plaça Pons i Clerch (93 268 78 78/www.museudelaxocolata.com). Metro Jaume I. **Open** 10am-7pm Mon, Wed-Sat; 10am-3pm Sun. **Admission** €3.80; €3.20 concessions; free under-7s. **Credit** MC, V. **Map** p345 C3.

Every Easter the master *pastissers* of Barcelona take part in a competition for the finest *mona* – an elaborate chocolate sculpture. The best are then displayed here, inside the diminutive and quirky Chocolate Museum. Most impressive, perhaps, is the large model of Ben-Hur, but the 2ft (60cm) heavily detailed replicas of Modernista buildings are also quite something to see. After a number of unfortunate incidents involving small and hungry children, exhibits are increasingly being kept in glass cases.

Palau de la Música Catalana

C/Sant Francesc de Paula 2 (93 295 72 00/www.palaumusica.org). Metro Urquinaona. **Open** *Box office* 10am-9pm Mon-Sat. **Guided tours** 10am-3.30pm daily. **Admission** €7; €6 concessions. **Credit** (minimum €20) MC, V. **Map** p344 B-C2.

Walk on Medieval trading

Duration: 45 minutes
From **Plaça de l'Àngel**, site of the Plaça del Blat, the grain market, cross Via Laietana to **C/Bòria**, a name that probably means 'outskirts' or 'suburbs', since it was outside the original city. C/Bòria continues into the evocative little **Plaça de la Llana**, the old centre of wool (*llana*) trading in the city, now an animated meeting place for the Dominican Republic community. Alleys to the left were associated with food trades: **C/Mercaders** ('traders', probably in grain), **C/Oli** ('olive oil') just off it, and **C/Semoleres**, where semolina was made. To the right on Bòria is **C/Pou de la Cadena** ('well with a chain'), a reminder that water was essential for textile working.

After Plaça de la Llana the Roman road's name becomes **C/Corders** ('ropemakers'), and then **C/Carders** ('carders' or combers of wool). Where the name changes there is a tiny square, Placeta Marcús, with an even smaller Romanesque chapel, the **Capella d'en Marcús**, built in the early 12th century.

The chapel was built to give shelter to travellers who arrived after the city gates had closed for the night. Bernat Marcús, who paid for it, is also said to have organised the first postal service in Europe, and it was from here that his riders set off north. If you carry on a little way along C/Carders to **Plaça Sant Agustí Vell**, where the architecture can be dated as far back as the Middle Ages and as recently as the 19th century. Just off it, **C/Basses de Sant Pere** leads away to the left where you'll find a 14th-century house.

Retrace your steps down C/Carders, then turn left into **C/Blanqueria** ('bleaching'). Here wool was washed before being spun. At **C/Assaonadors** ('tanners'), turn right. At the end of this street, behind the Marcús chapel, is a statue of John the Baptist, patron saint of the tanners' guild.

Now you are at the top of **C/Montcada**, one of Barcelona's great museum centres and a beautiful street in itself. The first of the line of medieval merchants' palaces you reach after crossing C/Princesa is the **Palau Berenguer d'Aguilar**, home of the **Museu Picasso**, which has also taken over four more palaces. Opposite is one of the finest and largest palaces, the **Palau dels Marquesos de Llió**, now the **Museu Tèxtil**, with a fine café. To the right is the milliners' street **C/Sombrerers**; opposite it is Barcelona's narrowest street, **C/Mosques** ('flies'), not even wide enough for an adult to lie across, and now closed off with an iron gate because too many people were pissing in it at night. C/Montcada ends at **Passeig del Born**, a hub of the city's trading for 400 years.

The façade of Domènech i Montaner's Modernista concert hall, with its bare brick, busts and mosaic friezes representing Catalan musical traditions and composers, is impressive enough, but it is surpassed by the building's staggering interior. Decoration erupts everywhere: the ceiling centrepiece is of multicoloured stained glass; 18 half-mosaic, half-relief figures representing the musical muses appear out of the back of the stage; and on one side, massive Wagnerian carved horses ride out to accompany a bust of Beethoven. The old Palau has been bursting under the pressure of the musical activity going on inside it, and an extension and renovation project by Oscar Tusquets in the 1980s is being followed by yet more alterations by the same architect. The ugly church next door has been knocked down to make way for the extension of the façade, a subterranean concert hall and a new entrance.

Guided tours are available in English, Catalan or Spanish every 30 minutes or so. They begin with a rather tedious video, which can make the remaining tour a bit rushed, and parts of the building (such as the exterior decoration) are not touched upon. Be sure to ask plenty of questions, particularly if there's something you really want to know – the guides are very knowledgeable, but usually they concentrate mainly on the triumphs of the renovation unless drawn out by customers. If you have a chance, an infinitely preferable way to see the hall is by catching a concert (*see p261*).

Parc de la Ciutadella

Passeig Picasso (no phone). Metro Arc de Triomf or Barceloneta. **Open** 10am-sunset daily. **Map** p343 E6.
In 1869, when General Prim announced that the area taken up by the loathed Bourbon citadel could be reclaimed for public use, the city's joy was boundless. Soon the park was to become the site of the 1888 Exhibition; Domènech i Montaner's Castell de Tres Dragons at the entrance served as the cafeteria, while the Arc de Triomf to the north, formed the main entrance. Prim is honoured with a large equestrian statue at the south end.

Surprisingly extensive, the park also contains a host of attractions: the Zoo, the Natural History Museum, a boating lake and an array of imaginative statuary. Beside the lake is the Cascade, an ornamental fountain on which the young Gaudí worked as assistant to Josep Fontseré, the architect of the

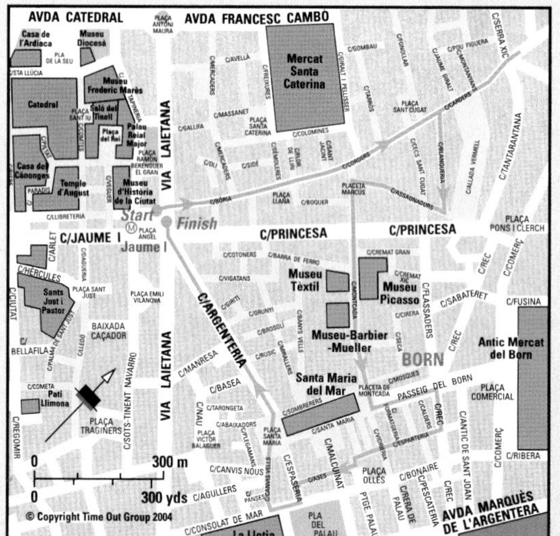

Turn left, and on the left is **C/Flassaders** ('blanket makers'), and to the right **C/Rec**, the old irrigation canal. Go down Rec to turn right into **C/Esparteria**, where *espart* (hemp) was woven. Turnings off it include **C/Calders**, where smelting furnaces would have been found, and **C/Formatgeria**, where one would have gone for cheese. After that is **C/Vidrieria**, where glass was stored and sold. Esparteria runs into C/Ases, which crosses **C/Malcuinat** ('badly cooked'). Turn left into **C/Espaseria** ('sword-making') to emerge out of ancient alleys on to the open space of Pla del Palau. Turn right, and then right again into **C/Canvis Vells** (or 'old exchange'). A tiny street to the left, **C/Panses**, has an archway above it, with an ancient stone carving of a face over the second floor. This face, called a *carabassa*, indicated the location of a legalised brothel.

At the end of Canvis Vells you come to **Plaça Santa Maria** and La Ribera's superb parish church, **Santa Maria del Mar**. The street on the left-hand side is **C/Abaixadors** ('unloaders'), where porters would unload goods, while, from the square **C/Argenteria** ('silverware') will lead you back to the Plaça de l'Àngel.

park. Not to be missed are Fontseré's Umbracle (literally, 'shade house'), which was built in the 1880s with a cast-iron structure reminiscent of his Mercat del Born on C/Comerç and then later restored to provide a pocket of tropical forest within the city, and the elegant Hivernacle ('winter garden'), which has a fine café, L'Hivernacle (*see p178*). Outside on the Passeig Picasso is Antoni Tàpies' *A Picasso,* a giant cubist monument to the artist.

Sala Montcada

C/Montcada 14 (93 310 06 99/www.fundacio.la caixa.es/salamontcada). Metro Jaume I. **Open** 11am-3pm, 4-8pm Tue-Sat; 11am-3pm Sun. **Admission** free. **Map** p345 C3.

This is a diminutive contemporary arts outpost of the CaixaForum (*see p111*), and is equally as ground-breaking in its own right. Each year three different curators develop excellent mixed programmes of Spanish and international artists.

Santa Maria del Mar

Plaça de Santa Maria (93 310 23 90). Metro Jaume I. **Open** 9am-1.30pm, 4.30-8pm Mon-Sat; 10am-1.30pm, 4.30-8pm Sun. **Admission** free. **Map** p345 C3.

This graceful basilica, named after Mary as patroness of sailors, was built on the site of a small church known as Santa Maria del Arenys (sand), for its position close to the sea. It was actually built remarkably quickly for a medieval building, and was entirely constructed between 1329 and 1384, with an unusual unity of style for structures from that period. Inside, two rows of slim, perfectly proportioned columns soar up to fan vaults, creating a wonderful atmosphere of space and a sense of peace. There's also some superb stained glass, particularly in the form of the great 15th-century rose window above the main door. It's perhaps thanks to the group of anti-clerical anarchists who set this magnificent church ablaze in 1936 that its superb features can be appreciated – without the wooden baroque images that clutter so many Spanish churches, the simplicity of its lines can emerge. The incongruous modern window at the other end was a 1997 addition, belatedly celebrating the Olympics. From June to September 2004, Santa Maria's 48 side chapels, along with the Museu Diocesà in Barri Gòtic (*see p85*) and the church of Sant Sever on C/Sant Sever, will house *Christus Splendor*, a collection of Spanish religious art.

Barceloneta & the Ports

Fish and ships.

Port Vell

It is often said of Barcelona that for the best part of 200 years the city turned its back on the sea, physically and figuratively. It's certainly true that a visitor returning after just 25 years away would struggle to recognise the waterfront, as the city has leapt to make the most of its coastal setting, realising once more that the water that bathes its eastern border is liquid gold.

Once the dominant power in the Western Mediterranean, the city's immense *drassanes* (shipyards) built state-of-the-art battleships for the Catalan navy, and the city became the military centre as well as the hub of trading routes between Africa and the rest of Europe. These same old shipyards now hold the interesting **Museu Marítim** (*see p106*). But the city's power was dealt a blow when Columbus sailed west and found what he thought was the East. The Atlantic became the important trade route, and Barcelona went into recession.

Prosperity returned in the 19th century when this became the base for the Spanish industrial revolution. The city spread inland to the mountains, and the shoreline was used for factories. The beach became a slum for the homeless, and a no-go area for everyone else. Only the docks, in what was later to become Port Vell, thrived.

In the 1960s mass tourism arrived in Spain, but Barcelona was slow to react to the vast commercial possibilities of its shoreline. It took the 1992 Olympics to get the urban planners really working – and they haven't stopped since. By the end of 2004, seven kilometres (four miles) of city coastline will be fully developed with new docks, beaches, marinas, hotels, conference centres and cruise and ferry harbours vying for space on the shoreline. New projects like the Diagonal-Mar area and Ricard Bofill's Nova Bocana harbour development (with a new maritime esplanade and a towering luxury hotel shaped like a sail) will change the seascape completely. Barcelona's coast will become a virtually continuous strip of modern construction designed to maximise income from the ocean. It might not be to everyone's taste, but you can't say it isn't progressive.

In 1888, at the height of the last great building frenzy in the city, the massive **Monument a Colom** (a bronze Columbus standing on a column, pointing out to sea, *see below*) was built at the end of the Rambla, as if to forgive the old adventurer for putting the city out of business now that it was rich again. It has been noted many times that his finger is not pointing west to the Americas at all, but eastwards, to Mallorca. A cynic might suggest that he is pointing in bemusement at the **World Trade Center**, a hulking, ship-shaped construction built on a jetty in 1999 to house offices and a five-star hotel. Or he could be pointing at the **Maremàgnum**, an island lumped into the old harbour with a US-style shopping mall with two dozen restaurants, 50 shops, mini-golf, a multiplex cinema for dubbed Hollywood movies, an **IMAX cinema** and the second-biggest **aquarium** in Europe (*see p223*).

You can take a lift up through the centre of Columbus' column to check out his view, or else you could jump aboard the rickety **cable car** (*transbordador aeri*). Below you, the **catamaran** and the **Golondrinas** (swallow boats) begin their excursions out to sea (for both, *see below*). To your right, beyond the ferry and cruise ports, you'll see the grandly named **Porta d'Europa**, a huge drawbridge (the biggest in Europe, whatever the Rotterdammers say) that masks the increasingly busy container port from view, and Andreu Alfaro's wacky ***Onas*** (*Waves*), an exuberant construction of curved aluminium tubes that brightens up gridlock time at the busy roundabout where it sits.

To Columbus' left, past the undulating **Rambla del Mar** bridge, you can see the newly refurbished palm-lined **Moll de la Fusta** (literally 'wood wharf') harbour front, leading to Roy Lichtenstein's pop art ***Barcelona Head***, the marina and its spanking yachts and the Palau de Mar, a converted warehouse that now hosts the **Museu d'Història de Catalunya** (*see below*) with its collection of artefacts that tell the tale of the history of this region. The truth about Columbus' finger is that in 1888 he was pointing at the only bit of the sea that could be seen from central Barcelona, reminding the citizens that their city was coastal. His persistence appears to have paid off.

Catamaran Orsom

Portal de la Pau, Port de Barcelona (93 441 05 37/ www.barcelona-orsom.com). Metro Drassanes. **Moll de la Fusta to Port Olímpic** (approx 1hr 20mins) *Mar-Oct* noon-8pm 3-4 sailings daily. All sailings subject to weather conditions. **Tickets** €12; €6-€9 concessions; free under-4s. **Credit** MC, V. **Map** p342 D7.

From its new moorings on the jetty in front of the Monument a Colom, this large catamaran chugs you out to sea round the Nova Bocana harbour development, then unfurls its sails and peacefully glides across the bay in front of Barcelona, giving you a bosun's-eye view of the city's rapidly changing seascape. It's a peaceful antidote to the bustle of the city, although less so if you board one of the 8pm jazz cruises (June-Sept). The catamaran can also be chartered for private trips to Sitges.

Las Golondrinas

Moll de Drassanes (93 442 31 06/www.las golon drinas.com). Metro Drassanes. **Drassanes to breakwater & return** (35mins) *July-late Sept* every 35-45mins 11am-8pm Mon-Fri. *Late Sept-June* hourly 11.45am-5pm Mon-Fri; every 35mins 11.45am-6pm Sat, Sun. **Tickets** €3.70; €1.80 concessions; free under-4s. **Drassanes to Port Olímpic & return** (1hr 30mins) *July-Sept* 11.30am, 1.30pm, 4.30pm, 6.30pm, 8.30pm daily. *Apr-June* 11.30am, 1.30pm, 4.30pm Mon-Fri; 11.30pm, 1.30pm, 4.30pm, 6.30pm Sat, Sun. *Oct-Mar* 11.30am, 1.30pm Mon-Fri; 11.30am, 1.30pm, 4.30pm Sat, Sun. **Tickets** €8.80; €3.85-€6.30 concessions; free under-4s. **Credit** MC, V. **Map** p342 C7.

Next to the Orsom catamaran, the double-decker 'swallow boats' pack them in, and then chug round the harbour, something they've done for more than 100 years. The glass-bottomed catamaran makes a return trip to the Port Olímpic.

Monument a Colom

Plaça Portal de la Pau (93 302 52 24). Metro Drassanes. **Open** *Oct-May* 10am-6.30pm daily. *June-Sept* 9am-8.30pm daily. **Admission** €2; €1.30 concessions; free under-4s. **No credit cards**. **Map** p345 A4.

A tiny lift takes you up the middle of the column, built in 1888 for the Great Exhibition, to a poky circular viewing bay from which you get a panoramic view of the city and port, moving at the pace of the snap-happy person in front of you. Claustrophobes and vertigo sufferers should stay away; the slight sway is particularly unnerving.

Museu d'Història de Catalunya

Plaça Pau Vila 3 (93 225 47 00/http://cultura.gen cat.es/museus/mhc). Metro Barceloneta. **Open** 10am-7pm Tue, Thur-Sat; 10am-8pm Wed; 10am-2.30pm Sun. **Admission** €3; €2.10 concessions; free under-7s. **Guided tours** noon, 1pm Sun. **Credit** (shop only) MC, V. **Map** p345 C4.

This museum is a must-see for anyone who wants to understand why Catalonia is so different from the rest of Spain. It is not so much a collection of old objects as the three-dimensional, two-storey book narrating the history of the region using text, photos, tape recordings, videos, computers, animated models, artefacts and reproductions of domestic scenes taking you from prehistoric times to the modern day. It takes in the Roman occupation, the feudal

The lie of the sand

Let it all hang out I

Platja de Sant Sebastià

Isolated by the swimming pools behind it and the building works of the new breakwater to its side, this isolated stretch of sand is the unofficial nudist beach and the hangout of assorted windsurfers, daytime dope smokers and any other eccentrics happy to swap an uninspiring background of industrial rubble for a bit more space. It's bound to change beyond recognition when the Bofill hotel complex is completed.

A bit of a Goa

Platja de Sant Miquel

A city beach if ever there was one – in the summer the streets of Barceloneta empty a constant flow of sunbathers out onto this narrow belt of sand. It's a great place for people-watching, with a high proportion of tattoos and dreadlocks: at night from May to October the *chiringuitos* (beach shacks) pump out garage and house music and revellers linger on the beach drinking beer until sunset.

Pebble dash

Platja de Barceloneta

This is a grubby family-oriented beach with slightly thinner crowds (as it's a bit of a walk from the metro station and the sand gets painfully pebbly where the sea breaks). Nearby are handy restaurants, nightclubs (including the hugely hip CDLC and the vulgar Baja Beach Club), and spaces for tables where wizened old men play topless dominoes. Boats from the sailing school gingerly tack this way and that just out beyond the line of yellow buoys.

Having a ball

Platja de Nova Icària

The first beach after the Port Olímpic and well served by Ciutadella-Vila Olímpica metro station, this wide stretch has a suburban feel to it after Barceloneta. Sheltered by the marina, the water is calm, if crowded in the summer by a nondescript mixture of local and *guiri* (foreign) yoof throwing balls, playing beach tennis and occasionally simply swimming. Three volleyball courts ensure a constant backdrop of whoops and high fives.

Rough stuff

Platja de Bogatell

A long and slightly narrower stretch of beach, this strip is less sheltered than Nova Icària, and so has rougher seas and, on the most stormy days, sand banked up into walls. The *chiringuito* in the wider stretch of the beach

system, the industrial revolution and the Spanish Civil War. There are hands-on exhibits, a waterwheel and wearable armour. Most of the text is in Catalan, but every section has an introduction in English that is sufficient for a rewarding overview. The museum also has space for two concurrent temporary exhibitions: 2004 will see a display of materials and information on the three great Mediterranean civilisations in medieval times (Islamic, Christian and Byzantine) and an analysis of the relationship between Federico Lorca and his friend Salvador Dalí. Upstairs there's a library (with some books in English) and a café with an unbeatable view of the marina and beyond.

Museu Marítim

Avda de les Drassanes (93 342 99 29/www.diba.es/mmaritim). Metro Drassanes. **Open** 10am-7pm daily. **Admission** €5.40; €2.70 concessions; free under-7s. *Temporary exhibitions* varies. *Combined ticket with Las Golondrinas (35mins)* €6.60; €4-€5.10 concessions; free under-4s. *(1hr30mins)* €10.10; €5.70-€7.70 concessions; free under-4s. **Credit** MC, V. **Map** p345 A4.

One of the finest examples of civil Gothic architecture in Spain, the medieval shipyards, or *drassanes*, are a wonderful setting for this spacious nautical museum, which leaves you in no doubt of the importance that the sea has had on shaping Barcelona's history, and, for its part, the impact Barcelona has had on maritime history. The mainstay of the collection is a full-scale replica of the Royal Galley, in which Don Juan of Austria led the Holy League to a resounding victory against the Turkish navy in the Battle of Lepanto in 1571. Stand on the platform over the poop deck with your audio-guide and like magic a group of ghostly galley slaves will appear in front of you. The original ship was built in the very same shipyards. The museum also shows you how shipbuilding and cartography techniques have developed over the years through an absorbing range of maps and models, and there is a curious collection of figureheads. The museum hosts two concurrent temporary exhibitions – 2004 will see one on the splendour of the Mediterranean in medieval times and another on the history of the fishing industry in Barcelona. A ticket to the museum also allows you access to the three-masted *Santa Eulàlia* schooner docked in the Moll de la Fusta.

Transbordador Aeri

Torre de Sant Sebastià, Barceloneta (93 441 48 20). Metro Barceloneta. Also Torre de Jaume I, Port Vell, to Avda Miramar, Parc de Montjuïc. Metro

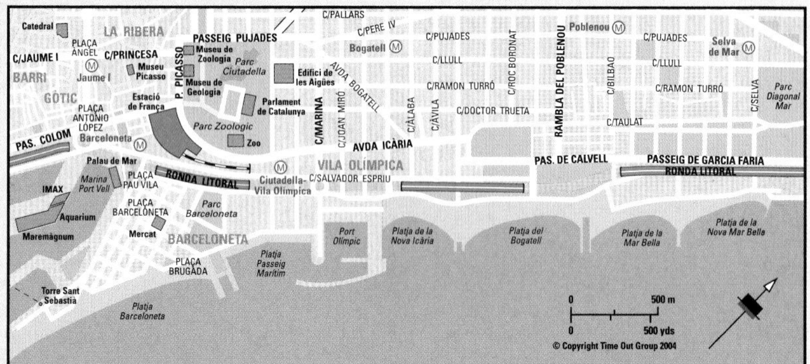

further north puts torches and deck chairs out at night from May to October for a more chilled experience than its hectic and bustling Barceloneta equivalent.

Let it all hang out II

Platja de Mar Bella

The official nudist beach, this stretch is protected from prying view by sand dunes, and flanked by the hip bar/restaurant Base Nautica (where the wearing of clothes is encouraged). Afternoons here are punctuated by yelps of triumph and pain from skateboarders, Rollerbladers and BMXers on the popular half-pipe behind.

A beach too far

Platja de Nova Mar Bella

Backed by a huge carpark and a forest of high-rise residential blocks, this short but quiet stretch at the end of the line is largely used by local families and by those who enjoy the techno music perpetually blasting out of the *chiringuito*.

Drassanes. **Open** *Mid June-mid Sept* 10.45am-7.15pm daily. *Mid Sept-mid June* 10.30am-5.45pm daily. **Tickets** €7.50 single; €9 return; free under-3s. **No credit cards**. **Map** p342 C/D7.

For an unparalleled view of the port area (not to mention the most exciting way to get up to Montjuïc), take the swaying, rickety old cable car from the Sant Sebastià tower at the top of Passeig Joan de Borbó or the Jaume I tower in front of the World Trade Center. Try to avoid busy times to get an unobstructed view.

Barceloneta

Cut off from the rest of the city by road and railway lines, the seaside *barrio* of Barceloneta has retained a distinctive, working-class identity, and famously exuberant local celebrations. The first plans for 'Little Barcelona' were drawn up by Flemish military engineer Prosper Verboom in order to address the problem of those living in makeshift shelters after the destruction of La Ribera neighbourhood in 1714 (*see p11*). The reality – 15 narrow streets of two-storey buildings running down a triangle of reclaimed marshland – was only to come about in the 1750s. The houses became home to the city's fishermen, who quickly built up to six further floors on top, so that the streets have become valleys decorated with washing hanging down from the balconies, somewhat claustrophobic but with a very distinct atmosphere.

In the summer the streets are teeming with sun-seekers heading for the beaches. Most come straight down Passeig Joan de Borbó, which has been converted from an industrial dockside street into an elegant restaurant-lined promenade running alongside the marina. At the top of the walkway is Juan Muñoz' disturbing sculpture of five bronze figures in a cage, known as ***Una habitació on sempre plou*** (*A Room Where it Always Rains*). Behind this somewhat gloomy piece is the city's hugely popular municipal **swimming pool** (*see p274*).

From this point, the road leads to the **Nova Bocana** development, which will soon be dominated by Ricard Bofill's controversial 100-metre, sail-shaped hotel. If you head the other way, you'll reach Barceloneta beach and Rebecca

Barceloneta beach.

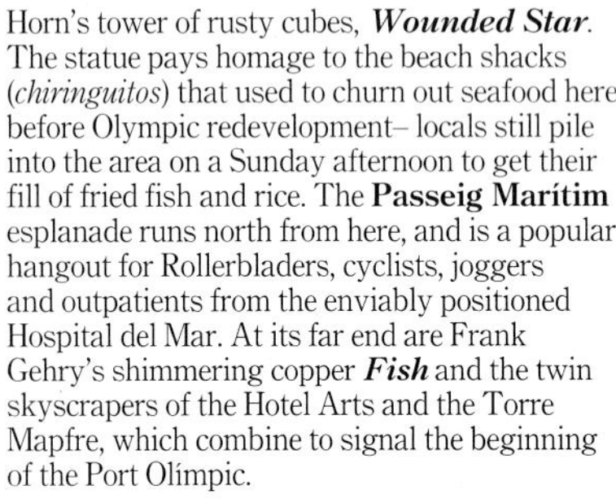

Horn's tower of rusty cubes, ***Wounded Star***. The statue pays homage to the beach shacks (*chiringuitos*) that used to churn out seafood here before Olympic redevelopment– locals still pile into the area on a Sunday afternoon to get their fill of fried fish and rice. The **Passeig Marítim** esplanade runs north from here, and is a popular hangout for Rollerbladers, cyclists, joggers and outpatients from the enviably positioned Hospital del Mar. At its far end are Frank Gehry's shimmering copper ***Fish*** and the twin skyscrapers of the Hotel Arts and the Torre Mapfre, which combine to signal the beginning of the Port Olímpic.

Vila Olímpica

The need to provide accommodation for 15,000 athletes in the 1992 Olympic Games led to a bold plan – to open the city up to the sea by building a whole new *barrio* in a space largely taken up by industrial wasteland. The fruit of that idea is 4.5 kilometre (2.8 mile) area known as the Vila Olímpica, which is home to 2,000 apartments, several parks, four beaches and the Port Olímpic leisure marina. On the far side are the Olympic beaches, which will eventually link up with the new Diagonal-Mar district to the north.

The area, built over a period of two years, was originally to be known as 'Nova Icària' to recall the socialist utopian society that once briefly existed here, but the name didn't stick. When it was constructed, developers hoped the apartments would provide low-cost housing after the athletes had gone, although economic realities have dictated otherwise. The design group for the project, headed by the company MBM (David Mackay, Oriol Bohigas and Josep Martorell) joined by Albert Puigdomènech, used a team of 30 prize-winning architects, hoping to build a model neighbourhood with all the amenities anyone could ever need. Remarkably, apart from the Hotel Arts, the whole project was completed on time.

The result is an odd place with some horrendous elements (the hellish pergola on Avda Icària, inspired by ripped-up railway tracks, is an unpleasant structure to walk under, especially at night) and a few comic touches – the six metre (20 foot) sculpture of the lower half of a human body by Basque sculptor Eduardo Úrculo has, of course, been dubbed *el culo de Úrculo* (Urculo's arse).

You can plan a place to perfection but you can't account for its soul and that's what the Vila Olímpica lacks. The bustling Port Olímpic is given over to the city's less imaginative tourists (there's even a mock Irish pub built into a tent) and its hinterland has plenty of public space but nobody to fill it up. It's well-connected, there are plenty of shops and even a vast multiplex cinema, but nevertheless the Vila Olímpica is essentially rather dull.

Montjuïc

Put your climbing shoes on for views, parks and history.

Montjuïc is Barcelona's most lively public park, blending gardens with museums and sporting facilities. Yet for centuries, before the city began to conceive of the mountain as a leisure zone, Montjuïc had more sombre connotations; mention the name, and *barcelonins* thought of death, frequently of a violent nature.

The name 'juïc' comes from a medieval Catalan word meaning 'Jewish'. Until the devastating pogroms of 1391, a thriving population of Jews used the mountain as a burial site (there is a counterpart 'Montjuïc' in Girona); according to their religious precepts, cemeteries had to be set apart from populated areas. The original tombs were located near the summit, and the dead were given a simple headstone with a Hebrew inscription. After the definitive expulsion of the Jews in 1492 many of these stones were grabbed for use in 'new' construction (as seen in the walls of the former Archive of the Crown of Aragon building just to the east of the cathedral, built in the 16th century). An entire room has been set aside for a number of these tombstones in the **Museu Militar**, including translations of the wordings.

The gloomy associations do not end there. In the 17th century a fortress was built at the top of the hill, and it soon became a symbol of the suppression of Catalan liberties, especially after Spanish troops overran Barcelona in 1714. As a prison and torture centre for rebels and radicals – or those deemed as such – it inspired fear and loathing for two centuries. Here many republicans were executed after the Civil War, including Generalitat President Lluís Companys, who now has a monument in the cemetery. Only at the end of the 19th century did the military cede its jealous control over its lands, allowing for the construction of housing on its lower slopes.

The 1929 Exposition (*see p20*) was the first attempt to turn the hill into a leisure area. Then in the 1940s thousands of immigrant workers from the rest of Spain settled on the hill. Some squatted in precarious shacks, while others rented brick and plaster sheds laid out along improvised streets that covered the hillside, then virtually treeless. These *barraques* thrived until the last few stragglers moved out in the 1970s. Energetic visitors can follow the same steep routes these residents once took home, straight up C/Nou de la Rambla or C/Margarit in Poble Sec: the stairway at the top leaves you just a short distance from the **Fundació Joan Miró** (*see p111*) and the Olympic stadium area.

The long axis from **Plaça Espanya** is still the most popular access to the park, with the climb now eased by a sequence of open-air escalators. Plaça Espanya itself is ennobled by the disused **Las Arenas** bullring with its Moorish arches, now to be remade into a shopping and leisure centre designed by the architect Richard Rogers. On the other side of the square, two Venetian-style towers announce the beginning of the **Fira**, the trade show area, with pavilions from 1929 and newer buildings

Font Màgica. *See p111.*

Sightseeing

Looking out from the tropical **Jardíns Mossèn Costa i Llobera**.

used for conventions and congresses. Further up, the rebuilt Mies van der Rohe **Pavelló Barcelona**, a modernist classic, contrasts sharply with the neo-classical structures nearby. Across the street, Puig i Cadafalch's Modernista factory has been converted into the excellent **CaixaForum** cultural centre (*see p111*). Further up the hill is the bizarre **Poble Espanyol** (*see p114*), a model village also designed in 1929 especially to showcase Spanish crafts and architecture.

Presiding over it all is the bombastic **Palau Nacional** (originally built as a 'temporary exhibition' for the expo), where the **Museu Nacional d'Art de Catalunya** is located (*see p114*). At nightfall the entire setting is illuminated by a water-and-light spectacular, the **Font Màgica**, still operating with its complex original mechanisms (*see p113*). Other nearby buildings erected for the 1929 expo have been converted into the **Museu d'Arqueologia de Catalunya** (*see p113*) and the **Ciutat del Teatre** (theatre city) complex. From the same period are the nearby **Teatre Grec** (Greek theatre), used for summer concerts during the Grec festival, and the beautifully restored **Jardíns Laribal**, designed by famed French landscape architect JCN Forestier. At the bottom of this garden is the still quite new **Font del Gat** information centre, opened in 2003. The **Museu Etnològic**, a typical 1970s construction, sits just above it (*see p114*).

If walking isn't your thing, another way up the hill is via the **funicular railway**, now integrated with the city's metro system, leaving from the Paral.lel station and then linking up with the **Telefèric** cable car (*see p115*) to the **castle**. Alternatively, a more circuitous way up is by way of the **Transbordador Aeri** cable car across the harbour to **Miramar**. But bear in mind that at Miramar work on a five-star hotel has begun; the former road in front of it has disappeared and a new tunnel channels traffic behind the hotel site, which will continue to be affected by messy construction into 2004.

Montjuïc's **Anella Olímpica** (Olympic Ring) is a convergence of diverse constructions all laid out for the 1992 Olympic Games. The **Estadi Olímpic** – home to the city's 'second' football team, Espanyol, until they move to a new stadium in 2005 – although entirely new, was built within the façade of a 1929 stadium by a design team led by Federico Correa and Alfonso Milà. The expressive horse sculptures are copies of the originals by Pau Gargallo. Next to it is the most original and attractive of the Olympic facilities, Arata Isozaki's **Palau Sant Jordi** indoor arena, with its undulating façade evoking Gaudí, and a high-tech interior featuring a transparent roof. It now regularly serves as a venue for concerts and other events. In the hard, white plaça in front rises Santiago Calatrava's remarkable, Brancusi-inspired **communications tower**.

Across the square is the city's best swimming pool, the **Piscina Bernat Picornell** (*see also p274*), while further down is the INEFC physical education institute, by architect Ricardo Bofill. Walk across the road and you look over a cliff on to a rugby pitch and an equestrian area, where children can take pony rides. The cliff itself is a favourite hang-out for rock-climbers.

The many parks and gardens include the **Jardíns Mossèn Costa i Llobera** (*see p113*), which abound in tropical plants, but particularly cacti, just below Miramar, on the steep flank nearest the port. Not far above are the **Jardíns del Mirador**, from where there is a spectacular view over the harbour. These gardens are also the starting point for a new path for pedestrians and cyclists, running precariously below the castle. Just below, the 1922 red and white lighthouse should be open to the public by late 2004. One of the newest parks is the nearby **Jardíns de Joan Brossa**, featuring humorous, hands-on contraptions where children can manipulate water-courses and do creative adventure sports. Walk down towards the funicular station and you will reach the **Jardíns Cinto Verdaguer**, with a quiet pond, water lilies and grassy slopes. All these gardens play an adjunct role to the creative biospheres of the **Jardí Botànic**, just above the Olympic Stadium, still too young to fully enjoy (*see p113*).

CaixaForum

Casaramona, Avda Marquès de Comillas 6-8 (93 476 86 00/www.fundacio.lacaixa.es). Metro Espanya. **Open** 10am-8pm Tue-Sun. **Admission** free. **Credit** (shop only) AmEx, DC, MC, V. **Map** p341 A5.

This former textile mill, designed by Puig i Cadafalch, has undergone a recent revamp to become La Caixa's main cultural centre. Its exterior is distinguished by creative brickwork, with an entrance plaza designed by Arata Isozaki. The massive interior floor space allows for key pieces of the permanent collection, such as installations by Joseph Beuys and Jannis Kounellis, to be viewed at all times. Catalonia's largest savings bank, La Caixa, has a high-profile cultural foundation with an excellent collection of international contemporary art and a Spain-wide exhibitions programme that also touches on ethnology and archaeology.

Temporary shows in 2004 include Dalí: Mass Culture, featuring his work in design, cinema, fashion and advertising, running until May; an exhibit on Confucius in the summer, and a solo show by contemporary American artist Doug Aitken from July into the autumn. The CaixaForum also houses Barcelona's best documentary centre for video and media art, and runs an excellent programme of music (early music in the spring, non-commercial world music in the autumn).

Cementiri del Sud-oest

C/Mare de Déu de Port, 54-8 (93 484 17 00). Bus 38. **Open** 8am-6pm daily. **Admission** free.

The entire south-west corner of Montjuïc is occupied by the stepped terraces of the cemetery. When it was opened in 1883 it was a quiet, out-of-the-way spot looking out over unused beaches; nowadays the bustling container port and noisy ring road below make it a far from peaceful site for other-worldly respite. Its saving graces are the numerous pantheons featuring fine neo-Gothic architecture and Modernista sculptures (a favourite theme is the disconsolate angel slumped over the tomb). A newer and more pleasant part of the Cementiri is set into the Fossar de la Pedrera, a memorial park in a former quarry. On the far end of the meadow the dead of the International Brigades from the Civil War are remembered, while another corner has a Holocaust memorial. This is also where the Catalan martyrs of the Civil War are honoured.

Font Màgica de Montjuïc

Plaça d'Espanya (93 291 40 42/www.bcn.es/fonts). Metro Espanya. **Fountain** *Mid May-Sept* 8pm-midnight Thur-Sun; music every 30mins 9.30pm-midnight. *Oct-mid May* 7-9pm Fri, Sat; music every 30mins 7-9pm. **Map** p341 A5.

Still using its original art deco waterworks, the 'magic fountain' works its wonders with 3,600 pieces of tubing and over 4,500 light bulbs. Summer evenings after nightfall, the multiple founts swell and dance to various hits ranging from Sting to the *1812 Overture*, showing off its kaleidoscope of pastel colours while searchlights play in a giant fan pattern over the palace dome.

Fundació Joan Miró

Parc de Montjuïc (93 329 19 08/www.bcn.fjmiro.es). Metro Paral.lel, then Funicular de Montjuïc/61 bus. **Open** *July-Sept* 10am-8pm Tue, Wed, Fri, Sat; 10am-9.30pm Thur; 10am-2.30pm Sun. *Oct-June* 10am-7pm Tue, Wed, Fri, Sat; 10am-9.30pm Thur; 10am-2.30pm Sun. **Guided tours** 11.30pm Sat, Sun. **Admission** *All exhibitions* €7.20; €3.90 concessions. *Permanent exhibitions* €3.60; €1.80 concessions. Free under-14s. **Discounts** Articket, BC, BT. **Credit** MC, V. **Map** p341 B6.

Josep Lluís Sert's Mediterranean design makes this one of the world's great museum buildings. The white walls and arches house a collection of more than 225 paintings, 150 sculptures and all Miró's graphic work, plus some 5,000 drawings. The permanent collection, highlighting Miró's trademark use of primary colours and simplified organic forms symbolising stars, the moon, birds and women, occupies the second half of the exhibition space. It begins with a large tapestry created with Josep

Montjuïc Card

An excellent new way for visitors to take full advantage of the park is with the Montjuïc Card, which for €20 (€10 for 6-12s) offers one-day use of the Tren Montjuïc and Telefèric, free bike rental, free access to the Jardí Botànic and the Bernat Picornell swimming pool and free admittance to the Poble Espanyol and all museums on the mountain. It also lets you choose an evening show at the Ciutat del Teatre theatre complex. The card is available every day except Monday, from the park information office at Font del Gat, as well as at tourist offices and via ServiCaixa (*see p212*).

Castle of crossed destinies

Most towns overlooked by a brooding castle are pleased to play up the noble charm of their silent sentinels. Not so in Barcelona. The Montjuïc castle was built first as a defensive fortress against invading armies, but its subsequent role was to hammer rebellious Catalans into submission and as an execution site for political upstarts.

Construction up high on Montjuïc began when the counts of Barcelona built a small castle there in the 11th century. In 1357 a small watchtower was added. This was converted into the city's first major military fortress, completed in 1640. After the invasion of Catalonia by Castilian troops in 1714, the decision was made to enlarge it, so the current castle with its thick walls and wide moats dates from 1751. Strong though it was, it was taken by the armies of Napoleon in 1808.

The castle's already dubious reputation went definitively sour in 1842 when General Baldomero Espartero, acting in the name of Queen Isabel II, decided to bomb the city from its heights to repress a bourgeois uprising against government policies. On 3 December of that year there came a 13-hour bombardment that Barcelona citizens would never forget. From then on the castle was repeatedly used to suppress workers' movements. Six anarchists were executed there in 1894 after the bombing of the Liceu opera house, and five more met the firing squad there in 1897. Converted into a centre for the torture of political prisoners, public outcry began to demand that the castle be handed over to the city, but to no avail. After protests over the war in Morocco led to the Setmana Trágica in 1909 (*see p19*), a farcical trial culminated in the execution of Francesc Ferrer i Guardia, a famed education reformer. Known as 'the Spanish Dreyfuss', his case provoked widespread protests across Europe. A copy of the sculpture erected in his memory by Brussels in his honour in 1911 now stands between the Olympic Stadium and the Palau Nacional.

After the Civil War, Franco was not one to conceive of the castle in a new light. Catalonia's republican president Lluís Companys was arrested in exile by the Gestapo in occupied France, extradited, summarily tried and executed, barefoot, by firing squad in the castle moat on 15 October 1940. His tragic end only reinforced the castle's negative symbolism for most Catalans, and its stones, collection and memories continue to this day to be under the control of the Spanish armed forces.

Today, the city is pushing for central government to hand control of the castle to local authorities, to convert it into an institution dedicated to peace, and yet it is somehow appropriate that it now holds a military museum (Museu Militar). A few years ago, though, its bad reputation was made even worse when its gift shop was found to be peddling Franco and Nazi paraphernalia. Still, the museum has made an occasional gesture toward cleaning up its act: an unpopular equestrian sculpture of Franco, for example, was recently stashed out of sight.

Royo, and then, on the way to the sculpture gallery, is Alexander Calder's lovely reconstructed *Mercury Fountain*, originally seen at the Spanish Republic's Pavilion at the 1937 Paris Fair. In other works, Miró is shown as a cubist (*Street in Pedralbes*, 1917), naïve (*Portrait of a Young Girl*, 1919) or surrealist (*Man and Woman in Front of a Pile of Excrement*, 1935). Downstairs are works donated to the museum by 20th-century artists. In the upper galleries large, black-outlined paintings from the final period precede a room of works with political themes.

In 2004 temporary shows include *Behind the Facts – Interfunktionen*, featuring international artists from the late '60s and early '70s; in the spring, *The Beauty of Failure/The Failure of Beauty*, a summer show of utopian and dystopian art of the 1950s and '60s and an autumn exhibition dedicated to Salvador Dalí, part of the Dalí centennial celebrations. The Espai 13 in the basement features young contemporary artists. Outside is a pleasant sculpture garden with fine work by contemporary Catalan artists.

Galeria Olímpica

Estadi Olímpic, Parc de Montjuïc (93 426 06 60/ www.fundaciobarcelonaolimpica.es). Metro Espanya/ bus all routes to Plaça d'Espanya. **Open** *Apr-Sept* 10am-2pm, 4-7pm Mon-Fri. *Oct-Mar* (by appt) 10am-1pm, 4-6pm Mon-Fri. **Admission** €2.50; €1.20 concessions. **Credit** AmEx, MC, V. **Map** p341 A6.

A hotchpotch of imagery and paraphernalia commemorating the 1992 Olympics, including costumes from the opening ceremony and the ubiquitous mascot Cobi. A larger, updated museum dedicated to the Olympic movement and the Barcelona Games has been announced for the north end of the stadium, though it will not be complete until well into 2005.

Inside, the collection of historical weaponry is excellent: ancient armour, lances and muskets share the immense space with fine displays of rare pistols and early automatic weapons. The castle's long hall features some 23,000 lead pieces depicting a full 1920s Spanish battalion in marching formation. One room has medieval Jewish tombstones from the former cemetery site, their inscriptions fully translated – it is a remarkable display, although the setting is clearly inappropriate. The airy ramparts offer an excellent view of the coastline and inland valleys flanking Barcelona, which acts as a particularly effective reminder of just how useful this site must have been in protecting the good folk below, before the castle's owners turned on them.

Museu Militar

Castell de Montjuïc, Crta de Montjuïc 66 (93 329 86 13). Metro Paral.lel, then funicular & cable car. **Open** *Apr-Oct* 9.30am-8pm Tue-Sun. *Nov-Mar* 9.30am-5pm Tue-Fri; 9.30am-8pm Sat, Sun. **Admission** €2.50; €1.25 concessions; free under-14s. **No credit cards. Map** p341 B7.

Jardí Botànic

Doctor Font i Quer (93 426 49 35). Metro Espanya. **Open** *Apr-Oct* 10am-8pm daily. *Nov-Mar* 10am-5pm daily. **Admission** €3; €1.50 concessions; free under-16s. Free last Sat of mth. **No credit cards. Map** p341 A6-7.

The Jardí Botànic was first opened in 1999, and still needs a few more growing years before its long, meticulously tailored slope of plantings will mature to its full, lush potential. A visit is still worthwhile, however, if only to take in the extensive array of unusual and typical species from the Mediterranean area and the Canary Islands. Plants also were brought in from other parts of the world compatible with the Barcelona climate – these include places such as Chile, California, Australia and South Africa. Many of the shrubs and flowers complement the truly beautiful tree varieties.

Jardíns Mossèn Costa i Llobera

Ctra de Miramar 1 (93 413 41 80). Metro Paral.lel or Drassanes. **Open** 10am-sunset daily. **Admission** free. **Map** p341 B7.

One of the lovelier gardens on Montjuïc in spite of traffic noise from the ring road below, dedicated to cacti and other dry climate species. The microclimate on the port side of Montjuïc sustains more than 800 species, including a 200-year-old Backeberg cactus native to the high Andes, its long white hairs punctuated by orange spines.

Museu d'Arqueologia de Catalunya

Passeig de Santa Madrona 39-41(93 423 21 49/56 01/www.mac.es). Metro Poble Sec. **Open** 9.30am-7pm Tue-Sat; 10am-2.30pm Sun. **Admission** €2.40; €1.80 concessions; free under-16s. **Credit** (shop only) MC, V. **Map** p341 B6.

Telefèric de Montjuïc. *See p115.*

The archaeological museum is filled with artefacts from digs in Mediterranean Spain. The time frame for the collection starts with the Palaeolithic period, and there are relics of Greek, Punic, Roman and Visigoth colonisers, up to the early Middle Ages. A massive Roman sarcophagus is carved with scenes of the rape of Persephone, and an immense statue of Aesculapius, the god of medicine, towers over one room. Upstairs, alongside small temporary exhibitions, a huge statue of a sexually charged Priapus stands threateningly. A few galleries are dedicated to the Mallorcan Talayotic cave culture, and there is a very good display on the Iberians, the pre-Hellenic, pre-Roman inhabitants of south-eastern Spain. An Iberian skull with a nail driven through it effectively demonstrates a typical method of execution from that time. The display ends with the marvellous, jewel-studded headpiece of a Visigoth king.

Museu Etnològic

Passeig de Santa Madrona s/n (93 424 68 07/ www.museuetnologic.bcn.es). Metro Poble Sec. **Open** 10am-2pm Tue-Sun. **Admission** €3; €1.50 concessions; free under-16s & pensioners. **No credit cards**. **Map** p341 A6.

The ethnology museum will be closed for renovations until June 2004. Afterwards a new display will show off its massive collection of artefacts from non-European cultures. Overall, it holds 30,000 pieces which are shown on a rotating basis.

MNAC (Museu Nacional d'Art de Catalunya)

Palau Nacional, Parc de Montjuïc (93 622 03 60/ www.mnac.es). Metro Espanya. **Open** 10am-7pm Tue-Sat; 10am-2.30pm Sun. **Admission** *All exhibitions* €6; €4.20 concessions; free under-7s. *Permanent exhibitions* €4.80; €3.30 concessions. *Temporary exhibitions* €4.20; €2.10-€2.90 concessions. **Credit** MC, V. **Map** p341 A6.

As art historians realised that scores of solitary 10th-century churches in the Pyrenees were falling into ruin – and with them were going extraordinary Romanesque mural paintings that had served to instruct doubting villagers in the basics of the faith – the laborious task was begun of removing murals intact from church apses. The display here features 21 mural sections in loose chronological order. The artworks are set into freestanding wood supports or in reconstructed church interiors. One highlight is the tremendous Crist de Taüll, from the 12th-century church of Sant Climent de Taüll. Even 'graffiti' scratchings, probably by monks, of animals, crosses and labyrinths, have been preserved.

The Gothic collection is also excellent, and includes altarpieces and alabaster sculptures pulled from churches in Barcelona. Highlights are the works of the indisputable Catalan masters of the Golden Age, Bernat Martorell and Jaume Huguet. Works from the Renaissance up to the early 20th century, including everything once seen in the Museum of Modern Art (due to close in March 2004), will be displayed in new upstairs galleries from December 2004. Expect some upheaval during this time, and call to confirm opening hours.

High-quality temporary shows are presented in the basement: in 2004 these include a springtime exhibition of English and French photography from the mid-19th century, and an exhibition (from April to July) of early Peruvian art, featuring Inca treasures, and, later, a selection of Bronze Age sculpture from the Museum of Shanghai.

Pavelló Mies van der Rohe

Avda Marquès de Comillas (93 423 40 16/www.miesbcn.com). Metro Espanya. **Open** 10am-8pm daily. **Admission** €3.50; €2 concessions; free under-18s. **Credit** (shop only) MC, V. **Map** p341 A5.

Mies van der Rohe built the Pavelló Alemany (German Pavilion) for the 1929 Exhibition not as a gallery, but as a simple reception space, sparsely furnished by his trademark 'Barcelona Chair'. The pavilion was a founding monument of modern rationalist architecture, with its flowing floor plan and a revolutionary use of materials. Though the original was demolished after the Exhibition, a fine replica was built on the same site in 1986, the simplicity of its design setting off the warm tones of the marble and expressive Georg Kolbe sculpture in the pond.

Poble Espanyol

Avda Marquès de Comillas (93 325 78 66/ www.poble-espanyol.com). Metro Espanya. **Open** 9am-8pm Mon; 9am-2am Tue-Thur; 9am-4am Fri,

Sat; 9am-midnight Sun. **Admission** €7; €4.40 concessions; €3.70 7-12s; €14 family ticket; free under-7s. **Credit** AmEx, MC, V. **Map** p341 A5.
Another legacy of the 1929 Exhibition, this time an enclosed area showing examples of traditional architecture from every region in Spain. A Castilian square leads to an Andalucian church, then on to village houses from Aragon, and so on. There are numerous bars and restaurants (including vegetarian), and 60-plus shops. Many are workshops in which craftspeople make and sell Spanish folk artefacts, such as ceramics, embroidery, fans, metalwork and candles. Some of the work is quite attractive, some tacky, and prices are generally high. Outside, street performers recreate bits of Catalan and Spanish folklore; there are children's shows, and the 'Barcelona Experience', an audio-visual presentation (available in English).

The Poble has an unmistakeable tourist-trap air about it, but it has been working to raise its cultural profile, as with the Fran Daurel collection of contemporary art and a quality gallery of Iberian arts and crafts that opened in 2003. It also partly functions as a popular nightspot, and bands perform regularly in the main square. One of the city's most popular clubs, La Terrrazza/Discothèque, is located at the back (*see p251*).

Telefèric de Montjuïc

Estació Funicular, Avda Miramar (93 443 08 59/ www.tmd.net). Metro Paral.lel, then funicular. **Open** *June-mid Sept* 11.15am-9pm daily. *Mid Sept-Oct, Apr, May* 11am-7.15pm daily. *Nov-Mar* 11am-7.15pm Sat, Sun. **Tickets** €3.40 single; €4.50 return; €3.70 child return. **No credit cards**. **Map** p341 B6.
These four-person cable cars run between the funicular station and the castle, giving superb if vertiginous views of the city. In late 2004, the Telefèric will close down for an unspecified period, for renovations. After that it will extend down to the port.

Tren Montjuïc

Plaça d'Espanya (information 93 415 60 20). Metro Espanya. **Open** *Mid Apr-mid June* 10am-9pm Sat, Sun. *Mid June-mid Sept* 10am-9pm daily. *Mid Sept-Oct* 10am-9pm Sat, Sun. Closed Oct-mid Apr. **Frequency** every 30mins daily. **Tickets** *All day* €3.20; €2-€2.55 concessions. **No credit cards**. **Map** p341 A/B5.
Not a train but an open trolley pulled by a truck that goes up Montjuïc to Miramar, passing all the hilltop sights along the way.

Poble Sec & Paral.lel

Poble Sec, the name of the neighbourhood between Montjuïc and the Avda Paral.lel, means 'dry village', which is explained by the fact that it was 1894 before the thousands of poor workers or the *barri* who lived on the flanks of the hill celebrated the installation of the area's first water fountain (which is still standing in C/Margarit).

The name Avda Paral.lel derives from the fact that it coincides exactly with 41° 44' latitude north, one of Ildefons Cerdà's more eccentric conceits. The avenue was the prime centre of Barcelona nightlife – often called the city's 'Montmartre' – in the first half of the 20th century, and was full of theatres, nightclubs and music halls. A statue on the corner with C/Nou de la Rambla commemorates Raquel Meller, a legendary star of the street who went on to equal celebrity around the world. She now stands outside Barcelona's notorious live-porn venue, the Bagdad. Apart from this, most of its cabarets have disappeared, although there are still theatres and cinemas along the Paral.lel. A real end of an era came in 1997 when El Molino, the most celebrated of the avenue's traditional, vulgar old music halls, suddenly shut up shop. It seemed to symbolise the change that had come to the neighbourhood.

Today, Poble Sec is a friendly, working-class area of quiet, relaxed streets and leafy squares. On the stretch of the Paral.lel opposite the city walls three tall chimneys stand amid modern office blocks. They are all that remain of the Anglo-Canadian-owned power station known locally as *La Canadença* ('The Canadian'). This was the centre of the city's largest general strike, in 1919. Beside the chimneys an open space has been created and dubbed the **Parc de les Tres Xemeneies** (Park of the Three Chimneys). It is now particularly popular with skateboarders and Pakistani expat cricketers.

Towards the Paral.lel are some distinguished Modernista buildings, which local legend has maintained were built for *artistas* from the nude cabarets by their rich sugar daddies. At C/Tapioles 12 is a beautiful, narrow wooden Modernista door with particularly lovely writhing ironwork, while at C/Elkano 4 is **La Casa de les Rajoles**, which is known for its peculiar mosaic façade. Incongruous in such a central area is the small neighbourhood of single family dwellings with quaint gardens, off the upper reaches of C/Margarit, which is worth seeing solely for the juxtaposition.

Refugi Antiaeri del Poble Sec

C/Nou de la Rambla 175 (93 319 02 22). Metro Paral.lel. **Open** (guided tour & by appt only) 11am-12.30pm 1st Sat of mth. **Admission** €3.30; free under-7s. **Meeting place** Biblioteca Francesc Boix, C/Blai 34. **Map** p341 B6.
About 1,500 Barcelona civilians were killed during the vicious air bombings of the Civil War, a fact that the government long silenced. As Poble Sec particularly suffered the effects of bombing, a large air-raid shelter was built partially into the mountain at the top of C/Nou de la Rambla; one of some 1,200 in the entire city. Recently rediscovered, and converted into a museum, it is worth a visit.

The Eixample

The architect's Arcadia, the shopper's Shangri-La.

The undulating façade of Gaudí's **Casa Batlló**. *See p117.*

La Rambla may be Barcelona's most famous street but the most beautiful has got to be **Passeig de Gràcia**. This grand, pampered boulevard is a glittering wonderland filled with Modernista masterpieces and glitzy shopfronts, and yet it also has an alter-ego as one of the city's most emotionally charged public spaces. Both the Gaudí and the Gucci are regular witnesses to religious parades and high-profile demonstrations, such as the May Day union marches and the now famous immense anti-war protest of February 2003.

Passeig de Gràcia is topped by the once-independent village of Gràcia and tailed by **Plaça Catalunya**, Barcelona's focal point, transport hub and home to the underground city tourist office (*see p319*). In the early 1800s, the street evolved from a dirt track connecting the city and Gràcia to a landlocked version of Blackpool pleasure beach with fairground rides, gardens, theatres and dance halls. By the middle of the century, the surrounding fields were ripe for development, while overcrowding, disease and civil unrest in the Old City were leading to the demolition of the medieval walls. With few major obstacles between the city and the satellite villages of Gràcia, Horta, Les Corts, Sant Gervasi and Sarrià, a huge area of land was suddenly up for architectural grabs.

Much debate ensued and after the central Madrid government had stuck its oar in, the city authorities opted to build the Eixample (which translates as 'expansion') based upon a uniform grid designed by Ildefons Cerdà, a pioneer of modern urbanism. Following a socialist philosophy of strict equality, he chopped the land into 500 uniform blocks crossed by three main avenues.The very antithesis of the Barri Gòtic's dim, cramped warren, it is almost impossible to get lost in the Eixample if you stick to the standard reference points of *mar* (sea) or *muntanya* (mountain) but many give it a big raspberry for its endless homogeneity, the annoyance of stopping for traffic lights at every intersection, and the depressing lack of open squares and parks.

Cerdà's geometry lesson is a perfect example of 19th-century rationalism on paper, but on foot it feels rather like being trapped inside a giant industrial waffle iron.

Yet there is some madness in the order: acting as an antidote to such a monotonous, unnatural landscape, the buildings are an avalanche of sensuous organic shapes, fantasy turrets, Moorish minarets and colourful tiling. They are the result of a bourgeoisie enriched by industrialisation and clamouring for prestige, keen to invest the sweat of their downtrodden mill workers in a more spectacular Modernista creation than that of their neighbour.

Unfortunately, this insatiable demand for housing meant that the more utopian features of Cerdà's plan – building on only two sides of each block, height limits of just two or three storeys, and gardens in the middle of the blocks – were quickly crushed by the realities of property speculation. Now fortress-like blocks of six or seven storeys create echoing gulleys for heavy traffic, and any extra space provided by the open chamfered corners is immediately clogged with double-parked cars. Most of the interior courtyards were covered over to make car parks and shopping centres, but in an effort to recover the spirit of Cerdà, the ProEixample project to reclaim the courtyards started up in 1985. Since then, 54 have been reclaimed for public use with 13 more under restoration; the goal is that everyone should be able to find an open space within 200 metres (650 feet) of their home. Two of the better examples are the palm-fringed mini beach around the **Torre de les Aigües** water tower (C/Llúria 56) and the patio at **Passatge Permanyer** (C/Pau Claris 120).

The overland railway that used to run down C/Balmes has traditionally been the dividing line through the middle of the Eixample: the fashionable **Dreta** ('Right'), which contains the most distinguished Modernista architecture, the main museums and shopping avenues, and the **Esquerra** ('Left'), which was built slightly later, and contains some great markets and less well-known Modernista sights.

The Dreta

The trees, ceramic benches and idle ramblers make the **Passeig de Gràcia** feel rather like a calmer Champs Elysées. The Eixample's central artery, it is most distinctive for its magnificent wrought-iron **lamp-posts** by Pere Falqués and for its designer **pavement** – hexagonal slabs decorated with intertwining nautilus shells and starfish that was first designed for the patio of Gaudí's **Casa Batlló** (*see p122* **For a fistful of lollies**), then repeated in **La Pedrera** (*see p121*), before spreading over the whole boulevard.

The importance that the Modernistas gave to decorative and fine arts is reflected in the ubiquitous sgraffito and ornate sculpture, nowhere more so than the cluster of three wildly clashing masterpieces known as the **Manzana de la Discòrdia**. This is a pun on *manzana*, which in Spanish means both 'block' and 'apple', and alludes to the fatal choice of Paris when judging which of a bevy of divine beauties would win the golden Apple of Discord. If the volume of camera-toting admirers is anything to go by, the fairest of these Modernista lovelies is undoubtedly Gaudí's Casa Batlló, permanently illuminated by the light of a hundred flash bulbs. Runners up are Domènech i Montaner's **Casa Lleó Morera**, a decadently melting wedding cake on the corner of C/Consell de Cent at No.35, and Puig i Cadafalch's **Casa Amatller** at No.41. Built for a chocolate baron, it has a stepped Flemish pediment covered in shiny ceramics that look good enough to eat, and a gallery of medieval grotesques sculpted by Eusebi Arnau. It also houses the **Centre de Modernisme**, which organises the Ruta del Modernisme.

The Passeig de Gràcia hit parade also includes the **Casa Casas** (No.96), once home to one of Barcelona's greatest painters, Ramon Casas, and now to design emporium **Vinçon** (*see p192*), with a Modernista interior on the first floor and a patio overlooking La Pedrera's rear façade. Enric Sagnier's neo-Gothic **Cases Pons i Pascual** (Nos.2-4) is also worth a look, while the **Casa Vídua Marfà** (No.66) has one of the most breathtakingly sumptuous entrance halls in the Eixample.

Casa Lleó Morera.

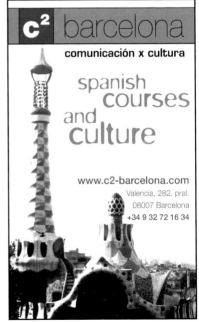

The section of the Eixample located between C/Muntaner and C/Roger de Flor has been labelled the **Quadrat d'Or** or 'Golden Square' of Modernisme, and plaques have been placed on 150 protected buildings. The most exalted of them all is the towering mass of the **Sagrada Família** (*see p121*), and whether you love it or hate it (and George Orwell called it 'one of the most hideous buildings in the world'), it has become the city's emblem and sine qua non of Barcelona tourist itineraries. A less well-known masterpiece bookends the northerly extreme of the Avda Gaudí in the shape of Domènech i Montaner's **Hospital de Sant Pau** (*see below*).

Other public buildings include the charming tiled **Mercat de la Concepció** on C/Aragó, designed by Rovira i Trias. Over to the right is the egg-topped **Plaça de Braus Monumental**, but the city's last active bullring is now mainly frequented by tour buses from the Costa Brava. Out-of-season, it hosts alternative animal abuse in the form of tatty travelling circuses.

The streets above the Diagonal are mainly residential, for the most part built after 1910, but with some striking Modernista buildings such as Puig i Cadafalch's 1901 **Palau Macaya**, now a cultural centre of the Fundació la Caixa (Passeig de Sant Joan 108, 93 476 86 00) and now temporary home to elements of the science museum until its completion in 2005.

Fundació Antoni Tàpies

C/Aragó 255 (93 487 03 15/www.fundaciotapies.org). Metro Passeig de Gràcia. **Open** 10am-8pm Tue-Sun. **Admission** €4.20; €2.10 concessions; free under-16s. **Discounts** Articket, BC, RM. **Credit** MC, V. **Map** p338 D4.

Founded in 1984, the Tàpies Foundation is dedicated to the study and appreciation of contemporary art. Antoni Tàpies himself has long been a polemic artist: when the director of the new MACBA entrusted him with the creation of a sculpture to decorate the museum's main hall, Tàpies – always a champion of society's ugly and discarded objects – proposed a 18m (60ft) dirty sock. It was not accepted.

Since 1990 his foundation has been housed in a masterpiece of early Modernista industrial design by Domènech i Montaner; the brick building's original function as a publishing house is evidenced by the decorative cogs and busts of Shakespeare and Cervantes. Floating above the façade is Tàpies' iconic *Núvol i Cadira* ('cloud and chair'). Created from a 305m (9,000ft) scribble of aluminium tubing, the sculpture reflects Tapies' lifelong interest in eastern mysticism but also serves to redress the height difference between this and the adjacent buildings. The permanent Tàpies collection is on the top floor along with a world-class contemporary art library. The ground floor and basement host lectures, films and temporary exhibitions which in 2004 include *Tour-ismes* – which explores the social influence of tourism.

Fundació Francisco Godia

C/Valencia 284 pral (93 272 31 80/www.fundacionfgodia.org). Metro Passeig de Gràcia. **Open** 10am-8pm Mon, Wed-Sun. **Admission** €4; €2.10 concessions; free under-5s. *Combined ticket with Museu Egipci* €8.50; €6.50 concessions. **Discounts** BC. **Credit** (shop only) MC, V. **Map** p338 D4.

This avid collector first came to fame as a successful Formula I driver for Maserati in the 1950s. Godia's private museum houses an interesting selection of medieval religious art, historic Spanish ceramics and modern painting. Highlights include Alejo de Vahía's medieval *Pietà* and a baroque masterpiece by Lucio Giordano, along with outstanding Romanesque sculptures, and 19th-century oil paintings by Joaquín Sorolla and Ramón Casas. The modern collection has works by Miró, Julio González, Tàpies and Manolo Hugué. Temporary exhibitions in 2004 include French art nouveau glassware from Gallé and Lalique.

Hospital de la Santa Creu i Sant Pau

C/Sant Antoni Maria Claret 167 (93 291 90 00/www.hspau.com). Metro Hospital de Sant Pau. **Map** p339 F4.

Domènech i Montaner's masterpiece – as well as Modernisme's greatest civil work – lies at the opposite end of the Avda Gaudí from the Sagrada Família. The hospital occupies the space of nine Eixample blocks inside the walls of a peaceful garden city; set at 45° from the rest of Cerdà's grid (which Domènech abhorred). Patients were spread over 18 pavilions, each boasting its own exuberant collection of sculpture, murals and mosaics and connected by underground galleries. Begun in 1901 as a long-overdue replacement for the original hospital in the Raval (*see p95*), this building was not finished until 1930, when it was completed by the architect's son.

Sadly, the complex is no longer considered suitable for modern medicine, so the pavilions are used for research and teaching while hospital facilities are gradually being transferred to the modern blocks at the far end of the grounds. The public has free access to the gardens, vestibules and waiting areas inside the pavilions; 20-minute guided tours in English can be arranged in advance (93 488 20 78).

Museu de Carrosses Fúnebres

C/Sancho de Avila 2 (93 484 17 20). Metro Marina. **Open** 10am-1pm, 4-6pm Mon-Fri; 10am-1pm Sat, Sun (weekends call to confirm). **Admission** free. **Map** p343 F5.

A deliciously creepy collection of funeral carriages hidden in a basement next to the municipal Sancho de Avila funerary services. Ask at the desk to see some 20 horse-drawn landaus and berlins dating from the late 18th century up to the city's first motorised hearses, including the Studebaker used for Generalitat President Francesc Macià in 1933. The pomp and circumstance of past funerals is recreated in interesting fashion, with teams of plumed plastic horses and top-hatted mannequins.

Walk on Modernisme

Duration: 1 hour 30 minutes

The tour begins with the splendid **Casa Comalat** by Valeri i Pupurull, which has the unusual distinction of two façades. The front (Avda Diagonal 442) has 12 voluptuously curvy stone balconies complete with whiplash wrought-iron railings, while the more radical back façade (C/Còrsega 316) is a colourful harlequin effect with curiously bulging green-shuttered balconies. Almost opposite on Avda Diagonal is Puig i Cadafalch's sombre **Palau Baró de Quadras** at No.373 and his **Casa Terrades** at Nos.416-20, known colloquially as *la Casa de les Punxes* ('House of Spikes') for its spiky turrets and gables. Look out for the individual entrances and staircases built for each of the family's three daughters.

Turn down C/Girona and then right onto C/Mallorca to see Barenys i Gambús' wedding cake fantasy **Casa Dolors Xiró** at No.302, followed by two Domènech i Montaner masterpieces: the **Casa Josep Thomas** at No.291, which is now home to the BD Design emporium (*see p192*), and the **Palau Ramón de Montaner** at No.278, which now houses government offices.

Double back a few steps and turn downhill on to C/Roger de Llúria. On the corner at No.80 is Fossas i Martinez's spike-topped **Casa Villanueva** and, just opposite at No.82, striking columns of stained-glass windows

There are also carriages, varying from ornate white hearses for children and virgins to a windowless black-velour mourning carriage that carried the unfortunate 'second wife' (mistress).

Museu del Perfum

Passeig de Gràcia 39 (93 216 01 21/www.museodelperfume.com). Metro Passeig de Gràcia. **Open** 10.30am-1.30pm, 4.30-8pm Mon-Fri; 11am-2pm Sat. **Admission** free. **Map** p338 D4.

In the back room of the Regia perfumery (*see p206*) Ramón Planas started gathering what is now nearly 5,000 scent bottles, cosmetic flasks and related vanity objects after he moved his shop here in 1961. The collection is divided into two parts; one shows all manner of unguent vases and essence jars in chronological order, from a tube of black eye make-up from pre-dynastic Egypt to Edwardian atomisers and a prized double flask pouch that belonged to Marie Antoinette; the second part exhibits perfumery brands including Guerlain and Dior, some with limited-edition bottles, such as a charming Dalí creation for Schiaparelli and a set of rather disturbing golliwog flasks for Vigny.

Museu Egipci de Barcelona

C/Valencia 284 (93 488 01 88/www.fundclos.com). Metro Passeig de Gràcia. **Open** 10am-8pm Mon-Sat; 10am-2pm Sun. **Admission** *Museum* €5.50; €4.50 concessions; free under-5s. *Combined ticket with Fundació Godia* €8.50; €6.50 concessions. **Discounts** BC. **Credit** AmEx, MC, V. **Map** p338 D4.

In addition to the art collection displayed in his Hotel Claris (*see p63*) Jordi Clos also owns this museum that reflects his lifelong fascination with ancient Egypt. Run by his prestigious archaeological foundation, there are two floors showcasing a well-chosen collection spanning 3,000 years of Nile-drenched culture. Exhibits include religious statuary such as the massive baboon heads used to decorate temples, everyday copper mirrors or alabaster headrests, and strangely moving infant sarcophagi. Outstanding pieces include some painstakingly matched fragments from the Sixth Dynasty Tomb of Iny, a bronze statuette of the goddess Osiris breastfeeding her son Horus, and mummified cats, baby crocodiles and falcons. The rooftop holds a wonderful café and terrace while the base-

decorate Granell i Manresa's **Casa Jaume Forn**. Just a few steps further down C/Roger de Llúria, the **Queviures Murrià** grocery at No.85 retains original decoration by painter Ramón Casas and, on the right at No.74, is the exceptionally lovely stained glass and floral decoration of the **Farmàcia Argelaguet**.

Retrace your steps up to the corner again and turn right onto C/València. Continue along for three blocks, and at No.339 is a stunning corner building by Gallissà i Soqué: the **Casa Manuel Llopis i Bofill**. The façade is a blend of red brick and white sgraffito by Gaudí's collaborator, Josep Maria Jujol, while the neo-Mudéjar turrets, ceramics and keyhole shapes take their inspiration from the Alhambra.

Backtrack a block and turn left on C/Girona. At No.86 is the **Casa Isabel Pomar**, Rubió i Bellver's eccentric sliver of a building that squeezes in a neo-Gothic pinnacle, lively red brickwork and a staggered gallery window on the first floor. This contrasts with the spacious feel of Viñolas I Llosas' **Casa Jacinta Ruiz** at No.54. Glass galleries are a characteristic feature of Modernista houses, but here the jutting windows form the pivot for the design and give a three-dimensional effect.

Further down, turn right on Gran Via, to another extravagant Modernista pharmacy, **Farmàcia Vilardell**, and Salvat i Espasa's elegant **Casa Ramon Oller** at No.658.

From there, turn left down C/Pau Claris and left again onto C/Casp. At No.22, **Casa Llorenç Camprubí**, Ruiz i Casamitjana's intricate stonework is a delight but the real treasure lies a little further along at No.48. Gaudí's **Casa Calvet** may look somewhat conventional for the master but closer study reveals characteristic touches: the columns framing the door and gallery allude to the bobbins used in the owner's textile factory while the intricate wrought iron depicts a mass of funghi surrounded by stone flowers. The corbel underneath the gallery interweaves the coat of arms of Catalonia with Calvet's initial 'C'. Should you peek inside at the excellent restaurant (*see p155*), lift the massive crucifix doorknockers to see the squashed bugs (a symbol of evil) beneath.

Turn right down C/Girona on to C/Ausiàs Marc, one of the most notable streets of the Quadrat d'Or. At Nos.37-9 are the **Cases Tomàs Roger** by prominent Modernista architect, Enric Sagnier, combining graceful arches with beautifully restored sgraffito. At No.31 is the **Farmàcia Nordbeck**, with a dark wood and stained-glass exterior. The last stop before reaching Plaça Urquinaona is the **Casa Manuel Felip** at No.20, designed by a little-known architect, Fernández i Janot, with sumptuous stonework and slender galleries connecting the first two floors.

Sightseeing

ment houses temporary exhibitions and a library (by appointment only). On Friday and Saturday nights there are dramatic reconstructions of popular themes such as the mummification ritual or the life of Cleopatra, for which reservations are essential.

Parc de l'Estació del Nord

C/Nàpols (no phone). Metro Arc de Triomf.
Open 10am-sunset daily. **Admission** free.
Map p343 E/F5/6.

A welcome oasis of calm, this park is enlivened by Beverly Pepper's Olympiad pieces of land art in glazed blue ceramic. *Espiral Arbrat* (*Tree Spiral*) is a spiral bench set under the cool shade of lime flower trees and *Cel Caigut* (*Fallen Sky*) is a 7m (23ft) high ridge rising from the grass, while the tiles recall Gaudí's *trencadís* technique.

La Pedrera (Casa Milà)

Passeig de Gràcia 92-C/Provença 261-5 (93 484 59 00/www.caixacatalunya.es). Metro Diagonal. **Open** 10am-8pm daily. **Admission** €7; €3.50 concessions; free under-12s. **Guided tours** (in English) 4pm Mon-Fri. **Credit** MC, V. **Map** p338 D4.

When they commissioned Gaudí to outdo every other apartment building on the Passeig de Gràcia, the newly wedded Pere Milà and Roser Segimon got somewhat more than they bargained for. The huge, rippling mass of rough-chipped stone resembles a coastal cliff or petrified wave and the marine feel is complemented by Jujol's tangled balconies, doors of twisted kelp ribbon, sea-foamy ceilings and interior patios as blue as a mermaid's cave. By the time of its completion in 1910, the public had gleefully nicknamed this craggy behemoth 'La Pedrera' ('the Stone Quarry') and it was the subject of mockery. The lack of straight lines and right angles prompted the painter Rusiñol to quip that a snake would be a more suitable house pet here than a dog, and much vexed Sra Segimon, who was reduced to hanging her priceless art collection on the backs of the doors.

These days the building is run by Fundació Caixa de Catalunya as a cultural centre and features three complementary exhibition spaces. The first-floor art gallery hosts temporary shows that frequently include some of the most important names in the history of art; 2004 exhibitions include Portuguese

For a fistful of lollies

The Casa Batlló project began in 1904 when textile baron Josep Batlló commissioned Gaudí to completely overhaul an existing apartment block. The result was one of the most unusual, expressive façades in the city and has inspired a host of symbolic interpretations. For some it is a representation of the translucent waters of a Costa Brava cove, for others it embodies the carnival spirit: the crested roof is a harlequin's cap, the balconies masks, and the polychrome tiles falling confetti. This interpretation gained further currency after the Civil War, when the ivory-coloured balconies were painted black until their restoration in 1984.

A more likely theme for a party-shy Catholic such as Gaudí is the patriotic allegory of Saint George killing the dragon: the humped, knobbly rooftop is the monster's spine, which is pierced by the tower topped with a three-dimensional cross that represents a lance. The rest of the façade is covered in dragon's scales with the balconies evoking the skulls of his victims and the lower window frames their femurs, tibias and fibulas.

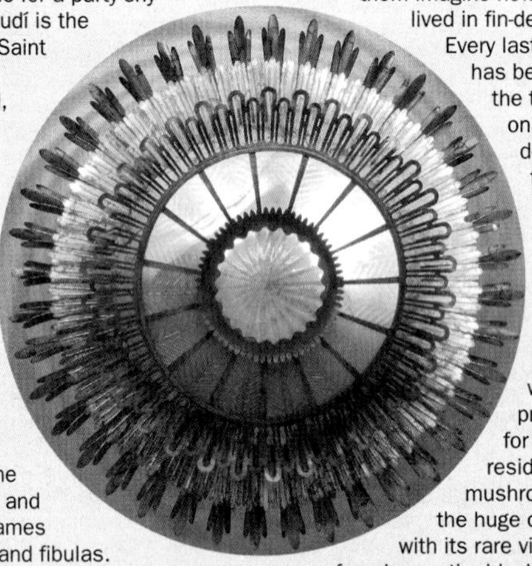

The owners of Gaudí's Casa Batlló are the local Bernat family – who just happen to be the inventors of the famous Chupa Chup lollipop. According to *El Mundo* newspaper, they shelled out nearly €22 million for the famous property in 1994 but the estimated worth has now shot up to around €75 million. Chupa Chups (which translates as something like 'suck-sucks') are the world's best-selling sweet on a stick, sucked by everyone from supermodels to the Russian Mir crew while in space. The flower power logo was designed by Salvador Dalí in 1969.

Unfortunately, the lolly industry has recently fallen on hard times and so the company has turned to its other piece of Gaudíana in its time of need, and Casa Batlló has been roped in to help. Coinciding with the 2002 Year of Gaudí – celebrating 150 years since the birth of the Barcelona tourist board's favourite son – they opened part of the building to the public for the first time.

Following massive popularity and over €2.5 million in entrance fees, it remained open throughout 2003. In 2004 yet another anniversary will come around: the centenary celebrations for Gaudí's work on the Casa Batlló itself. Ker-ching! What better excuse to crank up the cash registers?

The stiff €10 entrance fee includes an audio guide that leads visitors through some extraordinary, organic interiors that can help them imagine how the other half lived in fin-de-siècle Barcelona. Every last stick of furniture has been removed, so the tour concentrates on structural and decorational features, from the whipped-cream ceilings to the ergonomic doorhandles. Highlights include the dragon spine staircase, which was once the private entrance for the Batlló family residence, the squat mushroom fireplace and the huge ceramic patio with its rare view of all the rear façades on the block; in 2004 even more should be available after the attic and roof also are opened to the public.

Ever versatile, the Casa Batlló also hosts weddings, parties and bar mitzvahs, and the hiring of its conference rooms brings in a tidy profit for the company. Even so, in July 2003 Chupa Chups was forced to offer the house as a guarantee for an enormous loan, part of which they will invest in a last-ditch advertising blitz for their sweeties. Which might end up costing them an awful lot more lolly than they bargained for.

Casa Batlló

Passeig de Gràcia 43 (93 216 03 06/ www.casabatllo.es). Metro Passeig de Gràcia. **Admission** €10; €8 concessions; free under-7s. **Map** p338 D4.

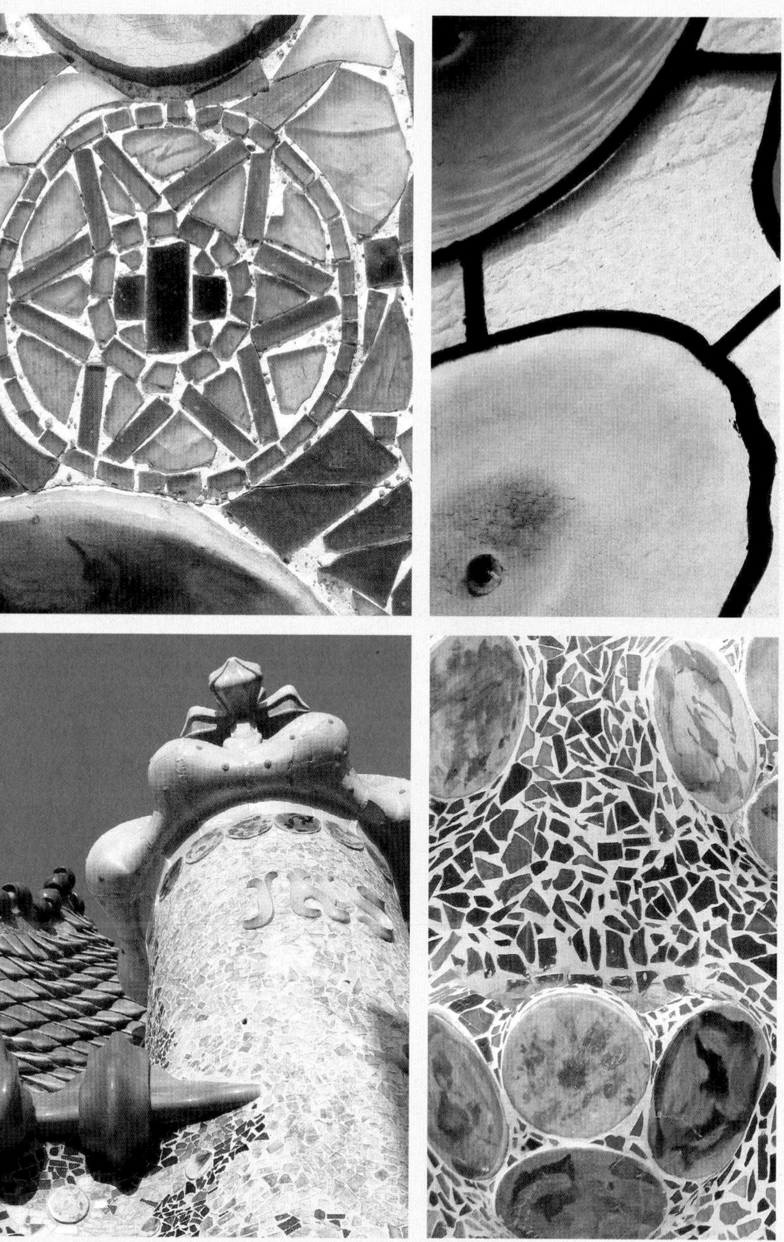

painters from the 1920s to the '70s, and Pre-Columbian Mexican art. The fourth-floor Pis de la Pedrera is a reconstructed Modernista apartment, worth a look for its sumptuous bedroom suite by Gaspar Homar and a minutely recreated nursery. In the attic space, originally intended for drying washing, the beautifully restored Espai Gaudí offers Barcelona's best overview of the architect's oeuvre with drawings, photos, models and audio-visual displays spread under the brick arches. Upstairs is the unmissable roof terrace with Escheresque stairways, centurion-helmeted ventilation shafts and 360° views of the city. This was Gaudí's last secular project but he wanted to top the building with a 12m (40ft) statue of the Virgin Mary, a plan hastily vetoed after the church burnings of the 1909 Tragic Week.

Sagrada Família

C/Mallorca 401 (93 207 30 31/www.sagradafamilia.org). Metro Sagrada Família. **Open** *Apr-Sept* 9am-8pm daily. *Oct-Mar* 9am-6pm daily. **Admission** €8; €5 concessions; free under-10s. Lift to spires €2. **Credit** (shop only) MC, V. **Map** p337 F4.

'The patron of this project is not in a hurry,' said Gaudí, and it is just as well: more than 120 years after the first stone was laid, the Temple Expiatori de la Sagrada Família is still nowhere near finished.

Barcelona's trophy building was begun under the direction of Francisco de Paula del Villar in 1882, but Gaudí took over just a year later and worked on it until his death in 1926, but only the crypt, the apse and the four towers of the Nativity façade (along C/Marina) were completed in his lifetime. Anarchists destroyed the few technical drawings he left behind, so its current continuation is a source of constant polemic. Many find the contemporary construction coldly clinical in comparison to the early period, while others condemn Josep Maria Subirachs' rigid sculptures on the Passion façade (on C/Sardenya) as contrary to Gaudí's spirit. Gaudí, however, saw the church as a collective effort, refusing to treat the endeavour as a question of individual authorship.

Laid out like the great Gothic cathedrals with a multi-aisled central nave and a transept defining a cross, the church is charged with symbolism. The 12 towers, representing the apostles, are topped with episcopal symbols such as bishops' rings and mitres and will eventually surround a monumental central spire of 170m (558ft) dedicated to Christ. Four more towers for each evangelist will flank it, and one topped with a star in honour of the Virgin Mary. Eventually, the blocks of flats facing the Glory façade on C/Mallorca will be demolished to make way for a wide entrance esplanade, with traffic sent along a tunnel below.

New additions to the exterior include baskets of coloured glass fruit by Etsuro Sotoo. The interior is a forest of columns, each made with stone from a different quarry. These hold up the vaults of the main nave, for the first time giving the Sagrada Família a substantial roof; the idea is to celebrate a mass inside on Saint Joseph's day (19 March) in 2007, the 125th anniversary of the beginning of construction. Officials from the church's foundation now venture that it all could be completed by 2015. The ticket price includes access to the Passion and the Nativity façades, the Nativity towers (walking only – the lift costs €2 extra), the cloister, exhibitions in the school building and the basement museum. Gaudí himself is buried beneath the nave of the basilica.

The Esquerra

The left side of the Eixample has more industrial origins than the right, and is also more liberally sprinkled with general city services along with some of the more unsavoury features of modern life that the middle classes just did not want to see on their doorsteps. For instance, a huge slaughterhouse was built in the extreme left of the area, but after years of local lobbying against the stench and noise, it was knocked down and replaced by the **Parc Joan Miró**. The **Hospital Clínic** takes up two blocks between C/Còrsega and C/Provença, and further out on C/Entença is the grim 1904 men's prison, **La Model**; it is scheduled for relocation outside the city in 2005 and the site will be used for subsidised housing and offices. Major academic institutions include the vast **Escola Industrial** on C/Comte d'Urgell – once the Can Batlló textile factory – and the original **Universitat** central building on Plaça Universitat, constructed in 1842.

There are two great markets, the **Ninot**, by the hospital, and the **Mercat de Sant Antoni**, on the edge of the Raval, which is taken over by a second-hand book market every Sunday morning. Modernista architecture does extend over into the Esquerra (as the Quadrat d'Or concept recognises), with a number of superb examples, such as the **Casa Societat Torres Germans** (C/Paris 180-2) from 1905 and the Moorish-influenced **Casa Golferichs** (Gran Via 491) which was built by Joan Rubió, one of Gaudí's chief collaborators, in 1901. Beyond the hospital the outer Eixample has no great sights, but it does lead up to **Plaça Francesc Macià**, which is the centre of the city's busy business district, and the main crossroads of affluent Barcelona.

Parc Joan Miró (Parc de l'Escorxador)

C/Tarragona (no phone). Metro Tarragona or Espanya. **Open** 10am-sunset daily. **Map** p341 B4/5.

The demolition of the old slaughterhouse provided some much-needed urban parkland, although there's precious little greenery here. The rows of stubby *palmera* trees and grim cement lakes are dominated by a library and Miró's towering phallic sculpture *Dona i Ocell* (*Woman and Bird*). Access will be limited throughout 2004 as work continues on a vast underground reservoir built to prevent floods.

Gràcia & Other Districts

Not all the jewels in Barcelona's crown lie in the centre.

The peaceful *barrio* of Gràcia started life as the Nostra Senyora de Gràcia convent in 1630. Soon a number of farmhouses sprang up around it, and later the area became popular with the middle classes, who arrived with the fortunes they made from the textile industry, building themselves large mansions, some of which are still evident today. The working classes moved in during a rapid 19th-century urbanisation (partially thanks to the construction of the Passeig de Gràcia which linked the village to Barcelona). The town's population rose from 2,608 in 1821 to 61,935 in 1897, making it the ninth largest town in Spain.

It was in 1897 that Gràcia was annexed to Barcelona, amid much opposition. There was opposition to just about anything in Gràcia at the time, and the area became a radical centre of Catalanism, republicanism, anarchism and, to a certain extent, feminism. It's still a politically active *barrio*, though the police have recently been waging a campaign to dislodge the radical Okupa squatter movement from the properties they have been inhabiting for years.

Those wanting to buy property in Gràcia have to fork out high prices; nevertheless the area still holds many workshops and artists' studios, and remains a firm favourite as a hangout for the city's bohemians – the many bars in the squares that punctuate its narrow streets are frequented by artists, designers and photographers, taking time off work for a coffee or a *caña*. As it's rich in small scruffy bars and reasonably priced restaurants, it's also a popular haunt for students.

Gràcia really comes into its own for a few days each August, when its famous *festa major* grips the entire city (*see p219*). The streets are festooned with startlingly original homemade decorations and all of Barcelona turns up in party mood. Open-air meals are laid on for the residents of Gràcia, and entertainment is laid on for everybody – from street parties for the old-timers singing along to *habaneros* (shanties) to amusements for the resident squatters who get to pogo to punk bands.

Of Gràcia's many squares **Plaça de la Virreina** is perhaps the most relaxing spot, silvered by the chairs and tables of bar terraces, and overlooked by Sant Joan church. **Plaça del Sol** is busier, home to half a dozen bars and restaurants and the main focus of the drinking crowd. Other favourites include **Plaça Rius i Taulet**, dominated by a 33-metre (108-foot) bell tower; the leafy **Plaça Rovira** (with a bronze statue of the neighbourhood's pensive planner, Antoni Rovira i Trias, sitting on a bench, his rejected plan for the Eixample at his feet); the rather rougher **Plaça del Diamant**, the setting for the Mercè Rodoreda novel *The Time of the Doves*, which has a peculiar sculpture to prove it; and then there's **Plaça John Lennon**, where the Liverpudlian singer is remembered with a huge model of the *Give Peace a Chance* single.

Much of Gràcia was built in the heyday of Modernisme, as is evident in the splendid main drag, the C/Gran de Gràcia. Many of the buildings are rich in nature-inspired curves and fancy façades, but the finest example is Lluis Domènech i Muntaner's **Casa Fuster** at No.2: the architect took four years to fashion its irregular form. Gaudí's disciple Francesc Berenguer was responsible for much of the civic architecture hereabouts – notably the **Mercat de la Llibertat** (Barcelona's oldest covered market) and the old **Casa de la Vila** (Town Hall) in Plaça Rius i Taulet. But the district's overwhelming Modernista gem is one of Gaudí's earliest and most fascinating works, the **Casa Vicens** of 1883-8, hidden away in C/Carolines. It is a private residence and thus not open to visitors, but the castellated red brickwork and colourful tiled exterior with Indian and Mudéjar influences should not be missed; see, too, the spiky wrought-iron leaves on the gates. And one of Gaudí's last works, the stunning **Park Güell**, is a walk away, across the busy Travessera de Dalt and up the hill, but well worth the effort, not only for the architecture, but for the magnificent view of Barcelona and the sea.

Park Güell

C/Olot (Casa-Museu Gaudí 93 219 38 11). Metro Lesseps/bus 24, 25. **Open** *Park* 10am-sunset daily. *Museum* Apr-Sept 10am-7.45pm daily. *Oct-Mar* 10am-5.45pm daily. **Admission** *Museum* €4; €3 concessions; free under-9s. **Credit** (shop only) MC, V. **Map** p339 E2.

A fantastical place, the most playful fruit of Gaudí's fertile imagination, and a must-see for any visit to the city. The two fairytale gatehouses were based on designs the architect made earlier for the opera *Hansel and Gretel*, one with a red and white mush-

Sightseeing

room for a roof. From here walk up a magnificent staircase flanked by multicoloured battlements, past the iconic mosaic dragon, to where a hundred palm-shaped pillars hold up a roof. On top of this is the esplanade, a circular concourse surrounded by undulating benches decorated with shattered tiles – a technique called *trencadís*, perfected by Gaudí's overshadowed but talented assistant Josep Maria Jujol. Like all Gaudí works, these seats are by no means a case of design over function, and are as comfortable as park benches come. The park is utterly magical, with twisted pathways and avenues of columns intertwined with the natural structure of the hillside. Gaudí lived for several years in one of the two houses built on the site (not designed by himself); it is now the Casa-Museu Gaudí. The park stretches well beyond the area designed by Gaudí, into the wooded hillside.

Based on the design of garden cities in England with which Gaudí's patron Eusebi Güell was fascinated (hence the spelling of 'park'), the Park Güell was intended to be an upmarket residential area overlooking the city. Gaudí was to design the basic structure and main public areas; the houses were to be designed by other architects. It was early days for Gaudí, however, and his ideas were still considered too radical for the city's bourgeoisie, few plots were sold, and the development was never finished. Guided tours are available, some in English. The best way to get to the park is on bus 24; if you go via Lesseps metro, be prepared for a steep uphill walk.

Sants

For many arriving by bus or train, Estació de Sants is their first sight of Barcelona – most take one look at the forbidding **Plaça dels Països Catalans** (which looks like it was designed with skateboard tricks in mind), and get the hell out of the area. It is perhaps not the most picturesque part of town – and be warned, the station is particularly popular among the city's bagsnatchers – but for those with time to spare, it's worth a few hours' investigation for historic if not aesthetic reasons.

Sants was originally built to service those who arrived after the town gates had shut at 9pm, with inns and blacksmiths to cater for latecomers. In the 19th century, it became the industrial motor of the city. Giant textile factories such as the **Vapor Vell** (which is now a library), **L'Espanya Industrial** (now a futuristic park) and **Can Batlló** (which is still a workplace) created the bourgeois wealth that the likes of Eusebi Güell spent on the Modernista dream homes that still grace more salubrious areas of the city. The inequality did not go unnoticed. The *barrio* has been a hotbed of industrial action – the first general strike in Catalonia broke out here in 1856, only to be violently put down by the infamous General Zapatero (known as the 'Tiger of Catalonia'). The left-wing nationalist ERC party (which now shares power in the Generalitat) was founded here, at C/Cros 9, in 1931.

Nearby **Plaça de Sants**, with Jorge Castillo's *Ciclista* statue, is the hub of the district, right in the middle of the C/Sants high street. Also worth checking out are the showy Modernista buildings at Nos.12, 130, 145 and 151 by local architect Modest Feu. The more humble workers' flats nearby in the narrow streets off C/Premià are more typical of this very working-class area. From there, C/Creu Coberta, an old Roman road once known as the Cami d'Espanya, 'the road to Spain', runs to Plaça d'Espanya.

Parc de l'Espanya Industrial

Passeig de Antoni (no phone). Metro Sants-Estació. **Open** 10am-sunset daily. **Map** p341 A4.

In the 1970s the owners of the old textile factory announced their intention to use the land to build blocks of flats; the neighbourhood put its collective foot down and insisted on a park, which was eventually built in 1985. The result is a puzzling space, designed by Basque Luis Peña Ganchegui, with ten watchtowers looking over a boating lake with a statue of Neptune in the middle, flanked by a stretch of mud mainly used for walking dogs. By the entrance kids can climb over Andrés Nagel's *Drac* – a massive and sinister black dragon.

Les Corts

Row after row of apartment blocks now obscure any trace of the rustic origins of Les Corts (literally 'cowsheds' or 'pigsties'), as the village itself was swallowed up by Barcelona in the late 19th century. But search and you will find **Plaça de la Concòrdia**, a quiet square that is dominated by a 40-metre (131-foot) bell tower. This is an anachronistic oasis housing the civic centre Can Deu, formerly a farmhouse and now home to a great bar that hosts jazz bands every other Thursday. The area is much better known, though, for what happens every other weekend, when tens of thousands pour in to watch FC Barcelona, whose **Nou Camp stadium** (*see below*) takes up much of the west of the *barrio*. At night the area is the haunt of transvestite prostitutes and their kerb-crawling clients.

Nou Camp – FC Barcelona

Nou Camp, Avda Arístides Maillol, access 9, Les Corts (93 496 36 00/08/www.fcbarcelona.com). Metro Maria Cristina or Collblanc. **Open** 10am-6.30pm Mon-Sat; 10am-2pm Sun. **Admission** €5.30; €3.70 concessions; free under-5s. *Guided tour* €9.50; €6.60 concessions. **Credit** (shop only) MC, V. **Map** p337 A3.

The Nou Camp, where FC Barcelona have played since 1957, is one of football's great stadiums, a vast cauldron of a ground that holds 98,000 spectators on

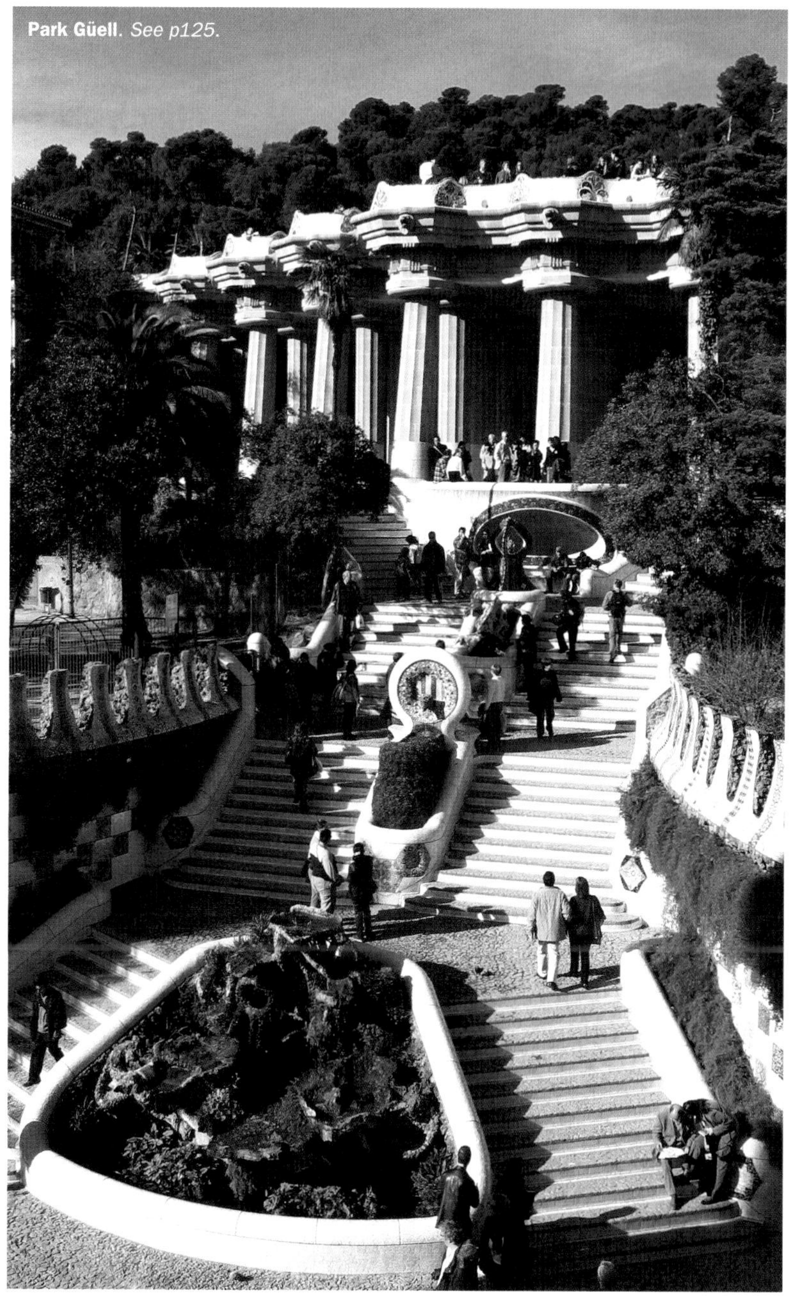
Park Güell. *See p125.*

The best Parks and gardens

Hemmed in between the mountains and the sea, the people of Barcelona live cheek by jowl, in a concentration far greater than in most European cities. Claustrophobes find relief on the beach or within the cooling, forested hills of Gràcia's Parc de Collserola (*see p129*), a short metro ride from the centre, while within the city itself there are many delightful parks and gardens. Here are some of the best.

Parc de la Ciutadella

In the Old City, on the far side of the Born market, this verdant paradise is named for Philip V's detested citadel, torn down to make way for it. It was laid out for the 1888 Exhibition, and houses the zoo and a boating lake. On Sundays it is taken over by the relentless beat of 100 djembés and tom toms as every man and his upturned box turn up to make some racket. *See p102.*

the odd occasion that it's full. That's a lot of noise when they're doing well, and an awful lot of silence when they aren't. If you can't get there on matchday (and you can usually pick up tickets if you try), but you love the team, it's worth a visit to the club museum. A guided tour of the stadium takes you though the players' tunnel to the dug-outs, and then, via the away team's changing room, on to the President's box, where there is a replica of the European Cup, which the team won at Wembley in 1992. The museum commemorates those glory years, making much of the days when the likes of Kubala, Cruyff, Maradona, Koeman and Lineker trod the hallowed turf, with pictures, video clips and souvenirs spanning the century that has passed since the Swiss business executive Johan Gamper first founded the club. *See also p269.*

Tibidabo & Collserola

During his temptation of Christ, the devil took him to the top of a mountain and offered him all before him, with the words '*tibi dabo*' (Latin for 'To thee I will give'). This gave rise to the name of the dominant peak of the Collserola massif, with its sweeping views of the whole of the Barcelona conurbation stretching out to the sea: quite a tempting offer, given the present day price of the city's real estate. The ugly neo-Gothic **Sagrat Cor** temple crowning the peak has become one of the city's most recognisable landmarks, and it is clearly visible for miles around. At the weekends thousands head up to the top of the hill in order to whoop and scream at the **funfair** – nowadays the only

Parc del Laberint

Try your luck in the maze, which is overlooked by neo-classical pagodas, or you can picnic in dappled woodland glades. It was originally designed as a private wonderland in 1791 and stayed in the same family until 1970, when it was restored and opened to the public. It's a little out of the way, but very atmospheric and you're likely to have the place to yourself. *See p136.*

Jardíns de Cervantes

Built on a gentle hill and providing much needed space between two busy roads, the Cervantes is notable for two things: its shimmering, suspended rhomboid sculpture *Dos Rombs* (by Andreu Alfaro) and its annual rose competition. Visit in early summer when the swathes of sweet-smelling flowers reach their blooming best. *See p130.*

Parc de la Creueta del Coll

An imaginative use for an old quarry, designed in 1987 by Josep Martorell, Oriol Bohigas and David Mackay, with shading palm trees and a bathing lake to take away the summer heat. A menhir by Ellsworth Kelly stands guard by the entrance while Chillida's sculpture, *In Praise Of Water*, is suspended over the top part of the lake. *See p132.*

Parc de Diagonal-Mar

The city's newest park, a step away from the site of the Fòrum 2004 and the nearby shopping centre, could do with a few years of growth. Enric Miralles' twisted trelliswork still lacks its hanging gardens but the two-tier lakes and the urns clad in post-Modernista *trencadís* (a tiling technique) are impressive. For the kids, there's a large, rustic playground built on sand, and a 'magic mountain' down which they can slide. *See p134.*

Park Güell

Gaudí's gingerbread-like gatehouses, emblematic dragon and undulating benches are the main draw. Further up the hill, past the master's troglodytic colonnades, there's peaceful shaded woodland with unspoilt views over the city towards the sea. *See p125.*

Jardí Botànic

This park doesn't intend to be a global catch-all like, say, Kew Gardens, but rather a more easily sustainable collection of plants from the five regions of the world with a Mediterranean climate. Still relatively young (it opened in 1999), the garden is maturing quickly and incorporates the Botanic Institute and educational facilities. *See p113.*

Parc de la Pegaso

The Pegaso lorry factory was renowned for the strength of its unions and it was therefore fitting that when it closed, the site became a public space. The old factory entrance remains, but it now leads into a beautiful, bucolic area with a boating lake, a children's playground and an exercise zone. On the small hill in the middle, there's a warren of overgrown pathways and secluded little nooks for wandering away an afternoon, forgetting you're in the middle of a big, bustling city. *See p134.*

Sightseeing

one in Barcelona – which has been running since 1921, and changed little since, with creaky, old-fashioned, but very quaint rides.

Getting up to the top on the clanking old **Tramvia Blau** (Blue Tram, *see p132*) and then the **funicular railway** (*see p130*) is part of the fun: Plaça Doctor Andreu between the two is a great place for an al fresco drink. For the best view of the city, either take a lift up the needle of Norman Foster's communications tower, the **Torre de Collserola** (*see p130*), or up to the *mirador* at the feet of Christ atop the Sagrat Cor.

The vast **Parc de Collserola** is more a series of forested hills than a park; its shady paths through holm oaks and pines open out to spectacular views. It is most easily reached by FGC train on the Terrassa-Sabadell line from Plaça Catalunya or Passeig de Gràcia, getting off at **Baixador de Vallvidrera** station. A ten-minute walk from the station up into the woods (there is an information board just outside the station) will take you to the **Vil.la Joana**, an old *masia* covered in bougainvillea and containing the **Museu Verdaguer** (93 204 78 05, open by appointment Tue-Fri, 10am-2pm Sat, Sun, admission free) dedicated to 19th-century Catalan poet Jacint Verdaguer, who used this as his summer home. Just beyond the Vil.la Joana is the park's **information centre** (93 280 35 52, open 9.30am-3pm daily) with basic free maps of the area, and more detailed maps for sale. Almost all the information is in Catalan but staff are very helpful. There is also a snack bar and an exhibition area.

Funicular de Tibidabo

Plaça Doctor Andreu to Plaça Tibidabo (93 211 79 42). FGC Avda Tibidabo, then Tramvia Blau. **Open** As funfair (*see p223*), but starting 30mins earlier. **Tickets** *Single* €2; €1.50 concessions. *Return* €3; €2 concessions. **No credit cards**.

This art deco vehicle offers occasional glimpses of the city below as it winds through the pine forests up to the summit. The service has been running since 1901, but only according to a complicated timetable. If it's not running, take the FGC line from Plaça Catalunya to Peu del Funicular, take the funicular up to Vallvidrera Superior, and take the 111 bus to Tibidabo (a process not half as complicated as it sounds). Alternatively, it's nearly an hour's (mostly pleasant) hike up from Plaça Doctor Andreu for those who are feeling energetic.

Museu d'Autòmates del Tibidabo

Parc d'Atraccions del Tibidabo (93 211 79 42). FGC Avda Tibidabo, then Tramvia Blau and Funicular de Tibidabo. **Open** As funfair (*see p223*). **Admission** €11 (includes 6 funfair rides). **Credit** MC, V.

This collection of fairground coin-operated machines from the early 20th century is inside the Tibidabo funfair (*see p223*), and contains some of the finest examples of automata in the world. Entertaining machines include a depiction of hell where, to the sound of roaring flames, repentant maidens slide slowly into the pit, prodded by naked devils. Then there's the saucy La Monyos, named after a famed eccentric who cruised the Rambla nearly a century ago: she claps her hands, shakes her shoulders and winks, pigtails flying. Unfortunately, you have to buy a ticket for the funfair to enter, and it doesn't come cheap.

Torre de Collserola. *See p129.*

Torre de Collserola

Ctra de Vallvidrera al Tibidabo (93 406 93 54/ www.torredecollserola.es). FCG Peu Funicular, then funicular. **Open** *Apr-May* 11am-2.30pm, 3.30-7pm Wed-Fri; 11am-7pm Sat, Sun. *Jun-Aug* 11am-2.30pm, 3.30-8pm Wed-Fri; 11am-8pm Sat, Sun. *Sept* 11am-2.30pm, 3.30-7pm Wed-Fri; 11am-8pm Sat, Sun. *Oct* 11am-2.30pm, 3.30-6pm Wed-Fri; 11am-7pm Sat, Sun. *Nov-Mar* 11am-2.30pm, 3.30-6pm Wed-Fri; 11am-6pm Sat, Sun. **Admission** €4.60; €3.90-€3.30 concessions; free under-7s. **Credit** AmEx, MC, V.

Five minutes' walk from the Sagrat Cor is its main rival as Barcelona's most visible landmark, Sir Norman Foster's communication tower, built in 1992 to transmit images of the Olympics around the world. Visible from just about everywhere in the city, and flashing at night, the tower is loved and hated in equal measure. Those who don't suffer from vertigo attest to the stunning view of Barcelona and the Mediterranean from the top.

Zona Alta

Zona Alta (the 'upper zone', or simply 'uptown') is the name given collectively to a series of smart neighbourhoods, including **Sant Gervasi**, **Sarrià**, **Pedralbes** and **Putxet**, that stretch out across the lower reaches of the Collserola hills. The handful of tourist sights around here includes the **Palau Reial**, with its lovely gardens and its brace of museums, the **Museu de Ceràmica** and **Museu de les Arts Decoratives**; the **Museu de la Ciència** and the remarkable **Pedralbes Monastery**, home, for now at least, to a selection of religious paintings from the **Thyssen-Bornemisza collection**, but well worth a visit in itself. The centre of Sarrià and the streets of old Pedralbes around the monastery still retain an appreciable flavour of the sleepy country towns these once were.

For many downtown residents, the Zona Alta is a place to relax in the parks and gardens that wind into the hills. At the end of Avda Diagonal, next to the functional Zona Universitària (university district), is the **Jardins de Cervantes**, with its 11,000 rose bushes, the striking *Dos Rombs* sculpture by Andreu Alfaro and picnicking students during the week. From the park, a turn back along the Diagonal toward Plaça Maria Cristina and Plaça Francesc Macià will take you to Barcelona's main business and shopping district. Here is the small **Turó Parc**, a semi-formal garden good for writing postcards amid inspirational plaques of poetry. The **Jardins de la Tamarita**, at the foot of Avda Tibidabo, is a pleasant dog-free oasis with a playground, while further up at the top of the tram line is the little-known **Parc de la Font de Racó**, full of shady pine and eucalyptus trees. A fair

Reflecting upon its own beauty, the **Palau Reial**. *See p130.*

walk to the north-east, an old quarry has been converted into a swimming pool, the **Parc de la Creueta del Coll**.

Gaudí fans are rewarded by a trip up to the **Pavellons de la Finca Güell** at Avda Pedralbes 15, with its extraordinary and rather frightening wrought-iron gate, featuring a dragon into whose gaping mouth the foolhardy can fit their heads. Once inside the gardens via the main gate on Avda Diagonal, there is a delightful fountain by the master. Across near Putxet is his relatively sober **Col.legi de les Teresianes** (C/Ganduxer 85-105), while up towards Tibidabo, just off Plaça Bonanova, rises his remarkable Gothic-influenced **Torre Figueres** or **Bellesguard**.

Monestir de Pedralbes Col.lecció Thyssen-Bornemisza

Baixada del Monestir 9 (93 280 14 34/www.museothyssen.org). FGC Reina Elisenda. **Open** 10am-2pm Tue-Sun. **Admission** *Monastery* €4; €2.50 concessions. *Col.lecció Thyssen* €3.50; €2.30 concessions. *Combined ticket* €5.50; €3.50 concessions; free under-12s; free 1st Sun of mth. **Credit** (shop only) AmEx, DC, MC, V. **Map** p337 A1.

In 1326 the widowed Queen Elisenda of Montcada used her inheritance to buy this land and build a convent for the 'Poor Clare' order of nuns, which she soon joined. The result is a jewel of Gothic architecture, with an understated single-nave church with fine (recently renovated) stained-glass windows and a beautiful three-storey cloister. The place was out of bounds to the general public until 1983 when the nuns, a cloistered order, opened it up as a museum in the mornings (they escape to a nearby annexe). It is a fascinating insight into life in a medieval convent, taking you through its well-preserved kitchens, pharmacy and refectory with its huge vaulted ceiling. To one side is the tiny chapel of Sant Miquel, with striking murals dating to 1343 by Ferrer Bassa, a Catalan painter and student of Giotto. Currently occupying a former dormitory on one side of the 14th-century cloister, the 90 or so religious paintings from the remarkable Thyssen art collection are sadly soon to leave this harmonious setting; the late Baron Thyssen's wife declared after his recent death that the public visiting hours for the convent were too limited and that the collection is to move to the MNAC on Montjuïc (*see p114*). At the time of writing little more had been decided.

The collection specialises in Italian painting from the 13th to the 17th centuries – an important influence in Catalonia – and European baroque works. There is one true masterpiece: Fra Angelico's *Madonna of Humility* (c1430s). Notable paintings include a small *Nativity* (c1325) by Taddeo Gaddi, a subtle *Madonna and Child* (1545) by Titian, and a Zurbaran crucifixion. Other highlights are the portraits of saints by Lucas Cranach the Elder and Tiepolo's *Way to Golgotha* (c1728), while the Velázquez portrait of *Queen Maria Anna of Austria* (1655-7) is also magnificent.

Museu de Ceràmica & Museu de les Arts Decoratives

Palau Reial de Pedralbes, Avda Diagonal 686 (93 280 16 21/www.museuceramica.bcn.es/www.museuartsdecoratives.bcn.es). Metro Palau Reial. **Open** 10am-6pm Tue-Sat; 10am-3pm Sun. **Guided tours** by appointment. **Admission** *Combined admission with Museu Tèxtil* €3.50; €2 concessions; free under-16s; free 1st Sun of mth. **No credit cards**. **Map** p337 A2.

These two collections, accessible, along with the Textile Museum, on the same ticket, are housed in the august Palau Reial originally designed for the family of Eusebi Güell, Gaudí's patron, and later used as a royal palace. The Museum of Decorative Arts is informative and fun, looking at the different styles

The **Vil.la Joana**. *See p129.*

informing the design of artefacts in Europe since the Middle Ages, from Romanesque to art deco and beyond. A second section is devoted to post-war Catalan design of objects as diverse as urinals and man-sized inflatable pens. The Ceramics Museum is equally fascinating, showing how Moorish ceramic techniques from the 13th century were developed after the Reconquista with the addition of colours (especially blue and yellow) in centres such as Manises (in Valencia) and Barcelona. Two 18th-century murals are of particular sociological interest – one, *La Xocolatada*, shows the bourgeoisie at a garden party, the other, by the same artist, depicts the working classes at a bullfight in the Plaza Mayor in Madrid. Upstairs there is a section showing 20th-century ceramics, including a room dedicated to works by Miró and Picasso. The two museums, along with the Textile Museum and several smaller collections, are to be merged in the future in a Museu de Disseny (Design Museum) as part of the cultural overhaul of the Plaça de les Glòries.

Museu de la Ciència

C/Teodor Roviralta 55 (93 212 60 50/www.fundacio.lacaixa.es). FGC Avda Tibidabo, then Tramvia Blau.

This popular museum, extravagantly advertised on the hill over the road by a black submarine and huge white Hollywood-style lettering, is scheduled to reopen in June/July 2004 after an extensive expansion that will make it the largest science museum in Europe. The original museum space, a boarding school-like Modernista block, has been increased fourfold by the construction of a huge underground chamber, and the museum has promised to sex up its content to move far away from traditional chemistry-physics-biology notions of science, and to encompass all knowledge. That's a pretty big subject. The museum's publicity machine promises interactive methods involving all five senses to explain the world around us, in four categories: inanimate matter, living matter, intelligent life and civilised life – and no dusty objects in glass cases.

Parc de la Creueta del Coll

C/Mare de Déu del Coll (no phone). Metro Penitents. **Open** 10am-sunset daily. **Admission** free.

Created from a quarry in 1987 – by the team that went on to design the Vila Olímpica, Josep Matorell and David Mackay – this park boasts a sizeable swimming pool complete with a 'desert island' and an interesting sculpture by Eduardo Chillida: a 50-ton lump of curly granite suspended on cables, called *In Praise of Water*. In 1998 three people were injured by this flying work of art when the cables snapped: view from a safe distance.

Tramvia Blau

Avda Tibidabo (Plaça Kennedy) to Plaça Doctor Andreu (93 318 70 74/www.tmb.net). FGC Avda Tibidabo. **Open** *Mid June-mid Sept* 10am-8pm daily. *Mid Sept-mid June* 10am-6pm Sat, Sun. **Frequency** 30mins Mon-Fri; 15mins Sat, Sun. **Tickets** single €2; return €2.90. **No credit cards**.

Barcelonins and tourists have been clanking 1,225m (4,000ft) up Avda Tibidabo in the 'blue trams' since 1902. In the winter months, when the tram only operates on weekends, a rather more prosaic bus takes you up (or you can walk it in 15 minutes).

Poblenou & beyond

Poblenou has been many things in its time: a farming community, a fishing port, the site of heavy industry factories and a trendy post-industrial suburb. Now it's also a burgeoning

What's in a name?

So successful has Barcelona's rebirth been, it's sometimes difficult to believe that this hasn't always been a comfortable city for fêted designers, keen-eyed developers and upmarket tourism. Yet behind the sleek façade lies another, more turbulent, past of upheaval and strife. As ideologies have fallen from favour and dictators toppled from power, statues have been ripped down and street names changed to blot out the past, and nowhere more so than in Gràcia, a *barrio* steeped in politics. Place names such as Mercat de la Llibertat, Plaça de la Revolució and C/Fraternitat speak volumes.

Take the Plaça Juan Carlos I at the top of Passeig de Gràcia. It was originally named in 1933 after Francesc Pi i Margall, a popular federalist who was to become President of the First Spanish Republic after the fall of Isabel II, if only for a couple of months. Pi i Margall's anarchist streak made him especially popular round these parts, thus Franco had no hesitation in renaming it Plaça de la Victoria ('victory') after the fall of Barcelona in 1939. Its current name is not just an empty gesture to Spain's monarch, but also specifically commemorates the King's actions in quashing an attempted military coup in 1981.

Avda Diagonal, which cuts through it, has been keeping the signwriters even busier. In 1914, it was called 'Agustín Argüelles', after another 19th-century politician, but in 1922 it changed to 'Nacionalitat Catalana' in celebration of the formation of the Mancomunitat (*see p19*). The advent of the dictatorship of General Primo de Rivera saw the name change back to Argüelles in 1924, but only for a year, after which it became known as Alfonso XIII, after the reigning monarch. In the aftermath of the 1931 elections, Alfonso stepped down and the Second Spanish Republic was euphorically proclaimed. The Second Republic was to be tragically short-lived, but the avenue was renamed after this historic day nonetheless: Avda 14 d'Abril. Naturally, Franco had other plans for it – in 1939, it became Avda Generalísimo Franco. The people of Barcelona were obstinate in their disgust, and it become popularly known as the 'Diagonal', a name it has held officially since 1979.

Further up into Gràcia, are two squares, Llibertat and Revolució de Setembre de 1868. Llibertat was originally known as Plaça del Rei, while Revolució was known as Isabel II before the unfortunate Bourbon queen was driven to exile in France by the same revolution. Again, Franco's people had no time for this, and during his regime it was known as Unificación. Isabel's other eponymous street became C/Mariana Pineda. A native of Granada, Pineda was executed in 1831 for giving aid to the liberals. She became a potent symbol for the struggle against repression.

Even apparently innocuous nomenclature fell prey to the whims of politicians. C/Torrent de l'Olla is so called because in centuries past torrents of water would rush down the street during storms. The name is as old as Gràcia itself and yet this too changed after 1939, to C/Menéndez Pelayo. The reasons for this are uncertain, although it is possible that Menéndez Pelayo, a 19th-century historian, philosopher and critic from Santander, was felt more suitable to represent the dictatorship's new dawn.

It's tempting to think that with Franco long dead and with Barcelona now one of Europe's most vibrant and prosperous cities, such upheaval will now end. It seems impossible to imagine that there could be a return to the barricades set up in Passeig de Gràcia during the Civil War, or the fierce fighting in Plaça Catalunya witnessed by Orwell. However, with politicians in at least six of Spain's autonomous communities keen to rewrite the constitution in the teeth of fierce opposition from Madrid, and with republican separatists now holding power in the Generalitat, it might be wise to remember that the signwriter's work is never really finished.

technology and business district, snappily tagged '22@'. In the 1960s many of the factories around here closed down; these days those buildings that have not already been torn down or converted into office blocks are used as schools, civic centres, workshops, open spaces or, increasingly, coveted lofts. The main drag, the pedestrianised **Rambla de Poblenou**, dating from 1886, is a much better place for a relaxing stroll than its busy central counterpart, and gives this still-villagey area a heart. Meanwhile, a bone's throw away, the city's oldest and most atmospheric cemetery, the **Cementiri de l'Est**, shows that most *barcelonins* spend their death as they did their life – cooped up in large high-rise blocks. Some were able to afford roomier tombs, many of which were built at the height of romantic-Gothic craze at the turn of the 19th century (check out the grave of Josep Soler, with its *El bes de la Mort* – or 'Kiss of Death' – statue, a masterpiece of erotic funerary art).

Nearby, **Plaça de les Glòries** finally seems about to fulfil its destiny. The creator of the Eixample, Ildefons Cerdà, planned for the square to become the new centre of the city, hoping his grid-pattern blocks would spread much further north than they did and shift the emphasis of the city from west to east; instead it became little more than a glorified roundabout on the way out of town. Now, with the hugely phallic **Torre Agbar** to landmark the area from afar, the *plaça* has become the gateway to Diagonal-Mar, and the new infrastructure being built around the Fòrum 2004. The tower, owned by the Catalan water board and designed by the French architect Jean Nouvel, has been a controversial project, and a bold one. A concrete skyscraper with a domed head, surrounded by a glass façade, it is not unlike London's famed 'Gherkin'. The architect says that it has been designed to reflect the Catalan mentality: the concrete represents stability and severity, the glass openness and transparency. At 144m (472ft), it is Barcelona's third-highest building (behind the two Olympic towers) and contains no fewer than 4,400 multiform windows. Remarkably, it will have no air-conditioning, as the windows will let the breeze do the job. Nouvel claims Gaudí as the inspiration for the multicoloured skin of a building that has already captured the public imagination, and has come to dominate the district.

One breath of fresh air in the rather stagnant area north of here is the **Parc del Clot**, and just beyond it, the **Plaça de Valentí Almirall**, with the old town hall of Sant Martí and a 17th-century building that used to be the Hospital de Sant Joan de Malta, somewhat at odds with the buildings that have mushroomed around them.

Further north, up C/Sagrera, the entrance to a former giant truck factory now leads to the charming **Parc de la Pegaso**. The area also has a fine piece of recent architecture, the supremely elegant **Pont de Calatrava** bridge. Designed by Santiago Calatrava, it links to Poblenou via C/Bac de Roda.

Diagonal-Mar

Barcelona's latest redevelopment, designed and built on the back of the **Fòrum 2004**, has stretched the Avda Diagonal all the way to the sea, and replaced old industrial land with skyscrapers, parks, a shopping centre and the Fòrum complex, continuing Barcelona's longstanding reputation as a city eager to find any excuse to renew itself.

Approaching from the city, the first sign of the new *barrio* is **Parc de Diagonal-Mar**, containing an angular lake decorated with scores of curling aluminium tubes and vast Gaudían flower pots, which will probably look better when the plants inside have grown. By Enric Miralles (of Scottish Parliament fame), the park may not be to most *barcelonins'* taste, but the local seagull population has found it to be an excellent roosting spot. Over the road is the Diagonal-Mar shopping centre, a three-storey mall of high-street chains, still woefully undervisited, and the grand Hotel Princesa, a triangular skyscraper by architect-designer-artist-local hero Oscar Tusquets.

Then comes the Fòrum site itself, nearing completion at the time of writing. After the international symposium, the complex is scheduled to be used for conferences and entertainment. Herzog and de Meuron's striking triangular **Edifici Fòrum** is the centrepiece, but the area also includes two parks, a marina, a new beach and the **Illa Pangea**, an island 60 metres (197 feet) from the shore, reachable only by swimming.

It's all a far cry from the local residential neighbourhood, **Sant Adrià de Besòs**, a poor district of tower blocks that includes the notorious La Mina neighbourhood, a hotbed of drug-related crime. It is hoped that the new development will help regenerate the area, which is best known for its Feria de Abril celebrations in April (*see p216*) the Andalucian community's version of the more famous annual celebrations in Seville. There's also a fine *festa major* in **Badalona**, just up the coast, in May, in which a large effigy of a devil is burned on the beach in a shower of whoops and fireworks.

Horta & around

Horta, to the far west of the blue metro line, is a picturesque little village that remains aloof from the city that swallowed it up in 1904. Originally a collection of farms (its name means 'market garden'), the *barrio* is still peppered with old farmhouses, such as **Can Mariner** on C/Horta, dating back to 1050, or the medieval **Can Cortada** at the end of C/Campoamor, now a huge restaurant in beautiful grounds. An abundant water supply also made Horta the place where much of Barcelona's laundry got done: a whole community of *bugaderes* (washerwomen) lived and worked in the lovely C/Aiguafreda, where you can still see their wells and open-air stone washtubs.

Parc de l'Espanya Industrial. *See p126.*

To the south, joined to Gràcia by Avda Mare de Déu de Montserrat, the steep-sided neighbourhood of **Guinardó**, with its steps and escalators, consists mainly of two big parks. **Parc del Guinardó**, a huge space designed in 1917 (making it Barcelona's third-oldest park) full of eucalyptus and cypress trees, is a relaxing place to escape. The smaller **Parc de les Aigües** shelters the neo-Arabic **Casa de les Altures** from 1890, Barcelona's most eccentrically beautiful council building.

The **Vall d'Hebron** is a leafy area located just above Horta in the Collserola foothills, in which formerly private estates have been put to public use, including the château-like **Palauet de les Heures**, now a university building. The area was one of the city's four major venues for the Olympics, so is rich in sporting facilities, including public football pitches, tennis, cycling and archery facilities at the **Velòdrom**. Around these venues there are a number of striking examples of street sculpture, including Claes Oldenberg's *Matches* and Joan Brossa's *Visual Poem* (in the shape of the letter 'A'). The area also conceals the rationalist **Pavelló de la República** and the delightfully zany **Parc del Laberint**, dating back to 1791, and surrounded by a modern park. More modern still is the **Ciutat Sanitària**, Catalonia's largest hospital where a good proportion of *barcelonins* first saw the light of day.

Parc del Laberint

C/Germans Desvalls, Passeig Vall d'Hebron (no phone). Metro Mundet. **Open** 10am-sunset daily. **Admission** €1.85; €1.20 concessions Mon, Tue, Thur-Sat; free under-6s, over-65s. Free Wed, Sun.

In 1791 the Desvalls family, owners of this marvellously leafy estate, hired Italian architect Domenico Begutti to design scenic gardens set around a cypress maze, with a romantic stream and a waterfall. The mansion may be gone (replaced with a 19th-century Arabic-influenced building) but the gardens are remarkably intact, shaded in the summer by oaks, laurels and an ancient sequoia. Best of all, the maze is still in use, an ingenious puzzle that still intrigues those brave enough to try it. Nearby stone tables provide a handy picnic site. On paying days, last entry is one hour before sunset.

Pavelló de la República

Avda Cardenal Vidal y Barraquer (93 428 54 57). Metro Montbau. **Open** 9am-8pm Mon-Fri. **Admission** free.

This austerely functionalist building now houses an interesting university library specialising in materials from the Spanish Civil War and the clandestine republican movement that operated continually during Franco's dictatorship. The structure was built in 1992 as a facsimile of the emblematic rationalist pavilion of the Spanish Republic, designed by Josep Lluís Sert for the Paris Exhibition in 1937 and later to hold Picasso's *Guernica*. It makes an interesting juxtaposition with Oldenberg's pop art *Matches* across the street.

The outer limits

L'Hospitalet de Llobregat lies beyond Sants, completely integrated within the city's transport system, but nevertheless a distinct municipality with its own very strong sense of separateness. Many of its inhabitants have Andalucian roots and this is Catalonia's main centre for flamenco (and not of the polka-dot-dress variety). One of the many flamenco *peñas* (clubs) is the **Tertulia Flamenca** (C/Calderon de la Barca 12, 93 437 20 44), which also offers guitar classes. The area has a number of bars and restaurants with a strong Andalucian flavour. It enjoys a rich cultural life, with good productions at the **Teatre Joventut** (C/Joventut 10, 93 448 12 10) and excellent art exhibitions at the **Tecla Sala Centre**.

Sant Andreu is another vast residential district, in the north-east of the city, and once was a major industrial zone. There's little reason to venture in to this area, unless you have a historical interest in Josep Lluis Sert's rationalist **Casa Bloc**, originally workers' residences from the brief republican era. A recently installed wine press in Plaça Xandri recalls Sant Andreu's pre-industrial rural past. The name of **Nou Barris**, on the other side of the Avda Meridiana, translates as 'nine neighbourhoods', but it is actually a collection of 11 former hamlets. The council compensates for the area's poor housing (many tower blocks were built in the area in the '50s and have fallen into disrepair) with the construction of public facilities such as the **Can Dragó**, a sports centre incorporating the biggest swimming pool in the city, and a **Parc Central**. The district centres on the roundabout at Plaça Llucmajor, which also holds Josep Viladomat's bold ***La República*** – a female nude holding aloft a sprig of laurel as a symbol of freedom. The renovation of the nearby **Seu de Nou Barris** town hall has brightened up an area that badly needed it, although it's not quite a tourist draw.

Tecla Sala Centre Cultural

Avda Josep Tarradellas 44, Hospitalet de Llobregat (93 338 57 71). Metro La Torrassa. **Open** 11am-2pm, 5-8pm Tue-Sat; 11am-2pm Sun. **Admission** free.

Tecla Sala is an old textile factory now housing a number of cultural concerns, including a vast library and this excellent gallery, which exhibits an eclectic mixture of international artists. The highlight of the 2004 season, from October to December, is an exhibition of Uruguayan painter Rafael Barradas, who lived in L'Hospitalet for a number of years.

Eat, Drink, Shop

Features

Restaurants

Goodbye deep-fried calamares, hello courgette parfait.

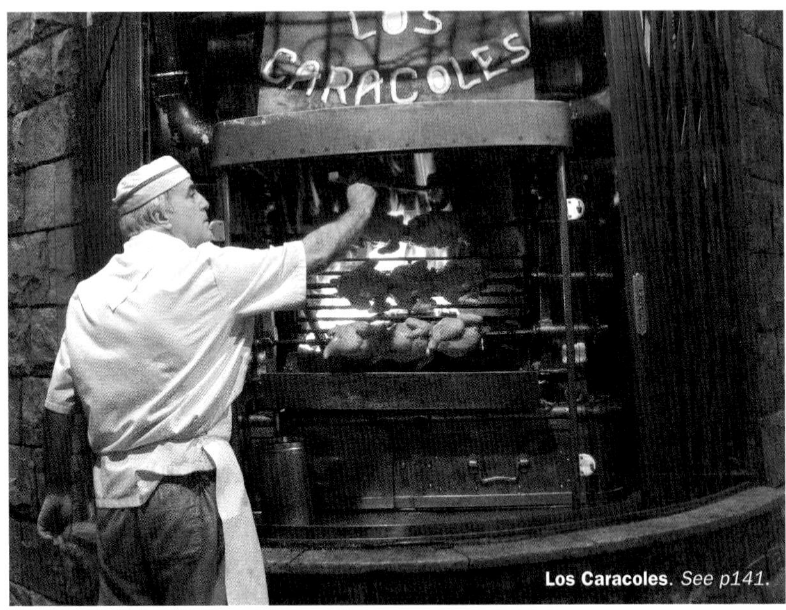

Los Caracoles. *See p141.*

'Spain is the new France!', declared the *New York Times* recently, to the bafflement of hacks and editors around the globe. A few frantic phonecalls later, and they agreed that, yes, if Gordon Ramsay et al consider Ferran Adrià to be the world's finest chef then Spain must indeed be the new France. The truth is rather more mundane. Although Adrià and his Costa Brava hideaway, **El Bulli** (*see p169*), have inspired hundreds of accomplished imitators, the renaissance of Spanish cooking is still in its early stages. Adrià aside, the country's culinary powerhouse is still the Basque country, which isn't so much the new France as virtually French to begin with.

What's happening in the lower echelons of Barcelona's culinary society is a less exciting fascination with all things miniature and foreign; like '80s food but without the element of surprise. Nouvelle cuisine and fusion appear to have found their spiritual home in Barcelona, where anything goes as long as it looks good and isn't too Spanish. Of course, there are plenty of restaurants that have been around forever, have a crowd of loyal regulars and a reputation that has lasted for generations, but there is little rising up to meet them. New restaurants open with concepts rather than cuisines, with DJs where once there were pianos and with kangaroo where once there was milk-fed lamb; which is all well and good until they dash your hopes for a 21st-century salad or professional service.

Authentic international cuisine is gaining ground only very slowly; unaccustomed local palates and the difficulty of sourcing key ingredients mean that it can be difficult to find really good Indian, say, or Italian food. Middle Eastern and Japanese restaurants have been rather more successful, along with a growing number of Latin American places.

Apart from the Pakistani restaurants that abound in the Raval, most of the ethnic variety is to be found in Gràcia. As they are relatively expensive, Japanese restaurants are mainly found in the Eixample or Zona Alta, where most of the top-end places are clustered, while seafood restaurants, for the most part, are in

For more detailed information on the city's eating and drinking scene, see Time Out's *Barcelona Eating & Drinking Guide.* Along with reviews of 300 bars, cafés and restaurants, the guide has location maps and details of opening times, prices and transport.

and around Barceloneta and the ports (with some notable exceptions). Catalan restaurants are evenly spread throughout the city, as is an impressive variety of vegetarian restaurants.

WHAT HAPPENS WHEN

Lunch starts around 2pm and goes on until about 3.30pm or 4pm, and dinner is served from 9pm until about 11.30pm or midnight. Some open earlier in the evening, but arriving before 9.30pm or 10pm generally means you will be dining alone or in the company of foreign tourists. Reserving a table is generally a good idea not only on Friday and Saturday nights, but also on Sunday evenings and Monday lunchtimes when few restaurants are open. Many also close for lengthy holidays, including about a week over Easter, two or three weeks in August or early September, and often the first week in January. We have listed closures of more than a week where possible, but restaurants are fickle, particularly on the issue of summer holidays, so call to check.

PRICES AND PAYMENT

Price guidelines used here are indications of the combined cost of an average starter, main course and dessert – not including wine, service or cover charge. € is used for under €20; €€ for €20-€30; €€€ for €30-€45; and €€€€ means the average meal will set you back more than €45. Eating out in Barcelona is not as cheap as it used to be, but low mark-ups on wines keep the cost relatively low for northern Europeans and Americans. All but the upmarket restaurants are required by law to serve an economical fixed-price *menú del día* (*menú* is not to be confused with the menu, which is *la carta*) at lunchtime – usually consisting of a starter, main course, dessert, bread and something to drink. The idea is to provide cheaper meals for the workers, and while it can be a real bargain, it is not by any means a taster menu or a showcase for the chef's greatest hits. It's also the case that since the euro came in, the average *menú* has rocketed up from around €7-€8 to around €10.

Laws governing the issue of prices are routinely flouted, but legally, menus must declare if the seven per cent IVA (VAT) is included in prices or not (it rarely is), and also if there is a cover charge (which is generally expressed as a charge for bread). Catalans, and the Spanish in general, tend to tip very little, but tourists let their conscience decide.

Barri Gòtic

Ateneu Gastronomic

Plaça de Sant Miquel 2 bis (93 302 11 98). Metro Jaume I or Liceu. **Open** 1-4pm, 8.30-11.30pm Mon-Thurs; 8pm-midnight Fri, Sat. Closed 3wks Aug. **Average** €€. Set lunch €7.81 Mon-Fri. Set dinner €12 Mon-Thur. **Credit** AmEx, DC, MC, V. **Map** p345 B3.

Epicurean Ernest Nuñez converted a second-hand anarchist bookshop into a 'gastronomic athenaeum' with the exalted aim of uniting culture and cuisine. Accordingly, the gourmet cigar bar, 500-strong wine list and library complement adventurous dishes such as pickled salt cod au gratin with quince *all i oli*, foie gras marinated in fortified wine or Moroccan pigeon pie. Even non-smokers can enjoy a sorbet flavoured with a Montecristo cigar marinated for a month in muscatel.

The best Restaurants

For dining like a prince

El Bulli (*see p169*); **Comerç 24** (*see p149*); **Espai Sucre** (*see p151*); **Gaig** (*see p168)* and **Jean Luc Figueras** (*see p159*).

For dining like a pauper

Bar Salvador (*see p149*); **Can Culleretes** (*see p141*); **L'Econòmic** (*see p151*); **Elisabets** (*see p146*); **Mercè Vins** (*see p141*); **Mesón David** (*see p146*); **Pla dels Àngels** (*see p147)* and **Pollo Rico** (*see p147*).

To see the beautiful at play

Alkimia (*see p155*); **Astoria** (*see p155*); **Bestial** (*see p166*); **Comerç 24** (*see p149*); **Lupino** (*see p146*) and **Noti** (*see p155*).

For sunshine

Agua (*see p163*); **Bestial** (*see p166*); **La Balsa** (*see p169*); **Café de l'Académia** (*see p141*); **Can Travi Nou** (*see p168*) and **La Venta** (*see p169*).

For seafood

Botafumeiro (*see p156*); **Cal Pep** (*see p149*); **Can Maño** (*see p164*); **Can Solé** (*see p164*); **Casa Leopoldo** (*see p146*) and **Passadís del Pep** (*see p151*).

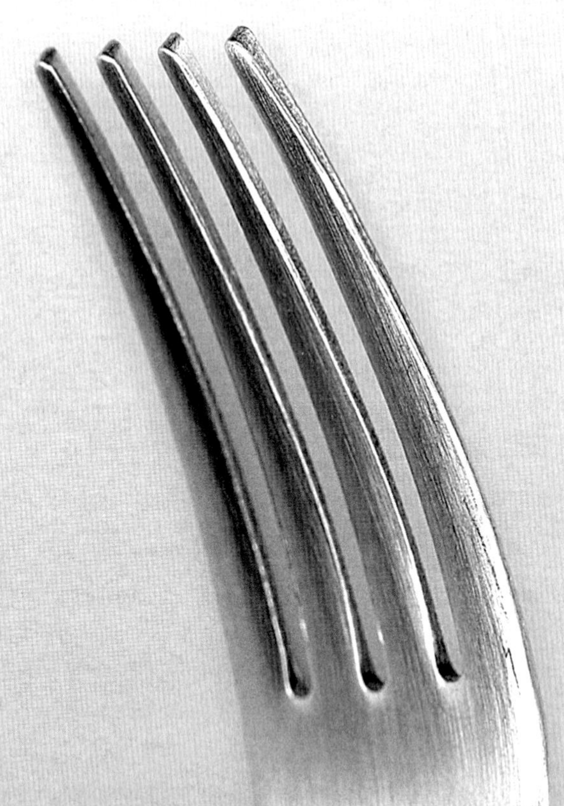
taxidermista...cafè restaurant
Plaça Reial 8   08002 Barcelona   tel. 93 412 45 36

Café de l'Acadèmia

C/Lledó 1 (93 319 82 53). Metro Jaume I. **Open** 9am-noon, 1.30-4pm, 8.45-11.30pm Mon-Fri. Closed 2wks Aug. **Average** €€. Set lunch €8.56-€12.30 Mon-Fri. **Credit** AmEx, MC, V. **Map** p345 B3.

At night these are some of the most sought-after tables in the city, especially those on the romantic little Plaça Sant Just in summer. By day it's a slightly different proposition, rammed with besuited workers from the nearby city hall, and with a lunch *menú* that offers no options. The regular menu offers superb value and has changed little over the years (if it ain't broke…), so you can expect a creamy risotto with duck foie, guinea fowl with a tiny tarte tatin, lots of duck and own-made pasta, delicious with shrimps and garlic.

Can Culleretes

C/Quintana 5 (93 317 30 22). Metro Liceu. **Open** 1.30-4pm, 9-11pm Tue-Sat; 1.30-4pm Sun. Closed July. **Average** €. **Credit** MC, V. **Map** p345 A3.

The 'house of teaspoons' is Spain's second oldest restaurant (with a framed certificate from Norris McWhirter to prove it) and its six dining rooms get so packed that reservations are essential. In 1786 you could eat here for just two pesetas and although prices have risen it's still an amazingly cheap spot for traditional Catalan scran. Under yellowing oil paintings and photos, diners munch sticky black boar stew, pork with prunes and dates, or sizzling garlic prawns all served fast and fresh from the oven in hot terracotta dishes.

Los Caracoles

C/Escudellers 14 (93 302 31 85). Metro Liceu. **Open** 1pm-midnight daily. **Average** €€€. **Credit** AmEx, DC, MC, V. **Map** p345 B3.

Venerated by the sort of people who take pictures of their food, Los Caracoles functions far better as a sight than a place to eat, its endless series of low-ceilinged characterful dining rooms adorned with heavy beams, pretty tiling and ancient fittings. The trick is to order conservatively – the food is acceptably unexceptional and not what you're here for. Best to stick with one of the chickens twirling outside on a spit, and avoid the fish dishes and eponymous snails, which come in a tomatoey gloop fizzing with e-numbers. The pricing is somewhat creative.

El Gran Café

C/Avinyó 9 (93 318 79 86). Metro Liceu. **Open** 1-4pm, 7.30-12.30am daily. **Average** €€. Set lunch €11.77 Mon-Fri. **Credit** AmEx, DC, MC, V. **Map** p345 B3.

El Gran Café blends a smart 1940s Parisian brasserie look with a crowd-pleasing menu. It covers all bases, from Catalan classic (*esqueixada* or *xató* salad), to modish Mediterranean (goose with mango chutney, skewered monkfish with king prawns) all adapted to the Anglo-Saxon palate (two veg with the main course, butter pats for the bread roll). Puddings and wines follow the same lines and on weekdays there's a good set lunch.

Mastroqué

C/Codols 29 (93 301 79 42). Metro Drassanes or Jaume I. **Open** 8.30pm-1am Tue-Sat. Closed 3wks Aug. **Average** €€. Set dinner €10. **Credit** MC, V. **Map** p345 B4.

For those willing to brave the urine-scented, back-alley location, Mastroqué offers a sweet-smelling haven of soft lighting, fresh flowers, exposed beams and scumbled, tawny walls. The small but sophisticated array of *platillos* (half portions) combine Gallic elements such as duck confit with ostrich tartar, gilt-head bream carpaccio, *cecina* (dried and cured ham) infused with rosemary or golden sorrel pie.

Mercè Vins

C/Amargós 1 (93 302 60 56). Metro Urquinaona. **Open** 8am-5pm Mon-Thur; 8am-5pm, 8.30pm-midnight Fri. **Average** €. Set lunch €7.90 Mon-Fri. **Credit** V. **Map** p344 B2.

Decorated in pretty pastels and terracotta, with green beams and fresh flowers, few places are as cosy as Mercè Vins. In the morning it functions as a breakfast bar, then switches to serving a set lunch *menú* (only), and on Friday nights becomes a *llesqueria,* where hams and cheeses are dished out with *pa amb tomàquet.* The standard of cooking can vary, but on a good day might include great salads with pasta and wild mushrooms or potato, bacon and spring onions, and the glass of muscatel with crispy *coca* to finish is a regular on the dessert choices.

Mesón Jesús

C/Cecs de la Boqueria 4 (93 317 46 98). Metro Jaume I or Liceu. **Open** 1-4pm, 8-11pm Mon-Fri. Closed Aug-early Sept. **Average** €. Set lunch €8.10 Mon-Fri. Set dinner €12.50 Mon-Fri. **Credit** MC, V. **Map** p345 A3.

The menu is limited and never changes, but dishes are reliably good and inexpensive to boot – try the sautéd green beans with ham to start, then superb grilled prawns or a tasty *zarzuela* (fish stew). The feel is authentic Castilian, with gingham tablecloths, oak barrels, cartwheels and pitchforks hung around the walls, while the waitresses are incessantly cheerful with a largely non Spanish-speaking clientele, and especially obliging when it comes to children. There are no reservations so it's wise to arrive early.

Pla

C/Bellafila 5 (93 412 65 52). Metro Jaume I. **Open** 9pm-midnight Mon-Thur, Sun; 9pm-1am Fri, Sat. **Average** €€. **Credit** MC, V. **Map** p345 B3.

If you're getting sick of all the ferociously hip Asian-Mediterranean fusion restaurants in Barcelona, then blame Pla. The much-imitated menu might include anything from seared tuna with seaweed and apple vinaigrette to ostrich with green asparagus, honey and grilled mango slices. Veggie options are clearly marked and desserts are rich and creative. As befits the vanguard of fashion, the lighting is nightclub dark, the music loud and the artwork louder.

Other locations: **Re-Pla** C/Montcada 6, Born (93 268 30 03).

Les Quinze Nits

Plaça Reial 6 (93 317 30 75). Metro Liceu. **Open** 1-3.45pm, 8.30-11.30pm daily. **Average** €. Set lunch €6.98 Mon-Fri. **Credit** AmEx, MC, V. **Map** p345 A3.

Combining fast-food speed and prices with tablecloths, potted palms and soft lighting has made this chain a legend in its own lunchtime. Waiting in line is a pain, but for many the rockbottom prices fully justify the inconvenience. The turnover is brisk as squadrons of harried waiters serve up good salads and local favourites such as meatballs with squid in black ink, grilled bream with asparagus, *botifarra* and beans, and *crema catalana*. For the best experience choose wisely: the quality of the steaks is variable and the paella can taste mass-produced.

Other locations: **La Fonda** C/Escudellers 10 (93 301 75 15) and throughout the city.

El Salón

C/Hostal d'en Sol 6-8 (93 315 21 59). Metro Jaume I. **Open** 8.30pm-midnight Mon-Sat. Closed 2wks Aug. **Average** €€. **Credit** AmEx, MC, V. **Map** p345 B4.

After flirting experimentally with a great lunch menu, the restaurant failed to pull in sufficient crowds to fill its quirky, baroque dining room, so now it's open evenings only. Inventive, frequently changing menus have included quail with *membrillo* (quince jelly); vegetable brochette with tikka sauce and yoghurty dressing, and prawn-filled filo pastry with a bitter orange chutney. Puddings are a highlight, with authentic blackcurrant crumble and tarte tatin. The only complaint might be the chest-height tables, uncomfortably reminiscent of childhood.

Taxidermista

Plaça Reial 8 (93 412 45 36). Metro Liceu. **Open** 1.30-4pm, 8.30-12.30am Tue-Sun. Closed 3wks Jan. **Average** €€. Set lunch €7.20 Tue-Fri. **Credit** AmEx, DC, MC, V. **Map** p345 A3.

The tourist-magnet location has not tempted this smart Franco-Catalan restaurant to compromise on quality. Its name commemorates a past incarnation as a taxidermist's, where Dalí famously purchased 200,000 ants and a stuffed rhino, but tastier offerings include artichoke ravioli in chicken broth, foie gras with quince jelly and sherry, duck breast with fig chutney, and, for dessert, a chestnut and chocolate parfait with baked pears in honey. The terrace is a great spot for afternoon coffee or a tipple from the very reasonable wine list.

International

La Locanda

C/Doctor Joaquim Pou 4 (93 317 46 09). Metro Jaume I or Urquinaona. **Open** 1.15-4.30pm, 8.15-midnight Tue-Sun. Closed Aug. **Average** €€. **Credit** MC, V. **Map** p344 B2.

This cosy restaurant serves up fresh, good quality Italian food amid potted palms, warm fittings and the odd mural of a Roman deity. The pizzas – divided into red (with tomato), white (with three cheeses) and calzone – continue the Roman theme: Vulcan (salami), Apollo (egg and parmesan), Poseidon (seafood) or Gladiator (a surprisingly fey combination of ricotta and mascarpone). There's a solid selection of classic salads, pastas, gnocchi, focaccia and risottos, and an all-Italian wine list.

El Paraguayo

C/Parc 1 (93 302 14 41). Metro Drassanes. **Open** 1-4pm, 8pm-midnight Tue-Sun. **Average** €€€. **Credit** AmEx, DC, MC, V. **Map** p345 A4.

The pleasures are exclusively carnal at this warm, wood-panelled little steakhouse, brightened with Colombian paintings of buxom madams and their dapper admirers. The cuts of beef are quite different to those in the north, and complicated to trans-

Biblioteca. *See p145.*

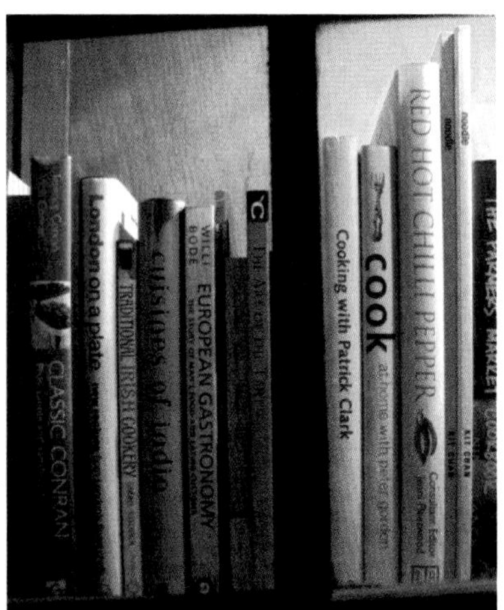

One for the road

The many all-Catalan wine lists take most visitors by surprise, to say nothing of the wine itself. A few tips on what to take home with you.

Best cava under €10

Rovellats Gran Reserva (€8.50)
Made in a beautiful 15th-century *bodega*, Rovellats is one of the best value small production cavas on the market. Aged for three years before release, it would fool many an expert blind taster into thinking they were judging a €20 wine.

Best premium cava

Llopart Brut Ex-Vite (€25)
From a family-run company that has been making cava since 1881, this is too good to wait for a celebration. Top-quality fruit from 40-year-old vines and five years' maturation in the bottle combine to produce a sparkling wine with complexity and class.

Best rosé

Gran Caus Rosado 2002 (€9.50)
Don't be put off by the dark glass bottle. Inside you'll find a rosé – made from 100 per cent merlot – with bags of colour and flavour.

Best white

Cervoles 1999 (€17.50)
Catalonia is still a region more renowned for its reds and, bar a few exceptions (Torres make consistently good whites), the hunt for top quality whites can be fraught with disappointment. Here is one of those rare exceptions. A blend of chardonnay and macabeo fermented in new oak with a lovely backbone of crisp acidity.

Best from undiscovered region

Ca N'Estruc (€6)
The wine revolution has touched almost every corner of Catalonia and barely a month goes by without news of another up-and-coming region . This impressive blend of cabernet sauvignon and tempranillo comes from Esparreguera, in the shadow of Montserrat.

Best new cult wine

Sof Lefriec 1999 (€62)
Allegedly this is the first so-called 'garage wine' – highly fashionable red wine made in tiny quantities – to be made in Catalonia. It may seem a high price to pay but the quality really is exceptional and compared to '*les garagistes*' in France, this is still relatively affordable.

Best Priorat under €20

Lauren Priorat 2001 (€19)
Most people would probably head straight to Alvaro Palacios' Les Terrasses (the third and most affordable of his excellent Priorat trio of wines) but Lauren is equal in quality and exclusivity. The second wine of Clos Erasmus – a label that American wine collectors fight over – Lauren is distinctive for being predominantly made from cabernet sauvignon rather than Spanish grape varieties.

Best Priorat under €40

Lo Givot 1999 (€40)
This is a blockbuster blend of garnacha, carignan, syrah and cabernet sauvignon, aged for 14 months in the finest oak barrels money can buy. To be put in a dark damp place for a few years and then uncorked on a dark damp night.

design: lacreativa.com
All of our chefs are besotted

late, but to try a range of *vacío*, *entraña*, *bife de cuadril*, *churrasco* and so on, the lunchtime tasting menu isn't a bad idea at €14. Baked potatoes are the standard side dish, but beyond that El Paraguayo is, like most South American restaurants, an unwitting pioneer of the Atkins Diet.

Peimong

C/Templers 6-10 (93 318 28 73). Metro Jaume I. **Open** 1-4.30pm, 8-11.30pm Tue-Sun. **Average** €. **Credit** MC, V. **Map** p345 B3.

There are no frills here (unles you count the wonky Inca village scenes) but this welcoming Peruvian restaurant certainly knows its spuds. Both the potato and yucca chips are gloriously fat, golden and abundant, and the *papas a la huancaina* (with cheese sauce) contrast wonderfully with the tongue-twanging lime and coriander ceviche or the creamy yellow *aji de gallina* (chicken with rice). If it's a party, order the two-litre bottles of Inca Cola or Arequipeña beer.

Polenta

C/Ample 51 (93 268 14 29). Metro Jaume I. **Open** 7pm-midnight Mon-Thur, Sun; 7pm-1am Fri, Sat; 1.30pm-midnight Sun. **Average** €. **Credit** AmEx, MC, V. **Map** p345 B4.

Bright stuccoed walls and eclectic music attract international diners out for an affordable tablecloth dinner. Global favourites include spaghetti with clams, Argentinian beef with chimichurri or yakitori with homespun standards like pralines or apple tart for dessert. More experimental food includes cod with creamed wasabi and squid ink or the salad of warm duck *gésiers*.

La Verònica

C/Avinyó 30 (93 412 11 22). Metro Liceu. **Open** 7.30pm-1.30am Tue-Fri; 12.30pm-2am Sat, Sun. Closed 2wks Feb, 2wks Aug. **Average** €. **Credit** AmEx, MC, V. **Map** p345 B3.

With plate-glass windows and high-exposure terrace, this bright orange, gay-friendly pizzeria makes the perfect posing gallery. Pizzas are as thin and well dressed as the clientele, with trendy toppings such as apple and gorgonzola along with the usual classics. Designer salads of rocket and ginger or parsnip, cucumber and poppy seeds take care of the vegetation and puddings are competent pan-EU standards of tiramisu, cheesecake and brownies.

Vegetarian

Govinda

Plaça Vila de Madrid 4 (93 318 77 29). Metro Liceu. **Open** 1-4pm Mon, Sun; 1-4pm, 8-11pm Tue-Thur; 1-4pm, 8-11.45pm Fri, Sat. Closed 2wks Aug. **Average** €. Set lunch €8.30 Mon-Fri; €12 Sat, Sun. **Credit** AmEx, DC, MC, V. **Map** p344 B2.

There's no alcohol at this Hindu vegetarian restaurant but there are plenty of interesting alternatives such as tamarind lassi, rose and lemon water or chai. The usual samosas, pakoras and biryanis are present and correct, along with more unusual offerings such as *gaja bada* (spicy carrot doughnuts), stuffed cabbage leaves or basmati with fresh fruit. The bargain, Mediterranean-influenced set lunch includes a go at the salad buffet.

Juicy Jones

C/Cardenal Casañas 7 (93 302 43 30). Metro Liceu. **Open** noon-midnight daily. **Average** €. **No credit cards. Map** p345 A3.

Wake up and smell the tofu at this Danish-owned juice bar where all the food – with the exception of honey in the soy milkshakes – is completely vegan. A staff of international backpackers serve the bargain all-day menu amid retina-wrenching graffiti and thumping eurotrance. If rice and couscous is too filling, try a baguette of roast beetroot, dill, apple and nuts or a salad of ginger, noodles, tofu and beansprouts. For nibbles to accompany organic wines and beers, there are tapas or freshly baked fruitcake and hazelnut cookies.

Raval

Ánima

C/Àngels 6 (93 342 49 12) Metro Liceu. **Open** 1-4pm, 9pm-midnight Mon-Sat. **Average** €€. Set lunch €8.50 Mon-Fri. **Credit** MC, V. **Map** p344 A2.

The crew behind Iposa (*see p175*) dips a toe in the water of serious food with this new venture, where Mediterranean food is served in a sharp-edged space with a thoughtfully positioned mirror to watch the chefs at work. A jumble of sautéd wild mushrooms, and rocket salad with crispy pear are tasty, and sea bass with crab bisque a smooth follow-up. Puddings sound better than they taste, though: apple crumble is actually a patty of apple, banana and crushed almonds, and pumpkin cake with peppermint ice-cream is just weird. Hit-or-miss, but mostly hit.

Biblioteca

C/Junta de Comerç 28 (93 412 62 21). Metro Liceu. **Open** 1-4pm, 9pm-midnight Tue-Sat. Closed 2wks Aug. **Average** €€. Set lunch €9.63 Tue-Fri. **Credit** AmEx, DC, MC, V. **Map** p345 A3.

A very zen-like space with minimal cream decor, Biblioteca is all about food. Food and books about food, that is. From Bocuse to Bourdain, they are all for sale, and their various influences collide in some occasionally sublime cooking. Beetroot gazpacho with live clams and quail's egg is a dense riot of flavour and endive salad with poached egg and *romesco* wafers superb. Mains aren't quite as head-spinning, but accomplished nonetheless. The set lunch offers more basic fare of pasta dishes and creative salads, and an excellent winelist offers a great Martivilli for €9 if the heavyweights don't appeal.

El Cafetí

C/Hospital 99 (end of passage)(93 329 24 19/www.elcafeti.com). Metro Liceu. **Open** 1.30-3.30pm, 8.30-11.30pm Tue-Sat; 1.30-3.30pm Sun. Closed 2wks Aug. **Average** €€. Set lunch €8 Tue-Sat. **Credit** AmEx, DC, MC, V. **Map** p342 C6.

A genteel hideaway at the end of a slightly insalubrious alley, with delicate lace curtains, polished mahogany sideboards, a gleaming brass beer pump and dried flower arrangements. It serves excellent renditions of Franco-Catalan classics such as steak tartar, *xató* salad or sole meunière, with a great lunchtime *menú*. The house speciality is paella in all its many forms, but don't miss out on the desserts before you get tempted into parlour games.

La Casa de la Rioja

C/Peu de la Creu 8-10 (93 443 33 63). Metro Catalunya. **Open** 1-4pm, 9-11pm Mon-Sat. Closed Aug. **Average** €. Set lunch €9 Mon-Fri; €12 Sat. **Credit** AmEx, MC, V. **Map** p342 C5.

Working overtime as a cultural centre and promoter for the region of La Rioja, this colourful, sharp-edged restaurant is not quite the jaw-dropping bargain it was when it opened a couple of years ago, but still provides some of the best-value food around, particularly in the abundant, honest nature of its lunch *menú*. Sturdy Rioja staples include steaks, chops and lamb with *patatas a la riojana* (potatoes with onions and pepper), and there's a long list of tapas available throughout the day.

Casa Leopoldo

C/Sant Rafael 24 (93 441 69 42). Metro Liceu or Paral.lel. **Open** 1.30-4pm, 9-11pm Tue-Thur; 1.30-4pm, 8.30-11pm Fri, Sat; 1.30-4pm Sun. Closed Aug. **Average** €€€. Set lunch €10.70 Tue-Fri. **Credit** AmEx, DC, MC, V. **Map** p342 C6.

Bullfighting paraphernalia, wooden fittings, tiles and red gingham give this Barcelona classic plenty of old-style charm, and traditional food is still the order of the day with generous and excellent fish, shellfish, steaks and homey stews. For some of the seafood, and particularly the fish of the day, you might want to put your bank manager on speed dial, however; the shabbiness of the surrounding area does little to affect the prices.

Dos Trece

C/Carme 40 (93 301 73 06). Metro Liceu. **Open** 1.30-4pm, 9pm-midnight Tue-Sun. **Average** €€. Set lunch €9 Tue-Sat. **Credit** AmEx, DC, MC, V. **Map** p344 A2.

Is it a bar? Is it a restaurant? Is it a nightclub? Where's my salad? Dos Trece caters to everyone from hangover victims (brunch on Sunday) to wannabe jazz musicians (a jam session on Tuesday). Apart from a little fusion confusion (Thai curry with nachos; cajun chicken with mash; curried sausage with baked apple, and all manner of things with yucca chips) the food's not half bad for the price, but the service could look a little livelier.

Elisabets

C/Elisabets 2-4 (93 317 58 26). Metro Catalunya. **Open** 7am-11pm Mon-Thur, Sat; 7am-2am Fri. Closed 3wks Aug. **Average** €. Set lunch €7.50 Mon-Sat. **No credit cards**. **Map** p344 A2.

A charming old neighbourhood restaurant where traditional and supercheap Catalan dishes are the order of the day; as well as a long list of generous *bocadillos*, there are rabbit stews, chicken cooked in beer, *botifarra* sausage with eye-watering *all i oli*, and so on. Look out especially for the *fesolet* beans fried up with onion and sausage. An unpretentious but friendly place to have lunch among the denizens of the Raval and those on their way to the MACBA.

Organic. *See p149.*

Lupino

C/Carme 33 (93 412 36 97). Metro Liceu. **Open** 1-4pm, 9pm-midnight Mon-Thur, Sun; 1-4pm, 9pm-1am Fri, Sat. **Average** €€. Set lunch €10 Mon-Fri. **Credit** AmEx, MC, V. **Map** p344 A2.

Like a retro-futuristic airport lounge with waiters dressed like mortuary attendants, Lupino is one of *the* places for the cool but impecunious to see and be seen. A hybrid of restaurant and cocktail club (with weekend dance sessions in the hands of the gloriously named DJ Gigi el Amoroso), it offers a difficult to categorise range of dishes from Japanese spinach soup with clams to roast lamb with chestnuts. Prices are pleasantly out of sync with the glamour quotient, especially for the lunch *menú*.

Mama Café

C/Doctor Dou 10 (93 301 29 40). Metro Catalunya or Liceu. **Open** 1pm-1am Mon-Sat. **Average** €. Set lunch €8 Mon-Fri. **Credit** DC, MC, V. **Map** p344 A2.

Very much of its *barrio*, with Rajasthani wallhangings, slide projections and trip hop, the Mama Café provides Mediterranean dishes to a wildly diverse crowd. Dreadlocks settle in next to blue rinses to chow down on dishes from healthy wok-fried vegetables to a diet-busting hamburger with mash and yucca chips. The Mama Café makes much of its policy to use nothing tinned or microwaved, and everything is bought fresh from the nearby Boqueria.

Mesón David

C/Carretas 63 (93 441 59 34). Metro Paral.lel. **Open** 1-4pm, 8pm-midnight Mon, Tue, Thur-Sun. Closed Aug. **Average** €. **Credit** AmEx, MC, V. **Map** p342 C6.

Loud, merry diners jam the wooden trestle tables, tended by even louder, merrier staff. The menu is a minefield of soggy salads and saltlick soups but three Galician specialities are consistently fantastic: the *lechazo* (treacly roast pork), *pulpo a feira* (tender slices of octopus) and *trucha navarra* (trout stuffed with cured ham and cheese). For dessert have almond *tarta de Santiago* or fresh pineapple doused in Cointreau. Tips are thrown into a large clog, and a ringing bell or shout of '*¡Bote!*' prompts everyone to cheer you out of the door.

Pla dels Àngels

C/Ferlandina 23 (93 329 40 47). Metro Universitat. **Open** 1.30-4pm, 9-11.30pm Mon-Thur, Sun; 1.30-4pm, 9pm-midnight Fri, Sat. **Average** €. Set lunch €5.35 Mon-Fri. **Credit** DC, MC, V. **Map** p342 C5.

The cheaper cousin of Semproniana (*see p156*) and Coses de Menjar (*see p149*) with a student-friendly €5 lunch menu of two courses. Otherwise the short menu includes rather self-consciously inventive but well-executed dishes of octopus carpaccio, gnocchi with gorgonzola and walnuts, carrot and orange soup or frogs' legs with caramelised vegetables and *all i oli*. The colourful décor resembles an installation from the MACBA opposite, with painted egg-box ceilings and a patio filled with white rocks.

Pollo Rico

C/Sant Pau 31 (93 441 31 84/www.polloricosl.com). Metro Liceu. **Open** 10am-1am Mon, Tue, Thur-Sat, Sun. **Average** €. Set lunch €6.60 Mon, Tue, Thur-Sat. **No credit cards**. **Map** p344 C6.

A Raval institution, the 'Tasty Chicken' has the best rotisserie fowl in the city twirling at its windows. Picnickers can take away a golden-skinned quarter for just €2 while local characters and tourists all troop upstairs for the €6.50 chicken menu, litre jugs of wicked sangria, or the €2.50 plate of *botifarra* and beans. The only downside, along with the supermarket lighting, is the droopy, greasy chips.

Silenus

C/Àngels 8 (93 302 26 80). Metro Liceu. **Open** 1.30-4pm, 8.45pm-12.30am Mon-Sat. **Average** €€. Set lunch €11 Mon-Fri. **Credit** AmEx, DC, MC, V. **Map** p344 A2.

The ghost of a clock is projected on a far wall; the faded leaves of a book float up high; the ceiling twinkles with little lights, and wisps of wild flowers sit in glass jars. Not the lair of the Faerie Queen, but a thoroughly modern restaurant, where the aesthetic reigns supreme. A lunchtime *degustación* (€14.80) affords tiny portions of every delight on the menu, bringing together doll's house paella; sea bass with rice cooked in squid ink, and duck magret with apple and foie gras. Feed your mind, meantime, with vibrant displays of local artists' work.

International

Fil Manila

C/Ramelleres 3 (93 318 64 87). Metro Catalunya. **Open** 11.30am-4.30pm, 8-11.30pm Mon, Wed-Sun. **Average** €. **No credit cards**. **Map** p344 A2.

There's practically a dish for every one of the 7,000 Philippine islands on this epic menu. Malay, Chinese and Spanish influences all contribute to the classic flavours of sour fish soup, *pancit* (noodles), chicken and pork adobo, fried *lumpia* (crispy vegetable or meat rolls) or a *halo-halo* dessert of fruits, crushed ice and milk. The bamboo-lined decor doesn't try too hard to be exotic and the faithful patronage of local Filipinos augurs well for the food's authenticity.

Moti Mahal

C/Sant Pau 103, (93 329 32 52/www.motimahal bcn.com). Metro Liceu. **Open** noon-4pm, 8pm-midnight daily. **Average** €. Set lunch €7 Mon-Fri. **Credit** AmEx, DC, MC, V. **Map** p342 C6.

In a city where 'curry' usually means a pinch of orange food colouring, this immaculate and courteous Indian restaurant by Sant Pau del Camp church

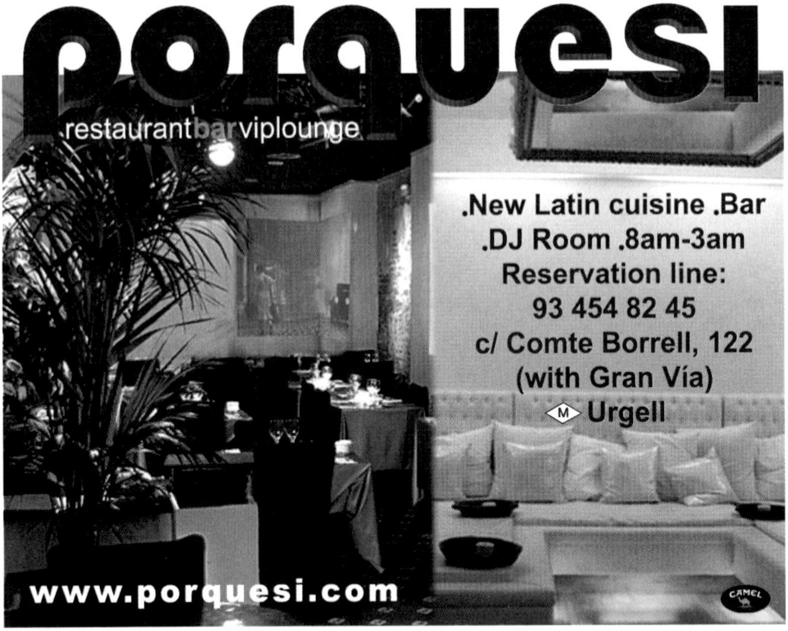
porquesi
restaurantbarviplounge
.New Latin cuisine .Bar
.DJ Room .8am-3am
Reservation line:
93 454 82 45
c/ Comte Borrell, 122
(with Gran Vía)
M Urgell
www.porquesi.com
CAMEL

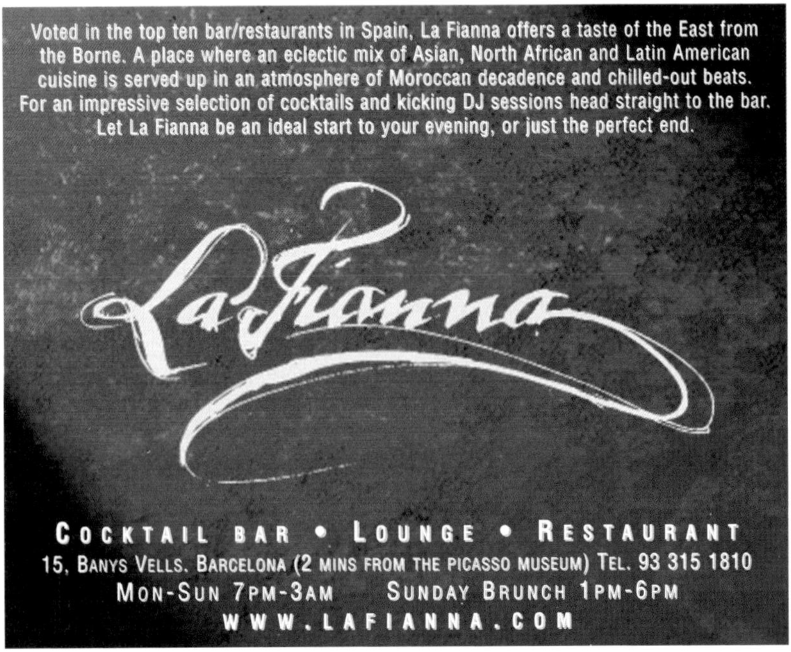
Voted in the top ten bar/restaurants in Spain, La Fianna offers a taste of the East from the Borne. A place where an eclectic mix of Asian, North African and Latin American cuisine is served up in an atmosphere of Moroccan decadence and chilled-out beats. For an impressive selection of cocktails and kicking DJ sessions head straight to the bar. Let La Fianna be an ideal start to your evening, or just the perfect end.
La Fianna
COCKTAIL BAR • LOUNGE • RESTAURANT
15, BANYS VELLS. BARCELONA (2 MINS FROM THE PICASSO MUSEUM) TEL. 93 315 1810
MON-SUN 7PM-3AM SUNDAY BRUNCH 1PM-6PM
WWW.LAFIANNA.COM

works hard to keep things authentic. Specialities include tandoori and a richly flavoured range of vegetable dishes served in lovely brass tureens, most notable among them the creamy dahl *makhni* and the *bhindi* (okra). For once, it comes hot as you dare but you can find relief in a glass of salty lassi.

Vegetarian

L'Hortet

C/Pintor Fortuny 32 (93 317 61 89). Metro Liceu. **Open** 1-4pm Mon; 1-4pm, 8.30pm-midnight Tue-Sun. **Average** €. Set lunch €7.75 Mon-Fri; €9.10 Sat, Sun. Set dinner €11 daily. **Credit** AmEx, MC, V. **Map** p344 A2.

The green gingham, pine fittings and horseshoes are very *Little House on the Prairie*, although the cooking might benefit from a little more of the pioneer spirit. Expect competent but no-frills renditions of all the veggie standards – lasagne, tortillas with guacamole, mushroom crêpes and pizzas – in hearty portions. The salad bar is tiny but always fresh.

Organic

C/Junta de Comerç 1 (93 301 0902) Metro Liceu. **Open** 12.30-5pm Mon-Thur, 12.30-5pm, 8pm-12.30am Fri, Sat. **Average** €. **Credit** MC, V. **Map** p345 A3.

Spacious and tastefully designed with its long rows of floating white lamps, Organic offers excellent value vegetarian food. The friendly and attentive staff will usher you in, seat you and give you a rundown on meal options: an all-you-can-eat salad bar (€4), a combined salad bar and main course (€5.50), or the full whammy – salad, soup, main course and dessert (€7.50). The superb main courses include tofu spring rolls, Pakistani and Indian dishes, spinach lasagnes and more. A decently stocked shop is located at the entrance.

Sésamo

C/Sant Antoni Abat 52 (93 441 64 11). Metro Sant Antoni. **Open** 1-4pm Mon; 1-4pm, 8.30-11.30pm Wed-Sun. **Average** €. Set lunch €8 Mon, Wed-Sat. **Credit** MC, V. **Map** p342 C5.

A funky café with mellow sounds and circuit-board lampshades segues into a relaxing back dining room serving Barcelona's most adventurous organic vegetarian food. Try 'jade pillars' (cucumber rolls stuffed with smoked tofu and mashed pine nuts), crunchy polenta with pesto and a haystack of peppery rocket or spicy curry served in popadom baskets with dahl and wild rice. Many dishes are vegan and at lunchtime there is a two-course lunch menu or a €6 *plato combinado*.

Sant Pere & the Born

Abac

C/Rec 79-89 (93 319 66 00). Metro Barceloneta. **Open** 8.30-10.30pm Mon; 1.30-3.30pm, 8.30-10.30pm Tue-Sat. Closed 2wks Aug. **Average** €€€€. **Credit** AmEx, DC, MC, V. **Map** p345 C4.

Sometimes it's hard to think much of a restaurant that thinks so much of itself. It is good, certainly, and Xavier Pellicer is undeniably a talented chef, but when diners aren't getting much change from €100 a head, expectations are pretty high. Classic French influences are still very evident in dishes such as red mullet with herb butter, rich venison with quince, or chocolate sablé, but things are lightening up of late with scallops, wild mushrooms and citrus fruit or brioche with mandarin and basil. The cheeses and petits fours remain a highlight. One for expense accounts, all told.

Bar Salvador

C/Canvis Nous 8 (93 310 10 41). Metro Jaume I or Barceloneta. **Open** 9am-5pm Mon-Fri. Closed Aug. **Average** €. **Credit** MC, V. **Map** p345 B4.

Much as it goes against the grain to publicise this unalloyed little gem, it would be a crime to keep it quiet. Providing breakfast and lunch for the workers, it also pulls in the local literati and their friends, who sit in large animated groups passing aloft glass *porrones* of beer. Daily-changing mains often include a sticky pork knuckle with fiery *all i oli*, duck with haricot beans or sardines in garlic and parsley, all nestling alongside fat, crisp potato wedges. As well as nearly-free house red from the barrel, there is Gotim Bru for a staggeringly low €9.75.

Cal Pep

Plaça de les Olles 8 (93 310 79 61). Metro Barceloneta. **Open** 8-11.45pm Mon; 1.30-4pm, 8-11.45pm Tue-Sat. Closed Aug. **Average** €€. **Credit** AmEx, DC, MC, V. **Map** p344 C4.

Pep's standing among local restaurateurs and the seafood cognoscenti is little short of regal. From creamy squid to pert little prawns and quivering razor clams, nobody selects and prepares them better. As much tapas bar as restaurant, Cal Pep is always packed: get here early for the coveted seats at the front and a bit more elbow room. There is a cosy dining room at the back, but it would be a shame to miss the show.

Comerç 24

C/Comerç 24 (93 319 21 02). Metro Arc de Triomf. **Open** 1.30-3.30pm, 8.30pm-midnight Tue-Fri. **Average** €€€. **Credit** MC, V. **Map** p345 C3.

A pioneer of nouvelle Catalan cuisine in the city, chef Carles Abellan plays with flavours and deconstructs traditional favourites (DIY tortilla: just dip the ingredients into a warm egg-yolk spume). A selection of tiny dishes roams the globe: tuna sashimi and seaweed on a wafer-thin pizza crust; Puy lentils with bacon and foie gras; or squid stuffed with *botifarra* and anise. Steel girders and jailhouse-grey paint punctuated with bursts of yellow and red provide some industrial chic.

Coses de Menjar

Pla de Palau 7 (93 310 60 01). Metro Barceloneta or Jaume I. **Open** 1.30-4pm, 9-11.30pm Mon-Thur, Sun; 1.30-4pm, 9pm-midnight Fri, Sat. **Average** €€. **Credit** AmEx, DC, MC, V. **Map** p345 C4.

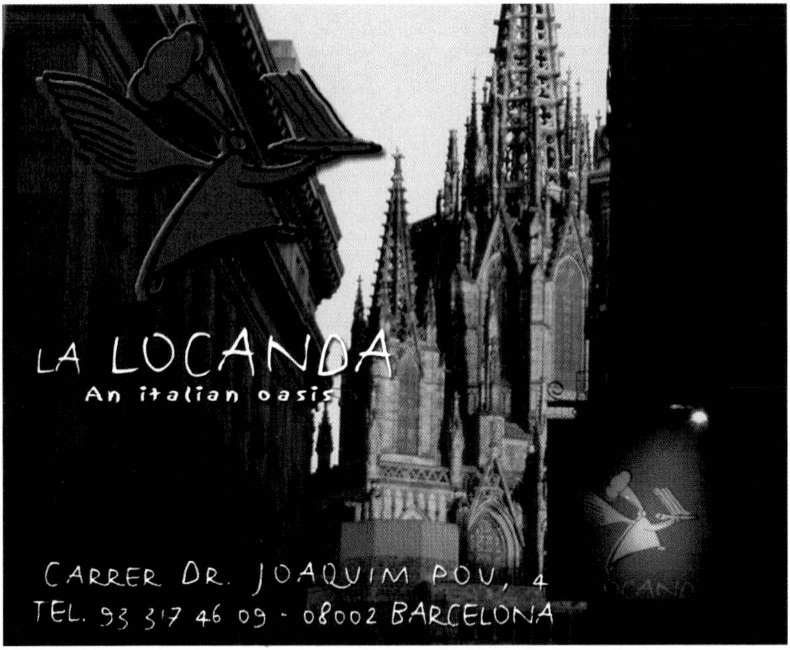
LA LOCANDA
An italian oasis
CARRER DR. JOAQUIM POU, 4
TEL. 93 317 46 09 - 08002 BARCELONA

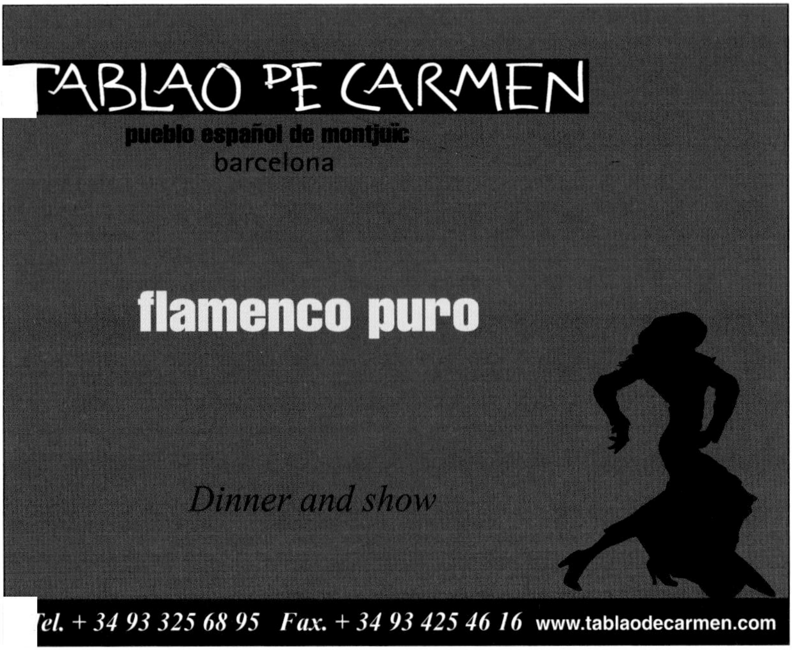
TABLAO DE CARMEN
pueblo español de montjuïc
barcelona
flamenco puro
Dinner and show
Tel. + 34 93 325 68 95 Fax. + 34 93 425 46 16 www.tablaodecarmen.com

The trademark quirkiness includes waiters in white pyjamas, flowers cut out of tin cans and cutlery candlesticks. The menu (which comes glued to a wine bottle) is almost a match: 'arm of a dark gypsy' translates to black pudding cannelloni, while 'classic pop rock' is a terrine (resembling, presumably, a rock) of octopus (*pop* in Catalan) with chilli sauce. At over 400 entries, the wine list is no light read either. For a cheaper experience, the lunch menu offers simpler fare for a third of the price – come early for a table on the summer terrace.

L'Econòmic

Plaça Sant Agustí Vell 13 (93 319 64 94). Metro Arc de Triomf. **Open** 12.30-4.30pm Mon-Fri. Closed Aug. **Average** €. **No credit cards**. **Map** p344 C2.

In some restaurants you go to eat, and in others you go to refuel. While L'Econòmic sidles into the latter category, the dining room is very charming: deep and narrow, lined with colourful tiles and oil paintings. The cheapest lunch deal around covers vegetable or fish soup, broad beans with ham and lettuce hearts with tuna to start, followed by unadorned fried pork or minute steak, lemon chicken, cod croquettes or fried hake. Getting hold of a table after 2pm is something of an ordeal.

Espai Sucre

C/Princesa 53 (93 268 16 30). Metro Jaume I. **Open** 9-11.30pm Tue-Sat. Closed Aug. **Average** €€€. **Credit** MC, V. **Map** p345 C3.

A diabetic deathtrap, the minimalist 'Sugar Space' is almost completely devoted to desserts. In Jordi Butrón's hands, 'soup' means lychee, celery, apple and eucalyptus juice while 'salad' is small cubes of spicy milk pudding resting on sticks of green apple with baby rocket leaves, peppery caramel – pause for a deep breath – dabs of kaffir lime and lemon curd with toffee squiggles. There are also familiar faces such as vanilla cream with coffee sorbet and caramelised banana. Every dish comes with a recommendation for an accompanying wine.

Mundial Bar

Plaça Sant Agustí Vell 1 (93 319 90 56). Metro Arc de Triomf or Jaume I. **Open** 11am-4pm, 8.30-11.30pm Tue-Fri; noon-4pm, 8.30pm-midnight Sat; noon-3.30pm Sun. Closed 2wks Aug. **Average** €. **Credit** MC, V. **Map** p344 C2.

Since 1925 this venerable family establishment has been dishing up no-frills platters of seafood, cheeses and the odd slice of cured meat. Colourful tiles and a marble trough of a bar add charm to rather basic decor, but it's not as cheap as it looks. People come for the steaming piles of fresh razor clams, shrimp, oysters, fiddler crabs and the like, but there's also plenty of tinned produce, so check the bar displays to see exactly which is which.

Passadís del Pep

Pla del Palau 2 (93 310 10 21). Metro Barceloneta. **Open** 1.30-3.30pm, 9-11.30pm Mon-Sat. Closed 3wks Aug. **Average** €€€€. **Credit** AmEx, DC, MC, V. **Map** p345 C4.

Acquired tastes

This little piggy

...went to market, along with the lamb and the calf, and so did their tongues (*llengues*), testicles (*turmes*), trotters (*peus*), brains (*cervellets*), snouts (*morros*), ears (*orelles*), tripe (*tripa*), cheeks (*galtes*), sweetbreads (*lletonets*) and bellies (*ventres*).

Rabbit face

Don't be surprised when a tiny jawbone, complete with teeth, fetches up in your rabbit casserole. This dates back to the days when rabbit was sold by the wriggling sackful, and unscrupulous traders might sneak in the odd cat. Thumper's gnashers are put into the pot to reassure you that you didn't get the one with the whiskers. Which brings us to...

Roast cat

OK, it's been a good couple of hundred years since anyone has eaten *gat rostit* round here, but should you wish to try one of Europe's earliest recipes, Coleman Andrew's fabulous *Catalan Cuisine* tells you how, and advises you to discard the brains. It is said they have the power to make men crazy .

Kokotxas

A Basque speciality, *kokotxas* are membranes found in the throats of cod and hake, with an elusive gelatinous texture, like licking a snail trail. Generally served with garlic and parsley, they are an expensive and rare delicacy. Long may they remain so.

Vichy Catalan

Ask for sparkling water in Barcelona and you will generally get Vichy Catalan. Laden with minerals it has a metallic tang, but its slight saltiness does grow on you. Should it not grow on you, it is at least good for you. Or tastes like it is.

Sea cucumbers

In fact the *espardenya* tastes just like very pricey squid, but its lifestyle choices are a little harder to swallow. It self-eviscerates when panicked, apparently, and, according to the *Oxford Companion to Food*, houses small fishes in its anus, which survive by 'nibbling at the host's gonads'. Bon appétit.

It's dinner at the captain's table in the classy yet convivial environs of this seafood restaurant, tucked down a long white corridor (which is unmarked, next to La Caixa). The complete lack of written menu (and, consequently, of prices) is not for wallet watchers, but if you can afford to play lucky dip with the bill, then follow the suggestions of the charming waiters and wait for a parade of superb shellfish, paellas and armadillo-sized lobsters all accompanied by the decent cava included in the price (which hovers at around €75 a head).

El Pebre Blau

C/Banys Vells 21 (93 319 13 08). Metro Jaume I. **Open** 8.30pm-midnight daily. **Average** €€. **Credit** MC, V. **Map** p345 C3.

This is a breathless gastronomic globetrot of Turkish lamb kebabs, Moroccan tajines, Indian curry, Greek salad and Mexican mole. The salad selection alone covers ten different countries. Stone floors and arches are warmed with buttery yellow lighting, and Born socialites wearing overly interesting spectacle frames nibble at goat cheese *timbal* with caramelised endives or peruse a large section entitled 'All we can do with a duck' – this includes sautéing its livers with sherry and apples or dousing it with banana, chocolate, yucca and ginger.

Other locations: L'Ou Com Balla C/Banys Vells 20, Born (93 310 53 78).

Pla de la Garsa

C/Assaonadors 13 (93 315 24 13). Metro Jaume I. **Open** 8pm-1am daily. **Average** €€. **Credit** AmEx, MC, V. **Map** p345 C3.

The antique-collector owner has graced this 16th-century dairy with a wrought-iron spiral staircase, painted mirrors and rustic tiling, not to mention some rather delicious food. One of the city's best wine lists complements fabulous pâtés, confit of duck thighs, sausages and Catalan goat's cheeses. Of the various taster menus, the €19 variety might include flat *coca* bread with *alboronia* (ratatouille); croquettes of courgette, beer and sea urchin; almogrote cheese; garum terrine and lamb *botifarra*.

Senyor Parellada

C/Argenteria 37 (93 310 50 94). Metro Jaume I. **Open** 1-3.45pm, 8.30-11.45pm Mon-Sat. **Average** €. **Credit** AmEx, DC, MC, V. **Map** p345 B3.

Senyor Parellada has been around forever, but after a makeover a couple of years back it now serves smaller dishes at lower prices, with only a slight dip in quality. Tasty Catalan favourites include plenty of seafood, or the ferociously good *xai a les dotze cabeces d'all* (lamb with 12 heads of garlic). Paellas and *fideuàs* are where the changes become more obvious, though, as those are not dishes that benefit from mass production.

Taberna Santa Maria

C/Abaixadors 10 (93 310 30 96). Metro Jaume I. **Open** 1-4pm Mon; 1-4pm, 9-11.30pm Tue-Fri; 1-4pm, 9pm-12.30am Sat. **Average** €. Set lunch €7.50 Mon-Fri. **Credit** AmEx, DC, MC, V. **Map** p345 B4.

An olde Castilian tavern straight from central casting, with bare bricks, Gothic arches and heavy iron chandeliers. The menu is completely in keeping, with a long, long list of *carnes a la brasa*, as well as boards of cheese and ham. Various good lunch deals involve thick soups (*caldo gallego* is a winner, with pork and cabbage), and maybe peppers stuffed with hake or roast pork knuckle (*codillo*) to follow. Puddings run the usual gamut of eggy comfort food. The real surprise is the wine list, which includes some top-of-the-range bottles from La Rioja and Ribera del Duero.

International

Bunga Raya

C/Assaonadors 7 (93 319 31 69). Metro Jaume I. **Open** 8pm-midnight Tue-Sun. **Average** €. **No credit cards. Map** p345 C3.

Expats flock to the tiny, bamboo-lined 'hibiscus flower' for the excellent Malaysian taster menu: a pile of coconut rice with curried squid rings, beef rendang, fried peanuts with coconut shavings, spicy pineapple, marinated beansprout salad, chicken and beef satay, and a bowl of chicken curry. Other good dishes include curried anchovies and a chokingly spicy shrimp tom yam soup, but avoid the uninspired vegetable dishes and puds. There is an airier room upstairs, but what you gain in space, you lose in waiter attentiveness.

El Celler de Macondo

C/Consellers 4 (93 319 43 72). Metro Jaume I. **Open** *Apr-Oct* 1pm-1am daily. *Nov-Mar* 6pm-1am Mon, Tue, Thur-Sun. **Average** €. **Credit** AmEx, DC, MC, V. **Map** p345 B4.

Macondo was the name of the imaginary village in *One Hundred Years of Solitude*, fans of which will recognise myriad other references from the butterflies on the menus to the names of the dishes. A speciality is 'arepizzas', made with an *arepa* (a Latin American corn cake) base and a variety of toppings. Ciabattas heaped high and generous salads are also good to pick at while sharing a bottle of intelligently sourced wine – the list is an interesting read, with plenty of Chilean and Argentinian offerings.

Dionisus

Avda Marquès de Argentera 27 (93 268 24 72). Metro Ciutadella. **Open** 1.30-4pm, 8pm-midnight Mon-Thur; 1.30-4pm, 8pm-12.30am Fri, Sat, Sun. **Average** €€. Set lunch €9 Mon-Fri. Set dinner €19.95 Mon-Fri. **Credit** MC, V. **Map** p345 C4.

Bottles of golden retsina filter the light like stained glass on to the Aegean blue walls at this excellent Greek restaurant. Filled pittas are served at the bar and and on the parkside terrace tables, while inside, diners go for the set lunch. À la carters should split a huge *pikilia megali* of houmous, *dolmadakia* (stuffed vine leaves), feta, tsatsiki and taramasalata, followed by *souvlaki* (skewers) of steak and seafood and lemon-roast potatoes. Finish off with halva or Greek yoghurt with honey.

Irrepressibly eccentric: **Coses de Menjar**. *See p149*.

Other locations: C/Torrent de l'Olla 144, Gràcia (93 237 34 17); C/Comte d'Urgell 90, Eixample (93 451 54 17).

Gente de Pasta

Passeig de Picasso 10 (93 268 70 17). Metro Ciutadella. **Open** 1-4pm, 9pm-midnight Mon-Wed, Sun; 1-4pm, 2pm-12.30am Thur-Sat. **Average** €€. Set lunch €9 Mon-Thur. **Credit** MC, V. **Map** p345 C3.

The look is high ceilings, chisel-jawed DJs, austere silver paint and dramatic spotlighting: loved by the under-25s and viewed a bit suspiciously by everybody else. By day the sunlight streams in, however, and the lunch menu offers a far happier deal than eating à la carte at night. A tangle of rocket with honeyed viniagrette and thick pats of mozzarella to start, perhaps, then a velvety rigatoni with mushrooms and ham. Carrot cake transpires to be simply carrot-coloured cake, but then again, most of the assembled Lolitas and their beaux don't do pudding anyway.

Habana Vieja

C/Banys Vells 2 (93 268 25 04). Metro Jaume I. **Open** 1.30-3.30pm, 8.30-11.30pm daily. **Average** €€. **Credit** AmEx, DC, MC, V. **Map** p345 C3.

With a menu that devotes as much space to cocktails as to food, this tiny Cuban restaurant is fun and laid-back, with plenty of *son* and rumba to get the evening going. The sharp taste of limes in the Mojitos and Caipirinhas complement the love-it-or-hate-it parade of Havana cuisine, which involves lots of meat, stodge and frying pans. Rice and beans accompany tender *ropa vieja* (shredded chilli beef), fried yucca with *mojo cubano* (garlic sauce), banana or *malanga* fritters (a taro-like root vegetable) with fresh guava for dessert.

Little Italy

C/Rec 30 (93 319 79 73). Metro Barceloneta or Jaume I. **Open** 1-4pm, 9pm-midnight Mon-Thur, Sun; 1-4pm, 9pm-12.30am Fri, Sat. **Average** €€. Set lunch €11 Mon-Fri. **Credit** AmEx, DC, MC, V. **Map** p345 C3.

The token pasta selection (pistachio gnocchi or penne with 'crystallised' tomato) is overshadowed by trendoid brasserie confections of grouper and crayfish supreme with vanilla oil, truffled beef carpaccio or even a gourmet New York hamburger. The great salads and fresh, if rather fussy food is as immaculately styled as the three-level dining space and the international yuppie crowd that grazes there. Live jazz on Wednesday and Thursday nights doesn't hurt either.

Al Passatore

Pla del Palau 8 (93 319 78 51). Metro Barceloneta. **Open** 1pm-12.30am Mon-Wed; 1pm-1am Thur-Sun. **Average** €. **Credit** MC, V. **Map** p345 C4.

No Gianni-come-lately, this chain – now with eight branches – completely dominates the market for budget Italian food. The service is entirely charmless but nowhere is faster – within ten minutes of ordering there's a pizza the size of a tractor tyre on

your plate. Cooked in an authentic Neapolitan wood-fired oven, they come in a whopping 40 varieties and not one of them costs over €9. Unfortunately, the rest of the food can be mediocre, with limp, watery salads and cheap cuts of meat.
Other locations: throughout the city.

Eixample

Alkimia

C/Indústria 79 (93 207 61 15). Metro Sagrada Família. **Open** 1.30-3.30pm, 9-11pm Mon-Fri; 9-11pm Sat. Closed 2wks Aug. **Average** €€€. **Credit** AmEx, DC, MC, V. **Map** p339 E3.
An excellent wine cellar and richly diverse menu comprising creative collages of taste and colour spun off from Catalan and Provençal standards make this a restaurant on the rise. Start with a salad of luxury lettuces, beetroot purée and warm sliced squid, and then expect main courses involving game, wild rice or baked fish in unexpected combinations. A great way to explore is the gourmet menu, with four savoury courses and a couple of desserts.

El Asador de Burgos

C/Bruc 118 (93 207 31 60). Metro Verdaguer. **Open** 1-4pm, 8.30-11pm Mon-Sat. Closed Aug. **Average** €€€. **Credit** AmEx, DC, MC, V. **Map** p339 D4.
If scurvy holds no fear for you, then try a veg-free meat feast from Old Castile. Best partnered with a heavy, potent Rioja, starters include *sopa burgalesa* (beef, potato and egg soup) or various *morcillas* (blood puddings), but the main event is the slow-roast meats, which must be ordered at least three hours ahead of time. Racks of lamb, roast sheep's heads, and whole suckling pigs cooked in wood-fired clay ovens are brought to the table still sizzling on their metal trays.

Astoria

C/Paris 193 (93 414 47 99). Metro Hospital Clínic. **Open** 9.30pm-midnight Mon-Sat. Closed Aug. **Average** €€. **Credit** MC, V. **Map** p338 C3.
Party like it's 1985 in this stunning converted theatre kitted out in red and blue neon and plush, black upholstery. The tables overlook the dancefloor from the glassed-in upper dress circle, and there's no danger of getting too stuffed for a boogie – the Thumbelina portions are clearly designed to maintain the cubist bone structure of the model/hairdresser clientele. What there is, though, is delectable: mango and tiger prawn salad, lobster claws on green beans, steak tartar, or médaillons of prime, pan-fried sirloin. All are a worthy precursor to the hot chocolate soufflé or sweet-and-sour truffles.

Casa Calvet

C/Casp 48 (93 412 40 12). Metro Urquinaona. **Open** 1-3.30pm, 8.30-11pm Mon-Sat. **Average** €€€. **Credit** AmEx, DC, MC, V. **Map** p344 C1.
This elegant restaurant sits inside Gaudí's Casa Calvet, one of his more understated projects, with an interior full of glorious detail in the carpentry, stained glass and tiles. The food is also a delight: modern Catalan dishes such as pea soup with little chunks of squid; smoked foie gras with mango sauce; succulent pigeon with Szechuan pepper and roast fennel, and tasty lamb meatballs with creamy risotto. Puddings are supremely good – try the pine nut tart with foamed *crema catalana* – and the wine list is encyclopaedic.

Cata 1.81

C/València 181 (93 323 68 18). Metro Hospital Clínic or Passeig de Gràcia. **Open** 6pm-midnight Mon-Thur; 6pm-1am Fri, Sat. Closed last 3wks Aug. **Average** €. **Credit** AmEx, DC, MC, V. **Map** p338 C4.
'Cata' means tasting, and is the raison d'être of this brightly lit and slightly austere-looking little place. Oenophiles flock to try 25cl decanters of whatever takes their fancy from the impressive wine list, with saucer-sized portions of food: dinky little hamburgers with tiny cones of chips, salted foie with strawberry sauce; miniature parcels of cheese and tomato, and treacly pigs' trotters with figs, walnuts and honey ice-cream. Hugely popular among Catalan gastronomic luminaries, who, sadly, also seem to get the best of the service.

Noti

C/Roger de Llúria 35 (93 342 66 73). Metro Passeig de Gràcia or Tetuan. **Open** 1.30-4pm, 8.30pm-midnight Mon-Fri; 8.30pm-midnight Sat. **Average** €€€. Set lunch €24.61 Mon-Fri. **Credit** AmEx, DC, MC, V.
At the very cutting edge of the vanguard, Noti is at once wildly glamorous and deadly serious about its food. Centrally positioned tables surrounded by reflective glass and gold panelling make celebrity-spotting unavoidable, but myriad other reasons for coming here include a rich and aromatic fish soup with velvety rouille; lobster carpaccio with crispy seaweed; smoky hunks of seared tuna, and a succulent lamb brochette with spiced couscous and spring vegetables. Modern jazz gives way to house as the night progresses and the restaurant becomes a bar for the city's most gorgeous.

El Racó d'en Baltà

C/Aribau 125 (93 453 10 44). FGC Provença/Metro Diagonal. **Open** 9-11pm Mon; 1-4pm, 9-11pm Tue-Sat. Closed 3wks Aug. **Average** €€. Set lunch €9 Tue-Fri. **Credit** MC, V. **Map** p338 C4.
This two-floor restaurant with a bar next door offers modern Catalan cuisine in original, vibrant surroundings. The best seats are in the airy upstairs room, where you can enjoy spring lamb in a reduction of brandy and honey, or a herbed goat's cheese salad, followed by a delicious banana *bavarois* trickled with golden syrup. The decor is a bizarre mix of '50s memorabilia (menus are presented on old record sleeves) and artist Steve Forster's sculptures incorporating spray-painted Marigolds and bathplugs. The clientele is generally young and up for it, and the service friendly and informal.

Semproniana

C/Rosselló 148 (93 453 18 20). Metro Hospital Clínic. **Open** 1.30-4pm, 9-11.30pm Mon-Thur; 1.30-4pm, 9pm-midnight Fri, Sat. **Average** €€. **Credit** MC, V. **Map** p338 C4.

The Old Curiosity Shop meets Tate Modern in this incredibly popular former printing house, wall-papered with old leaflets and book pages. The combination of antique furniture with arty mobiles made out of tortured kitchen utensils is as offbeat as the food: turbot with passion fruit and *escopinyes* (cockles); an all-white 'monochrome of cod and chickpeas', or a green salad that comes with a mad scientist's test-tube rack of 14 different aerosol dressings. The chocolate 'delirium tremens' fantasy dessert is not to be missed.

Tragaluz

Passatge de la Concepció 5 (93 487 01 96). Metro Diagonal. **Open** 1.30-4pm, 8.30pm-midnight Mon-Wed, Sun; 1.30-4pm, 8.30pm-1am Thur-Sat. **Average** €€€. Set lunch €21.40 Mon-Fri. **Credit** AmEx, DC, MC, V. **Map** p338 D4.

The stylish flagship for this extraordinarily successful group of restaurants (including Agua, *p163*, and Bestial, *p166*) has weathered the city's culinary revolution well, and is still covering new ground in Mediterranean creativity. Prices have risen a bit, and the wine mark-up is hard to swallow, but there's no faulting tuna tataki with a cardamom wafer and a dollop of ratatouille-like *pisto*; monkfish tail in a sweet tomato *sofrito* with black olive oil, or juicy braised oxtail with cabbage. Finish with cherry consommé or a thin tart of white and dark chocolate. **Other locations**: throughout the city.

Windsor

C/Còrsega 286 (93 415 84 83). Metro Diagonal. **Open** 1.15-4pm, 8.30-11pm Mon-Fri; 8.30-11pm Sat. Closed Aug. **Average** €€€. **Credit** AmEx, DC, MC, V. **Map** p338 D4.

The dishes on offer here are unreconstructed Catalan, consummately executed and wholly dependent on what's in season, from artichoke soup with cod mousse to venison cannelloni with black truffle sauce or pigeon risotto. The list of puddings, each accompanied by different suggestions for dessert wines, is a real highlight. La Selva Negra is a triumphant paean to current vogues – Black Forest gâteau presented as stacked slabs of chocolate cake next to swirls of cherry sorbet and vanilla cream foam. Very postmodern. Very good.

International

Al Diwan

C/València 218 (93 454 07 12). Metro Passeig de Gràcia. **Open** 8-11pm Mon-Thur; 8.30pm-midnight Fri, Sat. Closed Aug. **Average** €€. Set dinner €14.75 Mon-Thur. **Credit** AmEx, DC, MC, V. **Map** p338 C4.

Swagged ceilings, bright wool upholstery and dusky lighting simulate an Ottoman sultan's pleasure tent (*diwan*). It's quiet on week nights, but crowds come for the bejewelled belly dancers on Friday and Saturday nights, as well as the huge range of Lebanese meze including herby green *fattouch* salad, tabbouleh and stuffed vine leaves. After the national dish of kibe, finish off with honey-dripped baklava and a shot of aniseedy arak. Much of this features in an excellent all-day menu for €16.

Thai Lounge

C/València 205 (93 454 90 32). Metro Passeig de Gràcia. **Open** 1.30-4pm, 8-11.45pm Mon-Thurs, Sun; 1.30-4pm, 8pm-12.45am Fri, Sat. **Average** €€. Set lunch €10.72 Mon-Fri. **Credit** MC, V. **Map** p338 D4.

In tones of beige and deep-toasted mahogany, the minimalist interior may look like it's spent too long under the sunlamp but at least the food is done to perfection. Chef Supakan Tangsuwan's delicate rice paste ravioli with shrimp or *homok pla* (hake mousse and red curry in banana leaf origami) are infused with authentic Thai flavours of lemongrass, galangal and *naam pla* (salty fish paste). The set lunch offers good value and, unexpectedly for such a smart place, takeaways are also offered.

Ty-Bihan

Passatge Lluís Pellicer 13 (93 410 90 02). Metro Hospital Clínic. **Open** 1.30-3.30pm Mon; 1.30-3.30pm, 8.30-11.30pm Tue-Fri; 8.30-11.30pm Sat. **Average** €. Set lunch €8.50 Mon-Fri. **Credit** MC, V. **Map** p338 C3.

Functioning both as crêperie and Breton cultural centre, Ty Bihan has chosen a smart, spacious look over wheat sheaves and pitchforks. A long list of sweet and savoury galettes (crêpes made with buckwheat flour) are followed up with scrumptious little blinis – try them smothered in strawberry jam and cream – and crêpes suzettes in a pool of flaming Grand Marnier. The Petite menu takes care of *les enfants*, while a bowl or two of Breton cider takes care of the grown-ups.

Vegetarian

L'Atzavara

C/Muntaner 109 (93 454 59 25). Metro Diagonal or Hospital Clínic. **Open** 1-4pm Mon-Sat. Closed 3wks Aug. **Average** €. Set lunch €8.10 Mon-Fri. **Credit** MC, V. **Map** p338 D4.

Go all out sock-and-sandal at this worthy vegetarian lunch canteen. Despite the non-decor and stalag lighting, the three-course menu is a huge hit with local office workers, and it changes daily; it usually includes items from the vegan/vegetarian canon (alfalfa salads, lasagne, curry, tofu burgers) along with the odd piece of exotica like stuffed cabbage leaves or borscht. The €6.50 *plato combinado* also includes a choice of gooey cakes, pies and puds.

Gràcia

Botafumeiro

C/Gran de Gràcia 81 (93 218 42 30). Metro Fontana. **Open** 1pm-1am daily. **Average** €€€€. **Credit** AmEx, DC, MC, V. **Map** p338 D3.

Alkimia. *See p155.*

Mexi-terranean Cuisine
Evening Food
Bar with drinks and cocktails
basement with
Dj's residents
Shows
dance
RITA BLUE
3, Sant agusti sq. 08001 Barcelona
Hospital St & Ramblas 933424086

Out of China
Home-made Chinese food
Made with patience & excellent raw materials
No monosodium glutamate,
artificial colourings or flavouring
A wide range of vegetarian dishes
Muntaner, 100 (corner València)
08036 Barcelona
93 451 55 55

LITTLE ITALY
RISTORANTE
WEDNESDAY AND THURSDAY NIGHTS
LIVE JAZZ FROM 10:00 PM
LIVE MUSIC PLACE
MEDITERRANEAN GASTRONOMY
Open every day: 13 to 16 h. - 21 to 24 h.
Reservations: 93 319 79 73
Rec, 30. Passeig del Born. Barcelona

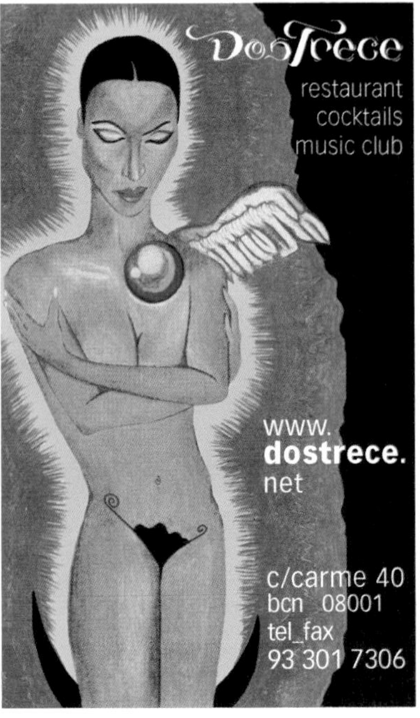
DosTrece
restaurant
cocktails
music club
www.
dostrece.
net
c/carme 40
bcn 08001
tel_fax
93 301 7306

Casa Calvet. *See p155.*

Reports both ecstatic and excoriating fly in on this legendary seafood restaurant, but we found the service excellent and the shellfish divine. The efficiency of the operation is staggering, but is also Botafumeiro's least likeable aspect. Squadrons of waiters wear white jackets with gold nautical trim to match the gilt-edged decor, and every last metre of space put to good use adds to the impersonal experience. However, the juicy lobster and shellfish salad is superbly fresh, as are fish dishes such as baked sea bass smothered in onions, mushrooms, garlic and flat-leaf parsley, or sole in a delicious buttery cava sauce with langoustines.

La Cova d'en Vidalet

C/Torrent d'en Vidalet 22 (93 213 55 30). Metro Fontana or Joanic. **Open** 1.30-3.30pm, 9-11pm Tue-Thur; 9pm-midnight Fri, Sat. Closed 3wks Aug. **Average** €€. Set lunch €6.60 Mon-Fri. **Credit** MC, V. **Map** p339 E3.

A quiet, understated little place with lace curtains, pale yellow walls and a French air to its decor, wonderful service and rich food. Duck breast, foie gras and entrecôte loom large on the menu, alongside monkfish ragoût, hake *en papillote*, partridge and gourmet burgers with Roquefort sauce. The lunch menu is exceptionally good value, if you can judge a place by the olive oil it leaves on the tables, then La Cova d'en Vidalet rates highly indeed.

Envalira

Plaça del Sol 13 (93 218 58 13). Metro Fontana. **Open** 1.30-4pm, 9pm-midnight Tue-Sat; 1.30-5pm Sun. Closed Aug. **Average** €€. **Credit** AmEx, MC, V. **Map** p338 D3.

Old-school Spain lives on as penguin-suited waiters solemnly hand out brown PVC menus at plastic teak effect tables under austere lighting. It's all worth it for the food (as traditionally brown as the decor), which runs the full gamut of hefty Iberian classics. Start with fish soups or lentils and go on to paellas, roast meats and seafood stews, followed by serious, own-made *crema catalana* or *tarta de Santiago*. Arrive early for the leather banquettes at the front.

Folquer

C/Torrent de l'Olla 3 (93 217 43 95). Metro Diagonal or Verdaguer. **Open** 1-4pm, 9-11.30pm Mon-Fri; 9-11.30pm Sat. Closed 3wks Aug. **Average** €€. Set lunch €9 Mon-Fri. **Credit** AmEx, DC, MC, V. **Map** p338 D3.

For anyone not artsy or Catalan or preferably both, walking into Folquer feels a little intrusive. Filled with an animated and older clientele, it is ultimately a welcoming space, however, with daffodil yellow wood panelling and huge splashy artworks. Inventive food is well executed and reasonably priced, never more so than in the various lunch deals: the 'Executive' is a sturdy main, such as entrecôte, with a salad, pudding and wine for €11, while the normal *menú* is cheaper and still creative, with a gourmet hamburger and wild mushrooms, or *suquet de pop* (octopus stew).

Jean Luc Figueras

C/Santa Teresa 10 (93 415 28 77). Metro Diagonal. **Open** 1.30-3.30pm, 8.30-11.30pm Mon-Sat. **Average** €€€€. **Credit** AmEx, DC, MC, V. **Map** p338 D4.

Spend it like Beckham at this superb Michelin-starred restaurant set in the palatial old atelier of fashion deity Balenciaga. Designer handbags rest on tiny tapestry stools as diners tuck into silver spoonfuls of Figueras' innovative Catalan-French cuisine. This might include fresh foie on fig bread with a reduction of anisette and ratafia, fried prawn and ginger pasta in mango and mustard sauce, or sea bass with cod and black pudding. Desserts, such as the parfait of peanuts and the caramelised banana with milk chocolate sorbet, are sumptuous combinations of temperature and texture.

Menu glossary

Essential terminology

Catalan	Spanish	
una cullera	*una cuchara*	a spoon
una forquilla	*un tenedor*	a fork
un ganivet	*un cuchillo*	a knife
una ampolla de	*una botella de*	a bottle of
una altra	*otra*	another (one)
més	*más*	more
pa	*pan*	bread
oli d'oliva	*aceite de oliva*	olive oil
sal i pebre	*sal y pimienta*	salt and pepper
amanida	*ensalada*	salad
truita	*tortilla*	omelette
(note: ***truita*** can also mean trout)		
la nota	*la cuenta*	the bill
un cendrer	*un cenicero*	an ashtray
vi negre/ rosat/blanc	*vino tinto/ rosado/blanco*	red/rosé/ white wine
bon profit	*aproveche*	Enjoy your meal
sóc vegetarià/ana diabètic/a	*soy vegetariano/a diabético/a*	I'm a vegetarian diabetic

Cooking terms

a la brasa	*a la brasa*	char-grilled
a la graella/ planxa	*a la plancha*	grilled on a hot metal plate
a la romana	*a la romana*	fried in batter
al forn	*al horno*	baked
al vapor	*al vapor*	steamed
fregit	*frito*	fried
rostit	*asado*	roast
ben fet	*bien hecho*	well done
a punt	*medio hecho*	medium
poc fet	*poco hecho*	rare

Carn i aviram/Carne y aves/ Meat & poultry

ànec	*pato*	duck
bou	*buey*	beef
cabrit	*cabrito*	kid
conill	*conejo*	rabbit
embotits	*embotidos*	cold cuts
fetge	*higado*	liver
gall dindi	*pavo*	turkey
garrí	*cochinillo*	suckling pig
guatlla	*codorniz*	quail
llebre	*liebre*	hare
llengua	*lengua*	tongue
llom	*lomo*	loin (usually pork)
oca	*oca*	goose
ous	*huevos*	eggs
perdiu	*perdiz*	partridge
pernil (serrà)	*jamón serrano*	dry-cured ham
pernil dolç	*jamón york*	cooked ham
peus de porc	*manos de cerdo*	pigs' trotters
pichón	*colomí*	pigeon
pintada	*gallina de Guinea*	guinea fowl
pollastre	*pollo*	chicken
porc	*cerdo*	pork
porc senglar	*jabalí*	wild boar
vedella	*ternera*	veal
xai/be	*cordero*	lamb

Peix i marisc/Pescado y mariscos/Fish & seafood

anxoves	*anchoas*	anchovies
bacallà	*bacalao*	salt cod
besuc	*besugo*	sea bream
caballa	*verat*	mackerel
calamarsos	*calamares*	squid

Laurak

C/Granada del Penedès 14-16 (93 218 71 65). FGC Gràcia. **Open** 1-4pm, 9-11.30pm Mon-Sat. **Average** €€€. **Credit** AmEx, DC, MC, V. **Map** p338 D3.

When Basques aren't eating or forming gastronomic societies, they're opening restaurants, and sleek, elegant Laurak is one of the finest. Living up to Basque cuisine's legendary reputation, dishes include a heavenly salad of tender pigs' trotters with octopus, caramelised suckling pig with pistachio mousse or a *porrusalda* (cod, potato and leek soup) deconstructed into foams, slices and swirls. The indecisive should try the five-course traditional menu or even the seven-dish taster. Laurak tends to be livelier at lunchtime

Octubre

C/Julián Romea 18 (93 218 25 18). FGC Gràcia or metro Diagonal. **Open** 1.30-3.30pm, 9-11pm Mon-Fri; 9-11pm Sat. Closed Aug. **Average** €€. **Credit** MC, V. **Map** p338 D3.

A lacy, characterful little dining room with only eight tables is presided over by Enric, whose mission in life is to produce good value, inventive Catalan food based on age-old recipes. The menu normally includes *corvall* (very similar to sea bass) on a bed of potatoes, onions and pepper, and occasionally wild mushroom meatballs on a bed of fresh pasta. On very good days there will be tender braised beef with a mustard sauce. *Crema catalana* tart is another regular, and is normally the best of the pudding options.

cloïsses	*almejas*	clams
cranc	*cangrejo*	crab
escamarlans	*cigalas*	crayfish
escopinyes	*berberechos*	cockles
espardenyes	*espardeñas*	sea cucumbers
gambes	*gambas*	prawns
llagosta	*langosta*	spiny lobster
llagostins	*langostinos*	langoustines
llamàntol	*bogavante*	lobster
llenguado	*lenguado*	sole
llobarro	*lubina*	sea bass
lluç	*merluza*	hake
moll	*salmonete*	red mullet
musclos	*mejillones*	mussels
navalles	*navajas*	razor clams
percebes	*percebes*	barnacles
pop	*pulpo*	octopus
rap	*rape*	monkfish
rèmol	*rodaballo*	turbot
salmó	*salmón*	salmon
sardines	*sardinas*	sardines
sípia	*sepia*	squid
tallarines	*tallarinas*	wedge clams
tonyina	*atún*	tuna
truita	*trucha*	trout

(note: ***truita*** can also mean an omelette)

Verdures/Legumbres/Vegetables

albergínia	*berenjena*	aubergine
all	*ajo*	garlic
alvocat	*aguacate*	avocado
bolets	*setas*	wild mushrooms
carbassós	*calabacines*	courgette
carxofes	*alcahofas*	artichokes
ceba	*cebolla*	onion
cigrons	*garbanzos*	chick peas
col	*col*	cabbage
enciam	*lechuga*	lettuce
endívies	*endivias*	chicory
espinacs	*espinacas*	spinach
mongetes blanques	*judías blancas*	haricot beans
mongetes verdes	*judías verdes*	French beans
pastanagues	*zanahorias*	carrot
patates	*patatas*	potatoes
pebrots	*pimientos*	peppers
pèsols	*guisantes*	peas
porros	*puerros*	leek
tomàquets	*tomates*	tomatoes
xampinyons	*champiñones*	mushrooms

Postres/Postres/Desserts

flam	*flan*	crème caramel
formatge	*queso*	cheese
gelat	*helado*	ice-cream
música	*música*	dried fruit and nuts, served with *moscatell*
pastís	*pastel*	cake
tarta	*tarta*	tart

Fruïta/Fruta/Fruit

figues	*higos*	figs
gerds	*frambuesas*	raspberries
maduixes	*fresas*	strawberries
pera	*pera*	pear
pinya	*piña*	pineapple
plàtan	*plátano*	banana
poma	*manzana*	apple
préssec	*melocotón*	peach
prunes	*ciruelas*	plums
raïm	*uvas*	grapes
taronja	*naranja*	orange

Ot

C/Torres 25 (93 284 77 52). Metro Diagonal or Verdaguer. **Open** 2-4pm, 9-11pm Mon-Fri; 9-11pm Sat. Closed 3wks Aug. **Average** €€€€. **Credit** MC, V. **Map** p339 E3.

It's the little extras that make the Ot experience memorable: an olive oil tasting to start; a shot glass of warm cauliflower soup speckled with herring eggs as an amuse-bouche, or the sweet and sour layers of coconut and hibiscus flower foam that accompany the coffee. Such assured cooking is in the hands of a surprisingly young team, working in colourful intimate environs, making for a funky atmosphere to boot. There is no à la carte menu, just a couple of set-price parades of dainty dishes, but these are very safe hands in which to leave yourself; when they say chocolate soufflé needs basil ice-cream, by Jove they're right.

International

Cantina Machito

C/Torrijos 47 (93 217 34 14). Metro Fontana or Joanic. **Open** 1-4pm, 7pm-1.30am daily. **Average** €. **Credit** MC, V. **Map** p339 E3.

One of life's perpetual mysteries is whether Mexican desserts are any good or not, given that no one has ever had room for them. Here, for example, 'your starter for ten' takes on a whole new meaning with the tasty but unfinishable *orden de tacos*, while mains

largely comprise *enmoladas* or *enchiladas* the size of wine bottles, beached next to a sea of thick mole sauce. Talking of wine, the mark-up on Raimat is almost negligible here, while for beer fans there's Coronita or dark, malty Negra Modelo. The tequila shots and Margaritas go without saying.

Figaro

C/Ros de Olano 4 bis (93 237 43 53). Metro Fontana. **Open** 1.30-4pm, 8.30pm-12.30am Mon, Wed-Fri; 1.30-4pm Tue; 8.30pm-12.30am Sat, Sun. **Average** €. Set lunch €8.50 Mon-Fri. **Credit** MC, V. **Map** p338 D3.

Romantic on a Tuesday night, crazy on a Saturday, this hip little hole-in-the-wall gets packed out with young couples munching on inexpensive Italian standards. Along with authentic salads and carpaccios, the pasta dishes include salmon tagliatelle or spaghetti ragu. Afterwards, there's panna cotta or *sottobosco* and cheeses include pecorino, gorgonzola, taleggio and fontina, all rounded off with *limoncello* or grappa. Wines are nearly all Italian and not one breaks the €13 barrier.

La Gavina

C/Ros de Olano 17 (93 415 74 50). Metro Fontana. **Open** 1pm-1am Tue-Thur, Sun; 1pm-2am Fri, Sat. Closed 2wks Aug. **Average** €. **No credit cards. Map** p338 D3.

This lovably kooky neighbourhood restaurant is the last word in thrift-shop chic, where a palimpsest of cherubs, pistols and Barbies passes for decoration. A scrum of young pizza hounds queue outside in the evenings, while inside, perfect thin-crust pizzas (and little else) are speedily served up on paper-covered wooden boards at tiny tables. The wine list is limited to house plonk, and the tiny selection of desserts normally includes a deliciously gloopy tiramisu.

Lahore

C/Torrent de l'Olla 159 (93 218 95 11). Metro Fontana. **Open** 8pm-midnight Mon; noon-4pm, 8pm-midnight Tue-Sun. Closed 2wks Aug. **Average** €. Set lunch €7.50 Mon-Thur. **Credit** MC, V. **Map** p338 D3.

No red flock wallpaper, no tapestries of maharajahs in compromising positions with doe-eyed lovelies, no sitar soundtrack; instead, grey tiling and formica, and a fabulously obliging Pakistani family who will rustle up anything you fancy whether it's on the menu or not. The offer is made redundant by the range of dansak, bhuna, mughlai, korma, biryani and tandoori dishes, alongside a few lesser-known treats.

Mesopotamia

C/Verdi 65 (93 237 15 63). Metro Fontana. **Open** 8.30pm-11.30pm Tue-Sat. **Average** €. Set dinner €25 daily. **No credit cards. Map** p339 D3.

The terracotta and adobe decor gives a *Temple of Doom* effect to Barcelona's only Iraqi restaurant, and you almost expect Indiana Jones to come bursting out from behind the wonderful ziggurat friezes. Owner Pius has done an equally excellent job with the menu, which is based on Arab 'staff of life' foods, such as yoghurt and rice. Best value is the enormous taster menu, which includes great Lebanese wines, a variety of dips for your *riqaq* bread – such as *tamr wa laban* (toffee-sweet date sauce with onion, cumin and walnuts) – aromatic roast meats, sticky baclawa and Arabic teas.

San Kil

C/Llegalitat 22 (93 284 41 79). Metro Fontana or Joanic. **Open** 1-4pm, 8.30pm-midnight Mon-Sat. Closed 2wks Aug. **Average** €. **Credit** MC, V. **Map** p339 E3.

If you've never eaten Korean before, it pays to gen up before you head to this bright and spartan little restaurant. *Panch'an* is the ideal starter: four little dishes containing vegetable appetisers, one of which will be tangy *kimch'i* (fermented cabbage with chilli). Then try mouth-watering *pulgogi* – beef served sizzling at the table and eaten rolled into lettuce leaves, and maybe *pibimbap* – rice with vegetables (and occasionally meat) topped with a fried egg. Just as you're finishing up with a shot of *soju* rice wine, the Korean telly sparks up and it's time to move on.

Vegetarian

L'Illa de Gràcia

C/Sant Domènec 19 (93 238 02 29). Metro Diagonal. **Open** 1-4pm, 9pm-midnight Tue-Fri; 2-4pm, 9pm-midnight Sat, Sun. Closed 2wks Aug. **Average** €. Set lunch €5.75 Tue-Fri. **Credit** DC, MC, V. **Map** p338 D3.

This rather stern-looking vegetarian restaurant has something of a modern prison canteen about it, with exposed brick and black plastic furniture. Porridge is off the menu, though, with 18 generous and interesting varieties of salad, along with tortillas, crêpes, pasta and chef's specials such as seitan with gorgonzola sauce and watercress. Add a great dessert list and you're on to a winner.

Barceloneta & the Ports

Agua

Passeig Marítim 30 (93 225 12 72). Metro Barceloneta. **Open** 1.30-4pm, 8.30pm-midnight Mon-Thur; 1.30-4pm, 8.30pm-1am Fri; 1.30-5pm, 8.30pm-1am Sat; 1.30-5pm, 8.30pm-midnight Sun. **Average** €€. **Credit** AmEx, MC, V. **Map** p343 F7.

Let down by front-of-house chaos that means a long wait even with a booking, Agua is otherwise one of the freshest, most relaxed places to eat in the city, with a large terrace smack on the beach and an animated, sunny interior. The menu rarely changes, but regulars never tire of the competently executed monkfish tail with *sofregit*, the risotto with partridge, and fresh pasta with juicy little prawns. Scrummy puddings include marron glacé mousse and sour apple sorbet. Wine mark-up is quite high for such reasonably priced food; a couple of very notable exceptions are white Creu de Lavit or red Añares.

Knights of the long knives

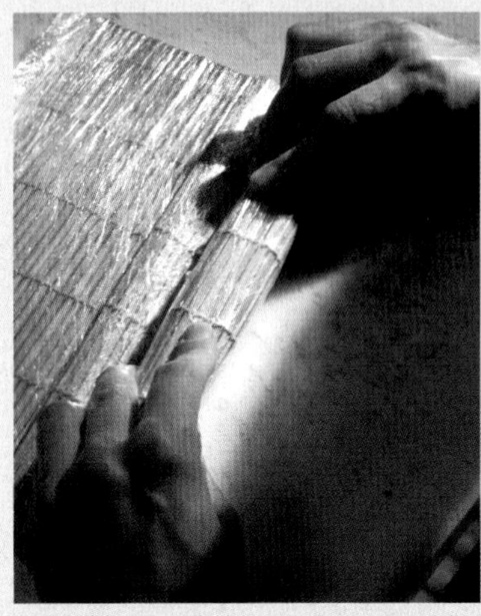

The city is riding a tsunami of tatami-mat minimalism and manga T-shirts nowadays, and along with all the futon shops and karaoke bars, there are now more Japanese restaurants than you can shake a chopstick at. As the antithesis of Catalonia's stout, brown country stews, sushi's sophistication and immaculate presentation mesh perfectly with Barcelona's hi-design urban aesthetic. It has become the fuel of choice for the gym bunny generation and even Catalan menus now include the odd stirfry.

Newcomers to this cuisine, many locals have a shaky grip on the chopsticks and still baulk at the sinus-searing wasabi, so restaurants don't always trouble to keep things completely authentic. As long as you don't expect exotica like beer-fed Kobe beef or blowfish sashimi, however, the following selection is pretty reliable.

One place where you'll see plenty of Japanese customers is **Shunka** (C/Sagristans 5, Barri Gòtic, 93 412 49 91). Book ahead for the sumo-sized €12.60 set lunch of rich miso soup, a leafy salad topped with salmon and punchy vinegar and teriyaki dressing followed by vegetable and shrimp tempura and six pieces of maki and nigiri sushi. For a less crowded experience, try the four-course lunch for €13.90 at **Tokyo** (C/Comtal 20, Barri Gòtic, 93 317 61 80). The muted but charming service makes up for the varnished stone-cladding and the speciality is Tokyo-style edomae (hand-rolled nigiri sushi). It also does a mean sukiyaki of paper-thin beef and vegetables cooked at your table.

If you've a yen to spend some serious euros, then go uptown to **Ken** (C/Benet i Mateu 53, Zona Alta, 93 203 20 44) where the speciality is meat and fish a la plancha. Be sure to get a ringside seat for the fabulous circus of fresh clams or squid being rapidly tossed and juggled over a firebreathing skillet. The nightclub-esque **Taira** (C/Comerç 7, Born, 93 310 24 97) channels Japan through a New York loft with arty kanji script projections, DJs and post-industrial iron furniture. Catwalk-perfect staff serve decent noodle and wok dishes along with a cook-it-yourself *shabu shabu* of beef and vegetables swished about in boiling broth, but don't expect to get much change from €40.

Can Majó

C/Almirall Aixada 23 (93 221 54 55). Metro Barceloneta. **Open** 1-4pm, 8-11.30pm Tue-Sat; 1-4pm Sun. **Average** €€. **Credit** AmEx, DC, MC, V. **Map** p342 D7.

One of the better seafood restaurants hereabouts, famous for its fresh-from-the-nets selection of oysters, scallops, Galician clams, whelks and just about any other mollusc you care to mention. In the summer there's seafood gazpacho while mains include stewy monkfish *suquets*, paellas and, for the flush, elvers (€48) or red Mediterranean lobster (€60 each). The smart yellow and green dining rooms and seafront terrace are packed with better-off tourists and migrant uptowners while harried waiters direct the overspill to the smart (though terrace-less) extension a few doors down at No.19.

Can Maño

C/Baluard 12 (93 319 30 82). Metro Barceloneta. **Open** 8am-4pm, 8-11.30pm Mon-Fri; 8am-5pm Sat. **Average** €. **No credit cards**. **Map** p343 E7.

With roaring telly, fruit machines and tables so cramped the waiters have to frisbee the food at you, this neighbourhood caff is a local institution. Catering principally to hungry local workers, the huge portions of market-fresh cuttlefish, red mullet or bream usually come with chips, although you can request fried tomatoes or aubergine (if you can keep the waiter's attention that long). Arrive early.

Can Solé

C/Sant Carles 4 (93 221 50 12). Metro Barceloneta. **Open** 1.30-4pm, 8-11pm Tue-Sat; 1.30-4pm Sun. Closed 2wks Aug. **Average** €€€. **Credit** AmEx, DC, MC, V. **Map** p343 E7.

Located in an old fisherman's cottage, this lavishly tiled restaurant has been serving traditional harbourside food for over a century. Regulars are usually of port-quaffing age, and tuck into giant red shrimp, wild mackerel, stewed lobster and superb paellas cooked under their noses in the bustling open kitchen. The decor is elegant yet not overboard, with lots of photos of former fans like Santiago Rusiñol and Joan Miró, but the occasionally lackadaisical service can take the edge off the charm.

Ruccula

World Trade Center, Moll de Barcelona (93 508 82 68). Metro Drassanes. **Open** 1.30-4pm, 8.30pm-midnight Mon-Sat; 1-4pm Sun. Closed 3wks Aug. **Average** €€. **Credit** AmEx, DC, MC, V. **Map** p342 C7.

Floor-to-ceiling observation windows dominate this huge restaurant, decorated in corporate beige to resemble a VIP airport departure lounge. This probably constitutes a home from home for the clientele – mostly expense account execs from the surrounding office and hotel complex. The real colour comes with the food, which might include an octopus terrine or smoked salmon ravioli with poached egg and a velouté of fennel and scallops among its starters, while mains showcase top quality meat and fish such as sea bass with artichokes and Jerez vinegar.

Set Portes

Passeig d'Isabel II 14 (93 319 30 33). Metro Barceloneta. **Open** 1pm-1am daily. **Average** €€. **Credit** AmEx, DC, MC, V. **Map** p345 C4.

The eponymous 'seven doors' open on to as many dining salons, all kitted out in elegant 19th-century decor. Long-aproned waiters bring regional dishes, served in enormous portions, including a stewy fish *zarzuela* with half a lobster, a different paella daily (shellfish, for example, or with rabbit and snails), and a wide array of fresh seafood or heavier dishes such as herbed black bean stew with pork sausage and *orujo* sorbet to finish off. There are no reservations, so expect long queues.

El Suquet de l'Almirall

Passeig Joan de Borbó 65 (93 221 62 33). Metro Barceloneta. **Open** 1-4pm, 9-11pm Tue-Sat; 1-4pm Sun. Closed 2wks Aug. **Average** €€. **Credit** MC, V. **Map** p342 D7.

One of the famous beachfront *chiringuitos* that was moved and refurbished in time for the '92 Olympic Games, El Suquet remains a friendly family concern despite the smart decor and mid-scale business lunchers. Fishy favourites range from *xató* salad to *arròs negre* plus a variety of set menus, including the 'blind' selection of tapas, a gargantuan taster menu and, most popular, the *pica-pica*, which includes roast red peppers with anchovies, a bowl of steamed cockles and clams, a heap of *fideuà* with lobster and much more.

Xiringuitó Escribà

Litoral Mar 42, Platja Bogatell, (93 221 07 29). Metro Ciutadella-Vila Olímpica. **Open** *June-Sept* 1-4.30pm, 9-11pm daily; *Oct-Mar* 1-4.30pm Tue-Sun. **Average** €€€. **Credit** MC, V.

An alfresco madhouse in summer, Escribà's prime beachfront terrace is so overcrowded it's a miracle anyone ever gets served, and indeed, sometimes they don't. The food is well worth the wait, though, with the speciality paellas and *fideuàs* complemented by dishes such as sea urchin soup au gratin, vichyssoise

Folquer. *See p159.*

with confit potatoes and vanilla oil or steamed cockles. The desserts, from Barcelona's foremost dynasty of pâtissiers, are never less than stunning.

International

Bestial

C/Ramón Trias Fargas 2-4 (93 224 04 07). Metro Barceloneta. **Open** 1.30-4pm, 8.30pm-midnight Mon-Wed; 1.30-5pm, 8.30pm-1am Thur-Sat. **Average** €€. Set lunch €16 Mon-Fri. **Credit** AmEx, MC, V. **Map** p343 F7.

The architecture here is something to behold; the planes of its low, stark structure extend seamlessly to a tiered wooden terrace on the beach, like a Le Corbusier holiday home. Bestial owes its name both to the peculiar animal-shaped splodges painted on its windows and the Spanish slang for 'fantastic', which is about right, with top-of-the-range Italian food: tuna with black olive risotto; crisp, salted red mullet; rocket salad with Parma ham and a poached egg; fabulous fresh pasta dishes and dainty, wafer-thin '*pizzetas*', followed by own-made tiramisu.

dZi

Passeig de Joan de Borbó 76 (93 221 21 82). Metro Barceloneta. **Open** 1-4pm, 8pm-midnight daily. **Average** €€. Set lunch €8.88 Mon-Fri. **Credit** AmEx, DC, MC, V. **Map** p345 C4.

This peaceful pan-Asian restaurant offers blessed respite from the harbourside mono-diet of paella. dZi's menu includes everything from Chinese dim sum and Cantonese spring rolls to spicy Thai soup and the lightest Japanese vegetable tempura in the city. Service is charmingly sweet and attentive but come early (or book) for the bargain €8.90 set lunch, as the small terrace and interior are quickly commandeered by the local yachting crowd.

Bestial.

Poble Sec & Sants

El Foc

C/Blasco de Garay 8 (93 442 22 53). Metro Parallel or Poble Sec. **Open** 8pm-midnight Mon, Wed-Sat; 1.30-5pm, 8pm-midnight Sun. Closed Sept. **Average** €€. **Credit** AmEx, MC, V. **Map** p341 B6.

It had to happen; the gastropub experience has arrived, and how. No smoky boozer this, but an inviting restaurant with bare-bricked walls, hessian table runners and expansive owners. As well as British cuisine at its protean best – leek and potato soup with chorizo, beef and Guinness pie, chicken curry, pork with tarragon and mushrooms – Mediterranean zest is added with char-grilled onion bread and own-made cheese floating in olive oil, all of it excellent and keenly priced. House wine is a sturdy, reliable Rioja, and the generous Sunday lunch with roast beef and Yorkshire pud is food for the soul.

La Parra

C/Joanot Martorell 3 (93 332 51 34). Metro Hostafrancs. **Open** 8.30pm-midnight Tue-Fri; 2-4.30pm, 8.30pm-midnight Sat; 2-4.30pm Sun. Closed Aug. **Average** €€. **Credit** MC, V. **Map** p341 A4.

Get your pound of flesh and more at this rustic 19th-century coaching inn with a charming vine-covered terrace. The open wood grill sizzles with various parts of goat, pig, rabbit and cow as well as a few more off-piste items such as deer and even foal. Steaks the size of a brontosaurus femur are slapped on to wooden boards and accompanied by baked potatoes, *calçots*, grilled vegetables and *all i oli* with jugs of local wines from the giant barrels.

La Tomaquera

C/Margarit 58 (no phone). Metro Poble Sec. **Open** 1.30-3.45pm, 8.30-10.45pm Tue-Sat. Closed Aug. **Average** €. **No credit cards. Map** p341 E6.

A world of red gingham and bright lighting, where staff will bark instructions at you, many of which are also reproduced on the walls. There is no booking and no telephone, there is only house wine, and there is only *a la brasa* meat – and if you don't like it, you can go elsewhere. *Barcelonins* obviously do like it, for they come in droves to tuck into huge portions of perfectly cooked meat served with weapons-grade *all i oli*.

International

La Bella Napoli

C/Margarit 14 (93 442 50 56). Metro Paral.lel. **Open** 1.30-4pm, 8.30pm-midnight Tue-Sun. **Average** €. **Credit** DC, MC, V. **Map** p341 B6.

Catalan specialities

Many dishes apparently from other cuisines – risotto, *canelons*, *raviolis* – are as entrenched in the Catalan culinary tradition as their own. One name borrowed from the French, that frequently appears on Catalan menus, is foie (as opposed to foie gras; or *fetge/higado* which just means liver), which has come to mean hare, duck or goose liver prepared with liqueur, salt and sugar.

a la llauna literally, 'in the tin' – baked on a metal tray with garlic, tomato, paprika and wine
all i oli garlic crushed with olive oil to form a mayonnaise-like texture, similar to aïoli
amanida catalana/*ensalada catalana* mixed salad with a selection of cold meats
arròs negre/*arroz negro* 'black rice', seafood rice cooked in squid ink
botifarra/*butifarra* Catalan sausage: variants include *botifarra negre* (blood sausage) and *blanca* (mixed with egg)
botifarra amb mongetes/*butifarra con judías* sausage with haricot beans
calçots a variety of large spring onion, available only from December to spring, and eaten char-grilled, with *romesco* sauce
carn d'olla traditional Christmas dish of various meats stewed with *escudella*
conill amb cargols/*conejo con caracoles* rabbit with snails
crema catalana custard dessert with burnt sugar topping, similar to crème brûlée
escalivada/*escalibada* grilled and peeled peppers, onions and aubergine
escudella winter stew of meat and vegetables
espinacs a la catalana/*espinacas a la catalana* spinach fried in olive oil with garlic, raisins and pine nuts
esqueixada summer salad of marinated salt cod with onions, olives and tomato
fideuà/*fideuá* paella made with vermicelli instead of rice
mar i muntanya a combination of meat and seafood in the same dish
mel i mató curd cheese with honey
pa amb tomàquet/*pan con tomate* bread prepared with tomato, oil and salt
picada a mix of nuts, garlic, parsley, bread, chicken liver and little chilli peppers, which is often used to enrich and thicken dishes
romesco a spicy sauce from the coast south of Barcelona, made with crushed almonds and hazelnuts, tomatoes, oil and a special type of red pepper (*nyora*)
samfaina a mix of onion, garlic, aubergine and red and green peppers (similar to ratatouille), often accompanies grilled meat and fish.
sarsuela/*zarzuela* fish and seafood stew
sípia amb mandonguilles/*sepia con albóndigas* cuttlefish with meatballs
suquet de peix/*suquet de pescado* fish and potato soup
torrades/*tostadas* toasted *pa amb tomàquet*
xató salad containing tuna, anchovies and cod, with a *romesco*-type sauce

A vast Gaudí-esque dome of a wood-fired pizza oven greets diners as they arrive, but aside from this the look is a more standard Chianti-in-a-basket trattoria vibe. Welcoming Neapolitan waiters can talk you through the long, long list of antipasti and pasta dishes, while you can't go wrong with the crispy baked pizzas. Portions are generous and everything is very fresh, bar the dull pudding menu of bought-in ice-cream desserts; for the own-made cheesecake and tiramisu you have to ask. Beer is Moretti and wine all-Italian.

Il Golfo di Napoli

C/Lleida 38 (93 423 53 83). Metro Plaça Espanya or Poble Sec. **Open** 1-4pm, 8pm-midnight Mon-Sat. Closed 3wks Aug. **Credit** AmEx, DC, MC, V. **Map** p341 B5.

Once you're past the mournful lobster peering through brackish water in the window and your eyes have adapted to the bright lighting things start to improve dramatically. Run by a family of Neapolitans, Il Golfo di Napoli offers some of the most authentic Italian food around, with fabulous own-made pasta, great crispy pizzas and a range of antipasti that would make meals in themselves.

Horta & Poblenou

Can Travi Nou

C/Jorge Manrique (93 428 03 01). Metro Horta or Montbau. **Open** 1.30-4pm, 8.30pm-midnight Mon-Sat; 1.30-4pm Sun. **Average** €€€. **Credit** AmEx, DC, MC, V.

In summer, diners sit on a vast covered terrace surrounded by dense vegetation, seemingly a million miles from the bustle of the city. In winter, the action (and tables) move inside the huge, beautiful, old farmhouse, perched on a hill above the former village of Horta. The food is traditional Catalan, with speciality *mar i muntanya* dishes, such as *sípia amb mandonguilles* and *cueta de rap amb all torrat* (monkfish tail with toasted garlic) with great traditional puddings that come accompanied by a decanter of dessert wine. Can Travi is difficult to reach by public transport (best to take a cab) but very worth finding.

Gaig

Passeig Maragall 402 (93 429 10 17). Metro Horta. **Open** 1.30-4pm, 9-11pm Tue-Sat; 1.30-4pm Sun. Closed 3wks Aug. **Average** €€€€. **Credit** AmEx, DC, MC, V.

Carles Gaig, to whose family this restaurant has belonged for over 130 years, believes that more than three elements on a plate is too much. But, oh, what elements! From the crayfish tempura *amuse-gueule*, served with a dip of creamed leek salted with a piece of pancetta, through to a shotglass holding layers of tangy lemon syrup, *crema catalana* mousse, caramel ice-cream and topped with burnt sugar (to be eaten by plunging the spoon all the way down), every dish is as surprising and perfectly composed as the last. If you treat yourself to one top-class restaurant in Barcelona, let it be this one.

Els Pescadors

Plaça Prim 1 (93 225 20 18). Metro Poblenou. **Open** 1-3.45pm, 8pm-midnight daily. **Average** €€€. **Credit** AmEx, DC, MC, V.

Smartly dressed members of the Catalan bourgeoisie sit at large, luxuriously laid terrace tables or in one of the two elegant dining rooms to enjoy some of the most imaginatively prepared seafood in the city. The house speciality is succulently fresh

El Foc. *See p166.*

La Venta.

cod, in dishes such as 'green' paella with *kokotxas* (tender throat flesh) or cod with garlic mousseline, while starters include the likes of sautéd green asparagus with foie gras or creamy leek soup with rock mussels. Service is impeccable, as are desserts such as warm fruit 'lasagne' with a chocolate sauce.

Zona Alta

La Balsa

C/Infanta Isabel 4 (93 211 50 48). FGC Avda Tibidabo. **Open** 9-11.30pm Mon; 2-3.30pm, 9-11.30pm Tue-Sat. **Average** €€€. Set lunch €20.33 Tue-Fri. **Credit** AmEx, DC, MC, V.

The location among the mansions of high society; the sniffy parking attendant; the award-winning building amid lush gardens ablaze with geraniums – all of this might lead you to expect fancy forkfuls of minimal food. Not so. The menu, like the restaurant, has a country feel to it, and is more likely to feature enormous portions of Catalan classics than itsy-bitsy polenta bites. On cold winter nights, a log fire crackles, while in summer nowhere is as pretty as the verdant, jasmine-scented terrace.

La Venta

Plaça Doctor Andreu (93 212 64 55). FGC Avda Tibidabo, then Tramvia Blau. **Open** 1.30-3.15pm, 9-11.15pm Mon-Sat. **Average** €€€. **Credit** AmEx, DC, MC, V.

Perched high above the city mayhem, La Venta's Moorish-influenced interior plays second fiddle to the terrace for every season: shaded by day and uncovered by night in summer, sealed and warmed with a wood-burning stove in winter. Complex starters include lentil and spider crab salad; sea urchins au gratin (a must), and langoustine ravioli, filled with leek and foie mousse. Simpler, but high quality mains run from rack of lamb to delicate monkfish in filo pastry with pesto. A millefeuille of red fruits wraps things up nicely.

Vivanda

C/Major de Sarrià 134 (93 205 47 17). Metro FGC Reina Elisenda. **Open** 9-11.30pm Mon; 1-3.30pm, 9-11.30pm Tue-Sat. **Average** €€. Set lunch €11.23 Tue-Fri. **Credit** DC, MC, V. **Map** 337 B1.

As if the peaceful, bosky garden, dappled with sunlight, weren't reason enough to come here, the waiters are completely charming and the chefs skilled. In keeping with the look of the place, starters are a light and healthy bunch, with crisp salads and baby vegetables, but mains are more traditionally Catalan. Oxtail is stuffed with cured duck with shallot 'jam', or there are more straightforward choices of pork with mustard sauce, hake, sea bass, bonito and, bizarrely, ostrich. Try the own-made pistachio ice-cream for a lighter finish.

Out of town

El Bulli

Cala Montjoi (972 15 04 57/www.elbulli.com). By car A7 or N11 north (7km/4.5 miles from Roses)/by train RENFE from Sants or Passeig de Gràcia to Figueres, then bus to Roses, then taxi. **Open** *Apr-June* 8-10pm Wed-Sun. *June-Sept* 8-10pm daily. Closed Oct-Apr. **Average** €€€€. **Credit** AmEx, DC, MC, V.

Darling of the Sunday papers, El Bulli is possibly the most talked-about restaurant in the world today, thus worthy of a mention here, despite its location up on the Costa Brava. There is only a *degustación*, and diners must arrive by 8.30pm if they are to finish the 34 or so courses by midnight. Dinner here is an extraordinary experience, occasionally exalted and frequently frustrating, where the diners are cossetted guinea pigs, their reactions scanned by the maître d' and the great Ferran Adrià himself. Raw quail's yolk in caramelised gold leaf; sautéd rabbit brains with a truffled cigar of veal marrowbone; edible clingfilm peppered with trout's eggs – every dish is as much food for the mind as the stomach. Love it or hate it, €135 was never so memorably spent.

Cafés, Tapas & Bars

Nibble, drink and be merry.

Quimet i Quimet. *See p181.*

The Spanish do not drink to get drunk. If, in Barcelona, you see someone crashing down the street knocking over dustbins and old ladies they will almost certainly be northern European. Which is not to say the locals don't enjoy a tipple. It's not uncommon to chase off the dawn with a *carajillo* (coffee with a shot of brandy), and breakfast in a bar often consists of a *bocadillo* (sandwich) and a glass of red wine. At lunch, too, you'll see plenty of wine drunk, but still no sign of anyone losing their balance or breaking into song. It's all about moderation – Catalans, in particular, can sit on a single drink for the best part of the evening.

THE GRAPE AND THE GRAIN

Generally speaking, if you ask for a *caña* you will be given a draught beer, and if you ask for a *cerveza* you will be given a bottle. A *caña* is usually around half a (UK) pint, and some places also serve *jarras*, which are more like a pint. Damm beer is ubiquitous in Catalonia, with Estrella, a strong lager, the most popular variety. Damm also produces an even stronger lager (Voll Damm) and a dark one (Bock Damm). Shandy (*clara*) is popular, and remains untouched by the stigma it has back home.

Among the wines, Rioja is well known, but in the north of Spain there are many excellent wines from other regions, such as the Penedès in Catalonia, Navarra or El Duero. Most wine drunk here is red (*tinto/negre*), but Galicia produces good whites, including a slightly sparkling and very refreshing wine called *vino turbio*. The Basques have a similar, clearer wine called Txacolí and, of course, Catalonia has its many cavas, running from *semi-sec* ('half-dry', but actually pretty sweet) to *brut nature* (very dry). Well-known Catalan brands such as Freixenet or Codorníu are much cheaper here

CAFFEINE KICKS

Spanish coffee is very strong and generally excellent. The three basic types are *café solo* (*cafè sol* in Catalan, also known simply as '*café*'), a small strong black coffee; *cortado/tallat*, the same but with a little milk; and *café con leche/cafè amb llet*, the same with more milk. Cappuccino has yet to really catch on, and whipped cream as a substitute for foam is not unheard of. Then there's *café americano* (a tall black coffee diluted with more water), and spiked coffee: a *carajillo*, which is a short, black coffee with a liberal dash of brandy. If you want another type of liqueur, you have to specify, such as *carajillo de ron* (rum) or *carajillo de whisky*. A *trifásico* is a *carajillo* with a layer of milk. Decaffeinated coffee (*descafeinado*) is widely available, but specify for it *de máquina* (from the machine) unless you want Nescafé. Decaff is surprisingly popular in Spain and consequently very good.

Tea, on the other hand, is pretty poor. If you cannot live without it, make sure you ask for cold milk on the side (*'leche fría aparte'*) or run the risk of getting a glass of hot milk and a teabag. Basic herbal teas, such as chamomile (*manzanilla*), lime-flower (*tila*) and mint (*menta*), are very common.

GOOD BEHAVIOUR

Except in very busy bars, or when sitting outside, you won't usually be required to pay until you leave. If you have trouble attracting a waiter's attention, a loud but polite '*oiga*' or, in Catalan, '*escolti*', is perfectly acceptable. Tipping is not obligatory, but it's customary to leave a few coins if you've been served at a table. On the vexed question of throwing detritus on the floor (cigarette ends, paper napkins, olive pits and so on), it's safest to keep an eye on what the locals are doing.

Barri Gòtic

Cafés

Arc Café

C/Carabassa 19 (93 302 52 04). Metro Drassanes or Jaume I. **Open** 10am-1am Mon-Thur; 10am-3am Fri; 11am-3am Sat; 11am-1am Sun. **Credit** MC, V. **Map** p345 B4.

Something of a nerve centre for the locals' campaign to save its historic street from the evil developers, this community-spirited café has recently become hugely popular with the expat crowd, particularly at night. By day, it's a great spot for breakfast or lunch, or simply to bask in the shafts of sunlight that pour in during the afternoon.

Bliss

Plaça Sant Just 4 (93 268 10 22). Metro Jaume I. **Open** 11am-midnight Mon-Sat. Closed Aug. **No credit cards**. **Map** p345 B3.

The good-value *menú del dia* is a thing of the past, but there are still daily lunch specials, as well as cakes and sandwiches throughout the day. The sunken lounge area is perfect for frittering away an afternoon, flicking through the selection of magazines. In summer there are also tables outside on the pretty Plaça Sant Just.

Café de l'Opera

La Rambla 74 (93 317 75 85/93 302 41 80). Metro Liceu. **Open** 8.30am-2.15am Mon-Thur, Sun; 8.30am-2.45am Fri, Sat. **No credit cards**. **Map** p345 B3.

Cast-iron pillars, etched mirrors and bucolic murals create an air of fading grandeur now incongruous among the fast-food joints and tawdry souvenir shops. A reasonable selection of tapas are served by attentive bow-tied waiters to a largely tourist clientele. Given the atmosphere (and the opposition), there's no better place for a coffee on La Rambla.

La Cereria

Baixada de Sant Miquel 3-5 (93 301 85 10). Metro Liceu. **Open** 10.30am-12.30pm Mon-Sat. Closed 1wk Aug, 1wk Easter. **No credit cards**. **Map** p345 B3.

Run by a left-leaning co-operative of different nationalities, La Cereria has turned a hippie philosophy into a thriving business. The tiny space and tables outside are always packed with fans of the healthy salads and pasta dishes, milkshakes, herbal teas and fresh juices, all made using fair-trade products.

La Granja

C/Banys Nous 4 (93 302 69 75). Metro Liceu. **Open** *Sept-July* 9.30am-9pm Mon-Fri; 9.30am-2pm, 5-9pm Sat; 5-10pm Sun. *Aug* 9.30am-2.30pm, 6.30-9pm Mon-Sat; 6.30-10pm Sun. **No credit cards**. **Map** p345 B3.

An old-fashioned café filled with yellowing photos and antiques and with its very own section of Roman wall. The tarry-thick hot chocolate and especially the *suis*, topped with whipped cream, will be too much for unaccustomed palates; but the *xocolata amb café*, a mocha espresso, or the *xocolata picant*, with chilli, pack a mid-afternoon energy punch.

Els Quatre Gats

C/Montsió 3 bis (93 302 41 40). Metro Catalunya. **Open** 9am-2am daily. **Credit** AmEx, DC, MC, V. **Map** p344 B2.

Set in a gorgeous building designed in 1897 by Puig i Cadafalch, this is a former hangout of the city's finest artists – including Picasso, who held his first

Terraces

Barri Gòtic

Bliss (*see left*); **Taller de Tapas** (*see p172*); **Vinissim** (*see p172*).

Raval

Bar Kasparo (*see p173*); **Iposa** (*see p175*); **Ra** (*see p175*); **Els Tres Tombs** (*see p175*).

Born

L'Hivernacle (*see p178*); **Tèxtil Cafè** (*see p178*).

Barceloneta

Bar Colombo (*see p181*); **La Miranda del Museu** (*see p181*).

Other areas

Bauma (*see p182*); **Merbeyé** (*see p185*).

exhibition here, and Modernistes Santiago Rusiñol and Ramón Casas, who painted pictures for it. The food served in the adjoining restaurant could be better, but the setting certainly couldn't.

Schilling

C/Ferran 23 (93 317 67 87). Metro Liceu.
Open 10am-2.15am Mon-Sat; noon-2.15am Sun.
Credit (over €12) MC, V. **Map** p345 A3.
Spacious and utterly elegant, with a particularly large gay clientele, Schilling is no longer as fashionable as it once was, although the supercilious waiters appear not to have realised. Nonetheless, it is an unbeatable place for meeting up, and the window seats remain the city's No.1 spot for budding travel writers to scribble in their journals.

Xocoa

C/Petritxol 11 (93 301 11 97). Metro Liceu. **Open** 9am-9pm Mon-Sat; 9am-2pm, 4-9.30pm Sun. Closed Aug. **Credit** V. **Map** p344 A2.
Chocoholics stand drooling at the windows of this buzzing little café and its sister shop next door, while inside ladies take a break from shopping to pick at scrumptious fruit tarts, cheesecake, tarte tatin and all manner of breakfasty pastries: croissants, *magdalenas*, brioche and huge Mallorcan *ensaimadas*. Cocoa (*xocoa*) is put to every available use from fondants to bath oil, and the 'chocolate survival kit' is the perfect gift for the family addict.

Tapas

Bar Celta

C/Mercè 16 (93 315 00 06). Metro Drassanes.
Open noon-midnight Mon-Sat. **Credit** MC, V.
Map p345 B4.
Along with the other *tascas* (traditional tapas bars) along this street, Bar Celta is a sea of screwed-up napkins, cigarette ends and toothpicks, with frighteningly bright lighting and deafening noise levels. For all that, the seafood tapas are good and cheap, and this is one of the most authentic experiences to be had in the increasingly sanitised Barri Gòtic.

Bar Pinotxo

La Boqueria 466-7, La Rambla 91 (93 317 17 31). Metro Liceu. **Open** 6am-7pm Mon-Sat.
No credit cards. Map 344 A2.
Bar Pinotxo may look like an ordinary spit 'n' sawdust market-stall bar, but the number of times Jean Paul Gaultier has been spotted here is perhaps some indication of the kind of food on offer. As well as superfresh tapas (you order it, they nip under the counter and buy it) there are daily specials ranging from duck magret to tuna stew. The queue for a bar stool is subject to an invisible but watertight monitoring system.

Onofre

C/Magdalenes 19 (93 317 69 37/www.onofre.net). Metro Urquinaona. **Open** 10am-12.30am Mon-Sat. Closed Aug. **Credit** DC, MC, V.
Artfully crafted into a stylish tapas restaurant, this long thin space sees a mix of ages and nationalities, drawn together by a love of good food. Generous portions of cheese, charcuterie, ham and carpaccio, (and a superb warm goat's cheese salad with tomato) and anchovy are served with *pa amb tomàquet*.

El Portalón

C/Banys Nous 20 (93 302 11 87). Metro Liceu.
Open 9am-midnight Mon-Sat. Closed Aug.
Credit MC, V. **Map** p345 B3.
When the city council was cleaning up the city in preparation for the Olympics, it demanded that this medieval-stables-turned-*bodega* be renovated. The warning was ignored, much to the regulars' relief, and El Portalón remains a pocket of authenticity, with traditional tapas and pitchers of wine to match.

Taller de Tapas

Plaça Sant Josep Oriol 9 (93 301 8020/www.tallerdetapas.com). Metro Liceu. **Open** noon-midnight daily. **Credit** AmEx, DC, MC, V. **Map** p345 A3.
Perfect for tongue-tied tourists and those who aren't prepared to eat standing three-deep at a bar, this sleek 'tapas workshop' has multilingual menus and plenty of seating, inside and out (but expect a 10% surcharge for out). The tapas are of reliable quality and are occasionally excellent – try the clams with haricot beans or spinach with pancetta and chickpeas.
Other locations: C/Argenteria 51, Born (93 268 85 59).

Txikiteo

C/Josep Anselm Clavé 7 (93 412 4157). Metro Drassanes. **Open** 1-4.30pm, 8pm-midnight Mon, Wed, Thur, Sun; 1-4.30pm, 8pm-1am Fri, Sat.
Credit MC, V. **Map** p345 A4.
A likeable Basque bar with a cider-house look. At €3 for three (plus a glass of Rioja) it would probably be churlish to complain that the *pintxos* weren't very exciting. And anyway perfectly nice food is available from a menu; *porrusalda* is a thick Basque soup with leek and cod, or try the *marmitako*: a stew of bonito, potatoes, onion, tomato and peppers.

Vinissim

C/Sant Domènec del Call 12 (93 301 45 75). Metro Jaume I. **Open** noon-11pm Mon-Thur; noon midnight Fri, Sat; noon-4pm Sun. Closed 2wks Aug.
Credit MC, V. **Map** p345 B3.
Owned by the same people as La Vinateria del Call across the road, and run with the same degree of knowledgeable enthusiasm for wine and good food, Vinissim is the daytime option. Painted in warm funky colours and bathed in sunlight, it also has tables outside on the bright Placeta Manuel Ribé.

Bars

El Bosc de les Fades

Passatge de la Banca 7 (93 317 26 49). Metro Drassanes. **Open** 10.30am-1.30am Mon-Thur, Sun; 11.30am-2.30am Fri, Sat. **No credit cards.**
Map p345 A4.

Time for reflection at the **Taller de Tapas**. *See p172.*

The 'fairies' forest' requires a very particular mood. As you grope in the semi-darkness you might chance upon a pointy-eared elf (an escapee from the nearby wax museum) kneeling in silent prayer at a waterfall. Or perhaps you'd care to sup in the castle kitchen, complete with inglenook and hanging cauldron. A very surreal drinking experience.

Ginger

C/Palma de Sant Just 1 (93 310 53 09). Metro Jaume I. **Open** 7pm-3am Tue-Sat. Closed 2wks Aug, 1wk Jan. **Credit** V. **Map** p345 B3.

Dangerously comfortable buttercup-leather chairs and a soothing mix of lounge and rare groove make Ginger one of the easiest places to while away an evening. An elegant cocktail bar on different levels, it also serves top-notch tapas – try the salmon tartare with horseradish or the wild mushroom filo pastry – and has an impressive selection of mainly Catalan wines by the glass.

Leticia

C/Còdols 21 (93 302 00 74). Metro Drassanes. **Open** 7pm-2.30am Mon, Wed, Thur, Sun; 7pm-3am Fri, Sat. **No credit cards**. **Map** p345 A4.

After a recent refurbishment, Leticia's quirky edge has been lost to a certain cookie-cutter kookiness. The cosy, hidden banquettes have been ripped out and replaced with mismatched chairs and tables, and where fruity vinyl tablecloths once provided wild splashes of colour, the inevitable slide projections have stepped in. It's still very chilled out, however, and there's no faulting the musical eclecticism.

La Palma

C/Palma de Sant Just 7 (93 315 06 56). Metro Jaume I. **Open** 8am-3.30pm, 7-10pm Mon-Thur; 8am-3.30pm, 7-11pm Fri; 7-11pm Sat. Closed 1wk Easter, Aug. **No credit cards**. **Map** p345 B3.

A bastion of old Catalunya, where service can seem brusque, and comes exclusively in Catalan. But this atmospheric old *bodega* has seen them all come and go, from the artists who used to meet here in the '50s to the Mayor's cronies from the nearby city hall who frequent it nowadays. Order some *pa amb tomàquet*, some own-made sausage and some wine from the barrel and be grateful you're not in Starbucks.

Pilé 43

C/Aglà (93 301 30 54/www.asociacioncultural pile.com). Metro Liceu. **Open** 9.30pm-2am Mon-Thur, Sun; 9.30pm-3am Fri, Sat. **No credit cards**. **Map** p345 A3.

From the '70s vinyl chairs and smoked glass coffee tables to the lava lamps and the pendant light fittings, almost everything in this bar is for sale. This is all well and good when it's busy, but at quieter moments there's no shaking off the feeling that you're just drinking in a shop.

Raval

Cafés

Bar Kasparo

Plaça Vicenç Martorell 4 (93 302 20 72). Metro Catalunya. **Open** *May-Aug* 9am-midnight daily. *Sept-Mar* 9am-11pm daily. Closed 2wks Dec/Jan. **No credit cards**. **Map** p344 A2.

A summer proposition (there is no indoor seating), with tables under shady arcades overlooking a playground for the kids. Run by two Australians, Kasparo has good, cheap food – plenty of soups, salads and pasta, curries Thai and Indian, stews and chilli, with tapas and *bocadillos* available all day.

Bar Mendizábal

C/Junta de Comerç 2 (no phone). Metro Liceu. **Open** 8am-midnight daily. **No credit cards**. **Map** p345 A3.

Little more than a colourful pavement stall, Mendizábal has been around for decades. More than two leaning on the bar is a crowd, so best to take a seat at the tables in the tiny square to enjoy fabulous juice combinations, milkshakes and soup, tortilla and *bocadillos*.

Buenas Migas

Plaça Bonsuccés 6 (93 319 13 80). Metro Liceu.
Open 9am-9pm daily. **Credit** MC, V. **Map** p344 A2.
Tables outside sprawl across the square in the shade of acacia trees, while inside has a rustic *Good Life* look, with plenty of pine and Kilner jars, that tells you everything you need to know about the food. Wholesome specialities include focaccia with various toppings, leek and potato or spinach tart, the usual vegetarian-approved cakes – carrot, pear and chocolate brownies – and herbal tea.
Other locations: Baixada de Santa Clara 2, off Plaça del Rei, Barri Gòtic (93 319 13 80); Passeig de Gràcia 120, Eixample (93 238 55 49).

El Café Que Pone Muebles Navarro

C/Riera Alta 4-6 (no phone). Metro Sant Antoni.
Open 6pm-1am Tue-Thur, Sun; 6pm-3am Fri, Sat.
No credit cards. Map p342 C5.
All kinds of furniture are stacked up in the rafters and fill the three long spaces merging on a grand circular bar. The style is battered '90s New York with Almodóvarian touches. Sandwiches and toasted bread are served with smoked salmon with onion and capers or avocado with chicken and dill, alongside more mainstream tapas and cold cuts.

Granja M Viader

C/Xuclà 4-6 (93 318 34 86). Metro Catalunya or Liceu. **Open** 5-8.45pm Mon; 9am-1.45pm, 5-8.45pm Tue-Sat. Closed 1wk Aug. **Credit** AmEx, MC, V. **Map** p344 A2.
The chocolate milk drink Cacaolat was invented in this old *granja* in 1931, and is still on offer, along with strawberry and banana milkshakes, *orxata* (tiger nut milk) and hot chocolate, among other things. It's an evocative, charming place with century-old fittings and enamel adverts, but the waiters will not be hurried. Popular with Catalan families on the way back from picking up the kids, and couples meeting after work.

Iposa

C/Floristes de la Rambla 14 (93 318 60 86). Metro Liceu. **Open** 1pm-2.30am Mon-Sat. **Credit** MC, V. **Map** p344 A2.
On a quiet, traffic-free square, Iposa keeps a row of tables outside throughout the year, while inside is a cosy, orange-walled space with Schiele-esque paintings, chilled-out music and a crowd of relaxed Raval regulars. The mainly Mediterranean food is a bit hit-or-miss, but the prices are unbeatable, especially the €5 lunch deal.

Ra

Plaça de la Gardunya 3 (93 301 41 63/ www.ratown.com). Metro Liceu. **Open** 10am-1am Mon-Sat; 10am-9pm Sun. **Credit** AmEx, V. **Map** p344 A2.
The queues snaking down the wall are becoming a thing of the past as erstwhile fans of Ra's lunch *menú* have despaired at the recent price hike (now €11.50), inexperienced waiting staff and the ill-matched technicolour ingredients increasingly thrown together as main courses. It is still just about worth seeking out, however, for the sunny terrace and the great selection of brunch dishes.

Tapas

Mam i Teca

C/Lluna 4 (93 441 33 35). Metro Sant Antoni.
Open 7.30pm-1am Mon, Wed-Fri; 1.30pm-1am Sat, Sun. **Credit** MC, V. **Map** p342 C5.
The name comes from an old Catalan expression meaning 'food and drink', and sums up the prevailing spirit of this little yellow and green tapas bar. All the usual tapas, from anchovies to cured meats, are rigorously sourced, and complemented by superb daily specials such as organic *botifarra*, pork confit and asparagus with shrimp. Excellent house wines are a robust Navarra or fruity Can Feixes.

Els Tres Tombs

Ronda Sant Antoni 2 (93 443 41 11). Metro Sant Antoni. **Open** 6am-2am daily. **No credit cards. Map** p342 C5.
Long the favoured meeting place for the Sunday morning book market scavengers, with great tapas and a line of tables outside in the sunshine. The *tres tombs* in question are the 'three circuits' of the area performed by a procession of men on horseback during the Festa dels Tres Tombs in January.

Valldonzella 52

C/Valldonzella 52 (mobile 647 643 449). Metro Universitat. **Open** 6pm-1.30am Mon-Thur; 8pm-2am Fri, Sat. Closed 3 wks Aug. **No credit cards.**
Aimed at the young and the funky (without the usual drop in standards that implies), Valldonzella offers a fresh take on tapas in a cosy, bare-bricked space. Try *papas arrugas con mojo picón* ('wrinkled' potatoes with a spicy sauce) or bitter orange biscuit with black sausage and onions, and be sure and leave room for mango cannelloni with mascarpone.

Bars

Bar Pastis

C/Santa Mònica 4 (93 318 79 80). Metro Drassanes.
Open 7.30pm-2.30am Tue-Thur, Sun; 7.30pm-3.30am Fri, Sat. **Credit** AmEx, DC, MC, V. **Map** p345 A4.
A quintessentially Gallic bar, which once served pastis to the visiting sailors and the denizens of the Barrio Chino underworld, this place has moved on, but not too much – it still has a louche Marseilles feel, floor-to-ceiling indecipherable oil paintings (painted by the original owner when drunk), Edith Piaf on the stereo and latterday troubadours most nights of the week.

Boadas

C/Tallers 1 (93 318 95 92). Metro Catalunya.
Open *Jan-June, Sept-Dec* noon-2am Mon-Thur; noon-3am Fri, Sat. *July, Aug* noon-3pm, 6pm-2am Mon-Thur; noon-3pm, 6pm-3am Fri, Sat. **No credit cards. Map** p342 C/D5

Eat, Drink, Shop

Fancy a pint?

Nobody in their right minds goes to southern Europe to throw darts, talk about the match and drink Foster's, do they? Well, yes, it would seem they do. Apparently sometimes a *caña* just isn't big enough, and, regardless of the weather outside or the customs of the land, some people just cannot resist forming groups with alliterative names in order to answer questions about George Lazenby and Jackie Charlton.

Barcelona's cannier innkeepers have been keeping an eye on this phenomenon, and recent years have seen an explosion of British and Irish theme pubs. One of the original and best is the Raval's **Quiet Man** (C/Marquès de Barberà 11, 93 412 12 19), a peaceful place with wooden floors and stalls, which eschews the beautiful game for occasional poetry readings and pool tournaments on its two tables in a backroom.

Finally the pressure of being 'so classic it's practically a stop on the tourist bus' proved too much for this tiny and well-loved cocktail bar, and in 2003 it was declared that to enter you must be appropriately dressed. If do you make the cut, this 1930s institution is elegant and relaxing, with sublimely cool barmen from another era.

Bodega Kenobi

C/Notariat 7 (no phone). Metro Catalunya or Liceu. **Open** 7-11pm Wed, Thur, Sun; 7pm-1am Fri, Sat. **No credit cards. Map** p342 A2.

Endearingly battered but painfully cool, Kenobi offers a long list of cocktails for a song. Coolhunters queue up next to Parka'd indie kids and bespectacled mullets for €3 Daiquiris, amid wallpapered pillars, 1960s tellies, Hawaiian garlands and Alpine snowscapes. Sofas and battered armchairs are there to catch the victims of this permanent happy hour.

Caribbean Club

C/Sitges 5 (93 302 21 82). Metro Catalunya. **Open** 7pm-2am Mon-Sat. Closed Aug. **No credit cards.**

The little sister to Boadas (*see p175*), hidden down a nearby sidestreet and known only to the cocktail cognoscenti. The prices are the same as Boadas', but, as the barmen will whisper conspiratorially, the measures are a dram more generous. The apparently closed door and the tiny space filled with nautical antiques make for a delightfully intimate atmosphere.

Casa Almirall

C/Joaquin Costa 33 (no phone). Metro Universitat. **Open** 7pm-2.30am Mon-Thur, Sun; 7pm-3am Fri, Sat. **No credit cards. Map** p342 C5.

Opened in 1860, the Almirall is the second oldest bar in the city after Marsella (*see p177*). It's a bar for all seasons, with Modernista woodwork, soft lighting and deep sofas giving it a cosy feel in winter, while its glass front opens up for a summer breeze. The jewellery occasionally displayed is for sale.

La Confitería

C/Sant Pau 128 (93 443 04 58). Metro Paral.lel. **Open** 7pm-3am Mon-Sat; 7pm-2am Sun. **No credit cards. Map** p342 C6.

This old sweetshop (*confitería*) has two distinct spaces, hinted at by the incongruous artistic creations (a broken guitar on a bed of coal, to name but

There is Guinness (properly pulled) and Murphy's, but you're as likely to find Catalans here as homesick expats.

The same cannot be said for **P Flaherty** (Plaça Joaquim Xirau, 93 412 62 63), a vast barn on the other side of La Rambla, however. Here you wonder why they bothered importing all the Oirish accoutrements and deep-fried breaded mushrooms, so transfixed are the punters by the behemoth of a plasma screen. This is not so much a pub as a football cinema. Still, there's pub grub for those who want it – bangers and mash, Irish stew, lasagne, filled baked potatoes and an Irish breakfast (like an English breakfast, but sounds healthier), washed down with Guinness and Murphy's.

Over in the Born are a couple of cosier options. The **Clansman** (C/Vigatans 13, 93 319 71 69; *pictured*) wants for nothing in the way of Scottish trappings, from tartan barstools to a decent range of malt whiskies. It recently had its licence for live music temporarily revoked, but a big screen was hastily installed, lest conversation should pall, plus there's a pub quiz on Tuesday nights. Beers include Beamish, Newcastle Brown and Bombardier, and a limited menu offers steak pie, chilli con carne, chicken curry and so on.

Nearby, and flying the flag for St George, is the **Black Horse** (C/Allada-Vermell 16, 93 268 33 38), whose four low-ceilinged, beamy rooms have a TV apiece. This, the bar staff proudly announce, is so that they can show four matches *at the same time!* Still, one man's meat, as they say. As well as a computerised dartboard and a PlayStation, there's a pub quiz every Sunday; John Smith's, Beamish, Boddington, and Tetley's on tap, and plenty of sickly tipples (Bacardi Breezers, Hooch and the like) in the fridge.

The Eixample's 'pubs' are mostly regular bars given wooden panelling and daft names (Bobby's Free, the Daily Telegraph), but the **Philharmonic** (C/Mallorca 204, 93 451 11 53) is worth a mention for its lindy hop on Monday, line-dancing on Tuesday, pub quiz on Wednesday, roast beef on Sunday and live music the rest of the week. The **Michael Collins** (Plaça de la Sagrada Família 4, 93 459 46 26) has captured the collective heart of the expat community, who pack out its three large bars for live Irish music from Thursday to Sunday, three screens of sport and yet more lasagne and curry. By night it can become something of a cattle market, but by day it's a shady oasis into which tourists from the nearby Sagrada Família can retreat for a refreshing six pints.

Eat, Drink, Shop

one) in the etched windows. Out front there is an art nouveau bar, with dusty bottles, old chandeliers and extravagantly carved wooden panelling, and, beyond, a backroom bedecked with modern art installations, but still cosy enough.

Granja de Gavà

C/Joaquín Costa 37 (93 317 58 83). Metro Universitat. **Open** 8am-8pm Mon; 8am-2am Tue, Wed; 8am-3am Thur, Fri; 8pm-3am Sat, Sun. Closed Aug. **No credit cards. Map** p342 C5.

A motley but affable crew hangs out in this old *granja*, known for its Wednesday evening recitals of slightly questionable poetry. The low but constant soundtrack of MOR classics – Phil Collins and Eric Clapton triumphant among them – appeals to an older crowd, but students tend to fill the backroom. Breakfasts are served with fresh fruit juices, milkshakes, and, later on, crêpes and salads.

London Bar

C/Nou de la Rambla 34 (93 318 52 61/ www.londonbarbcn.com). Metro Liceu. **Open** 7.30pm-4.30am Tue-Thur, Sun; 7pm-5am Fri, Sat. **Credit** AmEx, MC, V. **Map** p345 A3.

The London Bar hasn't changed its extravagant look (which is more Modernista than English pub) since it opened in 1910. It's popular among young resident expats and a mixed bunch of party-going *barcelonins*. There are regular live gigs, for which there's no entrance fee, but note that drink prices do go up accordingly.

Marsella

C/Sant Pau 65 (93 442 72 63). Metro Liceu. **Open** 10pm-2.30am Mon-Thur; 10pm-3.30am Fri, Sat. **No credit cards. Map** p345 A3.

A well-loved bar that's been in the same family for five generations. Jean Genet, among other notorious artists and petty thieves, used to come here – attracted, no doubt, by the locally made absinthe, which is still stocked. Dusty, untapped 100-year-old bottles sit in tall glass cabinets alongside old mirrors and faded William Morris curtains, and chandeliers loom over the cheerful, largely foreign crowd.

Merry Ant

C/Peu de la Creu 23 (no phone). Metro Sant Antoni. **Open** 9pm-2.30am Wed, Thur; 9pm-3am Fri, Sat. **Admission** free. **No credit cards. Map** p340 C5.

From the street, the mesmerising womblike glow of the red walls glimpsed through an extraordinary jumble of wooden furniture parts makes the Merry Ant slightly disturbing but very beguiling. Once inside, the ambience is nothing but friendly, however. Birds of all feathers gather under mobiles of hand-printed knickers, lightshades made of picnic cutlery, and plastic ants stapled to the walls.

Oddland

C/Joaquín Costa 52 (mobile 665 520 094). Metro Universitat. **Open** 7pm-2am Tue-Thur, Sun; 7pm-3am Fri, Sat. Closed 2wks Aug. **No credit cards**.
Small and unprepossessing from without, Oddland sure lives up to its name inside. The loos are especially whacky, with pebbles on the floor, a profusion of plastic ivy and Astroturf, an 'inspirational' blackboard with coloured chalks for your graffiti and cartoon characters aplenty. The bar serves great sandwiches, herbal teas, cheap cocktails and has listening posts for you to check out their favourite CDs.

Sifó

C/Espalter 4 (93 329 68 32). Metro Liceu. **Open** 9pm-2.30am Mon-Thur, Sun; 9pm-3am Fri, Sat. **No credit cards**. **Map** p342 C6.
There's a nod to every current Raval vogue (retro wallpaper, egg boxes on the ceiling, '70s lamps and trippy slide projections) along with rows of the eponymous soda siphons in this scruffy but likeable new bar. It doesn't really come into its own until the witching hour, however, much to the chagrin of the waterbombing neighbours.

Sant Pere & the Born

Cafés

Café Stockholm

C/La Ribera 12 (93 319 23 72). Metro Jaume I. **Open** 10am-1am Mon-Thur, Sun; 10am-2.30am Fri, Sat. **Credit** MC, V. **Map** p345 C4.
With missionary zeal, Café Stockholm reveals the wonders of Swedish cooking from this tranquil little spot beside the Born market. If you've never tried cured reindeer, this is where to start (it's exquisite), but there are also some of the best salads around, as well as gravadlax, own-made rye bread and other Scandinavian delights. An unbeatable lunch deal offers two courses and a drink for €5.

L'Hivernacle

Parc de la Ciutadella (93 295 40 17). Metro Arc de Triomf. **Open** 10am-midnight daily. **Credit** AmEx, DC, MC, V. **Map** p343 E6.
Sitting in the elegant late 19th-century iron and glass palmhouse at the entrance to the Ciutadella park, L'Hivernacle has three parts (one shaded room, one unshaded and a terrace). Occasionally, there are exhibitions and classical concerts, and – more frequently – live jazz bands. The food is nothing exciting, but kids are catered to, which makes this a perfect stop after the zoo or the rowing boats.

Tèxtil Cafè

C/Montcada 12-14 (93 268 25 98/www.textil cafe.com). Metro Jaume I. **Open** 10am-midnight Tue-Sun. **Credit** MC, V. **Map** p345 C3.
In the courtyard of a graceful 14th-century palace (which now houses the textile and Barbier-Mueller museums) is this peaceful oasis, an elegant place for a coffee in the shade, or under gas heaters in winter, with decent breakfast and lunch menus. The array of newspapers improves the lot of those waiting to be served, which can take forever.

Tapas

Euskal Etxea

Placeta Montcada 1-3 (93 310 21 85). Metro Jaume I. **Open** *Bar* 11.30am-4pm, 7pm-midnight Mon-Sat; 12.45-3.30pm Sun. *Restaurant* 1-4pm, 8.30-11.30pm Tue-Sat. Closed Aug. **Credit** AmEx, MC, V. **Map** p345 C3.
Doubling as a Basque cultural centre, Euskal Extea was one of the first *pintxo* bars in the city, and is still one of the best. Platters laden with dainty Basque morsels appear on the bar pre-lunch and dinner, while the restaurant at the back offers a good *menú del día*. It's worth asking for Txacolí wine just to see it poured from a height.

Mosquito

C/Carders 46 (93 268 75 69/www.mosquito tapas.com). Metro Arc de Triomf. **Open** 7pm-1am Wed-Thur, Sun; 7pm-2.30am Fri, Sat. **Credit** MC, V. **Map** p345 C3.
Heralding (say we) a turnaround in the fortunes of the hitherto unfashionable neighbourhood of Sant Pere, this new and fabulous tapas bar serves the very best Indian food in the city. Scrumptious little dishes from the subcontinent and elsewhere in Asia include spicy lentil fritters and sublime potato chaat for the veggies, mini skewers of chicken tikka for the cautious and pork with noodle cakes for the epicures.

Bars

Bar Upiaywasi

C/Allada-Vermell 11 (93 268 01 54). Metro Arc de Triomf or Jaume I. **Open** 6pm-2am Tue-Thur, Sun; 6pm-3am Fri, Sat. **No credit cards**. **Map** p345 C3.
Vibrant South American colours wash the walls and ceiling, Moroccan kilim cushions sit on baroque sofas, and candles flicker on the tables and drip from sconces on the walls. Thrown into the melting pot are Peruvian and Italian owners and – more prosaically – John Smith's bitter.

Espai Barroc

C/Montcada 20 (93 310 06 73). Metro Jaume I. **Open** 8pm-2am Tue-Sat; 6-10pm Sun. **Credit** MC, V. **Map** p345 C3.
A spectacular bar housed deep within the 17th-century Palau Dalmases (step through the heavy wooden doors to the back of the courtyard). Baroque

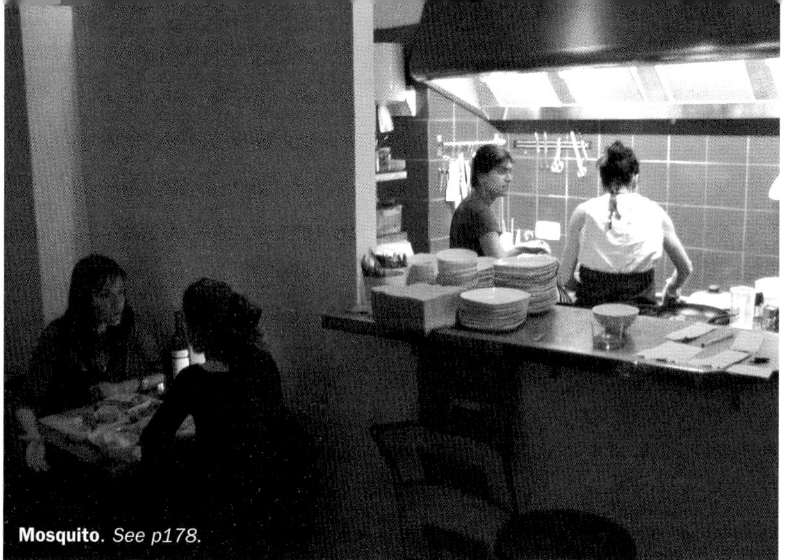

Mosquito. *See p178.*

furniture and paintings and displays of flowers, fruit and aromatic herbs give it the look of an Italian still life. Classical music enhances the experience, never more so than with Thursday night's live opera.

La Fianna

C/Banys Vells 15 (93 315 18 10). Metro Jaume I. **Open** 7pm-2am Mon-Thur; 7pm-3am Fri, Sat; noon-6pm, 7pm-2am Sun. **Credit** AmEx, MC, V. **Map** p345 C3.

Bedouin chic has swept across town like a sirocco wind, but La Fianna has made most dramatic use of it. Enter through heavy wooden doors into a high-arched medieval space, ablaze with diaphanous curtains, chandeliers and cushions, cushions everywhere. This Gothic seraglio also offers a reasonable selection of Mediterranean food in the evenings, and brunch from noon on Sundays.

Miramelindo

Passeig del Born 15 (93 310 37 27). Metro Jaume I. **Open** 8pm-2.30am Mon-Thur; 8pm-3am Fri, Sat; 7.30pm-2.30am Sun. **No credit cards**. **Map** p345 C3.

It's ironic that Miramelindo is considered such a Barcelona classic, and yet if you added a swirly carpet you'd have a London pub; mirrors, lots of wood, a fireplace of sorts, tables jostling for space and people three-deep at the bar. A short cocktail list and aproned waiters give it a little Mediterranean pzazz.

Mudanzas

C/Vidrieria 15 (93 319 11 37). Metro Jaume I. **Open** 10am-2.30am Mon-Thur, Sun; 10am-3am Fri, Sat. **Credit** AmEx, V. **Map** p345 C3.

An unpretentious and welcoming bar, with marble-topped tables and chequered tiled floor. There's a rack of newspapers and magazines, many in English, and some tables outside. In winter it's best to sit up on the mezzanine to avoid the smoky fug that pervades downstairs.

Supersanta

C/Sant Antoni del Sombrerers 7 (no phone). Metro Barceloneta or Jaume I. **Open** 6pm-midnight Mon-Thur; 6pm-2am Fri; 8pm-2am Sat; 6-10pm Sun. **No credit cards**.

Swathes of chicken wire hold pink satin slippers, silver coffee pots, feather boas, a mannequin's leg and diamante clutch bags, while Gothic chandeliers dripping with wax squat next to birdcages erupting with lurid plastic flowers, and empty gilt picture frames sit wonkily amid a collage of wallpapers. There is also beer, although this seems somehow incidental to the experience.

Va de Vi

C/Banys Vells 16 (93 319 29 00). Metro Jaume I. **Open** 6pm-1am Mon-Wed, Sun; 6pm-2am Thur; 6pm-3am Fri, Sat. **Credit** MC, V. **Map** p345 C3.

Run by an artist who has a taste for wine and an eye for Gothic extravagance, Va de Vi, with its 16th-century arches, candles and heavy drapery, mixes atmospheric sophistication with relaxed informality. The wine list includes numerous unusual bottles, many of which are available in a small tasting measure (*cata*), and accompanying tapas are of an equally high standard.

La Vinya del Senyor

Plaça Santa Maria 5 (93 310 33 79). Metro Barceloneta or Jaume I. **Open** noon-1am Tue-Thur; noon-2am Fri, Sat; noon-midnight Sun. **Credit** AmEx, DC, MC, V. **Map** p345 C4.

An elegant, timeless little wine bar with tables outdoors from which to contemplate the splendid lines of Santa Maria del Mar. Along with a superb and frequently changing list of more than 300 wines and selected cavas, sherries and *moscatells*, a huge number available by the glass, there are top-drawer tapas. The selection of five cheeses is one of the best you'll find anywhere.

CAREFULLY
SELECTED
AND PREPARED
· fusion food · creative tapas
· wines · cocktails · music
PREMIER
PROVENÇA 236
08008 BARCELONA
TEL. 93 532 1650
5 min. from the Pedrera
· Closed Mondays

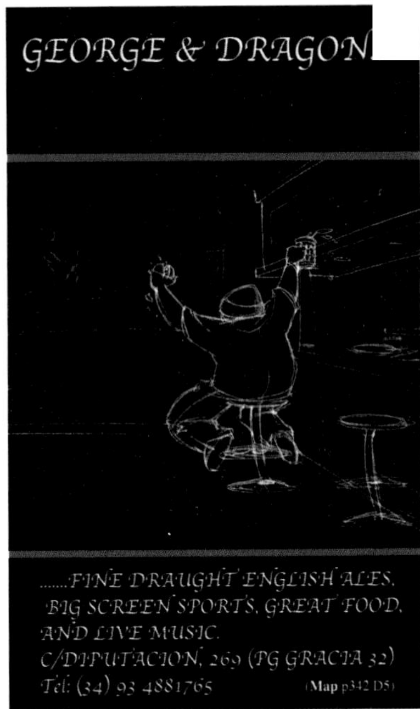
GEORGE & DRAGON
......FINE DRAUGHT ENGLISH ALES,
BIG SCREEN SPORTS, GREAT FOOD,
AND LIVE MUSIC.
C/DIPUTACION, 269 (PG GRACIA 32)
Tel: (34) 93 4881765
(Map p342 D5)

ménage
à trois
Alternative café
Terrace
Music
Creative food
House beer
brewed on premises
C/ d'En Bot, 4 (Pl. Vila de Madrid)
Tel. 93 301 55 42
Metro Pl. Catalunya Open 9.30am-2.30am

THE CLANSMAN
TV satellite for all sports.
Open every day 6pm-3am
c/ Vigatans 13 · BCN · Tel 93 319 7169
[near the Picasso Museum]
Port
Museu
Picasso
Montcada
Vigatans
Esquirol
Argenteria
Metro
Jaume I
Princesa
Via Laietana
Cathedral

El Xampanyet

C/Montcada 22 (93 319 70 03). Metro Jaume I. **Open** noon-4pm, 6.30-11.30pm Tue-Sat; noon-4pm Sun. Closed Aug. **Credit** MC, V. **Map** p345 C3.

Run by the same family since the 1930s, this little 'champagne bar' is one of the eternal attractions on this ancient street. It's lined with coloured tiles, barrels and antique curios, and there are a few marble tables; nearly always full. El Xampanyet has three specialities: anchovies, fresh cider and 'champagne' (a pretty plain cava, if truth be told, but very refreshing all the same).

Barceloneta & the Ports

Cafés

La Miranda del Museu

Museu d'Història de Catalunya, Plaça Pau Vila 3 (93 225 50 07). Metro Barceloneta. **Open** 10am-7pm Tue-Sat; 10am-2.30pm Sun. **Credit** MC, V. **Map** p345 C4.

In a city well known for its wonderful views, this top-floor café has one of the best, especially as the sun sinks down behind Montjuïc, bathing the city in a lustrous orange glow. The enormous terrace is perfect for young children to let off steam, and there is also a great value set lunch. You don't need a museum ticket; just take the lift to the top floor.

Tapas

Bar Colombo

C/Escar 4 (93 225 02 00). Metro Barceloneta. **Open** noon-3am daily. Closed 2wks Jan-Feb. **No credit cards. Map** p342 D7.

Deckshod yachties and moneyed locals stroll past oblivious to this unassuming little bar and its sunny terrace overlooking the port. In fact, nobody much seems to notice it, which is odd given its fantastic location and generous portions of *patatas bravas*. The only drawback is the nerve-jangling techno that occasionally fetches up on the stereo.

Can Paixano

C/Reina Cristina 7 (93 310 08 39). Metro Barceloneta. **Open** 9am-10.30pm Mon-Sat. Closed 3wks Aug/Sept. **No credit cards. Map** p345 C4.

It's impossible to talk, get your order heard or move your elbows, and yet the 'Champagne Bar', as it's invariably known, has a global following. People from every nation will tell you they discovered it first. Its narrow, smoky confines are permanently mobbed with Catalans and adventurous tourists making the most of dirt-cheap house cava and sausage *bocadillos* as necessary ballast (indeed you can't buy a bottle without a couple). A must.

La Cova Fumada

C/Baluard 56 (93 221 40 61). Metro Barceloneta. **Open** 8.30am-3.30pm Mon-Wed, Sat; 8.30am-3.30pm, 6-8.45pm Thur, Fri. **No credit cards.**

This cramped, chaotic little *bodega* is the birthplace of the potato *bomba*, served with a chilli sauce. Here, when they say spicy, they mean spicy. Especially tasty are the chickpeas with morcilla sausage, roast artichokes and marinated sardines. It needs no sign, and its enormous popularity with lunching workers means it's hard to get a table much after 1pm.

El Vaso de Oro

C/Balboa 6 (93 319 30 98). Metro Barceloneta. **Open** 9am-midnight daily. Closed Sept. **No credit cards. Map** p343 E7.

Its charm lies in the decor – like a bar on some down-at-heel 1950s cruise ship, with liveried staff, cramped layout and dark wooden fittings. It's always noisy and bustling and has some of the best tapas in town, especially the *patatas bravas*. Get there early for a seat in the wings, otherwise it's standing room only.

Bars

Port Olímpic has a strip of loud, overpriced, neon-lit bars with little to choose between them. Useful for stag nights, but not a great deal else.

Luz de Gas – Port Vell

Opposite the Palau de Mar (93 209 77 11/www.luzdegas.com). Metro Barceloneta or Jaume I. **Open** *Mar-Oct* noon-3am Mon-Sat; 11am-3am Sun. Closed Nov-Feb. **Credit** AmEx, MC, V. **Map** p342 D7.

Nobody's pretending it's not a bit cheesy, but this boat-cum-bar also has its romantic moments. By day, bask in the sun with a beer on the upper deck, or rest in the shade below. With nightfall, candles are brought out, wine is uncorked and, if you can blot out the Lionel Ritchie songs assailing your good taste, it's everything a holiday bar should be.

Poble Sec

Cafés

Fundació Joan Miró

Parc de Montjuïc (93 329 07 68). Metro Paral.lel, then Funicular. **Open** 10am-7pm Tue-Sat; 10am-2.30pm Sun. **Credit** MC, V. **Map** p341 B6.

One of very few decent places to have lunch or a coffee on Montjuïc, this place lies inside the Miró museum (you don't need to pay the entrance fee). In summer, sit in the grassy courtyard in the company of the artist's goblin ceramics and a bronze female statue, with a good choice of inventive sandwiches (like smoked salmon and avocado with radish sauce) or more substantial dishes at lunchtime.

Tapas

Quimet i Quimet

C/Poeta Cabanyes 25 (93 442 31 42). Metro Paral.lel. **Open** noon-4pm, 7-10.30pm Tue-Sat; noon-4pm Sun. Closed Aug. **Credit** MC,V. **Map** p341 B6.

The most is made of very limited space in this lovely old *bodega*: shelves reaching the ceiling are stocked with dusty bottles of wine, beer, liqueurs and cava, ranging from bargain-basement to the stuff of a connoisseur's dreams. There are only three tables and nowhere to sit, however, and it can get overwhelmingly crowded.

Bars

Bar Primavera

C/Nou de la Rambla 192 (93 329 30 62). Metro Paral.lel. **Open** *Apr-Oct* 8am-10pm Tue-Sun. *Nov-Mar* 8am-7pm Tue-Sun. **No credit cards. Map** p341 B6.

While this is emphatically not a destination bar, it does have its charm, and makes for a perfect pitstop on the climb up Montjuïc. Positioned on the edge of Poble Sec, it has a quiet, vine-covered terrace from which to look back over the city while munching on rather basic *bocadillos*. Winter is a different proposition, however, as there is no indoor seating.

Eixample

Cafés

Bauma

C/Roger de Llúria 124 (93 459 05 66). Metro Diagonal. **Open** 8am-midnight Mon-Fri, Sun. Closed 3wks Aug. **Credit** AmEx, MC, V. **Map** p338 D4.

An old-style café-bar, made for lazy Sunday mornings, with battered leather seats, ceiling fans and an incongruous soundtrack of acid jazz. This is one of few places in the Eixample with pavement seating. Along with well-priced, substantial dishes such as baked cod, wild boar stew and so on, there's an impressive list of tapas and sandwiches.

Café Berlin

C/Muntaner 240-242 (93 200 65 42). Metro Diagonal. **Open** 10am-1.30am Mon-Wed; 10am-3am Thur, Fri; 11am-3am Sat. **Credit** MC, V. **Map** p338 C3.

Downstairs soft, low sofas fill with amorous couples while upstairs all is sleek and light, with brushed steel, dark leather and a Klimtesque red and gold mural. A rack of newspapers and plenty of sunlight make it popular for coffee or snacks all day long; as well as tapas there are salads, pasta dishes, *bocadillos*, cheesecake and brownies, but beware the 20% surcharge for pavement tables.

Laie Libreria Cafè

C/Pau Claris 85 (93 302 73 10). Metro Passeig de Gràcia or Urquinaona. **Open** *Café* 9am-1am Mon-Sat. *Bookshop* 10am-9pm Mon-Sat. **Credit** AmEx, DC, MC, V. **Map** p344 B1.

An airy, spacious covered patio, decorated with photographs of last century's literary giants. There is a buffet breakfast of pastries, eggs, fruit and *bocadillos*, light lunches and more substantial restaurant fare at night. A fantastic selection of teas includes the Marrakech (green tea with fresh mint and pine nuts) and the Bali (black tea with rose petals.)

Tapas

La Bodegueta

Rambla de Catalunya 100 (93 215 48 94). Metro Diagonal/FGC Provença. **Open** 8am-2am Mon-Sat; 6.30pm-1am Sun. Closed 2wks Aug. **No credit cards. Map** p338 D4.

Dwarfed by the swanky designer palaces around it, this almost-subterranean bar is a much-loved classic of the *barrio*, with beautiful old tiles and stacks of charm. It's especially crowded around lunch, with, inevitably, more suits than overalls these days, but evenings see a mixed and cheerful crowd drawn uptown for the excellent tapas.

Casa Alfonso

C/Roger de Llúria 6 (93 301 97 83). Metro Urquinaona. **Open** 9am-1am Mon-Sat. **Credit** AmEx, MC, V. **Map** p344 C1.

Favoured by Catalans of a certain age and income, Casa Alfonso by night is a sea of beige. It has a refined, old-fashioned air; monochrome murals of early 20th-century Barcelona decorate the walls, and glass-fronted cupboards display bottles of oil and wine. The tapas are top quality, as are the cheese and charcuterie served on wooden slabs with hunks of *pa amb tomàquet*.

Cervesería Catalana

C/Mallorca 236 (93 216 0368). Metro Passeig de Gràcia. **Open** 7.30pm-1.30am Mon-Fri; 9pm-1.30am Sat, Sun. **Credit** AmEx, DC, MC, V. **Map** p338 D4.

The Catalan beerhouse lives up to its name with a winning selection of brews from around the world, but the real reason to come is the tapas. A vast array is yours for the pointing – only hot *montaditos*, such as bacon, cheese and dates, have to be ordered from the kitchen. Arrive early for a seat at the bar, and even earlier to sit at one of the pavement tables.

Bars

La Barcelonina de Vins i Esperits

C/València 304 (93 215 70 83). Metro Passeig de Gràcia. **Open** *Sept-June* 6pm-2am Mon-Fri; 7.30pm-2am Sat; 8pm-1am Sun. *July, Aug* 6pm-2am Mon-Fri; 7.30pm-2am Sat. **Credit** AmEx, V. **Map** p339 E4.

A brightly lit little wine bar, unconventional in that it's utterly unpretentious. The TV blares noisily, the clientele are as scruffy as the Eixample allows and you're not expected to know the first thing about wine, meaning there's no finer place to learn. There is also a selection of charcuterie and cheeses.

Dry Martini

C/Aribau 162-6 (93 217 50 72). FGC Provença. **Open** 1pm-2.30am Mon-Thur; 1pm-3am Fri; 6.30pm-3am Sat; 6pm-2.30am Sun. **Credit** AmEx, MC, V. **Map** p342 C5.

El Xampanyet. *See p181.*

All the trappings of a trad cocktail bar are present here – professional bow-tied staff, leather banquettes, the odd drinking antique and wooden cabinets displaying a century's worth of bottles – but none of the stuffiness; the music owes more to trip hop than middle-aged crowd pleasers, and the barmen welcome all comers. Mediterranean and Japanese food is now served at lunchtime in an adjoining dining room.

Santécafé

C/Comte d'Urgell 171 (93 323 78 32). Metro Hospital Clínic. **Open** 8am-3am Mon-Fri; 5pm-3am Sat, Sun. Closed 2wks Aug. **Admission** free. **No credit cards. Map** p336 C4.

Look out for the tangerine dream with goldfish tank windows on the corner of Rosselló. It's filled with a young, bespectacled crowd from the Jarvis Cocker school of cool, nursing cocktails to the tune of Parisian lounge from the Hôtel Costes, funkAfusion, downtempo and deep house. Conceived as a pre-club bar, but very chilled out during the day.

Gràcia

Cafés

Flash Flash

C/Granada del Penedès 25 (93 237 09 90). FGC Gràcia. **Open** 1pm-1.30am daily. **Credit** AmEx, DC, MC, V. **Map** p338 D3.

Opened in 1970, this bar was a design sensation in its day, with its white leatherette banquettes and walls imprinted with silhouettes of a life-size frolicking, Twiggyesque model. They call it a *tortilleria*, with more than 50 variations on the theme, including a handful of dessert tortillas.

Mos

Via Augusta 112 (93 237 13 13). FGC Plaça Molina. **Open** 7am-10pm daily. **Credit** V. **Map** p338 D3.

Oh, that all self-service cafés were like this elegant space. Colourful trays of superb hot and cold dishes that owe nothing to canteen cuisine; delectable

Eat, Drink, Shop

Tackling tapas

Along with bullfighting and flamenco, one of the many and oft-cited differences between Barcelona and other Spanish cities is the dearth of decent tapas bars. Tapas in Catalonia are a pale imitation, where they exist at all, and generally to be found in the bars belonging to immigrants from Andalucía, say, or Galicia. The custom of giving a free tapa, or just a saucer of olives, crisps or nuts, is almost unheard of in Catalonia, and hopping from bar to bar is not as popular as it is in other regions, so consequently a *caña/canya* (draught beer) comes in a larger measure. Instead the Catalans are happier to sit over a bottle of wine in a *llesqueria* – where *llesques* (slices) of *pa amb tomàquet* (bread rubbed with tomato) are served with cold meats and cheese. For convenience these places have been included here under 'Tapas'.

What has really caught on in Barcelona are *pintxo* bars – their Basque origin means that the word is always given in Euskera. A *pintxo* (not to be confused with the Spanish *pincho*, which is simply a very small tapa) consists of some ingenious culinary combination on a small slice of bread. Platters of them are generally brought out at particular times, often around 1pm and again at 8pm. *Pintxos* come impaled with toothpicks, which you keep on your plate, so that the barman can tally them up at the end. (The Brits hold the worst reputation for abusing this eminently civilised system by 'forgetting' to hand over all their toothpicks.)

Without a decent grasp of the language, tapas bars can be quite intimidating unless you know exactly what you want. Don't be afraid to seek guidance, but some of the more standard offerings will include *tortilla* (potato omelette), *patatas bravas* (fried potatoes in a spicy red sauce and garlic mayonnaise), *ensaladilla* (Russian salad), *pinchos morunos* (small pork skewers), *champiñones al ajillo* (mushrooms fried in garlic), *gambas al ajillo* (prawns and garlic), *mejillones a la marinera* (mussels in a tomato and onion sauce), *chocos* (squid fried in batter), *almejas al vapor* (steamed clams with garlic and parsley), *pulpo* (octopus) and *pimientos del padrón* (little green peppers, one or two of which will kick like a mule).

desserts and handmade chocolates. Simply point at what you want: it's weighed, marked on a ticket and you pay at the exit.

Salambó

C/Torrijos 51 (93 218 69 66). Metro Joanic. **Open** noon-2.30am Mon-Thur; noon-3am Fri, Sat. **Credit** MC, V. **Map** p339 E3.

The time-honoured meeting place for Verdi cinema-goers, Salambó is a large and ever so slightly staid split-level café serving coffee, teas and filled ciabatta to the *barri*'s more conservative element. At night those planning to eat are given preference when it comes to bagging a table.

Tapas

Bodega Manolo

C/Torrent de les Flors 101 (93 284 43 77). Metro Joanic. **Open** 9.30am-7.30pm Tue, Wed; 9.30am-11pm Thur, Fri; 12.30-4.30pm, 8.30pm-12.30am Sat; 10.30am-3pm Sun. Closed Aug. **No credit cards. Map** p339 E3.

Another old family *bodega* with a faded, peeling charm, barrels on the wall and rows and rows of dusty bottles, Manolo specialises not only in wine, but in classy food – try the foie gras with port and apple. At the other end of the scale, and also with its place, comes the 'Destroyer' hangover buster: eggs, bacon, sausage and chips. A €7 lunch *menú* can throw up some surprises.

Sureny

Plaça de la Revolució 17 (93 213 75 56). Metro Joanic. **Open** 8.30pm-midnight Tue-Thur; 8.30pm-1am Fri, Sat; 1-3.30pm, 8.30pm-midnight Sun. **Credit** MC, V. **Map** p338 D3.

One of the city's best-kept gastronomic secrets, Sureny boasts superb gourmet tapas and waiters who know what they're talking about. As well as a run-of-the-mill tortilla 'n' calamares, look out for tuna marinated in ginger and soy, partridge and venison in season, and a sublime duck foie with redcurrant sauce.

Bars

Casa Quimet

Rambla de Prat 9 (93 217 53 27). Metro Fontana. **Open** 6.30pm-2am Tue-Sun. Closed Feb, Aug. **No credit cards. Map** p338 D3.

Crumbling portraits and jazz posters cover every inch of wallspace, dozens of ancient guitars hang from the ceiling and ticking clocks compete to be heard over Billie Holliday. This other-worldly 'Guitar Bar' (as it's invariably known) occasionally springs to life with an impromptu jam session, but at other times is a perfect study in melancholy.

La Fronda

C/Verdi 15 (93 415 30 57). Metro Fontana or Joanic. **Open** 8.30pm-12.30am Mon, Wed, Thur, Sun; 8.30pm-2.30am Fri, Sat. Closed Aug. **Credit** MC, V. **Map** p338 D3.

Can Paixano. *See p181.*

As the name suggests, this is a leafy space, with a glassed-in garden at the back. The wicker furniture and travel magazines give it a low-key colonial look. It's a great place to eat after a visit to the Verdi cinema, with a great-value wine list and a selection of tapas. Excellent sandwiches include leek with feta cheese and anchovies, and *sobrassada* (a soft Mallorcan sausage) with honey and emmenthal.

Noise i Art

C/Topazi 26 (93 217 50 01). Metro Fontana. **Open** 6pm-midnight Mon-Thur, Sun; 6pm-2.30am Fri, Sat. **No credit cards. Map** p338 D3.

It's known locally as the 'IKEA bar', which, though some of the plastic fittings do look strangely familiar, doesn't really do justice to its colourful, pop art interior. A chilled and convivial atmosphere is occasionally livened up with a flamenco session, and Gràcia staples such as houmus and tabbouleh are served along with salads and pasta dishes. Mostly, though, it's a great place to sit and shoot the breeze.

Other areas

Bars

Merbeyé

Plaça Doctor Andreu, Tibidabo (93 417 92 79). FGC Avda Tibidabo, then Tramvia Blau/bus 60. **Open** noon-2.30am Mon-Thur; noon-3.30am Fri, Sat; noon-2am Sun. **Credit** MC, V.

A cocktail bar straight from central casting: moodily lit, plush with red velvet and hung with monochrome prints of jazz maestros. In summer there's also a peaceful, stylish terrace. The clientele runs the wealthy gamut from shabby gentility to flashy Barça players and their bling-encrusted wives.

Shops & Services

Seriously bad for your wealth.

This is a city where mega shopping malls co-exist with tiny neighbourhood shops trading in specialities as diverse as felt and coathangers. Where other cities have lost out to impersonal consumerist trends, the Barcelona shopping experience has become a delightful amalgam of the old and the new: buy a box of aspirin at the pharmacy and they still neatly wrap it in blue and white tissue paper; in the flashiest fashion store, browsers still say hello to the assistant when they enter and goodbye when they leave.

Whether steeped in tradition or right on the cutting edge, Barcelona's shops provide key insights into the personality of each district: the glitzy Gucci tribe in uptown **Eixample**, the young designer boutiques of the **Born**, the international chains around the **Plaça Catalunya** and the artisan treasure troves of the **Barri Gòtic** (*see p193* **Neighbourhood watch**). Even the **airport** has taken off as a shopping destination, with a brand new wing of high-street favourites and gift stores.

OPENING HOURS

Little gets going before 10am in Barcelona, and most shops close for a mid-afternoon siesta, so check opening times before a big shopping session. Although large shops and chains soldier through, smaller shops tend to close between about 2pm and 5pm on weekdays and – in a move that seems like financial suicide – quite a few close on Saturday afternoons and Mondays too. Markets open earlier, at 7-8am, and, except for some stalls in the Boqueria (*see p206*), are generally closed by 3pm.

The regulation of Sunday and holiday opening hours is complicated, but, generally speaking, restaurants, bakeries, flower stalls, convenience stores and shops in a tourist zone (like La Rambla or the Maremàgnum) may open seven days a week and nearly all stores open on the four Sundays before Christmas.

SALES, TAX AND REFUNDS

Unless you think of shopping as a contact sport, don't get in the way of the locals on the first day of the sales. *Rebaixes* (or *rebajas*) usually run from the second week in January to the end of February, and during July and August, but it's worth holding out a couple of weeks when there's a bigger markdown for second *rebaixes*, and finally *rematada* (or *remate*) – the final clearance sales.

The rate of sales tax (IVA) depends on the product: seven per cent on food and 16 per cent on most other items. In any of the 700 or so shops that display a Tax-Free Shopping sticker on their door, non-EU residents can request a Tax-Free Cheque on purchases of over €90.15. Before leaving the EU, these must be stamped at customs (in Barcelona airport this is in Terminal A by the Arrivals gate) and can be reclaimed in cash at La Caixa bank, by certified cheque or credited to a card.

Returning goods, even when they are faulty, can be difficult in all but the largest stores. But all shops are required to provide a complaints book (ask for an *hoja de reclamación*). The mere act of asking for it sometimes does the trick, but if not, take your copy of the completed form to the local consumer information office, OMIC (Ronda Sant Pau 43-5, 93 402 78 41/omic@mail.bcn.es), which may be able to help.

Note that if you're paying by credit or debit card in a shop, you have to show photographic ID, such as a passport or driving licence.

GETTING AROUND

Uptown shops are sparsely served by metro but there's a special shopping bus eerily named the **TombBús** (93 415 60 20). *'Tomb'* means 'round-trip' and it runs between Plaça de Catalunya (in front of Banc d'Espanya or El Corte Inglés) and Plaça Pius XII on Avda Diagonal. The blue buses make 28 stops along the way, and a single ticket costs €1.30, while a one-day travelcard is €5.20. Buses leave every seven minutes from 7am to 9.58pm on weekdays, and every 12 minutes from 9am to 9.58pm on Saturdays. Tickets are available on the bus or from tourist offices.

One-stop shopping

Barcelona Glòries

Avda Diagonal 208, Eixample (93 486 04 04/www.lesglories.com). Metro Glòries. **Open** *Shops* 10am-10pm Mon-Sat. **Map** p343 F5.

A sprawling shopping centre that faces a large, café-filled square. Over 200 mall favourites include a Carrefour hypermarket, H&M, Mango, Disney Store and so on. There's a plush multiplex cinema (films are mostly dubbed into Spanish) and kids love the pathways decorated with laser-triggered jets, play areas and entertainment such as bouncy castles, trampolines and live music on Saturday evenings.

BD Ediciones de Diseño is Barcelona's most prominent design centre. *See p192.*

Bulevard Rosa

Passeig de Gràcia 55, Eixample (93 378 91 91/ www.bulevardrosa.com). Metro Passeig de Gràcia. **Open** 10.30am-8pm Mon-Sat. **Map** p338 D4.

Populated by mall mavens and their handbag dogs, this chi-chi uptown arcade has over 100 clothes, jewellery and perfume stores. Ladies who lunch do so in the Jardí del Bulevard restaurant downstairs.

Diagonal-Mar

Avda Diagonal 3, Poblenou (900 90 09 55/ www.diagonalmar.com). Metro Besòs Mar. **Open** 10am-10pm Mon-Sat. *Food court* 10am-1am Mon-Thur, Sun; 10am-3am Fri, Sat. **Map** 343 F5.

Part of the 2004 Fòrum site, this three-level American-style mall is the largest in Catalonia. But despite opening amid great fanfare, Diagonal-Mar has yet to catch on with the public. No doubt this will change during the Fòrum, and as the area's new apartments gradually fill with families, the added custom will make the place feel like less of a ghost town. Big attractions include an 18-screen cinema, Alcampo supermarket, El Corte Inglés and FNAC; the second floor is devoted to fashion from chains such as Zara, Tous and Nine West, while culinary delights (of a sort) lurk on the third floor in places like Dunkin' Donuts and McDonald's.

El Corte Inglés

Plaça Catalunya 14, Eixample (93 306 38 00/www. elcorteingles.es). Metro Catalunya. **Open** 10am-10pm Mon-Sat. **Credit** AmEx, DC, MC, V. **Map** p344 B1.

Ask locals where to buy virtually anything and they are likely to send you here. Spain's only real department store may not be cheap but it's comprehensive, and its services cover everything, from an optician to a travel agent. The Plaça Catalunya branch has nine floors of fashion, beauty and homeware, a seventh-floor café and a supermarket in the basement. The branch on Portal de l'Àngel 19 (93 306 38 00) has six floors of music, electronics, mobile phone services, books and sporting goods.

Other locations: El Corte Inglés Avda Diagonal 471-3, Eixample (93 493 48 00); Avda Diagonal 617, Eixample (93 366 71 00); Hipercor Avda Meridiana 350-8, Sant Andreu (93 346 38 11); C/Salvador Dalí 15-19, Cornella de Llobregat, Outer Limits (93 475 90 00).

L'Illa

Avda Diagonal 545-57, Eixample (93 444 00 00/ www.lilla.com). Metro Maria Cristina. **Open** 9.30am-9.30pm Mon-Fri; 10am-9.30pm Sat. **Map** p345 B3.

This colossal avant-garde iceberg has over 100 big-name shops to attract the crowds, including Mandarina Duck, Bang & Olufsen and Decathlon. There are all manner of fast-food restaurants, a fresh food market on the ground floor and a hypermarket. The rest is taken up by a hotel, offices, a huge park and one of the largest car parks in the city centre.

Maremàgnum

Moll d'Espanya, Port Vell (93 225 81 00/www.mare magnum.es). Metro Drassanes. **Open** 10am-10pm daily. **Map** p342 D7.

A flashy mirrored leisure centre and mall designed by Viaplana and Piñon. In 1995 Maremàgnum's shops, discos, bars, restaurants and rooftop mini-golf course were once *the* places to hang out; nine years on, the gift shops are empty and the place only comes to life at weekends, when families come to visit the cinemas or the aquarium (*see p223*).

Antiques

An antiques market is held in front of the cathedral every Thursday and dealers set up stands at the **Port Vell** at weekends (*see p208*). C/Palla is the main focus for antique shops in the Barri Gòtic, and although they are of variable quality, it is fun to trawl through their dusty backrooms in search of that hidden Picasso. Dazzlingly expensive antiques are found on C/Consell de Cent in the Eixample but don't give up hope – there are more affordable shops around C/Dos de Maig near **Els Encants** fleamarket (*see p208*).

L'Arca de l'Àvia

C/Banys Nous 20, Barri Gòtic (93 302 15 98). Metro Liceu. **Open** 10am-2pm, 5-8pm Mon-Fri; 11am-2pm Sat. **Credit** AmEx, DC, MC, V. **Map** p345 B3.

Wannabe flappers and Gibson Girls will be in heaven at this treasure chest of high quality antique clothes. Look out for exquisite whalebone corsets, beaded silk bags, leg-of-mutton blouses, lace tea gowns and smocked nighties, but be warned that the prices have most definitely moved with the times.

Bulevard dels Antiquaris

Passeig de Gràcia 55, Eixample (93 215 44 99). Metro Passeig de Gràcia. **Open** *Jan-June, Oct-Dec* 10.30am-1.30pm, 4.30-8.30pm Mon-Sat. *July-Sept* 10am-1.30pm, 4.30-8.30pm Mon-Fri. **Credit** AmEx, MC, V. **Map** p338 D4.

Up a discreet stairway next to the Bulevard Rosa, this vast but little-visited arcade houses 73 shops selling all sorts of antiques at all sorts of prices, from exquisite art deco screens to archaeological finds, alabaster Virgin Marys and old tin toys.

Gothsland Galeria d'Art

C/Consell de Cent 331, Eixample (93 488 19 22). Metro Passeig de Gràcia. **Open** 10am-2pm, 4-8.30pm Mon-Sat. **No credit cards. Map** p342 D4-5.

The best of the antique shops in this area, Gothsland specialises in Modernista art with paintings by luminaries such as Santiago Rusiñol, Ramón Casas and Joaquim Mir, along with polychrome terracotta sculptures by Casanovas and alabaster by Cipriani. Another highlight is the original furniture by Gaspar Homar, and the decorative vases and mirrors.

Novecento

Passeig de Gràcia 75, Eixample (93 215 11 83). Metro Passeig de Gràcia. **Open** 10am-2pm, 4.30-8pm Mon-Sat. **Credit** AmEx, DC, MC, V. **Map** p338 D4.

This higgledy-piggledy antique jewellery shop is an anomaly among all the smart fashion stores on this street. Its windows are dripping with bijouterie from all eras including Victorian, art deco and belle époque, plus some glass and silver ornaments.

Bookshops

If you're seeking more in-depth city information than the ubiquitous photo books of Gaudí's greatest hits, try the excellent, multilingual selections at the **Palau de la Virreina** on the Rambla, the Generalitat's **Palau Robert** on Passeig de Gràcia and the shop in the main tourist office on **Plaça Catalunya** (for all, *see p319*). The **MACBA** bookshop (*see p95*) has a good collection of books and magazines (many in English) on architecture, art and culture, while **Laie Libreria Café** (*see p182*) has a more random selection.

Casa del Llibre

C/Passeig de Gràcia 62, Eixample (93 272 34 80/ www.casadellibro.com). Metro Passeig de Gràcia. **Open** 9.30am-9.30pm Mon-Sat. **Credit** AmEx, DC, MC, V. **Map** p338 D4.

This popular chain covers a variety of subjects including literature, anthropology and language learning courses. There's also English-language novels and non-fiction. The website has 500,000 titles.

FNAC

El Triangle, Plaça Catalunya 4, Eixample (93 344 18 00/www.fnac.es). Metro Catalunya. **Open** 10am-10pm Mon-Sat. **Credit** AmEx, MC, V. **Map** p344 A1.

A sweeping book selection and competitive prices ensure that the second floor of this French-owned megastore is always full of browsers. Books in English include a good range of bestsellers and classics, along with travel guides and books for children. There's CDs, DVDs, plasma screens and software, as well as a travel agency, film developing, a concert auditorium and an international newsstand.
Other locations: Diagonal-Mar, Avda Diagonal 3-35, Poblenou (93 502 99 00/50); L'Illa, Avda Diagonal 549, Eixample (93 444 59 00).

Specialist

Altaïr

Gran Via de les Corts Catalanes 616, Eixample (93 342 71 71/www.altair.es). Metro Universitat. **Open** 10am-2pm, 4.30-8.30pm Mon-Sat. **Credit** AmEx, DC, MC, V. **Map** p341 D4.
With a great range of travel books, Altaïr (Arabic for 'that which flies') is the first stop for globetrotters. As well as its stunning magazine, there are maps, anthropology and photography books and world music CDs. Many titles are in English.

BCN Books

C/Roger de Llúria 118, Eixample (93 457 76 92). Metro Passeig de Gràcia. **Open** 10am-8pm Mon-Fri; 10am-2pm Sat. **Credit** MC, V. **Map** p342 D4.
This three-story shop specialises in foreign-language books, including a huge range of titles in English. Stock mainly consists of teaching materials, but there's also a reasonable selection of novels, computer manuals, children's books and so on.
Other locations: C/Rosselló 24, Eixample (93 476 33 43).

Happy Books

Passeig de Gràcia 77, Eixample (93 487 00 31). Metro Passeig de Gràcia. **Open** 9.30am-9pm Mon-Sat. **Credit** AmEx, DC, MC, V. **Map** p338 D4.
This place is especially good for glossy photographic books on art history, cookery and culture. It's cheap and has a cheerfully confusing filing system. Go to the shelves tucked inside the entrance for a fair selection of English-language bonkbusters, Harry Potters and a few quality bestsellers.
Other locations: C/Pelai 20, Eixample (93 317 07 68); Portal de l'Àngel 5, Barri Gòtic (93 302 39 42).

Llibreria Quera

C/Petritxol 2, Barri Gòtic (93 318 07 43/ www.llibreriaquera.com). Metro Liceu. **Open** *Sept-July* 9.30am-1.30pm, 4.30-8pm Mon-Fri; 10am-1.30pm, 5-8pm Sat. *Aug* 10am-1.30pm, 4.30-8pm Mon-Fri. **Credit** MC, V. **Map** p344 A2.
Perfect for outdoorsy types, Llibreria Quera has an ample collection of books (including some that are in English) on everything from rock-climbing to archaeology, bike tours, folklore and mushroom hunting. There are good walking maps that cover the Catalan countryside and Pyrenees, along with every other part of the country, and staff are extremely helpful and well informed.

The best Shops

For dedicated swallowers of fashion
Lydia Delgado (*see p199*); **D409** (*see p193*); **R que R** (*see p196*).

For mall mavens
Diagonal-Mar (*see p187*); **L'Illa** (*see p188*); **El Corte Inglés** (*see p187*).

For your dentist's bank account
Papabubble (*see p203*); **Cacao Sampaka** (*see p202*); **Escribà** (*see p202*).

For frock rockin' flamenco beats
Casa Beethoven (*see p209*); **Discos Castelló** (*see p209*); **Wah Wah Records** (*see p209*).

For haggling
Els Encants (*see p208*); **Brocanters del Port Vell** (*see p208*); **Fira de Santa Llúcia** (*see p221*).

For a Beckham
Anthony Llobet (*see p208*); **La Pelu** (*see p208*).

For aromatic foodstuffs
Formatgeria La Seu (*see p203*); **Casa del Bacalao** (*see p203*); **Casa Gispert** (*see p203*).

For luxe that could kill
Loewe (*see p200*); **Bagués** (*see p199*); **Gothsland Galeria d'Art** (*see p188*).

Norma Comics

Passeig de Sant Joan 9, Eixample (93 244 84 20/www.normacomics.com). Metro Arc de Triomf. **Open** 10.30am-2pm, 5-8.30pm Mon-Thur; 10.30am-8.30pm Fri, Sat. **Credit** V. **Map** p343 E5.
A whole floor of European and US comics, another of Japanese manga, and hundreds of comic spin-offs, such as model kits, T-shirts, videos and posters.

Children

Clothes

The third floor of the Plaça Catalunya branch of **El Corte Inglés** (*see p187*) is devoted to kids. The **Galeries Maldà** (C/Portaferrissa 22) is a small shopping centre with plenty of children's shops. Larger branches of **Zara** (*see p196*) have reasonably priced kids' sections.

Du Pareil au Même

Rambla Catalunya 95, Eixample (93 487 14 49/ www.dpam.com). Metro Passeig de Gràcia. **Open** *Jan-July, Sept-Dec* 10.30am-8.30pm Mon-Sat. *Aug* 10.30am-2.30pm, 5-8.30pm Mon-Sat. **Credit** AmEx, MC, V. **Map** p338 D4.

Affordable well-designed clothes for babies and children up to 14. Young kids love the cords, embroidered berets, mouflon-lined booties and funky backpacks. Traditional *batas* (or pinafores) worn by Spanish primary schoolchildren are also stocked.

Menuts

C/Santa Anna 37, Barri Gòtic (93 301 90 83). Metro Catalunya. **Open** 5-8pm Mon; 11am-1.30pm, 5-8pm Tue-Fri; 11am-8.30pm Sat. **Credit** AmEx, MC, V. **Map** p344 B2.

The most committed child-hater would get broody at the sight of these diddy, handmade baby and toddler outfits in traditional styles: smocked tops, matinée jackets, crocheted hats and dangerously cute bootees. The very tiniest sizes are for dolls.

Prénatal

Gran Via de les Corts Catalanes 611, Eixample (93 302 05 25/www.prenatal.es). Metro Passeig de Gràcia. **Open** 10am-8.30pm Mon-Sat. **Credit** AmEx, DC, MC, V. **Map** p342 D5.

This ubiquitous but rather pricey French-owned chain has buggies, car seats, cots, feeding bottles and toys, plus a downstairs section full of unfrumpy maternity wear and clothes for kids aged up to eight. **Other locations**: throughout the city.

Toys

Drap

C/Pi 14, Barri Gòtic (93 318 14 87). Metro Liceu. **Open** 9.30am-1.30pm, 4.30-8.30pm Mon-Fri; 10am-1.30pm, 5-8.30pm Sat. **Credit** AmEx, DC, MC, V. **Map** p344 B2.

The doll's houses at Drap are probably more luxurious than your own home. Inside is everything a bourgeois doll's heart could desire, right down to tiny hand-carved bars of soap at the bathroom sink.

El Ingenio

C/Rauric 6, Barri Gòtic (93 317 71 38). Metro Liceu. **Open** 10am-1.30pm, 4.15-8pm Mon-Fri; 10am-2pm, 5-8.30pm Sat. **Credit** MC, V. **Map** p345 A3.

This old-fashioned shop is storybook stuff with its kaleidoscope of magic tricks, puppets, party decorations, wigs and juggling batons. The speciality is carnival outfits and masks, which range from warty noses to the pumpkin-like *capgrossos* (big heads).

Shopping tips

The lay of the land in Barcelona's retail jungle:

It's a wrap

Most shops will gift wrap an item for free if you tell them it's a present (*regal/regalo*).

Shrinking assets

This is a nation of shortish people with a mysterious tendency to sell trousers very long in the leg. Most places do on-site alterations, though, and your average chain store charges about €4 for hems with a two-day turnaround.

Smoke gets in your eyes

Be prepared that people think nothing of lighting up between perming rods at the hairdresser's and even in small clothes and music shops, although it is generally frowned upon in larger establishments.

Paying away

Shops will not accept travellers' cheques or even bank cheques as payment.

Bare-faced cheek

Small supply stores often operate on a two-tier price system. Try brazenly asking for *el precio especial* or *el descuento* and you may just get a ten per cent discount.

Try before you buy

Attempts to return or exchange items will usually receive short shrift, even if the items are faulty.

Blue Monday

Avoid shopping at the food markets on a Monday when stocks are low and there's no fish available.

Eat your greens

If you buy a reasonable amount of veggies, market sellers will often throw in a bunch of fresh parsley, mint or coriander for free.

Why are we waiting?

Rather than form an orderly queue at a bakery or market stall, you ask *'¿Qui es l'últim?'* or *¿Quién es el último?'* ('Who is the last?'). Whoever says *'Jo'* or *'Yo'* ('Me') is the one who should be immediately in front of you.

Slow food

Local shopping is very much seen as a social activity with lots of chit-chat and a distinct lack of urgency, so unclench your fists and just enjoy taking 15 minutes to buy that loaf of bread. It'll be worth it in the end.

All the best dolls head to **Drap**, for everything their hearts desire. *See p190.*

Joguines Monforte

Plaça Sant Josep Oriol 3, Barri Gòtic (93 318 22 85). Metro Liceu. **Open** 10am-1.30pm, 4.30-8pm Mon-Sat. **Credit** AmEx, MC, V. **Map** p345 A3.

This venerable old toy shop concentrates on life's quieter pursuits, stocking chess boards, jigsaw puzzles, wooden solitaire and croquet sets, hand puppets, kites and pile upon pile of board games.

Sardina Submarina

C/Cardenal Casanyes 7, Barri Gòtic (93 317 11 79). Metro Liceu. **Open** 10.30am-2pm, 4.30-8.30pm Mon-Sat. **Credit** MC, V. **Map** p345 A3.

A change from the semi-disposable plastic trash that usually passes for kids' toys, these beautiful wooden and fabric items (suitable for babies and children aged under six) include play mats, baby gyms, construction sets, nursery accessories and all manner of traditional Spanish board games.

Cleaning & repair

Any shop marked *'Rapid'* or *'Rápido'* does shoe repairs and key cutting; **El Corte Inglés** department store (*see p187*) also has shoe repair and key cutting in the basement.

La Laundry

C/Escudellers 44, Barri Gòtic (no phone). Metro Drassanes or Jaume I. **Open** 9am-10pm Mon-Sat. **No credit cards**. **Map** p345 B3.

Murky as a cave but redeemed by the friendly polyglot staff, great music and low prices. A self-service wash costs €3 (plus 50¢ for soap). Drop-off service is €7-€12. Internet costs €1 for an hour.

LavaXpres

C/Ferlandina 34, Raval (no phone). Metro Sant Antoni. **Open** 8am-11pm daily. **Map** p342 C5.

This is a fast, no-nonsense and fully automated self-service laundry where an 8kg (17.6lb) wash costs €3.50 and the dryer costs €3.50 for 30 minutes. Prices drop if you buy a LavaXpress club card.

Lavomatic

Plaça Joaquim Xirau 1, Barri Gòtic (93 342 51 19). Metro Drassanes. **Open** 10am-10pm Mon-Sat. **No credit cards. Map** p344 A4.

A funky self-service launderette just off the Rambla, where a 7kg (15lb) load costs €3.75, soap costs 75¢, and five minutes on the dryer cost 75¢. Drop-off service is €10 for collection the next day. The Born branch also offers a dry-cleaning service.

Other locations: C/Consolat del Mar 43-5, Born (93 268 47 68).

Mr Minit

L'Illa, Avda Diagonal 545-57, Eixample (93 419 94 89). Metro Maria Cristina. **Open** 10am-10pm Mon-Sat. **No credit cards**. **Map** p345 B3.

On-the-spot key cutting (from €1.45), shoe repairs (heels from €4.95) and other services such as personalised business cards or number plates, printed signs, rubber stamps and remote control keyrings.

Other locations: throughout the city.

Tintorería Ferran

C/Ferran 11, Barri Gòtic (93 301 87 30). Metro Liceu. **Open** 9am-2pm, 4.30-8pm Mon-Fri. **Credit** V. **Map** p345 A3.

Prices for laundry aren't cheap – 5kg (11lb) washed, dried and folded for the next day costs €15 – but the dry-cleaning service is good value at €10.75 for a man's suit, and €9 for a batch of five shirts. It can also clean awkward items, like rugs and duvets, and has an ironing and home delivery service.

Crafts & gifts

The sombreros and T-shirts of the La Rambla souvenir shops may be fun but they hardly qualify as crafts – you'll find more creative offerings near the big tourist sites such as C/Montcada by the Picasso museum. Some exceptionally good museum gift shops include the **Espai Gaudí** in La Pedrera (*see p121*) with all kinds of quality Gaudíana, from vases to mouse pads and reproduction pavement slabs from Passeig de Gràcia. The **Fundació Joan Miró** (*see p111*) stocks games and calendars in Miró's trademark primary colours, plus a good range of books, as does the **MACBA** (*see p95*), while the **Museu Tèxtil** (*see p101*) is great for quirky jewellery and scarves.

Art Escudellers

C/Escudellers 23-5, Barri Gòtic (93 412 68 01/ www.escudellers-art.com). Metro Drassanes. **Open** 11am-11pm daily. **Credit** AmEx, DC, MC, V. **Map** p345 A-B3.

Artisan Spanish products (mainly ceramics) are presented by region. There are everyday wares, like smashable clay *huchas* (piggy banks) or cooking pots, as well as more exclusive pieces and hundreds of Spanish wines, which can be sampled at the bar. Staff will ship anything that's too heavy to carry.

Baraka

C/Canvis Vells 2, Born (93 268 42 20). Metro Jaume I. **Open** 10am-2pm, 5-8.30pm Mon-Fri; 11am-2pm, 5-8.30pm Sat. **Credit** AmEx, DC, MC, V. **Map** p345 C4.

This dusky shop is stuffed with imported Moroccan leather babucha slippers, lamps, birdcages, tagines and rugs. Smaller items include CDs of Arabic music, books on Moroccan culture, kohl powder, henna, hookah pipe tobacco and incense.

Caixa de Fang

C/Freneria 1, Barri Gòtic (93 315 1704). Metro Jaume I. **Open** 10am-8pm Mon-Sat. **Credit** AmEx, DC, MC, V. **Map** p345 B3.

The fang refers to clay, not teeth, at this ceramics shop that shines with glassware, glazed *azulejos* (tiles), and cup-and-saucer sets inspired by Miró.

Design & household

BD Ediciones de Diseño

Casa Thomas, C/Mallorca 291, Eixample (93 458 69 09/www.bdbarcelona.com). Metro Passeig de Gràcia. **Open** *Sept-July* 10am-2pm, 4-8pm Mon-Fri; 10am-2pm, 4.30-8pm Sat. Closed Aug. **Credit** AmEx, DC, MC, V. **Map** p338 D4.

A Modernista masterpiece by architect Domènech i Muntaner is an appropriately lavish setting for Barcelona's most prominent design centre. Best known for its reproductions of classic pieces by design deities like Jujol or Charles Rennie Mackintosh, this is where a few thousand euros will buy Gaudí's curving Calvet armchair or Dalí's magenta Gala loveseat. The stunning art nouveau space also showcases new designers alongside contemporary big guns such as Javier Mariscal and the shop's co-founder Oscar Tusquets.

Dom

Passeig de Gràcia 76, Eixample, (93 487 11 81/ www.id-dom.com). Metro Passeig de Gràcia. **Open** 10.30am-8.30pm Mon-Fri; 10.30am-9pm Sat. **Credit** DC, MC, V. **Map** p338 D4.

The '70s live on at Dom with lava lamps, mirror-balls, chrome gadgets, PVC furniture and beaded feather curtains. The more upmarket branch in C/Avinyó even has an inflatable personal chill-out room (which basically resembles an outsize football).

Other locations: C/Avinyó 7, Barri Gòtic (93 342 55 91).

Gemma Povo

C/Banys Nous 5-7, Barri Gòtic (93 301 34 76/ www.gemmapovo.com). Metro Liceu. **Open** 10am-1.30pm, 4.30-8pm Mon-Fri; 10am-1.30pm, 5-8.30pm Sat. Closed Aug. **Credit** AmEx, MC, V. **Map** p345 B3.

Wrought iron is the speciality at this family-run artisan shop that has been going for three generations. Iron that is boldly twisted into unusual lamps, tables, bedsteads, wine racks and screens or combined with wicker, wood or glass to stunning effect.

Gotham

C/Cervantes 7, Barri Gòtic (93 412 46 47/ www.gotham-bcn.com). Metro Jaume I. **Open** 10.30am-2pm, 5-8.30pm Mon-Sat. **Credit** DC, MC, V. **Map** p345 B3.

Take a trip down nostalgia lane with Gotham's classic retro furniture dating from the '30s, '50s, '60s and '70s in warm cartoonish colours. Along with plastic moulded chairs, splay-legged cabinets and the like, there are fabulous lamps and bubble TVs.

Ici et Là

Plaça Santa Maria del Mar 2, Born (93 268 11 67/ www.icietla.com). Metro Jaume I. **Open** 4.30-8.30pm Mon; 10.30am-8.30pm Tue-Sat. **Credit** AmEx, MC, V. Closed 2wks Aug. **Map** p345 C3/4.

Quirky and reasonably priced handmade furniture and accessories by 40 artists. Check out the puffball fish lamps and animal furniture by Haillart, the horned and curlicued furniture from Pagart, and embroidered throws from Uzbekistan.

Pilma

C/València 1, Eixample (93 226 06 76/www.pilma.com). Metro Espanya. **Open** 10am-2pm, 4.30-8.30pm Mon-Sat. Closed 2wks Aug. **Credit** AmEx, DC, MC, V. **Map** p338 D4.

Catalonia's answer to Habitat started as a small cabinetmaker's workshop in the 1930s. Now a massive temple to interior design, the gleaming exhibition spaces are scattered with everything from sofas to spatulas by cutting-edge designers from 40 countries. Expect clean lines and minimalism.

Other locations: Avda Diagonal 403, Eixample (93 416 13 99).

Vinçon

Passeig de Gràcia 96, Eixample (93 215 60 50/ www.vincon.com). Metro Diagonal. **Open** 10am-8.30pm Mon-Sat. **Credit** AmEx, MC, V. **Map** p338 D4.

So cool that even its carrier bags are collector's items, Vinçon is the first stop for Catalan interior design. The ground floor is dedicated to lighting, kitchen, bathroom and knick-knacks ranging from a €15 'capitalist piggy bank' to a €184 paperweight

Neighbourhood watch

Vampy, villagey, fancy, sleazy... Barcelona's districts come in every flavour and they've all got the shops to match.

Barri Gòtic

For one-of-a-kind purchases nowhere beats the Barri Gòtic, where narrow streets are crammed with specialist shops that have often been in a family for generations. The city's oldest is **Cereria Subirá** (*see p210*) but other venerable establishments include **Herboristeria del Rei** (*see p211, pictured*), **La Manual Alpargatera** (*see p201*) and **L'Arca de l'Àvia** (*see p188*). Shops that are over 60 years old and have preserved their architectural heritage receive brass plaques from the Ajuntament. The Rambla itself offers a bizarre cocktail of flowers, cockerels, hamsters and porn but is also lined with irresistibly tacky souvenir shops, where you can haggle down football shirts, swords and the like to a reasonable price.

Born

The Born district still has plenty of speciality shops like **Casa Gispert** (*see p203*) or **El Rei de la Magia** (*see p210*), but is increasingly dominated by the almost daily influx of new fashion boutiques such as **Rouge Poison** (*see p202*), **Alea** (*see p199*) or **R que R** (*see p196*). At best these boutiques are cutting edge and innovative, at worst they cater only to professional zeitgeist surfers, and are reducible to a certain stereotype: post-industrial minimalist decor, a stock of three T-shirts (each priced at €100 and displayed in plastic eggs) and five beautiful assistants who sit around smoking cigarettes and completely ignoring you.

Raval

The Raval is at an interesting stage of its development: the section around the MACBA and C/Doctor Dou aspires to be the new Born, with its pricey designer cafés and boutiques like **Giménez y Zuazo** (*see p199*), while the rest of the area is holding fast to the seedy grunge aesthetic where **Discos Castelló** (*see p209*) and other small record shops along C/Tallers and C/Bonsuccès are still the first stop for music fanatics, and C/Riera Baixa is the epicentre of the second-hand scene with retro havens like **Smart & Clean** (*see p201*) and **Lailo** (*see p201*).

Eixample

The design-drenched Eixample boulevards are the habitat of beautiful people modelling Emporio's new clothes and the latest Nokias. Rambla de Catalunya, Passeig de Gràcia and the central part of Avda Diagonal sparkle with names like **Adolfo Domínguez** (*see p196*) and **Antonio Miró** (*see p196*), although chains like **Mango** (*see p195*) and **Zara** (*see p196*) have their flagship stores here. It's not just clothes, though: after snapping up antique gems at **Gothsland Galeria d'Art** (*see p188*) or a full set of Gaudí repro furniture at **BD Ediciones de Diseño** (*see p192*), you could have a designer cake at **Escribà** (*see p202*) or snaffle a jar of porcini mushrooms for a mere €275 at **Queviures Murrià** (*see p203*).

Gràcia

Further up the hill, things are more villagey. Independent stores, galleries and design studios throng the streets around Plaça del Sol, Plaça Rius i Taulet and C/Verdi, selling everything from jewellery to arty fashion. The pedestrianised area surrounding the **Mercat de la Llibertat** (*see p207* **Trading places**) has great food stores while high street chains live on Gran de Gràcia and Travessera de Gràcia.

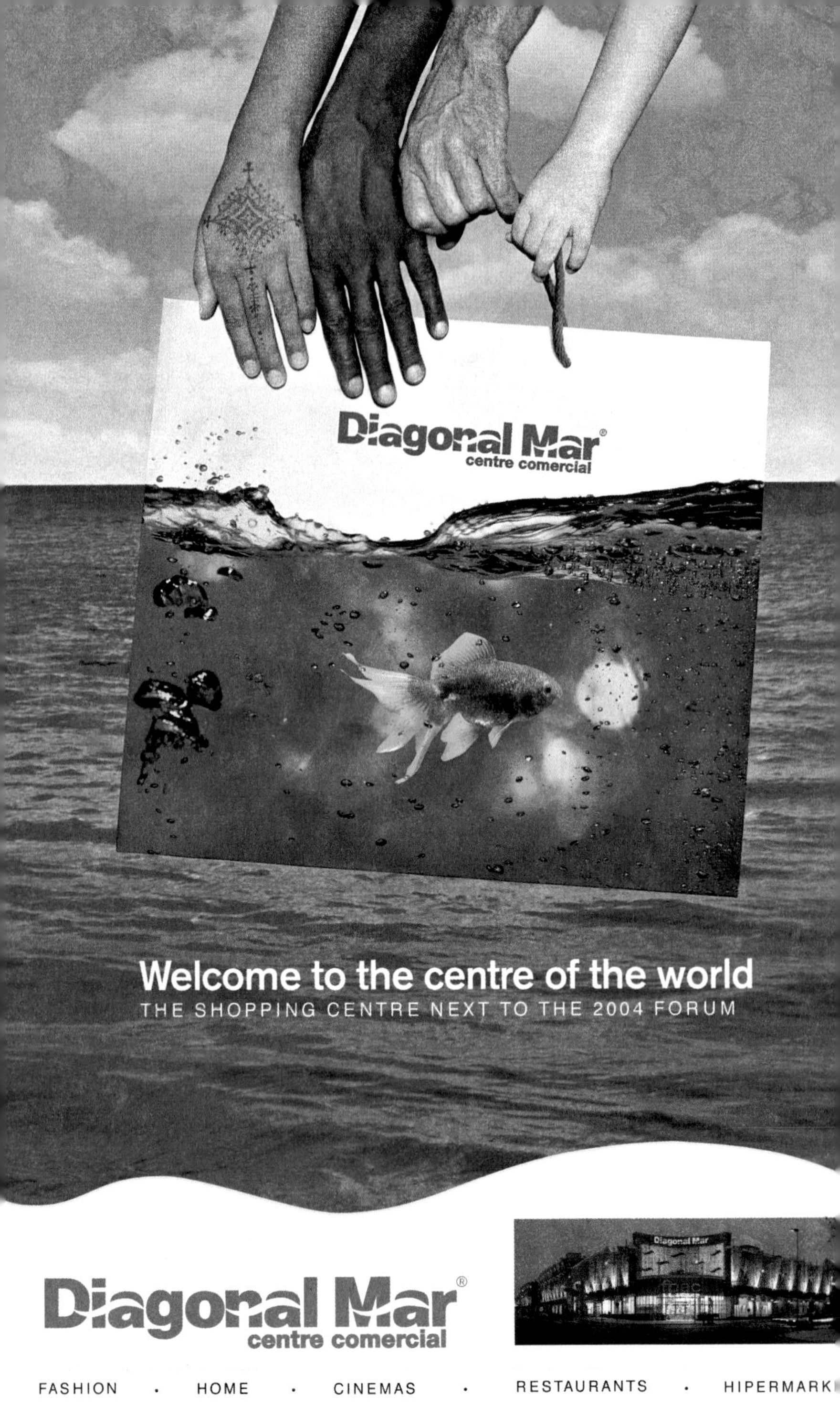
Diagonal Mar®
centre comercial
Welcome to the centre of the world
THE SHOPPING CENTRE NEXT TO THE 2004 FORUM
Diagonal Mar
Diagonal Mar®
centre comercial
FASHION · HOME · CINEMAS · RESTAURANTS · HIPERMARK

by Mariscal. Everything related to the bedroom is in a separate branch just around the corner called TincÇon (Catalan for 'I'm sleepy'), and the rest of the large furnishings are on the Modernista upper floor. Every December, Vinçon hosts Hipermercart, an art 'supermarket' with originals by young artists.
Other locations: **TincÇon** Rosselló 246, Eixample (93 215 60 50).

Fashion

By far the most dynamic area for fashion is the **Born** where hip new boutiques are springing up faster than you can say 'promising young designer'. Most of the high-street fashion chains are around C/Portaferrissa, C/Pelai and Portal de l'Àngel in the **Barri Gòtic**, while the serious money goes to uptown designer shops on Passeig de Gràcia and Avda Diagonal.

Black Jazz

C/Rec 28, Born (mobile 629 842 296). Metro Jaume I. **Open** 5-9pm Mon; 11am-2.30pm, 5-9pm Tue-Sat. **Credit** AmEx, MC, V. **Map** p345 C4.
Fearsomely hip new men's shop. Labels include industry standards like Dolce & Gabbana, Hugo Boss and Antoni Miró alongside harder-to-find pieces from Bikkembergs or Indian Rags.

D409

Avda Diagonal 409, Eixample (93 415 44 33). Metro Diagonal. **Open** 10am-8.30pm Mon-Sat. **Credit** AmEx, MC, V. **Map** p338 D3.
This is the archetypal Diagonal shopping experience: minimalist decor, large open spaces, nu-jazz on the stereo and ultra-discreet sales assistants. Labels include a wearable but still funky selection for well-to-do thirtysomethings from Paul & Joe, Antik Batik, Fairly, No-L-ita and Just Cavalli.

Jean-Pierre Bua

Avda Diagonal 469, Eixample (93 439 71 00/ www.jeanpierrebua.com). Bus 6, 7. **Open** 10am-2pm, 4.30-8.30pm Mon-Sat. **Credit** AmEx, DC, MC, V. **Map** p338 C3.
The city's original stockist of avant-garde international designer fashion is still going strong with exclusive selections for both men (upstairs) and women (ground floor) from Balenciaga, Jean-Paul Gaultier, Miu Miu and Stella McCartney and shoes and accessories by Alaïa and Marni.

Kwatra

C/Antic de Sant Joan 1, Born (93 268 08 04/ www.kwatra.com). Metro Barceloneta or Jaume I. **Open** 11am-2pm, 4-8pm Mon; 11am-9pm Tue-Sat. **Credit** AmEx, DC, MC, V. **Map** p345 C3.
Former Nike employee Robbie Pabla uses his connections to fill this fresh orange and white space with limited edition swoosh stuff. Along with clothes and bags are exclusive trainer lines like City Knife, Waffle and Speedsweep.
Other locations: **Bulevard Rosa**, Passeig de Gràcia 55, Eixample (93 488 04 27).

Loft Avignon

C/Avinyó 22, Barri Gòtic (93 301 24 20). Metro Jaume I or Liceu. **Open** 10.30am-2.30pm, 4.30-8.30pm Mon-Fri; 10.30am-8.30pm Sat. **Credit** DC, MC, V. **Map** p345 B3.
Fash mag luminaries such as Vivienne Westwood, Byblos and Gaultier, Cutler and Gross sunglasses and shoes by Bikkembergs, Hudson and A Guardiani.
Other locations: C/Boters 8, Barri Gòtic (93 301 37 95).

Mango

Passeig de Gràcia 65, Eixample (93 215 75 30/ www.mango.es/www.mangoshop.com). Metro Passeig de Gràcia. **Open** 10am-9pm Mon-Sat. **Credit** AmEx, DC, MC, V. **Map** p338 D4.
Phenomenally successful, this women's fashion store now has over 700 outlets worldwide. A small step up from Zara in price and quality, it's still noticeably cheaper than abroad for the tailored suits, clubwear, velveteen tracksuits, fragrance and excellent handbags. Many unsold items end up in the discount store, Mango 2 (C/Girona 37, 93 412 2935).
Other locations: throughout the city.

El Mercadillo

C/Portaferrissa 17, Barri Gòtic (93 301 89 13). Metro Liceu. **Open** 11am-9pm Mon-Sat. **Credit** AmEx, DC, MC, V. **Map** p344 B2.
Barcelona's lavishly pierced grunge kids gather at this fashion arcade for their new and second-hand leather, suede and denim. Other staples include piercing paraphernalia, Doc Martens and strikingly tacky outfits made of cheap materials. Pounding music and a life-size fibreglass camel mark the entrance, and on the second floor there's a café with a tranquil patio, indifferent service and coffee.

On Land

C/Princesa 25, Born (93 310 02 11/www.on-land.com). Metro Jaume I. **Open** 5-8.30pm Mon; 11am-2pm, 5-8.30pm Tue-Fri; 11.30am-5.30pm Sat. Closed 1wk Aug. **Credit** AmEx, MC, V. **Map** p345 C3.
Mercilessly cool urbanwear for men and women from On Land's own label plus an interestingly left-field selection from labels like Andayá, Que d'Alésia, Montse Ibañez and Gabriel Torres. The most accessibly priced pieces are spray-on stretch tops by Petit Bâteau and cheeky slogan T-shirts by popular local designers Divinas Palabras.
Other locations: C/Valencia 273, Eixample (93 215 56 25).

Overales & Bluyines

C/Rec 65, Born (93 319 29 76). Metro Barceloneta. **Open** *Jan-May, Oct-Dec* 10.30am-8.30pm Mon-Sat. *June-Sept* 11am-9pm Mon-Sat. **Credit** AmEx, DC, MC, V. **Map** p345 C3.
The perfect pair of jeans may well be lurking among these rails of vintage denim, Levi's Red Tab, Duffer, Diesel and Paul Smith, as well as O&B's own-label, which go for about €100 a pop. Look out for the Freitag bags made out of recycled seatbelts and tarpaulin, along with interesting jackets and T-shirts.

R que R

C/Rec 75 (93 268 84 98). Metro Jaume I. **Open** 11am-3pm Mon-Fri; 11am-9pm Sat. **Credit** AmEx, DC, MC, V. **Map** p345 C4.

An excellent new showcase for women's fashion. Lime-green crocheted minis, leather thong tops or quilted smoking jackets may not sound like the easiest things to wear, but advice from a helpful assistant makes it happen. Don't miss the back room filled with stretch tops and T-shirts by Orly Visuals.

Tactic

C/Enric Granados 11, Eixample (93 451 03 87). Metro Universitat. **Open** 10.30am-2pm, 5-8pm Tue-Sat. **Credit** AmEx, MC, V. **Map** p338 C4.

Custo Barcelona. *See p199.*

Fashion for surfers and skaters, from the likes of Quiksilver, Ripcurl, Volcom. It also specialises in snowboarding, windsurfing and kitesurfing, and has a range of accessories for dudes of all ages.

Tribu

C/Avinyó 12, Barri Gòtic (93 318 65 10/ www.tribubcn.com). Metro Jaume I. **Open** 11am-8.30pm Mon-Sat. **Credit** AmEx, MC, V. **Map** p345 B3.

A warren of showrooms for alternative clothes, shoes and accessories by internationally recognised names like Homeless, E-Play, Buffalo and Space Club, as well as local designers such as Spastor – remember the dress made out of real chicken skin?

Trip Shop

C/Duc de la Victoria 13, Barri Gòtic (93 412 67 11). Metro Catalunya. **Open** 10am-8.30pm Mon-Sat. **No credit cards**. **Map** p344 B2.

Trip Shop sells hip hop gear for B-boys and babes by Sir Benni Miles, South-Pole, Clench, Fubu and Phat Farm, among others. If you like it baggy round the booty and don't mind the other punters stinking of skunk, you'll be in heaven.

Zara

C/Pelai 58, Eixample (93 301 09 78). Metro Catalunya. **Open** 10am-9pm Mon-Sat. **Credit** AmEx, DC, MC, V. **Map** p344 A1.

No sooner do you see it on the catwalk, than an affordable copy appears on the heaving racks of your local Zara. The wait at the checkout and changing rooms may annoy, but it attests to the low prices, huge range of styles and almost weekly influx of new lines (top tip: queues are shorter in the children's department in the basement).

Other locations: throughout the city.

Designer

Adolfo Domínguez

Passeig de Gràcia 32, Eixample (93 487 41 70/ www.adolfodominguez.es). Metro Passeig de Gràcia. **Open** 10am-8.30pm Mon-Sat. **Credit** AmEx, DC, MC, V. **Map** p342 D5.

The sartorial equivalent of easy listening, Adolfo Domínguez specialises in safe, classic men's and women's designs aimed squarely at thirty- and fortysomethings. Expect lots of beige, navy and cream, although the new Línea U line includes fresher, more streetwise designs for younger people.

Other locations: Avda Diagonal 490, Gràcia (93 416 17 16); La Maquinista, C/Ciutat d'Asunción, Sant Andreu (93 360 8753); Passeig de Gràcia 89, Eixample (93 215 13 39).

Antonio Miró

C/Consell de Cent 349, Eixample (93 487 06 70/ www.antoniomiro.es). Metro Passeig de Gràcia. **Open** *Jan, Mar-July, Sept-Dec* 10am-2pm, 4.30-8.30pm Mon-Sat. *Feb, Aug* 11am-2pm, 5-8pm Tue-Sat. **Credit** AmEx, DC, MC, V. **Map** p338 D5.

Cheap tricks

The ultra-glam boutiques along Passeig de Gràcia are a tempting sight but the price tags (when indeed there are any) are enough to scare most people away. The antidote lies just a few streets away: a half-price haven of factory outlets and remainder stores that surprisingly few Catalans know about, despite their proverbial love of a *ganga* (bargain).

A cut-price tour of Barcelona starts on C/Girona, where the two blocks between C/Ausiàs Marc and Gran Via de les Corts Catalanes are crammed with remainder stores. Those marked *venta al mayor* or *venda a l'engròs* are wholesale only, but the rest are open to anyone. By far the most popular is **Mango 2** (*see p195, pictured*) with last season's stock from the successful high-street chain store. The presentation is pure bargain basement with supermarket lighting and tightly packed racks of clothes, but the girls aren't complaining as they snap up knee-length boots for €25 or skirts reduced from €35 to €5. A few doors down, the macho hunting-lodge decor at **Trading Post** (C/Girona 27, 93 342 43 99) houses imported American leather jackets and casual wear by Ralph Lauren and Dockers with prices reduced by 30 to 50 per cent. If you insist on Calvin Klein underwear, this is the only place in the city where you won't have to remortgage your house to buy it. Also going for the preppy Kennedy clan look is **Arrow** (C/Girona 36, 93 245 18 08), with plenty of stripy shirts, chinos and sweaters that are begging to be knotted around the shoulders.

Just around the corner, **Erre de Raso** (C/Casp 47, 93 301 14 85) caters to women past the first bloom of fashion victimisation but not yet ready for the twinset and pearls, with reduced overstock from small Spanish designers alongside full-price items. For sample, remainder and end-of-season footwear try **SBT 2** (C/Girona 31, 93 412 62 98), where both men's and women's styles tend to be plain and functional and a pair of chunky winter boots costs just €20.

The spacious layout in **E&P Store Factory** (C/Girona 40, 93 232 80 45) is an indication of higher prices, and although Etxart & Panno's girlie bustiers, corsets and frocks are slashed by up to 50 per cent, you'll still be paying €80 or so for a wisp of a dress. At the other end of the scale, **Factory Store** has several branches, all of them stunningly cheap; the one on C/Girona 38 has small-name women's casual wear, while around the corner (Plaça Urquinaona 5, 93 304 02 40), it stocks nothing but women's coats and jackets, with quilted nylon puffas for as little as €10. The largest branch (Ronda de Sant Pau 15, by Plaça d' Espanya) caters for both men and women.

Elsewhere in town, *ganga* wranglers can try old faithfuls like **Stockland** (*see p199*) or **Taxi Moda** (*see p199*), but the only decent store for high-end designers is **Contribuciones y Moda** (Riera San Miquel 30, 93 218 71 40). Here, you'll find 50 per cent off names like Dries Van Noten, Versace and Gaultier, but anyone really serious about designer bargains will need to go half an hour outside the city to **La Roca Village** (La Roca del Vallès, 93 842 39 00, www.larocavillage.com). This Disney-perfect, mock-Catalan village houses over 50 discount outlets such as Antonio Miró, Cacharel, Loewe or Camper with 25 to 60 per cent discounts on end-of-season merchandise.

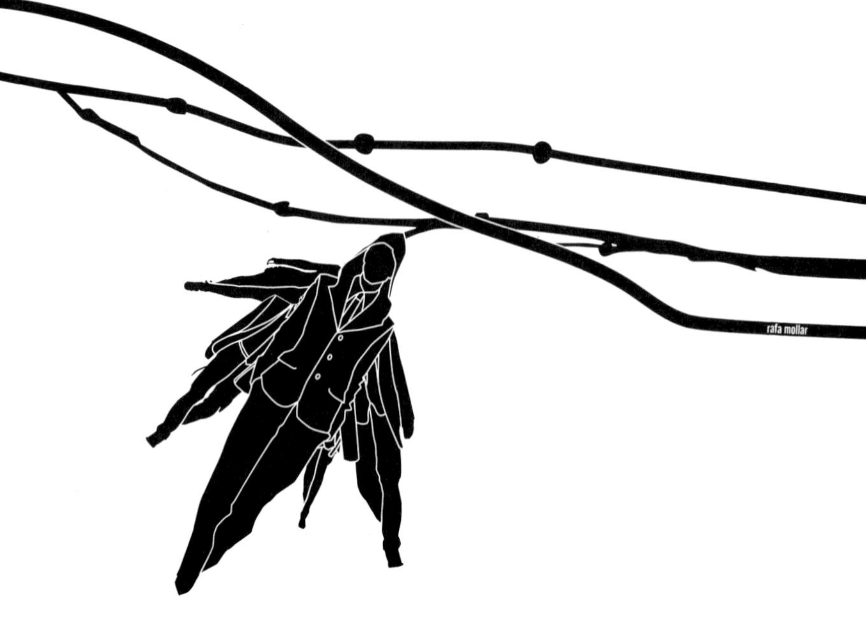
rafa mollar

The king of haute Catalan couture, Miró specialises in sublimely classic lines for both men and women, although his style can often be strangely androgynous. Hues are generally sober, with more black than a Cure concert, but he now has the funkier Miró Jeans label aimed at younger minimalists.
Miró Jeans: C/València 272, Eixample (93 272 24 91); C/Pi 11, Barri Gòtic (93 342 58 75). C/Vidrieria 5, Born (93 268 82 03).

Armand Basi

Passeig de Gràcia 49, Eixample (93 215 14 21/ www.armandbasi.com). Metro Passeig de Gràcia. **Open** 10am-8.30pm Mon-Sat. **Credit** AmEx, DC, MC, V. **Map** p338 D4.
This Spanish designer is famous for his jerseywear and jaquard knits and, although the flagship store also stocks his more traditional men's and women's classic collections, there's no shortage of more colourful, adventurous urban fashion influenced by anything from graffiti to magic realism. Famous aficionados include Tom Cruise, Jarvis Cocker and Davina McCall, and he's even dressed James Bond.

Custo Barcelona

Plaça de les Olles 7, Born (93 268 78 93/www.custo-barcelona.com). Metro Jaume I. **Open** 10am-10pm Mon-Sat; 1-8pm Sun. **Credit** AmEx, DC, MC, V. **Map** p345 C4.
Although Catalan designer Custodio Dalmau designs general couture, it's his instantly recognisable, stretchy cotton tops that everyone wants. Bearing strident designs and glamorous faces, they have become so popular that you can expect to pay anything from €58 for a tank top to €270 for a more ambitious creation. The shop has recently expanded to include a denim section.
Other locations: C/Ferran 36, Barri Gòtic (93 342 66 98).

Giménez y Zuazo

C/Elisabets 20, Raval (93 412 33 81/www.gimenez zuazo.com). Metro Catalunya. **Open** 10.30am-3pm, 5-8.30pm Mon-Sat. **Credit** AmEx, MC, V. **Map** p344 A2.
Since opening their first shop in 1999, Marta Giménez and Jorge Zuazo have gone from strength to strength with quirky urban fashion for men and women in bright, offbeat materials and knits. The biggest success has been the BoBa (*'bonito y barato'* or 'good and cheap') line of tops and T-shirts.
Other locations: C/Rec 42, Born (93 310 67 43).

Lydia Delgado

C/Minerva 21, Gracia (93 415 99 98). Metro Diagonal. **Open** 10am-2pm, 4.30-8.30pm Mon-Sat. **Credit** MC, V. **Map** p338 D4.
This award-winning Barcelona designer trained with Antoni Miró and has gone on to launch her own very wearable collection of shoes, clothes and bags for women. Bearing an uncanny resemblance to Audrey Hepburn, she also channels a modern version of her style with neat and feminine silhouettes in unusual and highly flattering materials.

Designer bargains

Stockland

C/Comtal 22, Barri Gòtic (93 318 03 31). Metro Urquinaona. **Open** 10am-8.30pm Mon-Sat. **Credit** AmEx, DC, MC, V. **Map** p344 B2.
Originally known as Preu Bo ('good price'), this popular discount outlet is still living up to its former name, with nicely presented end-of-line clothing by mostly Spanish designers including Jordi Cuesta, Purificación García and Jocomomola.

Taxi Moda

Passeig de Gràcia 81, Eixample (93 215 03 80). Metro Passeig de Gràcia/Bus22, 24, 28. **Open** 10.30am-8.30pm Mon-Sat. **Credit** MC, V. **Map** p338 D4.
Drastically reduced prices (at least 50%) on designer clothing, mostly by Italian fashion houses such as Valentino, Gazzarini or Pal Zileri. The men's section is especially strong on shirts, suits and coats, while the women's section concentrates on casual urbanwear by Guess Jeans, Liu Jo, Laltramoda and Miss Sixty with a good selection of larger sizes.

Fashion accessories

Jewellery

Alea

C/Argentería 66, Born (93 310 13 73). Metro Jaume I. **Open** 11am-2.30pm, 5-8.30pm Tue-Fri; 11am-3pm, 4-8.30pm Sat. Closed 2wks Aug. **Credit** AmEx, MC, V. **Map** p345 C3.
A funky little showroom with a fabulous collection of offbeat modern jewellery in gold and silver as well as more unusual materials like hessian, methacrylate and glass. Check out Felix Zuazu's matt gold wedding rings, Guigui Kohen's necklaces made out of tasselled passports and Ana Hagopian's lacy paper ruffs. Temporary displays by young designers feature in the new exhibition space.

Bagués

Passeig de Gràcia 41, Eixample (93 216 01 73/ www.bagues.es). Metro Passeig de Gràcia. **Open** 10am-8.30pm Mon-Fri; 10am-1.30pm, 5-8pm Sat. **Credit** AmEx, DC, MC, V. **Map** p338 D4.
Housed in Puig i Cadafalch's Casa Amatller, this distinguished jeweller and watchmaker is especially renowned for its art nouveau jewellery. The most breathtaking pieces (and prices – up to €10,000) come in the shape of winged nymphs and trembling insects in gold and translucent enamel by master jeweller Lluís Masriera. Watch out for the high security double entrance – you must close one door and wait a little before the other will open.
Other locations: C/Rambla de les Flors 105, Barri Gòtic (93 481 70 50).

MN

C/Sant Honorat 11, Barri Gòtic (93 325 15 36). Metro Jaume I or Liceu. **Open** 10am-1.30pm, 5-9pm Mon-Sat. **Credit** AmEx, MC, V. **Map** p345 B3.

Smart & Clean: remember this? *See p201.*

This tiny, highly specialised workshop and display room is devoted solely to fired enamel jewellery that has an unusual, arty appeal. Each piece sold at MN is unique with an unrepeatable pattern of swirling colours found in stunning wide, flat rings, pendants, brooches and bracelets.

Platamundi

C/Montcada 11, Born (93 268 10 94). Metro Jaume I. **Open** 10am-8pm Mon-Sat; 10am-3pm Sun. **Credit** AmEx, DC, MC, V. **Map** p345 C3.

Chunky silver pieces that mostly fall in the €20-€30 price range make Platamundi a highly popular choice for younger shoppers. For a splash of local colour, try the swirly Gaudí-inspired rings or a colourful Miró-style pendant, but the most popular lines combine silver with blue-hued enamels by local designers such as Ricard Domingo.

Other locations: C/Hospital 37, Raval (93 317 13 89); Plaça Santa Maria 7, Born (93 310 10 87); Galeries Maldà 40, Barri Gòtic (93 317 42 99).

Leather & luggage

Casa Antich SCP

C/Consolat del Mar 27-31, La Ribera (93 310 43 91/ www.casaantich.com). Metro Jaume I. **Open** 9am-8.30pm Mon-Fri; 9.30am-8.30pm Sat. **Credit** DC, MC, V. **Map** p345 B4.

Teetering stacks of hold-alls, briefcases, suitcases and metal steamer trunks big enough to sleep in can be found here. Designs are mostly big names such as Samsonite or Rimowa, but staff will also make bags to your personal specifications.

Loewe

Passeig de Gràcia 35, Eixample (93 216 04 00/ www.loewe.com). Metro Passeig de Gràcia. **Open** 10am-8.30pm Mon-Sat. **Credit** AmEx, DC, MC, V. **Map** p342 D5.

If you can convince youself that it's actually an investment to spend €1,000 on a handbag, then this top-of-the-range leather company is for you. Inside Domènech i Montaner's Casa Morera are two floors of exorbitantly priced clothes for men and women specialising, of course, in wonderfully supple leather and sheepskin items, along with bags, suitcases, scarves and other accessories of superb quality.

Other locations: Avda Diagonal 570, Eixample (93 200 09 20); Avda Diagonal 606, Eixample (93 240 51 04).

Lingerie & underwear

Look out for affordable swimwear and underwear, sold as mix-and-match separates, in high-street chains such as **Oyshu** (Rambla de Catalunya 77, Eixample, 93 488 36 01), from the same stable as Zara. Of the many underwear stores along the Rambla Catalunya, the most prestigious is the Italian firm **La Perla** (Rambla Catalunya, Eixample, 88, 93 467 71 49).

Janina

Rambla Catalunya 94, Eixample (93 215 04 84). Metro Diagonal/FGC Provença. **Open** *Sept-July* 10am-8.30pm Mon-Sat. *Aug* 10am-2pm, 5-8.30pm Mon-Sat. **Credit** AmEx, DC, MC, V. **Map** p338 D4.

A well-established shop that sells its own exclusive silk and satin underwear, nightwear and robes, as well as stockings by Risk and La Perla. A large selection of swimsuits and bikinis is also available.

La Perla Gris

Rambla Catalunya 118, Eixample (93 215 29 91). Metro Diagonal/FGC Provença. **Open** 10am-8.30pm Mon-Fri; 10am-2pm, 5 8.30pm Sat. **Credit** AmEx, DC, MC, V. **Map** p338 D4.

Large range of good quality Italian and French lingerie including labels like Cotton Club, Christian Dior, Barbara and Antigel. It also has silk stockings, nightwear and robes along with a large selection of swimsuits and bikinis in season.

Other locations: C/Balmes 285 (93 217 82 30); C/Rosselló 220 (93 215 29 91).

Women's Secret

C/Portaferrissa 7-9, Barri Gòtic (93 318 92 42). Metro Liceu. **Open** 10am-8.30pm Mon-Sat. **Credit** AmEx, DC, MC, V. **Map** p344 B2.

Whether you want seamless, strapless, skin-toned miracles of invisibility or a saucy lace seduction number, Women's Secret will have it. It also does a hot trade in funky bikinis, slippers, bathrobes, pyjamas, negligées, larger sizes, maternity underwear, socks and tights. Avoid trying things on at busy times when queues for changing rooms are very slow. **Other locations**: throughout the city.

Scarves & textiles

Textiles were once one of Barcelona's main industries; a legacy that can be seen in many of the street names of the Born, where the highest concentration of textile shops and workshops are to be found. Contact tourist offices (*see p319*) for information about taking a tour of the official 'Textile Itinerary'.

Almacenes del Pilar

C/Boqueria 43, Barri Gòtic (93 317 79 84). Metro Liceu. **Open** 9.30am-2pm, 4-8pm Mon-Sat. **Credit** AmEx, MC, V. **Map** p345 A3.

A quiet, old-fashioned shop with fabulous fringed silk *mantones de Manila* (shawls), lace *mantillas* to be worn over the high Spanish head combs, and bolts of the materials used in traditional costumes throughout Spain. Especially impressive are the encrusted brocades for the Valencian *fallera* outfits.

Rafa Teja Atelier

C/Santa María 18, Born (93 310 27 85). Metro Jaume I. **Open** 11am-9pm Mon-Sat; noon-3pm Sun. **Credit** AmEx, MC, V. **Map** p345 C3.

The rainbow-coloured racks of scarves, wraps and pashminas here come in an overwhelming range of materials, from embroidery-encrusted wool to swingy fringed silks. You can pick up a simple winter scarf for about €15 and there's also a small range of oriental tops, bags and jewellery.

Other locations: Conde de Salvatierra 10, Eixample (93 237 70 59).

Second-hand

Annie Hall meets Carnaby Street on **C/Riera Baixa** in the Raval, a concentration of second-hand shops and innovative boutiques. Whether your look is cowpunk, flapper, gypsy or dandy, you'll find it at **Lailo** at No.20 (93 441 37 49), which also stocks opera costumes, military jackets, '80s cocktail dresses and suits and leather jackets. **Leo Recicla** at No.13 (mobile 616 000 225) has more mainstream fashion items such as vintage Nike tracksuit tops and street gear. No.7 is a branch of **Smart & Clean** (*see below*). An alternative second-hand clothes **market** is held on the street every Saturday from May to September and in December, and on the first Saturday of every other month.

Produit National Brut

C/Avinyó 29, Barri Gòtic (93 268 27 55). Metro Drassanes or Jaume I. **Open** 11am-9pm Mon-Sat. **Credit** MC, V. **Map** p345 B3.

Retro chic looks like it's here to stay and this French outlet takes advantage with a selection of used army fatigues, slogan T-shirts (Iron Maiden, anyone?), velour tracksuit tops, leather jackets, wash'n'wear shirtwaisters and a truly terrifying rack of nylon paisley swimming trunks.

Smart & Clean

C/Xuclà 6, Raval (93 412 60 22/www.smartandclean.com). Metro Catalunya. **Open** 10.30am-1.30pm, 5-8.30pm Mon-Sat. **Credit** AmEx, MC, V. **Map** p344 A2.

Mods rule in this shrine to '60s and '70s UK fashion, although the Rockers do get a look in. Next to ska, punk and northern soul on vinyl, there are Fred Perry shirts, satchels, duffel bags, Sta Press hipster slacks, braces, drape jackets, penny loafers and Doc Martens – perfect for wearing to those Vespa runs.

Other locations: C/Riera Baixa 7, Raval (no phone).

Shoes

Traditional Catalan footwear is the *espardenya*, a stout beribboned espadrille. Although these have recently enjoyed a fashion renaissance, most shoppers prefer more modern delights found on the main shopping strips of Portal de l'Àngel or C/Pelai. Well-known chains include **Casas**, **Mar Bessas**, **Scarpa**, **Royalty**, **Querol** and **Vogue**, most of which hold similar stock.

Camper

C/Pelai 13-37, Eixample (93 302 41 24/www.camper.com). Metro Catalunya. **Open** 10am-10pm Mon-Sat. **Credit** AmEx, DC, MC, V. **Map** p344 A1.

These brightly coloured leather shoes may look like they belong in a school playground but everybody's wearing them. Camper means field worker, and the Mallorcan Fluxà family originally produced labourer's shoes made of recycled tyres and canvas; the most popular lines follow the basic philosophy of comfort and practicality and last for years.

Other locations: throughout the city.

Czar

Passeig del Born 20, Born (93 310 7222). Metro Jaume I. **Open** 5-9pm Mon; 11.15am-2.30pm, 4-9pm Tue-Sat. **Credit** DC, MC, V. **Map** p345 C3.

The best designer trainer shop in the city centre, this ferociously hip little selection includes trainers from Puma, Diesel and Paul Smith but also harder-to-find labels such as Rizzo, Fluxa and Le Coq Sportif.

La Manual Alpargatera

C/Avinyó 7, Barri Gòtic (93 301 01 72). Metro Liceu. **Open** *Jan-Sept, Dec* 9.30am-1.30pm, 4.30-8pm Mon-Sat. *Oct, Nov* 9.30am-1.30pm, 4.30-8pm Mon-Fri; 10am-1.30pm Sat. **Credit** AmEx, DC, MC, V. **Map** p345 B3.

The impressive stacks of traditional espadrilles include the ribboned Tabarner model that Catalans wear to dance the *sardana*, but staff will make whatever you want to order. Prices are low and customers famously include Jack Nicholson and the Pope.

Eat, Drink, Shop

Muxart

C/Rosselló 230, Eixample (93 488 10 64/ www.muxart.com). Metro Diagonal. **Open** 10am-2pm, 4.30-8.30pm Mon-Fri; 10am-2pm, 5-8.30pm Sat. **Credit** AmEx, MC, V. **Map** p338 D4.

Hermenegildo Muxart's shoes are created to be bought before the outfit rather than as mere accessories. Materials are refined, styles are sharp and avant-garde and not to be hidden under a pair of beige slacks. Lines for men and women are complemented by equally sexy bags and accessories.

Other locations: Rambla Catalunya 47, Eixample (93 467 74 23).

Rouge Poison

C/Flassaders 34, Born (93 310 55 46). Metro Jaume I. **Open** noon-2pm, 5-9pm Tue-Sun. **Credit** MC, V. **Map** p345 C3.

Presented in Barbarella-style plastic capsules, swings and flip-top boxes, a small but deadly selection of French and UK designs for men and women are snapped up by fashion cognoscenti and magazine stylists. Prices are off the charts.

Tascón

Avda Diagonal 462, Eixample (93 415 56 16). Bus 6, 7. **Open** 10.30am-9pm Mon-Thur; 10.30am-10pm Fri, Sat. **Credit** MC, V. **Map** p338 C3.

This selection of Spanish and international shoes concentrates on comfortable, good quality leather streetwear rather than teetering skinny stilettos and corn-inducing winklepickers. Brands at Tascón include Jocomomola, Camper, Vialis, Doc Martens, Timberland and Panama Jack.

Other locations: Rambla Catalunya 42, Eixample (93 487 44 47); Passeig de Gràcia 64, Eixample (93 487 90 84); Passeig del Born 8, Born (93 268 72 93).

U-Casas

C/Espaseria 4, Born (93 310 00 46). Metro Barceloneta. **Open** 10.30am-9pm Mon-Thur; 10.30am-10pm Fri, Sat. **Credit** MC, V. **Map** p345 C4.

Opened in 2003, with the usual plate glass and exposed ducts that are de rigueur in the Born, the novelty here is the seating: a huge wooden sandal. Use it as a slide, a bed or even to try on the ultra-hip squaw booties, trainers and fur clogs by Puma, Fly, Fornarina and Irregular Choice among others.

Vialis

C/Vidrieria 15, Born (93 319 94 91). Metro Jaume I. **Open** 11am-9pm Mon-Sat. **Credit** AmEx, MC, V. **Map** p345 B3.

Vialis uses buttery soft leather on supple soles that are bliss to walk on, whether in strappy sandals or chunky winter boots. Narrow, high-heeled clogs in a kaleidoscope of colours have proved a local hit.

Flowers

The flower stalls that have run along the **Rambla de les Flors** for 150 years came about when Boqueria market traders used to give a free flower to their customers. There are also stands at the **Mercat de la Concepció** on the corner of C/València and C/Bruc (map p339 E4), which are open all night. Barcelona has relatively few florist shops, however, and prices are correspondingly high.

Flors Navarro

C/València 320, Eixample (93 457 40 99). Metro Verdaguer. **Open** 24hrs daily. **Credit** AmEx, MC, V. **Map** p338 D4.

Fresh-cut blooms, dried flower arrangements, bouquets, baskets, wreaths, plants, and seedlings available 24 hours a day, plus a round-the-clock delivery service. A dozen red roses cost €18, or €24 to deliver anywhere in the city.

Food & drink

Pâtisseries & chocolate

Cacao Sampaka

C/Consell de Cent 292, Eixample (93 272 08 33/ www.cacaosampaka.com). Metro Passeig de Gràcia. **Open** 9am-8.30pm Mon-Sat; 5-8.30pm Sun. **Credit** AmEx, MC, V. **Map** p338 D5.

Curry chocolates, anchovy pralines and blue cheese bonbons are some of the more outlandish treats on offer at this luxury chocolate emporium. The lovely taster café at the back of the shop offers over 18 varieties of chocolate ice-cream, along with advice on chocolate fondue sets and which is the best cava or wine to drink with your goodies.

Caelum

C/Palla 8, Barri Gòtic (93 302 69 93). Metro Liceu. **Open** 5-8.30pm Mon; 10am-9pm Tue-Thur; 10.30am-midnight Fri, Sat. **Credit** MC, V. **Map** p344 B2.

An intriguing selection of edible gifts such as candied saints' bones, sugared egg yolks and gum-shrivellingly sweet herbal liqueurs made in the cellars and kitchens of some 30 monasteries and convents around Spain. Caelum stocks these delicacies and more, which you can sample in the downstairs café on the site of 15th-century Jewish thermal baths.

Escribà

Gran Via de les Corts Catalanes 546, Eixample (93 454 75 35). Metro Urgell. **Open** 8am-3pm Mon-Fri; 8am-9pm Sat, Sun. **Credit** MC, V. **Map** p342 C5.

Cakes with attitude, these cunning creations range from mechanised, musical Easter sculptures to chocolate photographs. As the celebrity-spangled walls of Antoni Escribà's shops attest, this local Willy Wonka has made cakes for everyone from Dalí to Bruce Springsteen, but also whips up plenty of more affordable treats. Catch the masters at work in the open kitchen or admire the Modernista decoration of the Antigua Casa de Figueras at the smaller Ramblas branch.

Other locations: La Rambla 83, Barri Gòtic (93 301 60 27).

Forn Boix

C/Xuclà 23, Raval (93 302 27 82). Metro Catalunya. **Open** 7am-9pm Mon-Sat. **No credit cards. Map** p344 A2.

In the land of refined white flour baguettes, a bakery specialised in wholewheat breads is a rare treat. Since 1920 the friendly Forn Boix has gradually expanded its range to include black German breads, Finnish 14-cereal bread, and loaves with lemon, chocolate and walnut, apple, vegetables, onion and even *sobrassada* sausage. For sweeter teeth, there are traditional *coques, polverons* and cream cakes.

General food stores

Colmado Afro-Latino

Via Laietana 15, Barri Gòtic (93 268 27 43). Metro Jaume I. **Open** 9am-9pm daily. **Credit** V. **Map** p345 B3.

Booming rumba on the stereo and shelves heaving with goodies from Latin America, Africa and Asia. Yucca, pulped papaya, dozens of tequilas and rums, Argentinian corned beef, sugar bread and arepa flour from Colombia, Cameroonian palm wine and sweet Ecuadorian soft drinks are all to be found.

Colmado Quilez

Rambla Catalunya 63, Eixample (93 215 23 56/ www.lafuente.es). Metro Passeig de Gràcia. **Open** *Jan-Sept* 9am-2pm, 4.30-8.30pm Mon-Fri; 9am-2pm Sat. *Oct-Dec* 9am-2pm, 4.30-8.30pm Mon-Sat. **Credit** MC, V. **Map** p338 D4.

Nearly 100 years old, this wonderful corner store is one of the monuments of the Eixample. The mirrored windows and walls are stacked high with a dazzling array of olive oils, sweets, preserves, cheeses and Jabugo hams, plus every type of alcohol from saké, whiskies, cava, and beers ranging from Trappist monk Chimay to Marston's Oyster Stout. It also stocks its own gourmet label, Quilez, which includes Iranian Beluga caviar, cava, Kenyan coffee, turrón, saffron and anchovies.

Queviures Murrià

C/Roger de Llúria 85, Eixample (93 215 57 89). Metro Passeig de Gràcia. **Open** 9am-2pm, 5-9pm Tue-Thur, Sat. 9am-2pm, 5-9.30pm Fri. **Credit** AmEx, MC, V. **Map** p338 D4.

Queviures is Catalan for provisions and there's enough here to feed the 5,000, all beautifully displayed against original tiled decoration by Ramon Casas. Delicacies include a superb range of individually sourced farmhouse cheeses and prime Scottish smoked salmon, along with more than 300 wines, including the family's own brut cava Murrià.

Food specialities

La Botifarrería de Santa María

C/Santa María 4, Born (93 319 91 23). Metro Jaume I. **Open** 8.30am-2.30pm, 5-8.30pm Mon-Fri; 8.30am-3pm Sat. **Credit** AmEx, MC, V. **Map** p345 C3.

This porcine shrine glistens with artisan pâtés, herb-coated country salami, tender chorizo, top quality *pata negra* hams from Jabugo and, the star of the show, gourmet *botifarra* sausages. Apart from garlands of plain *'botis'* and classics such as egg *botifarras* for Mardi Gras, Antoni Travé has stuffed his bangers with everything from Cabrales cheese and cider to asparagus, squid, lemon, cinnamon and even coffee. Though not all at once, naturally.

Casa del Bacalao

C/Comtal 8, Barri Gòtic (93 301 65 39). Metro Urquinaona. **Open** 9am-2.30pm, 4.30-8.30pm Mon-Sat. **Credit** AmEx, MC, V. **Map** p344 B2.

It definitely smells a bit fishy at the 'house of cod', where there's an off-white blizzard of the salted and dried pieces of cod central to so many Catalan dishes. The cheeks (*mejillas*) are served with a parsley and garlic sauce in Galicia; Catalan *esqueixada* uses narrow strips; and the soft throat membranes (*kokotxas*) are a Basque delicacy. Staff can vacuum-pack your fish to take home, but to transform it from a skateboard into something cookable you'll need to follow strict soaking instructions.

Casa Gispert

C/Sombrerers 23, Born (93 319 75 35/ www.casagispert.com). Metro Jaume I. **Open** *Oct-Dec* 9.30am-2pm, 4-7.30pm Mon-Fri; 10am-2pm, 5-8pm Sat. *Jan-Sept* 9.30am-2pm, 4-7.30pm Tue-Fri; 10am-2pm, 5-8pm Sat. **Credit** AmEx, DC, MC, V. **Map** p345 C3.

Still using the original 19th-century wood-burning stove, Casa Gispert has no better advert than its smell: roasted coffee, toasted hazelnuts, pistachios and almonds still warm in the sacks, and wooden shelves full of dried fruits, spices and teas. Wearing traditional aprons and huge smiles, the staff serve from behind a long counter laden with irresistible goodies. Their gourmet food baskets make perfect gifts and there are special DIY packs for local specialities, such as *calçot* sauce, *horchata* (tiger nut milk), Hallowe'en *panellets* and *crema catalana.*

Formatgeria La Seu

C/Dagueria 16, Barri Gòtic (93 412 65 48). Metro Jaume I. **Open** 10am-2pm, 5-8pm Tue-Fri; 10am-3pm, 5-8pm Sat. Closed Aug. **No credit cards. Map** p345 B3.

On site in Barcelona's first butter-making factory, big cheese Katherine McLaughlin sells a delectable range of individually sourced farmhouse olive oils and cheeses including rarities like a Cantabrian Pasiego or a Fierra de Cazorla from Jaén. On Saturdays from noon to 3pm there is a sit-down cheese and oil tasting for €5, but you can wash down three cheeses and a glass of wine anytime for €2 while Katherine explains her wares.

Papabubble

C/Ample 28, Barri Gòtic (93 268 86 25). Metro Barceloneta or Drassanes. **Open** 10am-2pm Tue-Fri; 10am-7.30pm Sat; 11am-7.30pm Sun. **Credit** MC, V. **Map** p345 pB4.

A permanent crowd of goggle-eyed spectators (mostly young children) stare at Australians Nigel and Chris as they stretch hot rock candy and roll it into lollipops, sticks and humbugs. The sweets are made to traditional recipes and sold in (refillable) glass jars or packets – 180g of bull's eyes costs €3.75, but they also make personalised giant lollipops for €12, along with candy jewellery, vases and bowls.

Tot Formatge

Passeig del Born 13, Born (93 319 53 75). Metro Jaume I. **Open** *Sept-May* 9am-2pm, 5-8pm Mon-Fri; 10.30am-2pm Sat. *June-Aug* 9am-2pm, 5-8pm Mon-Fri. **No credit cards. Map** p345 C3.

Lots of purple paintwork and a giant cheesy reinterpretation of Vermeer's *Milkmaid* decorate this international cheese shop. The selection concentrates mainly on Catalonia, Spain and France, and while desperate veggies will pounce on the rennet-free cheddar, there are also local specialities such as *garrotxa,* a creamy goat's cheese with a hint of hazelnut, *urgelia* from the Catalan Pyrenees or *mató*, a curd cheese typically eaten as dessert with honey.

Supermarkets

The most central of the hypermarkets is **Carrefour** in the Glòries shopping centre (*see p186*), but if you don't mind paying a little more, **El Corte Inglés** has a good basement supermarket and a 'gourmet' section featuring lavishly packaged local specialities along with imported delights like Heinz tomato soup.

Champion

Rambla dels Estudis 113, La Rambla (93 302 48 24). Metro Catalunya. **Open** 9am-10pm Mon-Sat. **Credit** MC, V. **Map** p344 A2.

On the plus side, Champion has an unbeatable location at the top end of La Rambla, is cheap, stays open late and has a high turnover, ensuring very fresh fruit and vegetables. In the minuses: the bakery out front is not recommended, and tourists fumbling with unfamiliar change make the queues sluggish.

Superserveis

C/Avinyó 11-13, Barri Gòtic (93 317 53 91). Metro Jaume I. **Open** 8.30am-2pm, 5-8.30pm Mon-Sat. **Credit** AmEx, DC, MC, V. **Map** p345 B3.

The strength of this shop is the range of hard-to-find imported food such as curry spices, poppadoms, burrito wraps, Marmite, soy sauce and the like.

Wine

Craft shop **Art Escudellers** (*see p192*) has a good selection of wines in its cellar.

La Carte des Vins

C/Sombrerers 1, Born (93 268 70 43/www.lacartedesvins.com). Metro Jaume I. **Open** 10.30am-9.30pm Tue-Sun. **Credit** AmEx, DC, MC, V. **Map** p345 C3.

La Carte des Vins has a small but user-friendly selection of 411 wines, champagnes and cavas that is clearly laid out and labelled by region and vintage. About 80% of the bottles are from Spain and cover all the important names from a L'Ermita '99 to organic wines by Catalan producers Albet i Noya. The friendly, multilingual assistants are happy to give guidance to customers, and there's a small collection of wine accessories and books on viticulture, available, including titles in English.

Lavinia

Avda Diagonal 605, Eixample (93 363 44 45/www.lavinia.es). Metro Maria Cristina. **Open** 10am-9pm Mon-Sat. **Credit** AmEx, DC, MC, V. **Map** p337 A2.

Lavinia has easily the largest selection of wine in the city. The modern, dramatically lit and enormous space houses thousands of wines, both local and international, including exceptional vintages and special editions at good prices. A very efficient online operation is also offered, along with a club, magazine and regular tasting events.

Vila Viniteca

C/Agullers 7-9, Born (93 310 19 56/www.vilaviniteca.es). Metro Jaume I. **Open** *Sept-June* 8.30am-2.30pm, 4.30-8.30pm Mon-Sat. *July-Aug* 8.30am-2.30pm, 4.30-8.30pm Mon-Fri; 8.30am-2.30pm Sat. **Credit** AmEx, DC, MC, V. **Map** p345 B4.

Now in its third generation, this friendly family business has built up a stock of over 3,500 wines since its beginnings in 1932. The selection is mostly Spanish and Catalan, but also takes in favourites from further afield in Italy, South Africa and California. If you visit, be sure to pick up one of the wonderful catalogues, or ask about the wine-tasting courses held across the road.

Hair & beauty

Beauty treatments

Bagua

Rambla de Catalunya 100, 4 1, Eixample (93 215 51 01). Metro Diagonal. **Open** 10am-8pm Mon-Fri. **Credit** MC, V. **Map** p338 D4.

As well as offering all the usual beauty treatments, such as facials, massages and anti-cellulite sessions, Bagua also specialises in reasonably-priced alternative therapies. These include lymphatic drainage, reiki and yogui-sui, and appointments in nutritional analysis and yoga classes.

Instituto Francis

Ronda de Sant Pere 18, Eixample (93 317 78 08). Metro Catalunya. **Open** 9.30am-8pm Mon-Fri; 9am-4pm Sat. **Credit** DC, MC, V. **Map** p344 B1.

Whether you want a manicure, moustache wax or teeth-whitening, this established institute has eight floors solely dedicated to pampering. But, be prepared that it ain't cheap.

Trading places

Of the 40 neighbourhood markets in Barcelona, the biggest and best of them all is **La Boqueria** on La Rambla. It evolved from a city wall trading spot for farmers and city dwellers, and became a fixed market in 1836. Its official name, Mercat de Sant Josep, comes from the 16th-century convent that originally occupied the site. Now under a canopy of vaulted glass and cast iron, it resembles a cavernous train station, and it reverberates with the raucous spectacle of buying and selling, chopping and skinning.

There is order in the madness: fruit and vegetables are around the outside, olives and pickles next; heading in from there are meat, offal and chicken stalls, then bakeries and egg stands; fish and seafood are in the centre. The beguilingly bright stalls down the main aisle trap tourists with their candy-coloured fruits and plastic-wrapped *pitaya* halves, chopped *higos chumbos*, and mini fruit salads complete with plastic fork and napkin for immediate consumption. All at a suitably outrageous price, of course.

Locals shop at the cheaper stalls further back from the main aisle, moving between orderly stacks of string beans, perfect peaches, rippling sheets of white tripe, chicken feet, slabs of cow tongues, sheep heads, struggling crayfish, fragrant bins of spices and, in the autumn, the colourful plumage of hanging game. The cheapest fruit and vegetable stalls are on the fringes of the market proper, in Plaça Sant Galdric. Also at the back is Llorenç Petras's woodland stall with wet sacks of snails, dried herbs and many varieties of wild mushroom unknown outside the Catalan Pyrenees.

Masajes a 1000

C/Mallorca 233, Eixample (93 215 85 85). Metro Diagonal/FGC Provença. **Open** *Jan-Apr, Oct-Dec* 8am-midnight daily. *Mar-Sept* 7am-1am daily. **Credit** AmEx, MC, V. **Map** p338 D4.

Defiantly holding on to its peseta-era name, this efficient and economic beauty centre charges by a ticket system. One ticket gets you a half-hour massage and siesta in an ergonomic chair, while 30 tickets buy a luxurious 90-minute 'four hand' massage. Pedicures, manicures, hair and skin care and tanning are also offered, with no need to book ahead.

Cosmetics & perfumes

A good selection is also to be found on the ground floor of **El Corte Inglés** (*see p187*).

Regia

Passeig de Gràcia 39, Eixample (93 216 01 21/ www.regia.es). Metro Passeig de Gràcia. **Open** 9.30am-8.30pm Mon-Fri; 10.30am-8.30pm Sat. **Credit** AmEx, DC, MC, V. **Map** p338 D4.

Regia was founded in 1928, and all six Barcelona branches have a good selection of upmarket per-

Ideal picnic foods to look out for are thinly sliced mountain ham, sausages like chorizo or the long, thin *fuet*, a creamy *garrotxa* goat's cheese, olives the size of golfballs, or little boxes of *seitons* (pickled anchovies).

If you can stand the noise, the market bars are wonderful places to eat; you can have tapas at the glossy wood and brass counter of **El Quim de la Boqueria** in the centre, or try the giant seafood platters at the excellent **Kiosko Universal** on the left-hand corner from the entrance. For **Bar Pinotxo**, *see p172.*

The Boqueria's closest rival for size and variety is **Mercat Sant Antoni** on the far side of the Raval, housed in an ornate cross-shaped iron building with a clothes and Sunday book market situated around the outside (*see p208*). One market that may eventually surpass it for beauty is the **Mercat Santa Caterina** (Passeig Lluís Companys 1-3, 93 319 57 40), which should be returning, with a dramatic new look, to its original site on Avda Francesc Cambó by the spring of 2004. The new market hall was designed by Catalan architect Enric Miralles shortly before his death in 2000.

Other markets worth looking at are the **Mercat de la Concepció** (C/Aragó 313-17, 93 457 53 29) with its famous flower stalls, the villagey charm of **Mercat de la Llibertat** (Plaça Llibertat 27, 93 217 09 95) and the **Mercat del Ninot** (C/Mallorca 133, 93 453 65 12), which has a tiny child (*ninot*) sculpted over the portal.

La Boqueria

La Rambla 91 (93 318 25 84). Metro Liceu. **Open** 8am-8.30pm Mon-Sat. **Map** p342 A2.

fumes and cosmetics as well as a house line of skin and hair products. What makes the Passeig de Gràcia outlet really special is the outstanding perfume museum hidden right at the back, past the offices (free entrance). Its collection ranges from eighth-century BC Corinthian perfume pots to ornate German porcelain or vintage Guerlain scent flasks.

Sephora

El Triangle, C/Pelai 13-39, Eixample (93 306 39 00). Metro Catalunya. **Open** 10am-10pm Mon-Sat. **Credit** AmEx, DC, MC, V. **Map** p344 A1.

An explosion of mirrors, red carpets and zebra stripes assault the eyes as viciously as thousands of scents assault the nose at this underground French perfume and cosmetic hypermarket. Gloved assistants prowl around to guide customers through the vast landscape of perfumes, make-up, accessories and hair and skin products, or to transform images with a makeover. Expect to see many international brands and few surprises.

Other locations: La Maquinista, C/Ciutat d'Asunción, Sant Andreu (93 360 87 21). Diagonal Mar, Avda Diagonal 3, Poblenou (93 356 23 19).

Hairdressers

Anthony Llobet

C/Sant Joaquim 28, Gràcia (93 415 42 10). Metro Fontana. **Open** 10.15am-3pm, 4-8pm Mon, Wed, Fri; 10.15am-3pm, 3-9pm Tue, Thur. Closed 2wks Aug. **Credit** MC, V. **Map** p338 D3.

A small, friendly salon, abuzz with a largely foreign clientele (Anthony and his staff speak English). Prices for a cut and dry are around €22-€26 for women and €11-€12 for men. Staff also do face and body massages, nail art and extensions.

Llongueras

Passeig de Gràcia 78, Eixample (93 215 41 75/ www.llongueras.com). Metro Passeig de Gràcia. **Open** 9am-7pm Mon-Sat. **Credit** AmEx, DC, MC, V. **Map** p338 D4.

A safe bet for all ages, this reassuringly pricey Catalan chain of hairdressers also has outlets in El Corte Inglés department stores. Stylists take the time to give a proper consultation, wash and massage, and the cuts themselves are up-to-the-minute but generally as natural as possible and free of the excesses of the trendier salons.

Other locations: throughout the city.

La Pelu

C/Argenteria 70-72, Born (93 310 48 07/ www.lapelu.com). Metro Jaume I. **Open** 11am-8pm Mon-Sat. **Credit** V. **Map** p345 C3.

The stylists here are a a slightly punky lot, bristling with dreads, badger streaks, shags, afros and, naturally, the mullet à la mode, which has become La Pelu's signature cut. It is also famous for its monthly Full Moon sessions when the branch in C/Argenteria is open from 11pm to 2am, offering special theme nights (tarot readings, live music and comedy, among other things), reduced prices and the added attraction of drinks. Booking essential.

Other locations: C/Tallers 35, Raval (93 301 97 73); C/Consell de Cent 259, Eixample (93 454 45 37).

Markets

Markets to look out for include the **Santa Llúcia Christmas market** (*see p221*), the annual **ceramics fair** at the top of Portal de l'Àngel held during the Mercè (*see p220*), and the **stamp and coin market** in the Plaça Reial on Sunday mornings. Of the city's many **artisan food fairs**, the most central is held on the first and third weekend of every month in the Plaça del Pi. For details of both the regular markets and the one-off events, such as book or record fairs, call 010 for the council information lines; for Barcelona's permanent food markets, *see p206* **Trading places**.

Antiques Market

Plaça Nova, Barri Gòtic (93 302 70 45). Metro Jaume I. **Open** 10am-8pm Thur. Closed Aug. **No credit cards**. **Map** p344 B2.

The location in front of the cathedral means tourist prices, so come prepared to haggle. The market itself dates from the Middle Ages but the antiques certainly don't, and generally consist of smaller items such as sepia postcards, Manila shawls, pocket watches, typewriters, feather quills, lace, cameras and jewellery among the bibelots and bric-a-brac. In December it transfers to Portal de l'Àngel.

Art Market

Plaça Sant Josep Oriol, Barri Gòtic (no phone). Metro Liceu. **Open** 11am-8.30pm Sat; 10am-3pm Sun. **No credit cards**. **Map** p345 A3.

About 50 local artists shoehorn their stands in to hawk art of very variable quality. Predictably, the 'bustling' Rambla is a favourite theme, as are mawkish nudes and Spanish balcony scenes, but a good burrow through the racks reveals some streaks of originality and even the odd treasure.

Book & Coin Market

Mercat de Sant Antoni, C/Comte d'Urgell 1, Eixample (93 423 42 87). Metro Sant Antoni. **Open** 8am-2pm (approx) Sun. **No credit cards**. **Map** p342 C5.

This ancient book fair has been traced back as far as 1573 when vendors sold to church-goers outside Santa Maria del Mar church. Now orbiting the Sant Antoni market, the scores of trestle tables heave with every manner of reading material from arcane old tomes to well-pawed bodice rippers and yellowing comics. This has expanded to include software, posters, music, stamps and stacks of plastic blister sheets filled with coins. Get there early as the market gets very crowded by late morning.

Brocanters del Port Vell

Moll de les Drassanes, Port Vell (93 317 61 35). Metro Drassanes. **Open** 11am-9pm Sat, Sun. **No credit cards**. **Map** p345 A4.

An upscale rag and bone market with a few antiques, popular with locals on the lookout for toys, china, coins, collectors' records, costume jewellery, military clothing and reproductions of archaeological finds. More recently the market has been invaded by stalls selling CDs and hippie gear.

Els Encants

C/Dos de Maig 186, Plaça de la Glòries, Eixample (93 246 30 30). Metro Glòries. **Open** 9am-6pm (auctions 7-9am) Mon, Wed, Fri, Sat. **No credit cards**. **Map** p343 F5.

The closest thing Barcelona has to a fleamarket like Madrid's Rastro, Els Encants has over 1,000 official stalls along with plenty of wandering hopefuls trying to sell you single shoes or rusty hairclips. The stalls sell heaps of fascinating junk, second-hand clothes and geriatric furniture along with modern and very cheap household and sports goods. Although the market is officially open in the afternoons, many stalls pack up at midday; for the best stuff, get there with the lark and be prepared to haggle. The auctions are best either at 7am (when the commercial dealers buy) or at midday, when unsold goods drop dramatically in price. Avoid Saturdays, when it's unpleasantly crowded, and be on your guard for pickpockets and shortchanging. As plans to relocate the market are under way, it may be wise to call before trekking out there.

Music

C/Tallers, C/Bonsuccès and C/Riera Baixa in the Raval are dotted with speciality shops that cater to all tastes and formats plus plenty of instruments and sheet music. Large mainstream music selections can be found in the huge Portal de l'Àngel branch of **El Corte Inglés** (*see p187*) and, often more cheaply, at **FNAC** (*see p188*).

Casa Beethoven

La Rambla 97 (93 301 48 26/www.casabeethoven.com). Metro Liceu. **Open** 9am-1.30pm, 4-7.45pm Mon-Fri, 9.30am-1.30pm, 5-7.45pm Sat. Closed 3wks Aug. **Credit** AmEx, MC, V. **Map** p344 A2.

The speciality at this beautiful old shop is sheet music and songbooks that cover the gamut from Handel to Bob Marley with a concentration on opera. Books cover music history and theory, while the CD collection is surprisingly diverse and particularly strong on modern and classical Spanish music.

Discos Castelló

C/Tallers 3, 7, 9 & 79, Raval (93 302 59 46/www.discoscastello.es). Metro Catalunya. **Open** 10am-8.30pm Mon-Sat. **Credit** AmEx, DC, MC, V. **Map** p344 A2.

This is actually a chain of small shops, each with a different emphasis. No.3 specialises in classical, while No.7 has rock, pop, heavy metal and jazz with a sprinkling of flamenco. The branch in C/Nou de la Rambla is good for ethnic music.

Other locations: C/Nou de la Rambla 15, Raval (93 302 42 36); **La Maquinista**, C/Ciutat d'Asunción, Sant Andreu (93 360 80 78).

New Phono

C/Ample 37, Barri Gòtic (93 315 13 61/www.newphono.com). Metro Jaume I. **Open** 9.30am-2pm, 4.30-8pm Mon-Fri; 9.30am-2pm Sat. **Credit** AmEx, DC, MC, V. **Map** p345 B4.

Budding Segovias will splurge on a fine Ramirez classical guitar while others will just want a dirt cheap Admira to strum on the beach. New Phono's cluster of display rooms hold a range of wind, string and percussion instruments and accessories while keyboards and recording equipment reside over the road. Check out its useful noticeboard for contacts.

Wah Wah Records

C/Riera Baixa 14, Raval (93 442 37 03). Metro Universitat. **Open** 11am-2pm, 5-8.30pm Mon-Sat. **Credit** AmEx, MC, V. **Map** p342 C6.

This charismatic hangout is divided into two spaces: the first is devoted to pop, rock, jazz and world music including second-hand, vinyl and first editions, while the back space is a dance DJ's delight with techno, house, drum 'n' bass and breakbeats along with the experimental pieces produced under its own label, Wah Wah Records Supersonic Sounds, which the clerk describes as 'bachelor pad space music'.

Opticians

Arense

Ronda Sant Pere 16, Eixample (93 301 82 90). Metro Catalunya. **Open** 10am-9pm Mon-Sat. **Credit** AmEx, DC, MC, V. **Map** p344 B1.

This full-service optician occupies a gorgeous Modernista space, built in 1874 as the art supply store Casa Teixidor. It sells big-name brands at reasonable prices and an optometrist works in the back behind a stained-glass window. The downstairs lab turns specs around within two days.

Grand Optical

El Triangle, Plaça Catalunya 4, Eixample (93 304 16 40). Metro Catalunya. **Open** 10am-10pm Mon-Sat. **Credit** AmEx, DC, MC, V. **Map** p344 A1.

English-speaking staff offer free eye-tests, and can provide new glasses within two hours (one hour if you have your prescription), or fit sunglasses with prescription lenses for only €50. Sunglasses are upstairs and frames downstairs, with over 3,500 models from designers such as Prada, Nike or Oakley, and staff will refund the difference if you can find the same glasses at a cheaper price. Ask downstairs about the full range of contact lenses.

Photography

Arpí Foto Video

La Rambla 38-40, Barri Gòtic (93 301 74 04). Metro Drassanes or Liceu. **Open** 9am-2pm, 4-8pm Mon-Sat. **Credit** AmEx, DC, MC, V. **Map** p345 A3.

Five floors of specialist equipment including projectors, underwater handycams, Polaroids and studio Hasselblads. For the happy snapper tourist, disposable cameras range from €2.80 to €10 and staff will develop 24 colour prints in 24 hours for about €8 and 36 prints for about €10. There is a basic repair centre here, but be prepared that service can be desperately slow.

Fotoprix

C/Pelai 6, Raval (93 318 20 36/www.fotoprix.es). Metro Universitat. **Open** 9.30am-8.30pm Mon-Fri; 10am-8.30pm Sat. **Credit** MC,V. **Map** p344 A1.

The distinctive canary yellow Fotoprix shops number more than 50 in the city, offering one-hour film developing and digital processing, frames, albums and basic selections of film and cameras. To develop 24 colour prints in 24 hours costs €9.19.

Speciality shops

Alonso

C/Santa Anna 27, Barri Gòtic (93 317 60 85). Metro Catalunya. **Open** 10am-8pm Mon-Sat. **Credit** DC, MC, V. **Map** 342 B2.

Who's who The image makers

If there is such a thing as a 'Barcelona look', it has been heavily influenced by the city's fashion troika: Custodio Dalmau, Antonio Miró and Jordi Labanda.

The **Custo Barcelona** fashion empire (*see p199*) was created in the 1980s after Catalan brothers Custodio and David Dalmau went on a round-the-world motorcycle trip and were inspired by California surf dudes. Back in Barcelona they started making colourful screen-printed cotton tops that were the fashion equivalent of a bag of Smartie-coloured Prozac pills. Relentlessly loud and happy, a typical top might combine screaming magenta and lime with foil, netting, metal paint and, of course, their trademark face-on-the-front printed panel, which might incorporate Japanese anime, 1970s pop art and drawings from famous illustrators (including some by the young Labanda, on whom more soon).

Custo shone out amid the grey minimalism of 1997's New York Fashion Week, and was suddenly on the most famous backs in FashionLand: the cast of *Sex and the City*, Penélope Cruz, Gwen Stefani... The line has now expanded to include denim and footwear, and although some of the current designs look like they've sprung from Austin Powers' wardrobe, Dalmau still managed to scoop the 2003 Italian Fashion Oscar. This most coveted of labels now has outlets across Spain and the US, and looks firmly set for world Custo-misation.

At the polar extreme is **Antonio Miró** (*see p196*), the long-established kingpin of grown-up Catalan fashion. Also starting out with his brother, he first blipped on the fashion radar back in the '60s, selling flowery shirts and cord flares in a whacky little beach boutique decorated with toilet seats. Now only the name remains: *Groc*, which means yellow in Catalan, and is a far cry from the austere palette for which he is famous. Catalonia's favourite doom and gloom merchant may occasionally dabble in browns or greys but this year, black is the new black. Again.

Still, nobody does it better, and his sober, elegant clothes manage to both embody the Catalan reverence for *seny* (common sense) and show the value of exquisite detailing and fabrics over gimmicky innovation. In his own defence, Miró has a theory that bright colours simply don't work in a vibrant landscape like Spain, and that cobalts and scarlets are best used to punctuate the drizzly greys of a country like Britain.

Perhaps the most influential force has not been a designer at all but 35-year-old commercial illustrator **Jordi Labanda**. Barcelona is completely saturated with his faux-naïf cartoons of swanky cocktail parties, jet-setting fashionistas and haute couture luxury (*pictured*), which decorate everything from sandwich bars to Zara perfumes, schoolgirl stationery and Font Vella water bottles.

Notable for its ornate Modernista façade, Alonso stocks every kind of glove, from chunky mittens to bridal ivory silks. It also stocks elegant accessories, such as traditional fringed shawls, lace *mantillas*, and fans that apparently speak their own language: fanning quickly means 'I'm engaged'; fanning slowly means 'I'm married'; if you handle to the lips, it means 'kiss me', although it's doubtful how successful this technique would be down the Dog & Whistle back home. Let us know how it goes.

Cereria Subirá

Baixada de Llibreteria 7, Barri Gòtic (93 315 26 06). Metro Jaume I. **Open** 9am-1.30pm, 4-7.30pm Mon-Fri; 9am-1.30pm Sat. **Credit** AmEx, MC, V. **Map** p345 B3.

Votive candles, wax beads, tapers and all manner of novelty creations are on display at this charming candle store that has beautifully preserved much of its original 1700s decor: steps swirl down from the mint-green balustraded gallery, heralded by two torch-bearing black maidens.

Flora Albaicín

C/Canuda 3, Barri Gòtic (93 302 10 35). Metro Catalunya. **Open** 10.30am-1pm, 5-8pm Mon-Sat. **Credit** AmEx, MC, V. **Map** p344 A-B2.

This is a fluffy ruffle of a shop that bursts with traditional flamenco dresses, shoes, combs, shawls and men's traditional *campero* suits and riding boots. Outfits are also stocked in children's sizes, and can even be made to measure for that special occassion.

Herboristeria del Rei

C/Vidre 1, Barri Gòtic (93 318 05 12/www.herboristeriadelrei.com). Metro Liceu. **Open** 5-8pm Mon; 10am-2pm, 5-8pm Tue-Sat. **Credit** MC, V. **Map** p345 A3.

Once the official herbalist to Queen Isabel II, this exquisitely restored herbal shop has ornate galleries, murals and a bust of the great Swedish botanist Linnaeus overlooking hundreds of tiny painted drawers and jars full of dried plants, spices, lotions and unguents. Popular choices for cooking are saffron and rosemary, while camomile tisanes aid sleep.

Born in Uruguay to a Catalan mother and Basque father, Labanda has been resident in Barcelona since the age of three; after a degree in industrial design he switched to commercial illustration, painting in gouache without the aid of computers. Like Custo, he made his name in the States before coming back home, and since 1994 has worked with newspapers and magazines including *Vogue*, *Cosmopolitan*, *Marie Claire*, the *New Yorker*, and *Wallpaper**. Although initially satirical, Labanda's visions of beautiful people enjoying decadent, privileged lifestyles ironically proved to be the ideal medium for commercial advertising, and he has been increasingly lured from the press by heavyweight corporate clients like American Express and Pepsi.

For a compilation of drawings, take a look at his glossy coffee table tome called *Hey Day*. It's selling out faster than he is.

El Rei de la Magia

C/Princesa 11, Born (93 319 39 20/www.elreidelamagia.com). Metro Liceu. **Open** 10am-2pm, 5-8pm Mon-Fri; 11am-2pm Sat. **Credit** AmEx, MC, V. **Map** p345 B3.

As well as the obligatory rubber chickens and fake turds, this wonderful old joke and magic shop – founded in 1881 – specialises in illusion for practitioners of all levels, and some tricks are made on site. The basic drawer box costs about €20 and co-owner Jack, a performing magician from New York, will teach you to use it in the shop's useful training space.

Sport

The tourist shops on La Rambla stock a huge range of football strips.

La Botiga del Barça

Maremàgnum, Moll d'Espanya, Port Vell (93 225 80 45). Metro Drassanes. **Open** 10am-10pm daily. **Credit** AmEx, DC, MC, V. **Map** p342 D7.

Now under the aegis of Nike, La Botiga has every permutation of Barça merchandise imaginable, from scarves (€11.20), balls and hats, to strips printed with your name, and a range of gifts including ashtrays, shield-embossed tankards and crested ties.

Other locations: Gran Via de les Corts Catalanes 418, Eixample (93 423 59 41); Museu del FC Barcelona, Nou Camp (93 490 68 43).

Decathlon

C/Canuda 20, Barri Gòtic (93 342 61 61/www.decathlon.es). Metro Catalunya. **Open** 10am-9.30pm Mon-Sat. **Credit** AmEx, DC, MC, V. **Map** p344 B2.

The city's most comprehensive sports shop has attire and equipment for every sport, from scuba diving to golf, and windsurfing to racquet sports. There's also a good repair service for bicycles, skis (winter only) and custom stamping for team shirts.

Other locations: Gran Via de les Corts Catalanes 2 & 75, Eixample (93 259 15 92); L'Illa, Avda Diagonal 549, Eixample (93 444 01 54).

Flora Albaicín. *See p210.*

Ticket agents

FNAC (*see p188*) has an efficient ticket desk for obtaining rock and pop concert tickets in advance, while concert tickets for smaller venues are often sold in record shops; look out for details on posters around the city. Alternatively, try the venues themselves, as they are often the best places to obtain advance tickets (for Barça tickets, *see p270*).

Servi-Caixa – La Caixa

902 33 22 11/www.servicaixa.com. **Credit** AmEx, DC, MC, V.

All larger branches of Catalonia's biggest savings bank, La Caixa, have yellow Servi-Caixa machines (some of which are combined with a cash dispenser). With a debit or credit card, you can use these machines to get T-10 and T-50/30 travel cards, local information and tickets to a great many attractions and events, including Universal Studios Port Aventura, Barça football games, the Teatre Nacional and the Liceu, 24 hours a day. You can also order tickets on the telephone (many staff speak some English) or by logging onto the website.

Tel-entrada – Caixa Catalunya

902 10 12 12/www.telentrada.com.
Credit MC, V.

Tel-entrada sells tickets for theatre productions, concerts, cinemas, museums and exhibitions over the counter at all branches of Caixa Catalunya. You can also book tickets over the telephone with a credit card (many of the staff speak English). You can phone from outside Spain (on 00 34 93 479 99 20) or alternatively, log onto the website.

Tobacco & cigars

L'Estanc de Laietana

Via Laietana 4, Born (93 310 10 34). Metro Jaume I. **Open** 9am-2pm, 4-8pm Mon-Fri; 10am-2pm Sat. **Credit** (gifts, not cigarettes) AmEx, MC, V. **Map** p345 B4.

This famous tobacconist stocks more than 100 brands of cigarettes and 100 types of rolling tobacco; the exceptional range of fine cigars are stored in an underground humidor at sea level.

Gimeno

La Rambla 100, Barri Gòtic (93 302 09 83). Metro Liceu. **Open** 9.30am-8pm Mon-Fri; 10am-8.30pm Sat. **Credit** (gifts, not cigarettes) AmEx, DC, MC, V. **Map** p345 A3.

The puff daddy of them all, Gimeno has been a shrine to the weed since it opened nearly a century ago. Cuban cigars are the speciality here, but of course there are lots of pipes, smoking accessories and every kind of cigarette.

Travel services

FNAC (*see p188*) also has a travel agency on the ground floor.

Halcón Viajes

C/Aribau 34, Eixample (93 454 59 95/90 230 06 00/www.halconviajes.com). Metro Universitat. **Open** 9.30am-1.30pm, 4.30-8pm Mon-Fri; 10am-1pm Sat. **Credit** AmEx, DC, MC, V. **Map** p342 C5.

Halcón moves quickly and therefore often has good, exclusive bargain deals with Air Europa for Spanish domestic and European flights. For hotels, cruises and car rental, it also has good deals with Globalia. In addition to this, it has a handy hotel booking service, and competative prices on travel insurance. Check out the website.

Other locations: throughout the city.

Viajes Zeppelin

C/Villarroel 49, Eixample (93 412 00 13/93 412 127 359/www.viajeszeppelin.com). Metro Urgell. **Open** 9am-8pm Mon-Fri; 10am-1pm Sat. **Credit** AmEx, DC, MC, V. **Map** p342 C5.

Viajes Zeppelin can get its hands on cheap schedule and charter flights. It also has some excellent special offers and good rates on the usual services such as car hire and travel insurance. Check out the easy-to-use website for more information.

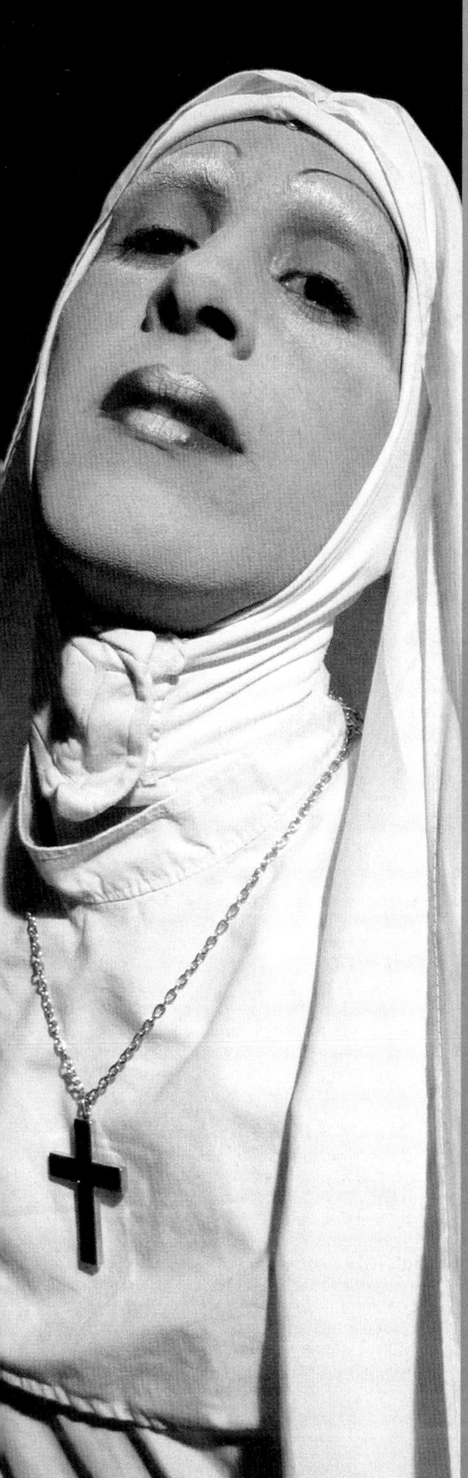

Arts & Entertainment

Features

Festivals & Events

24-hour party people.

Playing it cool at the **Festival International de Jazz**. *See p220.*

Barcelona is always up for a shindig and the flimsiest excuse will do: whether it's summer solstice or just that artichokes have come into season, somebody somewhere is throwing a party. In addition to the near-continuous cavalcade of festivals, fairs, parades and concerts throughout the year, the city gets an extra helping of entertainment between May and September 2004 from the mighty **Fòrum Universal de les Cultures**, which will stage hundreds of events across the city although many are cunningly appropriated from existing festivals. Anything involving the buzzwords 'multicultural' or 'international' made perfect Fòrum fodder: the **Grec** international theatre festival (*see p218*), **Sónar** (*see p216*) and the **International Poetry Festival** (*see p216*) will all present special Fòrum editions.

The customs and traditions of a Catalan festival are too many and far too varied to list here, but below are some of the most common you're likely to encounter. All of the following are staple ingredients of Sant Joan, the Mercè and the smaller neighbourhood *festes majors*. *See also p269* **Castellers**.

CORREFOC

After nightfall, pyromaniac pandemonium ensues when groups of horned devils do a *correfoc* (fire run) through the streets, brandishing tridents that spout industrial-strength fireworks at the shrieking crowd. The more daring onlookers, protected by cotton caps, long sleeves and scarves, try to stop the devils and touch the giant, firebreathing dragon being dragged in their wake. After flouting just about every safety rule in the book, the party goes on with more fireworks and dancing.

GEGANTS AND CAPGROSSOS

At the head of any procession come the regal, po-faced *gegants* (giants): richly dressed, five-metre (16-feet) tall papier-mâché and fibreglass figures that sway along on the shoulders of whoever is hidden up their skirts. The city's official *gegants* represent King Jaume I, Queen Violant and the apple-cheeked Santa Eulàlia, but each neighbourhood has its own figures; Poble Sec has a topless chorus girl atop a chimney stack to represent the area's old factory and music halls, while the beaches of Barceloneta have a crusty old fisherman. In total there are over 200 *gegants* in the city, usually joined by their skittering sidekicks colloquially known as *capgrossos* (fatheads). They live up to their name with grotesquely swollen bonces that caricature hapless public figures.

SARDANES

Watching the dancers executing their fussy little hops and steps in a large circle, it's hard to believe that Catalonia's sober folk dance once was banned as a vestige of pagan witchcraft. The music is similarly restrained and played by an 11-piece *cobla* band; to follow the steps of the dance, listen out for the piercing *flabiol* (recorder) flourishes, which mark counterpoints for the dancers. The *sardana* is much harder than it looks, and the joy lies in taking part rather than watching; it is a dance of solidarity not spectacle. To try your luck, check out the *sardanes* every weekend in front of the cathedral (6.30-8.30pm Sat, noon-2pm Sun) and in Plaça Sant Jaume (6-8pm Sun).

INFORMATION

Bear in mind that organisers are prone to change dates nearer the time. For more information, try tourist offices or the city's information phone line on 010, or the cultural agenda section at www.bcn.es. Newspapers also carry details, especially in their Friday or Saturday supplements. Events listed below that include public holidays (when many shops will be closed for the day) are marked *.

Spring

Festes de Sant Medir de Gràcia

Information: www.santmedir.org. Gràcia to Sant Cugat & back, usually via Plaça Lesseps, Avda República Argentina & Carretera de l'Arrabassada. **Starting point** Metro Fontana. **Date** early Mar. **Map** p338 D2/3.

Since 1830, decorated horses and carts have gathered bright and early around the Plaça Rius i Taulet to ride up into the Collserola hills. It's an hour's leafy walk from Sant Cugat or 25 minutes from Plaça Catalunya by FGC train to the procession which ends at the hermitage of Sant Medir, martyred by the Romans. Mass is celebrated, *sardanes* danced and barbecued *botifarres* eaten. At mid-morning and again in the evening, neighbourhood societies drive horse-drawn carts around the main streets of Gràcia; they heave 100 tons of blessed boiled sweets on to the crowds, who come armed with sharp elbows and plastic bags to reap the sticky goodies.

Setmana Santa* (Holy Week)

Date 5-12 Apr 2004.

Catalonia doesn't go in for the emotional religious processions of southern Spain, and the main Easter event is the blessing of the palms. On Palm Sunday dense crowds scrum around the cathedral clutching bleached palm fronds bought the week before from the stalls along Rambla de Catalunya and outside the Sagrada Família. Boys traditionally carry huge beribboned *palmons* up to 2m (6ft) long, while girls have graceful little *palmes* woven into intricate designs. On Good Friday, a series of small processions and blessings takes place in front of the cathedral, and a procession sets out from the church of Sant Agustí on C/Hospital at around 5pm and arrives at the cathedral a couple of hours later. On Easter Sunday it traditionally falls to the godparents to give kids a *mona*: originally a marzipan cake decorated with a boiled egg but now more likely to be an elaborate chocolate confection.

Sant Jordi

La Rambla & all over Barcelona. **Date** 23 Apr.

Sant Jordi (St George) is the patron saint of Catalonia, and on his feast day nearly every building bears the red and gold Catalan flag, while bakeries sell Sant Jordi bread streaked with red *sobrassada* pâté and yellow walnuts. Red roses decorate the Palau de la Generalitat and the city's many statues and paintings of Georgie in all his dragon-slaying glory. It is said that as the drops of the dragon's blood fell, they turned into red flowers, and for over five centuries this has been the Catalan version of St Valentine's Day. Men traditionally give women a rose tied to an ear of wheat with a stripy ribbon, and women reciprocate with a book, although in these enlightened times many now give both. The tradition of the book only dates back to the last century when it was announced Day of the Book due to the curious factoid that both Cervantes and Shakespeare died on 23 April 1616. This day accounts for 10% of Catalonia's annual book sales, and street stalls and bookshops give good discounts.

Festival de Música Antiga

CaixaForum, Avda Marquès de Comillas 6-8, Montjuïc (902 22 30 40/www.fundacio.lacaixa.es). Metro Plaça de Espanya. **Date** 18 Apr-8 May. **Concerts** €3-€9. **Map** p341 A5.

Plunking lutes, harpsichords and hurdy-gurdies are all part of the Festival of Early Music. Performers come from all over Europe and in 2003 included virtuoso soloists Gustav Leonhardt, Neal Peres da Costa, and Muhammed Faqir on the Pakistani suranthu, along with groups like Musicians of the Globe directed by Philip Pickett. The accompanying El Fringe festival offers young performers the chance to practise and perform alongside more established musicians. The atmosphere at the event is augmented by period performances that include such specialities as Renaissance cabaret, Venetian comedy and Shakespearean clowns.

Feria de Abril de Catalunya

Nova Mar Bella beach. Metro Besós-Mar, then special shuttle buses. **Information** Federación de Entidades Culturales Andaluces en Cataluña (93 488 02 95/ www.fecac.com). **Date** 30 Apr-9 May 2004.

Arts & Entertainment

It may be a pale imitation but this is the closest you'll get in Barcelona to Seville's famous ten-day fiesta – even the rainproof soil is imported from down south for the occasion. Dressed to frill and making a traditional grand entrance by horse and carriage, the city's Andalucian population gets down to some serious partying at a huge funfair with rows of decorated marquees proffering manzanilla sherry and flamenco shows. On the downside, the Portaloos are mobbed and filthy, and the food tents overpriced – so don't go with an empty stomach or a full bladder.

Dia del Treball* (May Day)

Date 1 May.

Committed trade unionists join organised marches, with main routes covering Passeig de Gràcia, Passeig Sant Joan and Plaça Sant Jaume. Attendance has dwindled in recent years, and the day has become a platform for anti-globalisation and anti-war protests.

Sant Ponç

C/Hospital, Raval. Metro Liceu. **Date** 11 May. **Map** p344-5 A2-3.

Sant Ponç is the patron saint of herbalists and beekeepers and was worshipped in the church of the Hospital de la Santa Creu. Since 1871, a charming fair of artisan food and alternative medicine has been held on his feast day, with aromatic and medicinal herbs, candied fruits, royal jelly and honey.

Festa de la Diversitat

Moll de la Fusta. Metro Drassanes. **Information** SOS Racisme (93 301 05 97/www.sosracisme.org). **Date** 3 days May/June. **Admission** €8; €4 concessions; free under-14s. **Map** p345 A-B4.

A laid-back celebration of the city's cultural and ethnic diversity with three days of alternative cinema, music, theatre, kids' activities and many concerts from names such as Ojos de Brujo or the James Taylor Quartet. Supported by nearly 100 NGOs, the many conferences and information stands are of limited interest to casual visitors, although local immigrant organisations also set up stalls with food, clothes and jewellery with daily exhibitions of *capoeira*, samba and the like. Profits go to SOS Racisme for its fight for racial equality.

Barcelona Poesia & Festival Internacional de Poesia

All over Barcelona. **Information** Institut de Cultura (93 301 77 75/www.bcn.es/icub). **Date** 1wk May 2004.

The city breaks out in a rash of couplets, limericks and haikus for this poetry extravaganza, which includes the International Poetry Festival held in the Palau de la Música Catalana on the last day. It all started as the courtly *Jocs Florals* (Floral Games) in 1393, which were named after the prizes: a silver violet as third prize; a golden rose as second prize and, naturally, a real flower for the winner. Having died out by the mid 15th century, the games were resuscitated in 1859 as a vehicle for the promotion of the Catalan language, and prizes went to the most suitably florid paeans to the motherland. Now Spanish is also permitted, along with the many foreign languages of the International Festival, which in 2003 included readings by Patti Smith and John Giorno.

Festival de Flamenco de Ciutat Vella

Information 93 443 43 46/www.tallerdemusics.com. **Date** 1wk late May.

Much of Barcelona's flamenco offerings are overpriced tourist bait replete with grubby frills, karaoke *coplas* and diluted sangria. For the real thing, try the newly expanded Old City flamenco festival with four days and nights of concerts, film exhibitions and children's activities, all centred around the CCCB (*see p95*). In 2003 the festival focused on the impact of flamenco fusions including jazz-flamenco from singer Chano Domínguez and rock 'n' flamenco from Enrique Morente in collaboration with Lagarjita Nick. The timing is designed to complement the Nou Barris Flamenco Festival (C/Doctor Pi i Molist 133) held a few days earlier.

Summer

Sónar

Information www.sonar.es. **Date** 17-19 June 2004.

This three-day International Festival of Advanced Music and Multimedia Art attracted over 90,000 visitors in 2003 and has become as overgrown and unwieldy as its title. Nowadays, a large part of the experience involves trekking between the many different stages and waiting in line. The event is divided into two parts: SónarDay is a techno-orgy of record fairs, conferences, exhibitions and soundlabs, while DJs play hip hop, chill out and indietronics for light relief. The CCCB (*see p95*), the patio of which is covered in fake grass and prone bodies, is the main hub of activity. SónarNight means a scramble for the desperately overcrowded SónarBus (from the bottom of La Rambla) out to the vast Polígon Pedrosa in L'Hospitalet de Llobregat. In this suitably post modern industrial wasteland, concerts and DJs are spread over three spaces and in 2003 included heavyweights like Björk, Aphex Twin and Carl Cox. Day passes cost around €17, night passes about €37 and the full pass about €95. Buy tickets in advance at the Palau de la Virreina, or by calling 902 888 902 or 34 902 150 025.

Marató de l'Espectacle

Mercat de les Flors, C/Lleida 59, Poble Sec. Metro Poble Sec or Espanya. **Information** Associació Marató de l'Espectacle (93 268 18 68/www.marato.com). **Date** 4-5 June 2004. **Map** p341 B6.

If you can stand the pace, Barcelona's anarchic performance marathon makes for an excellent night out. The audience wanders freely through the Mercat de Les Flors, Teatre Lliure and central Plaça Margarida Xirgu, where over 200 artists and productions try to win them over inside the stipulated time slot: three seconds up to a maximum of ten minutes. Theatre, circus acts and dance all feature but in principle anything is welcome, and the programme has broadened to include music, video and animation. The foyer hosts photography and art installations.

Festa de la Música

All over Barcelona. **Information** Institut de Cultura (93 301 77 75/www.bcn.es/icub). **Date** 21 June 2003.
Buskers bite back as amateur musicians from 100 countries take to the streets. The event is free, and you're as likely to see a kid slapping a bongo as a first-rate blues band, symphonic orchestra or choir.

Sant Joan*

All over Barcelona. **Date** night of 23 June.
The wildest night of the year is unquestionably the pagan pyromania of the eve of Sant Joan (St John the Baptist). Being summer solstice, it's traditional to stay up 'til dawn, munching *coca de Sant Joan* – a flat, crispy cake topped with candied fruit – with endless bottles of cava while faces glow orange by the light of huge bonfires all over the city. For a week beforehand, the June air is ripped apart by explosions, as every schoolkid spends their pocket money on bangers and chucks them about in an unnerving manner. Come the night itself, the city is a sonic boom of fireworks exploding from balconies and squares. The biggest displays are at Montjuïc, Tibidabo and L'Estació del Nord. Don't miss Barceloneta's *Nit del Foc* (Night of Fire) as devils dance about the bonfire under the setting sun and rising moon before everyone heads down to the sea for barbecues and dawn skinny-dipping. Special metro and FGC trains run through the night.

Curious customs

New Year knickers

For good luck over the year, underwear has to be bright red on 31 December. So street vendors hawk cheaply sewn scarlet scanties and it's a cheeky version of the red rose between couples.

The Man of the Noses

L'Home dels Nassos always appears on 31 December and has many noses as there are days in the year (it being the last day, the sly old fox only has one). If you're wandering around on the day, look out for an old sailor carrying a baby face to symbolise the coming of a new year.

Chocolate turds

Yuletide scatology carries on for Kings' Day (5 January), when bakeries sell traditional *tifas*: glistening turds made of chocolate cake, complete with sugar-spun flies on top.

Burying the sardine

The Enterrament de la Sardina marks Ash Wednesday, the last day of carnival before Lent. In Barceloneta children carry sardines on little fishing rods to be buried on the beach. They are usually followed by a bawdy mock funeral cortège for the ill-fated fish. Nobody really knows why any of this happens but it's awfully cute.

Flower carpets

Sitges smells sweet over Corpus Christi when the narrow streets of the old town are covered in swirling designs made from millions of flower petals. After a competition for best street, the final religious parade gets to trample it.

Dancing eggs

Over Corpus Christi, L'Ou Com Balla is a hollowed-out egg placed on the spout of a small fountain garlanded with flowers, where it spins on the jet of water. See it in all its glory at the Ateneu Barcelonès (C/Canuda 6), Casa de l'Ardiaca (C/Santa Llúcia 1) or the cathedral cloisters.

Christmas crappers

Known as the *caganer*, this small nativity scene figure crouches down behind the stable, trousers around the ankles, with a lovingly sculpted turd steaming below.

Shitting logs

The *caga tió* with smiling face and red Santa hat is filled with sweets and presents and covered with a blanket; children then quite literally beat the crap out of it while singing the log song. The violence is rewarded with a diarrhoeic slew of presents.

Farting fools

Cut-out paper figures, known as *llufes*, are attached to the backs of unsuspecting victims on 28 December. *Llufa* means a 'silent fart' and especially thorough pranksters follow up with a stinkbomb. It's also a day for spoof news headlines and practical jokes.

Saintly cakes

No fewer than 20 saints' days in Catalonia have cakes associated with them, from Sant Josep's *crema catalana* to Sant Joan's candied-fruit-laden *coca*. Santa Llucía, patron saint of dressmakers, is honoured with a cream-filled sponge in the shape of a pair of scissors.

Fòrum 2004

Barcelona's massively hyped, stellar event for 2004 looks at first glance like a standard world's fair. A vast site complete with flashy new architecture, squares, parkland and beachfront has been destined for a gallimaufry of exhibitions, debates, shows, markets and high-tech flourishes, like a huge photovoltaic panel promising to electrify the whole affair. But take a closer look. What? No national and regional pavilions vie for our attention on the long esplanades, trying to outdo one another with shameless jingoism? Well, no. After Barcelona's request to hold a universal exhibition was rejected, the city came up with a more contemporary way of interpreting the concept that avoids such clichés.

To be held from 9 May to 26 September, the Fòrum Universal de les Cultures represents not nations but ideas, putting the thematic triad of sustainable development, cultural diversity and conditions for peace front and centre. In other words, the institutional assimilation of myriad left-leaning ideals honed over scores of recent anti-globalisation and peace rallies. The 40 'Dialogues', each lasting anywhere from a day to a week, have titles such as 'Poverty, Microcredits and Social Development', 'Towards a World Without Violence' and 'Work Cultures'. The participant list for this latter Dialogue – intellectuals Susan George, Richard Sennet and Alain Touraine feature alongside former EU head Jacques Delors – gives an idea of the parade of illustrious minds convened. In other sessions the Clintons, Mandelas and Gorbachevs of the world will not be wanting.

The Fòrum also features an ambitious exhibitions programme. The four main on-site shows are 'Inhabiting the World' (on people and the environment), 'The Terracotta Warriors of Xi'an' (Chinese funerary art from the first Qin Dynasty), 'Voices' (languages in humankind) and 'Cities-Corners' (the city as cultural intersection). A further 16 smaller displays (on topics like biodiversity and ethical banking) will be complemented by exhibitions organised by area museums. China features strongly, with 'Confucius' at the CaixaForum and a show of ancient Chinese bronzes at the MNAC. Another project entitled 'The Outset of Inequality', at the Archaeology Museum, will deal with the origins of social and political discrimination in Mediterranean society.

If this all sounds a bit dry, the excellent and varied entertainment might help. Each of the Fòrum's 141 days and nights will offer theatre, concerts, shows, thematic markets, 'ethnic' days and participative games for children, as well as food stalls from around the world. Larger performance events will be in the two open 'sea auditoriums', each with a capacity of 3,000.

True to the model of the 1992 Olympics, the Fòrum is also the pretext for an ambitious urban planning extravaganza. The massive convention centre, a new leisure marina and even a small island off the coast – Pangea Island, 60 metres (197 feet) from a prefab beach – will transform the former industrial wasteland near the mouth of the Besòs River. It will be accessible only by swimming, and is expected to be a popular draw. Indeed, the Fòrum site works as the extension of the large new residential tracts that have taken up the lower part of Avda Diagonal, effectively merging into them. A worthwhile project to take the zoo out of the Ciutadella park and

Classics als Parcs

Information Parcs i Jardins (93 413 24 00/ www.bcn.es/parcsijardins). **Date** June-July.

A perfect start to a balmy summer evening is listening to some classical music in Barcelona's most beautiful parks. There is a wide-ranging programme for small ensembles and soloists, and usually two or three free concerts to choose from each week, in various parks around town.

Festival del Grec

Information Institut de Cultura (93 301 77 75/ www.bcn.es/grec). **Date** June-Aug 2004.

The whole city becomes a stage with performances at 30 venues around the city, while for sea dogs there's boat theatre aboard the *Santa Eulàlia* in Port Vell and swim-in movie showings at the Montjuïc pool. In 2003, the Grec staged everything from a Catalan version of Edward Bond's *Lear* to a saccharine selection from the simpering Nina (from Spain's *Popstars*); an English-language production of *The Tragedian* to a naked dance solo in the dark by Philippe Decouflé. The music selection is generally strongest on world, flamenco and jazz but last year united such diverse names as King Crimson, Morcheeba, Youssou N'Dour and Jane Birkin.

Dies de Dansa

Information Associació Marató de l'Espectacle (93 268 18 68/www.marato.com). **Date** 9-11 July 2004.

This three-day Festival of Dance aims to create what insiders like to call a 'dialogue' between public spaces and individual expression. This boils down to a Kids-from-Fame-style outbreak of pavement

fit it into a new shoreline location has been put off until after the event has run its course. Still, despite the impressive sound to it all, in the run-up to the Fòrum the criticism has been vociferous. Its aims and content are poorly defined – many residents still don't know what it's all about. At the same time, high ticket prices (€17.90 per day for adults) have effectively excluded many of those the Fòrum claims to represent.

Critics understandably wonder just how the Fòrum's monumental construction projects, with such drastic changes to the natural coastline, can ever be reconciled with its stated principle of supporting only sustainable development.

It's all something, Fòrum mandarins will surely reply, to sit down and talk about.
For tickets and further information, see **www.barcelona2004.org**.

pirouettes, lamp-post *lambadas* and phone-box flamenco by local troupes, along with some of Europe's best dance companies including names such as Mar Gómez and Josef Kiss. All shows are free and most centre around the terraces of the CCCB, MACBA, CaixaForum and Fundació Miró, including popular events such as dance-offs and the Spanish-Portuguese break-dancing championships.

Festa Major de Gràcia

All over Gràcia. Metro Fontana. **Information** 93 459 30 80/www.festamajordegracia.org. **Date** 3rd wk in Aug. **Map** p338 D/E2/3.

With little else going on in August, Gràcia's *festa major* receives everybody's undivided party energy and is most famous for its best-dressed street competition. Residents of some 25 streets put in hundreds of hours turning balconies and pavements into lavish underwater kingdoms or tropical rain forests. Each street lays on a dance and open-air meal for the neighbours, while residents flog Caipirinhas and beer to passers-by. The festival opens with giants and castles in Plaça Rius i Taulet, and climaxes on the last night with a *correfoc* and a *castell de focs* (castle of fireworks). In between, 600 activities, from concerts to *sardanes* and kids' bouncy castles, are centred around Plaça Rius i Taulet, Plaça de la Revolució, Plaça del Sol and Plaça de la Virreina.

Festa Major de Sants

All over Sants. Metro Plaça de Sants or Sants Estació. **Information** Federació Festa Major de Sants (93 490 62 14). **Date** 22-28 Aug 2004. **Map** p341 A4.

The stars of the **Festes de la Mercè**.

Hot on the heels of the Gràcia celebrations, its sister district of Sants starts putting up street decorations and trestle tables. This *festa* is less well known and more traditional, with floral offerings to images of Saint Bartholomew at the church and the market. Major events, such as the *correfoc* on the night of the 24th, are held in the Parc de l'Espanya Industrial; others are centred on Plaça del Centre, C/Sant Antoni, Plaça de la Farga and Plaça Joan Peiro, behind Sants station.

Autumn

Diada Nacional de Catalunya*

All over Barcelona. **Date** 11 Sept.

Catalan National Day commemorates Barcelona's capitulation to the Bourbon army in the 1714 War of the Spanish Succession, a bitter defeat that led to the repression of many Catalan institutions. It's lost some of its vigour, but is still a day for national re-affirmation, with the Catalan flag flying on buses and balconies, and displays of folk heritage such as *sardanes* and *castellers*. There are several marches throughout the city, and many make a pilgrimage to the monastery at Montserrat, the spiritual heart of the region and an important guardian of Catalan language and culture during the dictatorship.

Festes de la Mercè*

All over Barcelona. **Information** tourist offices or www.bcn.es. **Date** 20-26 Sept 2004.

It's a pretty safe bet that Barcelona's massive *festa major* will send the Fòrum out with a bang. For over a century, the frenzied, week-long celebrations have been dedicated to the patron saint of the city, Our Lady of Mercy, whose claim to fame was seeing off a plague of locusts in 1637. Ingredients include *castellers, gegants, capgrosses* and the diabolic *correfoc* on the Saturday night. The port area is a focus and there are dazzling fireworks on the beach, the seafront air show on the 26th and the solidarity festival around Port Vell. The main ingredient, though, is music, encompassing everything from traditional *sardanes* and *cobla*, to electronica, pop and jazz. The highlights are usually provided by Barcelona Acció Musical (BAM), a festival-within-a-festival of alternative music. Venues include the cathedral square, Plaça del Rei and La Rambla del Raval, and entrance is generally free.

Festa Major de la Barceloneta

Information 93 221 72 44. **Date** wk of 29 Sept. **Map** p345 C4.

Barceloneta's local celebrations are more picturesque than most with beach *correfocs* and lustily bellowed *habaneres* (sea shanties) forming part of the action but the *festa* especially stands out for its unusual opening ceremony. Since 1881, a wooden cannon has been paraded around the streets on 29 September, the feast day of the district's patron saint, Sant Miquel. Finally, a character known as General Bum Bum (pronounced Boom Boom) lights the cannon and, amid smoke and fireworks, shoots sweets and presents into the crowd. The party ends with dancing and fireworks on the beach.

Festival International de Jazz de Barcelona

Information The Project (93 481 70 40/www.theproject.net). **Date** Nov 2004.

This international festival is gradually growing in scope to include things such as gospel, Dixieland and marching bands, but jazz is still the heart of it all, and big names in 2003 included Chick Corea, Bobby McFerrin and jazz diva Abby Lincoln along with 20 other concerts at the Palau de la Música, Luz de Gas, Razzmatazz and L'Auditori. There are also big band concerts in the Ciutadella park with swing dancers providing the visuals.

Festival de Músiques del Món

CaixaForum, Avda Marquès de Comillas 6-8, Montjuïc (902 22 30 40/www.fundacio.lacaixa.es). Metro Plaça de Espanya. **Date** end Oct-early Nov 2004. **Map** p341 A5.

CaixaForum's annual World Music Festival hosts about 20 concerts, workshops and conferences over the month. Iranian, Palestinian and Kurdish music always feature strongly along with Asian and African music of various latitudes, including stars such as Rokia Traoré from Mali. Closer to home are melancholic *fados* from Portugal by singers like Argentina Santos, or Celtic folk fusion from local groups like Joglars e Senglars. Family concerts (tickets €3) are at 12.30pm at weekends.

La Castanyada*

All over Barcelona. **Date** 31 Oct-1 Nov.

All Saints' Day and the evening before are known as the Castanyada, after the tradition of eating *castanyes* (roast chestnuts), *moniatos* (sweet potatoes) and *panellets* – small almond balls covered in pine nuts. All Saints' is also known as the Dia dels Difunts (Day of the Dead), and nearly 90,000 people visited Barcelona's cemeteries over the weekend in 2003. For some, notably the gypsy community, the visit is an emotional affair with long vigils and lavish floral tributes. Hallowe'en is becoming increasingly popular and the witching hour sees several ghouls riding the metro to the next party.

Winter

Fira de Santa Llúcia

Pla de la Seu & Avda de la Catedral. Metro Jaume I. **Dates** end Nov-23 Dec. **Map** p338 B2-3.

Dating from 1786, this traditional Christmas fair has expanded to over 400 stalls, almost entirely blocking the square and streets around the cathedral. As you slowly shuffle past, you'll see all manner of handcrafted Christmas decorations and gifts, along with mistletoe, poinsettias and Christmas trees. The *pessebre* (nativity scene) is huge in Catalonia and a quarter of the stalls are devoted to figurines. There's also a nativity scene contest, musical parades and exhibitions, including the popular life-size nativity scene in Plaça Sant Jaume.

Nadal* & Sant Esteve* (Christmas Day & Boxing Day)

Dates 25 & 26 Dec.

Although Santa is catching on with the same speed as every other type of Americana, for most kids, Christmas only means little gifts from the long-suffering *caga tió*. The real booty arrives with the Three Kings on the night of 5 January. The Catalan equivalent of the Christmas midnight mass is the *missa del gall* (cockerel's mass) held at dawn. Later, the whole family enjoys a traditional Christmas feast of *escudella i carn d'olla* (a meaty stew with large pasta shells), seafood and roast truffled turkey, finishing off with great ingots of *turrón*.

Cap d'Any (New Year's Eve)*

Date 31 Dec & 1 Jan.

If you're turned off by the shamelessly hoiked-up entry prices at even the shabbiest disco, you can always head to the mass public celebrations around the city, principally La Rambla and Plaça Catalunya. Wherever you are at midnight you'll be expected to stop swilling cava and start stuffing 12 grapes into your mouth, one for every chime of the bell; you have to keep going until the New Year has been fully rung in or it's bad luck.

Cavalcada dels Reis

Kings usually arrive at Parc Ciutadella, then parade along C/Marquès de l'Argentera up Via Laietana to Plaça Catalunya & continue to Montjuïc. The detailed route changes each year. **Information** Centre d'Informació de la Virreina (010). **Date** 5 Jan, 5-9pm. **Map** p344-5 A/B1/4.

The day the kids have been waiting for. Melchior, Gaspar and Balthasar arrive aboard the *Santa Eulàlia* boat at the bottom of La Rambla, preceded by acrobats and circus clowns handing out paper crowns to the kiddies – either that or a lump of edible coal. The kings then drive around town on floats, throwing sweets. The route is published in the newspapers but the biggest crowds are always around the Ciutadella park and along C/Marquès de l'Argentera for the grand arrival ceremony.

Festa dels Tres Tombs

Sant Antoni. Metro Sant Antoni. **Date** 17 Jan. **Map** p341-2 B/C5.

Saint Anthony's day also marks the *festa major* of the district with all the usual ingredients of music and *gegants*, the most symbolic of which is a monstrous fire-breathing pig. The devil is supposed to have tempted the saint by taking the form of a pig and Sant Antoni is often depicted with a porker by his side. He thus became the patron saint of all domestic animals, and on his feast day it is still the custom to bring animals to the church of St Anthony to be blessed. Afterwards, horsemen in top hats and tails commemorate the occasion by riding three circuits (*tres tombs*) in a formal procession from Ronda Sant Antoni, through Plaça Catalunya, down La Rambla and along C/Nou de la Rambla.

Carnestoltes (Carnival)

All over Barcelona. **Date** 19-25 Feb 2004.

For six centuries the tradition of orgiastic overeating, overdrinking and underdressing prior to the privations of Lent have ruled the city, and although you'll have to hop on a Tuesday-night train to Sitges for the gayest (in every sense of the word) carnival experience, there's still plenty going on in Barcelona. The opening is presided over by Don Carnal and King Carnestoltes – the masked personifications of the carnival spirit – followed a few days later by the traditional parade of floats through the city carrying figures in stunning outfits, amid a confusion of confetti, blunderbuss salvos and fireworks. There's dancing in Plaça Catalunya, concerts and a huge *botifarrada* (sausage barbecue) on La Rambla, with most of the kids and market traders in fancy dress. The end, on Ash Wednesday, is marked by the burning of the effigy of Carnestoltes and the Burial of the Sardine (*see p217* **Top ten curious customs**).

Children

The kids are all right.

In general, the Catalans have a pretty laid-back attitude towards children. Noise is a given, and kids from toddlers to teens run amok on the city's squares without adult onlookers so much as batting an eyelid when firecrackers threaten to convert a residential area into a battlefield or footballs hurtle within inches of their *patatas bravas*. Your wee ones will usually be made welcome wherever they go, screaming tantrums notwithstanding. Little Catalans themselves are actually a pretty rare breed – Catalonia has one of the lowest birth rates in the EU – but those who do exist certainly get out and about.

With its colourful fairytale houses, magic fountains, beaches and mountains, the Barcelona cityscape is a playground. Just navigating the city's streets, waters and skies is half the fun, in open-top bus, the swallow boats (*golondrinas*), cable car (*telefèric*) or catamaran. The compact centre makes exploration on foot both feasible and, with a dollop of imagination, glorious fun.

The cloud over this candy-coloured metropolis is a distinct dearth of child-specific facilities and entertainments. Nappy-changing facilities are scarce, though branches of El Corte Inglés make a good standby. Shopping malls also tend to be well equipped; La Maquinista has a baby-changing room and a breastfeeding space. Public transport is only free for children under four, and only stations on line 2 and some on line 4 have lifts.

The city's beaches are fairly clean and have plenty of lifeguards, play areas, showers and ice-cream kiosks; but the beaches further out of town towards the south, such as Castelldefels or Sitges (*see p277*), have shallower waters. Unfortunately, none has many public toilets.

Attractions

La Rambla is a firm favourite, its stalls a jumble of hamsters, bunnies, chickens, goldfish and other animals, giving way to the brightly coloured blaze of flower stalls further down. There are caricaturists and countless mimes, not to mention dancing puppets, piano-playing frogs and a hilariously bad gorilla duo. Halfway down, the **Boqueria market** appeals for the sheer gross-out value of the meat stalls – complete with skinned rabbits, pigs' trotters and goats' heads. The **Maremàgnum** shopping centre is another magnet for families, with its shops, cafés, ice-cream and sea views.

For something a tad less commercial, the labyrinthine streets of the old city can be a welcome challenge for older kids with a penchant for discovery. The **Eixample** has fantastical multi-coloured Modernista buildings with dreamy turrets and ornate flourishes worthy of a fairytale palace. For its part, the **Poble Espanyol** (*see p115*) is twee but the glass blowers and frothy flamenco dresses can be amusing for the under-12s. Also cheesy but decidedly fun, the light and music show of the **Font Màgica** (*see p113*) goes down well with most age groups.

L'Aquàrium

Moll d'Espanya, Port Vell (93 221 74 74/ www.aquariumbcn.com). Metro Barceloneta. **Open** *July, Aug* 9.30am-11pm daily. *June, Sept* 9.30am-9.30pm daily. *Oct-May* 9.30am-9pm Mon-Fri. **Admission** €13-€15; €9-€11 concessions; free under-4s. **Credit** AmEx, DC, MC, V. **Map** p342 D7.

The pièce de résistance of this vast aquarium is the Oceanari, which contains the equivalent of three Olympic swimming pools and has an 80m (260ft) glass tunnel through which you are slowly transported on a conveyor belt through shark infested waters. Many of the signs and smaller tanks are at eye-level for kids, so that they can examine shark eggs at close hand, or find out for themselves who carries the eggs in seahorse society. The Explora! section has bags of activities for children from three to 12, while in the Planet Aqua exhibition they can stroll into the mouth of a model sperm whale or locate currents or the ruins of the *Titanic* on an interactive lit-up world map.

Tibidabo Funfair

Plaça del Tibidabo, Tibidabo (93 211 79 42). FGC Avda Tibidabo. **Open** *Nov-Feb* noon-6pm Sat, Sun. *Mar* noon-7pm Sun. *Apr* noon-7pm Sat, Sun. *May, June* noon-8pm Sat, Sun. *July* noon-8pm Wed-Fri; noon-11pm Sat; noon-10pm Sun. *Aug* noon-10pm Mon-Thur; noon-11pm Fri-Sun. *1st 2wks Sept* noon-8pm Wed-Fri; noon-9pm Sat, Sun. *2nd 2wks Sept* noon-9pm Sat, Sun. *Oct* noon-7pm Sat, Sun. **Admission** *Six rides* €11. *Unlimited rides* €22; €9 children under 1m10cm tall; concessions €5-€16. **Credit** MC, V.

Some of the rides at this pine-scented, mountain-top fairground date back to 1901. Disneyland it is not, but all the old favourites (bumper cars, big wheel, ghost train) are here, and it's worth trying Aero Magic – a short, breathtaking ride on a train that skirts the mountain suspended beneath a rail. There's a wonderful collection of old fairground machines and puppet shows on the hour from 1pm.

Zoo de Barcelona

Parc de la Ciutadella, Born (93 225 67 80/ www.zoobarcelona.com). Metro Barceloneta or Ciutadella-Vila Olímpica. **Open** (daily) *Mar* 10am-6pm. *Apr* 10am-7pm. *May-Aug* 9.30am-7.30pm. *Sept* 10am-7pm. *Oct* 10am-6pm. *Nov-Feb* 10am-5pm. **Admission** €12.50; €8 3-12s; €3.40-€7 concessions. **Credit** V. **Map** p343 E6.

This large and slightly shabby zoo is facing the end of an era, having just lost its star attraction (*see p224* **Animal magnetism**). Some of the enclosures are depressingly small, but generally, with its wide sprawling walkways, plentiful eating areas, pony rides and hundreds of residents from anteaters to zebras, it's good fun for most kids.

Babysitting & childcare

Canguravis i Nens

C/Provença 327, Eixample (93 208 06 43). Metro Verdaguer. **Open** 9am-2pm, 4-9pm Mon-Fri. **No credit cards**. **Map** p339 E4.

A flat rate of €6-€7 is charged regardless of whether it is a day or night shift, and the sitter's taxi home will usually have to be paid for if you return late at night. Rates are slightly higher at weekends.

Canguro Gigante

Passeig de Sant Gervasi 20, Sant Gervasi (93 211 69 61). FGC Avda Tibidabo. **Open** 9am-9pm Mon-Fri. **No credit cards**.

Daycare centre for kids aged one to ten. The basic rate is €4 per hour, and they can have a meal there if required. Some English is spoken.

Cinc Serveis

C/Pelai 50, 3º 1ª, Eixample (93 412 56 76/ 24hr mobile 639 36 11 11). Metro Catalunya. **Open** 9.30am-1.30pm, 4.30-8.30pm Mon-Fri. **No credit cards**. **Map** p344 A1.

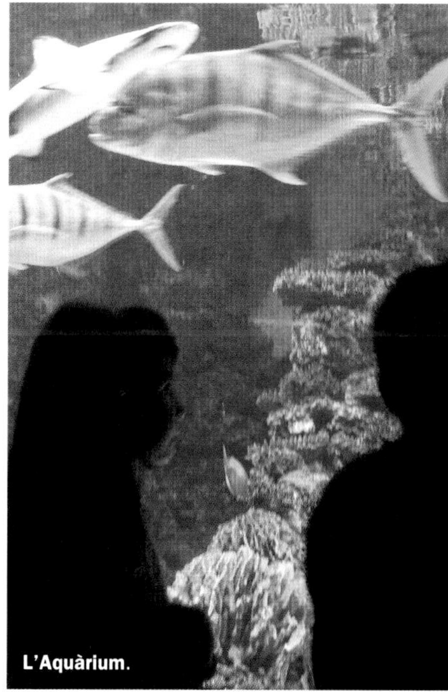
L'Aquàrium.

Animal magnetism

As 2003 drew to a close, the children of Barcelona were summoned to the zoo to say their goodbyes to Copito de Nieve (aka Snowflake), the legendary albino gorilla that has been synonymous with the city's animal attractions since the 1970s, but who finally succumbed, not unsurprisingly, to skin cancer.

Snowflake was unique in captivity – not many zoo residents have made the cover of *National Geographic* and featured in *Life* magazine. His scowling pink chops graced countless postcards and were the inspiration for many a stuffed toy or novelty pencil, and his sad demise heralds the end of an era.

So what will life after Snowflake bring? Barcelona's other animal citizens might get some attention, for a start. The Zoo de Barcelona (*see p223*) is home to big cats, rhinos, pygmy hippos, bears, giraffes, elephants, camels, snakes, crocodiles, black swans and so on. The dolphins are perennial favourites, although a recent feud between the two females involving a kidnapped baby dolphin, a put-upon mother and an uninterested father may have put paid to their erstwhile squeaky clean image.

Or maybe the answer to the lack of a city mascot lies at L'Aquàrium de Barcelona. Terenci the tiger-shark or Pili the Picasso fish make beguiling viewing, and there are hours of fun to be had making faces at the puffer fish or contemplating the vivid colours of the clownfish and the wispy silvery contours of the angelfish. The marine team has two clear contenders in the running for the title of new animal superstar: the delicate and mesmerising seahorses make the top five, but the Humboldt penguins are the most promising hopefuls for the top spot, while the sharks pull in the crowds but have less effect on the heartstrings.

This covert animal fever in a city not known for its animal-lovers isn't restricted to paying attractions. Even the Barcelona streets are dotted with animals, albeit representations. Check out the giant mammoth and herd of leaping deer in the Ciutadella park, the meditative bull and coquettish giraffe statues at opposite ends of Rambla de Catalunya, and the giant Fernando Botero cat on the Rambla del Raval. For live action on a small scale, the animal stalls on the Rambla have got domestic rodents, goldfish, terrapins and even the odd duckling, pigeon or hen. If you're careful you might spy a baby Japanese dwarf mouse. Still, no single beastie has a clear stake on Snowflake's throne. Who cares if he spent most of his time glowering at his

The basic babysitting rate after 8pm is €8.40 per hour, plus the cost of the sitter's taxi home. Day and long-term rates are cheaper and vary according to the age of the child. Some staff speak English.

Happy Parc

C/Pau Claris 97, Eixample (93 317 86 60/ www.happyparc.com). Metro Passeig de Gràcia. **Open** 5-9pm Mon-Fri; 11am-9pm Sat, Sun. **Rates** €3.60 per hr daily; 90¢ each subsequent 15mins. **No credit cards. Map** p342 D5.

Ball pools, twister slides and more at this giant indoor fun park and drop-in daycare centre for kids up to 11 (maximum height: 1m 45cm/4ft 7in.) It organises birthday parties for groups of ten or more. **Other locations**: C/Comte de Bell.lloc 74-8, Sants (93 490 08 35).

Entertainment

Most visits will coincide with some festival or other to take some of the work out of child entertainment. The carnival revelry is heavy on noise and colour, and sets the pace for the rest of the year. Older kids will enjoy the beach parties, bonfires and bangers of the Sant Joan summer solstice festival, although it's a bit hectic for smaller ones. In August, the streets of Gràcia are decked out in a vivid array of weird and wonderful decorations during the local *festa major*. The giants and street parties of **La Mercè** make for autumnal larks, and the fireworks display on Plaça d'Espanya ends the festivities with an almighty bang.

The various scatological implications of local Christmas traditions cannot fail to provoke the glee of any child; visit the Santa Llúcia market on the cathedral square for squatting pants-down figures and smiley-faced 'shitting' logs among the more familiar cribs and trees. If you are in town on 6 January, when little Catalans traditionally get their mitts on their pressies, you can take in the Three Kings' procession through town and be showered with sweets. For more info, *see p214-21*.

To catch a film in English, the best bet is the **Yelmo Icària** for mainstream blockbusters and purveyors of humungous ice-creams. The **Filmoteca** shows original-language children's films on Sundays at 5pm. On a rainy day, a good but pricey standby can be the **IMAX**

devotees or dignifying their pilgrimage with a view of his backside? To Barcelona, his matchlessness was marketing gold dust. As the city comes to terms with the emotional and financial loss, there's no doubt that local authorities will be scouring the horizon for the new animal idol of the 21st century. It's a hard act to follow.

cinema, although films are only shown in Spanish and Catalan, and tend to be rather dreary. For all, *see p227-30*.

Museums

While most child-specific activities at the city's museums are in Catalan, there is still plenty of scope for inquisitive minds. The **Museu de la Xocolata** (*see p101*) will appeal to just about all of them with its interactive touch-screen computers, quizzes and life-size Harry Potter chocolate statue in the entrance. There is a workshop at weekends in which kids from four to 12 can make chocolate figurines (€6.30 per child – reservation is required).

Young zoologists will lap up the children's exhibitions at the **Museu de Zoologia** (*see p99*), while budding Ronaldinhos will make a beeline for the **Museu del FC Barcelona** (*see p126*), where the guided tour includes a walk from the dressing rooms through the tunnel, a few steps on the pitch and a spell on the bench. At the **Museu Maritim** (*see p106*), the prize draw is the life-size Don Juan de Austria, on which the life of a galley slave is briefly re-enacted with the help of digital imaging. The **Museu de la Ciencia** (*see p132*) is to reopen in its new improved incarnation at some point in 2004/5, and the children's workshops, such as Clik de Nens (science through playing), Toca Toca (a pedagogical petting zoo) and the Planetarium will be resumed.

Many museums take part in the **Estiu als Museus** programme from June to September, which provides additional children's activities. Those aimed at young kids will be more accessible to non-Catalan-speakers.

Museu de Cera

Ptge de la Banca 7, Barri Gòtic (93 317 26 49/ www.museocerabcn.com). Metro Drassanes. **Open** *July-Sept* 10am-10pm daily. *Oct-May* 10am-1.30pm, 4-7.30pm Mon-Fri; 11am-2pm, 4.30-8.30pm Sat, Sun. **Admission** €6.65; €3.75 children; free under-5s. **No credit cards. Map** p345 A4.

The waxworks museum belongs to the so-bad-it's-good school of entertainment. Dramatisation reaches hilarious heights in the heterogeneous basement of doom, where severed heads and serial killers follow a trip through Neanderthal times and a spell under the sea in a submarine guarded by Jules Verne. Questions such as why ET sits on the Millennium Falcon next to R2D2, or if the monstrous proportions of Julia Roberts' mouth can anatomically be possible tend to eclipse the splashes of history throughout. It's more a giggle than an educational visit, though kids brought up on Disneyland and the *Matrix* might be underwhelmed. Finish off with a drink at the delightfully kitsch museum café next door.

Museu de la Màgia

C/Oli 6, Born (93 319 73 93/www.elreidela magia.com). Metro Jaume I. **Open** 6-8pm Fri. *Show* 8.30pm Thur; noon Sun. **Admission** €9 Thur; €6 Sun; free Fri. **Credit** MC, V. **Map** p345 B3.

This modest collector's gallery-cum-museum has a small assortment of objects and brightly coloured posters from the shop El Rei de la Màgia (*see p211*), dating from when it opened in 1881 to the 1950s. It is best to reserve for the Thursday or Sunday shows, as there are limited places. While the show is not in English, it's fairly accessible stuff.

Parks & playgrounds

The lovely **Jardins de la Tamarita** make a tranquil enclave of swings and slides hidden away next to the stop for the Tramvia Blau. **Parc de la Creueta del Coll** is a bit of a trek, but it can be worth it in the summertime, when the large artificial lake is filled up and acts as a public swimming pool (*see p132*). It also has a large playground, ping pong tables, a picnic area and great views of the city. Another park, Gaudí's wonderfully quirky **Park Güell** (*see p125*), is short on grass, but that is more than made up for by the bright gingerbread houses, winding coloured benches and stalactite caves. Similarly, the delightful **Parc del Laberint** (*see p136*) has hidden benches and elfin tables, picnic areas and a deceptively simple maze. But the star spot has got to be the **Parc de la Ciutadella**, where the shady gardens, giant mammoth, rowing boats and zoo combine to make for a relaxing day out in the city centre (*see p102*).

On **Plaça Vicenç Martorell** in the Raval and **Plaça de la Revolució** in Gràcia, you'll find pint-sized playgrounds situated on (almost) traffic-free squares close to café terraces.

Parc del Castell de l'Oreneta

Camí de Can Caralleu & Passatge Blada, Zona Alta (93 413 24 80/www.bcn.es/parcsijardins). By car Ronda de Dalt exit 9/by bus 30, 60, 66, 94. **Open** (daily) *May-Aug* 10am-9pm. *Apr, Sept* 10am-8pm. *Mar, Oct* 10am-7pm. *Nov-Feb* 10am-6pm.

This verdant park in the Collserola foothills has flowery fields and deliciously bosky glades. There are two signposted walks with wonderful views, plus picnic areas, pony rides for three- to 12-year-olds on Saturday and Sunday (10.30am-5pm, €5), ping-pong tables and various playgrounds. On Sundays, you can hop aboard the miniature steam train (11am-2pm, €1.20).

Restaurants & cafés

It is rare to find a children's menu in Barcelona, but many restaurants will provide smaller portions on request; although there's little need when children and tapas were so clearly made for each other. Remember that most restaurants don't serve lunch before 2pm or dinner before 8.30pm, which can be a little difficult for kids. If you're desperate for a snack, there are plenty of options; **Escribà** (*see p202*) is good for gooey cakes, while **Forn Boix** (*see p203*) offers more healthy wholegrain bread and the like.

Kids are more than welcome in **Bar Mendizábal** (*see p173*) for fresh milkshakes and fruit juices, or you can always plump for pizza at **Al Passatore** (*see p153*). For kicking back and relaxing in the sun, try the terraces of **Bar Kasparo** in the Raval (*see p173*) or **L'Hivernacle** in the Ciutadella park (*see p178*). And consider that, at noisy **Bar Celta**, nobody will hear them scream (*see p172*) .

Museum cafés are often child-friendly spots, and you don't necessarily have to visit the museum to enjoy them. **Miranda del Museu** (*see p181*) at the history museum, has fantastic views and plenty of terrace space to play in. The café of the **Fundació Joan Miró** (*see p111*) is a rare oasis of sustenance on Montjuïc; and **El Bosc de les Fades** (*see p172*) is a must after a visit to the waxworks museum.

Out of town

Some of the child-specific attractions in the area around Barcelona include the **Museu del Cinema** (972 412 777, www.museudelcinema.org) in **Girona**, and the toy museum (**Museu del Joguet de Catalunya**, 972 50 45 85, www.mjc-figueres.net) in **Figueres**. As well as the two water parks mentioned below, Catalonia has four others: **Aqua Brava** (in Roses), **Aquadiver** (Platja d'Aro), **Water World** (Lloret de Mar) along the Costa Brava and **Marineland** in Palafolls. *See also p284* for the endlessly popular **Port Aventura** theme park.

Catalunya en Miniatura

Can Balasch de Baix, Torrelles de Llobregat, Outer Limits (93 689 09 60/www.catalunyaenminiatura.com). By car NII south to Sant Vicens dels Horts, then left to Torrelles de Llobregat (10km/6 miles)/ by bus Soler i Sauret (info 93 632 51 33) from Travessera de les Corts. **Open** *Apr-Sept* 10am-7pm daily. *Oct-Mar* 10am-6pm Tue-Sun. **Admission** €9.50; €6.50 4-12s; free under-4s. **Credit** MC, V.

An appropriately munchkin-size train does a circuit of the park's meticulously recreated hit parade of scaled-down Catalan towns and monuments, from Montserrat to the Gaudí masterpiece of your choice. This is all an unparalleled opportunity for cheesy photos. A crew of clowns performs at 1pm every Sunday in the amphitheatre.

Isla de Fantasia

Finca Mas Brassó, Vilassar de Dalt (93 751 45 53/ www.islafantasia.com). By car NII north to Premià de Mar, then left (24km/15 miles). **Open** *June-Aug* 10am-7pm Mon-Fri, Sun; 10am-7pm Sat. Closed Sept-May. **Admission** €12; €9 2-10s; free under-2s. **Credit** AmEx, DC, MC, V.

Port Aventura on a budget, this water park has 22 attractions such as foam slides, kamikaze rides and rubber dinghy chutes, along with different pools, a restaurant, disco, supermarket and activities such as salsa and aerobics classes. A picnic/barbecue area in a pine grove allows you to bring your own food. The atmosphere is Spanish rather than touristy.

Parc de les Aus

Carretera de Cabrils, Vilassar de Mar, Outer Limits (93 750 17 65/www.elparcdelesaus.com). By car N11 north to Vilassar de Mar, then left to park (24km/ 15 miles)/by train RENFE from Sants or Plaça Catalunya to Vilassar de Mar, then taxi. **Open** 10am-sunset daily. **Admission** €10.50; €7.50 3-12s; free under-3s. **Credit** AmEx, DC, MC, V.

Over 300 species of local and exotic birds live in this colourful botanical park, which has grown into a full-scale nature reserve over the 30 years since the Viñals couple first started breeding canaries and parakeets. Budding ornithologists will have their fun cut out for them. For the younger children, there is a miniature train and trampolines, as well as a petting zoo and pony rides.

Film

Smoke and mirrors and banana skins.

With its atmospheric corners and acquiescent citizenry, Barcelona has become a popular place for film-making: though the filming in question is more often than not for car or bank commercials destined for pan-European airing. As a location for feature films and television series, it has a chequered history, certainly from an English-speaking perspective.

Whit Stillman used the city for his 1994 homage to Catalonia, *Barcelona*, producing a work that suffered from difficult second album syndrome coming, as it did, after the incisive *Metropolitan* and before *The Last Days of Disco*. More recently, the award for most inappropriate use of Gaudí and Gothic exteriors has gone to Susan Seidelman, director of *Desperately Seeking Susan*, for her misjudged 2002 feature *Gaudí Afternoon*, which even the talented Marcia Gay Harden could do nothing to salvage from ridicule and box-office oblivion. In contrast, when Pedro Almodóvar used Barcelona sets for *All About My Mother*, he topped the Spanish film charts for months and won the Oscar for best foreign picture.

At the other end of the scale, Filmax, another Barcelona-based production company, has carved a profitable niche in English-language film-making of an entirely different nature. Under the label Fantastic Factory, Filmax produces very low-budget gore and horror films shot in an unrecognisable Catalonia. Like, say, Toronto or Vancouver, parts of the region can pass for middle America for a fraction of the price. The results are unlikely to win any Oscars, and are usually destined for very brief releases before being consigned to video, but they have nevertheless contributed to Filmax's growth in a notoriously difficult industry.

Individually, several Catalan and Spanish directors have turned their hands to English-language cinema, generally emulating independent American cinema in style and content. Ventura Pons made his first film in English in 2001 (*Food of Love*, starring Juliet Stevenson), while Maria Ripoll (*If Only*) and Isabel Coixet (*Things I Never Told You*) have both recently released their second features, *Tortilla Soup* and *My Life Without You*. Top of the class, though, is Alejandro Amenábar, whose third film, *The Others* transformed him from geek wannabe to Spanish Tarantino virtually overnight.

Few other practising Spanish directors seem to get much screen time in subtitularly reluctant Britain, though British audiences might be familiar with the more innovative of them; Bigas Luna, Almodóvar and, increasingly, Julio Medem. Medem's outlook

Rex. *See p228.*

Arts & Entertainment

is more poetic and ethereal, although what started out as a fresh vision in his first film, *Vacas*, started to look a little formulaic in its insistent reliance on magical realism and whimsical charm by the time he reached *Lucia y el Sexo*. In contrast his feature-length 2003 documentary *La Pelota Vasca,* on the 'Basque question', won praise and reprobation in equal measure.

Another Spanish director making international waves is Álex de la Iglesia, who leaps with abandon from genre to genre: so far he's covered sci-fi (*Accion Mutante*), horror (*El Día de la Bestia*), melodrama (*La Comunidad*), westerns (*800 balas*) and soon the detective comedy (*Crimen Ferpecto*), and is showing no signs of flagging or a failing imagination. Look out, too, for Fernando León de Aranoa, a Spanish Ken Loach, who has won several Goyas (Spanish Oscars) for his feature films: *Barrio*, a hard-hitting but often hilarious look at life in a marginalised suburb of Madrid, and Spain's official entry for the 2003 Oscars, *Los Lunes al Sol*, a tender but amusing character study about friendship and unemployment starring the excellent Javier Bardem.

On the whole, the Spanish film industry is in reasonably good health, producing around 150 features a year, with an average budget of €2.5 million. Madcap comedy is particularly successful, with historical drama and contemporary issue-based drama sharing distant second. Around 40 per cent of films shown in Spain are American, compared to 22 per cent Spanish, though American cinema accounts for 70 per cent of box-office takings. Unusually, German films account for 15 per cent of output but only one per cent of box-office takings, an anomaly that is explained by the fact that most German films in Spain are destined for *Salas X* – porn cinemas.

SEEING FILMS

The variety of foreign independent cinema on offer has begun to shrink over the last couple of years in the face of the irresistible onslaught of Hollywood no-brainers. Release dates vary enormously. Many English and American films can take anything up to three years to reach Spain, and often fail to do so altogether. All types of cinema abound, from flea-pit to space-cruiser, though the relentless invasion by popcorn 'n' pap multi-screens is taking its toll on the smaller, more charming venues, one of which slips under every few years.

Newspapers carry full details of all cinema screenings, as does the weekly *Guía del Ocio*. Subtitled films are marked VO or VOSE (for *'versió original subtitulado en espanyol'*). Some of the larger cinemas open at 11am, though most open at around 4pm. Early-evening screenings start between 7.30pm and 8.30pm, and later screenings between 10.15pm and 10.45pm. Weekend evenings can be very crowded, especially for recent releases, so turn up early. On Fridays and Saturdays, many cinemas also have a late-night session starting around 1am. All cinemas have a cheap night, which is usually Monday, though in some cases Wednesday. Increasingly, you can buy tickets over the internet (www.cinentradas.com) or via **Servi-Caixa** (*see p212*).

Original-language cinemas

Icària Yelmo Cineplex

C/Salvador Espriu 61, Vila Olímpica (93 221 75 85/www.yelmocineplex.es). Metro Ciutadella-Vila Olímpica. **Tickets** €4.30 Mon, before 2pm Tue-Sun; €5.75 after 2.30pm Tue-Sun, late shows. **No credit cards**. **Map** p343 F7.

This 15-screen shopping-mall multiplex shows an unimaginative programme of mainstream films. Weekends are now seat-specific, so queues tend to be very slow-moving.

Maldà

C/Pi 5, Barri Gòtic (93 317 85 29). Metro Liceu. **Map** p344 B2.

The tatty but much-loved Maldà had been closed by council order at the time of writing, but may reopen sometime in 2004. The repertory programme involves thematically linked double bills of recent favourites.

Méliès Cinemes

C/Villarroel 102, Eixample (93 451 00 51). Metro Urgell. **Tickets** €2.70 Mon; €4 Tue-Sun. **No credit cards**. **Map** p342 C5.

A repertory, almost art-house cinema, the Méliès is run by and for film lovers, offering an eccentric combination of B&W classics, contemporary independents and whatever else the owner feels like. There are up to eight different films per week, with regular seasons organised by director, star or theme.

Renoir-Floridablanca

C/Floridablanca 135, Eixample (93 228 93 93/ www.cinesrenoir.es). Metro Sant Antoni. **Tickets** €4 Mon; €5.50, €4 concessions Tue-Sun; €4 late show Fri, Sat. **Credit** AmEx, MC, V. **Map** p342 C5.

The latest addition to Barcelona's VO scene, this four-screen branch of the Renoir chain features independent, off-beat American and British cinema, with occasional forays into European film. Programmes change less frequently than in other cinemas.

Other locations: Renoir-Les Corts C/Eugeni d'Ors 12 , Les Corts (93 490 43 05).

Rex

Gran Via de les Corts Catalanes 463, Eixample (93 423 10 60/www.grupbalana.com). Metro Rocafort. **Tickets** €5 Mon, Tue, Thur; €4 Wed; €5.50 Fri-Sun. **No credit cards**. **Map** p341 B5.

Spanish must-sees

Welcome Mister Marshall (1952)
Bardem and Berlanga's screwball satire on what Spanishness was reduced to under Franco. A gloriously life-affirming, two-fingered poke in the crossed-eyes of fate and fascism.

Death of a Cyclist (1955)
A damning fine thriller. Juan Antonio Bardem's generic jigsaw of melodrama and film noir is a condemnatory x-ray of the conscienceless middle classes under Franco.

Viridiana (1961)
Luis Buñuel's Bible-black comedy rails against faith, hope and charity as a novice nun fails to reconcile human frailties with her divinely naïve vocation. Once banned, still blasphemous, ever delightful. *The Sound of Music* for nihilists.

The Hunt (1965)
Carlos Saura's bleached and baking hunting trip with burnt-out old comrades from the Civil War. The start of New Spanish Cinema and, in its influence on Peckinpah's *The Wild Bunch*, the start of New Hollywood too.

The Spirit of the Beehive (1973)
A reasoned dream of monsters from the wide-eyed infant Ana, an innocent adrift in a guilty, post-Civil War world. Víctor Erice's poetic masterpiece: elusive, ambiguous and achingly frail, but forceful.

Law of Desire (1987)
Pedro Almodóvar's ravishing, ribald and romantic neo-noir/melodrama in which Antonio Banderas plays the bisexual, psychotic lover of a gay film-maker and his transexual brother/sister.

Lovers (1991)
Victoria Abril embodies all the carnal ferocity of a Spanish anti-Virgin in Vicente Aranda's dark and daring James M Cain with chorizo and *turrón*.

Días Contados (1994)
A rogue ETA terrorist falls for a junkie prostitute as Imanol Uribe replays *Carmen* out in the margins of Madrid. A gripping and controversial mix of adrenaline, testosterone, politics and myth.

Lovers of the Arctic Circle (1998)
Julio Medem's lyrical reflection on symmetry and chance (*pictured*). Fateful, tender and challenging in its emotional demands, narrative twists, and the intense look and voiceover of star Najwa Nimri.

Work in Progress (2001)
Balmy, dusty, impressionist documentary from José Luis Guerín on the revamping of Barcelona's red light district. A film that strolls, eavesdrops, squints and stares as it reaffirms the meaning of life.

This large '70s, single-screen cinema is a delight, with its red-plush seats and warm, womb-like interior. Films in VO, though, are increasingly rare.

Verdi

C/Verdi 32, Gràcia (93 238 79 90/www.cines-verdi.com). Metro Fontana. **Tickets** €4 Mon; €5.50 Tue-Thur; €5.80 Sat, Sun. **No credit cards. Map** p338 D3.

A long-standing champion of foreign cinema, the original five-screen Verdi, and its four-screen annexe Verdi Park on the next street over, offer a diverse programme of interesting, accessible cinema from around the world, particularly Asian and European, as well as some Spanish repertoire. At peak times chaos reigns, so arrive early and make sure you don't mistake the queue to go in for the ticket queue.

Other locations: **Verdi Park** C/Torrijos 49, Gràcia (93 238 79 90).

Specialist cinemas

Cine Ambigú

Sala Apolo, C/Nou de la Rambla 113, Paral.lel (93 441 40 01/www.retinas.org). Metro Paral.lel. **Shows** 8.30pm, 10.30pm Tue. **Tickets** €4 or €6 (incl 1 drink). **No credit cards. Map** p342 C6.

Taking over the Apolo music hall for one night a week (usually Tuesday), Cine Ambigú is a year-round festival of alternative and experimental film never likely to get a wider distribution. More like a cabaret than a cinema, with small tables, candles and a bar, it's not overly comfortable, but you're free to indulge a variety of vices as you watch, and the programme throws up some real gems.

Filmoteca de la Generalitat de Catalunya

Cinema Aquitania, Avda Sarrià 31-3, Eixample (93 410 75 90/http://cultura.gencat.net/filmo). Metro Hospital Clínic. Closed Aug. **Tickets** €2.70; €2 concessions; €33 20 films; €66 100 films. **Credit** (block tickets only) MC, V. **Map** p338 C3.

Funded by the Catalan government, the Filmoteca fulfils a key public service, and not just in keeping film nerds off the streets. Its extensive, esoteric programmes range from little-known auteurs to old favourites. Each spring it screens all films nominated for Goyas. Books of 20 and 100 tickets bring down the price per film to negligible. The Filmoteca also runs a library of film-related books, videos and magazines, round the corner from the Centre d'Art Santa Monica, at the bottom of La Rambla.

IMAX Port Vell

Moll d'Espanya, Port Vell (93 225 11 11). Metro Barceloneta or Drassanes. **Tickets** €7-€10. **Credit** AmEx, MC, V. **Map** p342 D7.

If anyone ever gets round to making a decent film for IMAX, this will be the place to go. In the meantime, the dazzling but still disappointing staple of nature documentaries (particularly strong on fish, for some reason) and gimmicks dominate – although as gimmicks go, 3D is a particularly good one.

VOID/Sala Zelig

C/Ferlandina 51, Raval (93 443 42 03/www.void-bcn.com). Metro Sant Antoni or Universitat. **Shows** 9pm Wed-Sun. **Tickets** (incl 1 drink) €3. **Credit** AmEx, MC, V. **Map** p342 C5.

As well as renting out art-house films on video and DVD, this branch of VOID has a small video projection room. On Sundays the audience turn up and choose what they want to see. The rest of the week consists of vaguely avant-garde classics from the catalogue. It is hoped that the newer branch in Gràcia will soon offer the same service.

Other locations: C/Santa Creu 1, Gràcia (93 218 99 34).

Festivals

Barcelona has recently woken up to the possibilities of open-air cinema, with various distributors operating short seasons July to September. Programming changes from year to year, but both the **CCCB** (*see p95*) and **Poble Espanyol** (93 508 63 00,www.poble-espanyol.com, €6, *see p114*) have run successful programmes of open-air cinema. The **Piscina Bernat Picornell** (www.grec.bcn.es, €6, *see p274*) runs massively successful late-night swimming and movie sessions at the Olympic pools. Most impressive, though, has been **Sala Montjuïc** (www.salamontjuic.com, €3), an impromptu, open-air cinema screened against the castle wall. Free buses from Plaça Espanya ferry hundreds of cinema-goers up to the grassy moat, suitably armed with booze, picnic blankets and smokables, for these dirt-cheap, twice-weekly sessions.

There are an increasing number of film festivals in Barcelona. Though none is as big or brash as Sitges (*see p277*), they all show interesting work unlikely to be screened elsewhere. Every year new events pop up, but the regulars include: **Asian** (April/ May), **Jewish** (May), **Women's** (June), **Gay and Lesbian** (July and October), **Open-Air Shorts** (September), **Documentaries** (October), **African** (November) and **Alternative Film** (November).

Festival Internacional de Cinema de Catalunya, Sitges

93 419 36 35/93 894 99 90/fax 93 439 73 80/www.sitges.com/cinema. **Advance tickets** from Tel-entrada. **Date** 2nd half of Nov.

Fed up with trying to compete with the Venice and San Sebastián festivals, the Sitges Film Festival has wisely chosen to relocate to late November, thus capitalising on misty evenings and empty hotel rooms. The formula remains otherwise unchanged: gore, horror and sci-fi beside the sea, with everything from the latest blood-lust blockbusters to Asian cyber-scream art-house and specky retrospectives.

Galleries

Barcelona's art scene is small but eager.

After years of fretting about where it stood in the pecking order of hip-to-art cities round the globe, Barcelona has finally decided to stop worrying about such things and get down to making art happen. A good part of the newfound confidence is due to the presence of strong local art institutions, especially those in the service of the contemporary scene. With a vibrant museum of contemporary art (**MACBA** *see p95*) leading the way, bolstered by excellent educational centres like the media art specialists MECAD and the artist-run **Hangar** (*see p234*), the city's institutional necessities finally seem to be taken care of. That is good for artists. With no more real or imaginary 'missing pieces' to gripe about, cultural politics has given way to cultural theory, cutting-edge training is paying off, and even the city's usually cautious established art dealers – and a bunch of new ones – have decided that it is time to take a few risks again.

The Barcelona gallery scene has had its ups and downs in recent years, not least because the ebullient local economy has not had a decisive impact on art collecting. That means that even the strongest commercial spaces are modest by international standards. Yet thanks to a few daring moves the gallery scene has proven itself able to stay on top of contemporary creativity. The best example is a new event called **Loop**, initiated in 2003 as the world's first commercial fair dedicated exclusively to video art; the second edition is slated for November 2004.

Barcelona was a minor hotspot of the early 20th-century avant-garde, with Picasso, Miró and Dalí the most luminous figures. The spirit that fostered them and many fine colleagues was all but quashed after the Civil War and the advent of dictatorship. Eventually, the art world recovered: the 1950s saw the emergence of *art informel* abstract painting, while conceptualism boomed in the '70s. With the city's reawakening in the 1980s and '90s, the Barcelona art scene fell into self-promotion, throwing money into museum construction and ill-defined events like the **Triennial** (coming up next in 2004). Fortunately, the health of art in the city is not dependent upon such government-led excesses.

Nowadays Catalonia has quite a few internationally successful artists, including granddaddy Antoni Tàpies, the senior generation of Antoni Muntadas, Francesc Torres and Susana Solano, the mid-career crop led by Eulàlia Valldosera, Antoni Abad and Josep Maria Martín, or younger lights like Martí Anson and Tere Recarens. This suggests local creation is heterogeneous, covering everything from abstract painting and sculpture to digital photography, audio-visual installation and web art. Catalan creators move comfortably on the international stage, without the inferiority complexes of former times. The new generation of artists has come to share the benefits of globalised culture, participating in biennials and museum shows worldwide, though perhaps without contributing anything specifically indicative of their culture of origin.

There is no definitive guide to galleries. Listings appear in the weekly *Guía de Ocio* and some newspapers, but are rarely comprehensive. The guides and websites of gallery associations are only partial. The simplest plan is to go to a gallery district and do the rounds. All private galleries are closed on Sundays and Mondays; a few are now open in August. Exhibition openings typically take place around 8pm midweek, and all are welcome.

Commercial galleries

The Barri Gòtic and the area centred on the Eixample's C/Consell de Cent are Barcelona's longest established gallery districts, but in recent years a new cluster of contemporary spaces has developed in the north of the Raval.

Barri Gòtic

In addition to those listed below, the **Galeria Segovia Isaacs** (C/Palla 8, 93 302 29 80) is also of some interest.

Antonio de Barnola

C/Palau 4 (93 412 22 14). Metro Liceu or Jaume I. **Open** 5-9pm Tue-Fri; noon-2pm, 5-9pm Sat. Closed Aug. **No credit cards**. **Map** p345 B3.

This handsome space presents interesting shows of works by known and new Spanish contemporary artists. It shows a particular passion for works with architecture themes. Regulars include Catalan installation artist Margarita Andreu, Argentine-born photographer Humberto Rivas, and young Basque artists including Itziar Okariz and José Ramón Amondarain. Barnola is respected for hanging the shows in his space with impeccable care.

Artur Ramon

C/Palla 10, 23 & 25 (93 302 59 70). Metro Liceu. **Open** *Oct-June* 10am-1.30pm, 5-8pm Tue-Sat. *July, Sept* 10am-1.30pm, 5-8pm Tue-Fri. Closed Aug. **Credit** MC, V. **Map** p344/5 B2/3.
The best of the local dynasties dealing in historic art and objects, the Artur Ramon family has several spaces on the same street. The finest shows are the exhibitions of historical Spanish and European arts and crafts, along with thematic shows pulled from private collections – Venetian glass, historical engravings, Spanish masters – sharply presented at No.23.

Sala Parés

C/Petritxol 5 (93 318 70 08/www.salapares.com). Metro Liceu. **Open** *Oct-May* 10.30am-2pm, 4.30-8.30pm Mon-Sat; 11.30am-2pm Sun. *June-Sept* 10.30am-2pm, 4.30-8.30pm Mon-Sat. Closed 3wks Aug. **Credit** V. **Map** p344 A2.
The Sala Parés opened in 1840 and has long been a symbol for the Catalan bourgeoisie, who still make up the majority of its rather cautious clientele. A century ago it promoted the Catalan avant-garde, and it was here that Picasso had his first one-man show. Now the spacious renovated gallery specialises in figurative and historical painting. The nearby Galeria Trama offers contemporary work.
Other locations: Galeria Trama, C/Petritxol 8, Barri Gòtic (93 317 48 77); **Galeria 18**, C/Jacinto Benavente 18, Barri Gòtic (93 201 99 06); **Edicions Margall**, Rambla Catalunya 116, Eixample (93 415 96 92).

Raval

The art scene in Raval is small but high quality. In addition to the galleries listed here, other galleries worth visiting include the paintings at **Galeria Ferran Cano** (Plaça dels Àngels 4, 93 310 15 48). Another good option is **Doque** (C/Joaquín Costa 47, 93 302 14 77), which is known for representing a new wave of South American artists. There's also the **Espai Vidre** (C/Àngels 8, 93 318 98 33) which has made its name specialising in quality glasswork. The **FAD** design centre also has regular shows (Convent dels Àngels, Plaça dels Àngels 5-6, 93 443 75 20, www.fadweb.com).

Galeria dels Àngels

C/Àngels 16 (93 412 54 54/www.galeriadels angels.com). Metro Catalunya. **Open** noon-2pm, 5-8.30pm Tue-Sat. Closed Aug. **No credit cards. Map** p344 A2.
A small gallery run hands-on by collector Emilio Álvarez, who has widened his tastes beyond painting to include shows in contemporary photography and video art. His exhibitions feature the abstract painting of Miquel Mont and Santi Moix, and the photography of Canadian Lynn Cohen and the team of Bleda + Rosa, who photograph historical battle sites. Young and rising Basque artist Naia de Castillo shows her textile sculptures.

Ras Gallery

C/Doctor Dou 10 (93 412 71 99/www.actar.es). Metro Catalunya. **Open** 11am-9pm Tue-Sat. **Credit** AmEx, MC, V. **Map** p344 A2.
Run by the Actar publishing house, Ras has a small arts bookshop fronting a gallery with fine shows often related to the contents of new publications. Especially interesting are exhibitions of original architectural drawings, photos and maquettes by contemporary masters, as a complement to Actar's thematic and historical volumes.

Born

A number of galleries have opened along narrow C/Flassaders, like **Galeria 44** (C/Flassaders 44, 93 310 01 82). Also worth visiting is funky and fresh **Cactus Art Gallery** (C/Assaonadors 29-31, 93 268 18 44, www.cactusartgallery.com).

Metrònom. See p98.

Galeria Maeght

C/Montcada 25 (93 310 42 45/www.maeght.com). Metro Jaume I. **Open** 10am-2pm, 4-8pm Tue-Sat. **Credit** AmEx, DC, MC, V. **Map** p345 C3.

The Paris-based Maeght gallery opened this handsome space in the 1970s. Occupying a Renaissance palace near the Picasso museum, with a lovely courtyard and staircase, it shows high-powered Spanish (Tàpies, Arroyo, Palazuelo) and European painters and sculptors. Despite its prestigious name and digs, though, the Maeght struggles for relevance on the crowded Barcelona scene.

Eixample

Other worthwhile galleries in the area include **Galeria Metropolitana Barcelona** (Rambla Catalunya 50, pral 1ª, 93 487 40 42, www.galeriametropolitana.com) and **Galeria Toni Tàpies** (C/Consell de Cent 282, 93 487 64 02, www.tonitapies.com), run with contemporary verve by the son of the famous painter.

Galeria Carles Taché

C/Consell de Cent 290 (93 487 88 36/www.carlestache.com). Metro Passeig de Gràcia. **Open** *Mid Sept-June* 10am-2pm, 4-8.30pm Tue-Sat. *July, 1st 2wks Sept* 10am-2pm, 4-8.30pm Tue-Fri. Closed Aug. **No credit cards. Map** p342 D5.

Carles Taché represents some of the most established senior Spanish painters, such as Arroyo, Broto and Campano. Blue-chip internationals such as Sean Scully and Tony Cragg can also be seen, along with Catalan sculptor Jordi Colomer and the clever pop of Carlos Pazos.

Galeria Estrany-de la Mota

Passatge Mercader 18 (93 215 70 51/www.estranydelamota.com). FGC Provença. **Open** *Sept-June* 10.30am-1.30pm, 4.30-8.30pm Tue-Sat. *July* 10.30am-1.30pm, 4.30-8.30pm Mon-Fri. Closed Aug. **No credit cards. Map** p338 D4.

This iron-columned basement gallery works well for Antoni Estrany's selection of neo-conceptualists, including the intelligent photo-montages of Montserrat Soto and the disarmingly simple comic-like drawings of Francesc Ruiz. International artists represented include Thomas Ruff, Jean-Marc Bustamante and Thomas Locher.

Galeria Joan Prats

Rambla Catalunya 54 (93 216 02 84/www.galeriajoanprats.com). Metro Passeig de Gràcia. **Open** *Sept-June* 10.30am-1.30pm, 5-8.30pm Tue-Sat. *July* 10.30am-1.30pm, 5-8.30pm Tue-Fri. Closed Aug. **Credit** AmEx, MC, V. **Map** p342 D4.

This gallery was born out of the 1920s friendship between Joan Prats, son of a fashionable hatmaker, and the artist Joan Miró. Nowadays, the only remnant of the original business is the name and the headgear motifs on the shopfront, as the Prats' excellent Miró collection is now in the Fundació Miró (*see p111*). Along with a crop of well-known painters, 'La Prats' represents artists like the high-profile Eulàlia Valldosera, and the quirky Catalan Perejaume. Shows in 2004 will feature the lush abstractions of José Maria Sicilia and the politically charged collages of Juan Ugalde. The nearby branch on C/Balmes has limited-edition prints.

Other locations: Joan Prats-Artgràfic, C/Balmes 54 (93 488 13 98).

Kowasa Gallery

C/Mallorca 235 (93 487 35 88/www.kowasa.com). FGC Provença. **Open** 11am-2pm, 5-8.30pm Tue-Sat. Closed Aug. **Credit** AmEx, MC, V. **Map** p338 D4.

This photography gallery is located above the excellent bookshop of the same name. Its two spaces are used to show the varied works of Spanish and international artists including the likes of Martí Llorens, Ramon David and the famed Civil War chronicler Agustí Centelles. The gallery has works by hundreds of photographers, among them Nadar, Cartier-Bresson and John Coplans.

aleria Toni Tàpies

C/Consell de Cent 282 (93 487 64 02/www.toni tapies.com). Metro Passeig de Gràcia. **Open** 10am-2pm, 4-8pm Tue-Fri; 11am-2pm, 5-8.30pm Sat. Closed Aug. **Credit** MC, V. **Map** p339 F4.

Run by the son of the prestigious Catalan painter, this gallery shows young Catalan artists Tere Recarens and Martí Anson, along with established creators Jaume Plensa and daddy Tàpies himself (showing in early 2003); there are shows by foreign artists as well, including Canadian Jana Sterbak. The gallery also produces limited-edition prints.

PROJECTESD

Ptge Mercader 8 (93 488 1360). FGC Provença. **Open** 11.30am-8.30pm Tue-Sat. Closed 2wks Aug. **No credit cards**. **Map** p338 D4.

Silvia Dauder has founded a handsome new space on either side of this tight Eixample courtyard. Exhibits exemplify her particular passion for new drawing, photography and film. Exhibits in 2004 include a group show featuring drawings by American artists David Brody, Gary Gissler, Marsha Cottrell, and a solo show by Kai Takeda, a young Japanese artist based in Barcelona.

Gràcia & Zona Alta

Fundació Foto Colectània

C/Julián Romea 6, D2 (93 217 16 26/www.colec tania.es). FGC Gràcia. **Open** 5-8.30pm Mon; 11am-2pm, 5-8.30pm Tue-Sat. Closed Aug. **Credit** AmEx, MC, V. **Map** p338 D3.

This private photography foundation is dedicated to the promotion of photography collecting. Shows in the large, handsome space emphasise collections of other important galleries and museums, including major Spanish and Portuguese photographers since the 1950s. In the spring of 2004, the space will exhibit a selection of its own outstanding collection.

Galeria Alejandro Sales

C/Julián Romea 16 (93 415 20 54/www.alejandro sales.com). FGC Gràcia. **Open** *Oct-June* 11am-2pm, 5-8.30pm Tue-Sat. *July, Sept* 11am-2pm, 5-8.30pm Tue-Fri. Closed Aug. **No credit cards**. **Map** p338 D3.

A winning combination of impeccable shows by international blue-chip artists with a solid Spanish stable. Work by emerging young creators and gallery regulars is also seen in a smaller room called Blackspace. The more interesting gallery artists you might seen include Madrid-based Marina Nuñez and local light Lluís Hortalà.

Galeria H_2O

C/Verdi 152 (93 415 18 01/www.h2o.es). Metro Lesseps. **Open** 11am-1pm, 5.30-8pm Tue-Fri; 11am-1pm Sat. Closed Aug. **Credit** V. **Map** p339 E2.

Architect/designer Joaquim Ruiz Millet and writer Ana Planella publish books and produce design objects (including works by Martí Guixé), while running a dynamic gallery out of this charming Gràcia home. Shows feature design (an exhibit by Eumo Gràfic is set for November 2004), architecture, photography (with Jesús Micó and Abby Robinson set for the 2004 Photography Spring) and contemporary art.

The fringe scene

Worth checking out in Poble Nou are the spacious **Centre Civic Can Felipa** (C/Pallars 277, 93 266 44 41), and the closely aligned **Theredoom Galeria** (C/Marina 65-7, 93 221 13 69, www.theredoom.com) and **La Santa Proyectos Culturales**, organiser of the free-flowing art festival BAC! in late autumn (C/Marina 65-67, 93 221 13 69, www.lasanta.org). Politically engaged projects emerge out of the **22A** group of artists and critics (93 441 84 81, www.22a.org), while **Barcelona Culture Studio** (C/Riereta 20 bis, 93 443 30 04, www.barcelonaculture.com) organises frequent shows, concerts and independent film events out of a Raval loft. In late spring 'Tallers Oberts' sees artists open their studios in Poblenou and the old city, with an information point at the **FAD** (Convent dels Àngels, Plaça dels Àngels 5-6, www.digiteca.com/tallersoberts).

Public centres complementing the fringe are **Metrònom** (*see p98*), the CaixaForum's **Mediateca** (*see p111*), and the **CCCB** (*see p95*). The alternative scene also blends into Barcelona's nightlife frontier, where many of the loose ends meet. If you're looking for somewhere to stay and study art, there are no residential art centres for visitors in Barcelona. The best and nearest option is **Can Serrat**, a converted farmhouse near Montserrat (mobile 699 487 866, www.canserrat.org).

Hangar

Passatge del Marqués de Santa Isabel 40, Poblenou (tel/fax 93 308 40 41/www.hangar.org). Metro Poblenou. **Open** *Information* 9am-2pm Mon-Fri. Closed Aug. **No credit cards**.

Besides being a multi-disciplinary centre with a number of artists' studios as well as facilities for the production of video and internet art, Hangar has now added some workshops, video screenings and debates that are open to the general public, while also offering a regular showroom of residents' work (which is generally not for sale). Run by the Catalan Visual Artists Association, Hangar also spearheads an open studio project for Poblenou artists in June. Visitors should call first.

La Xina A.R.T.

C/Doctor Dou 4 (93 301 67 03/www.laxinaart.org) Metro Catalunya. **Open** 5.30-8.30pm Mon-Fri; 11am-2pm, 5.30-8.30pm Sat. Closed Aug. **Map** p342 A2.

A group of mid-career artists runs this tiny space near the MACBA as a base for lively exchanges. Artists include Benxamín Álvarez and Luis Cadarso. La Xina also organises an open-air animated film festival in the summer, called Xinacittà.

Gay & Lesbian

Are you coming out tonight?

All types of diversity are famously greeted with enthusiasm in Barcelona, and sexuality is no exception. Being gay is simply not an issue and most of the places mentioned here cater to a mixed crowd. The gay scene is referred in Spanish as the *ambiente* – which can be deliberately ambiguous as the same word can be used in other contexts to mean 'atmosphere' – and a place can be *un poco de ambiente* (a bit gay), or more. The clubs may not have the technical sophistication of some London or New York clubs but they more than make up for it with an ebullient atmosphere, while bars really go the extra mile to bring the punters in, which means that many are worth visiting for the decor alone. But be prepared, it all starts late. Bars get going at midnight, and don't even think of going to a club before 2am unless you just want to get to know the DJ.

The lack of segregation means that there is not a gay ghetto as such, although the area bordered by the streets of Diputació and Aragó, Balmes and Villaroel in the Eixample is known as the 'Gaixample', and is where most gay venues are concentrated. Even this is not really a gayhood, because, although it has a certain buzz at night, the strict gridlines and wide streets make it anything but villagey.

Most outdoor cruising is done elsewhere, most popularly on Montjuïc, around the MNAC (*see p114*), but this area has undergone major changes recently, with much of the vegetation cut away and oh-so-unflattering floodlights installed, but there are still a couple of shadowy corners where it is business as usual.

Barcelona is short on listings magazines, but it's a good idea to pick up a copy of the free gay map or magazines such as *Nois* or *Shanguide* from various bars and gay shops. Websites worth checking out include www.mensual.com, www.naciongay.com and www.guiagay.com.

Cafés & bars

Gaixample

Note that the gay scene moves rapidly. Bars and clubs come and go at a dizzying pace. Also worth checking out are **Átame** (Consell de Cent 257, no phone), **Oui Café** (Consell de Cent 247, no phone) and **Escandalus** (Villarroel 86, 93 454 44 57). Unless otherwise stated women are mostly welcomed in the bars listed here.

Ambar

C/Casanova 71, Eixample (no phone). Metro Universitat. **Open** 6pm-3am daily. **No credit cards. Map** p338 C4.

A stylish bar, with classy Spanish pop art lining the walls and a cool, label-conscious crowd. In such a dimly lit atmosphere you might expect to stumble across a darkroom at the back, but surprise! Instead, it's a brightly lit room with eight full-sized pool tables. Seeing is believing.

Café Dietrich

C/Consell de Cent 255, Eixample (93 451 77 07). Metro Universitat. **Open** 10.30pm-2.30am Mon-Thur, Sun; 10.30pm-3am Fri, Sat. **No credit cards. Map** p342 C5.

A classic of the scene, Dietrich has become a victim of its own success, with attitude-laden staff, obnoxious doormen and expensive drinks. The atmosphere is camp-trendy with the strut-your-stuff crowd in a lighter mood before the serious trawling begins in the clubs. House music gives way to drag shows nightly at 1.30am.

Caligula

C/Consell de Cent 257, Eixample (no phone). Metro Universitat. **Open** 8pm-3am daily. **No credit cards. Map** p342 C5.

Resplendent with wonders of the Orient, Caligula hosts a drag cabaret nightly among its eastern artefacts and red drapes. Otherwise this is a quiet, cosy place with plenty of seating, attracting a more mixed crowd than neighbouring Dietrich.

D-Blanco

C/Villaroel 71, Eixample (93 451 59 86/www.d-blanco.com). Metro Urgell. **Open** 6pm-2am Mon-Wed; 11pm-3am Thur-Sat. **Credit** AmEx, DC, MC, V. **Map** p342 C5.

The keynote of this hip bar, as the name says, is white, but as a relief from the snowy rigours of the main bar, there is a riotously coloured salon privée. Well-heeled and well-muscled twenty-to-forties chow down on elaborate sandwiches and salads until 11.30pm, or, on Thursdays, tuck into a taster menu (€30) accompanied by cabaret.

Ironic Café

C/Consell de Cent 242 bis, Eixample (mobile 627 92 98 53). Metro Universitat. **Open** 7pm-midnight Tue-Sun. **No credit cards. Map** p342 C5.

Decorated in sleek, high-tech mode, with arty images shimmering across screens lining the walls, this is a relaxed place to sip a cocktail or two. The tiny stage at the back sees fewer performances nowadays, but the atmosphere still enjoys a buzz.

Big, red and throbbing – this is **Sweet**.

Punto BCN

C/Muntaner 63-5, Eixample (93 453 61 23). Metro Universitat. **Open** 6pm-2am Mon-Thur, Sun; 6pm-2.30am Fri, Sat. **No credit cards. Map** p342 C5.

One of Barcelona's oldest gay bars, this is also one of the few places that get busy early in the evening. It's not a place for design aficionados, but it is friendly and unpretentious, and attracts birds of many feathers, from besuited fiftysomethings to teenagers having their first drink out of the closet.

Sweet

C/Casanova 75, Eixample (no phone). Metro Universitat. **Open** 8pm-2.30am Tue-Thur, Sun; 8pm-3am Fri, Sat. **No credit cards. Map** p338 C3.

The newest and coolest in the Gaixample is this large, slick bar with red lighting, low seating and chill-out music in a relaxed atmosphere. Like any bar aspiring to be hip in Barcelona, it has the obligatory slide projections, but it also has friendly staff.

Z:eltas Club

C/Casanova 75, Eixample (93 454 19 02/www.zeltas.net). Metro Universitat. **Open** 11pm-3am Wed-Sun. **No credit cards. Map** p342 C5.

Z:eltas has the feel of a large cocktail bar, with stylish design accentuated by spectacular orange and green spotlighting. The DJ spins funky house for those warming up for the night on the tiny dancefloor.

Rest of the city

Along with those listed here, mixed bars like **Schilling** (*se p172*), **Ra** (*see p175*) and especially **La Concha** (*see p245*) are also worth checking out, though not gay per se.

The Eagle

Passeig de Sant Joan 152, Eixample (93 207 58 56/www.eaglespain.com). Metro Verdaguer. **Open** 10pm-2.30am Mon-Thur, Sun; 10pm-3am Fri, Sat. **No credit cards. Map** p339 E4.

The clientele here is over 30 and hirsute, and may well drop the stipulated leather once inside. A small bar gives off to a backroom with all manner of contraptions, including a bathtub for watersports. The videos and theme nights are pretty hardcore.

New Chaps

Avda Diagonal 365, Eixample (93 215 53 65). Metro Diagonal or Verdaguer. **Open** 9pm-3am Mon-Sat; 7pm-3am Sun. **No credit cards. Map** p338 D4.

A well-used bar for stockmen *d'un certain âge*, and true to its butch name. Steer horns on the wall, porn on the video, all sorts of goings-on in the labyrinthine darkroom downstairs and nary a dame to be seen.

Topxi

C/Valencia 358, Eixample (93 207 01 20/www.topxi.com). Metro Diagonal or Verdaguer. **Open** 11pm-5am Wed-Thur; 11pm-6am Fri, Sat; 7pm-5am Sun. **Admission** men €6, women €9. **No credit cards. Map** p339 E4.

A small bar for men over 40, with a busy darkroom showing porn films. Viper-tongued drag queens perform on Friday and Saturday around 1am. Real women pay more to get in.

Clubs

Other local clubs with gay followings include **La Terrrazza** and **Discothèque** (for both *see p251*), which attract a cheery suburban crowd.

Arena Classic

C/Diputació 233, Eixample (93 487 83 42/www.arenadisco.com). Metro Passeig de Gràcia or Universitat. **Open** 12.30am-5am Fri, Sat. **Admission** (incl 1 drink) €5 Fri; €10 Sat. **No credit cards**. **Map** p342 D5.

There are three discos called Arena offering variations on a well-worn theme. You can switch from one to another freely after getting your hand stamped. The Classic is the more light-hearted with plenty of anthems of the *Dancing Queen* genre; a campy-kitsch atmosphere and a healthy mix of the sexes.

Arena Madre

C/Balmes 32, Eixample (93 487 83 42). Metro Passeig de Gràcia or Universitat. **Open** 12.30am-5am Tue-Sat; 7pm-5am Sun. **Admission** (incl 1 drink) €5 Tue-Fri, Sun; €10 Sat. **No credit cards**. **Map** p342 D5.

Large and cavernous, Arena Madre has a spacious dancefloor, a darkroom and pounding house, along with current chart hits. It attracts a younger crowd than Arena Classic, and is more of a cattle market. Early in the week there are shows and strippers.

Arena VIP

Gran Via de les Corts Catalanes 593, Eixample (93 487 83 42). Metro Universitat. **Open** 12.30am-5am Fri, Sat. **Admission** (incl 1 drink) €5 Fri; €10 Sat. **No credit cards**. **Map** p342 D5.

The last and tackiest of the Arena troika is the most mixed and, again, a youthful venue with lots of space, but heaving nonetheless at weekends. Like the other Arenas, the VIP certainly does its bit for the Spanish retro pop industry, along with crooners Dion, Houston, Estefan et al.

La Luna

Avda Diagonal 323, Eixample (no phone). Metro Verdaguer. **Open** 11pm-3am Mon-Thur; 11pm-10.30am Fri, Sat. **Admission** €15; free before 5am. **No credit cards**. **Map** p339 E4.

Those who haven't had enough or simply haven't had anything at all head here after the clubs close, so this is the place to be between 6am and 8am on weekend mornings. It's a surprisingly friendly place, and its dancefloor is packed with a mixed bunch of survivors dancing to current club hits, followed later in the morning by older tunes. There is a quiet back bar and a very busy darkroom.

Martins

Passeig de Gràcia 130, Gràcia (93 218 71 67). Metro Diagonal. **Open** midnight-5am daily. **Admission** (incl 1 drink) €10. **Credit** MC, V. **Map** p338 D3/4.

A mere shadow of the pulsing nightspot it once was, Martins has three bars, a porno lounge, a shop selling accessories (that's harnesses and cockrings, not handbags) but is desperately low on punters. It does liven up a bit once the crowds from the Eagle and New Chaps turn out, when the action moves to a darkroom with so much history it should be listed.

Metro

C/Sepúlveda 185, Eixample (93 323 52 27). Metro Universitat. **Open** midnight-5am Mon-Thur, Sun; midnight-6am Fri, Sat. **Admission** (incl 1 drink) €9. **Credit** MC, V. **Map** p342 C5.

Metro continues to pull in men of all ages, but it has a slightly older feel. Both dancefloors are imbued with a real party atmosphere; the smaller plays

Find your dancing queen at **Salvation**'s La Madame. *See p238.*

Latin tunes interspersed with pop classics, while the packed main area focuses on disco greats. The maze of a darkroom gets rammed and it pays to watch your pockets. Check out the tiny individual screens showing porn over the urinal.

Salvation

Ronda Sant Pere 19-21, Eixample (93 318 06 86/ www.matineegroup.com). Metro Urquinaona. **Open** midnight-5am Fri, Sat; 6pm-5am Sun. **Admission** (incl 1 drink) €11. **No credit cards**. **Map** p342 D5.

One of Salvation's two large dancefloors sees disdainful barebacked Muscle Marys pumping to house among swirls of dry ice, while the other reverberates to cheesy disco. On Sunday nights, the club becomes La Madame, with a fun-loving gay/straight mix. Other events include an after-hours weekend party at Souvenir in Viladecans (admission includes coach transport from Salvation or Plaça Espanya). Again, watch your wallet in the claustrophobic darkroom.

Restaurants

In addition to those listed here, plenty of mixed restaurants in Barcelona have thriving gay followings. Among the most popular are **La Verònica** (*see p145*) and Barri Gòtic's **Venus Delicatessen** (C/Avinyó, 93 301 15 85).

La Bodegueta de Muntaner

C/Muntaner 64, Eixample (93 451 51 04). Metro Universitat. **Open** 9pm-midnight Tue-Sun. Closed 2wks Aug. **Average** €€. **Credit** MC, V. **Map** p338 C4.

A long bar leads to a cosy little space with stone walls, wooden beams and a friendly smiling staff. The menu comprises mostly good Mediterranean dishes and traditional Spanish stalwarts such as high quality *jamón*, sausages and pâté. Although it's open to all, it does become more predominantly gay/lesbian in the evening.

Café Miranda

C/Casanova 30, Eixample (93 453 52 49). Metro Universitat. **Open** 9pm-midnight Tue-Thur, Sun; 9pm-1am Fri, Sat. **Average** **Credit** DC, MC, V. **Map** p342 C5.

This flamboyant café has become a mecca for office parties and stag nights, with its elaborate decor, spectacular waiters, drag queens, singers and acrobats. When they pause for breath the music is loud and uptempo. The food here is generally nothing special, but the atmosphere certainly is, so booking is essential, particularly at weekends.

Castro

C/Casanova 85, Eixample (93 323 67 84). Metro Universitat. **Open** 1-4pm, 9pm-midnight Mon-Fri; 9pm-midnight Sat. **Average** €€. **Set lunch** €7.85 Mon-Fri. **Credit** MC, V. **Map** p338 C4.

If a restaurant can be hardcore, then this is it: a heavy chain curtain welcomes you into the black leather and grey metal interior and a soundtrack of unintrusive trip hop. But fear not, this is not a darkroom, but a dedicatedly gay eaterie with an imaginative menu. Among the delicacies on offer (which do not include the young and impressively gym-toned waiters) are kangaroo steak, duck with pears, and fresh beef carpaccio.

Cubaneo

C/Casanova 70, Eixample (93 454 31 88/ www.cubaneo.net). Metro Universitat. **Open** 1-5pm, 8pm-12.30am Tue-Sun. **Average** €€. Set lunch €6.50. Set dinner €12. **Credit** MC, V. **Map** p338 C4.

As you'd expect from the name and the flag, you can find some Cuban dishes – *arroz congri*, *frijoles negros*, etc – but this is also a good place to taste some traditional Catalan dishes including things like grilled vegetables with romesco sauce or *esqueixada de bacallà* (cod salad). Invigorating Mojitos and handsome muscled waiters complete the picture, along with an unholy mix of Cuban personalities (OK, just Castro) and gay icons gracing the walls.

Services

Saunas

An invigorating sauna may not be the main attraction at these places for all customers, but that is none of our business. We can say that at all of these establishments you will find enough showers, steam rooms and dry saunas to justify the name, along with bars and colourful porn lounges. On arrival you are supplied with locker key, towel and flip-flops. Listed here are some of the more popular places.

Sauna Casanova

C/Casanova 57, Eixample (93 323 78 60). Metro Urgell. **Open** 24hrs daily. **Admission** €12.50 Mon, Wed, Fri-Sun; €10 Tue, Thur. **Credit** AmEx, DC, MC, V. **Map** p342 C5.

This is by far the city's most popular sauna, attracting plenty of muscled eye-candy. It's busiest on Tuesday and Thursday evenings, every night after the clubs close and all day Sunday.

Thermas

C/Diputació 46, Eixample (93 325 93 46). Metro Rocafort. **Open** noon-2am Mon-Thur; noon Fri-2am Sun. **Admission** €12.50 Mon, Wed-Sun; €10 Tue. **Credit** MC, V. **Map** p341 B5.

A well-equipped set-up attracting sugar daddies for the young and very pretty regular fixtures.

Sex shops

The following are all aimed at the gay market, and all have viewing cabins for videos.

Nostromo

C/Diputació 208, Eixample (93 323 31 94). Metro Universitat. **Open** 11am-10pm Mon-Fri; noon-10pm Sat, Sun. **No credit cards**. **Map** p342 C5.

Sestienda

C/Rauric 11, Barri Gòtic (93 318 86 76/ www.sestienda.com). Metro Liceu. **Open** 10am-2pm, 3.30-8.30pm Mon-Sat. **Credit** AmEx, MC, V. **Map** p345 A3.

Zeus

C/Riera Alta 20, Raval (93 442 97 95). Metro Sant Antoni. **Open** 10am-9pm Mon-Sat. **Credit** MC, V. **Map** p342 C5.

Shops

Antinous Libreria Café

C/Josep Anselm Clavé 6, Barri Gòtic (93 301 90 70/ www.antinouslibros.com). Metro Drassanes. **Open** 10.30am-2pm, 5-8.30pm Mon-Fri; noon-2pm Sat. **Credit** AmEx, DC, MC, V. **Map** p345 A4.

This spacious and elegant bookshop has an ample stock of gay and lesbian literature, some in English,

Camp sites

If you covet the wardrobe of Elizabeth I, have pink furry cushions at home and own at least one piece of leopardskin underwear, then we have good news, darling. This city is just the place for you.

Barcelona's romance with camp is an old affair. At the turn of the century Domènech i Montaner started working on the **Palau de la Música** (*see p261*), a building so overblown with flowery mosaics and frolicking muses as to bring on a Julie Andrews moment in all who witness it. In fact, the whole Modernista movement presents enough extravagant decoration and vivid colour to warm the hearts of the queeniest among us.

The city also does a good line in gay icons and their imitators. The walls of **La Concha** (*see p245*) are papered from ceiling to floor with pictures of the perpetually pouting Spanish screen goddess Sara Montiel, who watches imperiously over the performances of the Sunday night drag queens. Nearby you'll find **El Cangrejo** (*pictured*) for more of the same (along with Spanish disco anthems of the '80s on Fridays and Saturdays). El Cangrejo is also one of the bars where Carmen de Mairena, an unclassifiable and much-loved 70-year-old transsexual, is a frequent visitor. Ask about her last porn film; it's becoming a cult hit in record time.

For all this, it is a municipally run squeaky-clean family attraction that towers over all other elements of Catalan camp. **Font Màgica de Montjuïc** (*see p113*) is quite simply unmissable. This colossal 'magic fountain' surges and dances to every tune that's ever stuck obstinately in your head, from Nana Mouskouri to Wagner and the theme from *Love Story*. The fountain is a stone's throw from what is left of Montjuïc's cruising area, which means you could conceivably get a quickie as pink and yellow streams of light dance over the trees and the Valkyries thunder on. Unforgettable.

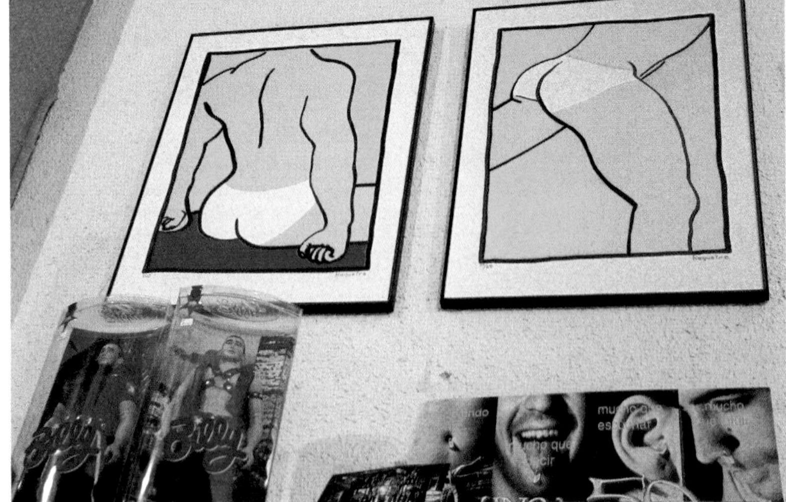

Art, books and gay dolls fill the shelves at **Antinous Libreria Café**. *See p239.*

as well as a large amount of other handy items including videos, postcards and a noticeboard displaying information on upcoming events and places to stay outside Barcelona. Once exhausted by browsing you can have your well-earned coffee and cake in the teashop at the back.

Complices

C/Cervantes 2, Barri Gòtic (93 412 72 83). Metro Jaume 1. **Open** 10.30am-8.30pm Mon-Fri; noon-8.30pm Sat. **Credit** AmEx, MC, V. **Map** p345 B3.

Two women run Barcelona's oldest gay bookshop, stocking women's books, magazines and videos on one side; men's on the other. Go downstairs for spicier material and a fair selection of books in English.

e-male

C/Consell de Cent 236, Eixample (93 454 08 72). Metro Universitat. **Open** 11.30am-2pm, 5-9pm Mon-Sat. **Credit** AmEx, MC, V. **Map** p342 C5.

This tiny shop sells all you need to dress according to your manly fantasies: leather jackets to ride your Harley, striped T-shirts to enlist in the navy, sporting strips and minimal underwear to display your toned self in the locker room.

M69

C/Muntaner 69, Eixample (93 453 62 69). Metro Universitat. **Open** 10am-2pm, 4.30-8.30pm Mon-Fri; 10.30am-2.30pm, 5-9pm Sat. **Credit** MC, V. **Map** p345 B3.

Jump over the doe-eyed golden retriever that guards the door to enter the hippest gay shop in the Eixample. Friendly shop assistants will guide you through sexy threads from the likes of Paul Smith, high-fashion trainers, swimming underwear, jewellery, a selection of design books and the very coolest CDs.

Ovlas

Via Laietana 33, Barri Gòtic (93 268 76 91). Metro Jaume I. **Open** 10.15am-8.30pm Mon-Fri; 10.15am-9pm Sat. **Credit** AmEx, MC, V. **Map** p345 B3.

This is a clothing emporium for the young at heart, or at least those with a sense of humour; it stocks a variety of attention-grabbing outer- and underwear and a good selection of footwear. There's also a bar at which to sip on a cocktail while pondering floral spandex leggings and the like.

Ritual

C/Consell de Cent, 255 Eixample (93 451 91 68). Metro Universitat. **Open** 11am-2pm, 5-8.30pm Mon-Sat. **Credit** MC, V. **Map** p342 C5.

Clothes in which a young man can make his mark when sweeping through the Gaixample night. Choose from Energie, Sixty, Bill Tornade as well as the shop's own label.

Lesbian Barcelona

The lesbian scene is a low-key one, centred around the C/Sèneca in Gràcia, where most dyke-friendly drinking spots are to be found. You'll also find lesbians in some places frequented by gay men, such as **Arena** (*see p237*), **La Luna** (*see p237*) or La Madame at **Salvation** (*see p238*).

Aside from gay bars, there are other options as well, of course. You'll find a friendly one-nighter at the largely straight bar **Risco** (*see p255*) if you go on Thursdays for Lesfatales. Regular events and parties are organised by a variety of groups: **Ca La Dona** (*see p320*) and **Casal Lambda** (*see p310*) are good places to get information, as is **Complices** (*see above*).

Aire

C/Valencia 236, Eixample (93 454 63 94/ www.arenadisco.com). Metro Passeig de Gràcia. **Open** *Sept-June* 11pm-3am Thur-Sat. *July, Aug* 11pm-3am Tue-Sat. **Admission** (incl 1 drink) €5 Tue-Fri; €6 Sat. **No credit cards**. **Map** p338 C4.

This is a vast and airy bar with a pool table, dancefloor and solid Egyptian columns to lend support to kissing couples. It attracts a multifarious crowd, and customers range from younger lesbians to thirtysomethings and a handful of their gayboy friends. Very busy at weekends.

Bahía

C/Sèneca 12, Gràcia (no phone). Metro Diagonal. **Open** 10pm-3am Mon-Thur, Sun; 6-9am, 10pm-3am Fri, Sat. **No credit cards**. **Map** p338 D3.

This is a friendly and welcoming little bar with a warm interior and a wide variety of music pumping from its speakers. It tends only to get busy at weekends, especially for its after-hours sessions on Saturday and Sunday mornings.

La Bata de Boatiné

C/Robadors 23, Raval (no phone). Metro Liceu. **Open** 10pm-3am Tue-Sun. **No credit cards**. **Map** p342 C6.

This battered and slightly grungy bar has recently become very popular among a young lesbian crowd, but is very mixed with gay and straight regulars. It is a good place to meet after midnight and to find out what's going on in the small hours.

D-Mer

C/Plató 13, Sant Gervasi (93 201 62 07/www.d-mer.com). Metro Lesseps/FGC Muntaner. **Open** midnight-3am Thur-Sat. **Admission** (incl 1 drink) €7. **No credit cards**. **Map** p338 C2.

At last! A stylish dyke bar with cool dance music, comfortable seating and pretty people on both sides of the long bar. The diverse clientele ranges from trendy young things to women in their 40s, but this is not really one to bring your male friends to.

La Singular

C/Francisco Giner 50, Gràcia (93 237 50 98). Metro Diagonal. **Open** 1-4pm, 9pm-midnight Mon-Fri; 1-4pm, 9pm-1am Sat, Sun. Closed 2wks Aug. **Average** €€. **Set lunch** €7.50. **Credit** MC, V. **Map** p338 D3.

A women-run restaurant with good tapas and home-cooked meals at very economical prices. The menu changes daily, so take the chef's recommendation on the best fare of the day.

Sitges

An easy half-hour's train ride down the coast is the predominantly gay resort of Sitges. A good deal of its old fishing village charm remains, but at night, and especially during summer, it comes alive with song, dance and a rowdy camaraderie. It's a pleasant place to while away a couple of days (*see also p277*).

The gay nudist beach to the south of town is not to be missed if you are up for the long walk (about an hour, and best attempted in trainers); the crowd is mellow and international and there is a bar that serves food. The cruising area is in the bushes behind.

Accommodation

For help with gay accommodation in Sitges, try Peter and Rico at **RAS** (mobile 607 149 451, www.raservice.com). One option is **La Masia Casanova**, which offers luxury suites with a pool, a bar and lots of tranquillity. Book well in advance for the minimum three-day stay (Passatge Casanova 8, 93 818 80 58, rates €120 incl breakfast). **Hotel Liberty** is a bright, airy, spacious hotel with modern, comfortable rooms and lush gardens (C/Illa de Cuba 35, 93 811 08 72, www.hotel-liberty-sitges.com, rates €67-€92 incl breakfast). Or there's the aptly named **Hotel Romàntic** – one of Sitges' most popular gay-friendly hotels. It's a beautifully restored 19th-century house with a palm-filled patio (C/Sant Isidre 33, 93 894 83 75, rates €80-€94 incl breakfast, closed Nov-Mar). Another option is **La Renaixença**, which is under the same management, with the same number and prices (C/Illa de Cuba 7). Finally, there's the central and friendly **Hostal Termes** (C/Termes 9, 93 894 23 43, rates €50-€72, closed Nov). *See also p278.*

Bars & clubs

There's a well-worn circuit to Sitges' nightlife, and it invariably begins at **Parrots Pub** (Plaça Indústria 2), along the main drag from the centre to the beach, known as 'Sin Street'. At around midnight, the crowd moves to **El Candil** (C/Carreta 9), followed by places like **Mediterraneo** (C/Sant Bonaventure 6); a stylish, spacious spot attracting the shirts-off loved-up techno crowd. After that it's time for a shimmy at **Organic** (C/Bonaire 15) or the busiest club of them all, **Trailer** (C/Angel Vidal 36), which stays open till 5am and pulsates to sounds from guest DJs.

Alternative drinking holes include **El Horno** (C/Joan Tarrida Ferratges 6), which attracts a more mature and hairier crowd, and **B Side Bar** (C/Sant Gaudenci 7), a busy venue with a darkroom and fewer foreigners.

Restaurants

Good food and a charming terrace can be found at **Flamboyant** (C/Pau Barrabeitg 16, 93 894 58 11, mains €10, closed Oct-Feb), while **Ma Maison** (C/Bonnaire 28, 93 894 60 54, mains €12, closed Wed) specialises in couscous and offers alfresco dining. There's a wide choice at **Can Pagés** (C/Sant Pere 24-6, 93 894 11 95, closed Mon, mains €12), while **Casa Hidalgo** (C/Sant Pau 12, 93 894 38 95, mains €16, closed Mon and 4wks Dec-Jan) offers a pleasant array of good traditional Spanish food.

Nightlife & Music

Shall we dance?

It is often said by the people who live here that when in Barcelona you can either soak up the sights by day, or you can turn yourself over to the creatures of the night, haunting bars and nightclubs until dawn. But you can't do both. At least, not at the same time; not unless you thrive on no sleep and have unlimited amounts of energy. Why? Because, going out in Barcelona happens late. People rarely meet for a drink much before 11pm. Bars don't shut until 3am, and it's not until they kick people out that the clubs (cutesily still known as *discotecas*) really get going. If you're still raring to go come 6am, if you keep your ear to the ground there's a good chance you'll find an after-party party for even more hedonism.

Like anywhere else, the biggest nights are Thursday, Friday and Saturday, with teatime chill-out sessions on Sundays fast catching on. It's all here, from superclubs hosting famed international celebrity DJs, to tiny little clubs specialising in the latest experimental electro, ear-bleeding drum 'n' bass and boom-busting techno. There are lounge-clubs and gilded ballrooms, *salsatecas* and Brazilian samba bars, alternative club nights offering anything from northern soul to Bollywood Bhangra, crooning drag queens and seductive tango emporiums. There are even bars with beds (**CDLC**, *see p249*), so why would you ever go home?

Traditionally, you had to head uptown to hit the posh clubs, but the Port Olímpic is putting out some serious competition with places like **Club Danzatoria** (*see p258*) and **CDLC** luring the *pijos* downtown. There are also nightly beach parties running up and down the coast from Bogatell (**El Chiringuito**, *see p249*) to Mataró through the summer. Meanwhile, you'll find smaller venues pulsating with life in the Barri Gòtic, particularly around the Plaza Reial and C/Escudellers. Across La Rambla, in the Raval, you can skulk the grittier, grungier places. If hippie chic, joints and chillums are your thing, Gràcia is good for hanging with the artsy crowd, though in truth, it's a far better place for bars than it is for serious nightlife.

LIVE MUSIC

In terms of live music you can hardly walk two steps in Barcelona without some kind of musical accompaniment, be it muzak on the metro, penny whistlers on La Rambla or the singing doughnut seller on Barceloneta beach, and although most beats in Barcelona come from DJs playing house and techno, there is still a strong live music scene here.

Although the smörgåsbord of local musical offerings is a varied feast, it's served up by only a very few venues. The occasional visits of pop-rock superstars can only be accommodated in one of the sports barns up on Montjuïc and Vall d'Hebron, or even way out in Badalona's Palau Olímpic. To see anyone else – from chart-toppers to newly signed flavours of the month – you have just three options. Top of the trio is the multi-faceted industrial space **Razzmatazz** (*see p259*), which plays host to museum pieces like Motörhead, elder statesmen of dance like the Chemical Brothers, and flavours of the month like the Datsuns. **Sala Apolo** (*see p251*) serves a similar constituency in a smaller space. Acts here may be weirder, less known, or slightly on the descendent. It's a good spot for an introduction to the local pop-rock scene, such as it is. **Bikini** (*see p258*) used to be the prime rock venue in the city before Razzmatazz surfed past it on the current wave. Now this too-slick venue, with its shopping mall architecture, has taken solid hold of the quality middle ground, hosting gigs by accomplished musicians at the funk, soul and bluesy end of rock, along with world music acts.

A few iconic jazz venues such as **Jamboree** (*see p244*) and **La Cova del Drac** (*see p258*), along with some metal-oriented sheds of noise on the outer limits, complete the major music venue roll call, although many clubs and bars, including places like **Sidecar** (*see p245*), **Maumau** (*see p251*) and **Magic** (*see p247*) – will host the occasional live band.

INFORMATION AND TICKETS

For concert information buy the weekly (out on Thursdays) listings guide *Guía del Ocio* or the Friday papers, which usually include listings supplements. Look in bars and music shops for free mags such as *Metropolitan*, *La Netro*, *Nativa*, *Go*, *AB*, *Mondo Sonoro* (all mostly independent pop/rock/electronica) and *Batonga!* (world music). *Punto H* and *Suite* are good for keeping yourself up to date on the club scene, or there is *Movin' BCN*, a monthly, bilingual publication available from news kiosks.

On the web, try listings sites www.atiza.com, www.salirenbarcelona.com, www.clubbing spain.com and barcelona.lanetro.com. For festivals try www.festivales.com and www.whatsonwhen.com. You can also get information and tickets from Tel-entrada and Servi-Caixa (*see p212*). Specialist record shops, such as the ones on C/Tallers in the Raval, are good for info and club flyers.

Barri Gòtic

Barcelona Pipa Club

Plaça Reial 3, pral (93 302 47 32/www.bpipaclub.com). Metro Liceu. **Open** 6pm-3am daily. **Admission** free. **No credit cards**. **Map** p345 A3.

One of Barcelona's best-loved late-night bars, where Catalan celebrities mingle with the bourgeoisie and American Erasmus students. Courses in the art of pipe smoking are offered along with live jazz and gastronomic evenings, but above all it's a great place for an after-hours drink. To get in, ring the buzzer next to the sign of the pipe: if there's no answer, it may be that there's just no room.

Café Royale

C/Nou de Zurbano 3 (93 412 14 33). Metro Liceu or Drassanes. **Open** 6pm-2.30am Mon-Thur, Sun; 6pm-3am Fri, Sat. **Admission** free (€1 drink min). **Credit** MC, V. **Map** p345 A3.

A little bit of rhythm, and a lot of soul. Café Royale opens every night to the sound of funk and rare groove. Small, intimate and reassuringly smoky, it has the air of a quirky house party – a huge vase of fresh flowers rattles away in the middle of the dance

Nightspots for...

Outdoor frolics

El Chiringuito for dancing barefoot in the sand (*see p249*); **La Terrrazza** for cruising the patio under a full moon (*see p251*).

Big names

The star-spangled line up at **Razzmatazz** for indie rock and DJ A-listers (*see p259*). Or you can find the internationally fabulous at **Bikini** (*see p258*). **Luz de Gas** attracts big names your parents would remember (*see p255*).

Lounge lizards

CDLC (*see p249*) or **La Fianna** (*see p179*) for sleeping on the job and looking cool while you're doing it; **Schomsky** for understated layabouts (*see p244*).

Pool parties

The one and only Cocobongo at **Liquid**, for moon-bathing and stars swimming (*see p259*).

Beautiful people

Mansion house glamour greets the glitterati at **Danzatoria** (*see p258*); famous faces smoulder over sex kittens at **Buda Barcelona** (*see p252*).

Music snobs

Anoraks spot obscure influences in the impenetrable electronica at **Maumau** (*see p251*); northern soul boys chalk the floor at **Sala Apolo's** Powder Room (*see p251*). And jazz beards nod knowingly over their coffee in **Jamboree** (*see p244*).

Maumau.

floor, battered leather sofas line the walls. It's packed to overflowing by 2am, and if this kind of music is your scene, it's one of the most reliable venues in town to get down and dirty with the in crowd.

Chez Popof

C/Aroles 5 (93 318 42 26). Metro Liceu. **Open** midnight-4am Wed-Sun. **Admission** free. **No credit cards. Map** p345 A3.

Presumably at some stage this bar was what it looks like: a rustically appointed cava emporium with gruffly appealing Catalan charm. For as long as anyone can remember, though, its sole selling point has been the fact that its wooden doors are ajar when everywhere else is closed: at 4am it's a haze of smoke and broken resolutions, supervised by unsmiling waiters of the old school.

Dot

C/Nou de Sant Francesc 7 (93 302 70 26/www.dotlightclub.com). Metro Drassanes. **Open** 11pm-2.30am Tue-Thur, Sun; 11pm-3am Fri, Sat. **Admission** free. **No credit cards. Map** p345 A4.

Dot manages to please with just two small rooms and an excellent playlist of hip hop, breakbeat, funk and house. A small red bar is joined to an even smaller blue dancefloor by what looks tantalisingly like a *Star Trek* teleporter. Standing in it and saying 'Beam me up, Scotty', though, is not cool.

Downstairs@Club13

Plaça Reial 13 (93 412 43 27). Metro Liceu. **Open** *Apr-Oct* 2pm-2.30am Mon-Thur, Sun; 2pm-3am Fri, Sat. *Nov-Mar* 6pm-2.30am Mon-Thur, Sun; 6pm-3am Fri, Sat. **Admission** free. **Credit** AmEx, MC, V. **Map** p345 A3.

Sounds glam, is glam. A relative newcomer to the scene, this little nightspot adds a touch of class to the grungy Plaça Reial, what with its glittering chandeliers and posh-nosh restaurant. The red flock wallpaper, exposed brick cellar and black leather sofas downstairs make an ideal backdrop for deep house and nu breaks. Good for posing and pulling; and Sunday nights are especially fun.

Fantastico

Ptge dels Escudellers 3 (93 317 54 11/www.fantasticoclub.com). Metro Drassanes or Liceu. **Open** 10.30pm-3.30am Wed-Sat. **Admission** free. **No credit cards. Map** p345 A4.

Friendly and laid-back, this is a great little spot to start or finish a night of bar hopping in the Barri Gòtic. Psychedelic swirls lend an air of 1970s cool, but the mood is more in the present with local DJs from BIPP (Barcelona Indie Pop Palace).

Fonfone

C/Escudellers 24 (93 317 14 24/www.fonfone.com). Metro Drassanes. **Open** 9.30pm-2.30am Mon-Thur, Sun; 9.30pm-3am Fri, Sat. **Admission** free. **Credit** MC, V. **Map** p345 A3.

A deep dark bar barely lit by the radioactive glow of its green and orange Lego-like brick decor, Fonfone packs in a mixed crowd of locals and tourists, dominated by fashion-savvy twenty- to thirtysomethings. Pop, electronica, house and breakbeats get well-clad bottoms swaying.

Harlem Jazz Club

C/Comtessa de Sobradiel 8 (93 310 07 55). Metro Jaume I. **Open** 8pm-4am Tue-Thur, Sun; 8pm-5am Fri, Sat. *Gigs* 10.30pm, midnight Tue-Thur, Sun; 11.30pm, 1am Fri, Sat. Closed 2wks Aug. **Admission** *Mon-Thur, Sun* (1 drink min) free. *Fri, Sat* (incl 1 drink) €5. **No credit cards. Map** p345 B3.

Squeeze past the narrow bar and the room opens up (slightly) to accommodate a small stage and a laid-back chatty crowd. Jazz and blues often make way for world music, particularly Afro-Caribbean sounds, and flamenco-fusion, as well as rock.

Jamboree/Los Tarantos

Plaça Reial 17 (93 301 75 64/www.masimas.com). Metro Liceu. **Open** 12.30pm-5.30am daily. *Gigs* 10pm Mon; 11pm Tue-Sun. **Admission** (incl 1 drink) €12. *Gigs* €7-€10. **Credit** V. **Map** p345 A3.

Every night there are jazz, Latin or blues gigs by mainly Spanish groups; then the beards wander off and the beatbox comes out. On Mondays, particularly, the outrageously popular What The Fuck (WTF) jazz jam session is crammed with a young local crowd waiting for the funk/hip hop night that follows. Upstairs, sister venue Los Tarantos stages flamenco performances, then joins forces with Jamboree as a smooth-grooves chill-out space.

Karma

Plaça Reial 10 (93 302 56 80). Metro Liceu. **Open** midnight-5am Tue-Sun. **Admission** €8 or 2-3 drinks min. **No credit cards. Map** p345 A3.

Cellar club Karma has long been the embarrassing old uncle on the Barcelona nightlife scene, steadfastly unhip, but always looking like it knows how to have a good time with its failsafe cocktail of booze and cheesy rock for backpackers and those who want to meet them. Time will tell whether its recent facelift will earn it any credibility points.

La Macarena

C/Nou de Sant Francesc 5 (93 317 50 70). Metro Liceu. **Open** *Apr-Sept* 11pm-5am daily. *Oct-Mar* 11pm-5am Mon-Sat. **Admission** free before 2.30am; €5 afterwards. **No credit cards. Map** p345 A4.

It's small, it's dark, it's open late and it's free. Electric grooves, elbows, knees and the odd splurge of funk are all equally in your face: it all makes for a frenetic atmosphere. On Fridays and Saturdays at 11pm there are flamenco shows.

Schomsky

C/Heures 6-10 (93 412 52 79). Metro Liceu. **Open** 7.30pm-3am Mon-Sat. **Admission** free. **Credit** V. **Map** p345 A3.

With two floors of deep sofas and armchairs, this has got to be one of the most comfortable late-night venues in town. On the ground floor, the DJ spins a variable mix of tunes while the grown-up crowd relaxes and sups on wine and cocktails. The upstairs lounge is fab for big groups, being one of few places in town that's likely not only to fit you in, but to find a place to seat you too.

Sidecar Factory Club

Plaça Reial 7 (93 302 15 86/www.sidecarfactory club.com). Metro Liceu. **Open** 8pm-4.30am Tue-Thur, Sun; 8pm-5am Fri, Sat. *Gigs* (Oct-July) 10.30pm Tue-Sat. **Admission** (incl 1 drink) €5. *Gigs* €5-€15. **No credit cards**. **Map** p345 A3.

There's a little bit of everything in this dungeoney, brick cellar, making it one of Barcelona's top spots for indie club nights, flamenco fusion and other new world music mixes along with live gigs. Upstairs, the newly furbished bar is sleek and modern, providing a slick contrast to the inferno raging below.

Raval

Aurora

C/Aurora 7 (93 442 30 44). Metro Paral.lel. **Open** 8pm-3am daily. **Admission** free. **No credit cards**. **Map** p342 C6.

An idiosyncratic little bar, just off the Rambla del Raval. Aurora used to be an unkempt ramshackle place inhabited by unkempt ramshackle arty types in the wee hours. It was renovated in summer 2003 and given a smarter, shinier look, but the clientele has shown no sign of scrubbing up.

Benidorm

C/Joaquín Costa 39 (93 317 80 52). Metro Universitat. **Open** 7pm-2am Mon-Thur, Sun; 7pm-2.30am Fri, Sat. **Admission** free. **No credit cards**. **Map** p342 C5.

This lively, smoky little place is a kitsch paradise of brothel-red walls, crystal lanterns and '80s disco paraphernalia, boasting the world's smallest toilet, dancefloor and chill-out room. The sounds being absorbed by the mass of humanity packed in here on weekends (watch your wallet) ranges from hip hop to '70s stuff, although mostly it's all variations on the same electronica theme.

Big Bang

C/Botella 7 (93 443 28 13). Metro Liceu or Sant Antoni. **Open** *Bar* 10.30pm-3am Wed-Sun. *Gigs* around 10.30pm Fri, Sat. *Jam sessions* around 10.30pm Wed, Thur, Sun. **Admission** *Bar & jam sessions* free. *Gigs* varies. **No credit cards**. **Map** p342 C5.

Compared to the Raval's usual seedy after-hours bar scene, Big Bang is pretty civilised. A long, chrome-encrusted bar with deep fridges keeps the beers cold, and there's table football and a small, silver club room for bizarre electronica. Expect to pay a surcharge of a couple of euros for it, though.

El Cangrejo

C/Montserrat 9 (93 301 29 78). Metro Drassanes. **Open** 9pm-4am Tue-Sun. **Admission** free. **Credit** MC,V. **Map** p345 A3.

The original Barcelona drag cabaret, this place attracts a mixed bag of old timers, honeymooners, gay couples and revellers. Tuesday and Wednesday feature DJ sessions, but otherwise the acts consist largely of mimed, golden-oldie Spanish ballads interspersed with raconteurs whose outrageous get-ups combine early Divine, Prince and the jolly green giant. You'd have to go a long way to find a more sequin-spangled line-up, and if you can imagine being sandwiched between a lemon meringue pie and a paella, you'll get some idea of the decor.

La Concha

C/Guàrdia 14 (93 302 41 18). Metro Drassanes. **Open** 5pm-2.30am Mon-Thur, Sun; 5pm-3am Fri, Sat. **Admission** free. **No credit cards**. **Map** p345 A3.

Manager Rashid has made such an impressive turnaround of this classic bar that these days it's talked about from Ronda to Rio, with as many in-the-know tourists as locals and doe-eyed drag queens taking up space along the bar. Spanish screen siren Sara Montiel remains immortalised behind the bar in a floor-to-ceiling black and white photo, while the exotic Arabic music mixes with flamenco.

DAF

Plaça dels Àngels 5-6 (93 329 00 21). Metro Universitat. **Open** 9pm-3am Wed-Sat. **Admission** free. **Credit** AmEx, V. **Map** p344 A1.

Design organisation FAD has converted part of its exhibition space into yet another restoclub – the multi-tasking venues spreading through Barcelona like SARS. The restaurant picks on the club theme by using guest chefs like clubs use guest DJs. After the last parmesan crisp has been swallowed, the floor is overtaken by a living design exhibition of a crowd, from white rastas to geek chic. Boys make passes at girls in glasses while nodding to obscure electronica. If you get there early (before 1am), you can escape to the ancient cloisters at the back.

DosTrece

C/Carme 40 (93 301 73 06/www.dostrece.net). Metro Liceu. **Open** 11pm-3am Tue-Sun. **Admission** (incl 1 drink) €3-€5 Tue-Thur, Sun; free Fri, Sat. **Credit** AmEx, DC, MC, V. **Map** p344 A2.

Restaurant, bar, club, music venue, cinema – this multi-functional space has rapidly become one of the most desirable hangouts around, attracting expats in search of a grown-up local, visiting film directors and media types. For all that, it's unpretentious, and the basement hosts sounds from tango and samba, to jam sessions and jazz quartets.

Jazz Sí Club

C/Requesens 2 (93 329 00 20/www.tallerde musics.com). Metro Sant Antoni. **Open** *Sept-July* 9am-11pm Mon-Fri; 6-11pm Sat, Sun. *Aug* 6-11pm Thur, Fri, Sun. **Admission** free (1 drink min) Wed; (incl 1 drink) €4 Mon, Sat; €5 Thur, Fri. **No credit cards**. **Map** p342 C5.

The nearby Barcelona contemporary music school runs this small studio-like bar (a decent café during the day) as a space for students, teachers and music lovers to meet, perform and listen. Each night is dedicated to a different musical genre: trad jazz on Mondays, pop/rock/blues jams on Tuesdays, jazz jams on Wednesdays, Cuban music on Thursdays, flamenco on Fridays, rock on Saturdays and Sundays. Entrance is either free or there's a small charge that includes a drink.

Kentucky

C/Arc del Teatre 11 (93 318 28 78). Metro Drassanes. **Open** 10pm-3am Tue-Thur; 10pm-4.30am Fri, Sat. Closed Aug. **Admission** free. **No credit cards**. **Map** p345 A4.

One-time pick-up bar and haunt of wayward US sailors and lowlifes of the old Barrio Chino, haven of lost souls and chancers steering by the wrong star, what epic lock-ins have unrolled behind that rattling shutter? What tales could be told of Kentucky? There must be a million, if only anyone could remember any of it...

Moog

C/Arc del Teatre 3 (93 301 72 82/www.masimas.com). Metro Drassanes. **Open** 11.30pm-5am daily. **Admission** €8. **Credit** V. **Map** p345 A4.

Moog has been programming electronic music for years with admirable consistency. Residents Omar, Robert X and Juan B share deck space with guest DJs on Wednesdays. Sunday's Affair guarantees eclecticism – entry is free, so what have you got to lose? A bar in the entryway, a few tables, a small downstairs dancefloor for house and techno and a chillout room (of sorts) upstairs combine to form a compact and scaled-down club.

La Paloma

C/Tigre 27 (93 301 68 97/www.lapaloma-bcn.com). Metro Universitat. **Open** 6-9.30pm, 11.30pm-5am Thur; 6-9.30pm, 11.30pm-2am; 2.30am-5am Fri, Sat; 6-9.30pm Sun. **Admission** (incl 1 drink) €3-€8. **No credit cards**. **Map** p342 C5.

This glamorous, gilded ballroom dates back to 1903, back when people knew a thing or two about atmosphere, and so it provides a stunning backdrop for one of the most varied experiences on the circuit – there's traditional dance-hall twirling during the first shift, then on Friday and Saturday, live orchestral music in the second shift, after which the DJs step up. Something for everybody. Late night, Thursday's Bongo Lounge continues loud and clear to a regular crowd, though sometimes the PA system isn't up to the demands of modern clubbing.

Rita Blue

Plaça Sant Agustí 3 (93 342 40 86/www.margaritablue.com). Metro Liceu. **Open** 7pm-2am Mon-Wed, Sun; 7pm-3am Thur-Sat. **Admission** free. **Credit** DC, MC, V. **Map** p345 A3.

Mexican fusion cooking, bubblegum cocktails and chilled out clubbing is the mix here. Dinner time grooves are funk, soul and house played comfortably low. All very civilised, you might say. It's a bit more brash in the steel-floored dungeon downstairs that serves as extra dining space until midnight, when, in true dungeon style, they strap the dining tables to the walls and make way for the crowds of groovers and shakers.

Salsitas

C/Nou de la Rambla 22 (93 318 08 40/www.salsitas.gruposalsitas.com). Metro Liceu. **Open** 8pm-3am daily. **Admission** free. **Credit** MC, V. **Map** p345 A3.

'Babes, babes, babes...' declares one happy visitor to this resto-club, which fills the gap at the more sophisticated end of the meat market. Dress code is fashion-conscious and dressed up, but don't try too hard – you'll never compete with the exotic decor of enormous white palm-tree pillars anyway. The house music from resident DJs Toni Bass and Joan Castelló almost seems secondary – this place is about looking, not listening.

Sant Pere & the Born

Astin Bar Club

C/Abaixadors 9 (93 442 96 69/www.nitsa.com/astin). Metro Jaume I. **Open** 11pm-3am Thur-Sat. **Admission** free. **No credit cards**. **Map** p345 B3.

Part of the same anagrammatic family as Nitsa at the Sala Apolo (*see p251*), this much smaller bar/club attracts the Born's cool army. They come to check out who's still wearing legwarmers and nod to experimental and eclectic electronica with a pop edge. German electropop DJs Le Hammond Inferno like to spin a few discs here now and then.

Bass Bar

C/Assaonadors 25 (mobile 699 326 594). Metro Jaume I. **Open** 7pm-2.30am Mon-Thur, Sun; 7pm-3am Fri-Sun. *Gigs* around 10-11pm Sat. **Admission** free. **No credit cards**. **Map** p345 C3.

After another refurbishment in autumn 2003, the tiny Bass Bar now has an extra postage stamp-sized space and buttercup-coloured walls. Nothing else

Footballers' wives dig **CDLC**. *See p249.*

has changed, however, and it's still the best place around for a very late beer, kooky exhibitions and a good, globally influenced selection of music. Most nights dreadlocked locals are to be seen attempting a little shuffle to the sounds of flamenco fusion.

Drop Bar

Via Laietana 20 (93 310 75 04). Metro Jaume I. **Open** 11pm-3am Thur-Sat. **Admission** free. **No credit cards**. **Map** p345 B3.

Long ignored at its corner of Via Laietana with C/Argenteria, Drop Bar sports unpromising '80s-style curved windows overlooking the street and has three different spaces inside, including an open-air area. Cool, cutting-edge programming includes the excellent collective X-per Fan Club (experimental electronic, dub and electro-pop) every first and third Saturday of the month, and equally fine local and international electronic talent on Thursday nights under the artistic direction of EDM.

Magic

Passeig Picasso 40 (93 310 72 67/www.magic-club.net). Metro Barceloneta. **Open** 11pm-5.30am Thur; 11pm-6.30am Fri, Sat. **Admission** *Gigs* varies. *Disco* (incl 1 drink) €10. **No credit cards**. **Map** p343 E6.

Magic reopened in autumn 2003 after an enforced six-month sabbatical, thanks to the council's noise abatement campaign. The new version is said to have better soundproofing. Sadly, the opportunity wasn't taken to turn this awkward, L-shaped and airless basement club into something more comfortable. Still, the pull for the quirky and cliquey locals who crowd in here is the music: a strange odds and sods mix of tribute bands and tongue-in-cheek pop-rock.

Nao Colón/Club Bamboo

Avda Marquès de l'Argentera 19, (93 268 76 33). Metro Barceloneta. **Open** 12.30-3am Thur-Sat. **Admission** free. **Credit** AmEx, DC, MC, V. **Map** p345 C4.

Brushed steel fittings and teak provide a slick, modern backdrop attracting a grown-up crowd for flash Mediterranean food and live music on Thursdays from 10pm. Expect anything from flamenco fusion to Dixieland to jazz quartets. Then at midnight, cue the metamorphosis from restaurant to club, and Bamboo kicks in with the organic rhythms of Afro-Brazilian, Latin house and funky soul.

Over the Club

C/Fusina 7 (93 268 10 80/www.overtheclub.com). Metro Barceloneta or Jaume I. **Open** 10.30pm-2.30am Thur; 11pm-3am Fri, Sat; 8pm-2.30am Sun. **Admission** free. **No credit cards**. **Map** p345 C3.

It had to happen. First restaurants were at it, then clothes shops and hairdressers, now internet cafés are doing a Cinderella and turning into a club at midnight. This one has relaxed, futuristic decor, and splits the space into two distinct areas: a chill-out zone of cube-shaped pouffes and lounge music and the dancefloor pounding to house.

República

Estació de França, Avda Marquès de l'Argentera 6 (mobile 699 636 888/www.republicaclub.com). Metro Barceloneta. **Open** midnight-6am Fri, Sat. **Admission** (incl 1 drink) €12; €15 Sat. **No credit cards**. **Map** p345 C4.

A low-ceilinged, labyrinthine space under the Estació de França. An easygoing but up for it, mixed crowd of gurning twenty-thirtysomethings sweat to

Keepin' it free

Ticket prices for Barcelona gigs have really skyrocketed over the last year – perhaps explained by the fact that the guest-list queue at most concerts is ten times longer than that for the ticket-buying public. So if you don't fancy joining the liggers, or compensating promoters for their freeloading, how else can you get your aural kicks?

One way of seeing gigging visitors pushing their latest CD is by going shopping. The books and music superstore **FNAC** (*see p188*) holds free music showcases at its Triangle and L'Illa Diagonal branches. Check in the stores and in listings mags for details. Another way to see international stars for no mo' money is by coming to Barcelona during the **BAM festival** in September (*see p220*). In 2003 hundreds of locals and tourists paid nada to hear dub legend Lee 'Scratch' Perry in the Rambla de Raval. The **LEM festival** in Gràcia has plenty of kooky electronica on the house, and the **Ribertardor festival** heralds the start of autumn in the Born by filling bars, restaurants and shops with live acts late into the night. Mostly, though, you get what you don't pay for: unknown jobbing musicians and young wannabes. However, these can often be more entertaining – and more talented – than big-name stars.

Bar Pastis (*see p175*) squeezes a lot of emotion on to its tiny stage for its tango (Tuesday) and chanson (Sunday) nights. The restaurant **Little Italy** admits non-diners (but must-drinkers) in to listen to fair quality jazz bands on Wednesday and Thursday nights. And **Harlem Jazz Club** (*see p244*), despite its misleading name, actually showcases an intriguing variety of roots sounds from gypsy music to Portuguese fado via Yiddish klezmer and a bit of swing-blues.

Bar Kabara (*pictured*) hosts an open mic night on Wednesdays – take your chances and you could hear top tunes from holidaying musicians or achingly earnest wailings from local crusty teens. The **London Bar** (*see p177*), despite its name, doesn't look much like an East End boozer, but it occasionally hosts gigs of a reasonable pub-rock standard. The many faux English, Irish and Scottish hostelries around town also do their bit to keep music alive (though sometimes you wish they'd put it out of its misery). The **Philharmonic**, the **George & Dragon** and the **Clansman** (*see p176*) operate some level of quality control, at least.

If you feel you do want to contribute a little something to Barcelona's more deserving musical underdogs, there are plenty of buskers to reward with your leftover coins. Some of the best can be heard behind the cathedral, particularly around the intersection of C/Bisbe and C/Pietat: from players of exotic Asian instruments to angel-voiced opera singers and string quartets, everybody seems to take up a square of pavement to have their chance at relative fame. Keep your ears open, too, for top trad jazz rhythms around the Col.legi d'Arquitectes in the cathedral square. If you're

various flavours of house amid swirling dry ice. There's the odd tattoo, a lot of naked male chests and an occasional international guest DJ, such as Manumission's David Seaman.

Suborn

Passeig Picasso 42 (93 310 11 10). Metro Barceloneta. **Open** 8.30pm-3am Tue-Sun. **Admission** free. **Credit** AmEx, MC, V. **Map** p345 C4.

With tables under the arches looking on to the Ciutadella park, this unassuming restaurant metamorphoses into a small and more successful club at some unspecified point in the evening, and the raised metal dancefloor fills to the beats of hectic techno and house. It's friendly, uninhibited and a bit cramped.

Port Vell & Port Olímpic

Around the right-angled quayside of the Port Olímpic, you'll find dance bars interspersed with seafood restaurants, fast-food outlets, ice-cream parlours, coffee shops and mock-Irish pubs; with video screens, glittery lights and go-go girls and boys in abundance, it makes little difference which one you choose.

Baja Beach Club

Passeig Marítim 34 (93 225 91 00/www.bajabeach.es). Metro Ciutadella-Vila Olímpica. **Open** *June-Oct* 1pm-3am Mon-Wed; 1pm-5am Thur, Sun; 1pm-6am Fri, Sat. *Nov-May* 1pm-5am Thur, Sun; 1pm-6am Fri, Sat. **Admission** (incl 1 drink) €12 Thur, Sun; €14 Fri; €15 Sat. **Credit** AmEx, MC, V. **Map** p343 E7.

The ineffable Baja attracts a mixed bunch of stag and hen groups, corporate weekenders and birthday parties. More circus than nightclub, this is the biggest act in Barcelona, with 130 buffed and beautiful staff, several different theme bars, performing cocktail tenders, playground rides and a cocktail of music that only Baja would get away with; pop favourites, movie theme tunes, the occasional sports anthem and, naturally, Freddie Mercury's *Barcelona*.

lucky, you might catch a talented band of ragamuffin-looking buskers, led by a frog-mouthed Russian banjo player, cranking out amazing, toe-tapping ragtime jazz tunes. They are Los Krokodillos and he is Mikha Violin. Which, we have to say, must be worth a céntimo or two for starters.

Bar Kabara *C/Junta de Comerç 20 (mobile 677 058 784).*
Little Italy *C/Rec 30 (93 319 79 73).*
The Philharmonic *C/Mallorca 204 (93 451 11 53).*
George & Dragon *C/Diputació 269 (93 488 17 65).*

El Chiringuito

Bogatell beach (no phone). Metro Llacuna. **Open** *May-Sept* 11pm-3am daily. **Admission** free. **No credit cards**.

There are now three *chiringuitos* strung together along the most happening night-time beach in Barcelona. The original – the one in the middle – offers Sunday night chill-out sessions, jazz on Mondays, bossa nova on Tuesdays and tango on Wednesdays, with an ambient mix of house and dance music on Friday and Saturday.

CDLC

Passeig Marítim 32 (93 224 04 70/www.cdlc barcelona.com). Metro Ciutadella-Vila Olímpica. **Open** noon-3am daily. **Admission** free Mon-Wed, Sun; €10 (incl 1 drink) Thur-Sat. **Credit** AmEx, MC, V. **Map** p343 E7.

Carpe Diem Lounge Club is the new darling of the Barça football team and other celebs staying at the Hotel Arts. By far the coolest new club on the circuit, with its swanky *sofa-camas* – large mattresses, bolstered with feather pillows and cordoned off by flowing white drapes for those in need of a little privacy – in lounge-lizard contrast to the fast-moving dancefloor and beachfront terrace. Rod Stewart's been, why shouldn't you?

Club Danzatoria

Marina Village, C/Ramon Trias Fargas s/n (93 221 61 61/www.clubdanzatoria.com). Metro Ciutadella-Vila Olímpica. **Open** midnight-6am Thur-Sat. **Admission** (incl 1 drink) €15. **Credit** MC, V. **Map** p343 F7.

It was the hippest thing to hit downtown Barcelona when it opened last year, but the crowd seems to get younger and younger with each passing month. If you have the stamina (and the looks to get in), there are two vast dancefloors, one slightly more techno than the other with brushed steel to match, bizarre plastic water bottle sculptures, and a couple of crowd-pleasing dance poles.

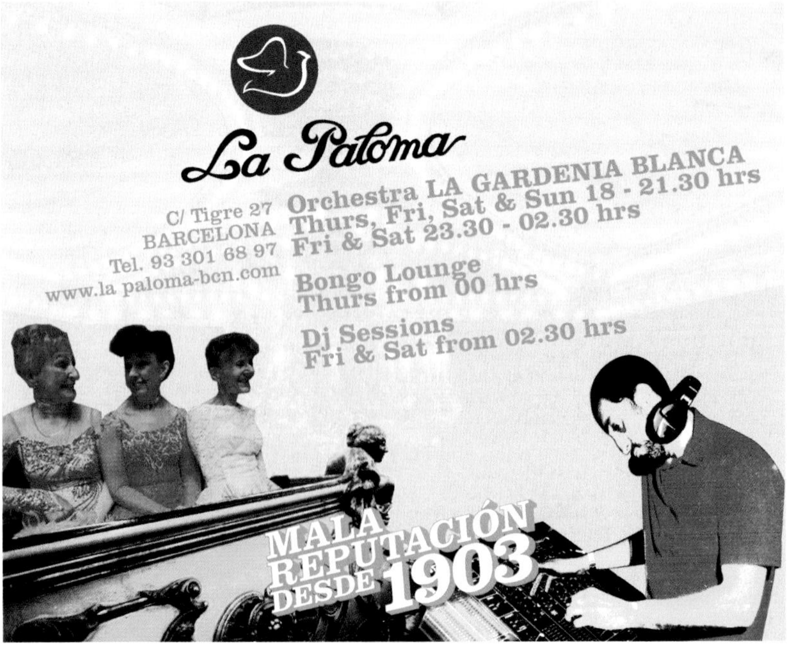

Le Kasbah

Plaça Pau Vilà (Palau del Mar) (93 238 07 22/ www.ottozutz.com). Metro Drassanes. **Open** 10pm-3am Tue-Sun. **Admission** free. **Credit** MC, V. **Map** p345 C4.

A white awning over terrace tables heralds the entrance to this louche bar beind the Palau de Mar. A cocktail-sipping crowd listens to lounge and chilled house, with the odd spot of techno to stop them falling asleep on the low tables and cushions that create the bar's North African look. Happy hour is 10pm and midnight on Tuesdays and Wednesdays.

Maremàgnum

Moll d'Espanya. Metro Drassanes. **Map** p343 D7.

This is a Jekyll and Hyde of a place, barely limping along during the day as a mall, with shoppers and tourists, and then turning into a monster by night as three levels of '80s-style bars and clubs flood with cocktail-guzzling hedonists. The row at ground level facing inland is ablaze with balloons, flashing disco balls, bright lights and neon, making for a party atmosphere even on a Monday night. The best of the bunch is probably Mojito, which has free salsa lessons every night from 10pm. But nothing gets going until after 1am, when the stags and hens start to turn up. *See also p188.*

Montjuïc & Poble Sec

Barcelona Rouge

C/Poeta Cabanyes 21 (93 442 49 85). Metro Paral.lel. **Open** 11pm-4am Tue-Sat. **Admission** free. **No credit cards**. **Map** p341 B6.

A slightly surreal place that's always rammed yet few have heard of. Ring the buzzer and shift around outside until someone lets you in – once inside, a long narrow corridor lined with velvet chairs draped with people from Planet Gorgeous leads into a large room strewn with battered sofas. The music's lounge, the cocktails hefty but the prices heftier.

Cube Club

Avda Paral.lel 37 (93 741 46 33/www.cubeclub.info). Metro Paral.lel. **Open** midnight-5am Fri, Sat. **Admission** (incl 1 drink) €9-€12. **No credit cards**. **Map** p342 C6.

This hardcore techno club changes its name and paint-job at least once a year. The current cornflower blue exterior is a jarring contrast to the red brick, industrial aesthetic of Paral.lel. Inside, it's rather handsome with a pillared dancefloor the size of a tennis court, a mezzanine and winding staircases worthy of a stately home. It's all in unnerving contrast to the supersonic soundsystem and unrelenting techno DJs.

Discothèque/La Terrrazza

Poble Espanyol, Avda Marquès de Comillas (93 423 12 85/www.nightsungroup.com). Metro Espanya/bus 50. **Open** *Mid Oct-mid May* midnight-6am Fri, Sat. **Admission** (incl 1 drink) €18 with flyer, €12 without. **Credit** MC, V. **Map** p341 A4.

Discothèque and La Terrrazza are the winter and summer faces respectively of the city's best-known club combo in the bizarre environs of the Poble Espanyol. Both are run by superclub promoters Nightsun Group, and have the same resident DJs (Sergio Patricio, Xavi VII and Peluca) playing house and techno. Both also have year-round queues of beautiful (or at least young, or at least gay) people out front. You don't have to dress to impress the door staff but you may skip the queue or the ticket price if you do. Projections, drag queens, podium dancers and an aspirational VIP bar all recreate the Ibiza-when-it-was-still-hot vibe.

Maumau

C/Fontrodona 33 (mobile 606 860 617/ www.maumauunderground.com). Metro Paral.lel. **Open** 11pm-2.30am Thur; 11pm-3am Fri, Sat; 7pm-midnight Sun. **Admission** (membership) €5. **No credit cards**. **Map** p342 C6.

Behind the anonymous grey door (ring the bell), first-timers to this likeable little chill-out club pay €5 to become members. In practice they rarely charge out-of-towners. Inside, a large warehouse space is humanised with colourful projections, sofas and a friendly, laid-back crowd. The music policy ranges from electronica to house to funk to post rock, and films are shown on Sunday evenings.

Sala Apolo

C/Nou de la Rambla 113 (93 441 40 01/www.sala-apolo.com/www.maumauunderground.com). Metro Paral.lel. **Open** *Nitsa* 12.30-6.30am Fri, Sat. *Powder Room* 12.30-5.30am Thur. **Admission** (incl 1 drink) Nitsa €12. Powder Room €6. **No credit cards**. **Map** p342 C6.

This 1940s dance hall is a curious and rather musty backdrop for some of the most eclectic alternative music programming in Barcelona. Local bands and international groups play from Thursday to Saturday before the club sessions kick off the night proper. Wednesday's Mundo Canibal night stretches the term Latin music to include hip hop and funk. Thursday is funk night in the Powder Room. Pick up a flyer for free entry at Maumau on Sundays. Friday and Saturday's Nitsa Club is now in its tenth year, an elder statesman of the techno scene.

Tinta Roja

C/Creu dels Molers 17 (93 443 32 43). Metro Poble Sec. **Open** 8pm-1am Wed, Thur, Sun; 8pm-3am Fri, Sat. **Admission** *Before midnight* (incl 1 drink) €8. *After midnight* free. Closed 2wks Aug. **No credit cards**. **Map** p341 B6.

Push through the bar's depths to be transported to a Buenos Aires bordello/theatre/circus/cabaret by the plush red velvet sofas, smoochy niches, ancient ticket booth and a stage overhung with trapeze bars. It's a cool and atmospheric place for a late-ish drink, or a distinctly different entertainment experience on Thursday, Friday and Saturday when there are live performances of tango, jazz and flamenco. Call to book tango classes on Wednesdays.

Eixample

Antilla BCN

C/Aragó 141 (93 451 45 64/www.antillasalsa.com). Metro Urgell. **Open** 11pm-4am Mon-Thur, Sun; 11pm-5.30am Fri, Sat. **Admission** free (1 drink min) Mon-Wed, Sun; (incl 1 drink) €10 Thur-Sat. **No credit cards**. **Map** p338 C4.

The Antilla prides itself on being a 'Caribbean cultural centre', hosting exhibitions and publishing its magazine *Antilla News*. But its true calling lies in being the self-claimed best *salsateca* in Barcelona, with dance classes (including acrobatic salsa and Afro-Cuban styles) and a solid programme of live music covering all Latin flavours from *son* to merengue via Latin jazz.

Astoria

C/París 193 (93 414 63 62/www.costaeste.com). Metro Diagonal. **Open** 9pm-3.30am Mon-Sat. Closed Aug. **Admission** free. **Credit** AmEx, MC, V. **Map** p338 C3.

From the same people who brought you Bucaro and the Sutton Club, Astoria offers a break from the norm. For a start, the club is housed in a converted 1950s cinema, which means the projections are big and actually watchable. There are three bars, so you're spared endless queues, there's plenty of comfortable seating along with a small dancefloor, and if you're very wonderful you may get to sit on a heart-shaped cushion in the tiny VIP area. With all this going for it, it has inevitably become the domain of Barcelona's moneyed classes.

La Boîte

Avda Diagonal 477 (93 419 59 50/www.masimas.com). Metro Hospital Clínic. **Open** *Jam session* 11pm Mon. *Gigs* midnight-2am Tue-Sat. *Club* 2-5am Mon-Sat. **Admission** *Club* (incl 1 drink) €12. *Gigs* €18. **No credit cards**. **Map** p338 C3.

The entrance to this purpose-built music venue and nightclub glows like a lighthouse cabin behind uptown office blocks and car parks off the Plaça Francesc Macià. You're then swallowed up into a rather dingy underground space with mirror-tiled pillars as the only concession to glamour. Regular gigs attract aficionados of blues and jazz, from greying rockers to college students. The crowd for the post-gig funk disco is an equally mixed bag.

La Bolsa

C/Tuset 17 (93 202 26 35). Metro Diagonal or FGC Provença. **Open** 8pm-2.30am Mon-Thur; 8pm-3am Fri; 7pm-3am Sat; 6pm-2.30am Sun. **Admission** free. **Credit** MC, V. **Map** p338 C6.

Buy? Sell? Keel over and cry? This place may not quite live up to the cut and thrust of big-city living, but it's a boozers' stock exchange. You have to figure out the system before you get started, and that isn't easy, as drink prices fluctuate according to what's selling at any particular time, so keep an eye on the in-house FTSE Index. DJs play mainly house and Spanish pop on Fridays and Saturdays.

Bucaro

C/Aribau 195 (93 209 65 62/www.costa-este.com). FGC Provença. **Open** 10.30pm-3.30am Mon-Wed; 10pm-4am Thur; 10pm-5am Fri, Sat. **Admission** free. **Credit** MC, V. **Map** p338 C3.

Looking a tad jaded these days, Bucaro's worn leather sofas and grubby pouffes still manage to pull a crowd of glamourpusses – those floor to ceiling mirrors allow plenty of preening space for Barcelona's peacocks. With the giant skylight looming above the dancefloor like a portal to another world, and a mezzanine for stalking your prey before swooping onto the dancefloor, this is a place that knows class when it sees it. Drinks are a couple of euros more expensive if you're sitting at a table.

Buda Barcelona

C/Pau Claris 92 (93 318 42 52/www.budabarcelona.com). Metro Catalunya. **Open** 9pm-3am daily. **Admission** free. **Credit** MC, V. **Map** p344 B1.

The centre of Barcelona is strangely devoid of glamorous nightspots, or at least it was until Buda came along and put sparkle back in the mix. There's lots of throne-style furniture and gilded wallpaper, topped off with a colossal chandelier. Proudly declaring itself the home of the beautiful people, it does seem to have earned its feathers among Spanish celebs like heart-throb Joaquín Cortes. Everyone else is equally gorgeous, but the laid-back nature of the staff (dancing on the bar seems completely acceptable) and upbeat house music make it excellent for drinks and an ogle.

City Hall

Rambla Catalunya 2-4 (93 317 21 77/www.ottozutz.com). Metro Catalunya. **Open** midnight-5am Tue-Thur, Sun; midnight-6am Fri, Sat. **Admission** (incl 1 drink) €7 Tue; €8-€12 Wed; €10 Thur; €12 Fri-Sun. **Credit** DC, MC, V. **Map** p344 A1.

You can rely on this well-established, central nightspot to come up with an excuse for a party, no matter what night of the week it is. This year it contrasts Zen Club garden parties on Sundays with Fucked on Tuesdays by Danish DJ Heidi Mortenssen. With several rooms and a candle-lit terrace, its huge popularity says it all.

Cocodrilo Club

Gran Via de les Corts Catalanes 770 (93 232 43 45). Metro Monumental. **Open** 11pm-5.30am Fri, Sat; 6.30-11pm Sun. **Admission** (incl 1 drink) €12 Fri, Sat; €9 Sun. **Credit** AmEx, MC, V. **Map** p343 F5.

Back in 1993, there was a popular radio show on Ona Catalana called the Cocodrilo Club, which played songs from the 1960s and '70s. This is its love child – a must for aficionados of the golden age of pop. It's worth phoning ahead before turning up here, as in 2003 it relocated three times.

Distrito Diagonal

Avda Diagonal 442 (mobile 607 113 602/www.distritodiagonal.com). Metro Diagonal. **Open** 10pm-3.30am Wed, Thur, Sun; 10pm-4.30am Fri, Sat. **Admission** free. **No credit cards**. **Map** p338 D4.

Astoria.

Housed in the stunning Casa Comalat, Distrito Diagonal attracts a slightly older crowd, with an easygoing atmosphere bathed in red light, sounds from nu jazz to deep house and plenty of chairs to sink into. It's become a sought-after venue for small promoters and one-off parties, which means the music can veer from Bollywood to hip hop. Fridays are Dub Family nights – dub, house and reggae.

Domèstic

C/Diputació 215 (93 453 16 61). Metro Universitat. **Open** 7.30pm-2.30am Mon-Thur; 7.30pm-3am Fri, Sat. **Admission** free. **Credit** AmEx, MC, V. **Map** 342 C5.

Domèstic is another multi-tasking venue, combining a rather half-hearted restaurant, a bar/club and an occasional live venue. The colours are bold, the crowd is studenty and the music is laid-back, from electropop to tribal house, with a new roster of DJs every month. It tends to be more of a meeting place rather than a destination, though the cosy, battered leather chairs can be hard to leave.

La Fira

C/Provença 171 (no phone). Metro Hospital Clínic. **Open** 10pm-3am Tue-Thur; 10.30pm-4.30am Fri, Sat. **No credit cards. Map** p338 C4.

A warehouse-sized space filled with an extraordinary haphazard collection of old funfair detritus, this place has merry-go-round horses, one-armed bandits, crazy mirrors and more. Out of their environment of childhood innocence, they can seem a little macabre; grotesquely smiling clowns' faces leer at the beefcake barmen, as they dish out drinks to a raucous studenty crowd to the sounds of tacky pop.

Luz de Gas

C/Muntaner 246 (93 209 77 11/www.luzdegas.com). FGC Muntaner. **Open** 11pm-5am daily. *Gigs* around 12.30am Mon-Sat; midnight Sun. **Admission** (incl 1 drink) €15. **Credit** AmEx, DC, MC, V. **Map** p342 C3.

This lovingly converted old music hall, garnished with chandeliers and classical friezes, occasionally hosts classic MOR acts: Kool and the Gang or Bill Wyman's Rhythm Kings. In between the visits from international 'names', you'll find nightly residencies: blues on Mondays, Dixieland jazz on Tuesdays, cover bands on Wednesdays, Saturdays and Sundays, soul on Thursdays and rock on Fridays.

The Pop Bar

C/Aribau 103 (93 451 29 58). Metro Hospital Clínic. **Open** 9pm-3.30am Wed-Sun. **Admission** free. **Credit** AmEx, DC, MC, V. **Map** p338 C4.

Balls to house, hip hop and the rest of it, when you can have pure, unadulterated pop and one-hit wonders that you never thought you'd hear again – we're talking early Kylie, Rick Astley and Donna Summer, here. The retro decor is appropriate to the sounds, with funky brown, orange and white, augmented by things like polka dot toilets, and deep orange sofa booths. This place also gets two thumbs up for its big screens showing FashionTV, a welcome change from all those darned projections that you find absolutely everywhere else these days.

Risco

C/Balmes 49 (93 423 12 85/www.nightsungroup.com). Metro Hospital Clínic. **Open** 11pm-3am Thur-Sun. **Admission** free Thur-Sat; (incl 1 drink) €9 Sun. **Credit** MC, V. **Map** p338 D4.

Past the grim carpark entrance, Risco opens up in a colourful '70s orange and yellow glow. A mixed under-thirty crowd comes here for the free entry, eclectic non-commercial house tunes and discount flyers for Discothèque/La Terrrazza (which is run by the same group). Sunday is the ever-popular Fuck Monday night (€6 entry) – a hip hop party led by local rap hero Mucho Muchacho.

Samba Brazil

C/Lepant 297 (93 456 17 98). Metro Sagrada Família. **Open** 7pm-2am Mon-Thur, Sun; 7pm-3am Fri, Sat. **Admission** free. **No credit cards. Map** p343 F5.

With its free samba and merengue classes, this place has a tropical taste with none of the faux palms and frippery supplied by other Caribbean-style bars. In fact, it's all very Brazil; travel agents' posters decorate the walls, last year's tinsel hangs in the corner, it's loud, it's too brightly lit. What bliss! Utterly unpretentious and zealous in the art of cocktail making, this is home-from-home for Brazil-o-philes.

Santa Locura

C/Consell de Cent 294 (93 487 77 22). Metro Passeig de Gràcia. **Open** midnight-6am Thur-Sat. **Admission** (incl 1 drink) €10; (incl 2 drinks) €15. **No credit cards. Map** p342 D5.

Perhaps the most extraordinary clubbing experience in Barcelona, Santa Locura has three floors of weird and wonderful, pseudo-religious, nocturnal pleasures; marry your honey at the bar, watch a Chippendale-style show, plead guilty at the confessional box, and hit the dancefloor to the music of Kylie and Sophie Ellis-Bextor.

Gràcia

Alfa

C/Gran de Gràcia 36 (93 415 18 24). Metro Diagonal or Fontana. **Open** 11pm-3am Thur-Sat. **Admission** free Thur; €4-€6 Fri, Sat (incl 1 drink). **No credit cards. Map** p338 D3.

This is a classic Gràcia nightspot, and one that keeps a low profile. People here are serious about dancing and leave their pretensions at the door. In other words, you come here to boogie, not to pose. The music is classic rock, pop and the odd smoochy number for the end of the evening.

Gusto

C/Francisco Giner 24 (no phone). Metro Diagonal. **Open** 10pm-2.30am Mon-Thur, Sun; 10pm-3am Fri, Sat. **Admission** free. **No credit cards. Map** p338 D3.

Gusto gets full to bursting on weekend nights, seemingly due to one rather bizarre feature – past the normal but attractive red-painted front bar,

Boogie nights

Lively as Barcelona's club scene is, it is still pretty limited in terms of alternative sounds, especially for older club-goers who hung up their techno whistles and bells ten years ago. The chicken korma of nightlife, it is perfectly enjoyable but unlikely to blow any heads off or leave anyone gasping for air. The good news is that in recent months, independent DJs and club promoters jaded by the last decade's electronica and the new century's obscure and inaccessible beats have returned to roots, offering a thoughtful platter of alternative and/or retro sounds for the more discerning (or simply bored, or maybe just ageing) clubber.

Scottish DJ Mr Stream heads a campaign called God Save the 45, where in true superhero style, his mission in life is to save the old 45 single through his increasingly popular northern soul parties, with guest DJs. Mr Stream's sessions evoke a social club atmosphere, with the same foptopped

where a DJ plays chilled electronica, a quirky backroom lures in a young crowd with a floor covered in sand and with sandbags as seats.

KGB

C/Alegre de Dalt 55 (93 210 59 06). Metro Joanic. **Open** 1-7am Fri, Sat. **Admission** (incl 1 drink) €9. **No credit cards. Map** p339 E3.

This aptly named place looks like it sounds – hardcore. A dark, intimidating space, it's long been Barcelona's top choice for ear-bleed techno. These days it's also experimenting with a wider music policy, including ska and reggae nights. Mostly, though, the promoters stick to the tried-and-tested recipe of any music that makes kids think they're hard: hip hop (Thursday's Project Jomeles), punk and nu-metal. Though anyone who saw Sigue Sigue Sputnik there in 2003 really deserves to be stripped of their tongue piercings.

Mond Bar

Plaça del Sol 21 (93 272 09 10/www.mondclub.com). Metro Fontana. **Open** 8.30pm-3am daily. **Admission** free. **No credit cards. Map** p338 D3.

Little brother to the Mond Club, this tiny split-level bar gets packed and sweaty, but you can always take a breather in the crusty-friendly Plaça del Sol and listen to some bongo playing. Inside, the music's classier – classic R&B, northern soul and Motown for Thursday's Ready, Steady, Bar! and God Save the 45 nights, and an eclectic mix of alternative rock and pop the rest of the week. The crowd's a young, hip mix of locals and tourists.

Mond Club

Sala Cibeles, C/Còrsega 363 (93 272 09 10/www.mondclub.com). Metro Diagonal. **Open** 12.30-6am Fri. **Admission** (incl 1 drink) €12. **No credit cards. Map** p338 D4.

modsters turning up time after time. Therein is the appeal of northern soul, after all: this dance culture is tribal, underground, but also enduring. Effectively, Mr Stream is doing for Barcelona what the Mecca and Wigan Casino did 30 years ago in the cold north of England for the rusty beachside town of Blackpool.

His particular brand of the genre is northern soul with a twist – blurring Motown-influenced tunes with anything with a soul groove from the '60s, '70s, '80s and '90s. Thrown into the mix are a whole lot of other musical styles spanning jazz, funk, rare groove and new electronica with a beat, and the result is something young, fresh and exciting, yet somehow nostalgic. *See p256* **Mond Bar**.

Appropriately enough, we're also seeing the revival of swing, a dance movement that predates northern soul by about 50 years. There are still no regular club nights, but watch this space, as we're quite sure that there will be. In the meantime fans of the do-wap-de-wap and the wap-de-da-doo can get together with other like-minded jive bunnies at a number of venues around town. There are regular classes at the **Philharmonic** pub on Monday evenings from 9.15pm where a mix of beginners and veteran dancers polish the floors with lindy hop, jitterbug and charleston moves. Plus there's also lindy hop in Parc Ciutadella on Sundays from noon.

For something a little spicier, **Club Masala** (pictured) hosts its Bollywood Bhangra nights twice a month at one of Barcelona's more salubrious venues, **Distrito Diagonal** (*see p252*). Masala began as a shop in Gràcia promoting everything from the Indian subcontinent and then morphed into a cultural centre, and from there into a club session. Musically, it offers a strong cross-section of traditional bhangra from India; it specialises particularly in sounds from the British-Asian underground bhangra scene mixed with UK garage, and the very latest Bollywood remixes. It is the only regular club night serving up bhangra (let alone Bollywood) in Spain. With its red walls, velvet curtains, chandeliers, big colourful projections from Bollywood movies and fashion stills from the latest Bollywood collections, Distrito Diagonal strikes just the right vibe for devotees of all things Indian. In addition, the truly smitten can get into it all by taking belly dancing classes on Tuesdays and Thursdays.

Northern soul

Mond Bar *(see also p256), one Thursday a month. Free.*

The Pop Bar at Razzmatazz *(see also p259), one Friday a month. €12. www.godsavethe45.co.uk.*

Swing

Parc de la Ciutadella *(see p102), Sundays. Free.*

The Philharmonic *(C/Mallorca 204, 93 451 11 53), Mondays. Free.*

Bollywood Bhangra

Distrito Diagonal *(see also p252), twice monthly. Mobile 639 825 207/www.club-masala.com.*

Another vintage dance hall, though this one's been upgraded with nasty floor tiles, with DJs playing old-school tunes from northern soul to '80s pop via new wave. It attracts downtown music enthusiasts who're willing to travel up here for their weekend of pop and rock nostalgia. Look out for occasional gigs from indie stars-turned-DJs like Jarvis Cocker.

Otto Zutz

C/Lincoln 15 (93 238 07 22/www.ottozutz.com). FGC Gràcia. **Open** midnight-4.30am Tue; midnight-6am Wed-Sat. **Admission** (incl 1 drink) €15. **Credit** AmEx, DC, MC, V. **Map** p338 D3.

This New York warehouse-style club has been around a while, and the absolute indifference with which the doorstaff usher in the desirables and charge the rest is getting outdated; Otto Zutz is hardly the cutting-edge clubbing experience it once was. The illusion of space on the downstairs dancefloor (Ibiza-style house) is due to an enormous mirror, the garage/hip hop/funk floor above is no bigger, and to get into the VIP room at the top you'll have to summon whatever reserves of glamour are left after getting in. Flyers around town offer discounts.

Sutton Club

C/Tuset 13 (93 414 42 17/www.thesuttonclub.com). Metro Diagonal. **Open** 11pm-5am Tue-Sun. **Admission** (incl 1 drink) €15. **Credit** AmEx, MC, V. **Map** p338 C3.

Glam, groovy and disco, in the truest sense of the word – with plenty of mirrors and chrome, and liveried waiters to bring your drinks to the table while sequinned podium dancers strut their stuff with feathers in their hair. The vibe is strictly *Saturday Night Fever* (unless you happen to go on a Wednesday night, when the joint is taken over by a herd of Catalan cowboys and girls, line-dancing).

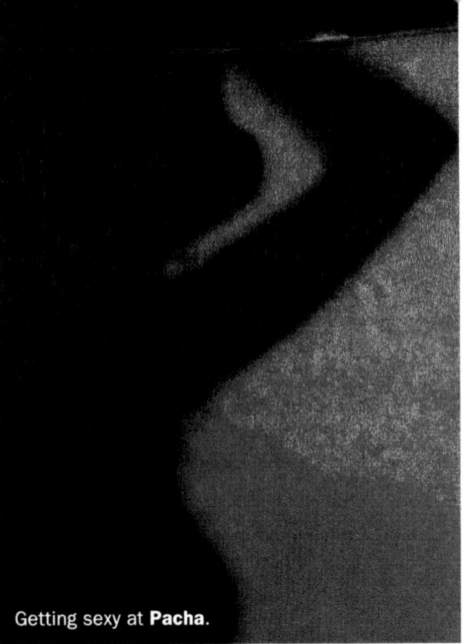
Getting sexy at **Pacha**.

Other areas

Bikini

C/Déu i Mata 105, Les Corts (93 322 08 00/ www.bikinibcn.com). Metro Les Corts or Maria Cristina. **Open** midnight-4.30am Tue-Thur; midnight-5.30am Fri, Sat. **Admission** *Women* free entry & drinks. *Men* (incl 1 drink) €11 Wed; €11 Thur; €12 Fri, Sat. **Credit** MC, V. **Map** p337 B3.

Bikini is well designed, with a long bar winding through three rooms. When it's not overrun with clubbers, the superbly equipped stage attracts an eclectic range of acts from Super Furry Animals to rapper Roots Manuva, as well as the best local talent, such as the Mogwai-esque Twelve. After the gig the main room runs through its paces with chart rock and pop; the Arutanga room plays salsa and Latin, while the Dry Room features a distinctly wet bar with plentiful seating.

La Cova del Drac/Jazzroom

C/Vallmajor 33, Zona Alta (93 319 17 89/ www.masimas.com). FGC Muntaner. **Open** *Club* 1-5am Fri, Sat. *Gigs* 11pm-12.30am Tue-Sat; 8.30-10pm Sun. **Admission** *Club* (incl 1 drink) €12. *Gigs* €7-€25 Tue-Thur; €9 Fri, Sat. **No credit cards**. **Map** p338 C2.

La Cova was a refuge for bohemians and intellectuals during Franco's rule, and it was also the only major jazz venue in town that regularly attracted big American stars. Its own star waned towards the end of the 1990s, but it has since been revitalised by the ubiquitous Mas siblings who've created a classy, if slightly clinical space downstairs and named it Jazzroom. This cellar bar features jazz concerts by mostly Spanish and Latin American musicians, with occasional Latin and blues artists spicing up the mix. There's also live comedy on Tuesdays for jazzaphobes. When the players pack up, the venue becomes a sophisticated uptown disco.

Danzatoria

Avda Tibidabo 61 (93 211 62 61/www.danzatoria. gruposalsitas.com). FGC Avda Tibidabo. **Open** 11pm-3am Wed-Sun. **Admission** free. **Credit** MC, V.

The uptown location attracts an upscale crowd to this spectacular converted manor house on a hill overlooking Barcelona. The top floor was recently converted to a restaurant, serving 'til midnight. The hipness factor goes up as you climb the club's glamour-glutted storeys. Preened *pija* flesh is shaken on hot-house dancefloors, or laid across sofas hanging from the ceiling in the chill-out lounges. We've had reports of snotty staff and snooty public, but who cares when you're lounging in one of the layers of palm-filled gardens, accompanied by some gorgeous creature and some (very expensive) champagne, gazing at the city lights below.

Mirablau

Plaça Doctor Andreu 1, Tibidabo (93 418 58 79). FGC Avda Tibidabo, then Tramvia Blau. **Open** 11am-4.30am Mon-Thur, Sun; 11am-6.30am Fri, Sat. **Credit** DC, MC, V.

Wander up the hill to the end of Avda Tibidabo after you've been kicked out of Danzatoria and you'll find the doors to one of the city's best views still open. If you've energy left to dance, cheesy Spanish pop music rules the dancefloor.

Universal

C/Marià Cubí 182 bis-184 (93 201 35 96). FGC Muntaner. **Open** 11pm-4.30am Mon-Sat. **Credit** MC, V. **Admission** free. **Map** p338 C3.

The production values of this well-established club on the corner of C/Marià Cubí and C/Santalo are unstinting, but the prices are steep. Multi-angled lights set up a flattering, cabaret-like semi-darkness on the ground floor, through which you shimmy up to the diagonal bar. Or you could float upstairs to the more laid-back first-floor bar, with its blue velvet seats, gleaming grand piano, heavy curtains and chandeliers like anchors wrapped in tulle and fairy lights. The usual weekend crowd is moneyed but not oppressively cool; the music policy is mainstream.

Poblenou

Oven

C/Ramon Turró 126 (93 221 06 02). Metro Poblenou. **Open** 1.30pm-3am Mon-Thur, Sun; 1.30-4pm, 9pm-3am Fri, Sat. **Credit** AmEx, MC, V. **Map** p343 F6.

The slickest outfit in the newly hip Poblenou, Oven is tiresome to get to but worth the effort, especially if you make a night of it by having cocktails and dinner first. The industrial interior segues into grown-up club land come midnight, when the tables are cleared to make way for dancing, and Barcelona's most famous DJ, Professor Angel Dust, hits the decks with his own brand of house.

Razzmatazz/The Loft/Razz Club

C/Pamplona 88 (93 272 0910/www.theloftclub.com). Metro Bogatell or Marina. **Open** 1-5am Fri, Sat. **Admission** (incl 1 drink) €12. **No credit cards**. **Map** p343 F6.

Razzmatazz is arguably Barcelona's top live venue of the moment, regularly hosting stars such as Orbital and Oasis, while also drawing in up-and-coming local and international acts from the ever-changing alternative rock and dance scene. One entry fee gets you quite a bit, as it allows entry to: Razz Club, the main dancefloor, which is the rock and pop zone; the Loft, its neighbouring hangar, specialising in eclectic electronica; Lo*li*ta, Loft's little sister next door with more of the same; the long thin Pop Bar with its nonstop pop sounds; and Temple Beat, a tomblike refuge for the goth crowd. Something for everyone then, which means everyone tries to get in – expect long queues.

Outer limits

Club Luna

Gran Hotel La Florida, Crta de Vallvidrera al Tibidabo 83-93 (93 259 30 00/www.hotellaflorida.com). By car A7, then take Ronda de Dalt. **Open** 11pm-3am daily. **Admission** €30. **Credit** AmEx, DC, MC, V.

Yet another jewel in the Salsitas group crown, Club Luna has eased itself into position as Barcelona's most exclusive nightspot. It's so exclusive, in fact, that for years you haven't been able to get in to the place unless you were either a member of the club or a guest at the hotel. However, this is due to change in 2004, when Luna has announced that it will at last admit normal people, albeit for a whopping big fee. For the money they'll get jazz bands, body-hugging chairs, an elegant cocktail bar and an ingenious fibre-optic ceiling that emulates the night sky. Call ahead to see if the admission rules have changed yet.

Liquid

Complex Esportiu Hospitalet Nord, C/Manuel Azaña (mobile 650 09 14 79/www.liquidbcn.com). Metro Zona Universitaria. **Open** *Mid June-mid Sept* 12.30am-5.30am Sun. **Admission** (incl 1 drink) €15. **No credit cards**.

This place's big attraction is the fact that it offers the only permanent pool party in town. Liquid has a huge, turquoise swimming pool and waterfall surrounded by swaying palms. Beware party-pooping bouncers – make sure your swimsuit looks like a swimsuit, as underwear will not be tolerated, and remember that skinny dipping will get you thrown out. Still, it's great fun in a group and unbeatable on a balmy night in August.

Pacha

Avda Gregorio Marañon 17 (93 334 32 33/www.clubpachabcn.com). Metro Zona Universitaria. **Open** midnight-7am Thur-Sat. **Admission** (incl 1 drink) €15. **Credit** MC, V.

The international *über*club lands in Barcelona and loses none of its charm in doing so. It's huge, brightly lit, and has one of the best sound systems in town – not a penny was spared in creating the club's six bars, two VIP areas, chill-out room and terrace. The crowd is a mix of nearby university students, ultra-cool uptowners and tourist punters from all over. Everyone from Roger Sanchez to Masters at Work has played here… or will do.

Performing Arts

All's well that vends well.

Palau de la Música. *See p261.*

Classical Music & Opera

Whether you prefer symphonies or sonatas, opera or electronica, Barcelona has music to accommodate all ears and allowances. The city boasts an embarrassment of venues, with no fewer than four being built (or in the case of the burnt-down opera house, rebuilt) in the last seven years: the hi-tech **Auditori**, the phoenix-like **Liceu**, the small **Winterthur** chamber hall and most recently a 600-seat subterranean auditorium to complement the Palau de la Música, due to open in spring 2004. Barcelona is still light arias away from, say, Vienna as a musical city, but it has a large concert-going public and dozens of concerts each month.

Classical music in Barcelona plays a constant waltz between the high brow, the low brow and the furrowed brow. Generally, audiences are drawn to a core repertoire, with only the occasional rash flirtation with more risqué work. They know what they like, and mostly it's Teutonic Goliaths, with the odd Hispanic David slung in for the home supporters. For many Stravinsky is still a dangerous renegade and Cage is where he should be locked.

Nevertheless, there are signs that things are changing. In addition to various cycles of contemporary music that take place each year, the new director of the **OBC**, the city orchestra, has programmed a regular series of short, modern works, offering hope to up-and-coming Catalan and Spanish composers. While the recent deaths of Xavier Montsalvatge and Frederic Mompou represented the end of an era, the podium is now clear for a younger wave of Catalan composer, lead by Albert Guinovart, Joan Guinjoan and Salvador Brotons, all of whom enjoy healthy reputations. Creative genius Carles Santos also enjoys a reputation, although healthy is not quite the word, specialising as he does in magnificent, surreal works that combine the best excesses of opera, circus, sex show and psychotherapy session.

The musical calendar is strictly seasonal, running from September to June. During this time the OBC plays weekly concerts at the Auditori, while the Liceu hosts a different opera every three or four weeks. Both the Auditori and the Palau de la Música hold several concert cycles of various genres. Several festivals take place, the foremost of which is the **Festival of Ancient Music** (*see p216*) in the spring.

In the summer, the focus of activity moves. Various museums – including the **Museu Marítim** (*see p106*), the **Fundació Miró** (*see p111*), the **Museu Barbier-Mueller** (*see p99*) and **La Pedrera** (*see p121*) – hold small, outdoor evening concerts, and there are weekly events in several of the city's parks (*see p218* **Classics als Parcs**). The more serious musical activity, though, follows its audience and heads up the coast, to major international festivals in the towns of Perelada, Cadaqués, Toroella de Montgrí and Vilabertrán.

In 2004 the usual musical midsummer drought will be assuaged by events linked to **Fòrum 2004** (*see p218*), with a range of concerts throughout the summer.

INFORMATION AND TICKETS

The most thorough source of info is the monthly leaflet *Informatiu Musical*, published by Amics de la Música (93 268 01 22), which details concerts across all genres. You can pick up a copy at tourist offices (*see p319*) and record shops. The weekly entertainment guide *Guía del Ocio* has a music section, while both *El País* and *La Vanguardia* list forthcoming concerts, and usually publish details for each day's more important concerts. Also check the council website at www.bcn.es. Tickets for most major venues can be bought by phone, or over the internet from the venue itself, or from Tel-entrada or Servi-Caixa (for both, *see p212*).

Venues

L'Auditori

C/Lepant 150, Eixample (93 247 93 00/www.auditori.org). Metro Marina. **Open** *Information* 9am-3pm, 4-6pm Mon-Fri. *Box office* noon-9pm Mon-Sat. *Performances* 8pm Mon-Thur; 9pm Fri; 7pm Sat; 11am Sun. **Tickets** varies. **Credit** MC, V. **Map** p343 F5.

Musically and architecturally, this state-of-the-art, 2,300-seater concert hall is excellent, if a little minimalist for some tastes. The hoped-for transformation to this dreary neighbourhood has yet to materialise and, together with the TNC next door, L'Auditori forms something of a cultural outpost, with few bars and restaurants nearby. A special bus service runs to Plaça Catalunya after concerts. Barcelona's main music school and the Museu de la Música are due to move here in 2005, which should liven things up. As well as the OBC's weekly concerts, the Auditori hosts dozens of other performances, covering not just classical music but also jazz, pop and world music.

Gran Teatre del Liceu

La Rambla 51-9, Barri Gòtic (93 485 99 13/www.liceubarcelona.com). Metro Liceu. **Open** *Information* 10am-10pm Mon-Fri. *Box office* 2-8.30pm Mon-Fri; 1hr before performance Sat, Sun. Closed 2wks Aug. **Tickets** varies. **Credit** AmEx, DC, MC, V. **Map** p345 A3.

In the four years since it reopened after a terrible fire, the Liceu has leapt from strength to strength. Gone is the rickety, 19th-century structure with outdated capabilities and a dry programme of tired operas. In its place has risen a modern, 2,340-seat pleasure palace that looks almost identical to the original (gold carvings and red plush), but is far better equipped. A large, subterranean foyer is used for talks, recitals, puppet shows and other events, and there is a new café. Also new are the seat-back subtitles, available in various languages, to complement the Catalan surtitles above the stage.

The 12 or so operas each season are rapturously received by a faithful audience, as are a similar number of recitals by high-profile soloists. As well as opera and concerts, the Liceu receives three or four touring dance companies each season, classical and contemporary. Nacho Duato is a frequent visitor with his Compañia Nacional de Danza, while the English National Ballet, Leipziger Ballet and Ballet de l'Opéra de Paris are all appearing in 2004.

Palau de la Música Catalana

C/Sant Francesc de Paula 2, Sant Pere (93 295 72 00/www.palaumusica.org). Metro Urquinaona. **Open** *Box office* 10am-9pm Mon-Sat; 1hr before performance Sun. **Tickets** varies. **Credit** MC, V. **Map** p344 B/C2.

Part wedding cake, part psychotropic vision (and possibly the result of overindulgence in absinthe), Domenech i Muntaner's sublime Modernista masterpiece is not to be missed, and there is no better way of appreciating its wild intricacies than during a concert. Acoustically the building has many shortcomings, but the Palau arouses loyalty among both concert-goers and performers. Its narrow auditorium means that most seats are rather far from the stage; try and avoid the rear half of the upper circle (here called the *segon pis*). The concert series Palau 100 brings top names from across Europe, as do private promoters Euroconcert and Ibercamera. A 600-seat, subterranean chamber hall and new entrance are due to be finished by spring 2004. *See also p102.*

Churches & smaller venues

A number of churches around Barcelona hold concerts. The most beautiful is probably **Santa Maria del Mar** (*see p103*) in the Born, with a tall, ghostly interior that exemplifies the Gothic intertwining of music, light and spirituality. Concerts include everything from Renaissance music to gospel singers. At the **cathedral** there is a monthly free organ concert, which usually, but not always, takes place on the second Wednesday of the month. Other churches with regular concerts include **Santa Maria del Pi**, **Sant Felip Neri**, **Santa Anna** and the monastery in **Pedralbes**. In May, keep an eye out for the **Festival de Música Antiga** (*see p216*), when concerts of early music are held in different locations in the Old City.

Auditori Winterthur

Auditori de l'Illa, Avda Diagonal 547, Les Corts-Sants (93 290 11 02). Metro Maria Cristina.
Open *Information* 8.30am-6.30pm Mon-Thur; 8am-2pm Fri. **Tickets & credit** varies. **Map** p345 B3.
This intimate, modern venue is a gem. It hosts only a dozen or so concerts, including an annual Schubert cycle and a series of song recitals.

Orchestras & ensembles

La Capella Reial de Catalunya, Le Concert des Nations & Hespèrion XXI

Information 93 580 60 69.
The indefatigable Jordi Savall is the driving force behind three overlapping early music groups. Together, they play an estimated 300 concerts a year worldwide, while also pursuing their own vigorous recording schedules. La Capella Reial specialises in Catalan and Spanish Renaissance and baroque music. Le Concert des Nations is a period instrument ensemble playing orchestral and symphonic work from 1600 to 1850, and Hespèrion XXI plays pre-1800 European music.

Orfeó Català

Information 93 295 72 00/www.palaumusica.org.
The Orfeó Català had its origins in the patriotic and social movements at the end of the 19th century; it was one of 150 choral groups that sprang up in Catalonia at that time and is inseparably identified with the Palau de la Música Catalunya. While it is certainly no longer as pre-eminent as it was, the Orfeó still stages around 25 performances a year, giving a cappella concerts as well as providing a choir for the OBC and other Catalan orchestras. The group is largely amateur, but includes a small professional nucleus, the Cor de Cambra del Palau de la Música, which gives some 50 performances a year.

Orquestra Simfònica de Barcelona Nacional de Catalunya (OBC)

Information 93 247 93 00/www.obc.es.
As the official Catalan national and Barcelona city orchestra, the OBC provides the bulk of orchestral music in Barcelona, with concerts at the Auditori most weekends from October to May, usually on Friday evening, then repeated on Saturday evening and again on Sunday morning. The many guest conductors to put in appearances during the season might explain the vagaries of the OBC's performance; in the right hands, they are a decent, jobbing orchestra, in the wrong ones, less so.

Orquestra Simfònica i Cor del Gran Teatre del Liceu

Information 93 485 99 13/www.liceubarcelona.com.
The Liceu currently offers around a dozen incredibly popular operas per season. To help meet demand, at least one performance of each opera is not covered by season tickets, and there's always a full run of a crowd-pleaser from the previous season to end the year. In 2003 this was a glittering *Aida* and in 2004 a wonderful production of Handel's *Giulio Cesare.* Highpoints of the 2003/4 season include a Royal Opera House production of Verdi's *Macbeth* (following a Swiss production of Ambroise Thomas's *Hamlet*), a couple of favourites (*Tosca* and *Cosi fan tutte*), Britten's troubling *Peter Grimes* and the two remaining operas in Wagner's ring cycle, *Siegfried* and *Götterdämmerung,* after 2003's excellent *Das Rheingold* and *Die Walküre,* all four produced by Deutsche Staatsoper Berlin.

Orquestra Simfònica del Vallès

Information 93 727 03 00/www.osvalles.com.
Though not quite at the level of the two main city orchestras, this country cousin from the neighbouring town of Sabadell performs regularly in Barcelona. It can often be found at the Palau de la Música Catalana, where it plays a dozen symphonic concerts each season.

Contemporary music

Avuimúsica

Associació Catalana de Compositors, Passeig Colom 6, space 4, Barri Gòtic (93 268 37 19/www.accompositors.com). Metro Drassanes. **Open** *Information* 9.30am-1.30pm Mon-Fri. *Tickets* €9; €4.50 concessions. *Book of 7 tickets* €31.50; €15.75 concessions. **No credit cards. Map** p344 B4.
A series of 14 small-scale concerts at various venues around town, predominantly featuring music by members of the Association of Catalan Composers, much of which is being played in public for the first time. A handful of pieces by well-known foreign composers and a couple of modern electronic offerings are usually thrown in for good measure.

Barcelona 216

Information 93 301 60 44.
A small ensemble with a strong commitment to contemporary music of all types, including serious 'written' compositions and more experimental and avant-garde work. Its activities are as energetic as they are varied, and always worth looking out for.

Finding flamenco

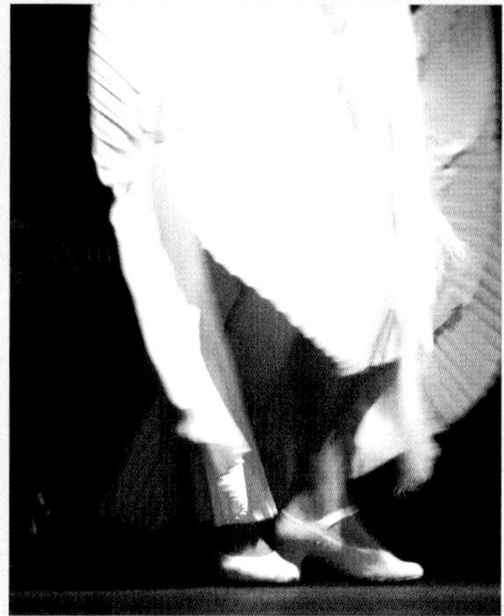

Coming to Barcelona for its flamenco scene would be a little like going to Sydney for the sushi – it's not the obvious place to visit, you have to really look for it, but it can also be very good. Flamenco was brought here by immigrants from much poorer southern Spain who settled in marginal suburbs of the city in the 1940s and '50s. The bulk of flamenco activity still happens in *peñas* (local associations) in these areas, making them the early training ground for most of the city's flamenco artists. Some of these, such as singers Miguel Poveda, Ginesa Ortega and Mayte Martin or the guitarist Chicuelo, occasionally tour and are worth looking out for.

Many local artists are managed by the Taller de Musics (93 443 43 46), responsible for a lot of the high-quality commercial flamenco events in the city. Look out particularly for its wonderful **Festival de Flamenco de Ciutat Vella** in May/June (*see p217*), which brings some of the best traditional and experimental flamenco to Barcelona each year.

The *tablaos,* or flamenco bars, cater almost exclusively to tourists and usually offer shows that are competent but uninspired, not to mention expensive. The three main *tablaos,* **Los Tarantos** (Plaça Reial 17, 93 318 30 67), **El Tablao de Carmen** (Poble Espanyol, 93 425 46 16; *pictured*) and **Tablao Cordobes** (La Rambla 35, 93 317 57 11) all offer dinner or drink and a show.

Flamenco is all about the unrepeatable combination of a moment, an artist, a space, an audience, and if you take the anything-can-happen element away what remains can seem noisy, melodramatic or simply tacky. A newly opened venue, **TiriTiTran** (C/Buenos Aires, 28, 93 363 05 91), is shaping up as a much-needed alternative, with performances currently only on Thursday nights, while the restaurant **Nervion** (C/Princesa 2, 93 315 21 03) has recently turned an upstairs room into a *tablao* on Friday nights, and seems to be aimed at curious tourists, but is a lot cheaper than the established *tablaos*.

The Taller de Musics also runs a small bar, the **Jazz Sí Club** (*see p245*), with live flamenco singing and guitar every Friday night. The atmosphere is authentic but performances are a bit of a lucky dip, ranging from nervous and unaccomplished students to memorable unannounced performances by visiting artists just dropping by.

Other bars in the city play flamenco music and sometimes host performances, but these are often short-term ventures due to inappropriate venues or noise regulations. The most reliable of these is **Soniquete** (C/Milans 5, mobile 639 382 354). Along with some of the seedier bars in nearby C/Gignas, this is a favourite hangout for local gypsies, who will sometimes put on a spontaneous performance, probably the most authentic to be found in the city.

CAT

Tvra de Sant Antoni 6-8, Gràcia (93 218 44 85). Metro Fontana. **Open** *Bar* 5pm-midnight daily. *Gigs* about 10pm Thur-Sat. Closed July, Aug. **Admission** €6-€9. **No credit cards. Map** p336 D3.

The Centre Artesà Tradicionàrius promotes traditional Catalan music and culture, hosting a number of music festivals, including the Festival Tradicionàrius, a showcase of folk music and dance held between January and April. Concerts, workshops and classes cover indigenous music from the rest of Spain and other countries. The centre also takes part in the LEM festival of experimental music (*see below*, Gràcia Territori Sonor).

Festival de Músiques Contemporànies

Information 93 247 93 00/www.auditori.com.

The content of Barcelona's most popular and mainstream contemporary music festival has fluctuated dramatically of late, covering a wide array of genres, including jazz and flamenco. The current focus is on big-name composers from the last few decades, and in 2004 includes performers such as Percussions de Barcelona, Barcelona 216, AMM, Bang on a Can, Octeto Ibérico de Violoncellos and the OBC.

Fundació Joan Miró

Parc de Montjuïc, Montjuïc (93 443 94 70/ www.bcn.fjmiro.es). Metro Paral.lel, then Funicular de Montjuïc/bus 50, 55. **Open** *(Mid June-July) Box office* 1hr before performance Thur. **Tickets** €5; €12 for 3 concerts. **Credit** MC, V. **Map** p341 B6.

The Miró runs a short but explosive series of concerts, with improvised music and a roster of well-regarded international musicians. The auditorium isn't the greatest in the world, but some concerts are held on the terrace overlooking the city.

Gràcia Territori Sonor

Information 93 237 37 37/www.gracia-territori.com.

The main focus of this dynamic, tirelessly creative collective is the LEM festival, held in various venues in Gràcia; a rambling, wonderfully eclectic series of musical happenings, much of it experimental, improvised and electronic, and most of it free. Ranging from the head-spinningly rarefied to the foot-tappingly contagious, it's almost irresistible in its reach and energy. Larger, more formal events are held at L'Espai and CaixaForum.

Metrònom

C/Fusina 9, Born (93 268 42 98). Metro Arc de Triomf or Jaume I. **Concerts** 10pm. **Admission** free. **Map** p345 C3.

Contemporary art space Metronòm complements its commitment to avant-garde art with a similar commitment to music whenever its exhibition schedule permits. The focus of activity is a hugely successful festival of experimental music in January, featuring everything from minimalist weirdos extracting sound from credit cards and wire loops, to extreme noisist types doing things to vinyl that would bring your average DJ out in a cold sweat.

Theatre & Dance

The Fòrum 2004's major draw will be its packed cultural entertainment programme, both on site and at venues all over town. Not that the Barcelona theatre scene needs any help: it is the most vibrant and varied in Spain, attracting more attention than ever. There were two million bums on seats in Barcelona's theatres last year – 22 per cent up on 2002 – and these figures look set to rise as the Fòrum pulls out all the cultural stops.

Although the local theatre scene has always been healthy, this spectacular growth in numbers has partly been sparked by a trend for using television actors as crowd bait and partly by an increase in high glitz moneyspinners with musical comedy at the forefront. Among 2003's biggest hits were *Sit* by mime trio Tricicle and musicals such as *Gaudí* and *Poe.* Meta-textual performance is key in much Catalan theatre, gaily leapfrogging language barriers with a festive blend of music, choreography, multimedia sleight-of-hand and slick production values.

Long queues and major venues for dance are still the exception, reserved for legendary performers such as Pina Bausch, but in general there is a lot more output and experimentation than audiences or venues are willing or able to absorb. Emblematic and highly influential companies such as Metros, Lanònima Imperial and Gelabert-Azzopardi are often better known outside Spain than locally and tend to spend a lot of their time touring, while a Dancers in Residence programme funded by the Catalan government means that newer or more experimental dancers such as Andres Corchero develop and perform their works mainly in theatres outside the city.

While contemporary dance manages to thrive against the odds in Barcelona, surprisingly, classical and modern ballet barely exist in the city. There are no major schools, no local companies and no consistent programming anywhere, and although rumours of a new project occasionally do the rounds, this is unlikely to change in the near future.

VENUES

Independent spaces receive some public funding but remain poor cousins to massive projects such as the Generalitat-sponsored Teatre Nacional de Catalunya, and the Ciutat del Teatre on Montjuïc, a rival project run by the Ajuntament. The Ciutat del Teatre brings together three buildings and seven stages around a common square: the innovative Mercat de les Flors, the Teatre Lliure, and the new Institut del Teatre, the city's most prestigious training ground for the performing arts. A number of local theatre companies and musicians participate in the Ciutat del Teatre, although programming there does not differ greatly from that at the TNC.

SEASONS AND FESTIVALS

The main performing arts season runs from September to June, but the hugely successful **Festival del Grec** (*see p219*) fills the gap in July and is the best time to gorge on visiting theatre and dance companies, both national and international. The fringe is best represented by the **Mostra de Teatre de Barcelona** (www.mostradeteatredebarcelona.com), which runs from the end of October to the end of November, while quality amateurs get their ya-yas out at the spring free-for-all **Marató de l'Espectacle** (*see p217*). The high-profile **Sitges Teatre Internacional** (www.sitges.co/teatre) is held in late May and early June while the annual **Dies de Dansa** (*see p219*) offers three days of national and international dance in various architecturally significant sites.

TICKETS AND TIMES

Main shows start late, around 9-10.30pm, although many theatres have earlier (and cheaper) shows at 6-7pm. There are also late shows on weekend nights. Be warned that most theatres are closed on Mondays and theatre box offices often accept cash only. Advance bookings are best made through the ticket sales operations of Servi-Caixa or Tel-entrada (*see p212*). The best places to find information are the *Guía del Ocio*, the *cartelera* (listings) pages of the newspapers and, for Tel-entrada theatres, the *Guía del Teatre*, free at Caixa Catalunya branches. Online, check out www.teatral.net and www.teatrebcn.com.

Associació dels Professionals de Dansa de Catalunya

Via Laietana 52, entl 7, Sant Pere (93 268 24 73/ www.dancespain.com). Metro Urquinaona. **Open** 10am-2pm Mon-Fri. **Map** p342 B2.

Acts as a clearing-house for the dance companies, with information on who is doing what at any time.

Major venues

Large-scale commercial productions are shown in the massive **Teatre Condal** (Avda Paral.lel 91, 93 42 31 32), the **Borràs** (Plaça Urquinaona 9, 93 412 15 82) and **Tívoli** (C/Casp 10-12, 93 412 20 63), while the ex-cinema **Club Capitol** (La Rambla 138, 93 412 20 38) hosts stand-up and quirkier numbers, such as *The Vagina Monologues* in 2003. The **Monumental** bullring (*see p119*) and the **Palau d'Esports** (C/Guàrdia Urbana s/n, 93 423 64 63) are used for mega-shows in the off-season. Ballet and modern dance troupes occasionally appear at the **Liceu** opera house and even the **Teatre Nacional**, while cultural centres such as the **CCCB** (*see p95*) and gallery **Metrònom** (*see p264*) are often used for contemporary dance.

L'Espai

Travessera de Gràcia 63, Gràcia (93 241 68 19). FGC Gràcia. **Box office** 6.30-9.30pm Tue-Sat; 5-7pm Sun. **Tickets** €11-€20; €8.25-€15 concessions. **Credit** AmEx, DC, MC, V. **Map** p338 C3.

The Catalan government's showcase for the performing arts is the best bet for seeing contemporary dance. Established companies often première new works here, and more experimental and improvised works are given space within the En Dansa festival in spring and Improvisa in autumn. In June 2004 a new festival around the theme of conflict, *Dansa i Conflicte*, will be held for the first time.

Teatre Nacional de Catalunya. *See p267.*

Who's who Calixto Bieito

Buñuel said that you can do anything you like except be boring. Calixto Bieito has surely taken that advice to heart. He is one of the world's most controversial opera geniuses, and whatever he does, he does not do boring. Over the last few years his unusual approach to classic operas and plays has shocked audiences from Spain to Britain and beyond, and he shows no sign of falling into line any time soon.

Bieito cites inspiration from Goya's 'black' pictures, and admires the surrealism of Buñuel and the violence of Tarantino. In literature his loves include Lorca, Lope de Vega and Cervantes. He takes all of these influences and pours them into classical works in bizarre ways that some find repugnant, and many find fascinating.

The former are often offended by his obsession with the scatological: on-stage urinating is a common device of his, recurring in both his *Die Fledermaus* and *Don Giovanni*. Bodily functions were also front and centre when Bieito took on Verdi's difficult *Un Ballo in Maschera*. The original story was based on the real King Gustav of Sweden, a homosexual who was shot with rusty bullets and then died a painful death. Verdi's version adapted the tale to that of a king in love with the wife of one of his courtiers, with no mention of man-on-man action. For his part, Bieito demanded a gay gang rape of a naked king (the first tenor cast in the role refused to do the scene). To make matters weirder, the scene in which conspirators from the court plan the king's murder was staged with the members of the English National Opera chorus, trousers around their ankles, sitting on a row of toilets.

He later had more fun with the storyline of Mozart's *Don Giovanni*. The production reduced most of the press to apoplexy when it appeared at the ENO in summer 2003, but some thought it brilliantly melded filmatic touches with the classic tale. There were constant Tarantino touches, and *Time Out* magazine described it as 'bloody, brutal and sexy... as we followed the long night of bonking, boozing and bloodshed, complete with an orgasmic Donna Anna whooping out the climax of her Act Two aria as Don Ottavio screwed her on a bar stool.'

The reaction, as you might expect, was mixed. This did not put Bieito off, naturally. In his latest slam at theatrical convention, his Hamlet brutally rapes Ophelia, to a tight-lipped response from the critics.

Bieito has no shortage of fans around the world, but there are many who think that if he knows better than Shakespeare, Mozart or Verdi, let him write his own plays and operas.

Institut del Teatre

Plaça Margarida Xirgú, Montjuïc (93 227 39 00/ www.diba.es/iteatre). Metro Poble Sec. **Box office** 2hrs before show Mon-Sat; 1hr before show Sun. **Tickets** normally free, but must be booked. **No credit cards. Map** p341 B6.

Every January and June, this leading theatre and dance school allows audiences in to watch final-year students' performances. The biannual Festival Internacional de Teatre Visual i de Titelles, a theatre and puppetry festival, is due in November 2004.

Mercat de les Flors

Plaça Margarida Xirgú, C/Lleida 59, Montjuïc (93 426 18 75/www.mercatflors.com). Metro Poble Sec. **Box office** 1hr before show. **Advance tickets** also from Palau de la Virreina. **Tickets** varies. **No credit cards. Map** p341 B6.

This is a huge converted flower market with three spaces. The smaller theatre will be closed for renovations during the first half of 2004, affecting mainly dance, but it's business as usual for the larger spaces, which continue to experiment with unusual formats and pieces that mix new technologies, popular culture and the performing arts, as well as regular film nights and an Asian festival in autumn.

Teatre Lliure

Plaça Margarida Xirgú, Montjuïc (93 289 27 70/ www.teatrelliure.com). Metro Poble Sec. **Box office** 11am-3pm, 4.30-8pm Mon-Fri; 4.30-8pm Sat; 4-6pm Sun. **Tickets** €15 Tue, Wed; €20 Thur-Sun; €9 concessions Tue-Sun. **Credit** MC, V. **Map** p341 B6.

The 'Free Theatre' group has a reputation for the quality of its classic and contemporary repertoire, which also includes dance and music. It still programmes in the original Gràcia venue (C/Montseny 47, 93 218 92 51) but the mothership is now the overhauled Palace of Agriculture. Highlights in 2004 include the latest piece by Els Joglars (as yet untitled), a Haydn opera and *Porno* by Dani Salgado.

Teatre Nacional de Catalunya (TNC)

Plaça de les Arts 1, Eixample (93 306 57 00/ www.tnc.es). Metro Glòries. **Box office** noon-3pm, 4-9pm Mon; noon-9pm Tue-Sat; noon-5pm Sun. **Tickets** €9.50-€25; concessions vary. **Credit** MC, V. **Map** p341 F5.

The Parthenon-like TNC was designed in 1996 by architect Ricard Bofill as a homage to Greek theatre. It has failed to supplant the more central theatres in popularity despite its three flawless performance spaces and state-of-the-art facilities. Naturally, the TNC gives great weight to Catalan theatre, along with Spanish classics and a full range of global theatre in translation plus all genres of dance and young people's theatre. The spring and summer programming in 2004 includes *Caligula* by Albert Camus, *Maria Rosa* by Àngel Guimerà and Sol Picó's flamenco exploration *Puntapà!*

Teatre Poliorama

La Rambla 115, Barri Gòtic (93 317 75 99/www.teatre poliorama.com). Metro Catalunya. **Box office** 5-8pm Tue; 5-9.30pm Wed-Thur; 5-10pm Fri, Sat; 5-7pm Sun. **Tickets** varies. **Credit** MC, V. **Map** p344 A2.

This large, comfortable theatre is now privately run, in conjunction with the Teatre Victòria (Avda Paral.lel 67, 93 443 29 29), by commercial producers 3xtr3s. The emphasis is on musicals and other big productions. The Poliorama's major spring/summer production this year is *Mayumana*, Israeli dance and percussion in the same vein as *Stomp!*

Other venues

Other spaces include **Artenbrut** (C/Perill 9-1, 93 457 97 05), **Nou Tantarantana** (C/Flors 22, 93 441 70 22), **Espai Escènic Joan Brossa** (C/Allada-Vermell 13, 93 310 13 64) and **Conservas** (C/Sant Pau 58, 93 302 06 30).

Sala Beckett

C/Alegre de Dalt 55 bis, Gràcia (93 284 53 12/www. salabeckett.com). Metro Joanic. **Box office** from 8pm Wed-Sat. **Tickets** €16; €12 concessions. **No credit cards. Map** p339 E3.

Founded by the Samuel Beckett-inspired Teatro Fronterizo group, and run by José Sanchis Sinistierra, one of Spain's finest contemporary playwrights, this small space offers challenging new theatre and dance, with occasional productions in English.

Theatre companies

Other companies to look out for include the satirical and camp **Chanclettes**, and the **Compañia Nacional Clásica** for versions of the Spanish masters. As for English-language theatre, **Josh Zamrycki** has a black comedy up his sleeve for 2004 with the **Jocular** theatre company; playwright and actor Christopher Hood, known for his television screenplay work in Britain, channels his projects through **Black Custard Theatre**. The **Teatre de la Riereta** (C/Reina Amalia 3, 93 442 98 44) hosts a few English works as does the **Teatre Llantiol** (C/Riereta 7, 93 329 90 09).

Els Comediants

This colourful troupe continues the *commedia dell'arte* tradition with a lively combination of mime, circus, puppetry and folklore, all wrapped up in vivid costumery and frequently performed in the open air. Fully plugged into the city's self-promotion machine, their main projects in 2004 are a tribute to the mustachioed one for the Year of Dalí celebrations, and a six-month stint of *L'Arbre de la Memòria* (*The Memory Tree*) at the Fòrum amphiteatre – a play starring a 12m (39 ft) high tree as imagined by the nature-starved occupants of a post-holocaust future.

La Cubana

Big, brash but amazingly slick, La Cubana's productions are painted with cartoonish colours and broad humour. Although it has now lost some of its best actors to television contracts, director Jordi Milán's version of Verdi's *Aida* at the Liceu in 2003 was highly successful. In 2004 they'll be touring with *Mamá, quiero ser famoso* (*Mummy, I Wanna Be Famous*), a spoof British TV show dedicated to converting ordinary folk into celebrities.

Dagoll Dagom

This group specialises in deliciously kitsched-up musicals in the old-time Broadway vein. They enjoyed a big hit in 2003 with *La Perritxola*, in which orchestra pit musicians and actors mixed roles. Their 30th anniversary in 2004 will be celebrated with a revival of their most emblematic work, *Mar i Cel* (*Sea and Sky*), Àngel Guimerà's story of irreconcilable culture clashes and thwarted love in the 17th century.

La Fura dels Baus

The name means 'ferret of Els Baus' (Els Baus de Moià being a ravine in the group's hometown), and raw meat, industrial techno, and more power tools than *Friday the 13th* are stock ingredients of a typical show. Call them daring provocateurs or shameless attention sluts, this local troupe has been a frontrunner of Catalan theatre since the mid '80s, and continued to fill theatres around Europe in 2003 with *XXX*, a porno cabaret inspired by the Marquis de Sade. In a grand theatre-boat tour in 2004, they will sail to 18 countries with a show based on the unlikely concepts of 'peace, dialogue and interculturality'. Could this mark the taming of the ferret?

Els Joglars

Els Joglars' director, Albert Boadella, is still spitting with fury at the repressive Franco regime in particular and political injustice in general. He was imprisoned for his outspokenness in the 1970s and has since made a career of ridiculing unscrupulous leaders with darkly sardonic gems, from *Ubú President* (spoofing former Catalan President Jordi Pujol) to the 2003 film *Buen viaje, excelencia!* about the last years of Franco. No doubt more egos will topple in 2004 when the group tours with their brand new interpretation (as yet untitled) of Cervantes' religious farce, *Los Retablos de Las Maravillas*.

Tricicle

Local boys Carles Sans, Paco Mir and Joan Gràcia founded this mime trio 25 years ago and their comedy *Sit* was Barcelona's biggest hit of 2003. The goofy, clean-cut humour appeals to the Spanish taste for slapstick and they are not above the odd Benny Hill moment of crossdressing or chase sequences.

Dance companies

Other groups worth looking out for include popular and established company **Metros**; the collective **La Caldera**; experimental collective **PA CK**, and newer groups like **Erre que erre**, **Projecte Gallina**, **Búbulus**, and **Lapsus**, as well as **Nats Nus** and its highly successful offshoot **Nats Nens**, which produces contemporary dance shows and workshops for children.

Andrés Corchero-Rosa Muñoz

This is the dance company that dancers love, but its experimental style based on improvisation and butoh can make it a little more difficult for the uninitiated. Very influential and highly respected, it's worth looking out for the company's collaborative works, as well as their own performances.

Gelabert-Azzopardi

www.gelabertazzopardi.com

After more than 30 years working as a dancer and choreographer, Cesc Gelabert's most recent works are an expression of that brief moment in time when mental maturity and physical ability exist in more or less equal measure. His emotional range and versatility can be seen in the works he will perform at the Teatre Lliure in April 2004, before touring to other Spanish cities.

Lanònima Imperial

One of the most emblematic of local companies, popular with audiences at home and all over Europe, this group has flashy production values, but all elements, including their fabulous dancers, are as good as they come and it's worth looking out for one of their increasingly rare performances in the city.

Mal Pelo

Mal Pelo have a particular Catalan sensibility, creating expressive, earthy and somewhat surreal choreographies. Their Utopian project *L'animal a l'esquena* is a farmhouse turned rehearsal/performance/accommodation/workshop space, where they explore links between dance and other disciplines.

Mudances

93 430 87 63/www.margarit-mudances.com

Director Àngels Margarit has been gaining in stature as a choreographer throughout the past decade, producing highly structured, work that involves a creative use of video. Mudances often programmes dance workshops and pieces for children.

La Porta

This is not a company but a showcase for new choreography and experimental dance, and it is responsible for some of the most interesting performances in the city, though the continuation of its regular programmes, such as *Nits Salvatges* at the CCCB or *Perversiones* at CaixaForum, is precariously dependent on the whims of venues and funding bodies.

Sol Picó

www.solpico.com

Through perserverance, charisma, hard work and lots of energy, Sol Picó and her company are probably the best known of the younger generation of dancers. The company's recent works have not always been completely successful, but Sol's energy, curiosity and willingness to explore are never dull. Her new, flamenco-inspired work, tentatively called *Puntapà!*, is at the TNC in June 2004.

Dance schools & workshops

Many of the major companies allow you to join their own classes for short periods, but call to check first. Some, like **Mudances** and **Lanónima Imperial,** also run special workshops. The **Institut del Teatre** runs summer classes but these are often expensive. A good place for contemporary dance classes at almost all levels is **Area Espai de Dansa i Creació** (C/Alegre de Dalt 55, 93 210 78 50), while the central **El Timbal** (C/Portaferrissa 13, 93 302 73 47) is an acting school that also has drop-in dance classes for students trained at many different levels and in a variety of performance styles. A more complete list of dance schools in Barcelona can be found at www.dancespain.com/schools.html.

Sport & Fitness

In Barcelona, they do sporty with style.

It's now 12 years since the Olympics were celebrated here, but the sporting infrastructure created for it is still in good condition – and even improving. The socialist city council has provided well-equipped gyms and pools for virtually every neighbourhood, the ever more modern beach provides an eventful place to jog, and there are plenty of facilities to ice skate or play tennis, go sailing or play *jai alai*. Just don't expect to find yourself an impromptu kickaround in the park: there isn't room.

Barcelona attracts several international sporting events, from Formula One Grand Prix to showjumping, from tennis to yachting regattas, but one sport dominates most Catalans' hearts and minds – football, and particularly the fortunes of FC Barcelona, 'Barça'. Barça claim to be 'more than just a club' and so they are, literally as well as spiritually, running basketball, roller hockey, handball and American football teams, too, all wearing the hallowed '*blaugrana*' (claret and blue) colours.

Spectator sports

Tickets can often be purchased by credit card with **Servi-Caixa** or **Tel-entrada** (*see p212*). Check www.agendabcn.com for event info.

Basketball

Spain hosts Europe's most competitive basketball league, the ACB, and basketball is the second most popular sport in the country by a long nose. **FC Barcelona** are the most powerful side, attracting high quality European players, and even exporting some to the USA; there are two other top clubs from the area, **DKV Joventut**, from Badalona, and **Basquet Manresa**. The season runs from September to early June: league matches are on weekend evenings, European matches are midweek.

FC Barcelona

Palau Blaugrana, Avda Arístides Maillol, Les Corts (93 496 36 75/www.fcbarcelona.com). Metro Collblanc or Maria Cristina. **Ticket office** 9am-1.30pm, 3.30-6pm Mon-Thur; 9am-2.30pm Fri; 2hrs before a game. (Tickets available from 1 day before match.) **Tickets** €7-€26. **No credit cards.**

In May 2003, at the sixth attempt, FC Barcelona finally won the European Cup, thanks largely to the wily coaching of Svetislav Pesic, the power of Slovene Gregor Fucka and the skill of Serb Dejan Bodiroga; victory sparked off a party from which the city centre took some time to recover. It is a good idea to book in advance to get a ticket in the atmospheric 8,000-capacity Palau Blaugrana.

Bullfighting

Plaza de Toros Monumental

Gran Via de les Corts Catalanas 749, Eixample (93 245 58 04/215 95 70). Metro Monumental. **Open** *Bullfights* Apr-Sept 5.30-7pm Sun. *Museum* Apr-Sept 11am-2pm, 4-8pm Mon-Sat; 10.30am-1.30pm Sun. **Advance tickets** also available from Servi-Caixa. **Admission** *Bullfights* €18-€95. *Museum* €4; €3 concessions. **No credit cards. Map** p343 F5.

Corridas (bullfights) take place on Sundays (April to September), but local interest is low and a card of the most prestigious *toreros* is needed to even half-fill it, and then with Andalucian immigrants and tourists, who often leave after the first bull gets killed. If you want to see a good bullfight, go west.

Castellers

The hardworking, unflamboyant nature of the Catalans is reflected in their preference for *castellers* (human castles) over bullfights. In this sport, a team of men, women and children all play their part in achieving the goal – a human castle up to ten storeys high, topped by a small child stretching out a hurried arm to 'crown' it. *Castellers* can be seen at fiestas every weekend from March to November all over Catalonia. They're a terrifying sight as they wobble, sway, and (occasionally) fall. Their season comes to a climax every two years with a massive competition in Tarragona in October: next in 2004. For more information, contact the group Coordinadora de Colles Castelleres de Catalunya (977 605 206, www.coordinadora collescastelleres.info).

Football

FC Barcelona represented the only legal way of expressing Catalan identity during the Franco years and the club became a symbol of Catalan nationalism. Though it's been going through a difficult period, it still attracts world-class players. **Espanyol**, the city's second team, perennially struggle to stay in the top flight, and have all but ceased being credible

Catalonia united

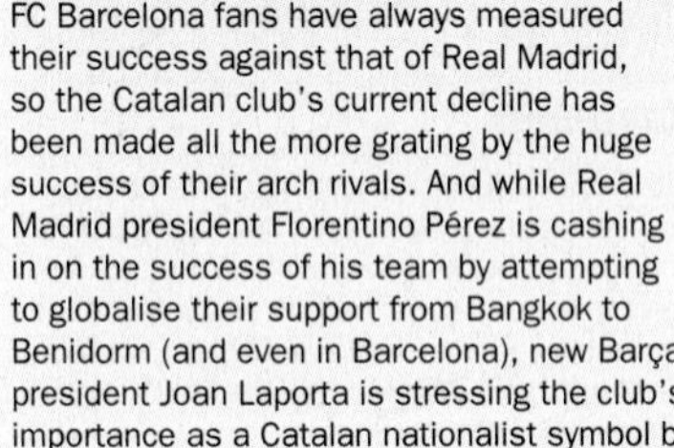

FC Barcelona fans have always measured their success against that of Real Madrid, so the Catalan club's current decline has been made all the more grating by the huge success of their arch rivals. And while Real Madrid president Florentino Pérez is cashing in on the success of his team by attempting to globalise their support from Bangkok to Benidorm (and even in Barcelona), new Barça president Joan Laporta is stressing the club's importance as a Catalan nationalist symbol by suggesting that every Catalan should support the club – and that 'Barça should be a symbol of Catalonia in the rest of the world'.

It's a curiously inward-looking approach, which will inevitably alienate Barça's large non-Catalan fan base. But it is not an original stance. The club was formed in 1899, its directors espousing Catalan causes and promoting the language. Both of Spain's 20th-century dictators, De Rivera and Franco, temporarily closed the club down upon

rivals to Barça, therefore it's easy to get tickets for their matches. Every weekend one or the other will be playing, usually on Saturday or Sunday evening (though check the press for details, and keep checking as kick-off times can change). **Europa** (based in Gràcia) and **Jupiter** (in Poblenou) are semi-pro teams worth a watch if you're starved of live action.

FC Barcelona

Nou Camp, Avda Arístides Maillol, Les Corts (93 496 36 00/www.fcbarcelona.com). Metro Maria Cristina or Collblanc. **Ticket office** 9am-1.30pm, 3.30-6pm Mon-Thur; 9am-2.30pm Fri; 2hrs before a game. (Tickets available 1wk before each match.) **Tickets** €19-€93. **Advance tickets** (league games only) Servi-Caixa. **Credit** DC, MC, V. **Map** p337 A3.

Barça have been in decline over the last five years while their bitter rivals Real Madrid have been winning trophy after trophy, so new president Joan Laporta's big ideas will need time to gel before the 98,000-capacity Nou Camp stadium fills again. When the team is in full flow, with Ronaldinho performing his tricks, the atmosphere is unbeatable. Around 4,000 tickets usually go on sale before the game – ring up to find out when, and join the queue an hour or so beforehand at the intersection of Travessera de les Corts and Avenida Arístides Maillol. 'Rented out' seats go on sale from these offices, and can also be bought through Servi-Caixa. If all else fails, go to the stadium before the game and buy a *'revendita'* ticket from touts at the gates. If you don't get to see Barça, it's always possible to watch their B team (a couple of divisions down the league system) in the mini stadium over the road (check press for fixtures).

RCD Espanyol

Estadi Olímpic de Montjuïc, Passeig Olímpic 17-19, Montjuïc (93 292 77 00/www.rcdespanyol.com). Metro Espanya then escalators, or Paral.lel then

gaining power. Real Madrid were seen as Franco's pet team, and the fight for supremacy between the two teams was to become representative of the centuries-old struggle between the centralised power in Madrid and the would-be autonomy of its richest province. Older Barça fans can remember a time when they could express their Catalan identity only on the terraces of the Nou Camp – using their support of the team as an act of defiance.

Nowadays the pendulum of repression has swung so far the other way that non Catalan speaking Spaniards feel hard done by in the region, and the Nou Camp remains a hotbed of nationalist sentiment. In 2003 Luis Figo, who moved from Barça to Real Madrid, was pelted with objects, including a whisky bottle and a pig's head. The truth is, Figo left a sinking ship. While Real Madrid (thanks to government help) cleared its debts, Barça was knee deep in it, having overstretched itself to pay the wages of pricey foreign stars.

Barça fans grew used to success in the '90s, when they won the Spanish League six times. But they've yet to win a trophy this millennium, and the announcement of a goal, any goal, against Real Madrid announced over the tannoy can stimulate more of a cheer than a home goal, and if Barça are doing badly '*la pitada*' (whistling) starts up and white handkerchiefs are waved at the players.

The club is in crisis, and Laporta's appeal to the nationalist sentiments of his fans – however it might alienate non-Catalan supporters – is a desperate act of a man who needs all the help he can get. Laporta promised in his election manifesto that he would bring David Beckham to the club. He failed of course, and now Beckham is the most powerful weapon in Real Madrid's push for global domination, selling Real Madrid shirts all over the world. Instead Laporta bought Brazilian ace Ronaldinho – and suggested he should learn Catalan.

Funicular de Montjuïc/50 bus. **Ticket office** 9.30am-1.30pm, 5-8pm Mon-Fri. *If match days* 8am-3pm Fri; 10am-1.30pm Sat; 10am-matchtime Sun. **Tickets** €20-€45. **Credit** V. **Map** p341 A6.
Espanyol are a provincial team in a capital city, attracting an average crowd of 20,000 in a stadium that holds 56,000, and struggling financially. Still, they have only spent two seasons out of the first division in 20 years. The team is currently homeless, playing its games in the rented Olympic stadium on Montjuïc, waiting for a new 'Sports City' to be built in Cornellà (for the 2005-6 season). Free buses ferry ticket holders from Plaça Espanya, starting 90 minutes before kick-off.

Other team sports

FC Barcelona's handball and roller hockey teams both will be challenging for national and European honours in 2004. Several other team sports have found fan bases outside the centre of town in the suburbs of Barcelona, such as **Santboiana**, Spain's oldest rugby team based in Sant Boi (93 640 07 26); **Terrassa Hockey**, a top-level field hockey team based in Terrassa (93 787 03 51), and **Viladecans**, Spain's dominant baseball team (93 424 02 25).

Special events

Barcelona Marathon

Information & entry forms *C/Jonqueres 16, 15°, Born (93 268 01 14/www.redestb.es/marathon_cat). Metro Urquinaona.* **Open** *Office* 5.30-8.30pm Mon-Fri. **Date** Mar. **Fee** €35-€40. **No credit cards. Map** p344 B1.
The Marató de Catalunya follows a flat, picture-postcard route that allows runners to clock up career-best times and a good deal of sightseeing to

boot. The course starts and finishes by the magic fountain in Plaça Espanya and takes in the Port Olímpic and the Rambla – about 3,500 runners take part. The city's biggest fun-run is La Cursa del Corte Inglés, which takes place in May, challenging over 50,000 runners, joggers and, yes, walkers, to take on the 11km (7-mile) course (contact El Corte Inglés, 93 270 17 30, www.elcorteingles.com).

Motor sports

Circuit de Catalunya, Carretera de Parets del Vallès a Granollers, Montmeló, Outer Limits (93 571 97 00/ www.circuitcat.com). By car C17 north to Parets del Vallès exit (20km/13 miles). **Times & tickets** vary according to competition; available from Servi-Caixa. **Credit** MC, V.

The success of newcomer Fernando Alonso has electrified Spain's interest in Formula One racing and hopes are high for his performance on 7-9 May 2004. The same circuit hosts the motorcycle racing Grand Prix in mid June. The track, which from above looks uncannily like a Space Invader, can also be used by the public driving their own cars on 12 weeks a year.

Tennis

Reial Club de Tennis Barcelona-1899, C/Bosch i Gimpera 5-13, Les Corts (93 203 78 52/www.rctb 1899.es). Bus 63, 78. **Open** (members only) 8am-10pm daily. **Ticket office** (during competitions) 8.30am-1.30pm, 3.30-6.30pm Mon-Fri; 9am-1pm Sat. **Tickets** €19.80-€64. **Credit** AmEx, MC, V.

The annual Comte de Godó tournament in Pedralbes is on the ATP circuit and is always attended by a number of top seeds, including the 'Spanish Armada' of Ferrero, Costa, Moya and so on, cheered on by 40,000 fans over the week. The 2004 tournament runs from 24 April to 2 May – the only time the club is open to non-members – and tickets can be bought through Servi-Caixa.

Active sports/fitness

The 237 municipally run facilities include a network of *poliesportius* (sports centres), most of which have a gym with fitness equipment, a hall for indoor sports and a covered swimming pool. Charges are low and you don't have to be a resident to use them. And there's always the beach: there's a free outdoor gym and ping-pong table at Barceloneta, and the sea is swimmable from May to October. All beaches have wheelchair ramps and most of the city's pools are fully equipped for disabled people. Check with the **Servei d'Informació Esportiva** for details.

Servei d'Informació Esportiva

Avda de l'Estadi 30-40, Montjuïc (information 93 402 30 00). Metro Espanya, then escalators, or Paral.lel, then Funicular de Montjuïc/bus 50. **Open** *25 Sept-23 June* 8am-2pm, 3.45-6pm Mon-Thur; 8am-2.30pm Fri. *24 June-24 Sept* 8am-2.30pm Mon-Fri. **Map** p341 A6.

The Ajuntament's sports information service is based in the Piscina Bernat Picornell building. Call for information on sports facilities (although not all the staff speak English), or consult the Ajuntament's very thorough listings on the Esports section of its website: www.bcn.es.

Bowling

Bowling Pedralbes

Avda Dr Marañón 11, Les Corts (93 333 03 52). Metro Collblanc. **Open** 10am-2am Mon-Thur; 10am-4am Fri, Sat; 10am-midnight Sun (Aug from 5pm only). **Rates** (per person per game) €1.50 until 5pm Mon-Fri; €2.05 from 5pm Mon-Thur; €2.70 until 5pm Sat, Sun; €3.70 from 9pm Fri, from 5pm Sat, Sun. **Credit** AmEx, MC, V.

Fourteen lanes to try for that perfect 300, or to loft all your throws into the moat, in an alley that hosts international tournaments. Early afternoons are quiet, otherwise sit at the bar and wait to be paged. Shoe hire is available (€1) plus pool, snooker and *futbolín* (table football).

Cycling

The city has striven to provide cycle routes around town – tourist offices (*see p319*) can provide maps. These make cycling just about viable as a mode of transport, though the major roads in the Eixample can get a bit hairy. The seafront is a good bet for leisure cycling, or try the spectacular **Carretera de les Aigües**, a flat gravel road that skirts along the side of Collserola mountain (to avoid a killer climb getting up there, take your bike on the FGC to Peu del Funicular station, then take the Funicular de Vallvidrera to the midway stop). For more serious mountain biking, try the excellent www.pangea.org/org/amicsbici, which also details when you can take your bike on public transport.

Probike

C/Villarroel 184, Eixample (93 419 78 89/ www.probike.es). Metro Hospital Clínic. **Open** 4.30-8.30pm Mon; 10.30am-2pm, 4.30-8.30pm Tue-Sat. **Credit** AmEx, MC, V. **Map** p338 C4.

A mecca for mountain bikers, with excellent equipment and service, as well as maps and information to help you find the route you need, whether it's historically interesting or just plain hilly. The Probike club organises regular excursions ranging from daytrips to a summertime cross-Pyrenees run.

Football

Barcelona International Football League

Information 93 218 67 31/649 261 328/ nicksimonsbcn@yahoo.co.uk.

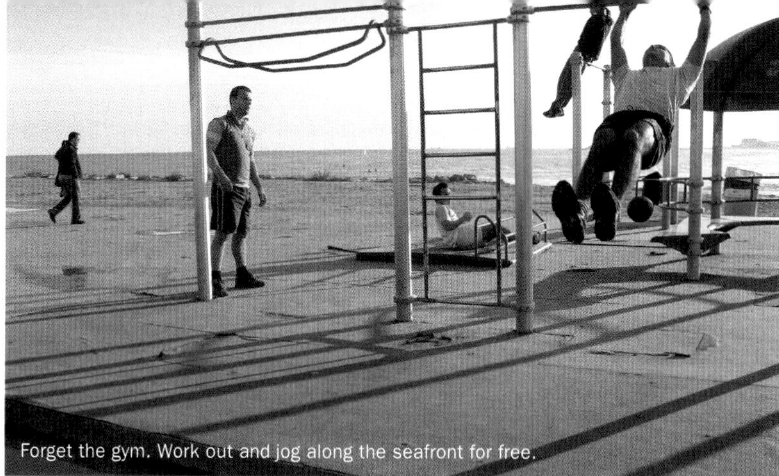
Forget the gym. Work out and jog along the seafront for free.

Matches are generally played at the weekend, among teams of expats and locals of a Sunday League standard. There is often room for new players.

Golf

Catalonia is one of the best emerging golfing holiday destinations. Visitors should book in advance. Courses can be full at weekends.

Club de Golf Sant Cugat

C/Villa, Sant Cugat del Vallès, Outer Limits (93 674 39 58). By car Túnel de Vallvidrera (C16) to Valldoreix/by train FGC from Plaça Catalunya to Sant Cugat. **Open** *June-Oct* 8am-8.30pm Mon; 7.30am-8.30pm Tue-Fri; 7am-9pm Sat, Sun. *Nov-May* 8am-5.30pm Mon; 7.30am-5.30pm Tue-Fri; 7am-5.30pm Sat, Sun. **Rates** (non-members) €55 Mon; €65 Tue-Fri; €150 Sat, Sun. Club hire €20. **Credit** MC, V.

Designed by Harry S Colt back in 1917 this is a tight, varied 18-hole course making the most of natural obstacles, challenging enough to host the Ladies' World Matchplay Tour. It has equipment hire, a restaurant, bar and swimming pool.

Club de Golf Terramar

Camí de la Carrerada, Sitges (93 894 05 80). By car C31 through Sitges, 3km towards Vilanova. By train RENFE from Sants or Passeig de Gràcia, then taxi. **Open** *July-Sept* 8am-10pm daily. *Oct-June* 8am-10pm Mon, Wed-Sun. **Rates** (non-members) €65 Mon-Fri; €90 Sat, Sun. Club hire €20. **Credit** DC, MC, V.

Another technically interesting 18-hole course, designed in 1922 in a beautiful setting, surrounded by forest and the Costa Daurada, with three lakes to devour your balls. You can hire equipment.

Gyms/fitness centres

Sports centres run by the city council are cheaper and generally more user-friendly than most of the private clubs. Phone the **Servei d'Informació Esportiva** (*see p272*).

Centres de Fitness DiR

C/Casp 34, Eixample (901 30 40 30/93 450 48 18/www.dirfitness.es). Metro Catalunya. **Open** 6.45am-10.15pm Mon-Fri; 9am-3pm Sat, Sun. **Rates** €30.10 for 7 days, then €3.90 per day. **Credit** V. **Map** p344 B1.

This large private chain has ten fitness centres scattered around the city, offering an excellent range of facilities as well as classes in a range of physical activities from spinning to 'mind-body'. Additional installations vary from a huge outdoor pool (at DiR Diagonal) to a squash centre (DiR Campus).

Branches: DiR Campus, Avda Dr Marañón 17, Les Corts (93 448 41 41); DiR Diagonal, C/Ganduxer 25-7 Eixample (93 202 22 02); and throughout the city.

Europolis

Travessera de les Corts 252-4, Zona Alta (93 363 29 92). Metro Les Corts. **Open** 7am-11pm Mon-Fri; 8am-8pm Sat; 9am-3pm Sun. **Rates** *Non-members* €9 per day. *Membership* approx €41 per mth plus €70 joining fee. **Credit** MC, V.

Municipally owned but run by British fitness chain Holmes Place, the Europolis sports centres are as large and well equipped as almost any private gym in town. Each has acres of shiny new exercise machines, as well as extensive pool areas, classes, private trainers and weight-lifting equipment.

Branch: Europolis C/Sardenya 549-51, Gràcia (93 210 07 66).

Ice skating

FC Barcelona Pista de Gel

Avda Arístides Maillol, Les Corts (93 496 3600/ www.fcbarcelona.com). Metro Maria Cristina or Collblanc. **Open** 10am-2pm, 4-5.45pm Mon; 10am-2pm, 4-7.15pm Tue, Thur; 10am-2pm, 4-7.30pm Wed; 10am-2pm, 4-8pm Fri; 10.30am-1.45pm, 4.30-9pm Sat, Sun. Closed Aug. **Rates** (incl skates) €6.30 Mon-Fri; €8 Sat, Sun. **No credit cards**. **Map** p337 A3.

Functional rink next to the Nou Camp complex, also used for ice hockey matches. It's perfect for the non-football fans in the family to kill 90 minutes or so.

Skating Roger de Flor

C/Roger de Flor 168, Eixample (93 245 28 00/ www.skatingbcn.com). Metro Tetuan. **Open** 10.30am-1.30pm Tue; 10.30am-1.30pm, 5-9pm Wed, Thur; 10.30am-1.30pm, 5pm-midnight Fri-Sun. **Rates** (incl skates) €9.50; glove hire (gloves are compulsory) €1.50. **Credit** MC, V. **Map** p343 E5.

A family-oriented ice rink in the Eixample. Any non-skaters in a group get in free and can use the café.

Jogging & running

The seafront is the easiest option for an enjoyable jog. If you can handle the initial climb, or use other transport for the ascent, there are scenic runs on Montjuïc, especially around the castle and Olympic stadium, the Park Güell/Carmel hills and Collserola. For the city marathon and other races *see p271*.

Sailing

Base Nàutica de la Mar Bella

Avda Litoral, between Platja Bogatell & Platja de Mar Bella, Port Olímpic (93 221 04 32/www.base nautica.org). Bus 36, 41. **Open** *June-Sept* 10am-8pm daily. *Oct-May* 10am-5pm daily. **Rates** 10hr windsurfing course €150; 16hr catamaran course €176; windsurf hire €15.50 per hr. **Credit** AmEx, DC, MC, V.

The scruffy but friendly Base Nàutica hires catamarans and windsurf equipment to those with experience. There's a proficiency test when you first get on the water (€12, but you only pay if you fail). You can hire a kayak without a test.

Skiing

See p298 **On the piste**.

Swimming

It's not difficult to go for a swim in Barcelona. The city has hundreds of municipal all-year swimming pools, and 25 open-air pools that are open from July to September. It also has five kilometres (three miles) of beach, patrolled by lifeguards during the summer. For a full list of pools, contact the **Servei d'Informació Esportiva** (*see p272*). Flip-flops and swimming caps must be worn by everyone.

Club de Natació Atlètic Barceloneta

Plaça del Mar, Port Vell (93 221 00 10). Metro Barceloneta, then bus 17, 39, 64. **Open** *Oct-Apr* 6.30am-11pm Mon-Fri; 7am-11pm Sat; 8am-5pm Sun. *May-Sept* 7am-11pm Mon-Sat; 8am-8pm Sun. **Admission** *Non-members* €7 per day. **Credit** AmEx, DC, MC, V. **Map** p342 D7.

This historic beachside centre – counting down to its centenary in 2007 – has an indoor pool and two outdoor pools (one heated) as well as sauna and gym facilities. There is a *frontón* if you fancy a go at the world's fastest sport, *jai alai*, a fierce Basque game somewhere between squash and handball.

Piscina Bernat Picornell

Avda de l'Estadi 30-40, Montjuïc (93 423 40 41/ www.picornell.com). Metro Espanya then escalators, or Paral.lel then Funicular de Montjuïc/bus 50. **Open** *June-Sept* 7am-midnight Mon-Fri; 7am-9pm Sat; 7.30am-8pm Sun. *Oct-May* 7am-midnight Mon-Fri; 7am-9pm Sat; 7.30am-4pm Sun. **Admission** €8; €4 under-15s. *Outdoor pool only* €4; €3 under-15s. Free under-6s. **Credit** MC, V. **Map** p341 A6.

The 50m (164ft) indoor pool here was the main venue for the Olympics; there is also a 50m outdoor pool, a climbing wall and a gym. During the annual Grec festival the centre offers special late-night sessions with swimming and film projections. There are also regular sessions for nudists (9-11pm Saturday all year, 4.15-6pm Sun Oct-May).

Poliesportiu Marítim

Passeig Marítim 33 (93 224 04 40/www.claror.org/ maritim). Metro Ciutadella-Vila Olímpica. **Open** 7am-midnight Mon-Fri; 8am-9pm Sat; 8am-5pm Sun. **Admission** (non members) €12.50 Mon-Fri; €15 Sat, Sun; 5-visit pass €52.50; 10-visit pass €94. **Credit** MC, V. **Map** p343 E7.

This luxurious spa centre specialises in the understandably popular treatment known to aficionados as thalassotherapy – hydrotherapy using seawater. There are eight saltwater pools of differing temperatures, including a huge jacuzzi with waterfalls to massage your shoulders. There is also a chilled plungepool, a sauna and a steam room. Other services include a freshwater pool, a gym and bike hire. The centre gives access to Barceloneta beach, so in the summer you can top and tail your day's sunbathing here, and leave your belongings in a locker.

Tennis

Barcelona Tenís Olímpic

Passeig de la Vall d'Hebron 178, Vall d'Hebron (93 427 65 00/www.fctennis.org). Metro Montbau. **Open** *Dec-Apr* 7.45am-11.45pm Mon-Fri; 7.45am-7pm Sat, Sun. *May-Nov* 9.45am-9pm Sat, Sun. **Rates** (non-members) courts €15.20 per hr; floodlights €4.40. **No credit cards**.

These tennis courts, which were originally built for the Olympics, are a little way from the city centre, but there's a good metro connection, and they are worth the trip. There are 24 tennis courts (mostly clay), as well as paddle courts and racquet hire.

Centre de Tennis Montjuïc

C/Foixarda, Montjuïc (93 325 13 48). Bus 50. **Open** 8am-11pm Mon-Fri; 8am-10pm Sat, Sun. **Rates** €126 per term (3mths). Non-members €9.65 per hr; €3.65 floodlights. **No credit cards**.

There are good rates for non-members at this pleasant club above the Poble Espanyol, with a wonderful view of Barcelona to put you off your returns. There are seven clay courts and you can hire racquets (€3).

Trips Out of Town

Features

Getting Started

There's more to life than Gaudí.

Occupying the north-east corner of Spain, bordered by the Pyrenees, the Med and the Aragonese plains, Catalonia's landscapes are nothing if not diverse. Its coastline is well known: the brash and blighted Costa Brava is much maligned, despite its hidden coves and rugged beauty, and the unassuming Costa Daurada, presided over by the historic hub of Tarragona, rings many bells with package tourists who remember the 1970s. Fewer people know about the small sierras running parallel to the Mediterranean coastline, or the wetlands to the south; the vast and varied nature reserves, or the villages huddled around Romanesque churches and monasteries.

The Generalitat (Catalan Government) has set about changing all that, promoting 'rural tourism' and providing all kinds of previously inaccessible information. Similar to the French *gîtes* system is the network of *casa de pagès* – country houses or old farmhouses (*masies*) where you can rent a room or a whole house. For details see the Generalitat's widely available guide *Residències – casa de pagès* (€5.30). For information on roads and public transport within Catalonia, see the Generalitat's **www.mobilitat.org**. The **Palau Robert** tourist centre (*see p319*) deals specifically with Catalonia and should be your first port of call.

On foot

Catalonia's hills and low mountain ranges make it hugely popular for walking. In many places this is made easier by GR (*gran recorregut*) long-distance footpaths, indicated with red and white signs. Good places for walking within easy reach of the city include the **Parc de Collserola** (*see p129*), **Montserrat** (*see p280*) and **La Garrotxa** (*see p300*). Another excellent Generalitat website, **www.gencat.net** (click on 'information centre' and 'routes'), has particularly good information on walks. For organised walks with an English speaker, try **Spain Step by Step** (93 302 76 29). For detailed walking maps, try Llibreria Quera or Altaïr (for both, *see p189*).

By bus

The **Estació d'Autobusos Barcelona-Nord**, C/Alí Bei 80 (map p343 E5) is the principal bus station for coach services around Catalonia. General information and timetables for all the different private companies are on **902 26 06 06**. The **Costa Brava** is better served by buses, however, than trains (with the **Sarfa** company), as is the high **Pyrenees** (with **Alsina-Graëlls**), though the latter region is beyond the scope of this guide.

By road

Roads beginning C1 run north–south; C2 run east–west; C3 run parallel to the coast. Driving in or out of Barcelona, you will come across either the **Ronda de Dalt**, running along the edge of Tibidabo, and the **Ronda Litoral** along the coast, meeting north and south of the city. They intersect with several motorways (*autopistes*): the C31 (heading up the coast from Mataró); the C33/A7 (to Girona and France) and C58 (Sabadell, Manresa), which both run into Avda Meridiana; the A2 (Lleida, Madrid), a continuation of Avda Diagonal which connects with the A7 south (Tarragona, Valencia); and the C32 to Sitges, reached from the Gran Via.

All are toll roads, but where possible, we've given toll-free alternatives in the following pages. Avoid the automatic ticket dispensers if riding a motorbike – in the 'Manual' lanes you will pay considerably less. The **Túnel de Vallvidrera**, the continuation of Via Augusta that leads out of Barcelona under Collserola to Sant Cugat and Terrassa, also has a high toll, as does the **Túnel de Cadí**, running through the mountains just south of Puigcerdà. For more information on tolls, call 902 20 03 20 or see www.autopistas.com.

By train

All **RENFE** (902 24 02 02/www.renfe.es) trains stop at **Barcelona-Sants** station, and some at **Passeig de Gràcia** (Girona, Figueres, the south coast), **Estació de França** (the south coast) or **Plaça Catalunya** (Montseny, Vic, Puigcerdà). RENFE's local and suburban trains (*rodalies/cercanías*) are now integrated into the metro and bus fares system (*see map p346*). Tickets for these are sold at separate windows. The Catalan Government Railways (**FGC**) also serve destinations from **Plaça d'Espanya** (including Montserrat) and **Plaça Catalunya** (Tibidabo, Collserola, Sant Cugat and Terrassa). FGC information is on 93 205 15 15/www.fgc.net.

Around Barcelona

Party like a devil in festive Sitges and atone like a martyr at regal Montserrat; heaven and the beaches are all within reach.

Caldetes. *See p279.*

South along the coast

Heading south out of Barcelona along the scenic C32, the first town of any interest is **Castelldefels**, just 20 kilometres (12 miles) away, and known for its wide, sandy beaches and cheap seafood restaurants. Castelldefels has a large recreational port, where you can rent sea kayaks and all classes of catamaran from the **Catamaran Center** (Port Ginesta, local 324, 93 665 22 11, www.catamaran-center.com).

More of the same, in a pretty horseshoe-shaped bay fringed with bright beach huts, lies in **Garraf**, a few miles along. The Gaudí-designed **Celler de Garraf**, a wonderful Modernista building, now home to an upmarket restaurant, is on the edge of town. Behind the town, the nature reserve of **Parc del Garraf** stretches inland, offering an endless variety of trails to hike or bike (you'll find that trail maps are available at tourist offices).

Most visitors, though, will head straight to **Sitges**, Catalonia's party town without equal in summer, and a quiet, picturesque getaway in winter. Known predominantly as a gay resort, with a carnival to wake the gods, Sitges has long been a magnet for artists, writers and plain old beach bums. The town took its first steps toward becoming an upscale tourist resort when those who made fortunes in trade with Cuba began building grand summer homes along its coast in the 18th century. Nearly 100 of these mansions are still standing and can be visited on guided tours (call **Agis Sitges**, Plaça Sota Ribes, mobile 619 793 199, for tour times and prices). Though it tends to get stiflingly crowded during the heat of summer, when the

Trips Out of Town

otherwise picturesque beaches are dirty and cramped, Sitges has a charm unmatched along the Costa de Garraf.

The centre of Sitges' famed nightlife is C/Primer de Maig, a short strip lined with bars and clubs that the locals affectionately refer to as the 'Carrer del Pecat' or 'Sin Street.' A long seaside promenade, the **Passeig de la Ribera**, passes numerous seafood restaurants and outdoor cafés and is crowned by 'La Punta', the town's pretty, 17th-century church, **Sant Bartomeu i Santa Tecla**, perched on a bluff. Near the church is the **Museu Cau Ferrat** (C/Fonollar s/n, 93 894 03 64, admission €3, closed Mon). The museum, which boasts works by El Greco, Picasso, Ramon Casas and others, was once Santiago Rúsiñol's home. During Rusiñol's life it was a meeting place for artists such as Picasso and Joan Miró. Across the street is the **Palau Maricel** (C/Fonollar, 93 894 03 64, admission €6, concerts July-Sept Tue-Thur 8pm), a hospital converted into a spectacular Modernista palace, with a collection of elaborate marble sculptures, ceramics and medieval and baroque art. During the day the Palau is often closed, but the doors open for concerts on summer evenings. Also worth a visit is the **Museu Romàntic** in the Casa Llopis (C/Sant Gaudenci 1, 93 894 29 69, admission €3, closed Mon) which portrays the lifestyle of an upper-class Sitges family through displays of furniture, clocks and antique dolls.

Many of Sitges' water activities centre around the Port Esportiu Aiguadolç. The **Centro Náutico Aiguadolç-Vela** (93 811 31 05, www.advela.net) rents sailboats and organises sailing excursions; a private one-hour lesson costs €40 (Mar-Nov only). The **Yahoo Motor Center** rents jet skis with guides (93 811 30 61, €40 for 15-min ride).

Cultural festivals and special events seem non-stop in Sitges. These include the anything-goes carnival, Sitges' loud and colourful *festa major* at the end of August, and the Sitges International Film Festival in October (*see p230*).

Where to eat

In Sitges, the **Hotel La Santa Maria** (Passeig de la Ribera 52, 93 894 09 99, rates €90.50-€109, mains €10, closed Christmas-mid Feb) is an elegant popular hotel, with a restaurant serving good seafood. **El Greco** (Passeig de la Ribera 70, closed Mon & Tue, mains €25) is one of the best seafood restaurants. For something less formal and more wide-ranging, try **Tribeca** (C/Nou 12, 93 894 56 58, closed Tue, closed Oct-June, mains €10), with dishes ranging from moussaka to sushi. For Catalan classics such as rabbit with snails and *xató* salad with cod and *romesco* sauce, head to **La Masia** (Passeig de Vilanova 164, 93 894 10 76, mains €14). Intimate, artistic and innovating, **Al Fresco** (C/Pau Barrabeig 4, 93 894 06 00, closed Mon, mains €16) is worth splashing out for.

In Castelldefels, there are several cheap seafront restaurants to choose from, or you could head to the more upmarket **Nàutic** (Passeig Marítim 374, 93 665 01 74, mains €28). In Vilanova i la Geltrú, **Peixerot** (Passeig Marítim 56, 93 815 06 25, closed Sun dinner Sept-June, mains €25) gets the pick of the day's fish, while there's excellent grilled meat at **Can Pagès** (C/Sant Pere 24, 93 894 11 95, closed Mon-Fri in Nov, closed Mon in Oct, closed Dec-Mar, set menu €30).

Tourist information

Oficina de Turisme de Castelldefels

C/Pintor Serrasanta 4 (93 635 27 27). **Open** *June-Sept* 10am-9pm daily. *Sept-mid June* 4-8pm Mon; 10am-2pm, 4-8pm Tue-Fri; 10am-2pm Sat.

Oficina de Turisme de Sitges

C/Sinia Morera 1 (93 894 42 51/www.sitges.org). **Open** *July-Sept* 9am-9pm daily. *Oct-June* 9am-2pm, 4-6.30pm Mon-Fri.

Getting there

By bus

Mon-Bus runs a hourly night service to Plaça Catalunya from Sitges between 12.12am and 3.12am.

By car

C32 toll road to Castelldefels, Garraf and Sitges (41km/25 miles), or C31 via a slow, winding drive around the Garraf mountains.

By train

Trains leave every 20mins from Passeig de Gràcia for Platja de Castelldefels (20min journey) and Sitges (30mins); not all stop at Castelldefels and Garraf. The last train back leaves Sitges at 10.26pm.

North along the coast

For a day on the beach away from the worst of the crowds, the strip of towns including **El Masnou**, **Caldetes** (also known as Caldes d'Estrac), **Sant Pol de Mar** and **Calella** is an pleasant train ride away.

El Masnou's long beaches are an easy 15-minute train journey from Barcelona, but as you'll find along much of the Costa Maresme, train tracks run right along the beach, somewhat spoiling the otherwise tranquil air. In Caldetes, the slightly incongruous Modernista houses are the legacy of wealthy summer visitors who flocked to the hot springs here at the turn of the 20th century. Sant Pol, where you'll find some of the prettiest beaches in the area, is a mostly unspoilt, though rather gentrified, fishing village. Calella, at the northern end of the Costa Maresme, is known for its **Parc Dalmau**, a large and lush garden in the town centre, and for its many examples of Gothic architecture.

Where to eat

In Caldes d'Estrac, the **Fonda Manau Can Raimón** is a small *pensión* that serves great food (C/Sant Josep 11 93 791 0459, mains €12, closed Tue Oct-May). Another good mid-price restaurant is **Can Suñe** (C/Callao 4, 93 791 00 51, closed Mon, closed Mon-Wed Oct-Jun, mains €18). In Sant Pol, **La Casa** (C/Riera 13, 93 760 23 73, closed Mon-Thur, mains €7) is a colourful, stylish place,or, for something more upmarket, head to the wonderful, Michelin-starred **Sant Pau** (C/Nou 10, 93 760 06 62, closed all Mon, Thur lunch and Sun dinner, closed 2 weeks May and Nov, mains €33).

Getting there

By car

NII to El Masnou (10km/6 miles), Caldes d'Estrac (36km/22 miles), Canet de Mar (42km/26 miles), Sant Pol (48km/30 miles) and Calella (52km/32 miles).

By train

RENFE trains leave every 30mins from Sants or Plaça Catalunya for El Masnou, Caldes d'Estrac, Canet, Sant Pol and Calella. Journey approx 1hr.

Colònia Güell & Montserrat

Just west of Barcelona next to Santa Coloma de Cervelló, the **Colònia Güell** (93 630 58 07, open daily, admission €4, guided tours €5-€8) was another of Eusebi Güell's ideas for Gaudí to build a Utopian garden city for the workers, this time built around a textile factory. Like the Park Güell, it was never finished, but is still worth a visit for the extraordinary crypt.

Further inland, the Benedictine monastery of **Montserrat** sits atop spectacular mountains surrounded by hermitages and tiny chapels, in a suitably dramatic setting for the spiritual heart of Catalonia. A top tourist attraction, and unbearably crowded in summer, the monastery is accessible by a steep and crowded road, mountain cable car or a new rack railway, all with breathtaking views.

In the Middle Ages, this important place of pilgrimage grew rich and powerful, while its remote position helped to ensure its political independence. During the Franco era, it became a bastion of non-violent Catalan nationalism. Today, the monastery itself is not particularly interesting, while the souvenir shop is unwittingly entertaining for its vast size and sheer tastelessness. The monastery's prize possession is La Moreneta, or the 'Black Virgin', a small Romanesque figure that was discovered in a nearby mountain cave in the 12th century. Queues of people wait to touch the statue of the virgin (8.30-10.30am, noon-6.30pm) inside the 16th-century **basilica** (7.30am-7.30pm), and pray. The basilica is most crowded at 1pm, when the monastery's celebrated boys' choir sings mass. The **museum** (10am-6pm, admission €5.50) houses a collection of liturgical gold and silverware, archaeological finds, gifts for the virgin, and works by Dalí, Monet, Picasso, Caravaggio and El Greco.

The views and walks around the monastery are spectacular. As well as **Santa Cova**, the cave where the virgin was discovered (a 20-minute walk or a €6.10 funicular ride), there are 13 hermitages, the most accessible of them being **Sant Joan**, reached by funicular from the monastery or a 20-minute walk with superb views. The tourist office has details of longer walks including a circuit of the hermitages and the (relatively easy) trek to the peak of **Sant Jeroni**, at 1,235 metres (4,053 feet).

There are several overpriced restaurants on Montserrat, but picnics are the most popular option: the mountain provides an abundance of quiet, scenic lunching spots.

Tourist information

Oficina de Turisme de Montserrat

Plaça de la Creu, Montserrat (93 877 77 77/ www.abadiamontserrat.net). **Open** *Apr-July* 9am-7pm daily. *July-Aug* 7.30am-9.30pm daily. *Sept-Mar* 9am-6pm daily.

Getting there

By bus

Montserrat: A Julià-Via (93 490 40 00) bus leaves at 9.15am from Sants bus station and returns at 6pm daily; journey time is approx 80mins.

By car

Colònia Güell: A2 to Sant Boi exit, then turn towards Sant Vicenç dels Horts (3 miles/5km).
Montserrat: Take the NII to exit km 59, or the A2 to the Martorell exit, then the C55 towards Monistrol (60km/37 miles).

By train

Colònia Güell: FGC trains go from Plaça Espanya, Journey takes 10-25mins.
Montserrat: FGC trains from Plaça Espanya hourly from 8.36am to the Aeri de Montserrat (approx 1hr) for the cable car (every 15mins); or Monistrol de Montserrat for the rack train (every hour) up to the monastery. Last cable car and rack train around 6pm.

Tarragona & the Costa Daurada

What the Romans have done for us.

Tarragona

Known in Roman times as Tarraco, this sleepy little Catalan city was unimaginably powerful as capital of over half the Iberian peninsula. Its hilltop location, port and grand buildings ensured its popularity and prosperity for hundreds of years, before it ceded much of its importance to Barcelona in the 14th century.

For a long time, the city was contained within its Roman walls. You can walk along the remains of these walls for a sense of past glories and wonderful views. The path is known as the **Passeig Arqueològic** (Avda Catalunya, 977 24 57 96, admission €1.94), and the entrance is at **Portal del Roser**, one of the remaining three towers, two of which were rebuilt in medieval times. Inside the walls, the superbly preserved Roman remains include the ancient **Pretori**, or praetorium (977 24 19 52), which has been used as a palace and government office and is rumoured to have been the birthplace of Pontius Pilate. From here you can walk to the ruins of the **Circ Romans**, the first-century Roman circus. Excavations suggest that chariot races were once held here. The **Museu Nacional Arqueològic**, home to an important collection of Roman artefacts and some stunning mosaics, is nearby.

To see all parts of the **Catedral de Santa Maria**, not to mention some wonderful religious art and archaelogical finds, you will need a ticket for the **Museu Diocesà** (Pla de la Seu, 977 23 86 85, closed Sun, admission €2.40).The majestic cathedral was built on the site of a Roman temple to Jupiter, and is Catalonia's largest. The cloister, built in the 12th and 13th centuries, is glorious, and the carvings alone are worth the trip.

Leading from the old town towards the sea, the **Passeig de las Palmeres** runs to the '**Balcó del Mediterrani**' overlooking the Roman **amphitheatre** (Parc del Miracle, 977 24 25 79). The same street also takes you to the bustling pedestrian **Rambla Nova**, from where you can follow C/Canyelles to the **Fòrum** (C/Lleida, 977 24 25 01) to visit the remains of the juridical basilica and Roman houses.

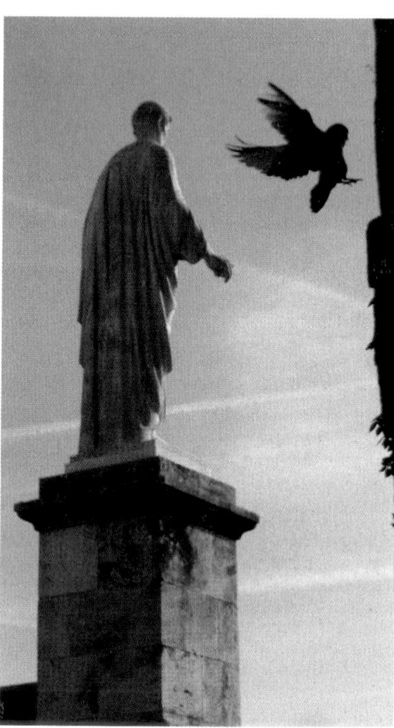

Tickets for the Museu Arqueològic also allow entry to the **Museu i Necròpolis Paleocristians** (Avda Ramón y Cajal 80, 977 21 11 75, closed Mon), on the site of an early Christian cemetery. Thousands of graves have been uncovered and the museum displays some interesting finds, including beautifully decorated sarcophagi. A couple of miles north of the city (but an unpleasant walk along a busy main road – take bus No.5 from the top of the Rambla Nova instead) is the spectacular **Pont del Diable** (Devil's Bridge), a Roman aqueduct built in the first century.

Entry to the Passeig Arqueològic, the praetorium and circus, the amphiteatre and the Fòrum costs €1.94 (60¢ concessions, free under-

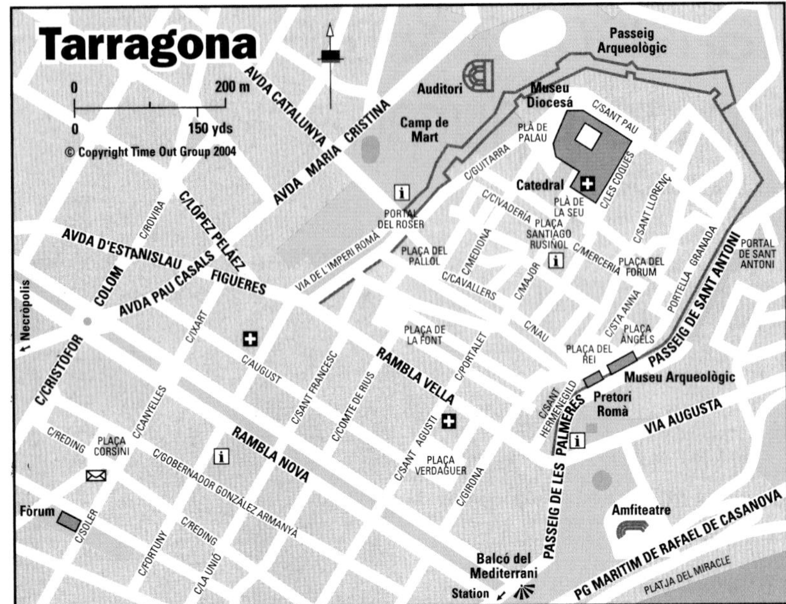

16s) each one, although entry is free to holders of **Port Aventura** tickets (*see p284*). Opening hours are the same for all: Easter-mid Oct 9am-9pm Tue-Sat; 9am-7pm Sun; mid Oct-Easter 9am-5pm Tue-Sat; 9am-3pm Sun.

Museu Nacional Arqueològic de Tarragona

Placa del Rei 5 (977 23 62 09/www.mnat.es). **Open** *June-Sept* 10am-8pm Tue-Sat; 10am-2pm Sun. *Oct-May* 10am-1.30pm, 4-7pm Tue-Sat; 10am-2pm Sun. **Admission** (incl entrance to Museu i Necròpolis Paleocristians) €2.40; €1.20 concessions; free under-18s, over-65s. **No credit cards**.

Where to eat

The fishing neighbourhood of El Serrallo is home to the best seafood restaurants: try the paella at **Cal Martí** (C/Sant Pere 12, 977 21 23 84, closed dinner Tue, closed Sept-June, mains €15). **La Puda**, opposite the site of the fish auctions, is another place to find exceptionally fresh fish (Moll Pescadors 25, 977 21 15 11, mains €20). Another place for good seafood, a little way out of the centre to the west, is **Sol-Ric** (Via Augusta 227, 977 23 20 32, closed dinner Mon, all Sun, mains €18). Those on a budget can fall back on the **Bufet el Tiberi** (C/Martí d'Ardenya 5, 977 23 54 03, closed Mon and dinner Sun, buffet €12.80), while just below the cathedral is **La Cuca Fera** (Plaça Santiago Rusiñol 5, 977 24 20 07, closed Mon, dinner Sun and Nov, set lunch €9.70), with especially good fish *suquet*. In the old town, **Palau del Baró** serves huge portions of Catalan classics in the colourful rooms of a former baronial mansion (C/Santa Anna 3, 977 24 14 64, closed Oct-May and dinner Sun, mains €13.50).

Where to stay

The smartest of the hotels is the towering **Imperial Tarraco** (Passeig de les Palmeres, 977 23 30 40, rates €79-€144). The **Lauria** (Rambla Nova 20, 977 23 67 12, rates €57.80-€68.50) is also good value, has a pool and gives hefty discounts at weekends out of season. Other mid-range hotels include the **Astari** (Via Augusta 95, 977 23 69 00, rates €63-€87), which has a pool, and the central **Hotel Urbis** (C/Reding 20 bis, 977 24 01 16, rates €62-€91.80). You'll find cheaper digs at the **Pensión Forum** (Plaça de la Font 37, 977 23 17 18, rates €32-€38) and the nearby **Pensión La Noria** (Plaça de la Font 53, 977 23 87 17, rates €31-€41), with little to choose between them.

Tourist information

Oficina de Turisme de Tarragona

C/Fortuny 4 (977 23 34 15). **Open** 9am-2pm, 4-6.30pm Mon-Fri; 9am-2pm Sat.

Getting there

By car

Take the A2, then A7 via Vilafranca (Tarragona 98km/60 miles); or the toll-free N340 (Molins de Rei exit from A2).

By train

RENFE from Sants or Passeig de Gràcia. Trains hourly (journey time 1hr 6mins).

The Wine Country

Current interest in Catalonia's many wine *denominaciones de origen* is bringing new wealth to struggling regions all over the country, but nowhere more so than in the **Penedès**. The town at the centre of the area, **Vilafranca**, is worth a visit, with some handsome medieval buildings and the elegant 14th-century **Basílica de Santa Maria**. Vilafranca's wine museum, the **Museu del Vi** (Plaça Jaume I 1-3, 93 890 05 82, closed Mon, admission €3) has old wooden presses and wine jugs, some dating back to the fourth century.

While Vilafranca itself is very easy to navigate on foot, a car is almost essential to explore the surrounding wine region. Penedès' largest winemaker, **Torres**, runs tours at its cellars outside town (not to be confused with its offices opposite the train station). Miguel Torres has long been one of Spain's most influential winemakers, responsible for introducing modern winemaking practices to the region. Torres' free tours include the obligatory visits to the cellars, bottling area and fermentation tanks, along with a train ride through a virtual reality tunnel that shows how the weather and soil create aromas in wine. **Jean León**, another pioneering brand, and now also owned by Torres, recently inaugurated its visitors' centre near Torrelavit, in a modern building with breathtaking views of a valley lined with vineyards.

Some six miles (nine kilometres) away is **Sant Sadurní d'Anoia**, the capital of Penedès' cava industry and Vilafranca's major rival. More than 90 per cent of Spain's cava, a sparkling wine traditionally made with local *parellada, macabeo* and *xarel.lo* grapes, is made in this tiny town. **Codorníu**, one of the largest producers, offers a wonderful tour of its Modernista headquarters, designed at the end of the 19th century by Puig i Cadafalch. A train takes visitors through part of the 16 miles (26 kilometres) of underground cellars. **Freixenet**, another mega-producer, is nearby.

The **Priorat** area south of here has gained fame in the past decade for making full-bodied (and pricey) red wines. Monks were producing wine in the Priorat as long ago as the 11th century, but the area had been all but abandoned when young winemaker **Alvaro Palacios** set up a tiny vineyard here in the late 1980s. He battled against steep hills and a sceptical wine industry, but within a few years he was winning international acclaim. Now the region is one of Spain's most popular among wine buyers.

The small **Alella** district, just east of Barcelona, is best known for whites. More important is **Terra Alta**, near the Priorat in Tarragona, with Gandesa as its capital. It is renowned for its heavy reds. The newly created *denominación de origen* **Montsant**, with Falset as its capital, is growing in popularity. Look out for the splendidly weird **Cooperativa Agrícola** in Gandesa, and the **Bodega Cooperativa** in Falset, designed by a disciple of Gaudí, César Martinell. The **Celler Capçanes**, also in Montsant, makes one of the world's top kosher wines.

Where to stay & eat

To try excellent and unusual local wines in Vilafranca, head to the wine bar and store **Inzolia** (C/Palma 21, 93 818 19 38). **El Purgatori** (Plaça Campanar, 93 892 12 63, open dinner only, closed Wed, mains €10) serves *pa amb tomàquet* with charcuterie and cheese in a tiny, secluded square. **Taverna Ongi Etorriak** (C/Sant Bernat 4, 93 890 43 54, closed Mon, tapas average €1.25) is a Basque bar with a wide variety of *pintxos* and a great wine list, many available by the glass. Try **La Fabrica** (C/Hermenegild Clascar 4, 93 817 15 38, closed Sun, mains €9) for finer dining, with an emphasis on Asian flavours. A good traditional restaurant in the region is **Sol i Vi**, a restaurant with a nice hotel between Vilafranca and Sant Sadurní (93 899 32 04, Ctra Sant Sadurní a Vilafranca, closed 2wks Jan, mains €15, rates incl breakfast €75). Another lodging option is the three-star **Hotel Pere III** (93 890 31 00, Plaça del Penedès 2, rates €58-€64), in the centre of Vilafranca. In Torrelavit is **Masia Can Cardús** (93 899 50 18, rates €36.66), a working farm and vineyard with rooms to rent.

Tourist information

Falset

C/Sant Marcel 2 (977 83 10 23). **Open** 9am-2pm, 4-7pm Mon-Fri; 10am-2pm Sat; 11am-2pm Sun.

Sant Sadurní d'Anoia

C/Hospital 26 (93 891 31 88). **Open** *Sept-July* 10am-2pm, 4.30-6.30pm Tue-Fri; 10am-2pm Sat, Sun. *Aug* 10am-2pm Tue-Sun.

Don't miss Vineyards

Caves Codorníu

Avda Codorníu, Sant Sadurní d'Anoia (93 818 32 32/www.grupocodorniu.com). **Open** 9am-5pm Mon-Fri; 9am-1pm Sat, Sun. **Admission** free Mon-Fri; 2 (incl free champagne glass) Sat, Sun.
Tour includes a short film, a mini-train ride through the cellars and a tasting.

Caves Freixenet

C/Joan Sala 2, Sant Sadurní d'Anoia (93 891 70 00/www.freixenet.es). **Tours** 11am, noon, 1pm, 4pm, 5pm Mon-Thur; 10am, 11am, noon Fri. **Admission** free.
The cellars are directly opposite the station.

Celler de Can Suriol del Castell

Castell Grabuac, Ctra de Vilafranca a Font Rubí (BV2127) km 6, Font Rubí (93 897 84 26/www.suriol.com). **Open** by appointment.
A limited quantity of very fine cava is made at this vineyard, centred on a historic *masia.*

Jean León

Pago Jean León, Torrelavit (93 899 55 12/ www.jeanleon.com). **Open** 9.30am-5pm Mon-Sat; 9.30am-1pm Sun. **Admission** 3.
Price includes a video, a tour through the museum and winery and a tasting.

Scala Dei

Rambla de la Cartoixa, Scala Dei (977 82 70 27). **Open** by appointment. **Admission** free.
Housed in a 12th-century monastery. Great reds, in particular the Cartoixa Scala Dei.

Torres

Finca El Maset, Pacs del Penedès (93 817 74 87/www.torres.es). **Open** 9am-5pm Mon-Fri; 9am-6pm Sat; 9am-1pm Sun. **Tours** hourly. **Admission** free.
Tour includes a video, train-ride through the vineyards, look at the cellars and a tasting.

Vilafranca del Penedès

C/Cort 14 (93 892 03 58). **Open** 4-7pm Mon; 9am-1pm, 4-7pm Tue-Sat.

Getting there

Alella

By bus Barcelona Bus (93 232 04 59) from Plaça Urquinaona. **By car** NII north to Montgat, then left turn to Alella (15km/9 miles).

Alt Penedès

By car A2, then A7 to Sant Sadurní (44km/27 miles) and Vilafranca (55km/34 miles), or A2, then toll-free N340 from Molins de Rei, which is much slower. **By train** RENFE from Sants or Plaça Catalunya; trains leave hourly 6am-10pm (journey time 45mins), then taxi for Torres, Jean León and Codorníu.

Falset, Scala Dei & Gandesa

By car A2, then A7 to Reus, and right on to N420 for Falset (143km/89 miles) and Gandesa (181km/112 miles). For Scala Dei take T710 from Falset, then turn right at La Vilella Baixa. **By train** RENFE from Sants or Passeig de Gràcia to Marçà-Falset. Six trains daily (journey time 2hrs). For Gandesa continue to Mora d'Ebre (20mins) and catch a local bus.

Costa Daurada

Beyond Sitges and Vilanova, the coastline offers little relief from the towering concrete rows of holiday apartments erected in a 1970s tourist boom. **Calafell** is worth half a day's mooch, with an Iberian citadel, a lively seafront and decent quiet beaches not far away at **Sant Salvador**. Really, though, there's not much of interest until **Altafulla**, a few minutes north of Tarragona on the train.

Altafulla is split into two parts; Altafulla Playa hugs the sea with a modern but elegant esplanade of low-rise houses and the stately **Tamarit castle** overlooking a sandy bay. The castle is under private ownership, but to get a better look, walk around to the far side where there is a lovely hidden sandy cove. Altafulla Pueblo, meanwhile, a jumble of narrow cobbled streets with a medieval feel, is a ten-minute walk inland. Local folklore has it that the old town has been home to a coven of witches for centuries. Further south along the coast towards the rather unlovely resort of **Salou** is the **Port Aventura** theme park.

Universal Mediterránea/ Port Aventura

977 77 90 90/www.portaventura.es. By car A2, then A7 or N340 (108km/67 miles)/by train fromPasseig de Gràcia (1hr 15mins). **Open** *Mid Mar-mid June, mid Sept-Oct* 10am-7pm daily. *Mid June-mid Sept* 10am-midnight daily. *Nov, Dec* 10am-6pm Fri; 10am-7pm Sat, Sun. **Admission** *Port Aventura* €33-€35; €26.50-€28 concessions; €18.50-€23 night ticket. Free

under-4s. *Costa Caribe* (mid June-mid Sept) €9-€18; €7.50-€14.50 concessions. *3 days combined ticket* €61; €49 concessions. **Credit** AmEx, DC, MC, V.
Port Aventura theme park is the main attraction of this beach resort, but there are also two hotels and the tropically landscaped Costa Caribe water park. Port Aventura has 90 rides spread over five internationally themed areas: Mexico, the Far West, China, Polynesia and the Mediterranean, while Popeye and the Pink Panther roam the time space continuum to hug your kids. The truly stomach-curdling Dragon Khan rollercoaster is one of the highlights, while for the little ones there is the usual slew of carousels and spinning teacups. There are also 100 daily live shows and a spectacular lakeside Fiesta Aventura with lights, music and fireworks .

Where to stay & eat

In Calafell the **Hotel Ra** is a new spa and thalassotherapy centre that has opened on the site of an old sanatorium (Avda Sanatori 1, 977 69 42 00, www.hotelra.com, rates incl breakfast €140-€240). In the old centre of the town is an eccentric, colourful bar-restaurant, **Angelitos Negros**, with a globe-trotting range of dishes and great salads (C/Vilamar 33, 977 693 402, mains €9.50, closed Mon-Wed). In Altafulla the **Hotel San Martín** has a pool, and is the only hotel in town to be open year-round (C/Mar 7, 977 65 03 07, www.hotelsanmartin, rates €51-€76). The **Faristol**, up in the old town, is a hotel, bar and restaurant in an 18th-century house run by an Anglo-Catalan couple, with a pleasant outdoor terrace (C/Sant Martí 5, 977 65 00 77, closed Mon-Thur and Oct-May, rates incl breakfast €60. The restaurant is particularly good (mains €11). To rent rooms in the old town, ask at **El Corral** bar (977 65 04 86) or the Faristol. For seafood tapas and grilled meats right on the seafront, try **Botigues de Mar** (C/Botigues de Mar 81, 977 652 560, mains €10, closed Mon-Thur from Sept-May). Another good, cheap eating option is **La Chunga** (C/Mar 13, 977 652 281, mains €8).

Tourist information

Oficina de Turisme de Altafulla

Plaça dels Vents (977 65 07 52). **Open** *Mid June-mid Sept* 11am-1pm Mon, Tue, Thur-Sun.

Getting there

By car

Take the A2, then A7 via Vilafranca; or the toll-free N340 (Molins de Rei exit from A2).

By train

RENFE from Sants or Passeig de Gràcia to Altafulla (1hr 15mins). Trains run hourly approx 6am-9.20pm.

The Cistercian Route

The three architectural gems of the area inland from Tarragona are the Cistercian monasteries: **Poblet**, **Santes Creus** and **Vallbona de les Monges**. A signposted path, the GR175, runs between them, and the trail has become known as **La Ruta del Cister** (the Cistercian Route). Not for the unfit, the distances covered add up to over 62 miles (100 kilometres), although there are plenty of places to stay en route. All three monasteries are also easily accessible by car from **Montblanc**, 70 miles (112 kilometres) due west of Barcelona, and a beautiful town in its own right. In the Middle Ages, Montblanc was one of Catalonia's most powerful centres, with an important Jewish community, a past that is reflected in its **C/Jueus** (Jews' Street), the magnificent 13th-century town walls (two-thirds of which are still intact), its many churches, the **Palau Reial** (royal palace) and the **Palau del Castlà** (chamberlain's palace).

Poblet, a few kilometres west of Montblanc, was founded in 1151 to be a royal residence as well as a monastery. The remarkable complex includes a 14th-century **Gothic royal palace**, the 15th-century **chapel of Sant Jordi** and the main **church**, housing the tombs of most of the Count-Kings of Barcelona. The monastery can be visited only on a guided tour. **Santes Creus**, founded in 1158 and perhaps still more beautiful than Poblet, grew into a small village when families moved into abandoned monks' residences in the 1800s. Fortified walls shelter the **Palau de l'Abat** (abbot's palace), a monumental fountain, a 12th-century church and a superb Gothic cloister and chapterhouse. Visits to Santes Creus include an audio-visual presentation.

Vallbona de les Monges, the third of these Cistercian houses, was, unlike the others, a convent of nuns. It was particularly favoured by Catalan-Aragonese queens, including Violant of Hungary (wife of Jaume I), who was buried here. It has a fine part-Romanesque cloister, but is less grand than the other two. Like them it still houses a religious community.

Monestir de Poblet

977 87 02 54. **Open** *Mar-Sept* 10am-12.15pm, 3-5.45pm daily. *Oct-Feb* 10am-12.15pm, 3-5.15pm daily. **Admission** €4.20; €2.40 concessions. **No credit cards**.

Monestir de Santa Maria de Vallbona

973 33 02 66. **Open** *Mar-Oct* 10.30am-1.30pm, 4.30-6.30pm Mon-Sat; noon-1.30pm, 4.30-6.30pm Sun. *Nov-Feb* 10.30am-1.30pm, 4.30-5.30pm Mon-Sat; noon-1.30pm, 4.30-5.30pm Sun. **Admission** €2.50; €2 concessions. **No credit cards**.

Trips Out of Town

Monestir de Santes Creus

977 63 83 29. **Open** *Mid Mar-mid Sept* 10am-1.30pm, 3-7pm Tue-Sun. *Mid Sept-mid Jan* 10am-1.30pm, 3-5.30pm Tue-Sun. *Mid Jan-mid Mar* 10.30am-1.30pm, 3-6pm Tue-Sun. **Admission** €3.60; €2.40 concessions. Free Tue. **No credit cards**.

Where to stay & eat

In Montblanc, you'll need to book in advance to secure a room at the popular **Fonda dels Àngels** (Plaça dels Àngels 1, 977 86 01 73, closed dinner Sun and 3wks Sept, rates €37, mains €14), which also has a great restaurant. Alternatively, the **Fonda Colom** is a friendly old inn behind the Plaça Major (C/Civaderia 5, 977 86 01 53, set lunch €14). If these are both full, try the **Hotel Ducal** (C/Francesc Macià 11, 977 86 00 25, rates €46.50-€50.29).

In L'Espluga de Francolí, on the way to Poblet, the **Hostal del Senglar** (Plaça Montserrat Canals, 977 87 01 21, rates €50-€59) is a great-value country hotel with gardens, a pool and an atmospheric if slightly overpriced restaurant (mains €12). Santes Creus is very well served for hotels and restaurants. The **Fonda La Plana del Molí** is set in extensive gardens, with a swimming pool (Avda Plana del Molí 21, 977 63 83 09, rates €51). Try the partridge broth or wild boar stew at its restaurant (closed Wed, mains €8). The **Hostal Grau** (C/Pere El Gran 3, 977 63 83 11, closed mid Oct-June, rates €38-€40) is another very reasonable option. Good Catalan food can also be had at the restaurant here (closed Mon and mid Dec-mid Jan, mains €12) or at the **Restaurant Catalunya** (C/Arbreda 2, 977 63 84 32, closed Wed, set lunch €10) further down the hill.

Tourist information

Oficina de Turisme de Montblanc

Antiga Esglesia de Sant Francesc (977 86 17 33). **Open** 10am-1.30pm, 3-6.30pm Mon-Sat; 10am-2pm Sun.

Getting there

By bus

Hispano Igualadina (93 488 15 63) runs a daily service to Montblanc from Sants station. There are more buses running from Valls and Tarragona.

By car

For **Montblanc**, take the A2, then A7, then back on the A2 to exit 9; or take the toll-free N340 to El Vendrell, then the C51 for Valls, and the N240 for Montblanc (112km/70 miles). For **Poblet**, take the N240 west from Montblanc and turn left in L'Espluga de Francolí. For **Vallbona de les Monges**, take the C14 north from Montblanc towards Tàrrega and turn left on to a signposted side road. For **Santes Creus**, turn off the C51 or A2 before Valls, following signs to Vila-rodona.

By train

RENFE trains leave from Sants or Passeig de Gràcia to Montblanc. There are 5 trains a day. Journey takes about 2hrs.

Tortosa & the Ebre Delta

About an hour further down the coast from Tarragona the railway dips inland to **Tortosa**, a little-visited town with a rich history evident in the fabric of its buildings. A magnificent Gothic **cathedral**, built on the site of a Roman temple, is surrounded by narrow medieval alleyways, and traces of the town's **Jewish** and **Arab quarters** can still be seen (and are clearly signposted). Interesting Modernista buildings around town include the colourful, Mudéjar-inspired pavilions of the former slaughterhouse (**Escorxador**), on the bank of the Ebre river.

East of here is the extraordinary **Parc Natural del Delta de l'Ebre**, an ecologically remarkable protected area.The towns of the delta are nothing special, but the immense, flat, green expanse of wetlands, channels, dunes and still productive rice fields are eerily beautiful. The town of **Deltebre** is the base for most park services. From there it's easy to make day trips to the bird sanctuaries, especially the remote headland of **Punta de la Banya**. The delta's flatness makes it an ideal place for walking or cycling (for bicycle hire, check at the tourist office in Deltebre). Small boats offer trips along the river from the north bank about eight kilometres (five miles) east of Deltebre.

It's also a hugely popular birdwatching destination, and home to nearly 300 of the 600 bird species found in Europe. The area is a vital breeding ground for birds who rest and feed in the delta during the winter migratory season. The flocks of flamingos make a particularly spectacular sight, and the wetlands are inundated with different species of herons, egrets, great crested grebes, spoonbills, marsh harriers and ducks. Even non-birdwatchers could hardly fail to be enthused by the evocatively named whiskered tern, moustached warbler, lesser short-toed lark and the red-necked nightjar.

Sadly, not all is well in the delta. The government has dreamt up a Plan Hidrológico Nacional (National Water Plan), a scheme to divert water from the northern Ebro (Ebre in Catalan) river to irrigate the south-east, creating dozens of dams, destroying entire villages in Aragón and Navarra, and sounding the death knell for the lower Ebre, and therefore the delta.

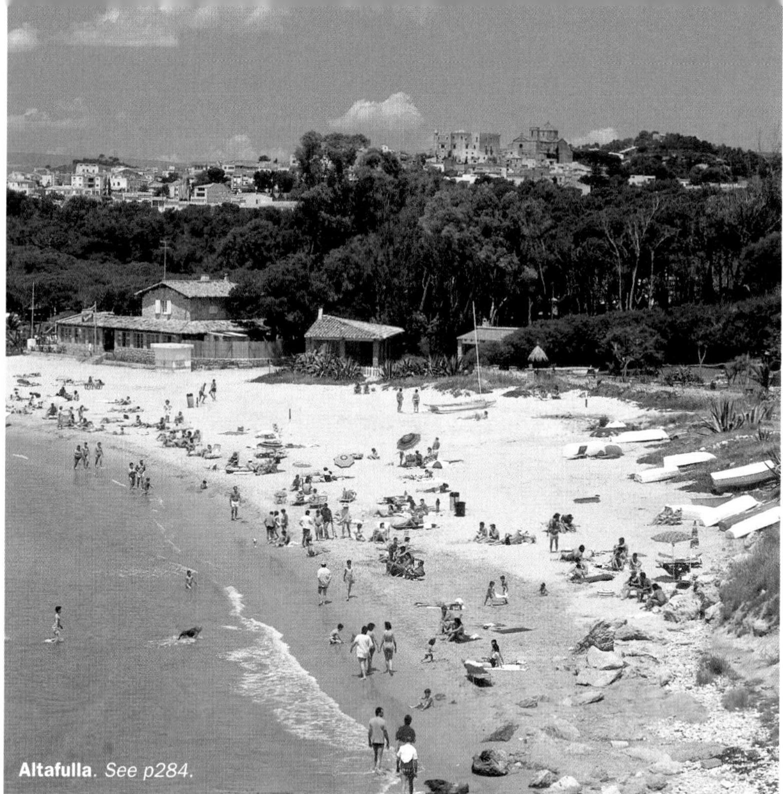

Altafulla. See p284.

Not only would the reserve be lost, but also the livelihoods of rice-growers and fishermen. Greenpeace and the Worldwide Fund for Nature have joined forces with thousands of smaller local groups and have been vociferous in their opposition; to what effect remains to be seen.

Where to stay & eat

Tortosa has a wonderful *parador*, **Castell de la Suda** (977 44 44 50, rates €90.60-€101), built on the site of a Moorish fortress with panoramic views. See www.paradors.es for occasional offers. On the eastern edge of the Ebre delta is a wide, sweeping beach, Platja dels Eucaliptus, where you'll find the **Camping Eucaliptus** (977 47 90 46, closed Oct-Apr, €3.95-€4.35 per person & per tent). In Deltebre the **Hotel Rull** is large but friendly, and organises free 'safaris' for guests on Saturdays (Avda Esportiva 155, 977 48 77 28, rates incl breafast €54.25-€87.74, mains €12). You can also stay and eat at the ecologically friendly **Delta Hotel** (Avda del Canal, Camí de la Illeta, 977 48 00 46, www.dsi.es/delta-hotel, rates €58-€79). Local specialities include dishes made with delta rice, duck, frogs' legs and the curious *chapadillo* (sun-dried eels). Try them all at **Galatxo,** at the mouth of the river (Desembocadura Riu Ebre, 977 26 75 03, mains €13).

Tourist information

Centre d'Informació Delta de l'Ebre

C/Doctor Martí Buera 22, Deltebre (977 48 96 79/www.parcsdecatalunya.com). **Open** 10am-2pm, 3-6pm Mon-Fri; 10am-1pm, 3.30-6pm Sat; 10am-1pm Sun.

Tortosa Oficina de Turisme

Parc Municipal Teodoro González (977 44 25 67). **Open** *Oct-Mar* 10am-1.30pm, 3.30-6.30pm Tue-Sat. *Apr-Sept* 10am-1.30pm, 4.30-7.30pm daily.

Getting there

By car

Take the A2, then A7 via Vilafranca; or the toll-free N340 (Molins de Rei exit from A2) to the delta, then the C42 to Tortosa.

By train & bus

RENFE from Sants or Passeig de Gràcia every 2hrs to Tortosa (2hrs) or L'Aldea (2hrs 30mins), then 3 buses daily (HIFE 977 44 03 00) to Deltebre.

Girona & the Costa Brava

Seek and ye shall find lovely coves and medieval corners amid the tourist tat.

Girona

The strength of this most Catalan of cities is legendary after it resisted 30 sieges during the last millennium. Looking at it on a map, it's easy to see why its oppressors wanted in. Neatly divided into old and new by the **River Onyar**, this is an elegant city with an intact medieval heart, which has always prospered from its strategically useful position at the gateway through the Pyrenees to France.

The Onyar, lined by buildings in red and ochre and spanned by some interesting bridges (including the **Pont de les Peixateries**, designed by Eiffel), is a good place to start a stroll round the town. A walk up the lively riverside **Rambla de la Llibertat** takes you towards the city's spiritual core and major landmark, the magnificent **cathedral**. Its 1680 baroque façade conceals a graceful Romanesque cloister and understated Gothic interior, which happens to boast the widest nave in Christendom. In the cathedral museum is the stunning 12th-century '**Tapestry of Creation**' and the **Beatus**, an illuminated 10th-century set of manuscripts.

Before their expulsion in 1492, the sizeable percentage of the city's population that was Jewish had their own district, the **Call**, whose labyrinthine streets around the C/Força are still beautifully preserved to this day. The story of this community is told in the excellent Jewish museum in the **Centre Bonastruc ça Porta** (C/Sant Lorenc, 972 21 67 61), built on the site of a 15th-century synagogue. Heading north from here, the *mudéjar* **Banys Àrabs** (C/Ferran el

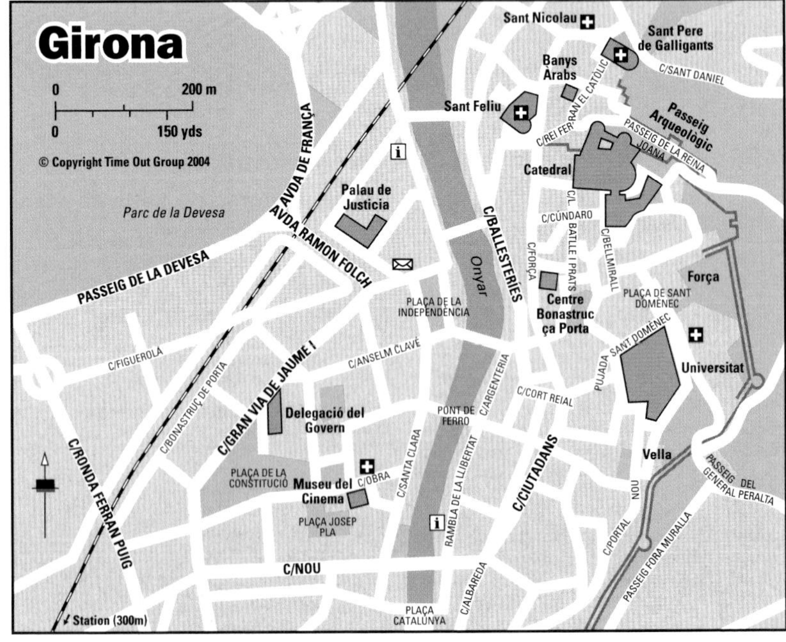

Catòlic, 972 21 32 62) is actually a Christian creation, a 12th-century bathhouse with a blend of Romanesque and Moorish architecture.

The nearby monastery of **Sant Pere de Galligants** is one of the finest of the countless examples of Romanesque architecture in Catalonia, with a beautiful 12th-century cloister, rich with intricate carvings. The monastery also houses the **Museu Arqueològic** (C/Santa Llúcia 1, 972 20 26 32), showing day-to-day objects from the Paleolithic to the Visigothic periods. Continuing from here the **Passeig Arqueològic** runs along what's left of the old city walls, intact until 1892.

Where to stay & eat

Girona offers plenty of mid-range sleeping possibilities, but not much else. **Pensión Bellmirall** (C/Bellmirall 3, 972 20 40 09, rates incl breakfast €56) is in a pretty 14th-century building with a shady breakfast courtyard. The **Hotel Peninsular** (C/Nou 3 & Avda Sant Francesc 6, 972 20 38 00, rates €56-€60) is good value. **Apartments Historic Barri Vell** (C/Bellmirall 4A, 972 22 35 83, rates €60) are fully equipped apartments, the old fourth-century stone walls are still visible downstairs. For undistinguished comfort, the modern **Hotel Carlemany** (Plaça Miquel Santaló, 972 21 12 12, rates €112.30) is top of the bill.

The locally cherished **Boira** (Plaça Independencia 7, 972 20 30 96, mains €7), in the 19th-century area over the river from the old town, has alfresco seating and offers mainly Catalan fare; try the baked duck with pears and cloves. In the same square you'll find Girona's oldest and possibly best value restaurant, **Casa Marieta** (Plaça de la Independència 5, 972 20 10 16, mains €8), while in the old Modernista flour factory is **La Farinera** (Passatge Farinera Teixidor 4, 972 22 02 20, mains €15), a good Basque restaurant with excellent tapas. La Crêperie Bretonne (C/Cort Reial 14, 972 22 35 83, mains €6) transports you to northern France with Breton crêpes, cider and towering salads. Halfway up a medieval flight of steps nearby is another francophile's delight, **Le Bistrot** (Pujada Sant Domènec 4, 972 21 88 03, mains €10), with a cheap (and good) set lunch in a gorgeous setting. For more typically Catalan dishes, and the occasional Jewish one (and even kosher wine) is **El Pou del Call** (C/Força 14, 972 22 37 74, mains €11).

Tourist information

Oficina de Turisme de Girona

Rambla de la Llibertat 1 (972 22 65 75). **Open** 8am-8pm Mon-Fri; 8am-2pm, 4-8pm Sat; 9am-2pm Sun.

Getting there

By bus

Barcelona Bus (93 232 04 59), approx 5 buses daily from Estació del Nord.

By car

A7 or toll-free NII.

By train

RENFE from Sants or Passeig de Gràcia (1hr15mins). Trains leave hourly approx 6am-9.15pm.

From Girona to the coast

The Catalans claim that after God created the world in one week, he spent the rest of the year perfecting the region known as the Empordà. The C66 takes you from Girona to the coast through the Baix (Lower) Empordà, whose strategic importance in medieval times is demonstrated by a legacy of castles and walled towns. The road splits in dignified **La Bisbal**, the administrative centre of the region, where you can buy no end of ceramic goods, and visit the **Terracotta Museum** (Sis d'Octubre de 1869 99, 972 64 02 67, open May-Sept, evenings only). Nearby **Verges** is the birthplace of protest singer Lluis Llach, and is most famous for its grotesque 'dance of death' procession on Maundy Thursday. Just up the road is the 12th-century **Castell de Púbol**, bought by Salvador Dalí to house (and eventually bury) his wife-muse Gala in her later years. Relations were strained by then; Dali had to book appointments to see her, and the tomb that he prepared for himself next to hers lies empty (he changed his mind), guarded by a stuffed giraffe. There are several spindly-legged concrete elephants in the beautiful gardens.

A few miles further east lies the walled, moated town of **Peratallada**, dominated by an 11th-century castle and famous for its good food. Nearby **Ullastret** takes you further back in time, with extensive ruins from a third-century BC Iberian settlement, explained in the small **Museu d'Arqueologia** (Puig de Sant Andreu, 972 17 90 58, closed Mon).

The friendly medieval town of **Pals**, with its imposing **Torre de les Hores**, has great views of the coast, as does **Begur**, a 14th-century town built around its castle. It acts as a gateway to the Costa Brava, and is a steep three-kilometre (two-mile) walk from the sea.

Castell de Púbol

Information: Teatre-Museu Dalí (972 67 75 00/ www.salvador-dali.org). **Open** *15 Mar-14 June, 16 Sept-1 Nov* 10.30am-5.30pm Tue-Sun. *15 June-15 Sept* 10.30am-7.30pm daily. Closed 2 Nov-14 Mar. **Admission** €5.50; €4 concessions. **No credit cards**.

Where to stay & eat

Medieval sleeping options abound, if you don't mind the jokes about ghosts. In **Peratallada**, the luxurious four-poster bed option is the 11th-century **Castell de Peratallada** (Plaça del Castell 1, 972 63 40 21, rates incl breakfast €120-€240); the **Hostal Miralluna** (Plaça de l'Oli 2, 972 63 43 04, rates €110-€120 incl breakfast) is a tranquil, 14th-century place filled with antiques. The charming **Ca l'Aliu** (C/Roca 6, 972 63 40 61, rates incl breakfast €49-€52) is probably the best value in town.

Pals has the **Barris** (C/Enginyer Algarra 51, 972 63 67 02, rates €36). In **Begur**, try the **Hotel Rosa** (C/Pi i Ralló 19, 972 62 30 15, closed Nov-Feb, rates incl breakfast €51.10-€73.30).

Locals travel from far and wide to eat in **Peratallada's** restaurants; try the famous *galtes de porc a l'empordanesa* (pigs' cheeks with artichoke and carrots) at the **Restaurant Bonay** (Placa de les Voltes 13, 972 63 40 34, closed Dec-Jan, mains €13). In Begur, **Els Patis de Begur** (C/Pi i Rallo 9, 972 62 37 41, closed Sun dinner & Mon, mains €15) specialises in paellas. In Pals, **Restaurant Sa Punta** (Urbanizació Sa Punta, 972 66 73 76, mains €21.50) serves excellent poolside Mediterranean dishes.

Tourist information

Oficina de Turisme de Begur

Avda 11 de Setembre 8 (972 62 45 20). **Open** *Apr-June* 9am-2.30pm, 5-8pm Mon-Fri; 10am-2pm, 5-8pm Sat; 10am-2pm Sun. *July-Sept* 9am-9pm daily. *Oct-March* 9am-2.30pm Mon-Fri; 10am-2pm Sat, Sun.

Oficina de Turisme de Pals

Plaça Major 7 (972 63 73 80). **Open** *June-Sept* 10am-2pm, 4-8pm daily. *Oct-May* 10am-2pm, 4-8pm Mon-Fri; 10am-2pm Sun.

Getting there

By bus

Barcelona Bus (93 232 04 59) to Girona from Estació del Nord. Sarfa (902 302 025) has 9 daily buses to Palafrugell (some continue to Begur), and regular buses to La Bisbal, which stop at Púbol.

By car

A7 or toll-free NII to Girona. For Peratallada, Pals and Begur take exit 6 from A7 or leave NII after Girona and take C66.

Costa Brava

Costa Brava means 'wild' or 'rugged' coast, a name, coined by a journalist in the early 1900s, that refers to its many rocky coves. It is these that have prevented the area from being swamped by the sort of high-rise monstrosities that plague the seaside just north of Barcelona, in home-from-home tourist traps like **Calella**, **Blanes** and **Lloret de Mar**. North of these, **Tossa del Mar** heralds the Costa Brava proper, and is just about worth stopping in (but only out of season). Once a haven for artists, it has a beachside medieval castle and pretty, narrow bar-filled streets.

The tortuous 20km (12mile) drive through coastal pine forests from here to **Sant Feliu de Guíxols** offers brief but unforgettable views of the sea. Sant Feliu itself has some fine Modernista buildings along the dignified Passeig Maritim, and the town museum has a wonderful collection of local ceramics. **Sant Pol** beach is three kilometres (two miles) north of the crowded town sands, and offers more towel room. You can explore further along the coast on foot – the **Camí de Ronda** slaloms its way along the undulating shoreline.

Further along the coast, **Platja d'Aro** and **Palamós** are worth avoiding (the latter has never recovered from an attack by the famous pirate Barba Roja (Redbeard) in 1543). Instead continue to **Palafrugell**, which has a great Sunday market and offers access to a number of picturesque villages built into the rocky coves. **Calella de Palafrugell** (not to be confused with its near namesake down the coast) is a charming, quiet town, even during its annual Cantada d'Havaneres song festival in July, while, a scenic 20-minute walk away, **Llafranc** offers a long curved beach from where you can swim between fishing boats at anchor in the bay. **Tamariu** is known for its good seafood, and is a base for waterskiing and fishing (between May and Oct to hire a boat call Paco Heredia (972 30 1310, www.gironautic.com) or Albert Muñoz (972 61 15 48). Next up is **Aiguablava**, with its modern *parador* and white sandy beach, and **Fornells**, both accessible from **Begur**, as is the small **Aiguafreda**, a cove sheltered by pines. Nearby **Sa Riera**, the northernmost cove, shelters two beaches, **La Platja del Raco**, where swimmers must wear bathing costumes, and **Illa Roja**, where they mustn't.

Beyond the Ter estuary and the Montgri hills, which divide the Baix and Alt Empordà, is the small resort town **L'Estartit**. This now makes much of its living catering for tourists interested in exploring the **Illes Medes**, a group of rocky limestone outcrops, of which only two are habitable (but uninhabited) islands. The biggest housed a British prison in the 19th century, but Les Illes are now only home to a unique ecosystem of flora and fauna; an underwater paradise in which divers can

Girona. *See p288.*

contemplate the colourful coral and hundreds of different species of sealife, including cat sharks. Glass-bottomed boats do tours in the summer months for the flipperless. For a view of the islands, and a sense of history, it's worth the 45-minute climb up to the 12th-century **Castell de Montgrí**.

Water sports

In Calella de la Costa, catamarans, kayaks and windsurfing equipment can all be hired at **Club Nàutic Calella** (Passeig Platja, 93 766 18 52). In L'Estartit, for diving around the Illes Medes, try the **Diving Center La Sirena** (C/Camping La Sirena, 972 75 09 54, www.la-sirena.net), **Unisub** (Ctra Torroella de Montgrí 15, 972 75 17 68, www.unisub.es), or **Quim's Diving Center** (Ctra Torroella de Montgrí, km 4.5, 972 75 01 63, www.quimsdivingestartit.com).

Where to eat

In **Sant Feliu de Guíxols** try the **Nàutic** in the Club Nàutic sailing club, for great views and superb seafood (Port Esportiu, 972 32 06 63, closed Mon and 2wks Nov, set lunch €24). **Calella** has the excellent **Tragamar** (Platja de Canadell s/n, 972 61 43 36, mains €11), a branch of the restaurant Tragaluz in Barcelona. In **Tamariu**, there's more good seafood at the **Royal** on the beachfront (Passeig de Mar 9, 972 62 00 41, mains €14), while in Aiguablava, the **Hotel Aiguablava** (Platja de Fornells, 972 62 20 58, closed Nov-Feb, mains €18) has an excellent restaurant in a beachfront setting.

Where to stay

If you don't mind flaking paint but love a bohemian atmosphere, try **Sant Feliu de Guixol's Casa Rovira** (C/Sant Amanç 106, 972 32 12 02/48 57, closed mid Oct-mid May, rates €46.80-€53.50), a rambling, leafy *hostal* frequented by painters and writers. Book in advance. Also in Sant Feliu, try the **Hotel Les Noies** (Rambla de Portalet 10, 972 32 04 00, closed late Oct-early June, rates €34.30), or the small, friendly **Hotel Plaça** (Plaça Mercat 22, 972 32 51 55, rates €64-€93) which is close to the beach and open all year. North of Sant Feliu, in **S'Agaró**, is the nearest luxury option, the **Hostal de la Gavina** (Plaça de la Rosaleda, 972 32 11 00, closed Nov-Easter, rates €176.80-€267.50), a five-star in the European grand hotel tradition. Llafranc has the **Hotel Llafranc** (Passeig de Cipsela 16, 972 30 02 08, rates €79-€123 with breakfast), or try the friendly **Hotel Casamar** (C/Nero 3-11, 972 30 01 04, closed Feb, rates incl breakfast €71.50-€88.50).

Tamariu is home to the relaxed **Hotel Tamariu** (Passeig de Mar 2, 972 62 00 31, closed Nov-Mar, rates incl breakfast €80-€110), while in **Aiguablava**, there's the pleasant local *parador,* **Platja d'Aiguablava** (972 62 21 62, www.parador.es, rates €83.80-€132.90) or the stately, family-run **Hotel Aiguablava** (rates incl breakfast €138-€183). **Sa Tuna** has the **Hostal Sa Tuna** (Platja Sa Tuna, 972 62 21 98, closed Nov-mid March, rates incl breakfast €96.30), with five rooms in a perfect spot by the sea. In **Sa Riera** is the **Hotel Sa Riera** (Platja de Sa Riera, 972 62 30 00, closed mid Oct-Easter,

Far out food festivals

There's nothing like a tour of Catalonia's towns and villages for uncovering some of the most arcane festivals imaginable. This being Spain, most of them involve food, and whether it's a grape-treading gala or a snail-cooking contest, Catalans are more than willing how to let their hair down and their belts out for the occasion.

One of the oldest and messiest food festivals in the region is **La Gran Festa de la Calçotada** in the so-called '*calçot* capital' of **Valls**. On the last Sunday in January, the *calçots* – sweetish jumbo spring onions – are chargrilled in the open air, and then draped through spicy *romesco* sauce of mashed almonds, olive oil and *nyora* peppers. There's music, dancing and parades along with a 45-minute *calçot* eating contest at midday; pretenders to the throne should know that the record stands at 300 well-sauced *calçots*. Plus bread. For more restrained appetites, though, the day usually ends with open-air *calçot* and sausage barbecues in Plaça de l'Oli and Plaça de la Zeta.

Lleida's Aplec del Caragol is Catalonia's most visited food festival, and over three days in mid May, 200,000 visitors each year chew their way through a whopping 12 tons of snails. The festivities are held in the fields on the banks of the river Segre and alongside the usual singing, dancing and drinking, some local clubs set up stands selling gastropod specialities, including the likes of snails stewed in cognac with cured ham.

Introduced in 2000, **La Carxofada** artichoke festival was an instant hit with the punters. It is held in the nearby town of **Sant Boi** on the first Sunday in April and involves fierce contests for the finest home-made artichoke dish and the best artichoke omelette along with tastings of popular local artichoke dishes such as 'chokes stuffed wth creamed cod and shrimp, or oven-roasted with *romesco* sauce. The event is so popular that, in 2003, crowds gobbled their way through 20,000 artichokes from barbecues set up along the beautiful Rambla de Rafael Casanova.

During Carnival, salad days come to Catalonia with the **Xatonada**. Enthusiasm over lettuce leaves is usually reserved for the higher ranks of the health Gestapo but this sultan of salads is reassuringly calorific; the basic ingredients of a *xató* are escarola lettuce with anchovies, salt cod, olives and tuna, all smothered in an artery-clogging sauce of almonds, hazelnuts, oil, *nyora* peppers and tomatoes, although each chef adds their own secret ingredients. The festival comprises a 'Xató route' spread out over eight towns between Barcelona and Tarragona, with the main stops being **Sitges** and **Vilanova i la Geltrú**. There are street competitions for the best salad and sauce, and many restaurants do a special *xató* menu, serving that all-important dish as the first course.

Something you rarely get to eat fresh from the waves are sea urchins (*garoines* or *garotes* in Catalan). When the water is cold enough, usually between late January and mid March, **La Garoinada** is celebrated in and around the coastal towns of **Palafrugell** where the spiky shells are expertly chopped open and the fat red eggs scooped out raw with a spoon. They are offered at the market or at beach-front stands and the better restaurants serve special menus with a dozen of the little critters as a starter. On Saturday nights during the festival, many bars host *habaneres* – old sea shanties accompanied by endless slugs of *cremat*. Literally meaning 'burnt', this is rum served aflame in a terracotta dish, with sugar, lemon peel, cinnamon and coffee beans.That'll warm your cockles.

rates incl breakfast €97.40-€113.60). L'Estartit is the **Santa Clara** (Passeig Marítim 18, 972 75 17 67, rates incl breakfast €41-€48).

Tourist information

Oficina de Turisme de L'Estartit

Passeig Marítim (972 75 19 10). **Open** *May* 9am-1pm, 4-7pm Mon-Fri; 10am-2pm Sat; 10am-2pm Sun. *June-Aug* 9.30am-2pm, 4-8pm Mon-Sat; 10am-2pm Sun. *Oct-Apr* 9am-1pm, 3-6pm Mon-Fri; 10am-2pm Sat.

Oficina de Turisme de Palafrugell

C/Carrilet 2 (972 30 02 28). **Open** *May-June, Sept* 10am-1pm, 5-8pm Mon-Sat; 10am-1pm Sun. *July, Aug* 9am-9pm Mon-Sat; 10am-1pm Sun. *Oct-Apr* 10am-1pm, 4-7pm Mon-Sat; 10am-1pm Sun.

Oficina de Turisme de Sant Feliu de Guixols

Plaça Monestir (972 82 00 51). **Open** *Mid June-mid Sept* 10am-2pm, 4-8pm daily. *Mid Sept-mid June* 10am-1pm, 4-7pm Mon-Sat; 10am-2pm Sun.

Getting there

By bus

Sarfa (902 302 025) has 15 buses daily to Sant Feliu from Estació del Nord (journey time 1hr20mins), and 9 to Palafrugell (2hrs); some continue to Begur. Change in Palafrugell or Torroella for L'Estartit.

By car

A7 north to exit 9 on to C35/C65 for Sant Feliu de Guíxols, then C31 for Palafrugell (123km/76 miles); or A7 exit 6 for Palafrugell and Begur via La Bisbal.

North to France

The seaside town of **L'Escala**, famous for its anchovies, provides a great place for refuelling with coffee and provisions before making the worthwhile 15-minute walk to **Empúries**. There you will find the well-preserved remains of an ancient city that dates back to 600 BC, when it was founded by the Phoenicians, before being recolonised by the Greeks and finally by the Romans in AD 2. Today, ruins from all three periods, as well as the layout of the original Greek harbour, are clearly visible. The whole site is picturesque and atmospheric, lending a rare immediacy to history in an ancient site right at the edge of the beach.

Just visible the other side of the huge Golf de Roses is the overcrowded tourist resort of **Roses**, which has little to recommend it apart from a 16th-century citadel and the nearby legendary restaurant **El Bulli** in Cala Montjoi. From Roses the road coils over the hills that form the **Cap de Creus** nature reserve, before dropping spectacularly down to **Cadaqués**. The town's relative isolation has made it a destination for the discerning. Picasso painted much of his early Cubist work here but it was Salvador Dalí who really put the place on the map. Dalí spent his childhood summers here, brought his surrealist circle to see it, and ended up building his home in **Port Lligat**, a short walk away. Cadaqués later became the resort for the Catalan cultural elite; it has kept its charm primarily thanks to a ban on the high-rise buildings that have blighted the rest of coastal Spain. Dalí's house, with much of its zany furniture, peculiar fittings and some impertinent stuffed animals, has been maintained as a museum, which gives great insight into the eccentric genius' strange lifestyle. Note that you should book some days before you visit as only eight people are allowed in at a time.

On the north side of the cape, **Port de la Selva**, looking towards France, is less touristy than Cadaqués and within hiking distance of the remarkable **Sant Pere de Rodes** fortified abbey, the most accomplished example of Romanesque architecture in the area. A further climb takes you up to the remarkable **Castell de Sant Salvador**, an imposing 10th century castle that seems to grow out of the rock. From here there are unparalleled views out over the Pyrenees to France, and back over the Gulf of Roses into Catalonia.

The capital of the Alt Empordà region is **Figueres**, where Dalí was born and is buried in his own museum in the city's old theatre, the **Teatre-Museu Dalí**. This is one of Spain's most-visited tourist spots and will doubtless be mobbed in 2004, being as it is the much hyped 100th anniversary of Dalí's birth. The artist donated many of his works to the museum, and redesigned the place, putting thousands of yellow loaves on the external walls and huge eggs on its towers. The highlight inside is the three-dimensional room-sized Mae West face, a collection of furniture arranged to look like the American film star when viewed from a certain angle. All of this rather overshadows the city's other two (rather good) museums, the **Museu de l'Empordà** (Rambla 2, 972 50 23 05), which gives an overview of the history of the area, and the **Museu del Joguet** (C/Sant Pere 1, 972 50 45 85), full of 19th-century toys, some of which belonged to Dalí and Miró.

Girona. *See p288.*

Between Figueres and the sea is the nature reserve of **Aiguamolls de l'Empordà**, a haven for rare species of birds who flock to the marshy lowlands at the mouth of the Fluvia river in spring and autumn. As well as flamingos, bee-eaters and moustached warblers, it is home to turtles, salamanders and otters.

Casa-Museu de Port Lligat

972 25 10 15/www.salvador-dali.org. **Open** *15 Mar-14 June, 16 Sept-6 Jan* 10.30am-5.30pm Tue-Sun. *15 June-15 Sept* 10.30am-8.30pm Tue-Sun. Closed 7 Jan-14 Mar. **Admission** €8; €5 concessions. **Credit** MC, V.

Sant Pere de Rodes

972 38 75 59. **Open** *June-Sept* 10am-8pm Tue-Sun. *Oct-May* 10am-5.30pm Tue-Sun. **Admission** €3.60; €2.40 concessions; free Tue. **No credit cards**.

Teatre-Museu Dalí

Plaça Gala-Salvador Dalí 5, Figueres (972 67 75 00/www.salvador-dali.org). **Open** *July-Sept* 9am-7.45pm Tue-Sun. *Oct-May* 10.30am-5.45pm Tue-Sun. *June* 10.30am-5.45pm daily. **Admission** €9; €6.50 concessions. **No credit cards**.

Where to stay & eat

Right next to the Greek ruins in **Empúries**, the **Hostal Ampurias** (Platja Portitxol, 972 77 02 07, rates €60-€95, set menu €20) offers sparse but clean rooms in a fantastic setting in front of the rocky beach, and does good Mediterranean food all year round. Fifteen minutes' walk away in the pretty little village of Sant Martí d'Empúries, is the comfortable **Riomar** (Platja del Riuet, closed mid Oct-Easter, 972 77 03 62, rates incl breakfast €60-€90). Over the bay, a twisting 7km (4.5mile) drive from Roses is the extraordinary world-famous restaurant **El Bulli** (*see p169*), where 32 courses are the rule of the day, and it's the best in Spain (for those who can afford it).

Cadaqués has few hotels, and most are closed in winter, so always call first. Try the friendly *pensión*/restaurant **Fonda Cala d'Or** (C/Sa Fitora 1, 972 25 81 49, rates €25, mains €9) or the **Hostal Marina** (C/Riera 3, 972 25 81 99, closed Jan-Easter, rates €48.20). **Playa Sol** (Platja Pianc 3, 972 25 81 00, closed Dec-Feb, rates incl breakfast €88.60-€156.30) has lovely sea views. The **Misty** (C/Nova Port Lligat, 972 25 89 62, closed Jan-mid Mar, rates €47.60-€72.90) has a pool, or try the **Llane Petit** (C/Doctor Bartomeus 37, 972 25 10 20, closed Jan, Feb, Nov, rates €70.30-€108).

Dining options include the pretty **Es Balconet** up a winding street back from the bay (C/Sant Antoni 2, 972 25 88 14, mains €13.50) for great paella, and **Ix!** (C/Horta Sanés 1, 972 25 87 33, mains €13), just off the main tourist drag but with tables outside overlooking the sea and a good-value *menú*. **Casa Anita** (C/Miguel Roset, 972 25 84 71, www.casa-anita.com, closed Feb & Mon, mains €12) is a very popular, family-owned place with excellent fresh seafood (according to the catch of the day) and long queues. Dalí used to eat here. At Cap de Creus, the **Restaurant Cap de Creus** (972 19 90 05, mains €14.50) serves an eclectic range from seafood to curry, from a spectacular setting on a headland jutting out to sea.

In Figueres, try the **Hotel Duran** (C/Lasauca 5, 972 50 12 50, rates €59-€63, mains €20), which exudes comfortable, battered elegance and was an old haunt of Dalí's. The restaurant serves excellent game and seafood. For clean, dull but well-equipped rooms there's **La Barretina** (C/Lasauca 13, 972 67 34 25, rates €38) and also the **Hostal Bon Repòs** (C/Villalonga 43, 972 50 92 02, rates €25). **President** (Ronda Firal 33, 972 50 17 00, closed Mon, set lunch €13) offers good, solid Catalan fare and excellent seafood. C/Jonquera is the main drag for cheap *menús del dia*, with alfresco tables. Just south of Figueres, off the C31 in Siurana, is **El Molí** (972 52 51 39, rates €48 incl breakfast), a beautifully restored farmhouse with six rooms to rent.

Tourist information

Oficina de Turisme de Cadaqués

C/Cotxe 2A (972 25 83 15). **Open** *June-Sept* 10am-1pm, 4-7pm Mon-Sat; 10am-1pm Sun. *Oct-May* 10am-1pm, 4-7pm Mon-Sat.

Oficina de Turisme de L'Escala

Plaça de les Escoles 1 (972 77 06 03). **Open** *mid June-mid Sept* 9am-8.30pm daily. *Mid Sept-mid June* 9am-1pm, 4-7pm Mon-Fri; 10am-2pm Sat.

Oficina de Turisme de Figueres

Plaça del Sol (972 50 31 55). **Open** *Mar-June, Oct* 9am-6pm Mon-Fri; 10am-1.30pm, 3.30-6.30pm Sat. *July-Sept* 9am-8pm Mon-Sat; 10am-3pm Sun. *Nov-Feb* 9am-6pm Mon-Fri.

Getting there

By bus

Barcelona Bus (93 232 04 59) has several buses daily to Figueres from Estació del Nord (2hrs30mins). Sarfa (902 302 025) has 2 buses daily to Roses and Cadaqués (2hrs15mins), and services to Roses, Port de la Selva, Cadaqués and L'Escala from Figueres.

By car

A7 or NII to Figueres (120km/74 miles). For Roses and Cadaqués, take the C260 from Figueres.

By train

RENFE from Sants or Passeig de Gràcia to Figueres (journey 2hrs). Trains leave every hour.

Tossa del Mar. *See p290.*

Vic to the Pyrenees

You'll need a wide-angle lens to take it all in.

Vic & around

Life in **Vic** revolves around the impressive arcaded square **Plaça Major**, and never more so than for its Saturday market, famed throughout the region and almost as old as the town itself. Vic began life as the capital of the Ausetian tribe, became a Roman city, and later fell briefly to the Moors, who lost it to Wilfred the Hairy, Count of Barcelona, in the ninth century. Since then it has remained just an administrative, artistic and religious centre, with an extraordinary number of churches.

Very few tourists pass through here, despite its many buildings of historic importance. In one corner of the market square is the Modernista **Casa Comella**, with sgraffiti depicting the four seasons designed by Gaietà Buïgas, who designed the Monument a Colom in Barcelona. The **Catedral de Sant Pere** contains Romanesque, Gothic and neo-classical elements, along with a set of dramatic 20th-century murals by Josep Lluís Sert, who is buried here. The **Museu Episcopal** (Plaça del Bisbe Oliva 3, 93 886 93 60, closed Mon, admission €4) is unmissable, with some magnificent 12th-century murals and a fascinating collection of Romanesque and Gothic art. The **Temple Romà** (Roman temple) was only discovered in 1882, when the 12th-century walls that surrounded it were knocked down – it has since been well restored and now houses an art gallery.

The picturesque countryside around Vic is full of interesting villages, and the tourist offices have useful detailed maps of the many hiking routes. Following the C153 road towards Olot, a remarkably beautiful stop is **Rupit**, an ancient village built on the side of a medieval castle, with a precarious hanging bridge across a gorge. Later building in the town was done so sympathetically to the style that it's difficult to tell the old from the new.

Where to stay & eat

In Vic itself there is very little in the way of accommodation; its only *pensión* is **Hostal Osona** (C/Remei 3, 93 883 28 45, rates €26.50). It does, however, have some great restaurants. The best is probably **Jordi Parramon** (C/Cardona 7, 93 886 38 15, closed Mon & dinner except Fri, Sat, closed 2wks Sept & Mar, mains €22), with a short but exquisite list of dishes. More affordable is the entrecôte *café de Paris* at **La Taula** (C/Sant Marius 8, 93 417 28 48, closed 2wks Feb & Sept, mains €12), or there's **Ca l'U** (Plaça Santa Teresa 4, 93 889 03 45, closed dinner Tue, Wed & Sun, all Mon and 3wks July-Aug, set lunch €11), a friendly traditional inn with fish and game dishes. The small, colourful **La Creperia** (Plaça Sant Felip Neri 9, 93 886 37 81, closed dinner Tue, mains €4) is the budget option, with cheap crêpes, waffles and salads.

Historic **Vic** has much to offer.

If you have transport (and a few quid), the nicest places to stay are actually outside Vic. The **Parador de Vic** is modern but comfortable, and sits in a fabulous location overlooking the Ter gorge (Paraje el Bac de Sau, 93 812 23 23, rates €92.90-€103.40) – take the C153 north and follow the signs (around 14km). In Tavèrnoles, just before it, **Mas Banús** (93 812 20 91) is a giant old farmhouse, where self-contained accommodation for six for the weekend costs €267.50. Also in Tavèrnoles is the **Fussimanya** (Ctra del Parador km 7, 93 812 21 88, closed all Wed and dinner Thur, mains €9), a rambling old restaurant famous for its fine sausages, and wildly popular at weekends. In Rupit, **Hotel Estrella** (Plaça Bisbe Font 1, 93 852 20 05, rates incl breakfast €89.70, set lunch €14) is a *pensión* with a huge and popular restaurant.

Getting there

By bus

Empresa Sagalès (93 231 27 56) from the Fabra i Puig bus station (near metro of same name) to Vic. For Rupit, take a local bus from Vic.

By car

Take the C17, signed for Puigcerdà, to Vic (65km /40 miles). For Rupit, take the C153 out of Vic (signposted to Olot).

By train

RENFE from Sants or Plaça Catalunya to Vic. Trains leave about every 90mins. Journey time is 1hr 20mins.

Tourist information

Oficina de Turisme de Vic

Plaça Major 1 (93 886 20 91). **Open** 9am-8pm Mon-Fri; 9am-2pm, 4-7pm Sat; 10am-1pm Sun.

Berga to Puigcerdà

To the west, on the most popular approach to the Pyrenees from Barcelona, is **Berga**, famous for the frenzied festival of La Patum, held in May. Just north from there the giant cliffs of the **Serra del Cadí**, one of the ranges of the 'Pre-Pyrenees' or Pyrenees foothills, loom above the town. Berga has a medieval castle, **Sant Ferran**, with a suitably storybook air, but the blight of endless holiday apartment blocks has taken its toll on the charm of Berga's old centre. Far prettier is the little town of **Bagà**, north of here along the C17. Bagà, with its partially preserved medieval walls around an atmospheric old quarter, marks the beginning of the **Parc Natural del Cadí-Moixeró**, a gigantic mountain park containing wildlife and forest reserves and some 20 or so ancient villages. All retain some medieval architecture, and many offer stunning views. Picasso stayed and painted in the village of **Gósol** in 1906.

Above Bagà the C16 road enters the Túnel del Cadí to emerge into the wide, fertile plateau of the **Cerdanya**. Described by writer Josep Pla as a 'huge casserole', the Cerdanya has an obvious geographical unity, but the French and Spanish border runs right through the middle. The capital of the area (on the Spanish side), **Puigcerdà**, is a lively, pretty town with a very French feel, populated mainly by skiing second-homers. With handsome buildings, it's a good base (and a memorable train journey from Barcelona) for exploring the area on foot – the tourist office has a decent selection of maps and itineraries. One of the more charming places to stay in the area is **Bellver de Cerdanya**, a pretty hilltop village with a lively market and Gothic church. The village has an information centre, and all over town noticeboards list hikes of varying degrees of difficulty.

Where to stay & eat

In Bagà, the **Hotel Ca L'Amagat** (C/Clota 4, 93 824 41 60, rates €41.20-€45.60) has rooms with large balconies and a restaurant serving dishes like trout with almonds or veal with red currants (mains €11). Puigcerdà has plenty of hotels in the town centre, including the small and charming **Avet Blau** (Plaça Santa Maria 14, 972 88 25 52, rates incl breakfast €75-€100). The **Hotel Rita-Belvedere** (C/Carmelites 6-8, 972 88 03 56, closed Nov-June, rates €39-€50) is a good deal and has a small garden and terrace. The **Hotel del Lago** (Avda Dr Piguillem 7, 972 88 10 00, www.hotellago.com, rates €85), with its terracotta paintwork and green shutters, is not quite so pretty inside, but it's staff and atmosphere are bothvery friendly. Excellent pizzas from a wood-fired oven, along with civet of hare and grilled meats, are to be had at **El Pati de la Tieta** (C/Ferrers 20, 972 88 01 56, closed Mon-Wed, closed mid June-mid July, mains €18) in a pretty old house with a terrace. For modern French-Mediterranean food try **La Col d'Hivern** (C/Baronia 7, 972 14 12 04, closed Mon-Wed, mains €11). A little further out in Bolvir, the sumptuous **Torre del Remei** (C/Camí Reial, 972 14 01 82, rates €203-€321) also has one of the best (and most expensive) restaurants in the area (main courses €68). In Bellver, the **Fonda Bianya** (C/Sant Roc 11, 973 510 475, rates €34.50 incl breakfast) is utterly charming, with its sweet cornflower blue woodwork, a sunny bar and a lively atmosphere. For sophisticated top-drawer dining, try **Picot Negre** (C/Cami Real 1, 973 51 11 98, mains €16.50).

Getting there

By bus

Alsina Graëlls (93 265 68 66) runs five buses daily to Berga from the corner of C/Balmes and C/Pelai; journey time is about 2hrs. Same company has daily buses to Puigcerdà from Estació del Nord; journey time is 3hrs.

By car

Take the C16 to Berga (118km/73 miles) and Bagà. From Bagà continue on the C16 through Túnel del Cadí (toll), after which take the N260

On the piste

If you're beginning to feel a little jaded by the charms of the design capital of the world, a day in the mountains could be just the ticket. Although the Pyrenees do not have the cachet of the Alps, and many resorts in the mountain chain are a good half-day's drive away from the city, there are one or two alternatives where the atmosphere is considerably less exclusive and more family-oriented than in France or Switzerland. Infrastructure in the Pyrenees has improved a great deal in recent years, with heavy investments being made on artificial snow machines and lifts.

One possibility is a day or weekend package organised by a travel agent, such as **Viatgi** (Ronda Universitat 1, 93 301 16 29). These normally include return bus transport, ski pass (known as the '*forfait*'), insurance and hire of ski equipment – skis, boots and sticks. A class from a ski instructor is meant to be included, but these are not given in English, and it can be very difficult to locate your guide once you reach the slopes and have hired your skis.

Most packages organised through travel agents head for resorts in **Andorra**, which can get very crowded. This is especially true at weekends, when the Pyrenean principality becomes packed, and it can take an hour or more to travel the few kilometres from the frontier to the slopes, such is the build-up of traffic. A much more comfortable alternative is a trip by railway to the resort of **La Molina** (972 89 20 31). The train fare is 7.20, and a bus covers the short distance between the station and the slopes. A day's *forfait* will set

east for Puigcerdà or west for Lles and Bellver. A scenic alternative is to take the C17 and N152 through Vic and Ripoll.

By train

RENFE from Sants or Plaça Catalunya to Puigcerdà. About one train every 2hrs, and the journey generally takes about 3hrs.

Tourist information

Oficina de Turisme de Berga

C/Angels 7 (93 821 13 84). **Open** 9am-2pm Mon-Thur; 9am-2pm, 5-8pm Fri; 10am-2pm, 5-8pm Sat.

Oficina de Turisme de Puigcerdà

C/Querol, baixos (972 88 05 42). **Open** *Mid June-mid Sept* 9am-2pm, 3-8pm Mon-Sat; 10am-2pm Sun. *Mid Sept-mid June* 9am-1pm Mon; 9am-1pm, 4-7pm Tue-Fri; 10am-1.30pm, 4.30-8pm Sat.

Ripoll to the Vall de Núria

Ripoll is best known for its extraordinary monastery, **Santa Maria de Ripoll**, founded in 879 by Wilfred the Hairy, who is buried here. The church has a superb 12th-century stone portal; its carvings are among the finest examples of Romanesque art in Catalonia.

you back 29. Note that this price does not include ski hire, although this can easily be arranged at the foot of the slopes. La Molina is around 3hrs from Barcelona, with trains leaving at 7.05am from Plaça Catalunya.

As resorts go, with six black, 15 red, 12 blue and seven green runs, La Molina is not the most challenging in the world, but is more than adequate for a day's skiing. There are six bars and restaurants on the slopes with rather basic menus, but the view and location more than make up for that. Trains head back at 5pm and 7.10pm; bear in mind that the slopes close at sunset, and if you are planning on catching the last train, there is not a great deal to do in La Molina after that.

The monastery museum, **Museu Etnogràfic** (972 70 31 44), due to reopen in 2004, traces the customs and history of the area with everyday objects. Wilfred also founded the monastery and town of **Sant Joan de les Abadesses**, ten kilometres (six miles) east up the C26, and worth a visit for its Gothic bridge as well as the 12th-century monastery. Neither town holds much charm outside its monastery.

Ribes de Freser, the next town on the N152 north of Ripoll, is an attractive base from which to travel to the pretty if slightly gentrified villages of **Campelles** and **Queralbs**. Ribes is also the starting point for the *cremallera*, or 'zipper train', a narrow-gauge cog railway that runs via Queralbs along the Freser river up to the sanctuary of **Núria**, affording incredible views. Many choose to walk back to Queralbs (around 2hrs), following the path through dramatic rock formations, crumbling scree, pine-wooded slopes and dramatic, crashing waterfalls.

Núria itself nestles by a lake on a plateau at over 2,000 metres (6,500 feet), and was the first ski resort on this side of the border. Home to the second most famous of Catalonia's patron virgins, a wooden statue of the Madonna carved in the 12th century, Núria was a refuge and a place of pilgrimage long before then. The mostly 19th-century monastery that surrounds the shrine is not especially attractive, but its location is spectacular. Here you can bury your head in a pot to gain fertility, or ring a bell to cure headaches, but most choose to hike, ski, row boats or ride horses (you can get maps and information from the tourist office).

Where to stay & eat

In Ribes de Freser, the family-run **Hotel Els Caçadors** (C/Balandrau 24-6, 972 72 77 22, closed Nov, rates €43.40-€48.80, mains €10) has good food and comfortable rooms. If this is full, try **Hostal Porta de Núria** (C/Nostra Senyora de Gràcia 3, 972 72 71 37, closed May, rates incl breakfast €53.50). In Queralbs, try **Calamari Hostal l'Avet** (C/Major 5, 972 72 73 77, closed Mon-Thur, closed Oct-May, rates €39 per person). The one good place to eat in Queralbs is **De la Plaça** (Plaça de la Vila 2, 972 72 70 37, closed Tue, closed 2wks July-Oct, set menu €13.37), for regional specialities.

In Núria, there's the three-star **Hotel Vall de Núria** (Estación vall de Sana, C/Santuari Mare de Dèu de Núria, 972 73 20 20, closed Nov, rates per person €44.30-€78.50 half-board), which has a minimum stay of two nights.

Getting there

By bus

TEISA (972 20 48 68) from the corner of C/Pau Claris and C/Consell de Cent to Ripoll, Sant Joan de les Abadesses and Camprodon.

By car

Take the C17 direct to Ripoll (104km/65 miles). For Sant Joan de les Abadesses, Camprodon, take the C26 out of Ripoll.

By train

RENFE from Sants or Plaça Catalunya, (journey time to Ripoll 2hrs). For Queralbs and Núria, change to the *cremallera* train in Ribes de Freser.

Tourist information

Oficina de Turisme de Núria

Estació de Montanya del Vall de Núria (972 73 20 20/www.valldenuria.com). **Open** *July-Sept* 8.20am-8pm daily. *Oct-June* 8.20am-6.15pm daily.

Oficina de Turisme de Ribes de Freser

Plaça del Ayuntamiento 3 (972 72 77 28). **Open** 10am-2pm, 5-8pm Tue-Sat; 11am-1pm Sun.

Besalú & Olot

The medieval fortified town of **Besalú** is one of the loveliest in Catalonia, with an impressive 12th-century fortified bridge spanning the Fluvià River to mark its entrance. Once home to a sizeable Jewish community, it boasts the only remaining Jewish baths (*mikveh*) in Spain. These extraordinary structures date back to the 13th century but were only discovered in the 1960s. Charmingly, if the doors are locked when you arrive, the tourist office will give you a key so that you can let yourself in. Also worth visiting are the Romanesque church of Sant Pere and the arcaded Plaça de la Llibertat.

West from here the N260 runs to **Olot**, past a spectacular view of **Castellfollit de la Roca**, a village perched on the edge of a precipitous crag. The town is prettier from below than it is once you really get inside, but the old section still makes for an interesting stroll. **Olot** was destroyed in an earthquake in 1427, and so lost much of its oldest architecture, but it still has some impressive 18th-century and Modernista buildings. In the last century it was home to a school of landscape painters; the local **Museu de la Garrotxa** has works by them and Ramon Casas, Santiago Rusiñol and other Modernista artists (C/Hospice 8, 972 27 91 30, closed Sun afternoon and all Tue, admission €1.80, 90¢ concessions, admission includes entrance to Casa dels Volcans, *see below*). The town is not especially interesting, however, and is mainly worth visiting because of its position amid the 30-odd inactive volcanoes and numerous lava flows of the volcanic region of **La Garrotxa**. Just south of town on the road to Vic is elegant **Casal dels Volcans** (Ctra Santa Coloma 43, 972 26 67 62, closed Tue, closed Sun afternoon, admission €1.80, 90¢ concessions), a combination information centre and museum where you can pick up maps for hiking.

Off the G1524 heading toward Banyoles is a delightful beech forest, the **Fageda d'en Jordà,** immortalised by Catalan poet Joan Maragall, and the pretty if heavily touristed village **Santa Pau**, with an impressive castle and arcaded squares.

Where to stay & eat

Overlooking Besalú, **Mas Pitre** (972 19 02 37, rates €60 incl breakfast) is an easygoing Dutch-run place with a swimming pool and great views. In town a 19th-century riverside inn, **Fonda Siqués** (Avda Lluís Companys 6-8, 972 59 01 10, rates incl breakfast €39.80-€57.80) offers clean but drab rooms and is located above a charming restaurant (closed Sun dinner, closed Mon Oct-May, closed all Jan, set lunch €9). For nicer, though still simple, rooms, try **Els Jardins de la Martana** (C/Pont 2, 972 59 00 09, rates €96.30). A couple of miles north of the town, in Beuda, is a pretty *masia* with a pool, **Mas Salvanera** (972 59 09 75, www.salvanera.com, rates €115 incl breakfast). In Olot, **La Perla** (Avda Santa Coloma 97, 972 26 23 26, rates €59) is a large hotel with a good restaurant, or **Pensión La Vila** (C/Sant Roc 1, 972 269 807, rates incl breakfast €38) is modern and very central.

Restaurants in Besalú include the **Pont Vell** (C/Pont Vell 24, 972 59 10 27, closed dinner Mon, Tue, closed Jan, mains €10) for traditional cooking with a twist. The terrace of the **Cúria Reial** (Plaça de la Llibertat 15, 972 59 02 63, closed dinner Mon, Tue, closed Feb, mains €16) is very popular, with good traditional cooking. In Olot, **Can Guix** (C/Mulleres 3-5, 972 261 040, closed Sun and 2wks July-Aug, mains €4) has great, cheap local dishes, or north of the town is the **Restaurant Les Cols** (Crta de la Canya, 972 26 92 09, closed Mon, dinner Tue & Sun, closed 2wks July-Aug, mains €18) set inside a picturesque *masia* with a terrace – try the house speciality of cabbage leaves stuffed with duck liver. Just south of Olot, in La Pinya, is **Mas Garganta** (972 27 12 89, rates €59 per person, half-board) – an 18th-century *masia* with magnificent views that has walking tours with two *masies* nearby, so you can stay in one place and walk without bags to the next.

Getting there

By bus

TEISA (972 20 48 68) to Besalú and Olot from the corner of C/Pau Claris and C/Consell de Cent.

By car

To Besalú, take the C66 from Girona, then N260 to Olot.

Tourist information

Oficina de Turisme de Olot

C/Hospici 8 (972 26 01 41). **Open** *Sept-June* 9am-2pm, 5-7pm Mon-Fri; 10am-2pm, 5-7pm Sat; 11am-2pm Sun. *July, Aug* 10am-2pm, 5-8pm Mon-Sat; 11am-2pm Sun.

Directory

Features

Directory

Getting Around

Barcelona's centre is compact and easily explored on foot. There are cheap, efficient metro and bus systems for longer journeys. Bicycles are good for the Old City and port, and there is a decent network of bicycle lanes throughout the city. Cars can be a hindrance, as there is very little parking space, and most of the city is subject to one-way systems. For transport outside Barcelona, *see p276*.

Arriving & leaving

By air

Barcelona's airport is at El Prat, just south of the city. Each airline works from one of the two main terminals (A or B) for all arrivals and departures. Both terminals have tourist information desks, and cash and currency exchange machines.

For airport info, call 93 298 38 38 (press 1, then 3 for an English-speaking operator). Updated flight info can be found at www.aena.es/ae/bcn/homepage.htm.

Aerobús

The airport bus runs from each terminal to Plaça Catalunya (with stops at Plaça Espanya, C/Urgell and Plaça Universitat). Buses to the airport go from Plaça Catalunya (in front of El Corte Inglés), stopping along the way at Sants station and Plaça Espanya. Buses run every 12 mins, leaving the airport from 6am to midnight Mon-Fri (6.30am-midnight Sat, Sun); and returns to the airport from Plaça Catalunya, 5.30am-11.15pm Mon-Fri (6am-11.15pm Sat, Sun). The trip takes 20 to 30mins, depending on traffic; a single ticket is €3.45. For nocturnal runs, a local bus, the 106, runs (starting after 10.15pm) between the airport and Plaça Espanya (starting at 10.55pm); it takes longer, but runs later (last departure from the airport 3.20am; from Plaça Espanya 3.50am).

Airport trains

The long overhead walkway between the terminals leads to the airport train station. Trains stop at Sants, Plaça Catalunya and Arc de Triomf, all of which are also metro stops. Trains leave the airport at 13 and 43mins past each hour, 6.13am-11.40pm Mon-Fri. Trains to the airport leave Plaça Catalunya at 8 and 38mins past the hour, 5.38am-10.11pm Mon-Fri (5mins later from Sants). Weekend times vary slightly, but there are still trains every 30mins. The journey takes 20-25mins and costs €2.20 one way. Be aware that tickets are only valid for 2hrs after purchase.

Taxis from the airport

The taxi fare to central Barcelona should be about €13-€25 (depending on traffic), including a €2 airport supplement. Fares are about 20% higher after 10pm and at weekends. There is an 85¢ supplement for each large piece of luggage placed in the car boot. All licensed cab drivers use the ranks outside the terminal.

Airlines

Terminals are shown in brackets.

Air Europa (B) 93 478 47 63 www.air-europa.com

British Airways (B) 902 111 333 www.british-airways.com

Easyjet (A) 902 299 992 www.easyjet.com

Iberia (B) 902 400 500 www.iberia.com

Virgin Express (A) 93 226 66 71 www.virgin-express.com

By bus

Most long-distance coaches (national and international) stop or terminate at **Estació d'Autobusos Barcelona-Nord** at C/Alí Bei 80, next to Arc de Triomf rail and metro station (general information 902 26 06 06). The **Estació d'Autobusos Barcelona-Sants**, between Sants mainline rail station and Sants-Estació metro stop, is only a secondary stop for many coaches, though some international Eurolines services (information 93 490 40 00) both begin and end their journeys at Sants.

By car

The easiest way into central Barcelona from almost all directions is the Ronda Litoral (the coastal half of the ring road). Take exit 21 (Paral.lel) if you're coming from the south, or exit 22 (Via Laietana) from the north. Motorways also feed into Avda Diagonal, Avda Meridiana and Gran Via, which all lead directly into the city centre. Tolls are charged on most of the main approach routes, payable in cash (the lane marked 'manual'; motorbikes are charged half) or by credit card ('automatic'). For more information on driving in Barcelona, *see p304*.

By sea

Balearic Islands ferries dock at the **Moll de Barcelona** quay, at the bottom of Avda Paral.lel; **Trasmediterránea** (902 45 46 45/www.trasmediterranea.es) is the main operator. There are also other ferries running three times a week between Barcelona and Genoa in Italy, from the **Moll de Ponent**, a few hundred metres further south (**Grimaldi Lines**; for information, phone its agent Condeminas on 93 295 70 00).

Cruise ships use several berths around the harbour. The PortBus shuttle service runs between them and the bottom of the Rambla when ships are in port.

By train

Most long-distance services operated by the Spanish state railway company **RENFE** run from **Barcelona-Sants** station, easily reached by metro lines 3 (green) and 5 (blue). Some international services from France terminate at the **Estació de França** in the Born, near the Barceloneta metro (line 4, yellow). Other trains stop between the two at **Passeig de Gràcia**, which can be the handiest for the city centre and also has a metro stop on lines 2, 3 and 4.

RENFE

902 24 02 02/www.renfe.es. **Open** 5.30am-11.30pm daily. **Credit** AmEx, DC, MC, V.
Some English-speaking operators. RENFE tickets can be bought at travel agents or reserved over the phone and delivered to an address or hotel for a small extra fee. For more information on non-Spanish European trains, call 93 490 11 22 (7am-11pm daily).

Maps

For street, local train and metro maps, see *pp332-48*. Tourist offices provide a reasonable free street map, or a better quality map for €1.20. Metro maps (ask for '*una guía del metro*') are available free at all metro stations, and bus maps can be obtained from city transport information offices (*see below*). Access points for the disabled are shown on the metro and bus maps. There is an excellent interactive street map at www.bcn.es/guia.

Public transport

The metro is generally the quickest, cheapest and most convenient way of getting around the city, while buses run throughout the night and to areas not covered by the metro system. Local buses and the metro are run by the city transport authority (**TMB**). Two underground train lines (from Plaça Catalunya to Les Planes or Avda Tibidabo; and from Plaça Espanya to Cornellà) connect with the metro but are run by Catalan government railways, the FGC, or **Ferrocarrils de la Generalitat de Catalunya**. Although it is run by different organisations, Barcelona public transport is now highly integrated, with the same tickets valid for up to four changes of transport on bus and metro lines as long as you do it within 75 minutes.

TMB information

Main vestibule, Metro Universitat, Eixample (93 318 70 74/www.tmb.net). **Open** 8am-8pm Mon-Fri. **Map** p344 A1. **Branches**: vestibule, Metro Sants Estació and Sagrada Família (both 7am-9pm Mon-Fri; Sants open 10am-2pm, 3-6pm Sat, Sun); vestibule, Metro Diagonal (8am-8pm Mon-Fri).

Fares & tickets

Travel in the Barcelona urban area has a flat fare of €1.10 per journey, but multi-journey tickets or *targetes* are better value. The basic ten-trip *targeta* is the T-10 (*Te-Deu* in Catalan), which can be shared by any number of people travelling simultaneously, with the ticket validated in the machines on the metro, train or bus once per person per journey.

The T-10, along with the other 'integrated' *targetes* listed below, gives you access to all four of the city's main transport systems (local RENFE and FGC trains, the metro and buses). To transfer, insert your card into a machine a second time, but unless 75 minutes have elapsed another unit will not be deducted. Single tickets do not allow free transfers.

You can buy your T-10 in newsagents, lottery shops, bakeries and Servi-Caixa cashpoints as well as on the metro and train systems, although not on buses. More expensive versions of all *targetes* take you to the outer zones of the metropolitan region, but the prices listed below will get you anywhere in central Barcelona, and to the key sights on the outskirts of the city itself.

Integrated targetes

- **T-10** Valid for ten trips; can be shared by two or more people. €6.
- **T-Familiar** Gives 70 trips in any 30-day period; can be shared. €36.70.
- **T-50/30** Gives 50 trips in any 30-day period; but can only be used by one person. €25.
- **T-Día** A one-day travelcard. €4.60.
- **T-Mes** Valid for any 30-day period. €38.80.
- **T-Trimestre** Valid for three months. €106.70.

Other targetes

- **2,3 & 5 Dies** Two-, three and five-day travelcards for one person on the metro, buses and FGC trains. Also sold at tourist offices. €8, €11.30 and €17.30.
- **Aerobús + Bus + Metro Unlimited** travel for one person on the metro and buses (not FGC), including a return trip to the airport. Two-day (€13.50), three-day (€16.75) and five-day (€22.35) passes are available. Sold on board the Aerobús.
- **Barcelona Card** A tourist discount scheme that gives unlimited travel on public transport, for up to five days.

Metro & FGC

The five metro lines are identified by a number and a colour on maps and station signs. At interchanges, lines are shown by the names of the station at the end of the line. Some suburban FGC trains do not stop at all stations.

All metro lines operate from 5am to midnight Monday to Thursday; 5am to 2am Friday, Saturday and nights before public holidays; 6am to midnight Sunday.

FGC information

Vestibule, Plaça Catalunya FGC station (93 205 15 15/www.fgc.net). **Open** 7am-9pm Mon-Fri. **Map** p344 A1. **Branches**: FGC Provença (open 9am-7pm Mon-Fri, closed Aug); FGC Plaça Espanya (open 9am-2pm, 4-7pm Mon-Fri).

Buses

Many city bus routes originate in or pass through the city centre, at Plaça Catalunya, Plaça Universitat and Plaça Urquinaona. However, they often run along different parallel streets depending on the direction of travel, due to the city's one-way system. Not all stops are labelled and street signs are not easy to locate, meaning that it is difficult to see where to get off.

Most bus routes operate between 6am and 10.30pm, Monday to Saturday, although many begin earlier and finish later. There is usually a bus at least every 10 to 15 minutes, but they are less frequent before 8am, after 9pm and on Saturdays. On Sundays, buses are less frequent still, and a few do not run at all.

Board buses at the front, and get off through the middle or rear doors. Only single tickets can be bought from the driver on board; if you have a *targeta,* insert it into the machine behind the driver as you board.

Useful routes

Buses that connect Plaça Catalunya with popular parts of town include:
22 via Gràcia to the Tramvia Blau up to Tibidabo and the Pedralbes monastery
24 goes up Passeig de Gràcia and is the best way to get to Park Güell
41, **66** and **67** go to the Plaça Francesc Macià area, which is not served by the metro
39 connects Gràcia, the town centre and the beach
41 also goes to Ciutadella and the Vila Olímpica
45 stops in Plaça Urquinaona and goes down to the beach near Port Olímpic.

Three good crosstown routes:
50 goes from north-east Barcelona past Sagrada Família, along Gran Via and then climbs Montjuïc from Plaça Espanya to Miramar
64 goes from Barceloneta beach, past Colom, Avda Paral.lel, Plaça Universitat to Sarrià and Pedralbes
7 runs the length of Avda Diagonal, from the Zona Universitària to Diagonal-Mar and along Passeig de Gràcia and Gran Via to Glòries.

Night buses

There are 16 urban night bus ('Nitbus') routes, most of which run from 10.30pm to 4.30am nightly, with buses every 20-30mins. Most pass through Plaça Catalunya. Fares and *targetes* are as for daytime buses. Plaça Catalunya is also the terminus for all-night bus services linking Barcelona with more distant parts of its metropolitan area.

TombBús

A special shoppers' bus. *See p186.*

Local trains

Regional trains to Sabadell, Terrassa and other towns beyond Tibidabo depart from FGC Plaça Catalunya, and those for Montserrat from FGC Plaça d'Espanya.

All trains on the RENFE local network ('Rodalies/ Cercanías') stop at Sants, but can also be caught at either Plaça Catalunya and Arc de Triomf (for Vic and the Pyrenees, Manresa, the Penedès and Costa del Maresme) or Passeig de Gràcia (for the southern coastal line to Sitges and the Girona-Figueres line north).

Taxis

Barcelona's 10,500 distinctive black and yellow taxis are usually easy to find at any time of day or night, and can be hailed on the street when they show a green light on the roof, and a sign saying *'Lliure/Libre'* (free) behind the windscreen. There are ranks at railway and bus stations, main squares and throughout the city. Fares are reasonable.

Fares

Current official rates and supplements are shown inside cabs on a sticker in the rear side window (in English). The current minimum fare is €1.80, which is what the meter should register when you set off. The basic rates apply 6am to 10pm Monday to Friday; at all other times (including midweek public holidays), the rate is about 20 per cent higher. There are supplements for luggage (85¢), for trips to the airport (€2.10) and to the port (€1.85), as well as a waiting charge. Taxi drivers are not required to carry more than €20 in change, and few accept payment by credit card.

Receipts & complaints

To get a receipt, ask for *'un rebut/un recibo'*. It should include the fare, the taxi number, the driver's NIF (tax) number, the licence plate, driver's signature and the date; if you have a complaint about a driver, insist on all these, and the more details the better (time, route). Call the Institut Metropolità del Taxi on 93 223 51 51 to file a complaint.

Radio cabs

The companies listed below take bookings 24 hours daily. Phone cabs start the meter as soon as a call is answered.
Barnataxi 93 357 77 55
Fono-Taxi 93 300 11 00
Taxi Col·lectiu 93 318 21 82
Ràdio Taxi '033' 933 033 033
Servi-Taxi 933 300 300
Taxi Groc 93 322 22 22
Taxi Miramar 93 433 10 20

Driving

Driving in Barcelona can be tiring, intimidating and time-consuming. It's only out in the country that a car becomes an asset. If you do drive in town, bear these points in mind:

- Tourists can drive in Spain with a valid driving licence from most other countries. An international driving licence or EU photo licence can be useful as a translation/credibility aid.
- Keep your driving licence, vehicle registration and insurance documents with you at all times.

- It is compulsory to wear seat belts and carry warning triangles, spares (tyre, bulbs, fanbelt) and tools to fit them.
- The speed limit is 50kmph in towns, 90kmph on most highways and 120kmph on motorways – although most drivers ignore these limits.
- Children under 12 may not travel in the front of a car except in a child car seat.
- Do not leave anything of value, including car radios, in your car. Foreign number plates can attract thieves.
- Be on your guard against thefts at motorway service areas, or thieves in the city who may try to make you stop and get out, perhaps by indicating you have a flat tyre.
- Bear in mind that Catalonia has one of the highest accident rates in Europe.

Car & motorbike hire

Car hire is relatively pricey, but it's a competitive market so shop around. Check carefully what's included: ideally, you want unlimited mileage, 16 per cent VAT (IVA) included and, especially, full insurance cover, rather than the third-party minimum (*seguro obligatorio*). You will need a credit card, although sometimes a cash downpayment will do. Most companies require you to have had a licence for at least a year.

EasyCar

Passeig Lluís Companys, 2nd level of underground car park (no phone/ www.easycar.com). Metro Arc de Triomf. **Open** 7am-11pm daily. **Credit** MC, V. **Map** p343 E6.

Online-only booking and payment. Basic rates for its Mercedes A-Class hatchbacks can be low (for example, two days for €60.82), but check the conditions carefully – such as only 100km of free mileage per day, and possible supplements for credit card payments, insurance and late return. There are also branches at Sants railway station and Maria Cristina (Parking Saba, Gran Via Carlos III, 97-105), both open 7am-11pm, renting Toyota Yaris and Mercedes cars respectively.

Europcar

Plaça dels Països Catalans, Sants (93 491 48 22/www.europcar.com). Metro Sants Estació. **Open** 7.30am-10.30pm Mon-Fri; 8am-1pm Sat. **Credit** AmEx, DC, MC, V. **Map** p341 A4.

A large international agency with several offices in Barcelona. Prices change daily – phone for details. **Airport branch**: 93 298 33 00.

Vanguard

C/Viladomat 297, Eixample (439 38 80/93 322 79 51/www.vanguard rent.com). Metro Hospital Clínic. **Open** 8am-2pm, 4-8pm Mon-Fri; 9am-1pm Sat, Sun. **Credit** AmEx, DC, MC, V. **Map** p341 B4.

Scooter and motorcycle hire, as well as cars at good rates. Prices range from a Honda (50cc) for €83.66 to a Yamaha (600cc) for €261. You must be 19 to hire a small bike and have had a licence for a year; 25 and three years for larger bikes.

Parking

Parking here is fiendishly complicated, and municipal police are quick to hand out tickets or tow away cars.

Don't park in front of doors with the sign *'Gual Permanent'*, indicating an entry with 24-hour right of access. In some parts of the Old City, access is limited to residents for much of the day. Be extremely careful about parking in streets in the Old City, as sometimes you may be able to get into a street but not out of it, as time-controlled bollards can be raised.

Pay & display areas

Many streets in the centre of the city and the Eixample are pay-and-display areas (*'zones blaves'*, or blue zones), with parking spaces marked in blue on the street. Parking restrictions apply 9am-2pm, 4-8pm Mon-Fri, when you can park for up to 2hrs; in the centre, the rate is €1.70/hr, less in other districts. If you overstay by no more than an hour, you can cancel the fine by paying an additional €6; to do so, press *Anul.lar denúncia* on the ticket machine, insert €6. Most machines accept credit cards (MC, V), and most do not give change.

Car parks

Car parks (*parkings*) are signalled by a white 'P' on a blue sign. **SABA** and public **SMASSA** both charge €1.70/hr. **SABA**: Plaça Catalunya, Plaça Urquinaona, Arc de Triomf, Avda Catedral, Passeig de Gràcia, C/Diputació-C/Pau Claris. **SMASSA**: Plaça dels Àngels-MACBA, Moll de la Fusta, Avda Francesc Cambó, Avda Paral.lel.

Metro-Park

Plaça de les Glòries, Eixample (93 265 10 47). Metro Glòries. **Open** 5am-11pm Mon-Thur; 5am-1am Fri, Sat. **Credit** AmEx, DC, MC, V. **Map** p343 F5.

A park-and-ride facility. Included in the €4.65 ticket is a day's unlimited travel on the metro and buses.

Towing away

Information 93 428 45 95. **Credit** AmEx, DC, MC, V.

If the municipal police have towed away your car, they will leave a triangular sticker on the pavement where it was. Call to find out which pound it has been taken to. Staff do not usually speak English. Recovering your vehicle within 4hrs of being towed costs €103, with each subsequent hour costing €1.65.

Petrol

Most *gasolineres* (petrol stations) have unleaded fuel (*sense plom/sin plomo*), regular (*super*) and diesel (*gas-oil*). Petrol is considerably cheaper in Spain than it is in most northern European countries.

Cycling

There is a growing network of bike lanes (*carrils bici*) along major avenues and by the seafront. However, weekday traffic is still risky for those used to more polite northern European drivers. Tourists should think twice before wheeling out. Rollerblading is popular along the seafront and the Diagonal and Rambla Catalunya.

Al punt de trobada (bicycle hire)

C/Badajoz 24, Poblenou (93 225 05 85/bicipuntrobada@hotmail. com). Metro Llacuna. **Open** *Apr-Sept* 9am-3pm, 5-9pm daily. *Oct-Mar* 9am-2pm, 4-8pm Mon-Sat; 9am-5pm Sun. **Credit** AmEx, MC, V.

This is a bike-hire place close to the beach. Mountain bikes cost €3.60/hr, €10.80/half-day and €15/day.

Resources A-Z

Addresses

Most apartment addresses consist of a street name followed by a street number, floor level and flat number, in that order. So, to go to C/València 246, 2º 3ª, find No.246; go up to the second floor and find the door marked as 3 or 3ª. Ground-floor flats are usually called *baixos* or *bajos* (often abbreviated 'bxs/bjos'); one floor up, the *entresol/entresuelo* ('entl'), and the next is often the *principal* ('pral'). Confusingly, numbered floors start here, first, second, up to the *àtic/ático* at the top.

Age restrictions

In Spain, you must be 18 to drive a car, 14 to drive a scooter (up to 75cc) and 16 to drink, smoke or have sex.

Business

Anyone wanting to set up shop in Barcelona needs to know the intricacies of local, Spanish and EU regulations. It's a waste of time trying to deal with this system alone. A visit to the **Cambra de Comerç** (*see p308*) is a must; some consulates can also refer you to professionals, and a *gestoria* (*see below*) will save you time and frustration.

Admin services

The *gestoria* is a very Spanish institution, the main function of which is to lighten the weight of local bureaucracy by dealing with it for you. A combination of book-keeper, lawyer and business adviser, a good *gestor* can be more than a little helpful in handling all of the paperwork and advising on various shortcuts, although *gestoria* employees rarely speak English.

LEC

Travessera de Gràcia 96, 2º 2ª, Gràcia (93 415 02 50). Bus 27, 31, 32. **Open** 9am-2pm, 4-7pm Mon-Fri. Closed Aug. **Map** p338 D3.
Offers business, social security, fiscal and general advice about financial procedures in Barcelona. Some English is spoken.

Tutzo Assessors

C/Aribau 226, Eixample (93 209 67 88/tutzoass-juridic@infonegocio.com). Bus 31, 58, 64. **Open** 8.30am-2pm, 4-7pm Mon-Fri. Closed 2wks Aug, Fri pm July, Aug. **Map** p338 C3.
Lawyers and economists as well as a *gestoria*. Some English speakers.

Conventions & conferences

Barcelona Convention Bureau

Rambla Catalunya 123, pral, Eixample (93 368 97 00/ www.barcelonaturisme.com). Metro Diagonal. **Open** *Sept-June* 9am-2.30pm, 4-7pm Mon-Thur; 9am-3pm Fri. July, Aug 8am-3pm Mon-Fri. **Map** p338 D4.
Specialist arm of the city tourist authority that assists organisations with conferences.

Fira de Barcelona

Avda Reina Maria Cristina, Montjuïc (93 233 20 00/www.firabcn.es). Metro Espanya. **Open** *Mid Sept-mid June* 9am-2pm, 4-6pm Mon-Fri. *Mid June-mid Sept* 9am-2pm Mon-Fri. **Map** p341 A5.
The Barcelona 'trade fair' is one of the largest permanent exhibition complexes in Europe. In addition to the main area at Plaça Espanya, it includes a huge site, Montjuïc-2, towards the airport, and administers the Palau de Congressos conference hall in the Plaça d'Espanya site, which can be let separately.

World Trade Center

Moll de Barcelona, Port Vell (93 508 88 88/www.wtcbarcelona.es). Metro Drassanes. **Open** 9am-2pm, 4-7pm Mon-Thur; 9am-3pm Fri. **Map** p342 C7.
The WTC rents 130,000 sq m of office space, with all the relevant infrastructure, in a modern complex in the old port. Both events and conferences can be arranged.

Courier services

Estació d'Autobusos Barcelona-Nord

C/Alí Bei 80, Eixample (93 232 43 29). Metro Arc de Triomf. **Open** 7am-9pm Mon-Fri; 7am-1.30pm Sat. **No credit cards. Map** p343 E5.
An inexpensive service available at the bus station for sending parcels on scheduled buses within Spain.

Missatgers Trèvol

C/Antonio Ricardos 14, La Sagrera (93 498 80 70/www.trevol.com). Metro Sagrera. **Open** 8.30am-7pm Mon-Fri. **No credit cards.**
Courier firm with bikes and vans. Delivering a package (weighing up to 6kg/13lb) by bike within the central area costs €3.45, plus tax.

Travel advice

For up-to-date information on travel to a specific country – including the latest news on safety and security, health issues, local laws and customs – contact your home country government's department of foreign affairs. Most have websites packed with useful advice for would-be travellers.

Australia
www.dfat.gov.au/travel

Republic of Ireland
www.irlgov.ie/iveagh

Canada
www.voyage.gc.ca

UK
www.fco.gov.uk/travel

New Zealand
www.mft.govt.nz/travel

USA
http://www.state.gov/travel

Seur

(*902 10 10 10/www.seur.es*). **Open** 8am-7pm Mon-Fri; 8am-2pm Sat. **No credit cards**.
A relatively efficient (though not always cheap) service, especially for international deliveries.

UPS

(*902 88 88 20/www.ups.com*). **Open** 8am-8.30pm Mon-Fri. **Credit** AmEx, MC, V. **Map** p337 C3.
Next-day delivery to many destinations, both Spanish and international. There are some English-speaking operators.

Office & computer services

Centro de Negocios

C/Pau Claris 97, 4° 1ª, Eixample (93 304 38 58/fax 93 301 69 04/www.centro-negocios.com). Metro Passeig de Gràcia. **Open** *Sept-July* 8am-9pm Mon-Fri. *Aug* 9am-3pm Mon-Fri. **Map** p342 D5.
Desks in shared offices, mailboxes, meeting rooms, secretarial services and a wide range of administrative services for hire.

GeoMac

Mobile 606 30 89 32/geomac@terra.es. **Open** by appt. **No credit cards**.
Experienced and Apple-certified American computer technician George Cowdery offers maintenance and trouble-shooting for Mac home and business computers.

Microrent

C/Rosselló 35, Eixample (93 363 32 50/fax 93 322 13 57/www.microrent.es). Metro Sants Estació or Entença. **Open** 9am-6pm Mon-Fri. **No credit cards. Map** p341 B4.
Computer equipment for rent: PCs, Macs, laptops, faxes, photocopiers.

Translators

DUUAL

C/Ciutat 7, 2° 4ª, Barri Gòtic (93 302 29 85/fax 93 412 40 66/www.duual.com). Metro Jaume I. **Open** *Oct-May* 9am-2pm, 4-7pm Mon-Thur; 9am-2pm Fri. *June-Sept* 8.30am-3pm Mon-Fri. Closed 3wks Aug. **No credit cards**. **Map** p345 B3.
Services in many languages, along with desktop publishing.

CMB Despacho Profesional de Traducciones

Gran Via de les Corts Catalanes 561 entl, Eixample (93 453 73 03). Metro Urgell. **Open** 9am-6pm Mon-Fri. **Map** p339 E3.
Legally certified translations ('*traducciones juradas*') of foreign-language documents into Spanish and Catalan. You will sometimes need a *traducción jurada* for official transactions.

Useful organisations

Ajuntament de Barcelona

Plaça Sant Miquel 4-5, Barri Gòtic (93 402 70 00/www.bcn.es). Metro Jaume I. **Open** *Sept-June* 8.30am-5.30pm Mon-Fri. *July, Aug* 8.15am-2.15pm Mon-Fri. **Map** p345 B3.

Up in smoke

If there's no smoke without fire, then Barcelona should be twinned with Beelzebub's back garden. Cigarettes are as common as concrete and no stigma whatsoever is attached to smoking: it's cool, it's clever and, above all, it's cheap.

In fact, it's the non-smokers who feel left out in a city where one in three is powered by the nicotine rush. Non-smoking areas do exist, but they're usually within three feet of an ember (and some even include ashtrays, just in case you change your mind). Even buying cigarettes is an experience here. Tobacconists in the city vary from steel-meshed holes in the wall to grand pre-war high-ceilinged museums with large wooden cabinets filled with all things inhaleable. As in other European countries, the *estanco* (*see p315*) is also the place where you can buy stamps and phonecards – and they're always shut during siesta time.

The choice is mind-boggling. Cigars from the Americas are both cheap and plentiful, but if you really want to blend in with the locals, the leading Spanish brand is Fortuna, available in different strengths. For people travelling from the UK or the USA, the price of carcinogenics will come as something of a pleasant surprise. The reason being that, while the Spanish government is desperate to increase tax on cigarettes and discourage smoking, it isn't allowed to. At the time of writing, a price rise would bring national inflation above the Euro-imposed limits. So until the deadlock is settled, prices stay firmly at a generous level and smoking tourists would be advised to leave a carton-sized space when packing their suitcase.

There are also differences in the way the government deals with soft drugs. Small amounts of marijuana for personal use have been all but legalised, though things get a little hazy when identifying when and where you can smoke it. Most bars and clubs frown on the practice, at least when done openly, but it's far from unusual for a herby aroma to waft across the dancefloor. The parks are the safest bet, particularly in the summer and at the weekend when few shops are open. This tradition is so established that Ciutadella park now has a great line in food sellers offering munchies to the desperate on those lazy Sunday afternoons. Suffice to say, '*¿Tienes papel?*' ('Do you have any papers?') is now as common a request as '*¿Tienes fuego?*' ('Do you have a light?').

The city council. Permits for new businesses are issued by the ten municipal districts.

Borsa de Valors de Barcelona

Passeig de Gràcia 19, Eixample (93 401 35 55/www.borsabcn.es). Metro Passeig de Gràcia. **Open** *Info* 9am-6pm Mon-Fri. *Library* 9am-noon Mon-Fri. **Map** p342 D5.
The stock exchange.

British Society of Catalunya

Mailing address: Lloyds TSB Bank, Rambla Catalunya 123 (tel/fax 93 688 08 66). Metro Diagonal.
Map p338 C2.
An informal group for expats that has been organising walks, drinks and other events since 1920. Annual membership is €9.

Cambra de Comerç, Indústria i Navegació de Barcelona

Avda Diagonal 452-4, Eixample (902 448 448/www.cambrabcn.es). Metro Diagonal/FGC Provença. **Open** 9am-5pm Mon-Thur; 9am-2pm Fri. **Map** p338 D4.
An important institution for businesses, the Chamber of Commerce offers information and advice.

Generalitat de Catalunya

General information 012/new businesses 902 20 15 20/ www.gencat.net.
The Catalan government provides a range of consultancy services.

Complaints

If you have a complaint that can't be cleared up on the spot, ask for an official complaint form (*hoja de reclamación/full de reclamació*), which many businesses and all shops are required to have available (in English). Fill out the form, and leave the pink copy with the business. Take your copy, along with any receipts, guarantees and so on, to an official consumer office.

Oficina Municipal d'Informació al Consumidor

Ronda de Sant Pau 43, Barri Gòtic (93 402 78 41/www.omic.bcn.es). Metro Paral.lel or Sant Antoni. **Open** *Mid Sept-mid June* 9am-2pm Mon, Wed, Fri; 9am-2pm, 4pm-6pm Tue, Wed. *Mid June-mid Sept* 9am-2pm Mon-Fri. **Map** p345 A/B3.
This is a municipally run official centre for consumer advice and complaints follow-up. You can file complaints in English through the useful website.

Telèfon de Consulta del Consumidor

012. **Open** 9am-6pm Mon-Fri.
A phoneline run by the Generalitat for consumer advice. Call the general info number and ask to speak to a consumer specialist.

Consulates

A full list of consulates is in the phone book under *'Consolats/Consulados'*. Most consultates have an emergency phone number as well.

Australian Consulate

Gran Via Carles III 98, Zona Alta (93 490 90 13/fax 93 411 09 04/www.embaustralia.es). Metro Maria Cristina or Les Corts.
Open *Sept-July* 10am-noon Mon-Fri. **Map** p344-5 A2/3.

British Consulate

Avda Diagonal 477, Eixample (93 366 62 00/fax 93 366 62 21/ www.ukinspain.com). Metro Hospital Clínic. **Open** *End Sept-mid June* 9.30am-1.30pm, 4-5pm Mon-Fri. *Mid June-mid Sept* 9am-1.30pm Mon-Fri. **Map** p338 C3.

Canadian Consulate

C/Elisenda de Pinós 10, Zona Alta (93 204 27 00/fax 93 204 27 01/ www.canada-es.org). FGC Reina Elisenda. **Open** 10am-1pm Mon-Fri. **Map** p338 D4.

Irish Consulate

Gran Via Carles III 94, Zona Alta (93 491 50 21/fax 93 411 29 21). Metro Maria Cristina or Les Corts. **Open** 10am-1pm Mon-Fri. **Map** p337 A3.

New Zealand Consulate

Travessera de Gràcia 64, 2º, Gràcia (93 209 03 99/fax 93 202 08 90). Metro Diagonal/bus 64, 58. **Open** Sept-June 9am-1pm, 4-6pm Mon-Fri. **Map** p338 C3.

US Consulate

Passeig Reina Elisenda 23, Zona Alta (93 280 22 27/fax 93 280 61 74/www.embusa.es). FGC Reina Elisenda. **Open** 9am-1pm Mon-Fri. **Map** p337 A1.

Customs

Customs declarations are not usually necessary if you arrive in Spain from another EU country and are carrying only legal goods for personal use. The amounts given below are guidelines only; if you approach these maximums in several categories, you may still have to explain your personal habits.

- 800 cigarettes, 400 small cigars, 200 normal cigars or 1 kilogram of loose tobacco
- 10 litres of spirits (over 22 per cent alcohol), 20 litres of fortified wine or alcoholic drinks with under 22 per cent alcohol, 90 litres of wine and 110 litres of beer.

Coming from a non-EU country, you can bring:

- 200 cigarettes, 100 small cigars, 50 regular cigars or 250 grams (8.82 ounces) of tobacco
- 1 litre of spirits (over 22 per cent alcohol) or 2 litres of any other alcoholic drink with under 22 per cent alcohol
- 50 grams (1.76 ounces) of perfume.

Visitors can also carry up to €6,000 in cash without having to declare it. Non-EU residents can also reclaim VAT (IVA) paid on some large purchases when they leave Spain.

Disabled

Institut Municipal de Persones amb Disminució

Avda Diagonal 233, Eixample (93 413 27 75/www.bcn.es/imd). Metro Glòries/7, 56 bus. **Open** *Mid Sept-mid June* 9am-2pm, later by appt, Mon-Fri. *Mid June-mid Sept* 8.30am-2.30pm Mon-Fri. **Map** p343 F5.
The city's organisation for the disabled has info on access to theatres, museums and restaurants.

Access to sights

Newer museums, such as the **MACBA** (*see p95*), have good access, but the process of converting older buildings is slow and difficult. Phoning ahead to check is always a good idea even if a place claims to be accessible: access might depend, for example, on getting a lift key in advance. Here are some wheelchair-friendly venues:

Museums & galleries

CCCB
Col.lecció Thyssen-Bornemisza (Monestir de Pedralbes)
Fundació Joan Miró
Fundacío Antoni Tàpies
MACBA
MNAC
Museu Barbier-Mueller d'Art Precolombi
Museu d'Arqueologia de Catalunya
Museu d'Art Modern
Museu de les Arts Decoratives
Museu del Calçat
Museu de Cera de Barcelona
Museu del Temple Expiatori de la Sagrada Família
Museu d'Història de Catalunya
Museu de la Xocolata
Museu Egipci de Barcelona
Museu Frederic Marès
Museu Futbol Club Barcelona
Museu Picasso
Museu Tèxtil i d'Indumentaria

Transport

Barcelona's transport facilities and access for disabled people still leave quite a lot to be desired, despite improvements. For wheelchair users, buses and taxis are usually the best public transport options. There is a special transport information phoneline, and transport maps, which you can pick up from transport information offices (*see below*), indicate wheelchair access points and adapted bus routes. You can also find information on the city's public transport website, www.tmb.net.

Centro de Informacion de Transporte

Information 93 486 07 52/fax 93 486 07 53. **Open** *Sept-July* 9am-9pm Mon-Fri; 9am-3pm Sat. *Aug* 9am-9pm Mon-Fri.
The TMB's disabled transport information department. English speakers are sometimes available.

Buses

All the Aerobús airport buses and the open-topped tourist buses are fully accessible to wheelchair users. Similar fully adapted buses also alternate with standard buses on all night bus routes and most daytime routes. Transport maps and bus stop signs indicate which routes use adapted vehicles.

Metro & FGC

Only L2 (purple) has lifts and ramps at all stations; on L1 and L3, a few stations have lifts. The Montjuïc funicular railway is fully adapted for wheelchairs. FGC stations at Provença, Muntaner and Avda Tibidabo are accessible.

RENFE trains

Sants, Estació de França, Passeig de Gràcia and Plaça Catalunya stations are accessible to wheelchairs, but trains are not. At Estació de Sants, if you go to the *Atenció al Client* office ahead of time, help on the platform can be arranged.

Taxis

All taxi drivers are officially required to transport wheelchairs and guide dogs for no extra charge, but their cars can be inconveniently small, and, in practice, the willingness of drivers to co-operate varies widely. Special minibus taxis adapted for wheelchairs can be ordered from the Taxi Amic service, as well as from some general taxi services, such as Barnataxi (93 357 77 55) and Radiotaxi 33 (93 303 30 33).

Taxi Amic

93 420 80 88. **Open** 7.30am-11pm Mon-Fri; 9am-10pm Sat, Sun.
Fares are the same as for regular cabs, but there is a minimum fare of €9 for Barcelona city, and more for surrounding area. Numbers are limited, so call well in advance to request a specific time.

Emergencies

Emergency services 112. The operator will connect you to the police, fire or ambulance services, as required.
Ambulance/*Ambulància* 061. For hospitals and other health services, *see p310.*
Fire Service/*Bombers/Bomberos* 080
Policia Nacional (first choice in a police emergency) 091
Guàrdia Urbana (city police; for traffic but also general law and order) 092. For more information on police forces, *see p314.*
Electricity (all companies) 900 77 00 77
Gas/*Gas Natural* 900 760 760
Water/*Aigües de Barcelona* 900 710 710
All are open 24 hours.

Drugs

Many people smoke cannabis very openly in Spain, but you should be aware that its possession or consumption in public places is illegal.

In private places, the law is contradictory: smoking is OK, but you can still be nabbed for possession. Enforcement is often not the highest of police priorities, but you could theoretically receive a hefty fine. Smoking in bars is also prohibited; proprietors are strict on this issue because it could cost them their licences.

Electricity

The standard current in Spain is 220V. A diminishing number of old buildings still have 125V circuits, and it's advisable to check before using electrical equipment in old, cheap hotels. Plugs are all of the two-round-pin type. The 220V current works fine with British-bought 240V products with a plug adaptor. If you have US (110V) equipment you will also need a current transformer to avoid a meltdown.

Gay & lesbian

Ca la Dona (*see p320*) is the main centre for women.

Casal Lambda

C/Verdaguer i Callís 10, Barri Gòtic (93 319 55 50/www.lambdaweb.org). Metro Urquinaona. **Open** 6-9pm Mon-Sat. **Map** p344 B2.

Gay cultural organisation that is the focus for a wide range of activities and publishes the magazine *Lambda* three times a year.

Coordinadora Gai-Lesbiana

C/Finlàndia 45, Sants (93 298 00 29/www.cogailes.org). Metro Plaça de Sants. **Open** 7-9pm Mon-Fri. **Map** p341 A4.

This gay umbrella organisation works with the Ajuntament on issues of concern to the gay, bisexual and transexual community.

Front d'Alliberament Gai de Catalunya

C/Verdi 88, Gràcia (93 217 26 69). Metro Fontana. **Open** 7-9pm Tue, Thur, Fri. **Map** p339 E3.

FAG is a vocal multi-group that produces the *Barcelona Gai* information bulletin.

Teléfon Rosa

900 601 601. **Open** 6-10pm daily.

The phoneline of the Coordinadora Gai-Lesbiana gives help or advice on any gay or lesbian issue.

Health

Visitors can obtain emergency care through the public health service (Servei Catalá de la Salut, often referred to as the 'Seguretat Social/Seguridad Social'). EU nationals are entitled to free basic medical attention if they have an E111 form (if you can get one sent or faxed within four days, you will be exempt from all charges; otherwise, you can be reimbursed in your country of residence). E111 also works for people from countries that have an agreement with Spain, such as Switzerland, Andorra, Chile, Peru, Ecuador, Brazil and Paraguay. For more information call 902 111 444.

For non-emergencies, it's usually quicker to use private travel insurance rather than the state system. Similarly, non-EU nationals with private medical insurance can also make use of state health services on a paying basis, but it will usually be simpler to use a private clinic.

Accident & emergency

In a medical emergency go to the casualty department (*Urgències*) of any of the main public hospitals. All listed below are open 24 hours daily. The most central are the **Clínic** or the **Perecamps**. If necessary, make an emergency call to 112 (and you will be put through to the appropriate service) or 061 (ambulance).

Centre d'Urgències Perecamps

Avda Drassanes 13-15, Raval (93 441 06 00). Metro Drassanes or Paral.lel. **Map** p345 A4.

Located near the Rambla, this clinic specialises in primary attention for injuries and less serious emergencies.

Hospital Clínic

C/Villarroel 170, Eixample (93 227 54 00). Metro Hospital Clínic. **Map** p338 C4.

The main central hospital, the Clínic also has a first-aid centre for less serious emergencies two blocks away at C/València 184 (93 227 93 00; 9am-9pm Mon-Fri, 9am-1pm Sat).

Hospital de la Creu Roja de Barcelona

C/Dos de Maig 301, Eixample (93 507 27 00). Metro Hospital de Sant Pau. **Map** p339 F4.

Hospital del Mar

Passeig Marítim 25-9, Barceloneta (93 248 30 00). Metro Ciutadella-Vila Olímpica. **Map** p343 E7.

Hospital de la Santa Creu i Sant Pau

C/Sant Antoni Maria Claret 167, Eixample (93 291 90 00). Metro Hospital de Sant Pau. **Map** p339 F4.

AIDS/HIV

The actual death rate from AIDS is falling in Spain, but the HIV virus continues to spread in many groups, particularly among young heterosexuals. Local chemists take part in a needle-exchange and condom-distribution programme for intravenous drug users. Antiretroviral drugs for HIV treatment are covered by Social Security in Spain. Free, anonymous blood tests for HIV and other sexually transmitted diseases are given at **CAP Drassanes** (*see p311*).

Actua

C/Gomis 38 bajos, Zona Alta (93 418 50 00/www.interactua.net). Metro Vallcarca/bus 22, 27, 73. **Open** 9am-2pm, 4-7pm Mon-Fri.

Support group for people with HIV.

AIDS Information Line

900 21 22 22. **Open** *Mid Sept-May* 8am-5.30pm Mon-Fri. *June-mid Sept* 8am-3pm Mon-Fri.

Complementary medicine

Integral: Centre Mèdic i de Salut

Plaça Urquinaona 2, 3º 2ª, Eixample (93 318 30 50/www.integralcentremedic.com). Metro Urquinaona. **Open** *Sept-July* 9am-9pm Mon-Fri (call for an appt). **Map** p344 B1.

Acupuncture, homeopathy and other forms of complementary medicine are offered at this well-established clinic. Some speak English.

Contraception & abortion

All pharmacies sell condoms (*condons/preservativos*) and other forms of contraception including pills, which can be bought without a prescription. Many bars and clubs also have condom vending machines.

Although abortion is legal, under certain circumstances, during the first 12 weeks of pregnancy for those aged 18 or over, it is usually easier to obtain at a private clinic than at a public hospital.

Centre Jove d'Anticoncepció i Sexualitat

C/La Granja 19-21, Gràcia (93 415 10 00/www.centrejove.org). Metro Lesseps. **Open** 12am-6.30pm Mon-Thur; 10am-2pm Fri. **Map** p339 E2.

A family planning centre aimed at young people (officially, under 25).

Free AIDS tests are given to people up to the age of 30. Pregnancy tests are available for a small fee.

Dentists

Not covered by EU reciprocal agreements, so private rates, which can be costly, apply.

Centre Odontològic de Barcelona

C/Calàbria 251 bajos, Eixample (93 439 45 00). Metro Entença. **Open** *Sept-July* 9am-8pm Mon-Fri. *Aug* 9am-1pm, 3-8pm Mon-Fri. **Credit** DC, MC, V. **Map** p341 B4.
Well-equipped clinics providing a complete range of dental services. Several of the staff speak English.
Other locations: Institut Odontològic de la Sagrada Família C/Sardenya 319, Eixample (93 457 04 53). Institut Odontològic C/Diputació 238, Eixample (93 342 64 00).

Doctors

A **Centre d'Assistència Primària** (CAP) is a local health centre where you can normally be seen fairly quickly by a doctor. Alternatively, you could go private.

CAP Casc Antic

C/Rec Comtal 24, Barri Gòtic (93 310 14 21/50 98). Metro Arc de Triomf. **Open** 9am-8pm Mon-Fri; 9am-5pm Sat (emergencies only). **Map** p344 C2.

CAP Doctor Lluís Sayé

C/Torres i Amat 8, Raval (93 301 24 82/27 05/emergencies 93 301 25 32). Metro Universitat. **Open** 8am-8pm Mon-Fri; 9am-5pm Sat (emergencies only). **Map** p344 A1.

CAP Drassanes

Avda Drassanes 17-21, Raval (93 329 44 95). Metro Drassanes. **Open** 8am-8pm Mon-Fri. **Map** p345 A4.

CAP Vila Olímpica

C/Joan Miró 17, Vila Olímpica (93 221 37 85). Metro Ciutadella-Vila Olímpica. **Open** 8am-9pm Mon-Fri; 8am-4.30pm (emergencies only). **Map** p343 F6.

Centre Mèdic Assistencial Catalonia

C/Provença 281, Bajos, Eixample (93 215 37 93). Metro Diagonal. **Open** 8am-9pm Mon-Fri. **Credit** V. **Map** p338 D4.
Dr Lynd is a British doctor who has been practising in Barcelona for many years. She can be seen at this surgery from 3.30pm to 7.20pm every Wednesday.

Dr Mary McCarthy

C/Aribau 215, pral 1ª, Eixample (93 200 29 24/mobile 607 220 040). FGC Gràcia/58, 64 bus. **Open** by appt only. **Credit** MC, V. **Map** p338 C3.
Dr McCarthy is an internal medicine specialist from the US. She will also treat general patients at American healthcare rates.

Opticians

See p209.

Pharmacies

Pharmacies (*farmàcies*) are signalled by large green and red crosses, usually in flashing neon. There are plenty about, and most are open from 9am to 1.30pm and 4.30pm to 8pm Monday to Friday, and 9am to 1.30pm on Saturdays. About a dozen pharmacies operate around the clock, while more have late opening hours; some of the most central are listed below.

The full list of chemists that stay open late (usually till 10pm) and overnight on any given night is posted daily outside every pharmacy door, and also given in the day's newspapers. You can call the 010 and 098 information phonelines (*see p319*). At night, duty pharmacies often appear to be closed, but knock on the shutters and you will be helped by the duty pharmacist.

Farmàcia Alvarez

Passeig de Gràcia 26, Eixample (93 302 11 24). Metro Passeig de Gràcia. **Open** 24hrs daily. **Credit** MC, V. **Map** p342 D5.

Farmàcia Cervera

C/Muntaner 254, Eixample (93 200 09 96). Metro Diagonal/FGC Gràcia. **Open** 24hrs daily. **Credit** AmEx, MC, V. **Map** p338 C3.
Will also do home deliveries.

Farmàcia Clapés

La Rambla 98, Barri Gòtic (93 301 28 43). Metro Liceu. **Open** 24hrs daily. **Credit** AmEx, MC, V. **Map** p345 A3.

Farmàcia Vilar

Vestibule, Estació de Sants, Sants (93 490 92 07). Metro Sants Estació. **Open** 7am-10.30pm Mon-Fri; 8am-10.30pm Sat, Sun. **Credit** AmEx, MC, V. **Map** p341 A4.

Helplines

Alcoholics Anonymous

93 317 77 77. **Open** 10am-1pm, 5-8pm Mon-Fri; 7-9pm Sat, Sun.
Among the local AA groups there are several that have dedicated English-speaking sections.

Telèfon de l'Esperança

93 414 48 48. **Open** 24hrs daily.
The staff at this local helpline service run by a private foundation can consult an extensive database to put you in contact with other specialist help groups – from psychiatric to legal. English is occasionally spoken, but not guaranteed.

ID

From the age of 14, Spaniards are legally obliged to carry their DNIs (identity cards). Foreigners are also meant to carry a national ID card or passport, but in practice it's usually OK to carry a photocopy of your passport, or a driving licence.

Insurance

For healthcare and EU nationals, *see p310*. Some non-EU countries have reciprocal healthcare agreements with Spain, but for most travellers it's usually more convenient to have private travel insurance – which will also, of course, cover you in case of theft and flight problems.

Internet

Many ISPs (such as **Wanadoo**, 902 011 902/ www.wanadoo.es) offer free basic access, while others offer a slightly better service for a monthly fee (such as **Auna**, 902 500 090/www.iddeo.com).

Broadband (ADSL) is still experiencing monumental teething problems. Companies such as **Telefónica** (www.telefonicaonline.es), **Ya** (www.ya.com), Wanadoo and **Terra** (www.terra.es) offer ADSL lines with 24hr access for a flat monthly rate of approximately €25-€45. However, all of them are known to have serious flaws in their technical and customer service.

Internet access

There are internet centres all over Barcelona. Some libraries (*see below*) have internet points.

Ciberopción

Gran Via de les Corts Catalanes 602, Eixample (93 412 73 08). Metro Universitat. **Open** 9am-1am Mon-Fri; 10am-1am Sat; 11am-1am Sun. **No credit cards. Map** p338 D4.
Cheap and very fast internet connection with 130 terminals. It costs 60¢ for each 30min online.

Click Center

Ronda de Sant Antoni 32-4 (93 324 80 79/www.click-center.net). Metro Sant Antoni. **Open** 10am-midnight Mon-Thur, Sun; 10am-1am Fri, Sat. **Credit** AmEx, MC, V. **Map** p342 C5.
Internet access, as well as sale of computers and accessories, and photo development.
Other location: C/Verdi 9 (93 415 88 39).

Cybermundo

C/Bergara 3 & C/Balmes 8 (93 317 71 42). Metro Catalunya. **Open** 9am-1am Mon-Thur; 9am-2am Fri; 10am-2am Sat; 11am-1am Sun. **No credit cards. Map** p344 A1.
Centrally located, with some English/American keyboards. Prices vary according to the time of day, and can be quite cheap.

easyEverything

La Rambla 31, Barri Gòtic (93 318 24 35/www.easyeverything.com). Metro Liceu. **Open** 8am-2.30am daily. **No credit cards. Map** p345 A3.
There are 330 terminals here and 240 at Ronda Universitat 35 (93 412 10 58). Prices vary according to demand: €1.20 can get you as much as 3hrs if it's empty, but only about 30mins when it's busy (usually from around noon-9pm). Connection is slow.

Left luggage

Aeroport del Prat

Terminal B. **Open** 24hrs daily. **Rates** €4 per day.
If you've left it at the airport.

Estació d'Autobusos Barcelona-Nord

C/Alí Bei 80, Eixample. Metro Arc de Triomf. **Open** 24hrs daily. **Rates** €3, €4.50 per day. **Map** p343 E5.

Train stations

There are lockers at Sants (open 6am-11pm) and França (6am-11.45pm daily), but not the smaller stations. Rates are around €6-€7 per day.

Legal help

Servicio d'Orientació Jurídica

C/València 344, Eixample (93 567 16 44/www.gencat.es/justicia/dgraj/soj.htm). Metro Verdaguer. **Open** 9am-2pm Mon-Fri. **Map** p339 E4.
A legal advice service run by the Generalitat's justice department. The lawyers at the centre will not write any document or become involved themselves, but those who qualify through low income can be appointed a legal-aid lawyer.

Libraries

Some libraries offer novels in English and free internet access. Call 010 for library addresses.

Ateneu Barcelonès

C/Canuda 6, Barri Gòtic (93 343 61 21/www.ateneu-bcn.org). Metro Catalunya. **Open** 9am-11pm daily. **Map** p344 B2.
This venerable old cultural and philosophical society has the best private library in the city, plus a peaceful interior garden patio and a quiet bar. It also organises cultural events, exhibitions and films. Membership costs €120.20, and €14.15 per month.

Biblioteca de Catalunya

C/Hospital 56, Raval (93 270 23 00/www.gencat.es/bc). Metro Liceu. **Open** 9am-8pm Mon-Fri; 9am-2pm Sat. **Map** p344 A2.
The Catalan national collection is housed in the medieval Hospital de la Santa Creu and has a wonderful stock reaching back centuries. Readers' cards are required, but one-day research visits are allowed (take your passport). The library has internet terminals.

British Council/ Institut Britànic

C/Amigó 83, Zona Alta (93 241 97 11). FGC Muntaner. **Open** *Oct-June* 9.30am-12.30pm, 3.30-9pm Tue-Fri; 10.30am-1.30pm Sat. *July, Sept* 9.30am-2pm, 4-8.30pm Mon-Fri. **Map** p338 C2.
UK press, English books, satellite TV and a big multimedia section oriented towards learning English. (Access is free; borrowing costs €55 a year).

Mediateca

CaixaForum, Avda Marquès de Comillas 6-8, Montjuïc (902 22 30 40/www.mediatecaonline.net). Metro Plaça d'Espanya. **Open** 10am-8pm Tue-Sat; 10am-2pm, 4-8pm Sun. **Map** p341 A5.
A high-tech art, music and media library in the arts centre of Fundació la Caixa. Most materials are open-access, and you can borrow books, magazines, CDs, etc. Membership is €6 (€3 concessions).

Lost property

If you lose something at the airport, report the loss immediately to the **Aviación Civil** office in the relevant terminal, or the lost property centre (*Oficina de objetos perdidos,* Terminal B, 93 298 33 49). If you have mislaid anything on a train, look for the *Atención al Viajero* desk or *Jefe de Estació* office at the nearest main station to where your property went astray, or call ahead to the destination station of the train. Or call station information and ask for *Objetos Perdidos*.

Municipal Lost Property Office

Oficina de Troballes, C/Ciutat 9, Barri Gòtic (lost property enquiries 010). Metro Jaume I. **Open** 9am-2pm Mon-Fri. **Map** p345 B3.
All items found on city public transport and taxis, or picked up by the police in the street, should eventually find their way to this office near the Ajuntament, within a few days. Call 010 for information. Within 24hrs of the loss you can also try ringing the city transport authority on 93 318 70 74, or, for taxis, the Institut Metropolità del Taxi on 93 223 40 12.

Media

Spanish and Catalan newspapers tend to be stuffy, with few large photographs and easy-on-the-eye fonts of their British counterparts. There are no sensationalist tabloids in Spain – for scandal and salaciousness, the *prensa rosa* ('pink press' – gossip magazines) is the place to look. Television channels, though, go straight for the mass market, with *telebasura* (junk television) prevalent.

Catalan is the dominant language in both radio and television, less so in print.

Daily newspapers

Free daily papers of a reasonable quality, such as *Barcelona@Más*, *20 Minutes* and *Metro,* are handed out in the city centre every morning. Articles in these papers jump between Spanish and Catalan with no apparent reason.

Avui

A conservative, nationalist Catalan-language newspaper, now suffering from declining readership numbers.

El País

This serious, socialist-leaning paper is the only one extensively read across Spain. There is a daily Catalonia supplement.

El Periódico

A tabloid layout with serious content, and often critical of the Partido Popular government in Madrid. In Catalan or Spanish.

La Vanguardia

Barcelona's top-selling daily. It's conservative in tone, with a Barcelona supplement every day. Written in Spanish, it often includes the work of syndicated international correspondents throughout the world.

English language

Foreign newspapers are available at most kiosks on La Rambla and Passeig de Gràcia.

Barcelona Business

A monthly paper combining business and political stories with city news.

b-guided

Quarterly bilingual style magazine in Spanish and English for bars, clubs, shops, restaurants and exhibitions; sold at hip venues and in FNAC.

Metropolitan

A free monthly general interest magazine for English-speaking Barcelona residents, distributed in bars, embassies and other anglophone hangouts.

Movin' BCN

A well-designed bilingual monthly covering concerts, movies, food, theatre, nightlife and cultural events.

Listings & classifieds

The main newspapers have daily 'what's on' listings, with entertainment supplements on Fridays (television schedules usually appear on Saturdays). For monthly listings, see *Metropolitan* and freebies such as *Mondo Sonoro, AB* and *Go* (found in bars and music shops). Of the dailies, *La Vanguardia* has the best classified section, especially on Sundays.

Anuntis

The largest of the classified-ad magazines, *Anuntis* (www.anuntis.com) is published on Mondays, Wednesdays and Fridays.

Guía del Ocio

This weekly listings magazine (www.guiadelociobcn.es) is available at any kiosk, but its listings are not always up to date.

Television

Spanish TV – its audience dominated by the country's ageing population – may come as something of a shock, with tedious variety shows, comedians telling mother-in-law jokes and interminable ad breaks. Programme start times are unreliable and films are mainly dubbed. Some of the private channels scrape the barrel still further with soft porn. Undubbed films are shown by 'VO' in listings or, on 'dual' TVs, the dual symbol at the top of the screen.

TVE1

The heavily in debt Spanish state broadcaster, 'La Primera', is controlled by the government and has a corresponding bias. Do not expect cutting edge television.

TVE2

Also state-run, TVE 2, 'La Dos' offers more highbrow fare with some good late-night movies and documentaries.

TV3

Programmes are entirely in Catalan, with generally mainstream subject matter. Often has good films in original version or 'dual'.

Canal 33

Also regional and in Catalan, with documentaries, sports programmes and round table discussions.

Antena 3

A private channel providing a mixture of chat programmes and American action films.

Tele 5

Also private, and part-owned by Silvio Berlusconi. Its main recent attraction has been *Gran Hermano* (Big Brother), as well as various celebrity gossip programmes.

Canal +

A subscription channel offering films and sport, with some programmes, such as the news, *Los 40 Principales* (Spain's Top 40) and *Las Noticias de Guiñol* (an excellent daily news spoof using puppets) shown unscrambled to whet your appetite.

BTV

The young staff of the Ajuntament's city channel (who can be seen hard at work through their office windows on Via Laietana) produce Barcelona's most ground-breaking TV.

City TV

A private channel, cloned from a Toronto city station. Magazine-style programmes and soft porn.

Satellite & cable

Satellite and cable are becoming increasingly popular in Barcelona. The leader is Digital+.

Radio

There are vast numbers of local, regional and national stations, with Catalan having a high profile. **Catalunya Mùsica** (101.5 FM) is mainly classical, while **Flaix FM** (105.7 FM) provides news and music. For something a little more alternative, there is **Radio Bronka** on 99 FM, or **Radio 3** (98.7), with an eclectic music policy. You can listen to the **BBC World Service** on shortwave on 15485, 9410 and 6195 KHz, depending on the time of day.

Money

Spain's currency is the euro.

Banks & foreign exchange

Banks (*bancos*) and savings banks (*caixes d'estalvis/cajas de ahorros*) usually accept travellers' cheques for a commission fee, but often refuse to cash any kind of personal cheque except one issued by that bank. Some foreign exchange bureaux (*cambios*) don't charge commission, but these generally offer you a lower rate. Obtaining money through an ATM machine – which are everywhere – with a debit or credit card is often the easiest option despite the fees often charged for withdrawals.

BANK HOURS

Banks are normally open from 8.30am to 2pm Monday to Friday. From 1 October to 30 April most branches also open on Saturday mornings from 8.30am to 1pm. Hours vary a little between banks. Savings banks, which offer the same exchange facilities as banks, open from 8.30am to 2pm Monday to Friday. From October to May many are open late on Thursdays, from 4.30pm to 7.45pm.

OUT-OF-HOURS SERVICES

Outside normal hours there are foreign exchange offices open at the airport (both terminals, 7am-10.30pm daily) and Sants station (8am-10pm daily), and more in the city centre. Some on La Rambla are open until midnight (and until 3am from July to September). At the airport, Sants and outside some banks there are automatic exchange machines that accept notes in major currencies.

American Express

La Rambla 74 (93 342 73 11). Metro Liceu. **Open** 9am-9pm Mon-Sat. **Map** p345 A3..
All the usual AmEx card services, along with currency exchange and money transfers.

Western Union Money Transfer

Loterías Manuel Martín, La Rambla 41 (93 412 70 41/www.westernunion.com). Metro Liceu or Drassanes. **Open** 9.30am-11.30pm daily. **Map** p345 A3.
The quickest, although not the cheapest, way of having money sent from abroad.
Other location: Mail Boxes, C/València 214, Eixample (93 454 69 83).

Credit cards

Major credit cards are widely accepted in hotels, shops, restaurants and other places (including metro ticket machines, and pay-and-display on-street parking machines). However, American Express and to a certain extent, Diner's Club cards are less accepted than MasterCard and Visa.

You can withdraw cash with major cards from ATMs, and banks will advance cash against a credit card.

Note: you need photo ID (passport, driving licence or similar) when using a credit or debit card in a shop, but usually not in a restaurant.

Lost/stolen credit cards

All lines have English-speaking staff and are open 24hrs daily.
American Express 902 37 56 37
Diners Club 901 10 10 11
MasterCard 900 97 12 31
Visa 900 99 12 16

Tax

The standard rate for sales tax (IVA) is 16 per cent, although this drops to seven per cent in hotels and restaurants, and four per cent on books. IVA may or may not be included in listed prices in hotels and restaurants. If it's not, the expression *més/más* IVA (plus sales tax) or IVA *no inclòs/incluido* (sales tax not included) must appear after the price. Beware of this when getting quotes on expensive items. In shops displaying a 'Tax-Free Shopping' sticker, non-EU residents can reclaim tax on large purchases when leaving the country.

Opening times

Most shops open from 9 or 10am to 1 or 2pm and then from 4 or 5pm to 8 or 9pm, Monday to Saturday, though many do not reopen on Saturday afternoons. All-day opening is becoming increasingly common.

Markets open earlier, at 7 or 8am, and most stalls are shut by 2pm. The Ajuntament has recently ordered that some stallholders at each municipal market should remain open in the afternoons, in an effort to compete with supermarkets.

Major stores, shopping centres and a growing number of shops open all day, from 10am to 9pm Monday to Saturday. Larger shops are allowed to open for Sundays and a few holidays, mostly around Christmas.

In summer, shops closing for weeks at a stretch has become less common, although many restaurants and shops still shut for all or part of August. Some businesses work a shortened day from June to September, from 8 or 9am till 3pm. Most museums close one day each week, usually on Mondays.

Police

Barcelona has several police forces. The **Guàrdia Urbana** wear navy and pale blue, and are concerned with traffic and local regulations, but also help to keep general law and order, and deal with noise complaints. The **Policía Nacional**, in darker blue uniforms and white shirts (or blue, combat-style gear), patrol the streets, and are responsible for dealing with more serious crime. The Catalan government's police, the **Mossos d'Esquadra**, in navy and light blue with red trim, are gradually increasing their remit, and are now responsible for traffic control in Barcelona province, but not in the city itself. The **Guàrdia Civil** is a paramilitary force with green uniforms. It polices highways, customs posts and some government buildings.

REPORTING A CRIME

If you are robbed or attacked, report the incident as soon as possible at the nearest police station (*comisaría*), or dial 112. In the centre, the most convenient is the Guàrdia Urbana station on the Rambla, which often has English-speaking officers on duty. Elsewhere, contact the Policía Nacional (the 24-hour operator on 091 can connect you to the closest *comisaría*).

If you report a crime, you will be asked to make an official statement (*denuncia*). It is highly improbable that you will recover your property, but you need the *denuncia* to make an insurance claim.

Guàrdia Urbana Ciutat Vella

La Rambla 43, Barri Gòtic (092). Metro Liceu or Drassanes. **Open** 24hrs daily. **Map** p345 A3.

Postal services

Letters and postcards weighing up to 20g cost 26¢ within Spain; 51¢ to the rest of Europe; 76¢ to the rest of the world. It's usually easiest to buy stamps at *estancs* (*see below*).

Mail sent to other European countries generally arrives in three to four days, and to the USA in about a week.

Postboxes in the street are yellow with a white horn insignia. Postal information is on 902 197 197 or at www.correos.es.

Correu Central

Plaça Antonio López, Barri Gòtic (93 486 80 50). Metro Jaume I or Barceloneta. **Open** 8.30am-9.30pm Mon-Sat. **Map** p341 B4.

Take a ticket from the machine in front of you as you enter and wait your turn. Apart from the typical services, fax sending and receiving is offered at all post offices (more expensive than at fax shops, but with the option of courier delivery in Spain, using the Burofax option). To send something express, say you want to send it *'urgente'*. Some post offices close in August.

Other locations: Ronda Universitat 23; Eixample; C/Aragó 282, Eixample. Open 8.30am-8.30pm Mon-Fri, 9.30am-1pm Sat.

Estancs/Estancos

The ubiquitous government-run tobacco shop, known as an *estanc/estanco* (sometimes just as 'tabac'), and identified by a brown and yellow sign, is a very important Spanish institution. As well as cigarettes and tobacco, they also supply postage stamps and envelopes, public transport *targetes* and phonecards.

Post boxes

A PO box (*apartado postal*) address costs €43.25 annually.

Poste restante

Letters sent poste restante should be addressed to Lista de Correos, 08070 Barcelona, Spain. Pick-up is from the main post office, and you'll need your passport to collect them.

Queuing

Contrary to appearances, Catalans have an advanced queuing culture. While they may not stand in an orderly line, they are normally very well aware of when it is their turn, particularly at market stalls and in small shops. The standard drill is to ask when you arrive, *'¿Qui es l'últim/la última?'* ('Who's last?') and get behind whoever answers. Say *'jo'* ('me') to the next person who asks the same question.

Religion

Anglican: St George's Church

C/Horaci 38, Zona Alta (93 417 88 67/www.st-georges-church.com). FGC Avda Tibidabo. **Main service** 11am Sun.

An Anglican church with a multicultural congregation, weekly women's club, bridge and Bible study.

Catholic mass in English: Parròquia Maria Reina

Carretera d'Esplugues 103, Zona Alta (93 203 41 15). Metro Maria Cristina. **Mass** Call for times. **Map** p337 A1.

Jewish Orthodox: Sinagoga de Barcelona & Comunitat Israelita de Barcelona

C/Avenir 24, Zona Alta (93 209 31 47). FGC Gràcia. **Prayers** call for times. **Map** p338 C3.

A Sephardic, Orthodox synagogue.

Jewish Reform: Comunitat Jueva Atid de Catalunya

C/Castanyer 27, Zona Alta (93 417 37 04/www.atid.info). FGC Putxet or Avda Tibidabo. **Prayers** 8.15pmFri, Sat 10.30am.

Reform synagogue.

Muslim: Mosque Tarik Bin Ziad

C/Hospital 91, Raval (93 441 91 49). Metro Liceu. **Prayers** 2pm Fri. Call for other times.

Safety

Pickpocketing and bag-snatching are epidemic in Barcelona, with tourists a prime target. Be especially careful around the Old City, and particularly La Rambla, as well as on public transport and at stations. However, thieves go anywhere tourists go, including parks and beaches. Most street crime is aimed at the inattentive, and can be avoided by taking a few simple common-sense precautions:

- Avoid giving invitations to thieves: don't keep wallets in accessible pockets, keep your bags closed and in front of you. When you stop, put your bags down right beside you, where you can see them and where they cannot be easily snatched.
- In busy streets or crowded places, keep an eye on what is happening around you. If you're suspicious of someone, don't hesitate to move somewhere else. Paranoia can be good.
- As a rule, Barcelona street thieves tend to use stealth and surprise rather than violence. However, muggings and knife threats do sometimes occur. Avoid deserted streets in the city centre if you're on your own at night, and offer no resistance when threatened.

Through the keyhole

Buying property in Spain no longer conjures up images of dodgy timeshare deals on the Costa del Crime, as thousands of Europeans join the rush to buy flats in Barcelona, Madrid and elsewhere. As Spain has become more closely integrated with Europe, prices have risen steeply, however – as much as 125 per cent since 1997, according to a study by La Caixa bank. In Barcelona particularly, only a few years ago there were plenty of ramshackle flats available at low prices, but this is no longer the case.

Most flat sales take place via the services of an estate agent, and all require a lawyer. Be careful when choosing the former, as no licence or authorisation is required to sell properties in Spain, although licensed operators do adhere to a set of professional standards. Proof of membership of the Official College of Estate Agents (the *Col·legi Oficial d'Agents de la Propietat Immobiliària*) may assuage your doubts in this respect. Estate agents in Spain usually charge a fee of between one and two per cent of the eventual price of the flat, which is payable by the vendor.

Once you have found your dream home, the procedure is fairly simple. Having agreed upon the price, the purchaser and the vendor sign what is known as a *contrato de arras*, or deposit contract. Under the terms of this contract, you hand over a nominal sum, in the region of around ten per cent of the purchase price, for the vendor to take it off the market. This contract stipulates the conditions of sale and the date for final completion before a public notary. The money you hand over is ultimately deducted from the eventual sale price. Here's where it gets interesting: if you then pull out of the sale, the vendor keeps that money. If the vendor pulls out, he or she has to pay the buyer double the amount paid in the *arras*.

In Spain, there is no legal requirement to arrange a survey of the property. Once you have arranged your mortgage, you will have to sign the deed either in person or by proxy in front of a notary, the state-appointed official who supervises the whole process and certifies that everything that is happening is legally OK and above board. Which, in Spain, it usually isn't, as there is almost always an agreement between purchaser and vendor to declare the sale price as being lower than it really is for tax purposes – the vendor is thus subject to less capital gains tax and the purchaser doesn't have to pay so much in stamp duty. Things usually get a little surreal when the deeds are signed, with the *'negro'* ('black') money changing hands – bank managers and notaries affect to look the other way, or need to use the bathroom, or have to make an urgent phone call and so on while the cash is counted.

This is all culturally taken for granted by most Spaniards, and indeed, many vendors will not sell you their property if you do not acquiesce to a little tax fraud. Finally, bear in mind that notaries' fees, registration fees and other bureaucratic business – transfer tax, VAT and stamp duty – will mean that you should add around 12 per cent to the cost of the property.

Once you have become a property owner, you will then become a member of the *comunidad de vecinos* of your building, which is like a residents' association. This allows you to attend interminable annual meetings at which heated debate over painting the hall, lighting the common areas and noise levels is enough to make you want to sell the place – but that's another story.

- Despite precautions, sometimes you can just be unlucky. Don't carry more money and valuables than you need to – use your hotel's safe deposit facilities if available, and take out travel insurance.

Smoking

Despite signs telling them not to do so, it seems as if people in Barcelona still smoke wherever they want to. They smoke in banks, in shops and in offices. In fact, there are very few non-smoking areas in restaurants, although bans in cinemas, theatres and on trains are generally respected.

Smoking is banned on the metro system and FGC, although smoking on station platforms (but not on trains) is still quite common. *See p307*, **Up in smoke**.

Study

Catalonia is pro-European, and the vast majority of foreign students in Spain under the EU's Erasmus scheme are studying at Catalan schools. Catalan is usually spoken in these universities, although lecturers are often relaxed about use of Castilian in class for the first few months.

Accommodation & advice

Barcelona Allotjament

C/Pelai 12, pral B, Eixample (tel/fax 93 268 43 57/www.barcelona-allotjament.com). Metro Universitat or Catalunya. **Open** *Sept-June* 10am-2pm, 5-7pm Mon-Thur; 10am-2pm Fri. *July, Aug* 5-7pm Mon-Thur. **No credit cards. Map** p342 A1.
Rooms with local families and in shared student flats can be booked through this agency, aimed mainly at students. Short-term B&B rates start at €18 per day (for students); longer-term B&B stays cost €331 upward per month, plus a €103 agency fee.

Centre d'Informació i Assessorament per a Joves (CIAJ)

C/Ferrán 32, Barri Gòtic (93 402 78 00/fax 93 402 78 01/www.bcn.es/ciaj). Metro Liceu. **Open** *Sept-July* 10am-2pm, 4-8pm Mon-Fri. *Aug* 10am-2pm Mon-Fri. **Map** p345 A/B3.
Centrally located youth info centre run by the city council, with information on work, study, accommodation, travel and more. Also noticeboards and free web terminals (not for email).

Secretaria General de Joventut – Punt d'Informació Juvenil

C/Calabria 147-C/Rocafort 116, Eixample (93 483 83 83/fax 93 483 83 00/www.bcu.cesca.es). Metro Rocafort. **Open** *Oct-May* 9am-2pm, 3-5.30pm Mon-Fri. *June-Sept* 9am-2pm Mon-Fri. **Map** p341 B5.
Generalitat-run centre providing a number of services: information for young people on travel, work and study and internet access. Other services include Habitatge Jove (93 483 83 92/www.habitatge jove.com), an under-35s accommodation service.

Language classes

If you plan to stay in bilingual Barcelona for a while, you may want (or need) to learn some Catalan. The city is also a very popular location for studying Spanish. There's plenty on offer: for full course lists, try the youth information centres listed above.

Babylon Idiomas

C/Bruc 65, Eixample (93 488 1585/www.babylon-idiomas.com). Metro Girona or Passeig de Gràcia. **Open** 9am-8pm Mon-Fri. **Credit** MC, V. **Map** p343 E5.
Small groups run at all levels of Spanish in this friendly school, which also provides good business courses and intensive residential courses in the country. Helpful staff can also arrange accommodation.

Consorci per a la Normalització Lingüística

C/Quintana 11 1° 1ª, Barri Gòtic (93 412 72 24/www.cpnl.org). Metro Liceu. **Open** 9am-1pm, 4-5.30pm Mon-Thur; 9am-2pm Fri. **No credit cards. Map** p345 A3..
The Generalitat organisation for the promotion of the Catalan language has centres around the city offering Catalan courses for non-Spanish speakers at very low prices or for free. Courses start in October and February, with intensive courses in summer. Classes are very big and queues to enrol are long.

Escola Oficial d'Idiomes

Avda Drassanes, Eixample (93 324 93 30/www.eoibd.es). Metro Drassanes. **Open** Information *Oct-May* 10.30am-12.30pm Mon, Thur, Fri; 10.30am-12.30pm, 4-7pm Tue, Wed. *June-Sept* 10.30am-12.30pm Mon, Thur, Fri; 10.30am-12.30pm Tue, Wed. **Map** p341 A4.
This state-run school has semi-intensive three-month courses, starting in September and February, at all levels in Catalan, Spanish and other languages. It's cheap, and has a good reputation, so demand is high and classes are big. It also has summer courses, a self-study centre and a good library. It may be easier to get a place in the Escola Oficial at Avda del Jordà 18, Vall d'Hebrón (93 418 74 85). Metro Vall d'Hebron.

International House

C/Trafalgar 14, Eixample (93 268 45 11/www.ihes.com/bcn). Metro Urquinaona. **Open** 8am-9pm Mon-Fri; 10am-1.30pm Sat. **Map** p344 C1.
Intensive Spanish courses all year round. IH is also a leading TEFL teacher training centre.

Universitat de Barcelona

Gran Via de les Corts Catalanes 585, Eixample (information 93 403 54 19/www.ub.es/ieh/hisp.etm). Metro Universitat. **Open** *Information* (Pati de Ciències entrance) 9am-2pm, 3.30-6pm. Closed afternoons in Aug. **Map** p342 C-D5.
This school offers a series of intensive, three-month and year-long Spanish courses. Enrolment continues all year round.

Universities

The Erasmus student exchange scheme and Lingua project (specifically concerned with language learning) are the main parts of the EU's Socrates programme to help students move between member states. Interested students should contact the Erasmus co-ordinator at their home college. Information is available in Britain from the UK Socrates-Erasmus Council, R&D Building, The University, Canterbury, Kent CT2 7PD (01227 762712/fax 01227 762 711/www.ukc.ac.uk/erasmus).

Universitat Autònoma de Barcelona

Campus de Bellaterra, (93 581 10 00/student information 93 581 11 11/www.uab.es). FGC or RENFE Universidad Autonoma/by car A18 to Cerdanyola del Valles. **Open** *Information* 10am-1.30pm, 3.30-4.30pm Mon-Fri.
A 1960s campus outside the city at Bellaterra, near Sabadell. Frequent FGC train connections to the centre.

Universitat de Barcelona

Gran Via de les Corts Catalanes 585, Eixample (information 93 403 55 19/www.ub.es/ieh/hisp.etm). Metro Universitat. **Open** *Information* (Pati de Ciències entrance) 9am-2pm, 3.30-6pm Mon-Fri. Closed afternoons in Aug. **Map** p342 C-D5.
This is Barcelona's oldest and biggest university, with faculties in the main building on Plaça Universitat, as well as in the Zona Universitària at the top of the Avenida Diagonal, and in other parts of town. Intensive, three-month and year-long Spanish courses. Enrolment all year round.

Universitat Pompeu Fabra

Student information 93 542 22 28/www.upf.es. Information offices: La Rambla 30-32, Barri Gòtic; C/Ramon Trias Fargas 25-7, Vila Olímpica. **Open** *Both* 9am-9pm Mon-Fri.
Founded in 1991, this social sciences-based university has faculties conveniently in various parts of central Barcelona, many of them in the Old City.

Universitat Ramon Llull

C/Claravall 1-3, Zona Alta (93 602 22 00/www.url.es). FGC Av Tibidabo. **Open** *Information* 9am-2pm, 4-6.30pm Mon-Fri. Closed 2wks Aug.
Private university bringing together a number of previously separate institutions, including the highly prestigious ESADE business school (93 280 29 95/www.esade.edu).

Telephones

Competition in the Spanish phone market has led to a drop in prices, and new options are constantly appearing. Former state operator **Telefónica** still has a monopoly on the infrastructure, however. Phone cards, and the phone centres that sell them, generally give cheaper rates than Telefónica.

Dialling & codes

Normal Spanish phone numbers have nine digits, as the area code (93 in the province of Barcelona) must be dialled with all calls, both local and long-distance. Spanish mobile phone numbers always begin with 6. Numbers beginning 900 are freephone lines, while other 90 numbers are special-rate services.

International & long-distance calls

To make an international call, dial 00 and then the country code, followed by the area code (omitting the first zero in UK numbers) and number. To call Barcelona from abroad, dial 00 34 for Spain.

Country codes:
Australia 61
Canada 1
Irish Republic 353
New Zealand 64
United Kingdom 44
USA 1

Mobile phones

The mobile phone, or *móvil*, is omnipresent in Spain. Calls are paid for either through a monthly direct debit or by by using prepaid phones, charged with vouchers available in newsagents or via any cash machine. Costs vary widely, but are expensive compared to Britain or the US. Many mobile phones from other countries can be used in Spain, but you may need to set this up with your service provider before you leave home. This can be expensive and it may well be cheaper to buy or rent a Spanish mobile.

Rent a Phone

C/Numància 212, Eixample (902 200 908/www.rphone.es). Metro Drassanes. **Open** 9.30am-2pm, 4-7.30pm Mon-Fri. **Credit** AmEx, MC, V. **Map** p337 B2.
Mobile phones and accessories for rent, either for use in Spain or to take to other countries. Daytime Spanish calls are charged at around €1.20/min.

Public phones

The most common model of payphone accepts coins (from 5¢ up), Telefónica phonecards and credit cards. There is a multilingual digital display (press 'L' to change language) and written instructions in English and other languages.

For the first minute of a daytime local call, you'll be charged around 11¢; to a mobile phone around 35¢; to a 902 number, around 18¢. If you are still in credit at the end of your call, you can make further follow-on calls by pushing the 'R' button underneath where the handset rests before hanging up. Bars and cafés often have phones for public use, but these are often more expensive than street booths.

Telefónica phonecards (minimum €6) are sold at post offices, newsstands and *estancs* (*see p315*). Other cards sold at phone centres, shops and newsstands give cheaper rates on all but local calls. These give a toll-free number to call from any phone. You are told how many minutes you have (time varies according to where you are calling) and then connected with the number you want.

Operator services

Operators normally speak Catalan and Spanish only – except for international operators, most of whom speak English.

General information 010 (from 8am to 10pm)
International directory enquiries 025
International operator for reverse charge calls Europe & North Africa 1008; rest of world 1005
Medical emergencies 061
National directory enquiries 11818
National operator for reverse charge calls 1009
Telephone faults service 1002
Time 093
Wake-up calls 096 (After the recorded message key in the time at which you wish to be woken, in the 24hr clock, in four figures: for example, 0830 if you want to be called at 8.30am.)
Weather 932 211 600

Phone centres

Phone centres (*locutorios*) also offer cheap calls, and avoid the need for change. Most private centres offer international call rates that are cheaper than Telefónica's for all countries. Concentrated particularly in streets such as C/Sant Pau and C/Hospital in the Raval, and along C/Carders-C/Corders in Sant Pere, they occasionally offer other services, including international money transfer, currency exchange and internet access.

Oftelcom

C/Canuda 7, Barri Gòtic (93 342 73 70). Metro Catalunya. **Open** 11am-11pm daily. **Map** p344 B2.

Locutorio

C/Hospital 17, Barri Gòtic (93 318 97 39). Metro Liceu. **Open** 9.30am-11.30pm daily. **Map** p344 B2.

Time

Local time is one hour ahead of GMT, six hours ahead of US Eastern Standard Time and nine ahead of Pacific Standard Time. Daylight saving time runs concurrently with the UK.

Tipping

This is up to you. In bars and restaurants, you are not expected to leave anything other than a little loose change. In taxis, however, around five per cent is fair, depending on the service. It's also usual to tip hotel porters.

Toilets

Public toilets are not common in Barcelona, although the Ajuntament is making noises about introducing more of them as the problem of people urinating alfresco in the Old Town becomes more and more acute. Most of the main railway stations have clean toilets, and the beach at Barceloneta has pay-on-entry cubicles that cost 15¢. Bar and café owners do not usually mind if you use their toilets, although you may have to ask for the key first. Fast food restaurants are, of course, the old standbys.

Tourist information

The city council (Ajuntament) and Catalan government (Generalitat) both run tourist offices. Information about what's on in theatre, music, galleries, sport and so on can be found in local papers as well as listings magazines.

Oficines d'Informació Turística

Plaça Catalunya, Eixample (93 368 97 30/ www.bcn.es/www.barcelona turisme.com). Metro Catalunya. **Open** 9am-9pm daily. **Map** p344 B1.
The main office of the city tourist board is underground on the Corte Inglés side of the square (look for big red signs with 'i' in white). It has information, money exchange, a shop selling souvenirs and books, a hotel booking service and internet access.
Other locations: Plaça Sant Jaume (in Ajuntament building), Barri Gòtic; Sants station; Palau de Congressos (Trade Fair office), Airport (Terminals A & B).

Temporary offices & 'Red Jackets'

Information booths located at Passeig de Gràcia, Plaça d'Espanya & Sagrada Família. **Open** *Late June-late Sept* 10am-8pm daily. **Map** p339 F4.
In summer, Turisme de Barcelona usually opens these temporary booths. Red jacketed information officers also roam the Barri Gòtic and La Rambla during the summer, ready to field questions in a heroic variety of languages from 10am to 8pm daily.

Palau Robert

Passeig de Gràcia 107, Eixample (93 238 40 00/www.gencat.es/probert). Metro Diagonal. **Open** 10am-7.30pm Mon-Sat; 10am-2.30pm Sun.
Map p338 D4.
The Generalitat's lavishly equipped information centre is at the junction of Passeig de Gràcia and the Diagonal. It has maps and other essentials for the city itself, but the speciality is a huge range of information in different media on other parts of Catalonia. It occasionally hosts interesting exhibitions on local art, culture, gastronomy and nature.
Other locations: Airport Terminal A (93 478 47 04) 9.30am-3pm Mon-Sat; Airport Terminal B (93 478 05 65) 9.30am-8pm Mon-Sat.

Centre d'Informació de la Virreina

Palau de la Virreina, La Rambla 99, Barri Gòtic (93 301 77 75). Metro Liceu. **Open** 10am-8pm Mon-Sat; 11am-3pm Sun. **Ticket sales** 11am-8pm Tue-Sat; 11am-2.30pm Sun.
Map p344 A2.
The information office of the city's culture department, with details of concerts, exhibitions and special events. Also home to an excellent bookstore specialising in books about Barcelona.

010 phoneline

Open *General information* 8am-10pm Mon-Sat.
City-run information line aimed mainly at local citizens, but which does an impeccable job of answering all kinds of queries. Ask for an English operator.

Visas & immigration

Spain is one of the European Union countries covered by the Schengen agreement, which led to common visa regulations and limited border controls. However, neither the UK nor the Republic of Ireland are signatories, and so nationals of those countries will need their passports. Most EU citizens, as well as Norwegian and Icelandic nationals, only need a national identity card.

Visas are not required for US, Canadian, Australian and New Zealand citizens for stays of up to 90 days that are not for purposes of work or study. Citizens of South Africa and many other countries do need visas to enter Spain, which can be obtained from Spanish consulates and embassies in other countries (or from those of other Schengen countries that you are planning to visit).

Visa requirements are subject to change, so check the latest information with your country's Spanish embassy before leaving home.

Water

Barcelona tap water is drinkable, but tastes strongly of chlorine. Bottled water is what you will be served if you ask for *'un aigua/agua'* in a bar or restaurant.

When to go

Barcelona is marvellous all year round, and the weather is usually very agreeable. The humidity in summer can be debilitating, however, and the city is definitely not running at full steam then, with many shops and restaurants closed.

Climate

Spring is unpredictable, and warm sunny days can alternate with cold winds and showers; May and June temperatures are perfect, and the city is very lively around 23 June, when locals celebrate the beginning of summer with fireworks and fiestas. July and August can be unpleasant, as the summer heat and humidity kick in, making many locals leave town. Autumn weather is generally warm and fresh, with heavy downpours common around October. Crisp, cool sunshine is normal from December to February. Snow is very rare.

Public holidays

Almost all shops, banks and offices, and many bars and restaurants, close on public holidays (*festivos/festius*), and public transport runs a limited service. And many locals take long weekends whenever a major holiday comes along. The city's official holidays are:

New Year's Day/Any Nou 1 Jan
Three Kings/*Reis Mags* 6 Jan
Good Friday/*Divendres Sant*
Easter Monday/*Dilluns de Pasqua*
May (Labour) Day/*Festa del Treball* 1 May
Sant Joan 24 June
Verge de l'Assumpció 15 Aug
Diada de Catalunya 11 Sept
La Mercè 24 Sept
All Saints' Day/*Tots Sants* 1 Nov
Constitution Day/*Día de la Constitución* 6 Dec
La Immaculada 8 Dec
Christmas Day/*Nadal* 25 Dec
Boxing Day/*Sant Esteve* 26 Dec.

Women

Ca La Dona

C/Casp 38, pral, Eixample (93 412 71 61/http://caladona.pangea.org). Metro Catalunya or Urquinaona. **Open** *Office* 10am-2pm, 4-8pm Mon-Thur. Closed Aug. **Map** p344 B1.
A women's centre hosting several political, artistic and social groups, with a bar and meeting space. It also has a magazine with event listings.

Centre Municipal d'Informació i Recursos per a Dones

Avda Diagonal 233, 5ª, Eixample (93 413 27 22/93 413 27 23/ www.cird.bcn.es). Metro Glòries or Monumental. **Open** *Oct-June* noon-2pm Mon-Fri, 4-7pm Tue, Thur. Closed Aug. **Map** p343 F5.
The Ajuntament's women's resource centre. Provides a women-related information service, with publications including a monthly events guide, *Agenda Dona.*

Institut Català de la Dona

Information: C/Portaferrissa 1-3, Barri Gòtic (93 317 92 91). Metro Jaume I or Liceu. **Open** *Oct-May* 9am-2pm, 4-6pm Mon-Fri. *June-Sept* 8.30am-2.30pm Mon-Fri. **Map** p344 A2.
The women's affairs department of the Catalan government.
Other location: Document centre/library, C/Viladomat 319, entl, Eixample (93 495 16 00/www.gencat.net/icdona). Metro Entença. Open 9am-2pm, 3-5.30pm Mon-Thur; 9am-2pm Fri. Map p337 B3.

Working

Common recourses for English-speakers here is to find work in the tourist sector (although these jobs are often seasonal and outside the city), bar work or English-language teaching – still the best chance of finding work quickly.

EU CITIZENS

New rules introduced in March 2003 mean that citizens of the EU have the right to live, work and study in Spain for an indefinite period without having to apply for residency. If you want to make a voluntary application for a residency card for any reason, you should in theory be able to do this at any police station.

NON-EU CITIZENS

The legal situation is tougher than ever for people from the rest of the world. First-time applicants officially need a special visa, obtained from a Spanish consulate in your home country, although you can start things moving in Spain if you don't mind making at least one trip home. Getting good legal advice from a *gestor* (*see p306*) is very important given the length and complicated nature of the process, as well as possible changes in regulations. This may explain why Spain is home to a thriving undeclared, under-the-table labour market. It is, apparently, more than possible to live for months in the country without resorting to the bureaucratic jungle of the government offices, although in the end this may be more hassle, even if you don't get caught.

Delegación del Gobierno – Oficina de Extranjeros

Avda Marquès de l'Argentera 2, Barceloneta (93 482 05 44/ appointments 93 482 05 60 8am-3pm Mon-Fri/phoneline 8.30am-2.30pm Mon-Fri). Metro Barceloneta. **Open** 9am-2pm Mon-Fri. **Map** p345 C4.
Given the popularity of living in Barcelona, arrive very early, make sure you're in the right queue before you start, and expect a long wait.

Average monthly climate

	Max temp (C°/F°)	Min temp (C°/F°)	Rainfall (mm/in)	Rain (days/month)
Jan	13/56	6/43	44/1.7	5
Feb	15/59	7/45	36/1.4	6
Mar	16/61	8/47	48/1.9	6
Apr	18/64	10/50	51/2	7
May	21/70	14/57	57/2.2	7
June	24/76	17/63	38/1.5	5
July	27/81	20/67	22/0.9	3
Aug	29/84	20/67	66/2.6	5
Sept	25/78	18/64	79/3.1	6
Oct	22/71	14/57	94/3.7	6
Nov	17/63	9/49	74/2.9	6
Dec	15/59	7/45	50/2.5	6

Spanish Vocabulary

Spanish is generally referred to as *castellano* (Castilian) rather than *español*. Although many locals prefer to speak Catalan, everyone in the city can speak Spanish, and will switch to it if visitors show signs of linguistic jitters. The Spanish familiar form for 'you' – *tú* – is used very freely, but it's safer to use the more formal *usted* with older people and strangers (verbs below are given in the *usted* form).

For food and menu terms, *see p167*.

Spanish pronunciation

c before an **i** or an **e** and **z** are like **th** in **th**in
c in all other cases is as in **c**at
g before an **i** or an **e** and **j** are pronounced with a guttural **h**-sound that doesn't exist in English – like **ch** in Scottish loch, but much harder;
g in all other cases is as in **g**et
h at the beginning of a word is normally silent
ll is pronounced almost like a **y**
ñ is like **ny** in ca**ny**on
a single **r** at the beginning of a word and **rr** elsewhere are heavily rolled

Stress rules

In words ending with a vowel, **n** or **s**, the penultimate syllable is stressed: eg *barato, viven, habitaciones*.
In words ending with any other consonant, the last syllable is stressed: eg *exterior, universidad*.
An accent marks the stressed syllable in words that depart from these rules: eg *estación, tónica*.

Useful expressions

hello *hola*; **hello** (when answering the phone) *hola, diga*
good morning, good day *buenos días;* **good afternoon, good evening** *buenas tardes;* **good evening** (after dark), **good night** *buenas noches*
goodbye/see you later *adiós/ hasta luego*
please *por favor;* **thank you** (very much) *(muchas) gracias*;
you're welcome *de nada*
do you speak English? *¿habla inglés?;* I **don't speak Spanish** *no hablo castellano*
I don't understand *no entiendo*
can you say that to me in Catalan, please? *¿me lo puede decir en catalán, por favor?*
what's your name? *¿cómo se llama?*
speak more slowly, please *hable más despacio, por favor;* **wait a moment** *espere un momento*
Sir/Mr *señor (sr);* **Madam/Mrs** *señora (sra);* **Miss** *señorita (srta)*
excuse me/sorry *perdón;*
excuse me, please *oiga* (the standard way to attract someone's attention, politely; literally 'hear me')
OK/fine/(to a waiter) **that's enough** *vale*
where is...? *¿dónde está...?*
why? *¿porqué?;* **when?** *¿cuándo?;*
who? *¿quién?;* **what?** *¿qué?;*
where? *¿dónde?;* **how?** *¿cómo?*
who is it? *¿quién es?;* **is/are there any...?** *¿hay...?*
very *muy;* **and** *y;* **or** *o;* **with** *con;* **without** *sin*
open *abierto;* **closed** *cerrado;*
what time does it open/close? *¿a qué hora abre/cierra?*
pull (on signs) *tirar;* **push** *empujar*
I would like *quiero;* **how many would you like?** *¿cuántos quiere?;*
how much is it *¿cuánto es?*
I like *me gusta;* **I don't like** *no me gusta*
good *bueno/a;* **bad** *malo/a;* **well/ badly** *bien/mal;* **small** *pequeño/a;*
big *gran, grande;* **expensive** *caro/a;* **cheap** *barato/a;* **hot** (food, drink) *caliente;* **cold** *frío/a;*
something *algo;* **nothing** *nada*
more/less *más/menos;* **more or less** *más o menos*
do you have any change? *¿tiene cambio?*
price *precio;* **free** *gratis;* **discount** *descuento;* **bank** *banco;* **to rent** *alquilar;* **(for) rent, rental** *(en) alquiler;* **post office** *correos;*
stamp *sello;* **postcard** *postal;* **toilet** *los servicios*

Getting around

airport *aeropuerto;* **railway station** *estación de ferrocarril/ estación de RENFE* (Spanish railways); **metro station** *estación de metro*
entrance *entrada;* **exit** *salida*
car *coche;* **bus** *autobús;* **train** *tren;*
a ticket *un billete;* **return** *de ida y vuelta;* **bus stop** *parada de autobus;*
the next stop *la próxima parada*
excuse me, do you know the way to...? *¿oiga, señor/señora/etc, sabe cómo llegar a...?*
left *izquierda;* **right** *derecha*
here *aquí;* **there** *allí;* **straight on** *recto;* **to the end of the street** *al final de la calle;* **as far as** *hasta;* **towards** *hacia;* **near** *cerca;* **far** *lejos*

Accommodation

do you have a double/single room for tonight/one week? *¿tiene una habitación doble/para una persona/para esta noche/una semana?*
we have a reservation *tenemos reserva;* **an inside/outside room** *una habitación interior/exterior*
with/without bathroom *con/sin baño;* **shower** *ducha;* **double bed** *cama de matrimonio;* **with twin beds** *con dos camas;* **breakfast included** *desayuno incluído;* **air-conditioning** *aire acondicionado;*
lift *ascensor;* **pool** *piscina*

Time

now *ahora;* **later** *más tarde;*
yesterday *ayer;* **today** *hoy;*
tomorrow *mañana;* **tomorrow morning** *mañana por la mañana*
morning *la mañana;* **midday** *mediodía;* **afternoon/evening** *la tarde;* **night** *la noche;* **late night** (roughly 1-6am) *la madrugada*
at what time...? *¿a qué hora...?;*
at 2 *a las dos;* **at 8pm** *a las ocho de la tarde;* **at 1.30** *a la una y media;*
at 5.15 *a las cinco y cuarto;* **in an hour** *en una hora*

Numbers

0 *cero;* **1** *un, uno, una;* **2** *dos;* **3** *tres;*
4 *cuatro;* **5** *cinco;* **6** *seis;* **7** *siete;*
8 *ocho;* **9** *nueve;* **10** *diez;* **11** *once;*
12 *doce;* **13** *trece;* **14** *catorce;* **15** *quince;* **16** *dieciséis;* **17** *diecisiete;*
18 *dieciocho;* **19** *diecinueve;* **20** *veinte;* **21** *veintiuno;* **22** *veintidós;*
30 *treinta;* **40** *cuarenta;* **50** *cincuenta;* **60** *sesenta;* **70** *setenta;*
80 *ochenta;* **90** *noventa;* **100** *cien;*
200 *doscientos;* **1,000** *mil;*
1,000,000 *un millón*

Date & season

Monday *lunes;* **Tuesday** *martes;*
Wednesday *miércoles;* **Thursday** *jueves;* **Friday** *viernes;* **Saturday** *sábado;* **Sunday** *domingo*
January *enero;* **February** *febrero;*
March *marzo;* **April** *abril;* **May** *mayo;* **June** *junio;* **July** *julio;*
August *agosto;* **September** *septiembre;* **October** *octubre;*
November *noviembre;* **December** *diciembre*
spring *primavera;* **summer** *verano;*
autumn/fall *otoño;* **winter** *invierno*

Catalan Vocabulary

Over a third of Barcelona residents use Catalan as their predominant everyday language, around 70 per cent speak it fluently, and more than 90 per cent understand it. If you take an interest and learn a few phrases, it is likely to be appreciated.

Catalan phonetics are significantly different from those of Spanish, with a wider range of vowel sounds and soft consonants. Catalans use the familiar (*tu*) rather than the polite (*vosté*) forms of the second person very freely, but for convenience verbs are given here in the polite form.

For food and menu terms, *see p167.*

Pronunciation

In Catalan, as in French but unlike in Spanish, words are run together, so *si us plau* (please) is more like *sees-plow*.

à at the end of a word (as in Francesc Macià) is an open **a** rather like **ah**, but very clipped
ç, and **c** before an **i** or an **e**, are like a soft **s**, as in sit; **c** in all other cases is as in cat
e, when unstressed as in *cerveses* (beers), or Jaume I, is a weak sound like centre or comfortable
g before i or e and **j** are pronounced like the s in pleasure; **tg** and **tj** are similar to the **dg** in badge
g after an i at the end of a word (Puig) is a hard ch sound, as in watch; **g** in all other cases is as in get
h is silent
ll is somewhere between the **y** in yes and the **lli** in million
l.l, the most unusual feature of Catalan spelling, has a slightly stronger stress on a single **l** sound, so paral.lel sounds similar to the English parallel
o at the end of a word is like the **u** sound in flu; **ó** at the end of a word is similar to the **o** in tomato; **ò** is like the **o** in hot
r beginning a word and **rr** are heavily rolled; but at the end of many words is almost silent, so *carrer* (street) sounds like carr-ay
s at the beginning and end of words and **ss** between vowels are soft, as in sit; a single **s** between two vowels is a **z** sound, as in lazy
t after **l** or **n** at the end of a word is almost silent
x at the beginning of a word, or after a consonant or the letter **i**, is like the **sh** in shoe, at other times like the English expert
y after an **n** at the end of a word or in **nys** is not a vowel but adds a nasal stress and a y-sound to the n

Basics

please *si us plau*; **very good/ great/OK** *molt bé*
hello *hola*; **goodbye** *adéu*
open *obert*; **closed** *tancat*
entrance *entrada*; **exit** *sortida*
nothing at all/*zilch res de res* (said with both s silent)
price *preu*; **free** *gratuït/de franc*; **change, exchange** *canvi*
to rent *llogar*; **(for) rent, rental** *(de) lloguer*

More expressions

hello (when answering the phone) *hola, digui'm*
good morning, good day *bon dia*; **good afternoon, good evening** *bona tarda*; **good night** *bona nit*
thank you (very much) *(moltes) gràcies*; **you're welcome** *de res*
do you speak English? *parla anglès?*; **I'm sorry, I don't speak Catalan** *ho sento, no parlo català*
I don't understand *no entenc*
can you say it to me in Spanish, please? *m'ho pot dir en castellà, si us plau?*
how do you say that in Catalan? *com se diu això en català?*
what's your name? *com se diu?*
Sir/Mr *senyor (sr)*; **Madam/Mrs** *senyora (sra)*; **Miss** *senyoreta (srta)*
excuse me/sorry *perdoni/disculpi*; **excuse me, please** *escolti* (literally 'listen to me'); **OK/fine** *val/d'acord*
how much is it? *quant és?*
why? *perqué?*; **when?** *quan?*; **who?** *qui?*; **what?** *qué?*; **where?** *on?*; **how?** *com?*; **where is...?** *on és...?*; **who is it?** *qui és?*; **is/are there any...?** *hi ha...?/n'hi ha de...?*
very *molt*; **and** *i* or *o*; **with** *amb*; **without** *sense*; **enough** *prou*
I would like... *vull...* (literally, 'I want'); **how many would you like?** *quants en vol?*, **I don't want** *no vull*; **I like** *m'agrada*; **I don't like** *no m'agrada*
good *bo/bona*; **bad** *dolent/a*; **well/badly** *bé/malament*; **small** *petit/a*; **big** *gran*; **expensive** *car/a*; **cheap** *barat/a*; **hot** (food, drink) *calent/a*; **cold** *fred/a*
something *alguna cosa*; **nothing** *res*; **more** *més*; **less** *menys*; **more or less** *més o menys*
toilet *el bany/els serveis/el lavabo*

Getting around

a ticket *un bitllet*; **return** *d'anada i tornada*; **card expired** (on metro) *títol esgotat*
left *esquerra*; **right** *dreta*; **here** *aquí*; **there** *allí*; **straight on** *recte*; **at the corner** *a la cantonada*; **as far as** *fins a*; **towards** *cap a*; **near** *a prop*; **far** *lluny*; **is it far?** *és lluny?*

Time

In Catalan, quarter- and half-hours can be referred to as quarters of the next hour (so, 1.30 is two quarters of 2).

now *ara*; **later** *més tard*; **yesterday** *ahir*; **today** *avui*; **tomorrow** *demà*; **tomorrow morning** *demà pel matí*
morning *el matí*; **midday** *migdia*; **afternoon** *la tarda*; **evening** *el vespre*; **night** *la nit*; **late night** (roughly 1-6am) *la matinada*
at what time...? *a quina hora...?*
in an hour *en una hora*
at 2 *a les dues*; **at 8pm** *a les vuit del vespre*; **at 1.30** *a dos quarts de dues/a la una i mitja*; **at 5.15** *a un quart de sis/a las cinc i quart*; **at 22.30** *a vint-i-dos-trenta*

Numbers

0 *zero*; **1** *u, un, una*; **2** *dos, dues*; **3** *tres*; **4** *quatre*; **5** *cinc*; **6** *sis*; **7** *set*; **8** *vuit*; **9** *nou*; **10** *deu*; **11** *onze*; **12** *dotze*; **13** *tretze*; **14** *catorze*; **15** *quinze*; **16** *setze*; **17** *disset*; **18** *divuit*; **19** *dinou*; **20** *vint*; **21** *vint-i-u*; **22** *vint-i-dos, vint-i-dues*; **30** *trenta*; **40** *quaranta*; **50** *cinquanta*; **60** *seixanta*; **70** *setanta*; **80** *vuitanta*; **90** *noranta*; **100** *cent*; **200** *dos-cents, dues-centes*; **1,000** *mil*; **1,000,000** *un milló*

Date & season

Monday *dilluns*; **Tuesday** *dimarts*; **Wednesday** *dimecres*; **Thursday** *dijous*; **Friday** *divendres*; **Saturday** *dissabte*; **Sunday** *diumenge*
January *gener*; **February** *febrer*; **March** *març*; **April** *abril*; **May** *maig*; **June** *juny*; **July** *juliol*; **August** *agost*; **September** *setembre*; **October** *octobre*; **November** *novembre*; **December** *desembre*
spring *primavera*; **summer** *estiu*; **autumn/fall** *tardor*; **winter** *hivern*

Further Reference

Books

Food & drink

Andrews, Colman: *Catalan Cuisine* A mine of information on food and much else (also with usable recipes).
Davidson, Alan: *Tio Pepe Guide to the Seafood of Spain and Portugal* An excellent pocket-sized guide with illustrations of Spain's fishy delights.

Guides & walks

Amelang, J, Gil, X & McDonogh, GW: *Twelve Walks through Barcelona's Past* (Ajuntament de Barcelona) Well-thought-out walks by historical theme. Original, and better informed than many walking guides.
Güell, Xavier: *Gaudí Guide* (Ed. Gustavo Gili) A handy guide, with good background on all the architect's work.
Pomés Leiz, Juliet, & Feriche, Ricardo: *Barcelona Design Guide* (Ed. Gustavo Gili) An eccentrically wide-ranging but engaging listing of everything ever considered 'designer' in BCN.

History, architecture, art & culture

Burns, Jimmy: *Barça: A People's Passion* The first full-scale history in English of one of the world's most overblown football clubs.
Elliott, JH: *The Revolt of the Catalans* Fascinating, detailed account of the Guerra dels Segadors and the Catalan revolt of the 1640s.
Fernández Armesto, Felipe: *Barcelona: A Thousand Years of the City's Past* A solid, straightforward history.
Fraser, Ronald: *Blood of Spain* A vivid oral history of the Spanish Civil War and the tensions that preceded it. It is especially good on the events of July 1936 in Barcelona.
Hooper, John: *The New Spaniards* An incisive and very readable survey of the changes in Spanish society since the death of Franco.
Hughes, Robert: *Barcelona* The most comprehensive single book about Barcelona: tendentious at times, erratic, but beautifully written, and covering every aspect of the city up to the 1992 Olympics.
Kaplan, Temma: *Red City, Blue Period – Social Movements in Picasso's Barcelona* An interesting book, tracing the interplay of avant-garde art and avant-garde politics in 1900s Barcelona.
Orwell, George: *Homage to Catalonia* The classic account of Barcelona in revolution, as written by an often bewildered, but always perceptive observer.
Paz, Abel: *Durruti, The People Armed* Closer to its theme, a biography of the most legendary of Barcelona's anarchist revolutionaries.
Solà-Morales, Ignasi: *Fin de Siècle Architecture in Barcelona* Large-scale and wide-ranging description of the city's Modernista heritage.
Tóibín, Colm: *Homage to Barcelona* Evocative and perceptive journey around the city: good on the booming Barcelona of the 1980s.
van Hensbergen, Gijs: *Gaudí* A thorough account of the life of the architect.
Vázquez Montalbán, Manuel: *Barcelonas* Idiosyncratic but insightful reflections on the city by one of its most prominent modern writers.
Zerbst, Rainer: *Antoni Gaudí* Lavishly illustrated and comprehensive survey.

Literature

Calders, Pere: *The Virgin of the Railway and Other Stories* Ironic, engaging, quirky stories by a Catalan writer who spent many years in exile in Mexico.
Català, Victor: *Solitude* This masterpiece by female novelist Caterina Albert shocked readers in 1905 with its open, modern treatment of female sexuality.
Marsé, Juan: *The Fallen* Classic novel of survival in Barcelona during the long *posguerra* after the Civil War.
Martorell, Joanot, & Martí de Gualba, Joan: *Tirant lo Blanc* The first European prose novel, from 1490, a rambling, bawdy, shaggy-dog story of travels, romances and chivalric adventures.
Mendoza, Eduardo: *City of Marvels* and *Year of the Flood* A sweeping, very entertaining saga of Barcelona between its great Exhibitions in 1888 and 1929; and a more recent novel of passions in the city of the 1950s.
Oliver, Maria Antònia: *Antipodes and Study in Lilac* Two adventures of Barcelona's first feminist detective.
Rodoreda, Mercè: *The Time of the Doves* and *My Cristina and Other Stories* A translation of *Plaça del Diamant*, most widely read of all Catalan novels. Plus a collection of similarly bittersweet short tales.
Vázquez Montalbán, Manuel: *The Angst-Ridden Executive* and *An Olympic Death* Two thrillers starring detective and gourmet extraordinaire Pepe Carvalho.

Music

Angel Molina Leading Barcelona DJ with an international reputation and various remix albums released.
Barcelona Raval Sessions Dance/funk compilation of local artists, famous and unknown, conceived as a soundtrack to the city's most dynamic and multicultural barrio.
Lluís Llach An icon of the 1960s and early '70s protest against the fascist regime combines a melancholic tone with brilliant musicianship. One of the first to experiment with electronic music.
Maria del Mar Bonet Though from Mallorca, del Mar Bonet always sings in Catalan and specialises in her own compositions, North African music and traditional Mallorcan music.
Ojos de Brujo Current darlings of world music awards everywhere and leading proponents of rumba catalana fused with flamenco.
Pep Sala Excellent musician and survivor of the extremely successful Catalan group Sau. Sala now produces his own music, much of which shows a rockabilly and country influence.

Barcelona online

www.barcelonaturisme.com Information from the city's official tourist authority. Painfully slow.
www.bcn.es The city council's information-packed website.
www.catalanencyclopaedia.com Comprehensive English-language reference work covering Catalan history, geography and 'who's who'.
www.diaridebarcelona.com Local online newspaper with good English content.
www.lecool.com Excellent weekly round-up of offbeat and interesting cultural events in the city.
www.mobilitat.net Generalitat's website getting from A to B in Catalonia, by bus, car or train.
www.renfe.es Spanish railways' website, with online booking.
www.timeout.com/barcelona The online city guide, with a select monthly agenda.
www.vilaweb.com Catalan web portal and links page; in Catalan.

Index

Note Page numbers in **bold** indicate section(s) giving key information on a topic; *italics* indicate photographs.

Index

Index

Where to stay

Restaurants

Cafés, Tapas & Bars

Advertisers' Index

Please refer to the relevant sections for contact details

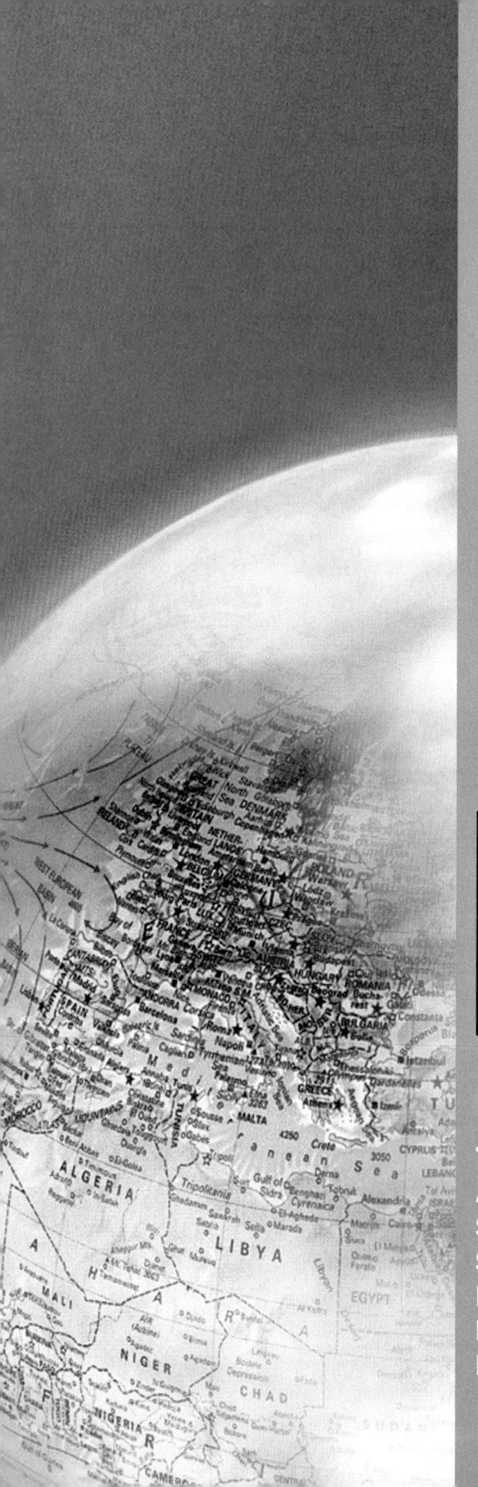

Place of interest and/or entertainment	
Hospital or college	
Pedestrianised zone	
Railway station	
Metro station, FGC station	
Area name	BARRI GÒTIC

Maps

Trips Out of Town

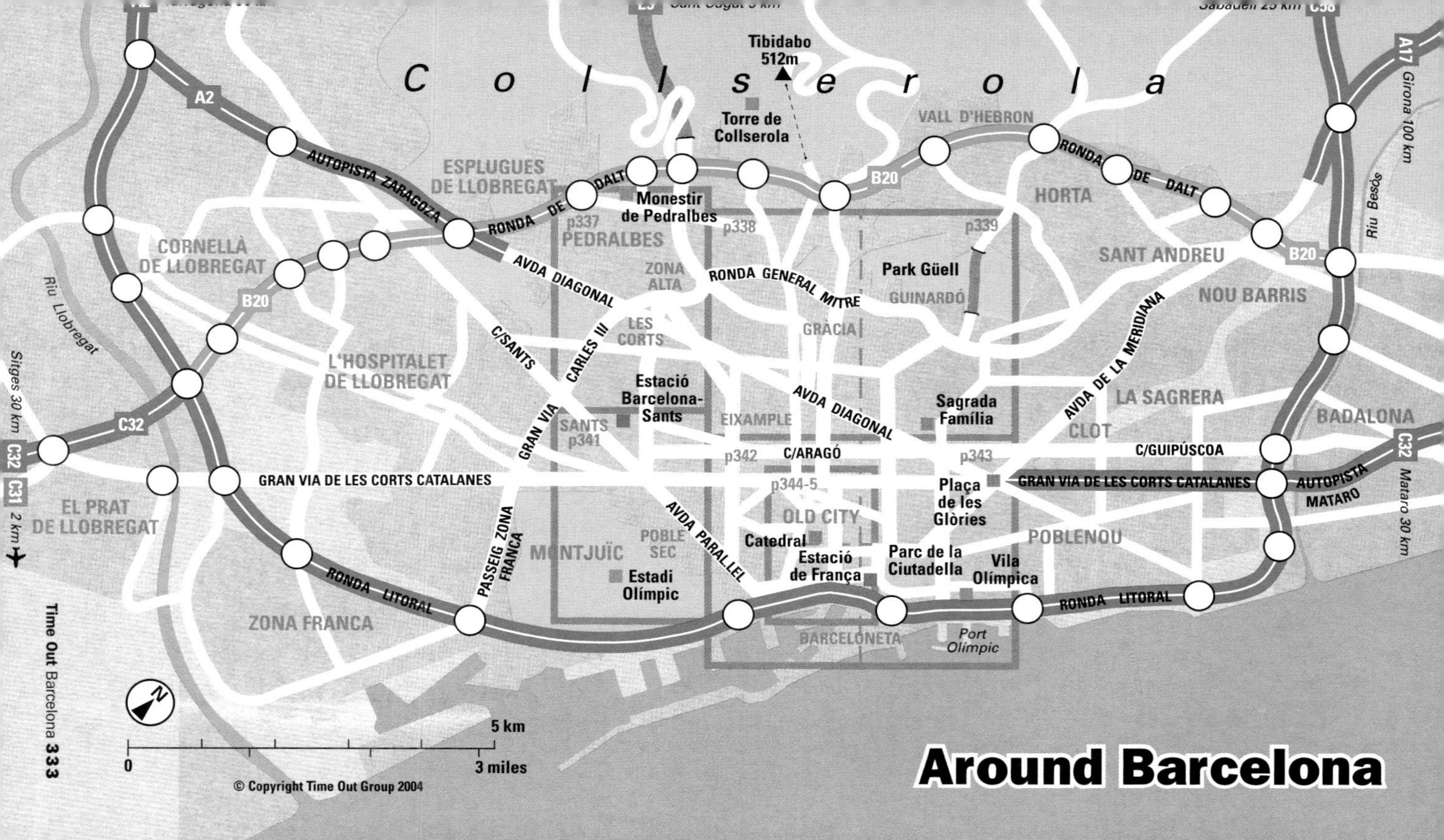
Around Barcelona
Collserola
Tibidabo 512m
Torre de Collserola
Vall d'Hebron
Esplugues de Llobregat
Cornellà de Llobregat
L'Hospitalet de Llobregat
El Prat de Llobregat
Zona Franca
Pedralbes
Zona Alta
Les Corts
Sants
Gràcia
Guinardó
Horta
Sant Andreu
Nou Barris
La Sagrera
Badalona
Clot
Poblenou
Eixample
Old City
Poble Sec
Montjuïc
Barceloneta
Port Olímpic
Vila Olímpica
Monestir de Pedralbes
Park Güell
Sagrada Família
Estació Barcelona-Sants
Plaça de les Glòries
Catedral
Estació de França
Parc de la Ciutadella
Estadi Olímpic
Ronda de Dalt
Ronda Litoral
Ronda General Mitre
Autopista Zaragoza
Autopista Mataro
Avda Diagonal
Avda de la Meridiana
Avda Paral.lel
Gran Via de les Corts Catalanes
Gran Via
Carles III
C/Sants
C/Aragó
C/Guipúscoa
Passeig Zona Franca
A2
A17
B20
C32
C31
Girona 100 km
Mataro 30 km
Sitges 30 km
2 km
Riu Llobregat
Riu Besòs
p337
p338
p339
p341
p342
p343
p344-5
5 km
3 miles
0
© Copyright Time Out Group 2004

Street Index

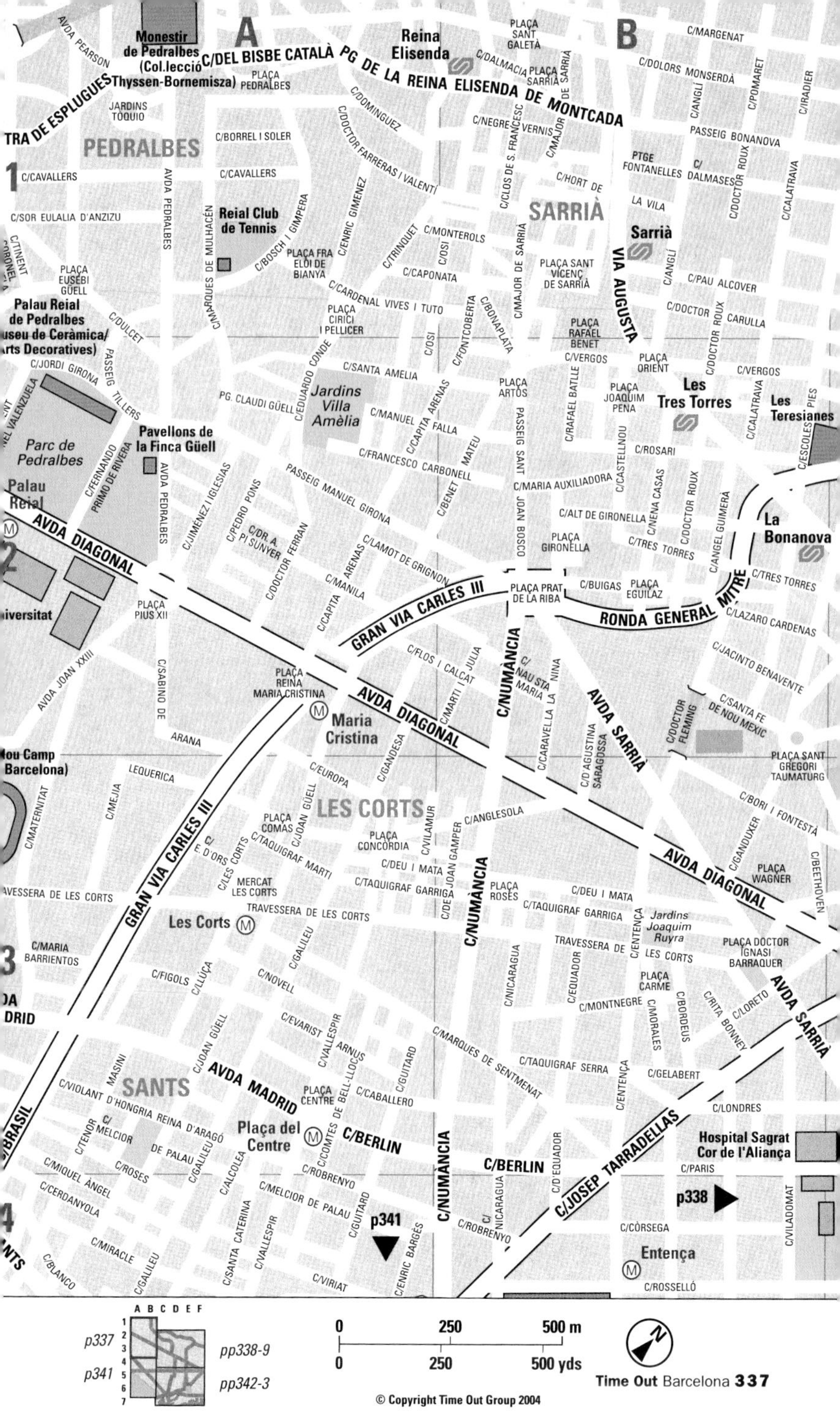

A
B
1
2
3
4
Monestir de Pedralbes (Col.lecció Thyssen-Bornemisza)
AVDA PEARSON
C/DEL BISBE CATALÀ
PLAÇA PEDRALBES
Reina Elisenda
PG DE LA REINA ELISENDA DE MONTCADA
PLAÇA SANT GALETÀ
C/DALMACIA
PLAÇA SARRIÀ
C/MAJOR DE SARRIÀ
C/MARGENAT
C/DOLORS MONSERDÀ
C/POMARET
C/IRADIER
C/ANGLÍ
PASSEIG BONANOVA
TRA DE ESPLUGUES
JARDINS TÒQUIO
PEDRALBES
C/BORREL I SOLER
C/CAVALLERS
C/DOMINGUEZ
C/DOCTOR FARRERAS I VALENTÍ
C/NEGRE
VERNIS
C/CLOS DE S. FRANCESC
PTGE FONTANELLES
C/ DALMASES
C/DOCTOR ROUX
C/CALATRAVA
C/HORT DE LA VILA
SARRIÀ
Sarrià
C/SOR EULALIA D'ANZIZU
AVDA PEDRALBES
Reial Club de Tennis
C/MARQUES DE MULHACÉN
C/BOSCH I GIMPERA
PLAÇA FRA ELOI DE BIANYA
C/ENRIC GIMENEZ
C/TRINQUET
C/MONTEROLS
C/OSI
C/CAPONATA
PLAÇA SANT VICENÇ DE SARRIÀ
VIA AUGUSTA
C/PAU ALCOVER
C/TINENT CORONEL
PLAÇA EUSEBI GÜELL
Palau Reial de Pedralbes
useu de Ceràmica/
rts Decoratives)
C/DULCET
C/CARDENAL VIVES I TUTO
PLAÇA CIRICI I PELLICER
C/FONTCOBERTA
C/BONAPLATA
PLAÇA RAFAEL BENET
C/DOCTOR CARULLA
C/JORDI GIRONA
PASSEIG TILLERS
C/EDUARDO CONDE
C/SANTA AMELIA
C/VERGOS
PLAÇA ORIENT
PLAÇA ARTÓS
Jardins Villa Amèlia
PG. CLAUDI GÜELL
C/MANUEL FALLA
C/CAPITA ARENAS
PASSEIG SANT JOAN BOSCO
C/RAFAEL BATLLE
PLAÇA JOAQUIM PENA
Les Tres Torres
Les Teresianes
C/ESCOLES PIES
Parc de Pedralbes
Pavellons de la Finca Güell
C/FERNANDO PRIMO DE RIVERA
C/FRANCESCO CARBONELL
C/BENET MATEU
C/ROSARI
C/CASTELLNOU
C/MARIA AUXILIADORA
Palau Reial
AVDA DIAGONAL
C/JIMÉNEZ I IGLESIAS
C/PEDRO PONS
C/DR. A. PI SUNYER
C/DOCTOR FERRAN
PASSEIG MANUEL GIRONA
C/NENA CASAS
C/ALT DE GIRONELLA
PLAÇA GIRONELLA
C/TRES TORRES
C/ANGEL GUIMERA
La Bonanova
C/LAMOT DE GRIGNON
C/MANILA
GRAN VIA CARLES III
PLAÇA PRAT DE LA RIBA
C/BUIGAS
PLAÇA EGUILAZ
RONDA GENERAL MITRE
iversitat
PLAÇA PIUS XII
C/LAZARO CARDENAS
AVDA JOAN XXIII
C/SABINO DE ARANA
C/FLOS I CALCAT
C/MARTI I JULIA
C/NUMÀNCIA
C/NAU STA MARIA
C/CARAVELLA LA NINA
AVDA SARRIÀ
C/JACINTO BENAVENTE
PLAÇA REINA MARIA CRISTINA
Maria Cristina
C/DOCTOR FLEMING
C/SANTA FE DE NOU MEXIC
ou Camp Barcelona)
LEQUERICA
C/GANDESA
C/EUROPA
C/D'AGUSTINA SARAGOSSA
PLAÇA SANT GREGORI TAUMATURG
C/MATERNITAT
C/MEJIA
LES CORTS
C/JOAN GÜELL
PLAÇA COMAS
C/VILAMUR
C/ANGLESOLA
C/BORI I FONTESTÀ
C/ E. D'ORS
C/LES CORTS
C/TAQUIGRAF MARTI
PLAÇA CONCORDIA
C/DEU I MATA
C/DE JOAN GAMPER
C/GANDUXER
PLAÇA WAGNER
C/BEETHOVEN
AVESSERA DE LES CORTS
MERCAT LES CORTS
C/TAQUIGRAF GARRIGA
PLAÇA ROSÉS
TRAVESSERA DE LES CORTS
Les Corts
Jardins Joaquim Ruyra
C/ENTENÇA
C/MARIA BARRIENTOS
C/GALILEU
C/NICARAGUA
C/EQUADOR
PLAÇA CARME
PLAÇA DOCTOR IGNASI BARRAQUER
DA DRID
C/FIGOLS
C/LLUÇA
C/NOVELL
C/MONTNEGRE
C/MORALES
C/BORDEUS
C/RITA BONNEY
C/LORETO
C/EVARIST ARNUS
C/VALLESPIR
C/MARQUES DE SENTMENAT
C/TAQUIGRAF SERRA
C/GELABERT
SANTS
AVDA MADRID
MASINI
C/VIOLANT D'HONGRIA REINA D'ARAGÓ
PLAÇA CENTRE
C/CABALLERO
C/GUITARD
C/LONDRES
/BRASIL
C/TENOR
C/MELCIOR DE PALAU
Plaça del Centre
C/COMTES DE BELL-LLOC
C/BERLIN
C/JOSEP TARRADELLAS
Hospital Sagrat Cor de l'Aliança
C/ROSES
C/MIQUEL ANGEL
C/CERDANYOLA
C/ALCOLEA
C/ROBRENYO
C/PARIS
C/D'EQUADOR
C/VILADOMAT
C/SANTA CATERINA
C/MIRACLE
C/BLANCO
C/ENRIC BARGÈS
C/CÒRSEGA
Entença
C/ROSSELLÓ
C/VIRIAT
NTS
p341
p338
p337
pp338-9
pp342-3
0 250 500 m
0 250 500 yds
N

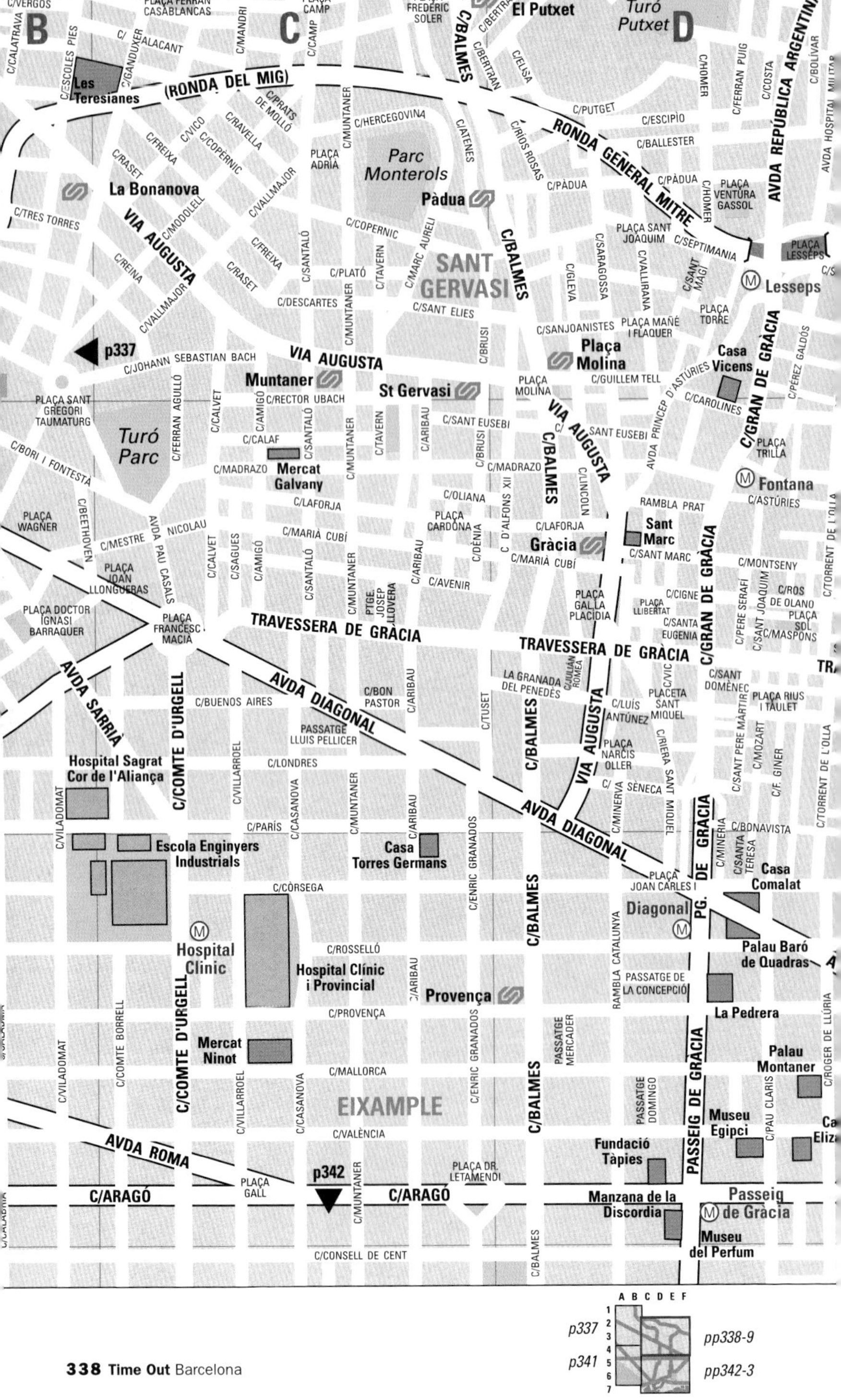
B
C
D
El Putxet
Turó Putxet
Les Teresianes
RONDA DEL MIG
La Bonanova
VIA AUGUSTA
Parc Monterols
Pàdua
SANT GERVASI
C/BALMES
RONDA GENERAL MITRE
AVDA REPÚBLICA ARGENTINA
Lesseps
PLAÇA LESSEPS
Plaça Molina
Muntaner
St Gervasi
Casa Vicens
Turó Parc
Mercat Galvany
Fontana
Gràcia
Sant Marc
C/GRAN DE GRÀCIA
PLAÇA FRANCESC MACIÀ
TRAVESSERA DE GRÀCIA
AVDA DIAGONAL
AVDA SARRIÀ
C/COMTE D'URGELL
Hospital Sagrat Cor de l'Aliança
Escola Enginyers Industrials
Casa Torres Germans
Casa Comalat
Diagonal
Palau Baró de Quadras
Hospital Clínic
Hospital Clínic i Provincial
Provença
La Pedrera
Mercat Ninot
EIXAMPLE
Palau Montaner
Museu Egipci
Fundació Tàpies
AVDA ROMA
C/ARAGÓ
Manzana de la Discordia
Passeig de Gràcia
Museu del Perfum
PASSEIG DE GRÀCIA
C/CONSELL DE CENT
p337
p342
p341
pp338-9
pp342-3

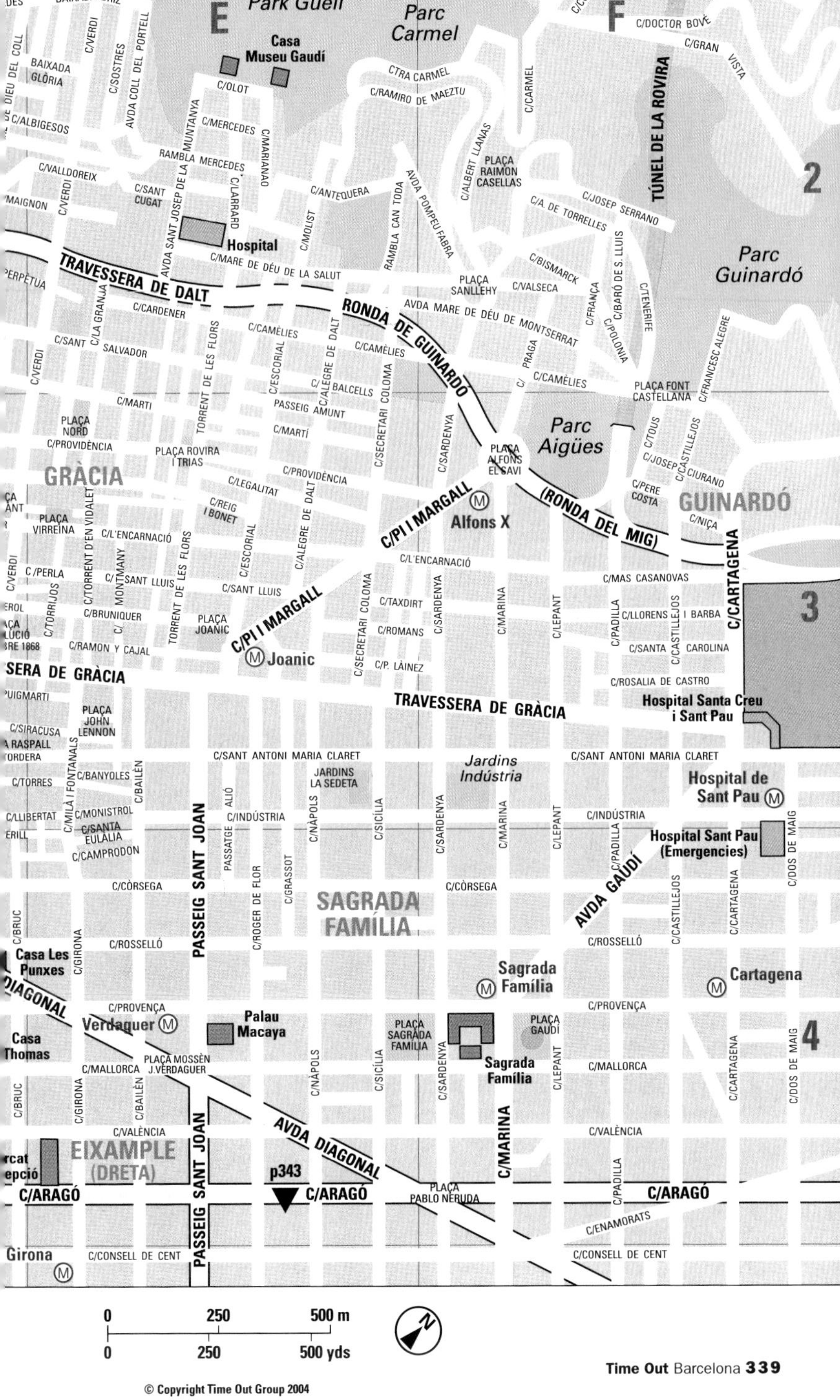

E
F
2
3
4
Park Güell
Parc Carmel
Casa Museu Gaudí
Parc Guinardó
Parc Aigües
GRÀCIA
GUINARDÓ
SAGRADA FAMÍLIA
EIXAMPLE (DRETA)
BAIXADA BRIZ
BAIXADA GLÒRIA
C/VERDI
C/SOSTRES
AVDA COLL DEL PORTELL
C/ALBIGESOS
C/OLOT
C/MERCEDES
C/MARIANAO
RAMBLA MERCEDES
C/VALLDOREIX
C/SANT CUGAT
AVDA SANT JOSEP DE LA MUNTANYA
C/LARRARD
Hospital
C/MARE DE DÉU DE LA SALUT
TRAVESSERA DE DALT
C/CARDENER
C/LA GRANJA
C/SANT SALVADOR
C/CAMÈLIES
C/ESCORIAL
C/ALEGRE DE DALT
RONDA DE GUINARDÓ
C/BALCELLS
PASSEIG AMUNT
C/SECRETARI COLOMA
C/MARTÍ
PLAÇA NORD
C/PROVIDÈNCIA
PLAÇA ROVIRA I TRIAS
TORRENT DE LES FLORS
C/LEGALITAT
C/REIG I BONET
PLAÇA VIRREINA
C/L'ENCARNACIÓ
C/TORRENT D'EN VIDALET
C/PERLA
C/MONTMANY
C/SANT LLUIS
C/BRUNIQUER
C/TORRIJOS
PLAÇA JOANIC
C/RAMON Y CAJAL
Joanic
C/PI I MARGALL
Alfons X
PLAÇA ALFONS EL SAVI
(RONDA DEL MIG)
CTRA CARMEL
C/RAMIRO DE MAEZTU
C/ANTEQUERA
C/MOLIST
RAMBLA CAN TODA
AVDA POMPEU FABRA
C/ALBERT LLANAS
PLAÇA RAIMON CASELLAS
C/CARMEL
C/A. DE TORRELLES
C/JOSEP SERRANO
TÚNEL DE LA ROVIRA
C/DOCTOR BOVÉ
C/GRAN VISTA
C/BISMARCK
C/VALSECA
PLAÇA SANLLEHY
AVDA MARE DE DÉU DE MONTSERRAT
C/FRANÇA
C/BARÓ DE S. LLUIS
C/POLONIA
C/TENERIFE
C/PRAGA
PLAÇA FONT CASTELLANA
C/FRANCESC ALEGRE
C/TOUS
C/JOSEP CIURANO
C/CASTILLEJOS
C/PERE COSTA
C/NIÇA
C/CARTAGENA
C/MAS CASANOVAS
C/LLORENS I BARBA
C/SANTA CAROLINA
C/ROSALIA DE CASTRO
C/SARDENYA
C/MARINA
C/LEPANT
C/PADILLA
C/TAXDIRT
C/ROMANS
C/P. LÀINEZ
TRAVESSERA DE GRÀCIA
Hospital Santa Creu i Sant Pau
PLAÇA JOHN LENNON
C/SIRACUSA
C/TORRES
C/BANYOLES
C/MILÀ I FONTANALS
C/BAILÈN
C/LLIBERTAT
C/MONISTROL
C/SANTA EULÀLIA
C/CAMPRODON
C/SANT ANTONI MARIA CLARET
JARDINS LA SEDETA
Jardins Indústria
Hospital de Sant Pau
C/INDÚSTRIA
PASSATGE ALIÓ
C/NÀPOLS
C/SICÍLIA
Hospital Sant Pau (Emergencies)
C/DOS DE MAIG
AVDA GAUDÍ
C/CÒRSEGA
PASSEIG SANT JOAN
C/ROGER DE FLOR
C/GRASSOT
C/BRUC
C/GIRONA
C/ROSSELLÓ
Casa Les Punxes
Sagrada Família
Cartagena
DIAGONAL
C/PROVENÇA
Verdaguer
Palau Macaya
Casa Thomas
PLAÇA SAGRADA FAMÍLIA
PLAÇA GAUDÍ
PLAÇA MOSSÈN J.VERDAGUER
C/MALLORCA
C/VALÈNCIA
AVDA DIAGONAL
p343
C/ARAGÓ
PLAÇA PABLO NERUDA
C/ENAMORATS
Girona
C/CONSELL DE CENT
0
250
500 m
0
250
500 yds
N

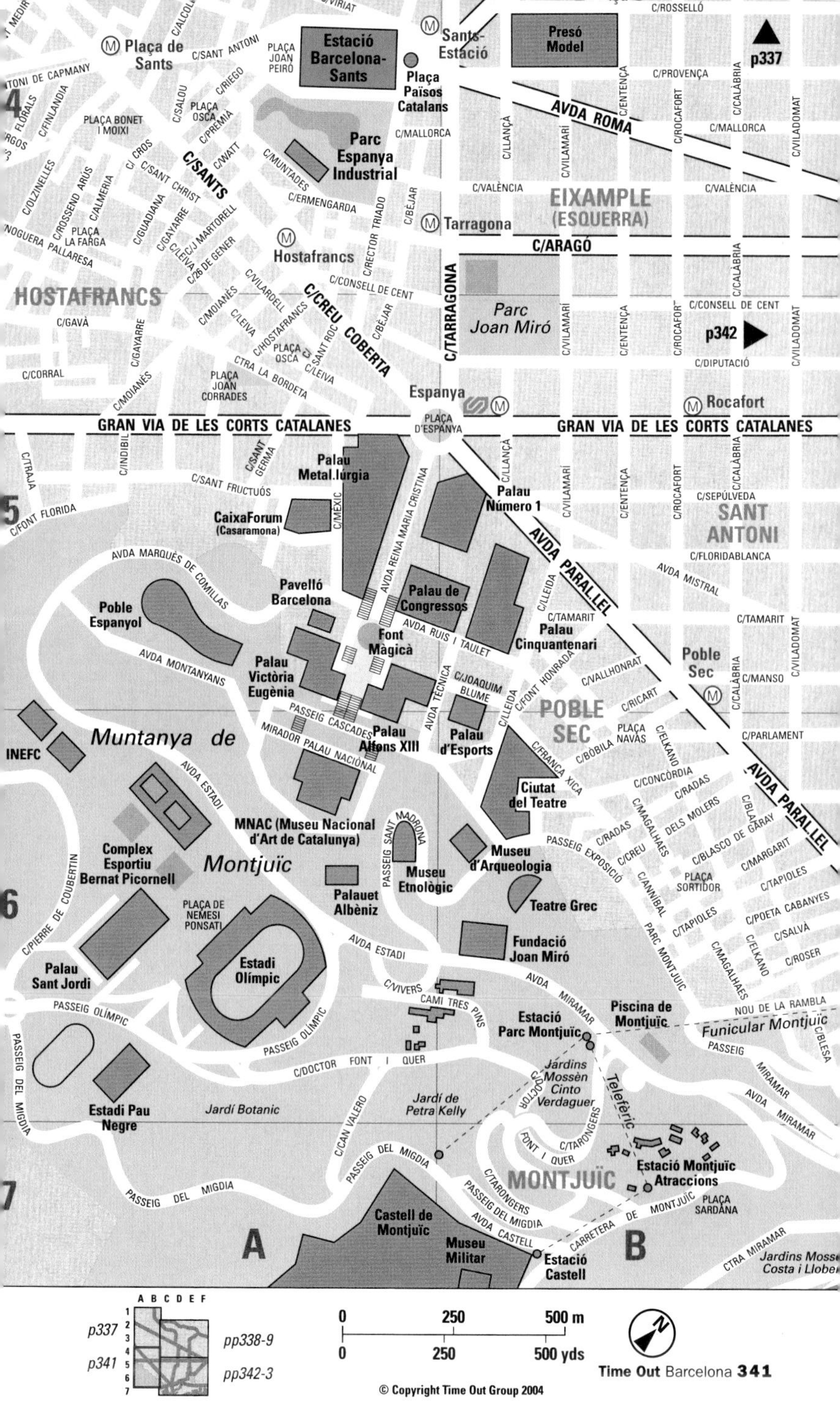

Plaça de Sants
C/SANT ANTONI
PLAÇA JOAN PEIRÓ
Estació Barcelona-Sants
Sants-Estació
Plaça Països Catalans
Presó Model
C/ROSSELLÓ
p337
C/PROVENÇA
AVDA ROMA
C/MALLORCA
C/VALÈNCIA
C/CALÀBRIA
C/VILADOMAT
C/ROCAFORT
C/ENTENÇA
C/VILAMARÍ
C/LLANÇÀ
TONI DE CAPMANY
C/FINLANDIA
FLORALS
PLAÇA BONET I MOIXÍ
C/SALOU
C/RIEGO
PLAÇA OSCA
C/PREMIÀ
C/WATT
C/SANTS
C/ CROS
C/SANT CHRIST
C/ALMERIA
C/ROSSEND ARÚS
C/OLZINELLES
PLAÇA LA FARGA
NOGUERA PALLARESA
C/GUADIANA
C/GAYARRE
C/J MARTORELL
C/LEIVA
C/26 DE GENER
Parc Espanya Industrial
C/MUNTADES
C/ERMENGARDA
C/RECTOR TRIADÓ
C/BÈJAR
Hostafrancs
Tarragona
EIXAMPLE (ESQUERRA)
C/ARAGÓ
HOSTAFRANCS
C/VILARDELL
C/CREU COBERTA
C/CONSELL DE CENT
C/TARRAGONA
Parc Joan Miró
p342
C/DIPUTACIÓ
C/GAVÀ
C/MOIANÈS
C/HOSTAFRANCS
C/LEIVA
PLAÇA OSCA
C/SANT ROC
C/CORRAL
PLAÇA JOAN CORRADES
CTRA LA BORDETA
Espanya
Rocafort
PLAÇA D'ESPANYA
GRAN VIA DE LES CORTS CATALANES
C/TRAJA
C/INDÍBIL
C/SANT GERMÀ
C/SANT FRUCTUÓS
C/FONT FLORIDA
Palau Metal.lúrgia
CaixaForum (Casaramona)
C/MÈXIC
AVDA REINA MARIA CRISTINA
Palau Número 1
C/SEPÚLVEDA
SANT ANTONI
AVDA PARAL.LEL
C/FLORIDABLANCA
AVDA MISTRAL
AVDA MARQUÈS DE COMILLAS
Poble Espanyol
Pavelló Barcelona
Palau de Congressos
C/LLEIDA
C/TAMARIT
Palau Cinquantenari
Font Màgica
AVDA RUIS I TAULET
AVDA MONTANYANS
Palau Victòria Eugènia
C/VALLHONRAT
Poble Sec
C/MANSO
C/FONT HONRADA
C/JOAQUIM BLUME
AVDA TÈCNICA
C/RICART
POBLE SEC
PASSEIG CASCADES
Palau Alfons XIII
Palau d'Esports
PLAÇA NAVAS
C/ELKANO
C/BÒBILA
C/PARLAMENT
Muntanya de Montjuïc
INEFC
MIRADOR PALAU NACIONAL
C/FRANCA XICA
C/CONCÒRDIA
C/RADAS
AVDA ESTADI
Ciutat del Teatre
MNAC (Museu Nacional d'Art de Catalunya)
PASSEIG SANT MADRONA
C/MAGALHAES
DELS MOLERS
C/BLAI
C/BLASCO DE GARAY
Complex Esportiu Bernat Picornell
Museu Etnològic
Museu d'Arqueologia
PASSEIG EXPOSICIÓ
C/CREU
C/ANNÍBAL
C/MARGARIT
PLAÇA SORTIDOR
C/TAPIOLES
Palauet Albèniz
Teatre Grec
C/PIERRE DE COUBERTIN
PLAÇA DE NEMESI PONSATI
C/POETA CABANYES
PARC MONTJUÏC
C/SALVÀ
Estadi Olímpic
Fundació Joan Miró
C/ROSER
Palau Sant Jordi
C/VIVERS
CAMI TRES PINS
AVDA MIRAMAR
Piscina de Montjuïc
NOU DE LA RAMBLA
PASSEIG OLÍMPIC
Estació Parc Montjuïc
Funicular Montjuïc
C/BLESA
C/DOCTOR FONT I QUER
Jardins Mossèn Cinto Verdaguer
Telefèric
PASSEIG MIRAMAR
PASSEIG DEL MIGDIA
Jardí Botànic
Jardí de Petra Kelly
C/CAN VALERO
Estadi Pau Negre
C/TARONGERS
FONT I QUER
MONTJUÏC
Estació Montjuïc Atraccions
PLAÇA SARDANA
CARRETERA DE MONTJUÏC
PASSEIG DEL MIGDIA
AVDA CASTELL
Castell de Montjuïc
Museu Militar
Estació Castell
CTRA MIRAMAR
Jardins Mossèn Costa i Llobera
A
B
4
5
6
7
A B C D E F
p337
p341
pp338-9
pp342-3
0 250 500 m
0 250 500 yds

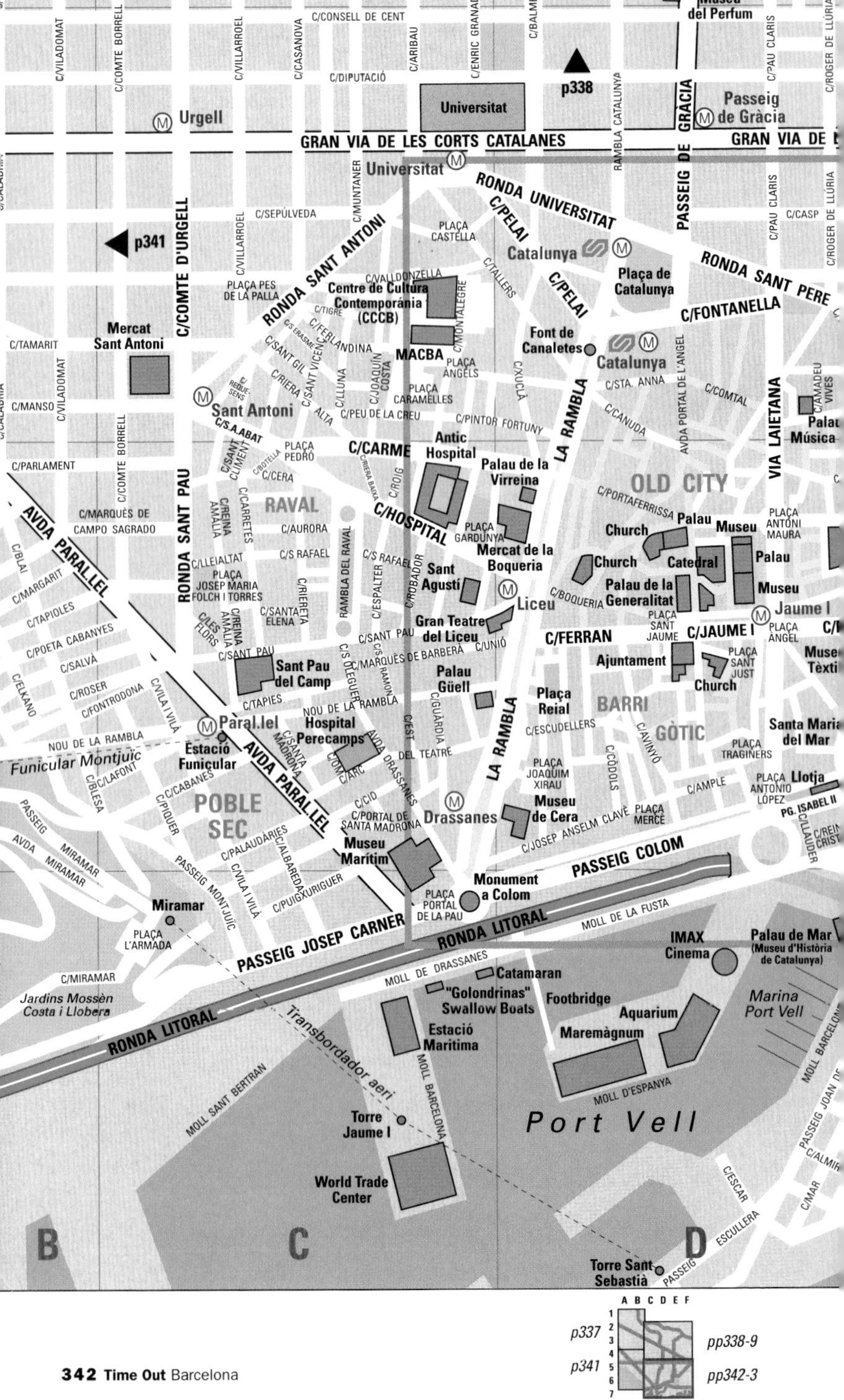
Museu del Perfum
C/CONSELL DE CENT
C/VILADOMAT
C/COMTE BORRELL
C/VILLARROEL
C/CASANOVA
C/ARIBAU
C/ENRIC GRANADOS
C/BALMES
C/PAU CLARIS
C/ROGER DE LLÚRIA
C/DIPUTACIÓ
Universitat
p338
Passeig de Gràcia
Urgell
GRAN VIA DE LES CORTS CATALANES
GRAN VIA DE
RAMBLA CATALUNYA
PASSEIG DE GRÀCIA
Universitat
C/MUNTANER
RONDA UNIVERSITAT
C/SEPÚLVEDA
C/CASP
p341
C/COMTE D'URGELL
PLAÇA CASTELLA
C/PELAI
Catalunya
RONDA SANT ANTONI
C/TALLERS
Plaça de Catalunya
RONDA SANT PERE
PLAÇA PES DE LA PALLA
C/VALLDONZELLA
Centre de Cultura Contemporània (CCCB)
C/FONTANELLA
C/TIGRE
C/MONTALEGRE
Mercat Sant Antoni
C/FERLANDINA
Font de Canaletes
C/TAMARIT
MACBA
Catalunya
C/SANT GIL
C/SANT VICENÇ
C/JOAQUÍN COSTA
PLAÇA ÀNGELS
C/XUCLÀ
C/STA. ANNA
C/MANSO
C/RIERA ALTA
C/LLUNA
PLAÇA CARAMELLES
C/COMTAL
AVDA PORTAL DE L'ÀNGEL
C/AMADEU VIVES
Sant Antoni
C/PEU DE LA CREU
C/PINTOR FORTUNY
C/CANUDA
LA RAMBLA
Palau Música
C/S.A.ABAT
PLAÇA PEDRÓ
C/CARME
Antic Hospital
VIA LAIETANA
C/PARLAMENT
C/SANT CLIMENT
C/BOTELLA
C/CERA
Palau de la Virreina
C/ROIG
OLD CITY
C/REINA AMÀLIA
C/CARRETES
RAVAL
C/PORTAFERRISSA
RONDA SANT PAU
C/MARQUÈS DE CAMPO SAGRADO
C/HOSPITAL
PLAÇA ANTONI MAURA
AVDA PARAL.LEL
C/AURORA
PLAÇA GARDUNYA
Palau
Church
Museu
C/BLAI
C/LLEIALTAT
C/S RAFAEL
RAMBLA DEL RAVAL
C/S RAFAEL
Mercat de la Boqueria
Church
Catedral
Palau
C/MARGARIT
PLAÇA JOSEP MARIA FOLCH I TORRES
C/RIERETA
C/ESPALTER
C/ROBADOR
Sant Agustí
Liceu
C/BOQUERIA
Palau de la Generalitat
Museu
C/TAPIOLES
C/SANTA ELENA
Jaume I
C/LES FLORS
Gran Teatre del Liceu
PLAÇA SANT JAUME
C/JAUME I
PLAÇA ÀNGEL
C/POETA CABANYES
C/SANT PAU
C/FERRAN
C/UNIÓ
C/SALVÀ
C/SANT PAU
C/MARQUÈS DE BARBERÀ
Ajuntament
PLAÇA SANT JUST
Museu Tèxtil
C/ELKANO
C/ROSER
Sant Pau del Camp
C/S OLEGUER
C/S RAMON
Palau Güell
Church
C/FONTRODONA
C/VILA I VILÀ
C/TAPIES
NOU DE LA RAMBLA
C/GUÀRDIA
Plaça Reial
BARRI GÒTIC
NOU DE LA RAMBLA
Paral.lel
Hospital Perecamps
C/EST
C/ESCUDELLERS
C/AVINYÓ
Santa Maria del Mar
Estació Funicular
C/SANTA MADRONA
AVDA DRASSANES
DEL TEATRE
Funicular Montjuïc
C/LAFONT
C/ARC
LA RAMBLA
C/CÒDOLS
PLAÇA TRAGINERS
AVDA PARAL.LEL
PLAÇA JOAQUIM XIRAU
C/BLESA
C/CABANES
POBLE SEC
C/AMPLE
PLAÇA ANTONIO LÓPEZ
Llotja
PASSEIG MIRAMAR
C/PIQUER
C/CID
Museu de Cera
PG. ISABEL II
C/PORTAL DE SANTA MADRONA
Drassanes
PLAÇA MERCÈ
AVDA MIRAMAR
C/PALAUDÀRIES
C/ALBAREDA
C/JOSEP ANSELM CLAVÉ
C/LLAUDER
C/REINA CRISTINA
PASSEIG MONTJUÏC
Museu Marítim
PASSEIG COLOM
C/VILA I VILÀ
C/PUIGXURIGUER
Monument a Colom
Miramar
PLAÇA PORTAL DE LA PAU
PLAÇA L'ARMADA
PASSEIG JOSEP CARNER
RONDA LITORAL
MOLL DE LA FUSTA
IMAX Cinema
Palau de Mar (Museu d'Història de Catalunya)
C/MIRAMAR
MOLL DE DRASSANES
Catamaran
"Golondrinas" Swallow Boats
Footbridge
Marina Port Vell
Jardins Mossèn Costa i Llobera
Aquarium
RONDA LITORAL
Transbordador aeri
Estació Marítima
Maremàgnum
MOLL BARCELONA
MOLL SANT BERTRAN
MOLL D'ESPANYA
PASSEIG JOAN DE BORBÓ
Torre Jaume I
MOLL BARCELONA
Port Vell
C/ALMIRALL
World Trade Center
C/ESCAR
C/MAR
B
C
D
ESCULLERA
Torre Sant Sebastià
PASSEIG
A B C D E F
1
2
3
4
5
6
7
p337
p341
pp338-9
pp342-3

C/CONSELL DE CENT
C/BRUC
C/GIRONA
C/BAILÈN
C/DIPUTACIÓ
C/ROGER DE FLOR
C/NÀPOLS
C/SICÍLIA
C/SARDENYA
p339
Monumental
AVDA DIAGONAL
C/CASTILLEJOS
C/CARTAGENA
C/DOS DE MAIG
Plaza de Toros Monumental
PLAÇA TETUAN
GRAN VIA DE LES CORTS CATALANES
PLAÇA DE LES GLÒRIES
Tetuan
See p344-345
Teatre Nacional
Glòries
C/CASP
C/RIBES
C/LEPANT
C/PADILLA
Auditori
C/AUSIÀS MARC
C/BOLÍVIA
C/ÀVILA
PASSEIG SANT JOAN
C/MARINA
AVDA MERIDIANA
RONDA SANT PERE
C/ALÍ BEI
Arc de Triomf
Estació d'Autobusos Barcelona-Nord
C/TÀNGER
C/ÀLABA
Marina
C/TRAFALGAR
AVDA VILANOVA
C/SANCHO DE ÁVILA
C/PAMPLONA
Parc de l'Estació del Nord
PLAÇA SANT PERE
C/ALMOGÀVERS
C/ZAMORA
C/CORTINES
C/PORTAL NOU
LLUÍS COMPANYS
Palau Justícia
C/BUENAVENTURA MUÑOZ
C/JOAN D'AUSTRIA
C/PALLARS
C/PERE IV
Jutjats
PLAÇA SANT CUGAT
C/COMERÇ
PASSEIG PUJADES
C/PUJADES
Museu de Zoologia
Parc Ciutadella
C/WELLINGTON
Bogatell
C/LLULL
Museu Picasso
PASSEIG PICASSO
Museu de Geologia
Edifici de les Aigües
C/RAMON TURRÓ
AVDA BOGATELL
Antic Mercat del Born
Parlament de Catalunya
C/DOCTOR TRUETA
C/MARQUÈS DE L'ARGENTERA
Estació de França
Parc Zoologic
C/RAMON TRIAS FARGAS
C/JOAN MIRÓ
C/ROSA SENSAT
C/ARQUITECTE SERT
C/MARQUESA
Zoo
AVDA ICÀRIA
PASSEIG CIRCUMVAL.LACIÓ
Barceloneta
VILA OLÍMPICA
C/DOCTOR AIGUADER
RONDA LITORAL
Ciutadella-Vila Olímpica
C/SALVADOR ESPRIU
PLAÇA CAMPIONS
C/BALBOA
AVDA LITORAL
PASSEIG MARÍTIM NOVA ICÀRIA
Parc Barceloneta
Hospital del Mar
C/TRELAWNY
PASSEIG MARÍTIM PORT OLÍMPIC
C/GINEBRA
C/MAQUINISTA
C/BALUARD
MOLL MESTRAL
PLAÇA FONT
Mercat
BARCELONETA
MOLL MARINA
Port Olímpic
MOLL GREGAL
Platja Nova Icària
PLAÇA POETA BOSCÀ
C/ANDREA DÒRIA
C/SANT CARLES
PLAÇA BRUGADA
C/CERVERA
PASSEIG MARÍTIM
Platja Passeig Marítim
Platja Barceloneta
E
F
5
6
7
0
250
500 m
0
250
500 yds
N

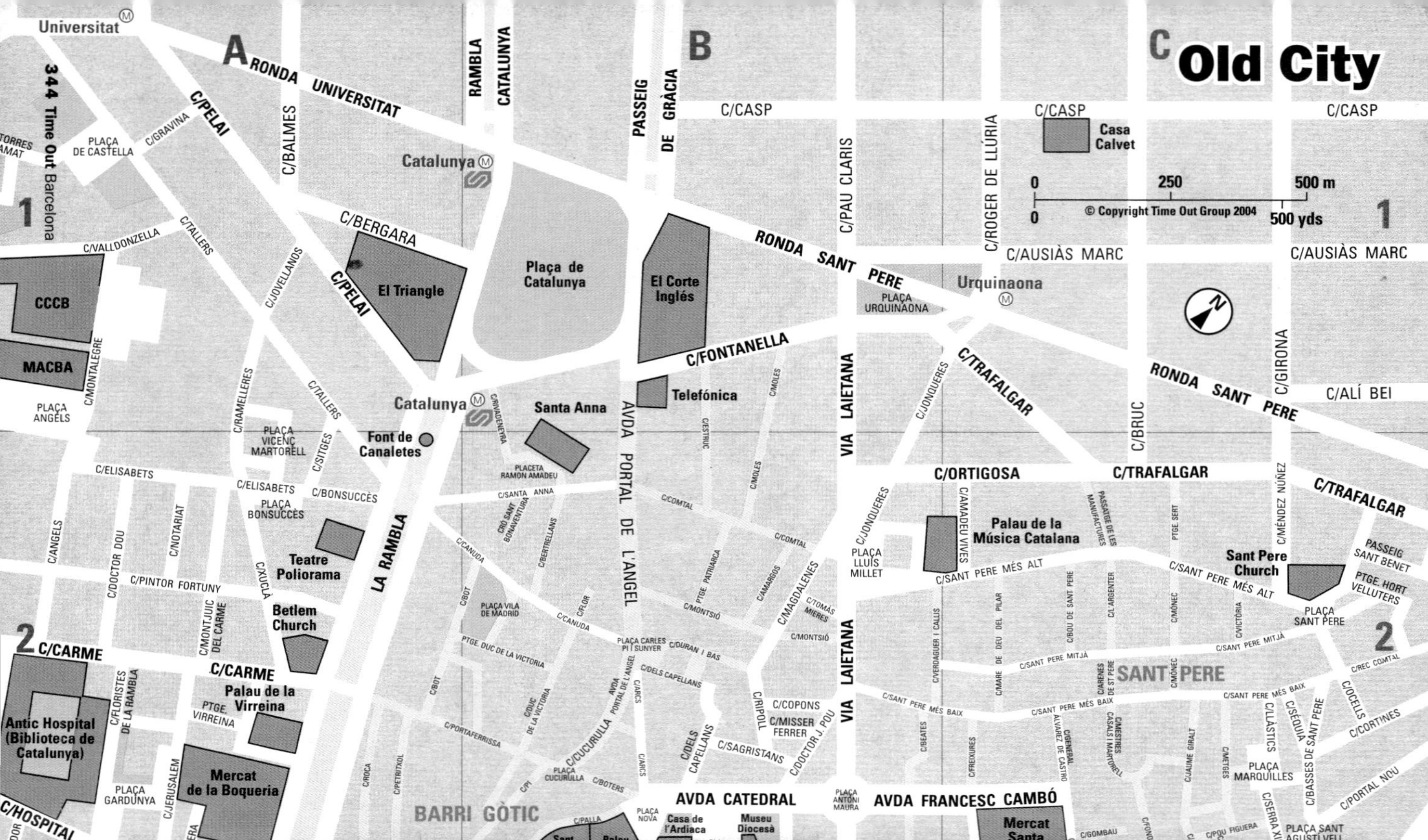
Old City
A
B
C
1
2
Universitat
Ronda Universitat
C/Pelai
C/Balmes
Rambla Catalunya
Passeig de Gràcia
C/Casp
Casa Calvet
0
250
500 m
0
500 yds
© Copyright Time Out Group 2004
C/Pau Claris
C/Roger de Llúria
C/Ausiàs Marc
C/Bruc
C/Girona
C/Alí Bei
Ronda Sant Pere
Urquinaona
Plaça Urquinaona
C/Trafalgar
C/Fontanella
Catalunya
Plaça de Catalunya
El Corte Inglés
Telefónica
El Triangle
C/Bergara
C/Gravina
Plaça de Castella
Torres Amat
C/Valldonzella
C/Tallers
C/Jovellanos
CCCB
MACBA
C/Montalegre
Plaça Angels
C/Ramelleres
Plaça Vicenç Martorell
C/Sitges
Font de Canaletes
C/Rivadeneyra
Santa Anna
Placeta Ramon Amadeu
C/Santa Anna
Cró Sant Bonaventura
C/Bertrellans
C/Elisabets
C/Bonsuccès
Plaça Bonsuccès
Teatre Poliorama
La Rambla
C/Angels
C/Doctor Dou
C/Notariat
C/Pintor Fortuny
C/Xuclà
C/Montjuïc del Carme
Betlem Church
C/Carme
Palau de la Virreina
Ptge. Virreina
Antic Hospital (Biblioteca de Catalunya)
C/Floristes de la Rambla
C/Hospital
Plaça Gardunya
C/Jerusalem
Mercat de la Boqueria
C/Roca
C/Petritxol
C/Bot
C/Portaferrissa
Barri Gòtic
C/Canuda
Plaça Vila de Madrid
Ptge. Duc de la Victoria
C/Duc de la Victoria
C/Flor
C/Pi
Plaça Cucurulla
C/Cucurulla
C/Boters
C/Palla
Avda Portal de l'Angel
C/Arcs
Plaça Nova
Casa de l'Ardiaca
Museu Diocesà
Avda Catedral
Plaça Carles Pi i Sunyer
C/Duran i Bas
C/Dels Capellans
C/Comtal
Ptge. Patriarca
C/Montsió
C/Estruc
C/Moles
C/Amargós
C/Magdalenes
C/Tomàs Mieres
C/Copons
C/Misser Ferrer
C/Ripoll
C/Sagristans
C/Doctor J. Pou
Via Laietana
Plaça Antoni Maura
Avda Francesc Cambó
Mercat Santa
C/Jonqueres
C/Ortigosa
Plaça Lluís Millet
C/Amadeu Vives
Palau de la Música Catalana
C/Sant Pere Més Alt
Passatge de les Manufactures
Ptge. Sert
C/Méndez Núñez
Sant Pere Church
Passeig Sant Benet
Ptge. Hort Velluters
Plaça Sant Pere
C/Verdaguer i Callis
C/Mare de Deu del Pilar
C/Bou de Sant Pere
C/L'Argenter
C/Mónec
C/Victòria
C/Sant Pere Mitjà
Sant Pere
C/Arenes de St Pere
C/Sant Pere Més Baix
C/Beates
C/Freixures
C/General Álvarez de Castro
C/Mestres Casals i Martorell
C/Jaume Giralt
C/Metges
C/Llàstics
Plaça Marquilles
C/Sèquia
C/Basses de Sant Pere
C/Rec Comtal
C/Ocells
C/Cortines
C/Portal Nou
C/Gombau
C/Pou Figuera
C/Serra Xic
Plaça Sant Agustí Vell

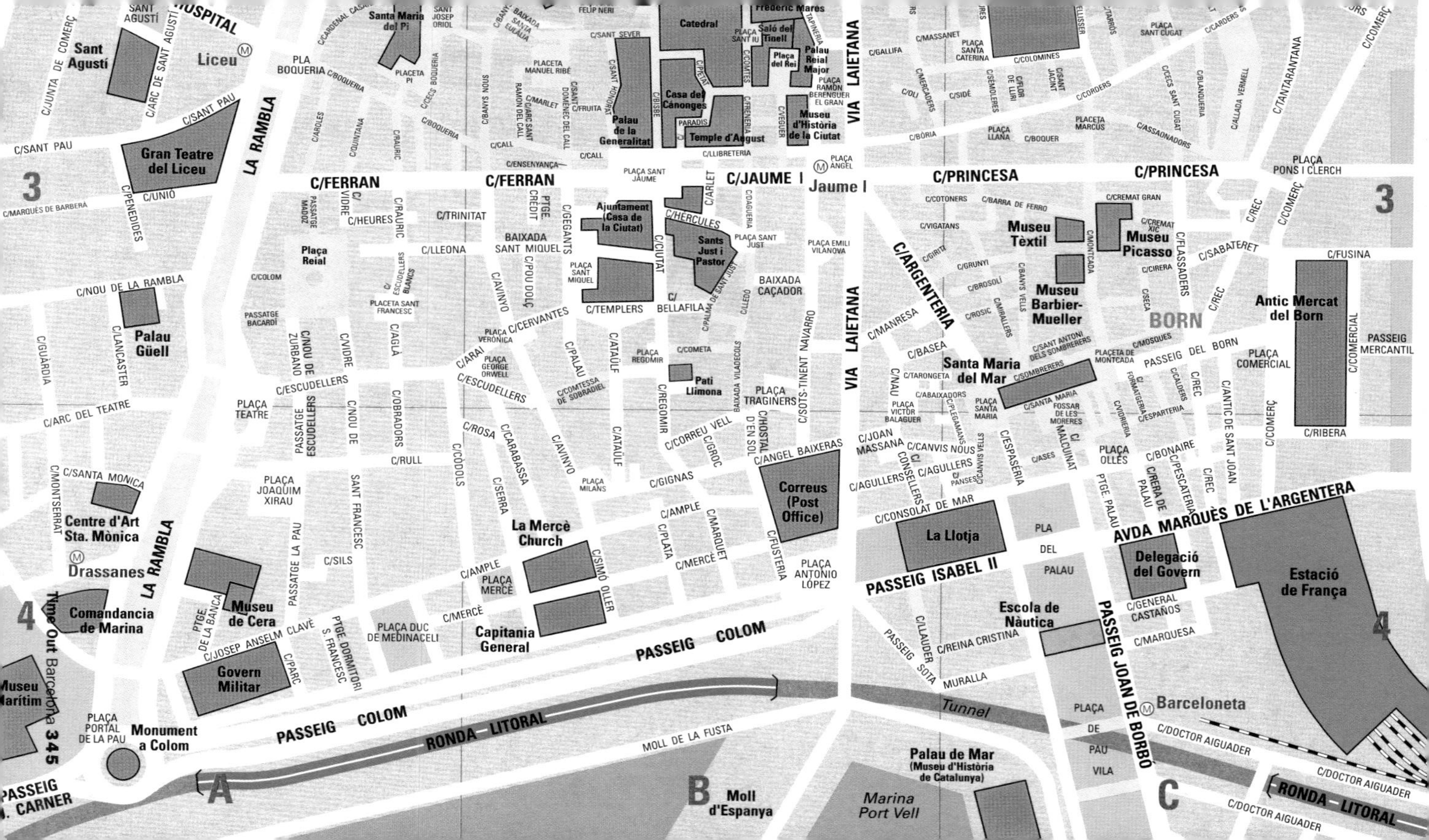

Estació de França
Antic Mercat del Born
Museu Picasso
Museu Barbier-Mueller
Museu Tèxtil
Santa Maria del Mar
Delegació del Govern
Escola de Nàutica
La Llotja
Palau de Mar (Museu d'Història de Catalunya)
Marina Port Vell
Correus (Post Office)
Moll d'Espanya
Catedral
Casa dels Canonges
Temple d'August
Palau de la Generalitat
Ajuntament (Casa de la Ciutat)
Sants Just i Pastor
Pati Llimona
Museu d'Història de la Ciutat
Palau Reial Major
Plaça del Rei
Saló del Tinell
La Mercè Church
Capitania General
Santa Maria del Pi
Plaça Reial
Gran Teatre del Liceu
Palau Güell
Sant Agustí
Museu de Cera
Govern Militar
Centre d'Art Sta. Mònica
Comandancia de Marina
Monument a Colom
Barceloneta
Jaume I
Liceu
Drassanes
BORN
C/PRINCESA
C/ARGENTERIA
VIA LAIETANA
C/JAUME I
C/FERRAN
LA RAMBLA
PASSEIG COLOM
RONDA LITORAL
PASSEIG JOAN DE BORBÓ
AVDA MARQUÈS DE L'ARGENTERA
PASSEIG ISABEL II
PASSEIG MERCANTIL
PASSEIG DEL BORN
PLA DEL PALAU
MOLL DE LA FUSTA
PASSEIG SOTA MURALLA
Tunnel
C/DOCTOR AIGUADER
C/COMERÇ
C/REC
C/MONTCADA
C/AVINYÓ
C/ESCUDELLERS
C/NOU DE SANT FRANCESC
C/BOQUERIA
C/SANT PAU
C/UNIÓ
C/PENEDIDES
C/NOU DE LA RAMBLA
C/LANCASTER
C/ARC DEL TEATRE
C/SANTA MONICA
C/MONTSERRAT
C/GUÀRDIA
PLAÇA PORTAL DE LA PAU
3
4
A
B
C

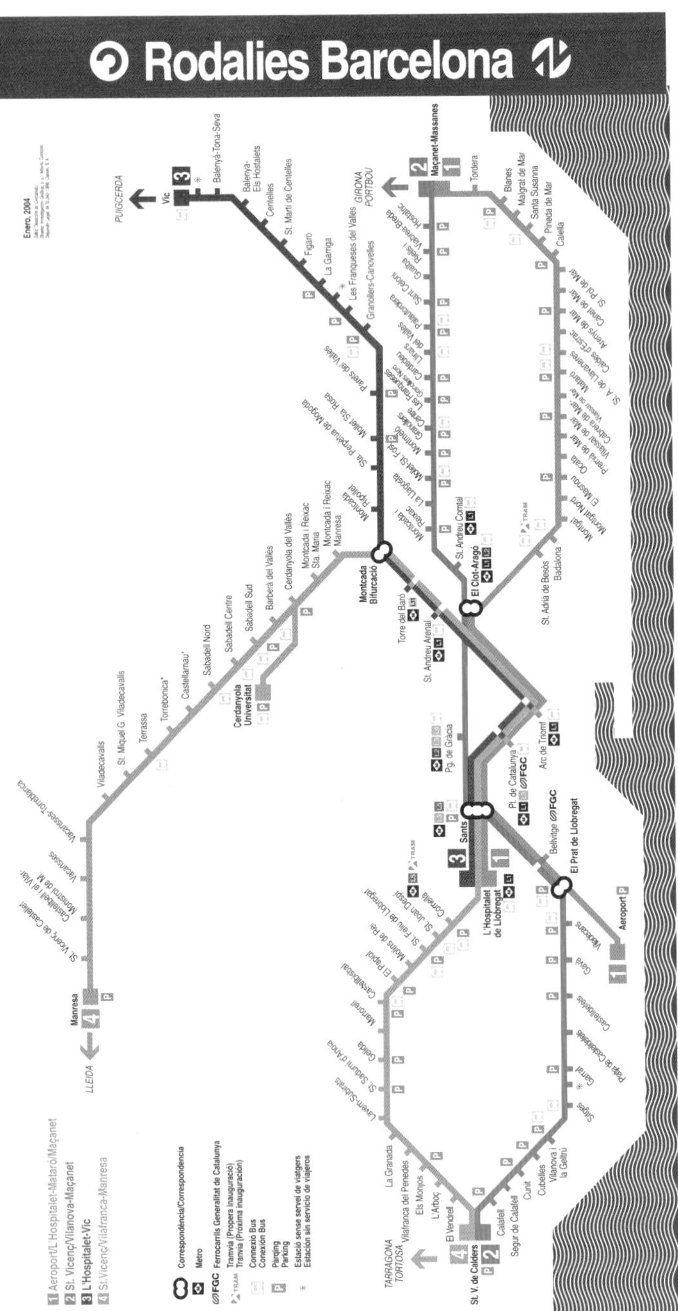
Rodalies Barcelona
Enero, 2004
1 Aeroport/L'Hospitalet-Mataró/Maçanet
2 St. Vicenç/Vilanova-Maçanet
3 L'Hospitalet-Vic
4 St. Vicenç/Vilafranca-Manresa
Correspondència/Correspondencia
Metro
FGC Ferrocarrils Generalitat de Catalunya
Tramvia (Propera inauguració)
Tranvía (Próxima inauguración)
Connexió Bus
Conexión Bus
Parquing
Parking
Estació sense servei de viatgers
Estación sin servicio de viajeros
PUIGCERDÀ
GIRONA PORTBOU
LLEIDA
TARRAGONA TORTOSA
Vic
Maçanet-Massanes
Manresa
St. V. de Calders
Aeroport
Montcada Bifurcació
El Clot-Aragó
Sants
L'Hospitalet de Llobregat
El Prat de Llobregat
Pg. de Gràcia
Pl. de Catalunya
Arc de Triomf
Cerdanyola Universitat
Mataró
Granollers-Canovelles
Terrassa
Sabadell Centre
Vilanova i la Geltrú
Sitges
Castelldefels
Vilafranca del Penedès
Martorell
Badalona
Blanes
Calella
Tordera

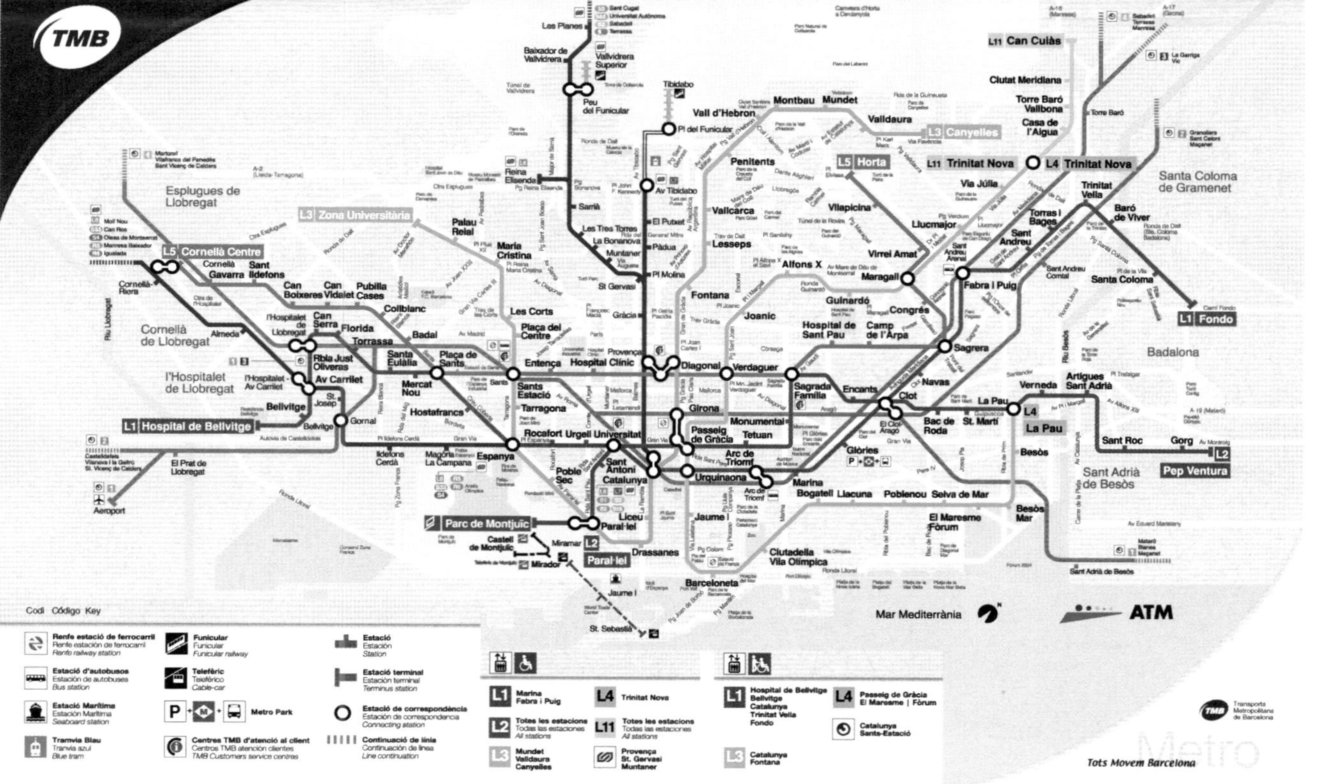
TMB
L1 Hospital de Bellvitge
L1 Fondo
L2 Paral·lel
L2 Pep Ventura
L3 Zona Universitària
L3 Canyelles
L4 Trinitat Nova
L4 La Pau
L5 Cornellà Centre
L5 Horta
L11 Trinitat Nova
L11 Can Cuiàs
Parc de Montjuïc
Santa Coloma de Gramenet
Badalona
Sant Adrià de Besòs
Esplugues de Llobregat
Cornellà de Llobregat
l'Hospitalet de Llobregat
El Prat de Llobregat
Riu Llobregat
Riu Besòs
Mar Mediterrània
ATM
Aeroport
Les Planes
Baixador de Vallvidrera
Vallvidrera Superior
Peu del Funicular
Tibidabo
Pl del Funicular
Av Tibidabo
El Putxet
Pàdua
Pl Molina
St Gervasi
Muntaner
La Bonanova
Les Tres Torres
Sarrià
Reina Elisenda
Maria Cristina
Palau Reial
Les Corts
Plaça del Centre
Badal
Collblanc
Can Boixeres
Can Vidalet
Pubilla Cases
Sant Ildefons
Gavarra
Cornellà
Cornellà-Riera
Almeda
Bellvitge
l'Hospitalet - Av Carrilet
Av Carrilet
Rbla Just Oliveras
l'Hospitalet de Llobregat
Can Serra
Florida
Torrassa
Santa Eulàlia
Mercat Nou
Plaça de Sants
Hostafrancs
Espanya
Magòria La Campana
Ildefons Cerdà
Gornal
St. Josep
Sants
Sants Estació
Tarragona
Entença
Hospital Clínic
Provença
Diagonal
Gràcia
Rocafort
Urgell
Universitat
Catalunya
Sant Antoni
Poble Sec
Paral·lel
Liceu
Drassanes
Miramar
Mirador
Castell de Montjuïc
Jaume I
Barceloneta
St. Sebastià
Ciutadella Vila Olímpica
Arc de Triomf
Urquinaona
Passeig de Gràcia
Girona
Verdaguer
Tetuan
Monumental
Sagrada Família
Marina
Bogatell
Llacuna
Poblenou
Selva de Mar
El Maresme Fòrum
Besòs Mar
Besòs
Glòries
Clot
El Clot-Aragó
Encants
Navas
Sagrera
Bac de Roda
St. Martí
La Pau
Verneda
Artigues Sant Adrià
Sant Roc
Gorg
Fabra i Puig
Sant Andreu
Sant Andreu Arenal
Torras i Bages
Trinitat Vella
Baró de Viver
Santa Coloma
Sant Andreu Comtal
Casa de l'Aigua
Torre Baró Vallbona
Ciutat Meridiana
Via Júlia
Llucmajor
Maragall
Congrés
Camp de l'Arpa
Hospital de Sant Pau
Guinardó
Alfons X
Joanic
Fontana
Lesseps
Vallcarca
Penitents
Vall d'Hebron
Montbau
Mundet
Valldaura
Virrei Amat
Vilapicina
Codi Código Key
Renfe estació de ferrocarril
Renfe estación de ferrocarril
Renfe railway station
Estació d'autobusos
Estación de autobuses
Bus station
Estació Marítima
Estación Marítima
Seaboard station
Tramvia Blau
Tranvía azul
Blue tram
Funicular
Funicular
Funicular railway
Telefèric
Teleférico
Cable-car
Metro Park
Centres TMB d'atenció al client
Centros TMB atención clientes
TMB Customers service centres
Estació
Estación
Station
Estació terminal
Estación terminal
Terminus station
Estació de correspondència
Estación de correspondencia
Connecting station
Continuació de línia
Continuación de línea
Line continuation
L1 Marina
Fabra i Puig
L2 Totes les estacions
Todas las estaciones
All stations
L3 Mundet
Valldaura
Canyelles
L4 Trinitat Nova
L11 Totes les estacions
Todas las estaciones
All stations
Provença
St. Gervasi
Muntaner
L1 Hospital de Bellvitge
Bellvitge
Catalunya
Trinitat Vella
Fondo
L3 Catalunya
Fontana
L4 Passeig de Gràcia
El Maresme | Fòrum
Catalunya
Sants-Estació
Transports Metropolitans de Barcelona
Metro
Tots Movem Barcelona

Barcelona Areas
Barri Gòtic (pp80-90)
Raval (pp91-96)
Sant Pere & Born (pp97-103)
Ports & Shoreline (pp104-108)
Montjuïc (pp109-115)
The Eixample (pp116-124)
Gràcia & Other Districts (pp125-136)
PEDRALBES
AVDA DIAGONAL
SANT GERVASI
RONDA GENERAL MITRE
Park Güell
Parc del Guinardó
HORTA
GUINARDÓ
LES CORTS
GRÀCIA
Hospital de Sant Pau
AVDA DE LA MERIDIANA
SANT ANDREU
AVDA JOSEP TARRADELLAS
GRAN VIA CARLES III
Estació Barcelona-Sants
C/TARRAGONA
EIXAMPLE (ESQUERRA)
PASSEIG DE GRÀCIA
AVDA DIAGONAL
Sagrada Família
LA SAGRERA
SANTS
C/ARAGÓ
C/GUIPÚSCOA
EIXAMPLE (DRETA)
CLOT
Plaça d'Espanya
GRAN VIA DE LES CORTS CATALANES
Plaça de les Glòries
Plaça Catalunya
POBLE SEC
AVDA PARAL.LEL
SANT PERE
RAVAL
Catedral
BORN
MONTJUÏC
LA RAMBLA
BARRI GÒTIC
Parc de la Ciutadella
POBLENOU
Estadi Olímpic
Estació de França
VILA OLÍMPICA
RONDA LITORAL
PORT VELL
PORT OLÍMPIC
BARCELONETA
0
2 km
1 mile
© Copyright Time Out Group 2004